amazons of the avant-garde

alexandra exter,
natalia goncharova,
liubov popova, olga rozanova,
varvara stepanova, and
nadezhda udaltsova

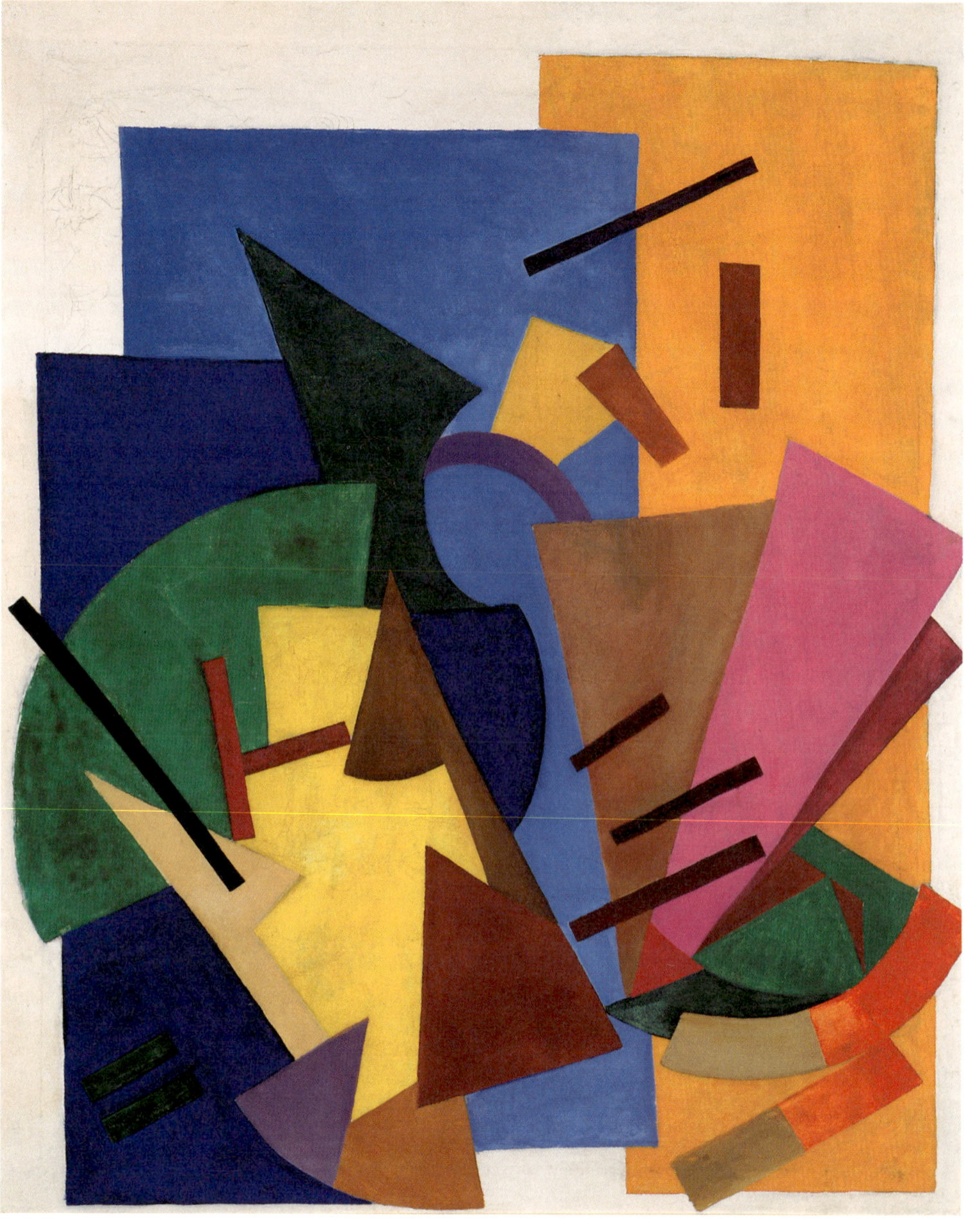

OLGA ROZANOVA
Non-Objective Composition (Flight of an Airplane), 1916
Oil on canvas, 118 x 101 cm
Art Museum, Samara

amazons of the avant-garde

alexandra exter,
natalia goncharova,
liubov popova, olga rozanova,
varvara stepanova, and
nadezhda udaltsova

edited by john e. bowlt and matthew drutt

royal academy of arts, 1999

Published on the occasion of the exhibition

AMAZONS OF THE AVANT-GARDE: ALEXANDRA EXTER, NATALIA GONCHAROVA, LIUBOV POPOVA, OLGA ROZANOVA, VARVARA STEPANOVA, AND NADEZHDA UDALTSOVA

Curated by John E. Bowlt, Matthew Drutt, and Zelfira Tregulova

Deutsche Guggenheim Berlin, 10 July–17 October 1999
Royal Academy of Arts, London, 13 November 1999–6 February 2000
Peggy Guggenheim Collection, Venice, 29 February–28 May 2000
Solomon R. Guggenheim Museum, New York, 21 June–1 October 2000

The Royal Academy of Arts is grateful to Her Majesty's Government for its help in agreeing to indemnify the exhibition under the National Heritage Act 1980, and to the Museums and Galleries Commission for its help in arranging this indemnity.

British Library Cataloguing-in-Publication Data
A catalogue record for this book is available from the British Library

ISBN 0-900-94681-4

Guggenheim Museum Publications
1071 Fifth Avenue
New York, New York 10128

Royal Academy of Arts
Burlington House
Piccadilly
London W1V 0DS

Printed in Germany by GZD

Design: DESIGN/WRITING/RESEARCH

Cover: Natalia Goncharova, *Peasants Gathering Grapes*, 1912 (plate 19)

CONTENTS

Lenders to the Exhibition

Art Co. Ltd. (George Costakis Collection)
Art Museum, Samara
Solomon R. Guggenheim Museum, New York
Krasnodar District Kovalenko Art Museum
Moderna Museet, Stockholm
Elena Murina and Dmitrii Sarabianov, Moscow
Museo Thyssen-Bornemisza, Madrid
Museum Ludwig, Cologne
Museum of History and Architecture, Pereiaslavl-Zalesskii
Museum of Private Collections,
Pushkin State Museum of Fine Arts, Moscow
Museum of Visual Arts, Ekaterinburg
National Art Museum of Ukraine, Kiev
National Gallery of Canada, Ottawa
National Museum and Gallery, Cardiff
Private Collection
Private Collection, Courtesy Gallery Gmurzynska, Cologne
Regional Art Museum, Ulianovsk
Regional Picture Gallery, Vologda
Rostov Kremlin State Museum Preserve
Slobodskoi Museum and Exhibition Center
Staatsgalerie, Stuttgart
State Art Museum of Bashkkortostan, Ufa
State Museum of History, Architecture, and Art, Smolensk
State Museum of the Visual Arts of Tatarstan, Kazan
State Museum of Visual Arts, Nizhnii Tagil
State Picture Gallery, Perm
State Radischev Art Museum, Saratov
State Russian Museum, St. Petersburg
State Tretiakov Gallery, Moscow
State Unified Art Museum, Kostroma
Carmen Thyssen-Bornemisza Collection
Vasnetsov Regional Art Museum, Kirov
Yale University Art Gallery, New Haven

PRESIDENT'S FOREWORD

SIR PHILIP DOWSON CBE,
PRESIDENT, ROYAL ACADEMY OF ARTS

The Royal Academy now has a long-standing tradition of celebrating the phenomenal achievements of the early twentieth-century Russian avant-garde. In 1983 we were one of the first institutions in the West to show the remarkable collection of Russian avant-garde art belonging to George Costakis; since then we have also held two major exhibitions of the art of Marc Chagall, in 1985 and 1998 respectively, and this year we showed the first retrospective of Vasily Kandinsky ever mounted in this country. It is with great pleasure that we are now able to present *Amazons of the Avant-Garde*. The exhibition features the work of six Russian women artists, Alexandra Exter, Natalia Goncharova, Liubov Popova, Olga Rozanova, Varvara Stepanova and Nadezhda Udaltsova, each of whom in their different ways contributed to the great Utopian dream of Russian art in the early decades of the twentieth century. Their art challenged traditional aesthetic values and redefined the boundaries between art and life. Unlike many previous exhibitions of Russian avant-garde art, this exhibition focuses on the vital and unprecedented role that women played in the evolution of modern art in Russia. Today, we take for granted the role that women play within the arts. Although numerous important women artists contributed to the history of art, never, before these pioneering Russian women, had a group had such an impact and shared equal status with their male colleagues.

The exhibition has been organised by the Solomon R. Guggenheim Museum in New York and we are very grateful to our colleagues there for sharing this exhibition with us. In particular we would like to thank the Director, Thomas Krens, the Deputy Director and Chief Curator, Lisa Dennison, the Curator, Matthew Drutt, and the Guggenheim's European Representative, Nicolas Iljine. We also extend our thanks to the co-curators of *Amazons of the Avant-Garde*, John Bowlt, Matthew Drutt and Zelfira Tregulova, for the thoughtful way in which they have prepared this important exhibition and the catalogue that accompanies it. At the Royal Academy the exhibition has been steered by our Exhibitions Secretary, Norman Rosenthal, with assistance from Simonetta Fraquelli, Curator, and Susan Thompson, Senior Exhibitions Organiser.

Finally, we would like to express our gratitude to all those museums and private collectors who have generously lent their treasured works, many of which have not been shown outside Russia before.

Preface

Thomas Krens
Director, The Solomon R. Guggenheim Foundation

The Guggenheim Museum has a distinguished history in collecting and presenting the art of the Russian avant-garde. In 1929, Solomon R. Guggenheim met Vasily Kandinsky in his Bauhaus studio, beginning a relationship that would result in this pioneering Russian abstract painter becoming closely associated with the museum's permanent collection. Masterpieces by Russians Marc Chagall, Natalia Goncharova, Mikhail Larionov, El Lissitzky, and Kazimir Malevich were acquired by the museum early on, and remain some of our most treasured works.

Over the years we have mounted many exhibitions devoted to Russian artists, with no fewer than nineteen since 1945 devoted to Kandinsky alone. Other Russian masters so honored by the Guggenheim include Malevich (1973), Chagall (1975 and 1992), and Naum Gabo (1986). In 1981, the Guggenheim organized the now-legendary *Art of the Avant-Garde in Russia: Selections from the George Costakis Collection*; a sweeping survey, it resulted in two publications that remain central to the scholarship on the subject. In 1992, we presented *The Great Utopia: The Russian and Soviet Avant-Garde, 1915–1932*, which remains the most comprehensive investigation of the subject anywhere in the world to date.

It is within this illustrious context that we are very pleased to organize another historic exhibition of Russian art. *Amazons of the Avant-Garde: Alexandra Exter, Natalia Goncharova, Liubov Popova, Olga Rozanova, Varvara Stepanova, and Nadezhda Udaltsova* is a model of scholarship and curatorial acumen. It brings together some of the most distinguished masterpieces of the period, including many not shown in the West since they were created, and offers a fresh and insightful approach to the subject. The exhibition could have no better starting point than Berlin, which was a breeding ground for Russian art in the early twentieth century.

Curators John E. Bowlt, Matthew Drutt, and Zelfira Tregulova deftly organized this complex project, and we are most grateful to them for their cooperation and hard work. We are indebted to the lenders to this exhibition, not only because they allowed us to borrow their treasured works, but because they have made important contributions to the scholarship of this publication. Finally, we are deeply grateful to Dr. Rolf-E. Breuer, Spokesman of the Board of Managing Directors of Deutsche Bank, for his ongoing support of the unique collaboration between our institutions. This exhibition marks the first traveling exhibition organized for the Deutsche Guggenheim Berlin; we are thankful for Deutsche Bank's unwavering enthusiasm for the project as well as its sponsorship of the tour.

ACKNOWLEDGMENTS

We have been very fortunate to work with a large network of associates, all of whom have contributed invaluably to this project. Foremost, we thank Nicolas V. Iljine, European Representative of the Solomon R. Guggenheim Foundation, for his steadfast support and advice throughout the exhibition. It was he who suggested the idea for this project, and his enthusiasm and passion combined with his experience and diplomatic skills made him a critical member of our team.

We would also like to express our deepest gratitude to Pavel Khoroshilov, Deputy Minister of Culture of the Russian Federation, who also stood at the beginning of the curatorial process, proposing its special focus, taking a personal interest and assisting us far beyond his call of duty.

We are most grateful to our Russian colleagues, whose help with this exhibition was indispensable. At the Ministry of Culture of the Russian Federation Department of Museums: Vera Lebedeva, Director, and Anna Kolupaeva, Deputy Director. At the State Tretiakov Gallery, Moscow: Valentin Rodionov, Director; Lidia Iovleva, Deputy Director of Academic Research; Natalia Avtonomova, Head of the Department of Twentieth-Century Art; Tatiana Gubanova of the International Department; Alla Lukanova, Liudmila Bobrovskaia and Tatiana Mikhienko, Curators of the Department of Twentieth-Century Art; Natalia Kobliakova and Elena Churakova of the Department of Restoration. At the State Russian Museum, St. Petersburg: Vladimir Gusev, Director; Evgenia Petrova, Deputy Director of Academic Research. At the State Pushkin Museum of Fine Arts, Moscow: Irina Antonova, Director. At the "Rosizo" State Museum Exhibition Center, representing 16 Russian regional museums: Oleg Shandybin, Director; Victoria Zubravskaia, Head of the Exhibition Department. Furthermore, we thank Faina Balakhovskaia for her archival research, coordination of loans from Russian regional museums and assistance with curatorial issues; Ekaterina Drevina for granting access to the Nadezhda Udaltsova archive; and Alexander Lavrentiev and Varvara Rodchenko for their generous help with artworks and documents from the Rodchenko-Stepanova Archive. We also extend our gratitude to Aliki Kostaki in Athens, Norman W. Neubauer, Philippa Delancey, and the Hellenic Republic Ministry of Culture for their assistance with loans from Art Co. Ltd. (the George Costakis Collection).

For their scholarly contributions, we are deeply grateful to the catalogue's authors: Natalia Adaskina, Charlotte Douglas, Ekaterina Dyogot, Laura Engelstein, Nina Gurianova, Georgii Kovalenko, Alexander Lavrentiev, Olga Matich, Nicoletta

Misler, Vasilii Rakitin, Dmitrii Sarabianov, and Jane A. Sharp.

Special mention goes to our colleagues at the Royal Academy of Arts, London. In particular, we thank Norman Rosenthal, Exhibitions Secretary, and Simonetta Fraquelli, Curator, for their support. Philip Rylands, Deputy Director of the Peggy Guggenheim Collection in Venice, was central to the early stages of organizing this project. We also thank Dr. Ariane Grigoteit and Friedhelm Hütte, curators of the Deutsche Bank Collection; Svenja Simon, Gallery Manager, and Sara Bernshausen, Gallery Assistant, both of the Deutsche Guggenheim Berlin.

The expertise of different staff members at the Solomon R. Guggenheim Museum was indispensable. The leadership of Thomas Krens, Director, and Lisa Dennison, Deputy Director and Chief Curator, must be recognized for nurturing the exhibition. We are most grateful to Vanessa Rocco, Project Curatorial Assistant, who managed all aspects of this endeavor. Luz Gyalui, curatorial intern, provided valuable assistance. Marion Kahan, Exhibition Program Manager, oversaw the transport of loans. Thanks must be given to our liaisons with Deutsche Guggenheim Berlin, Paul Pincus, Director of International Planning and Operations, and Anne Leith, Planning and Operations Manager. Also helpful were: Max Hollein, Executive Assistant to the Director; Scott Gutterman, Director of Public Affairs; Ben Hartley, Director of Corporate Communication and Sponsorship; Jane DeBevoise, Deputy Director for Program Administration; Karen Meyerhoff, Director of Exhibition and Collection Management and Design; Sean Mooney, Exhibition Design Manager and Alexis Katz, Architectural CAD Coordinator; Jessica Ludwig, Chief Graphic Designer/Exhibition Design Coordinator; and Gail Scovell, General Counsel, Julie L. Lowitz, Associate General Counsel, and Maria Pallante, Assistant General Counsel.

For the catalogue design, we thank J. Abbott Miller and Santiago Piedrafita of Design/Writing/Research. Anthony Calnek, Director of Publications, Elizabeth Levy, Managing Editor/Manager of Foreign Editions, Esther Yun, Assistant Production Manager, Meghan Dailey, Assistant Editor, and Liza Donatelli, Editorial and Administrative Assistant, were integral to every step of producing this publication. We are grateful to David Frankel, Stephen Robert Frankel, Jennifer Knox-White, and Tim Mennel. We would also like to extend our deep thanks to Elizabeth Franzen, Manager of Editorial Services, for her skillful management and organization.

We further thank: Barbara Lyons of Harry Abrams, Inc., Simon Taylor at Art Resource; J. Frank Goodwin for his translations from the Russian; Aneta Zebala for photography in Los Angeles; and Mariia Zubova. We appreciate the input of Jared Ash, Dimitri P. Dourdine-Mak, Krystyna Gmurzynska, Alexandra Ilf, Gérard Lob, Nikita D. Lobanov-Rostovsky, Nina Lobanov-Rostovsky, Ira Menshova, and Alik Rabinovich. Finally, and most importantly, we extend our deepest thanks to all of the lenders to the exhibition.

—John E. Bowlt, Matthew Drutt, Zelfira Tregulova

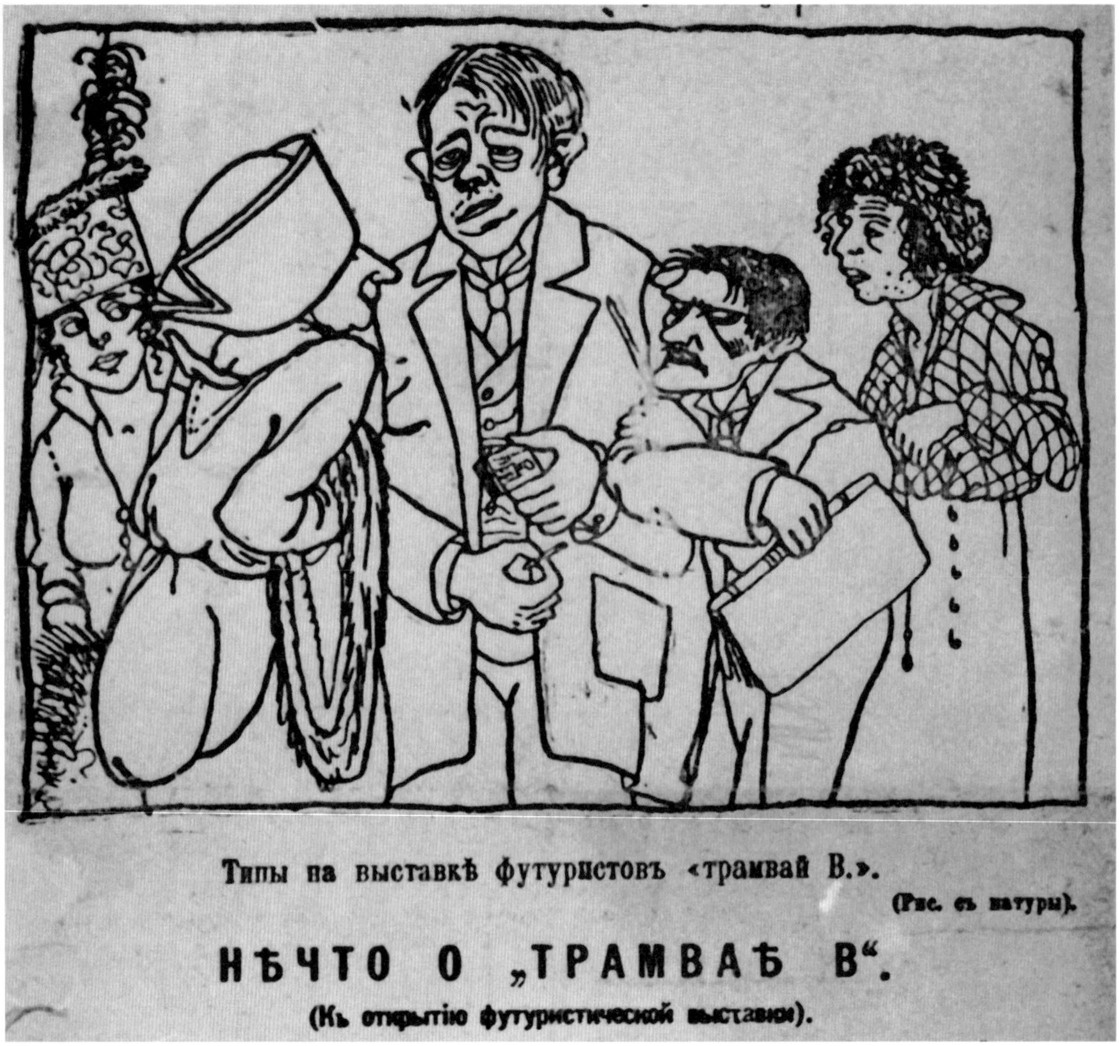

figure 1. anonymous
Types at the "Tramway V" Exhibition of Futurists, caricature published in the newspaper *Golos Rusi* (Petrograd), 1915. The drawing shows (left to right) Ksenia Boguslavskaia, Alexandra Exter, Vladimir Tatlin, Ivan Puni, and Olga Rozanova at the *Tramway V* exhibition. Courtesy of Puni-Archiv, Zurich.

Introduction

Matthew Drutt

Amazons of the Avant-Garde is modest in scale yet ambitious in scope. It marks a departure from previous endeavors that have taken a broad view of the Russian avant-garde, mapping the breadth of its interdisciplinary activities through an encyclopedic array of artists.[1] The exhibition celebrates the evolution of modern Russian painting from the 1900s through the early 1920s exemplified by six artists who were at the center of that history: Alexandra Exter, Natalia Goncharova, Liubov Popova, Olga Rozanova, Varvara Stepanova, and Nadezhda Udaltsova. Despite its tight focus, *Amazons of the Avant-Garde* has been a challenging undertaking. Some five years of planning and research have brought together more than seventy carefully selected paintings and drawings from international public and private collections. Many of the works have been lent by Russian institutions, some appearing in the West for the first time since the early twentieth century.

The narrower path charted by this exhibition is not taken at the expense of the complexity of the art or its milieu. Rather, it allows that complexity to fall under close examination. The present publication is more than a catalogue; it is a collection of interpretive essays and primary documents that delves deeply into its subject and offers a range of viewpoints. New research has concentrated directly on the paintings and drawings. Because a number of them were originally exhibited without dates and under generic names or simply as "untitled," questions of provenance have attended many of the works throughout their history. However, after extensive investigation in Russian archives, and with the assistance of colleagues at the different lending institutions, more precise titles and dates have been assigned to several key works. Some of these adjustments represent a subtle refinement of previous scholarship, while others may necessitate a reexamination of a given artist's stylistic evolution. In cases where questions remain, we have retained the currently accepted information and follow it with a newer suggestion in brackets. This invaluable documentation, along with a careful scrutiny of provenance and exhibition history for each work, has been assembled with the assistance of scholars Faina Balakhovskaia, Liudmila Bobrovskaia, Nina Gurianova, Alexander Lavrentiev, Alla Lukanova, and Tatiana Mikhienko.

The first section of the book consists of six essays on a range of subjects. In some cases, these contributions depart from the subject at hand, offering historical background and insight into topics inspired by this enterprise that make the book an extension of the exhibition rather than merely its companion. How and why such a great number of women artists became so prominent during a relatively confined period are questions that recur throughout this volume. Through an investigation of art criticism, artistic practice, and the art market in early twentieth-century Russia, John E. Bowlt considers the conceptual and historical context in which this question is posed. His essay, "Women of Genius," reflects on the ambivalence and enthusiasm alternately directed toward female artists in Russia from the turn of the century through the early 1930s. Bowlt also demonstrates that, by the 1910s, the women were quite firmly a part of the Russian art world, and that without them, future avant-garde trajectories would have been impossible. Women artists regularly participated in key exhibitions and wrote for major publications, and in many cases their contributions formed the foundations for pioneering conceptual developments of the period.

In her essay, Charlotte Douglas looks closely at the personal and professional lives of Russian women artists, describing the dynamic of camaraderie and independence that operated between them, their position in the European avant-garde, and their involvement within Russian artistic circles. Douglas reminds the reader that painting was but one facet of their creative output (which also included stage and textile design among other disciplines) and touches upon the complex amalgam of indigenous traditions and foreign influences that informed the art and writings of the six artists.

The roots of their confidence and prominence may be better understood when considered against the intricate historical fabric of Russia. In her essay "Between Old and New: Russia's Modern Women," Laura Engelstein provides a comprehensive foundation for understanding the social, historical, and political conditions that gave rise to the "new woman" in Russia. The country's labyrinthine culture and politics are laid bare as the author charts the ebb and flow of female political economy from the eighteenth through the early twentieth century. Engelstein moves deftly between high and low culture, sociology and cultural history, and economics and politics, considering elements as varied as the palace intrigues of the tsarist period to the fashion trends that made women appear more masculine long before the Russian Revolution proclaimed the sexes equal.

Olga Matich's essay may be viewed as building upon Engelstein's historical framework. The problematic relationship between power and sexuality — one implicit in the title of this exhibition — is traced through a close reading of Russia's fin-de-siècle cultural landscape and the question of gender identity. The essay investigates the ways in which women were depicted in the visual, literary, and performing arts, and in particular, how they represented themselves. While primarily concerned with examples from Symbolist art, literature, and theater, Matich's ideas provide another lens through which the viewer might look at the works in this exhibition. The notion of self-presentation is taken up by Nicoletta Misler in "Dressing Up and Dressing Down: The Body of the Avant-Garde," which examines the impact Exter, Goncharova, Popova, Rozanova, Stepanova, and Udaltsova had on fashion and design. "Dressing Up and Dressing Down" is another reminder that painting was part of a larger ideological and artistic structure, and that significant avant-garde practices of the period went beyond painting.

Finally, Ekaterina Dyogot's analysis of male and female creativity, and the dynamics of gender, recognition, and exclusion in Modernism, is a sensitive yet pointed discussion of the close personal and professional partnerships that the artists in this exhibition shared with their male contemporaries. Dyogot demonstrates how those relationships presented both means for empowerment and obstacles to the artists' maintaining their independence.

This volume also includes biographical essays profiling each artist, written by leading scholars — Georgii Kovalenko (Exter), Jane A. Sharp (Goncharova), Natalia Adaskina and Dmitrii Sarabianov (Popova), Nina Gurianova (Rozanova), Alexander Lavrentiev (Stepanova), and Vasilii Rakitin (Udaltsova). These contributions offer critical insight into, and new information about, specific works and shed further light on the artists' respective biographies. Some adjustments to the chronologies of the artists' activities have also been made; thus, the information here may in some cases differ from that in previous publications. Such changes have been made only after careful consideration of recently discovered information. The reproductions that follow each of these essays are arranged chronologically; however, this is not meant to suggest that, within a given year, one painting definitely preceded or followed another; and, further, certain works have been arranged according to stylistic considerations.

The final part of the book contains a selection of original writings by the artists themselves. These documents not only provide insight into the critical thinking and aesthetic concerns of each artist, but also reveal their personal struggles, highlighting both their affinities and their fierce competitiveness. While several of these primary sources have previously appeared elsewhere, most have been newly translated from Russian and published here for the first time. Every attempt has been made to preserve the original spirit of these tracts, diary entries, and letters. The polemical writing of the avant-garde demonstrates its support of radical cultural production and provides commentary on the relationship between these artists' work and the art of the past. These selections are as fascinating, revelatory, and central to the history of the avant-garde as the works of art themselves.

1. *The Great Utopia: The Russian and Soviet Avant-Garde, 1915–1932*, organized by the Solomon R. Guggenheim Museum in 1992, has become the exemplar of this approach.

editorial note

The transliteration of the Russian used in this book modifies the Library of Congress system, so that the Russian soft and hard signs have either been omitted or indicated with an "i" (e.g., Grigoriev). This system is also used throughout the footnotes and where bibliographical references involve Russian-language sources. Since this book is meant for the lay reader as much as for students and scholars, we have avoided the academic transliteration systems that can render a familiar name unrecognizable (e.g., whereby "Chekhov" becomes "Cexov"). Many Russian artists and writers spent time in Europe or the United States and often their names received various, even contradictory, transliterations from the original Russian into the language of their adopted home. For the sake of uniformity, names have been transliterated in accordance with the system described above, except when a variant has been long established and widely recognized, such as Alexandre Benois instead of Alexandr Benua, and El Lissitzky, rather than Lazar Lisitsky.

Dates referring to events in Russia before January 1918 are in the Old Style. If a given date falls during the nineteenth century, it is twelve days behind the Western calendar; if it falls between 1900 and 1918, it is thirteen days behind.

Finally, the city of St. Petersburg was renamed Petrograd in 1914; Leningrad in 1924; and then St. Petersburg again in 1992. However, both Petrograd and Petersburg continued to be used freely in common parlance and publications until 1924. As a general rule, Petrograd has been retained here to denote the official name of St. Petersburg from 1914–24. —*J.E.B.*

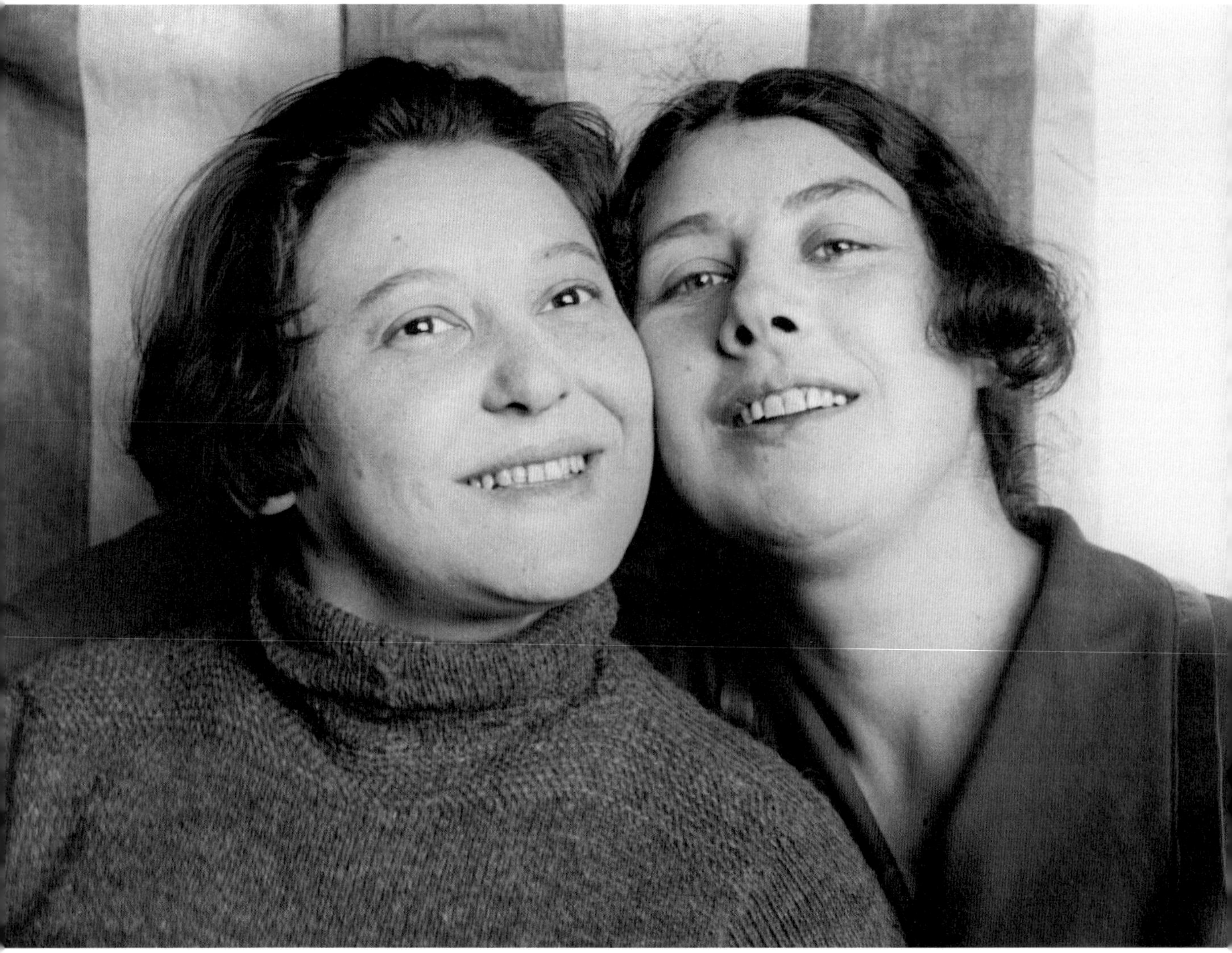

figure 2. Varvara Stepanova and Liubov Popova, photographed by Alexander Rodchenko, Moscow, 1924.

women of genius[1]

john e. bowlt

The triumph of the Russian avant-garde is unthinkable without the participation of the six women in this exhibition, each of whom contributed directly to its development. Benedikt Livshits, the Cubo-Futurist poet and friend of Alexandra Exter and Olga Rozanova, was the first to describe them as "real Amazons, Scythian riders."[2] The bold diapason of aesthetic ideas represented by the original and dazzling works in this exhibition — from Natalia Goncharova's evocation of traditional Russian culture in *Mowers*, 1907–08 (plate 14) to Liubov Popova's hard-edge abstraction in *Construction*, 1920 (plate 38), from Exter's Simultanism in *City*, 1913 (plate 3) to Varvara Stepanova's visual poetry of 1918 (plates 55–64), and from Rozanova's non-objectivity compositions (see e.g. plates 19–53) to Nadezhda Udaltsova's Suprematist ornaments (e.g. plates 86–89) — documents the stylistic history of the Russian avant-garde. For all the accomplishments of the "other avant-garde" in Europe and the United States, an analogous exhibition that defines entire movements in such a decisive and comprehensive manner through the work of women artists could hardly be undertaken for French Cubism, Italian Futurism, or German Expressionism. Obviously, this is not to deny the merits of Hannah Höch, Marie Laurencin, Benedetta Marinetti, Gabriele Münter, Sophie Täuber-Arp, or their numerous colleagues, but their total contribution still pales before the pictorial splendor of the work of these six Russian *avangardistki.* Perhaps Vladimir Bekhteev, a friend of Goncharova, and Georgii Yakulov, a friend of Sonia Delaunay, Exter, and Rozanova, had this strength and energy in mind when, at the height of the avant-garde, each painted his own version of the allegorical *Battle of the Amazons*.[3]

Certainly, the idea of grouping together a number of important Russian women artists and assembling their works into an exhibition is not new: in 1883 Andrei Somov, Curator of Paintings at the Hermitage in St. Petersburg and father of the fin-de-siècle artist Konstantin Somov, published a long article about the "phenomenon" of nineteenth-century Russian women painters and engravers[4]; in his 1903 history of Russian art, Alexei Novitsky included a special section on Russian women artists[5]; in 1910 the St. Petersburg journal *Apollon* (*Apollo*) organized an exhibition of Russian women artists in its editorial offices; and in the late 1910s — remarkably in the wake of World War I — the Russian press gave increasing space to the role of women artists and writers, both conservative and radical. More recently there have been many exhibitions and publications concerned with Russian women artists, all of which have posed the complicated question as to why these women were able to live, work, and play in such an unrestricted manner in such an apparently restricted society as Imperial Russia. In 1976–77 Linda Nochlin and Ann Sutherland Harris organized the impressive *Women Artists 1550–1950* — shown at the Brooklyn Museum, the Los Angeles County Museum of Art, and the University of Texas at Austin — which placed Exter, Goncharova, Popova, and Udaltsova in a rich panorama that started with Levina Teerline and ended with Dorothea Tanning. The first exhibition to concentrate on the women of the Russian avant-garde, however, was *Künstlerinnen der russischen Avantgarde/Women-Artists of the Russian Avant-Garde 1910–30*, organized by the Galerie Gmurzynska, Cologne, in 1979–80; this exhibition and its catalogue remain a cornerstone in current research on the history of the Russian avant-garde. Exhibitions that followed — such as *L'altra metà dell'avanguardia 1910–1940*, organized by Lea Vergine and shown at the Comune di Milano, Milan, in 1980, and *L'Avant-Garde au Féminin: Moscou, Saint-Petersbourg, Paris (1907–1930)*, organized by Valentine and Jean-Claude Marcadé and shown at Artcurial, Centre d'Art Plastique Contemporain, Paris, in 1983 — added to the basic sources presented in the Galerie Gmurzynska exhibition, reinforcing the already powerful position of women in histories of Russian art. Subsequent publications by Miuda Yablonskaya (*Women Artists of Russia's New Age: 1900–1935* [1990]) and Beat Wismer (*Karo Dame. Konstruktive, konkrete und radikale Kunst von Frauen von 1914 bis heute* [1995]) have expanded our knowledge of the subject still further.

Amazons of the Avant-Garde concentrates on studio paintings at the expense of the applied arts in which the six women also excelled, including designs for books, textiles, fashion, ceramics, and the stage. Inevitably, the focus reconfigures the total silhouette of their artistic careers, communicating some of the truth but not the whole truth, and inviting us to assume that studio painting was their most important activity (though ultimately, it probably was). Space limitations, availability of major works, and the exhibition's complex itinerary (four venues in as many countries) also dictates its scope and prompts an emphasis on the dramatic achievements of Cubo-Futurism and Suprematism rather than a loose survey of the life and work of each respective artist; for the same reasons, early and late works are missing from the exhibition, lacunae that are to be regretted, given the strong commitment of these women to Impressionism, Symbolism, and the return to order — in the form of European "Neo-Classicism" or Soviet Socialist Realism — in the 1920s through the 1940s. Ultimately, the selection of works was driven by the effect of the whole rather than that of the parts, and the idea of creating an applied-arts section or of including, say, six early and six late paintings paled before the vision of an iconostasis of iconoclastic paintings.

Dedicated to their art, these six women rarely formulated or championed particular social and political ideologies, although Goncharova, certainly, had strong opinions about traditional perceptions of women and the need for them to raise their voices, as she demonstrated in her "Open Letter" (see Documents section). While the force of their pictorial experimentation, their "career-mindedness," and their often unorthodox behavior might be interpreted as a protest against the status quo, we should be wary of imposing later political constructs upon them. They supported the idea of cultural renewal and rejected what they considered to be outmoded aesthetic canons, but apart from Goncharova's "Open Letter" their private statements contain few concrete references to the role of women vis-à-vis that of men in Russian society. In fact, their relationships with their male colleagues — Alexander Drevin, Mikhail Larionov, Kazimir Malevich, Alexander Rodchenko, Vladimir Tatlin, and Alexander Vesnin among them — seem to have been remarkably harmonious, collaborative, and fruitful, except perhaps in the case of Rozanova and poet Alexei Kruchenykh, whose romance was rocked by emotional and sentimental tempests.

At the same time, the ostensible ethical and social freedoms of these women cannot be regarded as typical of the conditions in Russia just before the October Revolution. They lived and worked within a small circle of relatives and friends and, however genuine their passion for national Russian culture (such as Goncharova's fascination with rural ritual and folklore), they had little to do with the "real" Russia — the peasants, urban workers, and revolutionaries — preferring to mix with the gilded youth of Moscow's bohemia or, paradoxically, with the rich and powerful of St. Petersburg.[6] It is also wrong to conclude that, if these Amazons enjoyed the respect of their advocates, friends, and lovers, all Russian men were just as unbiased and as unpatronizing in their assumptions about women. The traditional attribution of the qualities of ingenuousness, infantility, and innocence to women certainly continued through the 1910s: women were still expected to avert their gaze from "male shame" in statues that were considered too explicit,[7] and reviewers remarked that young ladies found the new art to be amusing (whereas, presumably, sensible citizens did not).[8] When one male reporter declared of Goncharova's 1913 retrospective that the "most disgusting thing is that the artist is a woman,"[9] he was expressing not only sexist shock at the fact that these overpowering Neo-Primitivist and Cubo-Futurist paintings were made by a woman, but also a profound despair at the need to suspend disbelief and invent a new critical language that would accommodate this implied displacement of criteria.

The Romantic attitude toward women and women artists as carriers of grace, beauty, and gentility — supported by critics such as Fedor Bulgakov[10] — quickly gave way to the newer metaphor of the creative virago and the militant Amazon. This inevitably evoked direct political associations with the so-called "Moscow Amazons" of the 1870s — women of the All-Russian Social Revolutionary Organization who had believed in violence, even assassination, as a real political instrument.[11] At the beginning of World War I, some Russians were asking why this Amazonian detachment could not be trained for military purposes: "Why can a woman be a doctor, an engineer, or an aviator, but not a soldier?" asked Vasilii Kostylev in an article entitled "Our 'Amazons'" in the Moscow *Zhurnal dlia khoziaek* (*Journal for Housewives*).[12] Other authors were perturbed by what they saw as the consequent "incurable disease of dichotomy, a disease that has appeared together with the so-called woman question, a dichotomy between the behests of reason and the profound essence of the purely female nature."[13] Such questions were discussed in the many lectures on the "woman question" that were held in Moscow and St. Petersburg. "Fables and Truth about Woman," presented by the actress Alexandra Lepkovskaia at the Polytechnic Museum, Moscow, on February 17, 1914, and its accompanying debate can be perceived as a summary of the new attitude toward women as an artistic force in Russian society at that time. She argued that the myth of woman as an enigmatic and mysterious creature had led men to the "most contradictory inferences and opinions,"[14] but that equal rights would cancel this image and a collective physiognomy would emerge, cleansed of "low intentions and impure passions."[15] Such thoughts may have seemed progressive to some of Lepkovskaia's respondents, but for the avant-garde poets and painters David Burliuk and Vladimir Mayakovsky, Lepkovskaia's speech was merely the "perfumed, boudoir logic of philistines," for neither man nor woman enjoyed real creative freedom, except in the bedroom.[16]

The strong contribution of women artists to Modern Russian art was soon noticed by critics outside Russia. Hans Hildebrandt, for example, emphasized the role of women artists in both studio painting and design in his *Die Frau als Künstlerinn* (1928),[17] and most of the early surveys of Russian Modernism draw attention to this fact. Writing in 1916, for example, Mikhail Tsetlin, a friend of Goncharova, claimed that "women have bequeathed to Humanity's Treasury of Art incomparably more than might be supposed. It is they who have been the unseen, unknown collaborators of art. It is they who made the lace, embroidered the materials, wove the carpet. They raised the artistic level of life by their aesthetic aspirations."[18] This plea for public and professional recognition of the anonymous artistic labor carried out by countless women as they sewed, stitched, and knitted is echoed in the attention that the Amazons gave to the applied arts, especially haberdashery. Malevich acknowledged his debt to this forgotten tradition when he declared, in describing the clothes and fabrics produced by Ukrainian peasant girls, that "art belonged to them more than to the men."[19]

The intention of *Amazons of the Avant-Garde* is not to imply that Exter, Goncharova, Popova, Rozanova, Stepanova, and Udaltsova supported a single artistic style, a single cultural tradition, or a single political ideology. On the contrary, just as the Russian avant-garde was a collective of disparate avant-gardes, so these artists were of different philosophical schools and had different social aspirations and aesthetic convictions. Here are six personalities, often in conflict, that do not constitute a homogeneous unit (even if Kruchenykh identified all modern Russian women as "half cats, combinations of tinplate and copper, domestic stuff and machines").[20]

Inevitably, this exhibition raises the often-asked question of why the women artists of the Russian avant-garde were ready, willing, and able to play such a primary role in the development of their culture. There have been many attempts to grapple with this issue and to expose the underlying causes for the freedoms that Exter, Goncharova, and Stepanova in particular enjoyed — in artistic belief, in everyday behavior, in geographical movement, and in sentimental relationships. But no critical commentary seems to be comprehensive or satisfactory, in part because the criteria that may function when applied to Europe and the United States fail when applied to Russia. That many women artists "were] dismissed as acolytes, seldom published their theories and allowed male colleagues to be their spokesmen"[21] may be true of the Western predicament, but certainly not of the Russian Amazons. Similarly, their creative energy cannot be explained by an alleged acceptance of the "initial support of the revolutionary forces,"[22] because these artists produced most of their avant-garde work before 1917 and at that point, at least, were not especially committed to raw political change. In many respects the Russian Amazons run counter to Western assumptions concerning the creative freedom of women artists and writers. If the Russian avant-garde can be accepted as a creative polemic between the two masculine poles of Malevich (composition) and Tatlin (construction), then Exter, Goncharova, Popova, Rozanova, Stepanova, and Udaltsova can be accommodated easily between these two poles and regarded as their strongest missionaries. Malevich referred to Udaltsova as the "best Suprematist," and invited her, not Ivan Kliun or Rodchenko, to teach with him at Vkhutemas; and when, in an issue of *Sinii zhurnal* (*Blue Journal*), he stated that he hoped "all artists would lose their reason," Exter promptly seconded his motion.[23]

Judging from circumstantial evidence, there seems to have been no professional jealousy between the male and the female factions in general or between partners in particular (Ksenia Boguslavskaia and Ivan Puni, Goncharova and Larionov, Popova and Alexander Vesnin, Rozanova and Kruchenykh, Udaltsova and Drevin). They painted and exhibited together, cosigned manifestoes, illustrated the same books, spoke at the same conferences, and seemed almost oblivious of gender differences and gender rivalry. Women were not discriminated against in the principal exhibitions, such as *Jack of Diamonds*, *The Donkey's Tail*, *Target*, *0.10*, and *Tramway V*, and in some cases the number of female participants was equal to or even greater than the number of men. (Six of the thirteen participants in *The Store* exhibition and three of the five in *5 x 5 = 25* were women.) Larionov not only encouraged Goncharova to paint and experiment with Cubism and Rayism, but he also played a practical role in the organization of her one-person shows in 1913 and 1914, gave her "exactly half the huge hall"[24] at *The Donkey's Tail* exhibition in 1912, and intended to devote the exhibition to follow *No. 4* of 1914—that is, *No. 5*—to another retrospective of her, not his, paintings.[25] True, in his *Manifesto to Woman* of September 1913, Larionov stated that he hoped women would "soon be going around with breasts totally bare, painted or tattooed" and that some would turn up like this at Goncharova's Moscow venue (which does not seem to have happened), but to be fair, he also distributed the onus of fashion, for he wanted men to shave asymmetrically, show their legs painted or tattooed, and wear sandals.[26] How different is this apparently serene and mutual respect from the attitude that the Italian Futurists advocated, with their explicit championship of masculinity and their "scorn for woman."[27] Not that the women associated with Futurism accepted this position, as they demonstrated in their *Manifesto della Donna futurista* of 1912: "Women, for too long diverted between morals and prejudices, turn back to your sublime instinct: to violence and cruelty."[28] As we can sense from Goncharova's *Letter to Filippo Tommaso Marinetti*, the Russian Amazons may well have subscribed to this same view, even if Popova did dedicate her *Italian Still-Life*, 1914 (plate 29) "to the Italian Futurists."

While Larionov helped Goncharova with practical advice, their mutual friend Ilia Zdanevich produced an outrageous fictional biography for her, delivering this as a lecture in St. Petersburg in March 1914, to coincide with her one-person show there. According to this fantasy, Goncharova met Claude Monet and Paul Cézanne, lived in a nunnery, and traveled in the East and to Madagascar to meet the bushmen before going on to the Cape of Good Hope, India, Persia, Armenia, and returning to Russia via Odessa.[29] But on other occasions Zdanevich also did much to explain the importance of Goncharova's painting, her attitude toward Cubism and Divisionism, and her integration of East and West, and urban and rural cultures.[30] The St. Petersburg physician, painter, and protector of the avant-garde Nikolai Kulbin supported Zdanevich, reasoning that the Realist works of Ilia Repin had once seemed as "savage" as the paintings of Goncharova did then.[31] Malevich was just as amenable to his female colleagues, inviting Popova, Rozanova, and Udaltsova to play major organizational and editorial roles in his unpublished journal *Supremus*, while Kruchenykh became Rozanova's diligent student as he composed his abstract collages for *Vselenskaia voina* (*Universal War*) in 1916 (see fig. 97).

How can the cultural prominence and social tolerance of the Amazons be explained? One answer to this question is to be found in the tradition of comparative freedom that Russian women artists had been enjoying toward the end of the nineteenth century. In 1871, for example, the Imperial Academy of Arts in St. Petersburg began to admit women students, welcoming thirty young ladies during that academic year, while the Moscow Institute of Painting, Sculpture, and Architecture quickly followed suit. These measures contributed directly to the formation of the first generation of professional Russian women painters in the 1880s, which included the silhouettist Elizaveta Bem (to whom Elizaveta Kruglikova was much indebted), Ekaterina Krasnushkina, Alexandra Mayakovskaya (sister of the celebrated *pompiers* Konstantin, Nikolai, and Vladimir), Olga Lagoda-Shishkina (wife of the landscapist Ivan Shishkin), and Emiliia Shanks, all of whom painted or etched in a competent, if not brilliant, manner. The legendary Mariia Bashkirtseva also belongs to this new generation of women artists, even though she spent most of her short creative life in France.[32]

The kind of narrative and didactic Realism that distinguished Russian art and literature in the 1880s and 1890s was soon replaced by a concern with decorative and aesthetic demands, an impulse that informed the development of the movement known as Neo-Nationalism or the Neo-Russian style, with its emphasis on the applied arts and industrial design. Russian women were largely responsible for the rapid expansion of this movement, stimulating the restoration of Russian arts and crafts, such as weaving, embroidery, wood carving, and enameling. For example, a principal stimulus of the diverse cultural achievements at Abramtsevo, Savva Mamontov's art retreat near the Orthodox center of Zagorsk, and, indeed, to the preservation and conservation of Russian antiquities in general, came from Mamontov's wife, Elizaveta Mamontova. By drawing attention to the Russian applied arts, Mamontova, together with the artists Natalia Davydova, Elena Polenova, and Mariia Yakunchikova, restored and appraised an entire cultural legacy and helped to build a platform upon which famous designers such as Lev

Bakst and Goncharova would launch the spectacular success of Russian stage, book, and fashion design in the 1910s and 1920s.

In this respect, the parallel accomplishments of the artist, collector, and patroness Princess Mariia Tenisheva deserve particular praise. Beginning in the late 1890s Tenisheva welcomed many distinguished artists, including Nicholas Roerich and Mikhail Vrubel, to her art colony, Talashkino, near Smolensk. As the Mamontovs had done to Abramtsevo, Tenisheva collected traditional arts and crafts, established workshops, designed and constructed a church, and financed her own intimate theater. A talented enameler and historian of the discipline,[33] Tenisheva promoted the patterns and leitmotifs of local Russian ornaments, integrating them with the sinuosity of Western Art Nouveau, a striking combination that was well in evidence in the Talashkino section at the Paris World's Fair in 1900.

Natalia Dobychina ran Russia's foremost private art gallery, the Art Bureau, between 1911 and 1919.[34] Situated on the field of Mars in St. Petersburg, the Art Bureau became a focus of contemporary artistic life, presenting many exhibitions and promoting numerous styles, from the extreme right to the extreme left. Dobychina herself was a no-nonsense manager who "dealt with the artistic Olympuses of both capitals as she would with her household ménagerie."[35] While profitting from fashionable painters such as Bakst, Alexandre Benois, and Somov, she did not hesitate to indulge in more provocative ventures. For example, the Art Bureau sponsored the Goncharova retrospective in 1914 and *0.10* the following year; included works by Chagall, Exter, Rozanova, and other radicals in its regular surveys; and supported soirées that included musical performances and poetry declamations. True, Dobychina was a merchant for whom material investment was perhaps more important than aesthetic commitment, but, nevertheless, she can be regarded as one of several important Russian patronesses or "facilitators" of the Modernist era whose activities exposed and publicized new ideas about painting, poetry, and music. Moreover, she stood up for her rights, protesting vociferously, for example, when "twelve paintings offending the religious feeling of visitors" were removed from the Goncharova show by the civic authorities.[36]

The Amazons of the avant-garde were distinguished by a similar championship of the new, as well as by a common sense and organizational spirit often lacking in their male colleagues. They expressed this synthetic talent not only in their disciplined, analytical paintings, but also in their ready application of ideas to functional designs such as books, textiles, and the stage.

Goncharova turned her very life into a work of art, painting her face and bosom, challenging the public, and exhibiting paintings that the Moscow censor deemed sacrilegious. "How great that, instead of Léon Bakst, you will become Russia's ambassador," declared Zdanevich, in a letter to Goncharova just before she left Russia for Paris, having been invited there by Diaghilev to design sets and costumes for his Ballets Russes.[37] Obviously, personal interaction with the public, whether provincial philistines or Parisian balletomanes, was of vital importance to her, and the performance of her life generated the most diverse responses. The reviews of her 1914 St. Petersburg retrospective indicate just how provocative Goncharova, as a woman artist, had become by then. On the one hand, Viktor Zarubin saw in her paintings "the disgusting, cross-eyed, crooked, green and red mugs of peasants,"[38] while on the other, Georgii Vereisky spoke of her "magnificent gift of color"[39]; Yakov Tugendkhold steered a middle course between violent censure and unmitigated praise, in one review identifying Goncharova as a "woman who lacks the ability and tenacity to bring things to their logical completion and who flitters from one easy victory to the next,"[40] and in another referring to her trials and tribulations as the "concentrated biography of the whole of contemporary Russian art."[41] In some sense Tugendkhold was right, for before she went to Paris and devoted her energies to stage design, Goncharova worked rapidly and impulsively, assimilating and refracting the most diverse aesthetic concepts. She left the "huge strength of Russia" for a "dry and pale Europe"[42] in 1914, at the apex of her career, before she had fully developed her interpretation of Rayism and abstract painting, which she left for her fellow Amazons Exter, Popova, and Rozanova to do.

Although Exter lived for extended periods in France and Italy, she maintained constant contact with the avant-garde in Moscow, St. Petersburg, and Kiev, and from the outset was an important intermediary between French Cubism and Simultanism and between Italian Futurism and Russian Cubo-Futurism, Suprematism, and Constructivism. As early as 1908, her paintings at David Burliuk's *Link* exhibition in Kiev stimulated a response that was typical of prejudices then and now: "Mr. Exter has daubed his canvas with unrelieved blue paint, the right corner with green, and signed his name."[43] While intended as a disparagement, this review emphasizes both the ultimate "transsexuality" of the Russian avant-garde and the real accomplishment of Exter's artistic system — that is, her almost physical love of color and paint. Even if tinged by the formal restraints of French Cubism and the linear dynamics of Italian Futurism, Exter's paintings manifest an extraordinary sensitivity to color and hence to the new concept of studio painting as an independent exploration of color consonance, dissonance, rhythm, and arhythmicality. As a follower of Suprematism from 1916 on, the "very bold" Exter[44] painted non-objective works that depended exclusively on spectral, planar contrasts for their effect.

Certainly, Exter was an accomplished studio painter, but her interest in pictorial construction and three-dimensional spatial resolution also brought her to the medium of the stage. Yet unlike many other artists — especially those who worked for Diaghilev's Ballets Russes, such as Bakst and Goncharova — Exter was drawn less to the illustrative or narrative functions of set and costume, regarding the latter, for example, as a "living moving relief, a living colored sculpture."[45] It was the whole idea of material construction, of space as a component of the composition, that attracted her, as is manifest in her designs for Alexander Tairov's 1916 production of *Thamira Khytharedes* and costumes for Yakov Protozanov's 1924 film *Aelita* (fig. 84). In her stage designs, Exter de-emphasized ornament, employed colored lights for dynamic effect, and attempted to transfer the kinetic element of Suprematist painting — the intersection and collision of colored geometric units — to the stage. It is easy to understand why she was so drawn to the cinema, with its kinetic denominator, its continuous interfusion of planes and volumes, and its formal definitions via gradations of light. Exter also tried to transmit this sensation of malleable space to her other design enterprises — marionettes, clothes, interiors, and books, all of which can be regarded as architectural exercises in the combination of volume, color, and tactility. As her Kiev student Alexander Tyshler said: "In her hands, a simple paper lampshade turned into a work of art."[46]

Like Exter, Rozanova was well aware of Italian Futurism, although unlike Exter, she did not travel in Italy and did not have an Italian companion (Exter and Ardengo Soffici were close friends). In her careful application of the Italian Futurist evocation of mechanical speed, explosivity, and mobility, Rozanova followed the same path as Malevich (as in his *Knife-Grinder,* 1912) and Kliun (as in his *Ozonator,* 1912–14), and her concurrent writings suggest, she regarded Futurism to be a key phase in the artistic evolution toward Suprematism. Rozanova expressed this impulse not only in her vivid, dynamic paintings, but also in what Yurii Annenkov described as the "black plumes of her drawing."[47] She used these "plumes" to decorate some of the most radical books of the Cubo-Futurists, especially those of Kruchenykh, including *Vzorval* (*Explodity*, 1913), *Vozropshchem* (*Let's Grumble*, 1913), and *Te li le* (1914); her drawings for these projects inspired Kruchenykh to call her the "first woman artist of St. Petersburg."[48]

Rozanova's visual deductions were calculated and formal, and she avoided the puns and puzzles that Goncharova applied to her Futurist paintings, such as *Bicyclist*, 1912–13 (fig. 54). In their force lines and collisions, Rozanova's evocations of the city in works such as *Man on the Street (Analysis of Volumes)*, 1913, and *Fire in the City (Cityscape)*, 1914 (plate 43) bring to mind Exter's parallel experiments, as in *Cityscape (Composition)*, ca. 1916 (plate 8). This process of deduction led Rozanova to her remarkable Suprematist pieces of 1916 on. As a leading advocate of a nonfigurative art form, she had no sympathy with those who remained behind: "Only the absence of honesty and of a true love of art provides some artists with the affrontery to live on stale cans of artistic economics stocked up for years, and, year in year out, until they are fifty, to mutter about what they had first started to talk about when they were twenty."[49] Rozanova was consistent and rational in her methodology, whether she was working on paintings, drawings, or book designs. Her premature death in 1918, said Annenkov, left "one less world in the universe."[50] Kliun wrote: "Her ever-searching soul, her exceptionally developed sense of intuition could never compromise with the old forms and always protested against all repetition, whether in everyday life or in art."[51]

If Rozanova traced her pictorial discipline to Italian Futurism, Popova and Udaltsova saw French Cubism as their main stylistic laboratory. Not interested in messianic philosophy or narrative anecdote, they regarded painting as painting. Even before their apprenticeship to Henri Le Fauconnier and Jean Metzinger in Paris, they accepted the aesthetic principles of one of their first Moscow teachers, Konstantin Yuon, for whom the important elements in painting were "architecture because of its definiteness, contrast, precision, and constructiveness . . . light because of its peculiar magical force . . . space because of its ability to transform, to universalize, to absorb everything tangible."[52] Popova's and Udaltsova's tenure at La Palette reinforced these basic assumptions, for they were now encouraged to perceive the object only in terms of form, texture, and coloration, to break the object into facets and to reassemble it, and to apply extraneous details of collage and verbal language in order to enhance the composition. A comparison of Popova's *Guitar*, 1914 (plate 30) and Udaltsova's *Guitar Fugue*, 1914–15 (plate 77) demonstrates how diligently and mechanically these two women learned their Cubist lessons.

French Cubism, of course, had an impact on many Russian artists, from Robert Falk to Malevich, from Vera Pestel to Tatlin, but Udaltsova was perhaps its most faithful practitioner. More than Popova, who "didn't understand much of what Le Fauconnier was saying,"[53] Udaltsova assimilated the formulae that Le Fauconnier and Metzinger were teaching: she accepted the Cubist vocabulary of guitars, violins, and nudes, repeated the restrained color schemes, and applied the faceting and foreshortening with fluency and ease. For Udaltsova, form, structure, and composition were the essence of studio painting, and she explored the Cubist style precisely as an exercise in analysis and "deconstruction," sometimes distributing Cyrillic characters to provide a Russian identity, as in *New*, 1914–15 (plate 79).

Like Popova, Udaltsova was aware of Italian Futurism, and her representation of rapid movements through space in *Seamstress*, 1912–13 (plate 74) — as in Goncharova's concurrent *The Weaver (Loom + Woman)*, 1912–13 (plate 21) — tell us that she was aware of Umberto Boccioni in particular. With their repeated lines, articulations, and dynamic trajectories, Udaltsova's larger canvases of the mid-1910s, such as *At the Piano*, 1915 (plate 76) come close to Popova's works (such as *Traveling Woman*, 1915 [plate 33]), and they already contain the linear emanations and collisions that she applied to her decorations for fabrics and accessories of 1916–18. Udaltsova's infrequent sallies into Suprematist painting are also distinguished by an emphasis on purely formal resolutions rather than by the cult of color that we associate with Malevich and Rozanova — in spite of her assertion that the "artists of today have arrived at the fundamental principle of painting: color (color-painting)."[54] Indeed, Udaltsova's role in the promotion of the Suprematist cause and the Supremus circle seems to have been more that of a theoretical custodian than that of a visual producer; while she welcomed "the freedom of pure creativity,"[55] she maintained her Cubist system, and her modest Suprematist compositions in watercolor and gouache can hardly compete with her major Cubist oils, such as *Kitchen*, 1915 (plate 84). It is surprising, therefore, that Udaltsova made an abrupt turn toward a kind of narrative Expressionism in the early 1920s, producing figurative works — portraits and landscapes — that rely upon new structures beneath heavy impasto and pulsating texture. After years of Cubist asceticism, Udaltsova suddenly discovered the density and consistency of paint. Pursuing a restrained table of color, Udaltsova and her husband, Drevin, came to share a common vocabulary and style, and by the 1930s they were painting in a very similar manner.

The formal discipline that Popova acknowledged in French Cubism was a clear inspiration to her architectonic paintings of 1916 on, although again it may have been Yuon who suggested the denotation to her, for he maintained that Modern art had returned to the "forgotten culture of the statics of form, i.e., painterly architectonics."[56] In any case, Popova's architectonic paintings are important for two reasons in particular: they are laboratory experiments in texture, weight, color density, and rhythm; and they are a modular series of exercises that both interconnect organically and seem to anticipate Popova's wider application of their forms to textile designs and book covers in the early 1920s. After all, these two qualities prompted Popova and her colleagues to organize *5 x 5 = 25* in 1921, and Vsevolod Meierkhold to recognize Popova's potential as a stage designer as soon as he saw her contributions to that exhibition.

Like Popova, Stepanova explored numerous stylistic formulae — from Art Nouveau to Suprematism — before reaching her interpretation of Constructivism, but her importance lies primarily in her theoretical and practical contributions to early Soviet culture. She was an active member of Inkhuk and Lef, taught at Vkhutemas, and participated in the radical exhibitions of 1919–21, such as *Tenth State Exhibition: Non-Objective Creativity and Suprematism*, *Nineteenth State Exhibition*, and *5 x 5 = 25*. Stepanova's writings indicate a vigorous curiosity and bold provocativeness that questioned and undermined conventional attitudes toward the fine arts, especially the established hierarchies of "high" and "low," fine and applied. Her participation in the ongoing debate at Inkhuk on construction ("centripetal" form) versus composition ("centrifugal" form), her ideas on texture, tectonics, and rhythm, her immediate recognition of utilitarian design as the only legitimate extension of abstract painting, and her commitment to book and textile design as primary elements of the new Soviet "look" make Stepanova one of the most uncompromising and aggressive champions of Soviet Constructivism.

As Stepanova herself asserted, she owed much to her husband Rodchenko, and her artistic career cannot be understood without reference to his concurrent inventions. But it would be misleading to regard her as merely a student or apprentice; rather, Stepanova and Rodchenko — like Goncharova and Larionov — should be accepted as an artistic team that functioned by interchange and interaction rather than by dominance and subservience. As a result, Stepanova's and Rodchenko's respective artworks are often similar in conception and medium, because they tended to share the same work space, fulfill the same commissions, use the same materials, and visit with the same friends (among them the filmmaker Esfir Shub and her husband, Alexei Gan; Vladimir Mayakovsky and Osip and Lilya Brik; and Popova and Alexander Vesnin). The formal parallels are especially striking in their collages and linocuts of 1918–20 (which often contain fragments from the same postcards and newspapers) and in their propaganda albums of the 1930s.

Even so, Stepanova's aesthetic and emotional approaches to the artistic process were very different from Rodchenko's, for she did not share his enthusiasm for minimal painting, the non-objective three-dimensional construction, or even photography (not that she avoided these mediums altogether). Rather, Stepanova advocated the primacy of the handmade or machine-made object, advocating a public art that could communicate and benefit its audience, such as book and stage design, textiles, and *prozodezhda* (professional clothing), even if her (and Popova's) projects for industrial production underwent substantial changes at the hands of the factory collective.[57] Perhaps this is why Stepanova emphasized the human figure, even in what she saw as her most radical paintings, such as *Dancing Figures on White*, 1920 (plate 65), for if these moving figures are streamlined and robotic, they still relate to a world of people working, playing, and dancing.

Symptomatic of Stepanova's outreach program was her reinvention and manipulation of verbal and visual language, in the combinations of phonic and semiotic systems that she constructed in her graphic or visual poetry of 1917–19. In her application and exploration of a transrational order of neologisms, as in *Rtny Khomle*, Stepanova was paying homage to the Cubo-Futurist *zaum* poetry practiced by Velimir Khlebnikov and Kruchenykh well before the Revolution and investigated also by avant-garde painters, including Pavel Filonov, Malevich, and Rozanova.[58] In fact, some of Stepanova's graphic designs are intended as illustrations of — or, rather, as complements to — Kruchenykh's *zaum* poetry (such as "Gly-Gly," see figs. 72, 102). In giving visual shape to Kruchenykh's and her own "words at liberty," Stepanova was creating an Esperanto that was universally (in)comprehensible in the same way that a baby's babbling or a dog's barking might be. The phonemes that Stepanova assembled in jazzy, kinetic compositions — "sherekht zist kigs mast kzhems usdr azbul gaguch chir gu za," and so on — elicit a savage primal sound from the dawn of civilization. Hers is a linguistic and visual Neo-Primitivism, consistent in its incomprehensibility, whose harsh and bewildering sounds — like a battle cry, a warning sign, or a siren — force us to listen and to look. These miniature syntheses of transrational verse and non-objective painting are among Stepanova's most audacious experiments in communication, and they undoubtedly prepared the way for her more celebrated applications of color to word in the form of her stage designs for Meierkhold's 1992 production of *The Death of Tarelkin* and Vitali Zhemchuzhnyi's *Evening of the Book* (1924).

After the October Revolution, the world of monumental propaganda and agit-design attracted many women artists. Sofia Dymshits-Tolstaya, wife of the writer Alexei Tolstoy and a student of Tatlin, helped with the decoration and illumination of Moscow for the first anniversary of the Bolshevik coup. Pestel, Udaltsova, and Elizaveta Yakunina also contributed to the decoration of the city streets and squares. Beatrisa Sandomirskaia, then a Cubist sculptress, designed a concrete statue of Robespierre for Lenin's Plan of Monumental Propaganda, but it was promptly destroyed by a grenade allegedly thrown by counterrevolutionaries. In some respects, the activities of the Blue Blouse theaters in the mid-1920s can also be regarded as an extension of agit-design, and Nina Aizenberg's simple, workaday costumes, like Tatiana Bruni's, must have appealed to the proletarian audiences.

But if women artists had been at the very center of the Russian avant-garde, they retired to the periphery of its counter-movements, Heroic and Socialist Realism, in the late 1920s and 1930s. Many accepted the doctrine of Socialist Realism and extended its directives in their works, among them Serafima Riangina's painting *Higher! Ever Higher!*, 1934, and Mukhina's enormous statue *Worker and Collective Farm Woman* on top of the Soviet Pavilion at the Paris World's Fair in 1937 (fig. 10). But these statements were the exception rather than the rule, for, by force of circumstances, the female Socialist Realists followed rather than led, illustrated rather than dictated. Their artistic victories were secondary and their works distant from the radicalism of Exter, Goncharova, Popova, Rozanova, Stepanova, and Udaltsova. Soviet women artists operated in a very different ambience from the women of the avant-garde, for the matriarchy of the Amazons was now replaced by a new hierarchical patriarchy, in which the male artist — whether Iosif Brodsky as Stalin's court painter or Alexander Gerasimov as president of the Academy — was again the person of privilege and power. But there is a historical and mythological consistency in this volte-face: after all, the Amazons had been the female warriors who had warred against the Greeks, the robust outsiders who had threatened and undermined the precise boundaries of a classical civilization. Obviously, with the abrupt return to order and the new classicism of Soviet art, such vandalous viragos, "primitive and childish,"[59] could no longer be tolerated — and they were not.

1. "Women of Genius" is the translation of *Genialnye zhenshchiny*, the title of an anonymous book on Mariia Bashkirtseva, Eleonora Duze, Sofia Kovalevskaia, and other Russian women (St. Petersburg: Vecherniaia zaria, ca. 1900).
2. Benedikt Livshits, *Polutoraglazyi strelets* (Leningrad: Izdatelstvo pisatelei v Leningrad, 1933), p. 143; Benedikt Livshits, *The One and a Half-Eyed Archer*, trans. John E. Bowlt (Newtonville, MA: Oriental Research Partners, 1977), pp. 128–29.
3. Bekhteev's *Battle of the Amazons*, 1914–15, is in a private collection in Paris; Yakulov's painting of the same title (1912) is in the collection of the State Picture Gallery, Erevan.
4. Andrei Somov, "Zhenshchiny-khudozhnitsy," in *Vestnik iziaschnykh iskusstv* (St. Petersburg: 1883), vol. 1, pp. 356–83, 489–524.
5. Alexei Novitsky, *Istoriia russkogo iskusstva* (Moscow: Mamontov, 1903), vol. 2, pp. 514–32.
6. The relationship between the Russian avant-garde and the "establishment" was an intricate and ambivalent one. While artists such as David Burliuk, Goncharova, and Larionov wanted to "shock the bourgeoisie," they also relied upon it for material support, promotion, and camaraderie. This is indicated not only by the fact that pillars of the establishment looked after the interests of the avant-garde (for example, the leading Moscow lawyer Mikhail Khodasevich defended Goncharova against accusations leveled by the Moscow Justice of the Peace in 1909), but also by the fact that avant-garde artists often had themselves photographed next to the rich and the titled.
7. According to Valentin Kurdov, even in 1918 the "naturalistic details" of Stepan Erzia's *Liberated Man* caused women to cover their faces and the local authorities to remove the statue. Kurdov, *Pamiatnye dni i gody* (St. Petersburg: Arsis, 1994), p. 15.
8. Boris Lopatin, "Futurizm-suprematizm" (1915), in Herman Berninger and Jean-Albert Cartier, *Pougny* (Tübingen: Wasmuth, 1972), p. 56.
9. Quoted by Mikhail Larionov in his review of Goncharova's one-day exhibition at the Society of Free Aesthetics, Moscow, March 24, 1909, at the opening of which three of her pictures were "confiscated" on grounds of "pornography": "Gazetnye kritiki v roli politsii nravov," *Zolotoe runo* (Moscow), nos. 11–12 (1909, appeared spring 1910), p. 97.
10. See, for example, Fedor Bulgakov, *Venera i Apollon* (St. Petersburg: Suvorin, 1899), and *Zhenshchina v iskusstve* (St. Petersburg: Suvorin, 1899).
11. See Richard Stites, *The Women's Liberation Movement in Russia* (Princeton: Princeton University Press, 1978), p. 141.
12. Vasilii Kostylev, "Nashi 'amazonki,'" *Zhurnal dlia khoziaek (Journal for Housewives)* (Moscow), no. 19 (October 1, 1914), p. 24.
13. *Genialnye zhenshchiny*, p. 2.
14. Quoted in "Skazki i pravda o zhenshchine," *Rannee utro* (Moscow), February 18, 1914.
15. Ibid.
16. Quoted in "Disput o zhenshchine," *Russkie vedomosti* (Moscow), February 18, 1914.
17. Hans Hildebrandt, *Die Frau als Künstlerin* (Berlin: Mosse, 1928).
18. Amari [Mikhail Tsetlin], "Natalia Goncharova," in Winifred Stephens, ed., *The Soul of Russia*

(London: MacMillan, 1916), p. 76.

19. Kazimir Malevich, "Glavy iz avtobiografii khudozhnika," in Vasilii Rakitin and Andrei Sarabianov, eds., *N. I. Khardzhiev. Stati ob avangarde* (Moscow: RA, 1997), vol. 1, p. 114.

20. Alexei Kruchenykh, *O zhenskoi krasote* (Baku: Literaturno-izdatelskii Otdel politotdela Kasflota, 1920), unpaginated.

21. Donna Stein, "The Turbulent Decades," in Stein, et al., *Women Artists in the Avant-Garde: 1910–1930*, exh. cat. (New York: Rachel Adler Gallery, 1984), unpaginated.

22. Rebecca Cunningham, "The Russian Women Artist/Designers of the Avant-Garde," *Theatre Design and Technology* (London), spring 1998, p. 50.

23. Malevich's and Exter's statements accompanied a photograph captioned "Paskha u futuristov" (Easter with the Futurists) in *Sinii zhurnal* (Petrograd), no. 12 (March 21, 1915), p. 9.

24. Varsanofii Parkin, "Oslinyi khvost in mishen," in Parkin et al., *Oslinyi khvost i mishen* (Moscow: Miunster, 1913) p. 55.

25. Mikhail Larionov, letter to Ilia Zdanevich, 1914, State Russian Museum, St. Petersburg, Manuscript Section (call no.: f. 177, ed. khr. 88, l. 12, verso). In the same letter Larionov writes that the exhibition after that, *No. 6*, would be devoted to Rayism.

26. "Manifest k muzhchine i manifest k zhenshchine," *Stolichnaia molva* (Moscow), no. 327 (September 15, 1913), p. 5.

27. Filippo Tommaso Marinetti, "Manifesto of Futurism" (1909), in Charles Harrison and Paul Wood, *Art in Theory 1900–1990* (Oxford: Blackwell, 1992), p. 147.

28. Valentine de Saint-Point, "Manifesto della Donna futurista" (1912), in Lea Vergine et al., *L'altra metà dell'avanguardia 1910–1940*, exh. cat. (Milan: Comune di Milano, 1980), p. 78.

29. Ilia Zdanevich, "N. S. Goncharova i vsechestvo" (October 1913), lecture delivered on March 31, 1914; State Russian Museum, St. Petersburg, Manuscript Section (call no.: f. 177, ed. khr. 15, ll. 1, 19, 22, 26).

30. See Ilia Zdanevich, untitled lecture on the occasion of Goncharova's retrospectives in Moscow and St. Petersburg; State Russian Museum, St. Petersburg, Manuscript Section (call no.: f. 177, ed. khr. 24).

31. Nikolai Kulbin, "Garmoniia, dissonans i tesnye sochetaniia v iskusstve i zhizni," in Ilia Repin et al., *Trudy Vserossiiskogo Sezda khudozhnikov v Petrograde 1911–1912* (St. Petersburg: Volike and Gilborg, 1914), vol. 1, p. 39.

32. For further information on Bashkirtseva's involvement in the movement for women's rights, see Colette Cosnier, *Marie Bashkirtseff: Un portrait sans retouches* (Paris: Horay, 1885), pp. 215–30. I would like to thank Tatiana Mojenock for providing me with this information.

33. Tenisheva wrote a dissertation on the subject of enameling, which was published as *Emal i inkrustasiia* (Prague: Seminarium Kondakovianum, 1930).

34. During the 1910s Dobychina also conducted a busy correspondence with Russian artists both at home and abroad, including Marc Chagall, Exter, Vasily Kandinsky, Kulbin, Larionov, and Rodchenko; see Russian National Library, Moscow, Manuscript Section (call. no.: f. 420, op. 13, ed. khr. 60). Apart from an anonymous article, "Slava zhizni," *Muzykalnaia zhizn* (Moscow), no. 3 (1993), p. 30, little else has been published on Dobychina.

35. Livshits, *The One and a Half-Eyed Archer*, p. 116.

36. "Udalenie kartin s vystavki," *Den* (St. Petersburg), March 17, 1914; unpaginated copy in Russian National Library, Moscow, Manuscript Section (call. no.: f. 420, o. 1, ed. khr. 32).

37. Ilia Zdanevich, undated letter to Natalia Goncharova, State Russian Museum, St. Petersburg, Manuscript Section (call. no.: f. 177, ed. khr. 57, l. 7).

38. Viktor Zarubin, "Futurizm i koshchunstvo," *Severnyi listok* (St. Petersburg), March 16, 1914; unpaginated copy in Russian National Library, Moscow, Manuscript Section (call no.: f. 420, o. 1, ed. khr. 32).
39. G. V. [Georgii Vereisky], "Vystavka Goncharovoi," *Teatr i iskusstvo* (St. Petersburg), no. 15 (April 13, 1914), p. 339.
40. Yakov Tugendkhold, "Vystavka kartin Natalii Goncharovoi," *Apollon* (St. Petersburg), no. 6 (1913), p. 71.
41. Yakov Tugendkhold, "Sovremennoe iskusstvo i narodnost," *Severnye zapiski* (St. Petersburg), November 1913, p. 153.
42. Natalia Goncharova, letter to Sergei Bobrov, February 13, 1917, Russian State Archive of Literature and Art, Moscow (call no.: f. 2554, op. 1, ed. khr. 28, l. 5).
43. Savenko, quoted in Alexei Filippov, "O vystavkakh," *V mire iskusstv* (Kiev), nos. 2–3 (1908), p. 30.
44. I. Chuzhanov, "Vystavki," *V mire iskusstv* (Kiev), nos. 14–16 (1908), p. 21.
45. "Kostiumy i dekoratsii Alexandry Exter," *Teatr-iskusstvo-ekran* (Paris), January 1925, p. 19.
46. Quoted in Olga Voronova, *V. I. Mukhina* (Moscow: Iskusstvo, 1976), p. 43.
47. Yurii Annenkov, "Teatr chistogo metoda" (ca. 1920), Russian State Archive of Literature and Art, Moscow (call. no.: f. 2618, op. 1, ed. khr. 14, L. 173).
48. Quoted in Vera Terekhina et al., *Olga Rozanova 1886–1918*, exh. cat. (Helsinki: Helsinki City Museum, 1992), p. 36.
49. Olga Rozanova, "Osnovy novogo tvorchestva i prichiny ego neponimaniia," *Soiuz molodezhi* (St. Petersburg), March 1913, p. 20; translated in John E. Bowlt, *The Russian Avant-Garde: Theory and Criticism, 1902–1934* (London: Thames and Hudson, 1988), p. 109.
50. Annenkov, "Teatr chistogo metoda."
51. Ivan Kliun, untitled essay, in *Pervaia Gosudarstvennaia vystavka. Katalog posmertnoi vystavki kartin, etiudov, eskizov i risunkov O.V. Rozanovoi*, exh. cat. (Moscow: Kushnerev, 1919), p. III.
52. Konstantin Yuon, *Avtobiografiia* (Moscow: GAKhN, 1926), p. 46.
53. Nadezhda Udaltsova, quoted in Voronova, *V. I. Mukhina*, p. 27.
54. Nadezhda Udaltsova, untitled article for *Supremus* (1917).
55. Ibid.
56. Yuon, *Avtobiografiia*, p. 24.
57. D. Aronovich, "Desiat let iskusstva," *Krasnaia nov* (Moscow) 11 (November 1927), p. 236.
58. For examples of this experimental poetry and commentary on it, see Jutta Hercher and Peter Urban, eds., *Erstens, Zweitens*, vol. I: "Dichtungen russischer Maler" (Hamburg: Material-Verlag, 1998).
59. The critic Osip Beskin used these terms in his description of Udaltsova's painting; see Beskin, *Formalizm v zhivopisi* (Moscow and Leningrad: Vsekokhudozhnik, 1933), p. 9.

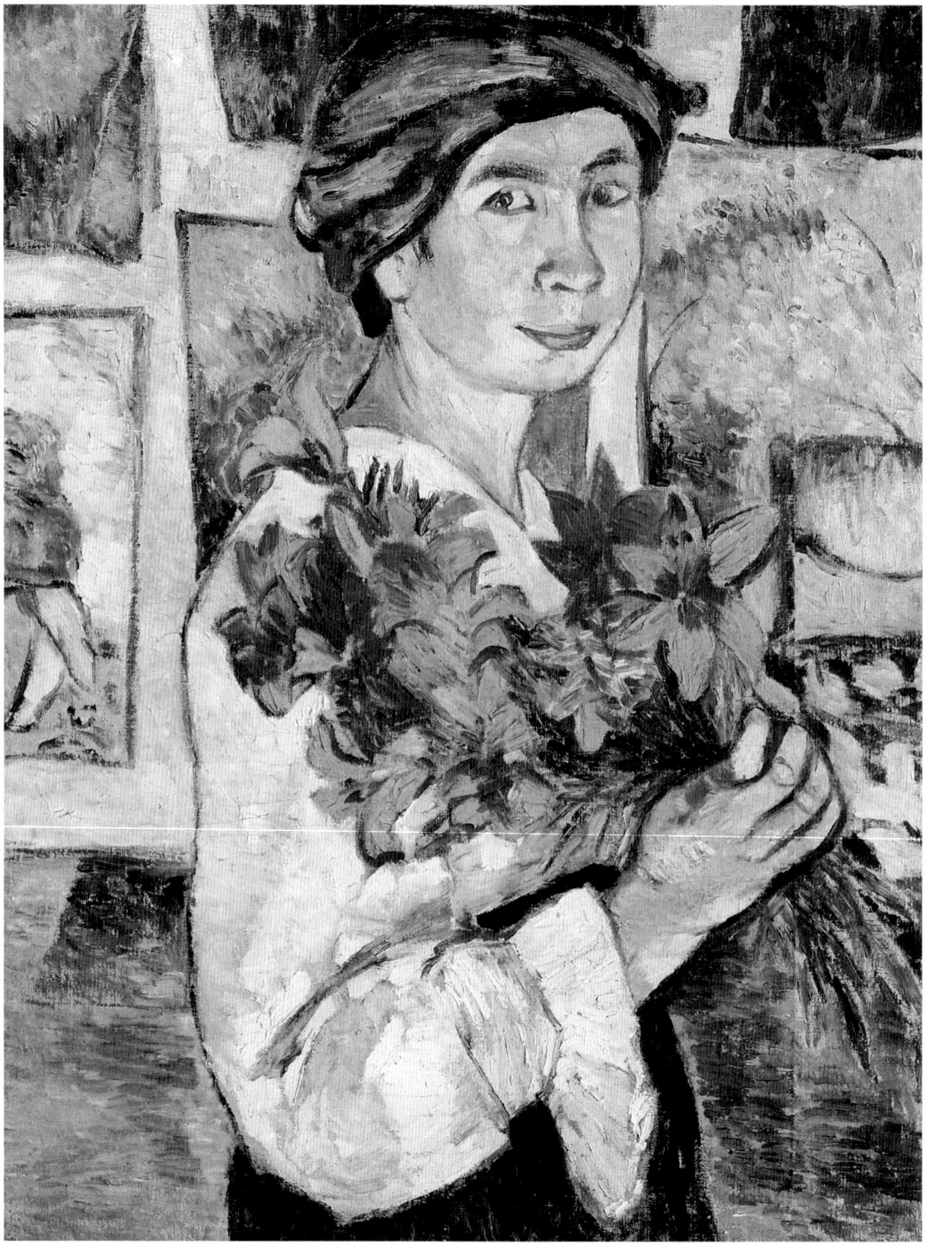

figure 3. NATALIA GONCHAROVA
Self-Portrait with Yellow Lilies, 1907
Oil on canvas, 77 x 58.2 cm
State Tretiakov Gallery, Moscow

six (and a few more) russian women of the avant-garde together

charlotte douglas

In Natalia Goncharova's *Self-Portrait with Yellow Lilies*, 1907 (fig. 3. plate 13) the painter stands before a wall chock-full of work, holding a bouquet of tiger lilies. She confronts the viewer without pretense, withholding nothing, directly and openly pleased with the paintings behind her. We see her plain, her hair held close to her head by a scarf. The feminine ruffle on her sleeve is countered by the awkward, muscular right hand emerging from it, a powerful hand, which seems only temporarily to have exchanged the painter's brush for orange flowers.

Goncharova gives us here a splendid image of the women of the Russian avant-garde: like the artist looking out at us from *Self-Portrait with Yellow Lilies*, most of these women were vital and direct, hardworking, competitive, and uncompromising in their view of themselves. As the subject of an exhibition they would seem the ideal group — women artists who lived in the same time and place, who knew each other, and whose art is substantial enough to merit the attention of even a male-privileged history.

Yet in looking at this exhibition the viewer should be cautious, for the show raises certain interpretive questions. On what basis can we treat these six artists as a "group"? There is no evidence that they considered themselves a separate category — "female artists" — and in fact they would certainly have considered such a distinction a form of marginalization. Their letters, diaries, and memoirs, as far as we know them, reveal little consciousness of gender identity, at least in terms of their art.[1]

Perhaps the best reason for isolating these women from their male colleagues is to enable us to consider in detail their striking successes and the centrality of their work in their time, which seem so unusual in the experience of the rest of the Western art world. Why, we want to ask — for our own sake — these women at this time in this place? It is an interesting historical question. Even so, we should not lose sight of the fact that the artists themselves would have felt it artificial to single them out, and quite beside the point. They accepted and worked almost completely within the male exhibition-and-sales paradigm, and they considered themselves artists first, zealous participants in a great aesthetic revolution. In this, a gendered identity seems to have played hardly any role at all.

But the viewer should take care not to judge these women — their identities as modern artists or their summary artistic merit — on the basis of paintings alone. As we view the exhibition we should remember that in no case did their artistic record consist only of painting; like many of their vanguard peers, they responded to the demands and interests of their times with a variety of artistic forms. True Modernists, who felt they could and should change the look of the world at large, they were stage designers, sculptors, photographers, and designers of books, textiles, and clothing. Therefore, I include here the activities of Alexandra Exter, Natalia Goncharova, Liubov Popova, Olga Rozanova, Varvara Stepanova, and Nadezhda Udaltsova beyond their engagement with the tradition of studio art.

An important question is how the women interacted. Did they know and identify with one another? Did they work together? Share artistic or other interests? Have similar experiences? Influence each other? Most shared a social class. Of the six artists in the exhibition, four were financially and socially secure. In their artistic activities Goncharova, Exter, Udaltsova, and Popova exercised the self-assuredness of the urban middle class; their male counterparts, by contrast, were more likely to be less well off and from the provinces. The friends and connections of the women undoubtedly offered certain advantages — in the reception of their exhibitions, in publicizing their work, and in the recruiting of potential patrons.

Goncharova was the oldest. A year older than Exter, four years older than Sonia Delaunay, five years older than Udaltsova and Rozanova, she served as a role model and set the stage for the others. Behind the deceptively demure exterior that looks out at us from old photographs of her was a delightfully irreverent, sexy woman, passionately outspoken about artistic matters. Goncharova sometimes favored an extremely low décolleté, sported trousers on occasion, and without any thought of marriage lived openly with the painter Mikhail Larionov. Her exuberance and directness scandalized society, and she often outraged critics and official guardians of public morals, who expectantly examined her art for evidence of hidden meanings. Such attention more than once hindered the progress of her career.

Goncharova's connection with future members of the avant-garde dates from

1906, when she was associated with the Symbolist journal *Zolotoe runo* (*Golden Fleece*) and also met the future impresario Sergei Diaghilev, who facilitated her entry into the Russian section of the Paris *Salon d'Automne*. The next year she joined a group of Symbolist painters, Venok-Stephanos (a coupling of the Russian and Greek words for "wreath"). With Larionov; Aristarkh Lentulov; Liudmila, David, and Vladimir Burliuk; Goncharova exhibited Impressionist still lifes and landscapes in December 1907 at the gallery of the Stroganov Art Institute in Moscow, an exhibition that moved to St. Petersburg the following spring. A year later, in November 1908, she, the Burliuks, and other colleagues from Venok-Stephanos joined with Exter, a graduate of the Kiev Art Institute, to produce an exhibition in Kiev that brought together young artists from Russia and Ukraine. Appropriately called *Zveno* (*The Link*), this exhibition was one of the first to unite key participants in the future avant-garde. Here, for the first time, works by Goncharova appeared with those of Exter.

The Link had significance beyond the presence of these two major women artists; it created an important connection between the Art Nouveau–inspired arts-and-crafts movement in Russia (associated with Maria Tenisheva's school in St. Petersburg) and the fledgling Russian and Ukrainian avant-garde. Over the next ten years, this early connection was to condition the association of applied-art and avant-garde styles. The number of women artists in *The Link* is remarkable: of a total of twenty-six artists, eleven were women. The group from St. Petersburg, led by Liudmila Burliuk, included Agnessa Lindeman and Erna Deters, already recognized for their Art Nouveau embroidery, and Natalia Gippius, a sculptor and one of the three talented sisters of the flamboyant and well-known Symbolist poet Zinaida Gippius. Other participants included the graphic artist Mariia Chembers (recently married to the artist Ivan Bilibin) and Evgenia Pribylskaia, like Exter a graduate of the Kiev Art Institute. Pribylskaia soon began to direct workshops in the Ukrainian village of Skoptsy that produced women's handwork, reviving traditional patterns and producing new folk designs.[2] In *The Link* Exter showed still lifes, pointillist scenes of Western Europe, and embroidery, an art form in which she also had a strong interest. From this time on she regularly exhibited embroidery and designs for embroidery alongside her painting. In succeeding years, she organized a group of women to produce abstract embroidery for avant-garde artists, including Sofia Karetnikova, Popova, Rozanova, and Kazimir Malevich.[3]

Both Exter and Goncharova pursued an active exhibition schedule with avant-garde groups in the major cities. Unlike Goncharova, who early in her career had personal and professional friendships with a variety of established artists, Exter from the first was drawn primarily to the developing avant-garde. After her graduation from the Kiev Art Institute and subsequent marriage to Nikolai Exter, a prominent Kievan lawyer, she threw her energies into a life of art both at home and abroad. The actress Alisa Koonen describes in her memoirs how different in nature and appearance the two women were, Goncharova seeming very Russian, Exter more Western. But they were similarly militant, she notes, when the conversation turned to questions or principles of art.[4]

Exter was part of *The Salon*, an exhibition of Russian and Western artists that opened in Odessa in December 1909, moved to Kiev in February 1910, and then on to St. Petersburg and Riga. Although Goncharova was not initially among the exhibitors, she managed to be added to the show when it reached St. Petersburg. In the spring of 1910, both women took part in the inaugural show of the Union of Youth, an association of progressive artists in St. Petersburg.[5] The Union, which included the female artists Elena Guro, Anna Zelmanova, and, from 1911, Rozanova, had wide-ranging interests, following German developments especially.[6] The direct emotion, economy of means, and bright color of painters such as Erich Heckel, Ernst Kirchner, Max Pechstein, and Kees van Dongen (a Dutch-born artist who exhibited with Die Brücke) particularly appealed to them. Up until 1912, when many Russian painters began to develop styles inspired by Cubism and Futurism, the German painters were an important source of inspiration for this wing of the avant-garde. Both Exter and Goncharova were also represented in the December 1910 exhibition of the Moscow Jack of Diamonds, an ad-hoc exhibition group organized late that year.

Goncharova would not travel abroad until 1914, but Exter was a consummate traveler, and beginning in 1908 she lived abroad for months at a time. Her frequent travels between Russia and the West — Switzerland, France, Italy — provided subjects for the Post-Impressionist studies of the Swiss countryside and the Paris streets that she brought to exhibitions in Kiev and St. Petersburg. It was Exter who was often responsible for the Russian avant-garde's almost instantaneous information about the contents of the most recent Paris shows, or about the latest discussions on Cubism. In Paris she worked at the studio of Carlo Delvall, at the Académie de la Grande Chaumière, and maintained her own studio as well. She came to know everyone — Guillaume Apollinaire, Georges Braque, Fernand Léger, Pablo Picasso, Ardengo Soffici — and was readily accepted in Western exhibitions. During her time in Paris, Exter also met Sonia Delaunay, who moved in the same circles. Delaunay too had been born in Ukraine, but as a child she had been adopted by a wealthy aunt and uncle and was then brought up in St. Petersburg. After her marriage to Robert Delaunay, she maintained a household in Paris that was particularly welcoming to Russian and Ukrainian artists, who visited the Delaunays and sometimes stayed with them for lengthy periods.

After the first *Jack of Diamonds* exhibition closed, in January of 1911, several of its organizers filed the documents necessary to incorporate the "Jack of Diamonds" as an official artists' organization.[7] Goncharova and Larionov withdrew, however, sensing their lack of control of the group, and instead began plans for a new organization that would emphasize their particular interests, and in which they would clearly be the leaders. David Burliuk and Lentulov took over as the organizers of the Jack. Neither Goncharova, Exter, nor for that matter any other woman was among the signatories of the Jack's registration papers.

Exter sent seven works to the second *Jack of Diamonds* exhibition, which opened late in January 1912. The show also included the German artist Gabriele Münter and other contributors to the contemporaneous second exhibition of the Blaue Reiter group in Munich. In connection with the Moscow exhibition, Burliuk arranged evenings of lectures and debates,[8] and toward the end of the first of these, as audience members were participating in a discussion, Goncharova made a dramatic entrance and objected loudly to the artist Nikolai Kulbin's characterization of her as a member of the Jack of Diamonds. In fact, she declared, she belonged to the "Donkey's Tail"! The audience burst into laughter. "There is no reason to laugh at the name. First see the exhibition when it opens — then laugh. To laugh now is ignorant."[9] Goncharova then gave a long disquisition on the origins of Cubism and its relation to primitivism, and claimed to have been the first Russian Cubist. She also criticized the Jack of Diamonds for artistic conservatism, excessive theorizing, and weakness of subject matter. A few days later she repeated her accusations in long letters sent to several newspapers.

Goncharova's performance was smart publicity: a month later, when The Donkey's Tail group exhibited for the first time, at the Moscow Institute of Painting, Sculpture, and Architecture, there was great anticipation. The exhibition, a combined show with fifteen members of the Union of Youth, included some half a dozen women, most notably Rozanova. Goncharova was the only woman in The Donkey's Tail section of the show, but this was compensated for by the size of her contribution — she exhibited fifty-four works.

The alliance of The Donkey's Tail and the Union of Youth brought Goncharova and Rozanova into many of the same exhibitions. Rozanova had sent eight works to the Union of Youth section of *The Donkey's Tail* exhibition that March, and Goncharova participated in The Donkey's Tail section of the Union of Youth's December show in St. Petersburg. Both artists contributed strong paintings, yet radically different ones: Goncharova was then pursuing an interest in peasant themes and naïve art, while Rozanova's style was quick and expressive, and her subjects were urban.

Goncharova and Larionov introduced Rayism (sometimes known as Rayonism), their new, near-abstract style of painting, at *The Target* exhibition in March 1913. Anecdotal history says that the Rayist Manifesto, though written by Larionov, had been instituted by Goncharova.[10] At the same time, Goncharova was preparing a solo exhibition, a survey of her works from the preceding ten years.

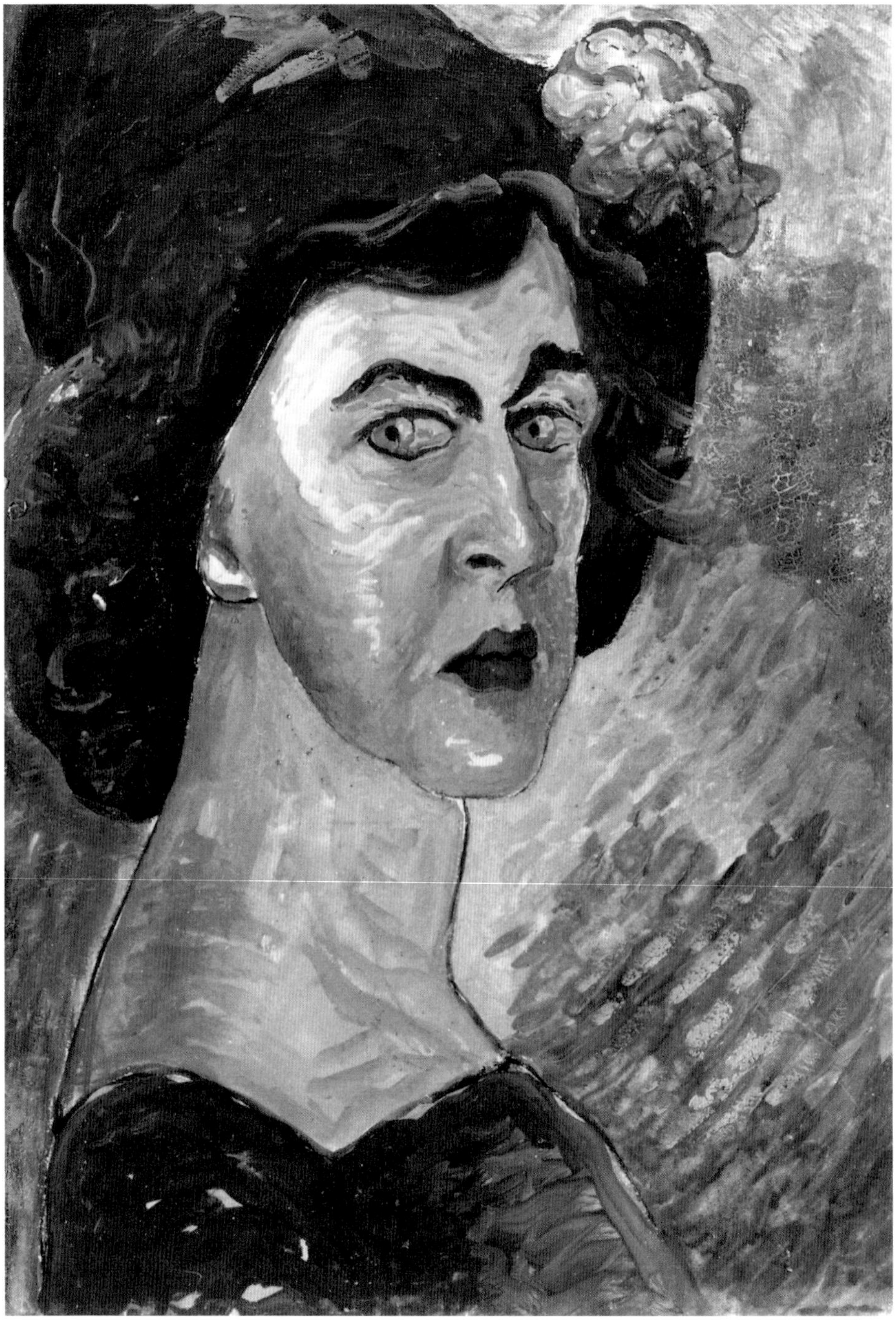

figure 4. MARIANNE WEREFKIN
[Marianna Verevkina]
Self-Portrait I, 1910
Tempera on cardboard, 51 x 34 cm
Städtische Galerie im Lenbachhaus, Munich

Opening in fall 1913, the show presented a staggering 760 artworks in a variety of media and styles — oils, pastels, tempera, primitive, Rayist, Cubo-Futurist, Egyptian.[11] The following spring, 250 of the works went to St. Petersburg for another solo show. The exhibitions were a highlight of the season, and impressive enough to reverse critical opinion of the avant-garde in general and Goncharova in particular. Goncharova, Diaghilev wrote, "has all St. Petersburg and all Moscow at her feet."[12]

The years 1912 to 1914 were also successful in terms of exhibitions abroad for Goncharova, and for Exter as well. Both had good contacts in Western Europe, Exter through the French, the Italians, and many Russians living in Paris, Goncharova through Vasily Kandinsky, Diaghilev, and, in London, the artist Boris Anrep. For these two years Exter led an active life divided between Russia and Western Europe, contributing to at least sixteen exhibitions in Kiev, Moscow, Paris, Brussels, and Rome. In March 1912, she was exhibiting at the Salon des Indépendants in Paris, and in October half a dozen of her works could be seen in the same city at the *Section d'Or* exhibition at the Galerie de la Boëtie. While Exter's work was on view at the Salon des Indépendants, Goncharova was exhibiting at the Hans Goltz gallery in Munich, the second Blaue Reiter exhibition; that same year, she also showed in Berlin (at Der Sturm) and in London, in the *Second Post-Impressionist Exhibition*, which opened in October at the Grafton Galleries.[13] In April 1913, works by Goncharova and Marianne Werefkin (Marianna Verevkina) were shown at the *Post-Impressionism* exhibition in Budapest, and both artists, as well as Delaunay and Münter, took part in the first *Herbstsalon*, which opened in Berlin in September. Exter and Delaunay appeared together at the March 1914 Salon des Indépendants show; a month later Exter and Rozanova, along with Kulbin and Archipenko, sent work to Rome for an exhibition at the Galleria Futurista.

Such frequent exposure gave Goncharova and Exter currency as members of the Western art world as well as the Russian one. Most certainly, their reception abroad influenced their later decisions to emigrate. The younger women artists were less well-known in the West; in fact, with the exception of Rozanova's single entry in the Rome exhibition, World War I and subsequent political upheavals prevented them from showing their work in Western Europe for the next eight years.

Goncharova and Exter began their careers unknown to one another; Popova and Udaltsova were close friends from their student days. Together with several other young women artists — Vera Mukhina, Vera Pestel, Liudmila Prudkovskaia (Udaltsova's sister), and Sofiia Karetnikova (born Til) — they now formed an alliance of female artists, which had its beginnings in Moscow's studio schools.

Private studios were crucial to the history of Russian art. For a major part of the future avant-garde, they were places of incubation, places where aspiring artists in their late teens and early twenties — middle-class women in particular — not only got to know one another but found common purpose, supported and inspired one another, and developed into mature artists. Between 1905 and 1908, Udaltsova (her last name was then still Prudkovskaia), her sister Liudmila, Popova, Pestel, and Mukhina attended the Moscow school run by the talented artist Konstantin Yuon and his colleague Ivan Dudin.[14] (Udaltsova and Pestel arrived first, in 1905 and 1906 respectively, and were followed in 1908 by Liudmila Prudkovskaia, Popova, and Mukhina.)[15] At the school Popova became a close friend of Prudkovskaia, and the two sometimes spent summers together. When the urbane Hungarian artist Károly Kiss arrived in Moscow (from Munich, in 1909) and opened a studio school, Udaltsova, Pestel, and Karetnikova immediately transferred to his tutelage.[16]

The women were an intense and energetic group. Yuon was a great admirer of the Post-Impressionists, and his students were *au courant.* They attended Moscow and St. Petersburg exhibitions, read the latest journals, and studied Post-Impressionism as it became possible to see it in Russian exhibitions and private collections. They were well acquainted with Sergei Shchukin's famous collection;[17] Udaltsova was particularly attracted to Gauguin. There is no doubt that the women developed together during this period, provoking and influencing one another. Mukhina, for example, credits Popova with deepening her basic aesthetic understanding:

> It was Popova, who first began to reveal to me the essence of art. Until then I conveyed only what I saw. But if an artist conveys only what s/he sees, s/he is a naturalist. One has to convey what one feels and knows. She made me understand that. She taught me to look at color, at the relationship of colors in the Russian icon, for example. Everything new touched her. She loved to talk about a work of art. I began to see.[18]

Even early in their lives and careers these artists were far from untraveled provincial young women; while still teenagers they had been exposed to the sights and major museums of Western Europe. In 1904, when she was just fifteen, Mukhina had traveled throughout Germany; Pestel traveled to Italy and Germany in 1907; Udaltsova in 1908 went to Berlin and Dresden; Popova had gone with her family to Italy in 1910. So it is not surprising to find Yuon's former students assembling on their own in 1912 for the winter season in Paris. Popova, Pestel, Udaltsova, and Karetnikova left Moscow for Paris late in 1912. (Liudmila Prudkovskaia missed the trip because she was ill.) The women stayed at a pension run by one Madame Jeanne, where Exter was already living.[19] Their apparent freedom, which may seem to us somewhat surprising, was due in part to the fact that

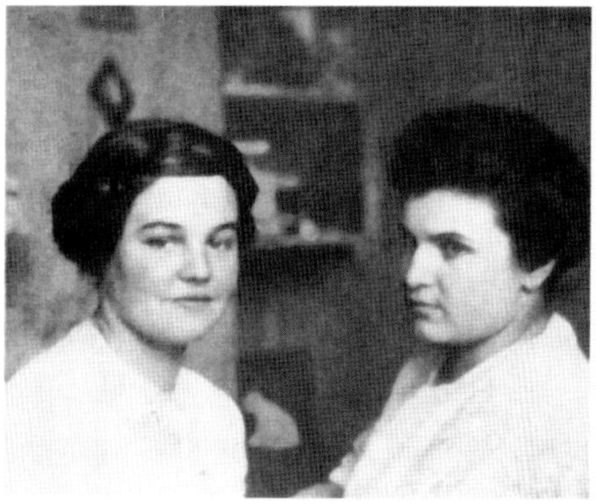

figure 5. Vera Mukhina with Iza Burmeister, Paris, 1912–13.

three of the four — Udaltsova, Pestel, and Karetnikova — were by that time already married.[20] They were young matrons of means, and marriage afforded them a certain independence: not only did their reputations no longer require very close supervision, but it was assumed that a married woman had the social protection of her husband. Perhaps equally important, it was common for women of propertied families to receive their inheritance and investment income upon their marriage. For the sake of propriety, as well as to help the women with domestic chores, the unmarried Popova brought along on the trip her former governess, Adelaida Dege.

Popova, Karetnikova, and Udaltsova enrolled at La Palette, where Henri Le Fauconnier, Jean Metzinger, and André Dunoyer de Segonzac gave lectures and weekly criticism. There the artists acquired the basis of the Cubist construction that would mark their mature work. Strangely enough, however, they had not made the trip with this in mind. Udaltsova would remember, "Our intention had been to work with Matisse, but his school was already closed, so we went over to Maurice Denis's studio. But there we ran into an Indian with feathers sitting against a red background and we fled. Someone then told us about La Palette, the studio of Le Fauconnier. We went there and immediately decided that it was what we wanted." [21] They studied the work of Picasso, Renaissance artists at the Louvre, and applied art at the Musée Cluny; and they made the obligatory visit to Gertrude Stein.

Mukhina also came to Paris at this time, and studied sculpture with Émile-Antoine Bourdelle at the Académie de la Grande Chaumiére.[22] Under Popova's influence she took time from her sculpting at Bourdelle's to learn Cubist drawing at La Palette: "Popova talked a lot about the Cubists, praised them, and grew quite excited. Behind it you could feel something great. I was bothered by the question, whence and why? Why do people think in a certain way?" [23] In the spring of 1913, Popova and Udaltsova returned to Moscow; but first Popova and Mukhina made a brief trip to Palus, in Brittany, to take advantage of Madame Jeanne's summer accommodations. They were accompanied by Boris Ternovets — another resident of Madame Jeanne's, and Mukhina's fellow student at Bourdelle's.[24]

Udaltsova would not return to Paris. Her mother died in September 1913, and she was left with the care of her younger sisters, including Liudmila, who was by

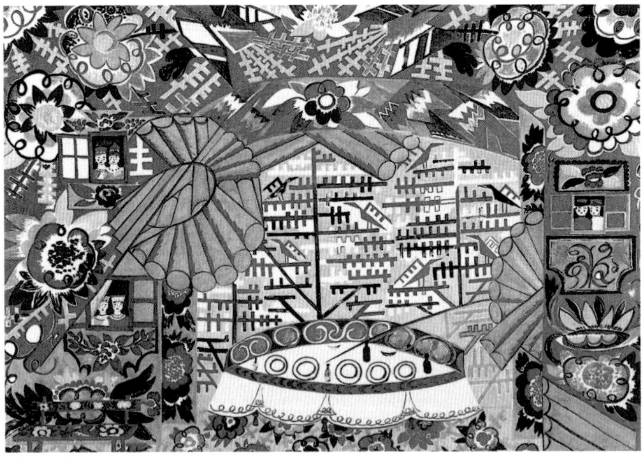

figure 6. NATALIA GONCHAROVA
Curtain design for *Le Coq d'Or*, 1914
Watercolor on paper, 53.3 x 73.7 cm

that time seriously ill. Popova, however, was back in Paris by mid-April the next year, to join Mukhina and sculptor Iza Burmeister on a tour of France and Italy.[25] The three women traveled to Nice, Menton, Genoa, Naples, Paestum, Florence, and Venice, and spent two weeks in Rome, everywhere sketching, painting, and exploring Gothic and Renaissance architecture.

While they were away, Goncharova arrived in Paris to attend the gala opening of *Le Coq d'Or* at the Opéra. It was her first time in the city, and the spectacular sets and costumes she had created for this ballet-opera were a dazzling success. They were her first theater designs; the commission had been a direct result of her ambitious 1913 retrospective. Within a month after the opening of *Le Coq d'Or*, an exhibition of more than fifty of Goncharova's paintings, along with a smaller number of works by Larionov, opened at the Galerie Paul Guillaume.[26] Apollinaire, in his catalogue essay, called her art "a revelation of the marvelous decorative freedom that has never ceased to guide Oriental painters amid their sumptuous treasure of forms and colors."[27] Apparently Goncharova chose not to go to London with the company to attend the English premiere at the Theatre Royal in Drury Lane.[28] At the outbreak of the war, she and Larionov were taking a holiday, and her boldly orchestrated move into the Western art world was cut short by their hasty departure for home.

The wartime isolation of Russian artists had an enormous effect on avant-garde art there; now denied any possibility of travel and any firsthand knowledge of Western art activities, their aesthetic lives seemed to concentrate and intensify. During the disastrous military campaigns of 1915 and 1916, women made significant innovations in artistic style and character. With the exception of Goncharova, who suddenly left for Switzerland in response to a summons from Diaghilev, and Stepanova, who had not yet penetrated avant-garde artistic life in Moscow, the women showed together for the first time in the *Tramway V* exhibition, which opened in Petrograd early March 1915. Exter, Popova, Rozanova, and Udaltsova exhibited their very personal varieties of Cubo-Futurist work. The following

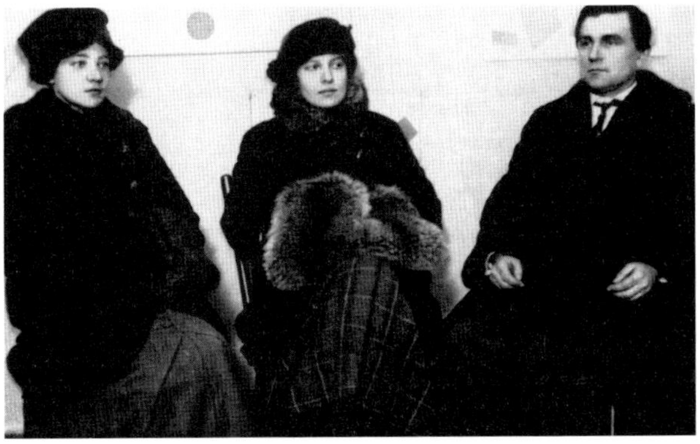

figure 7. Olga Rozanova, Ksenia Boguslavskaia, and Kazimir Malevich seated in front of Malevich's Suprematist paintings at the *0.10* exhibition, Petrograd, 1915.

December, Pestel, Popova, Rozanova, and Udaltsova were four of the six women in the historic *0.10* exhibition in Petrograd, and in February, Exter, Pestel, Popova, and Udaltsova were shown in the storefront space of *The Store* in Moscow. Surely a habitual gallery-goer, by this time, might mistakenly have consolidated them into a female "group."[29]

World War I was an impetus to work in applied art. Rural villages were hit extremely hard by the war, and women attempted to lessen the burden through the production and sale of handwork. At the same time, the design of fabric by professional artists also increased. In November of 1915, when the *Exhibition of Contemporary Decorative Art* opened at the Lemercier Gallery in Moscow, it showed forty items designed by Exter; embroidery by Ksenia Boguslavskaia; embroidered pillows and scarves by Boguslavskaia's husband, Ivan Puni; four handbags and eleven designs for embroidery and other items by Georgii Yakulov (who may have been inspired to take up this work by his prolonged visit with the Delaunays in Paris two years previously, just when Sonia was working on her Simultanist clothing); and handwork by Natalia Mikhailovna Davydova and Evgenia Pribylskaia. Malevich contributed designs for two scarves and a pillow. Most of the needlework was done by the women from Skoptsy and Verbovka.

At the *Exhibition of Industrial Art* in Moscow in late 1915–early 1916, avant-garde designs appeared together with the Symbolist and Style Moderne work of the Abramtsevo and Talashkino art colonies. These included Art Nouveau fabric designs by Lindeman and others; Abramtsevo's Art Nouveau and neo-folk dishes, vases, and ceramic mythological creatures; and dress designs, pillows, lampshades, handbags, and decorative appliqué by Pribylskaia, Exter, and Boguslavskaia. The catalogue points out the artists' ambitious plans to produce wallpaper, printed textiles, and book endpapers.

In Russia, 1916 was a difficult year, and the means for producing cloth became increasingly unavailable. Handwork was still possible, however, and throughout 1916 and 1917 the avant-garde continued to create designs for needlecraft.

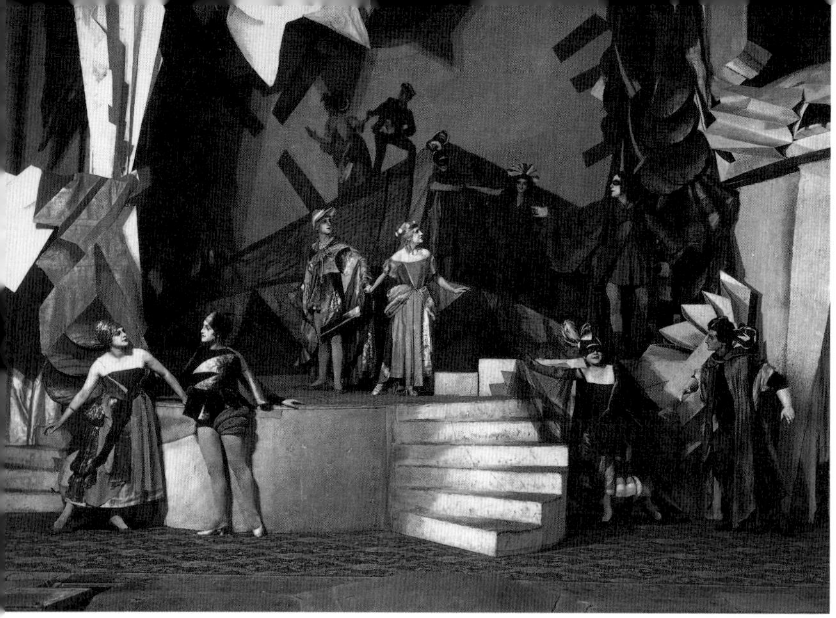

figure 8. Act I of *Romeo and Juliet*, Chamber Theater, Moscow, 1921, with sets and costumes designed by Alexandra Exter.

Hundreds of handwork designs appeared in 1916, produced by virtually every member of the avant-garde. Several major exhibitions included this work. After the *0.10* show closed at the beginning of the year, Davydova, Pestel, Popova, Rozanova, and Udaltsova joined Malevich in an attempt to propagate Suprematism through a journal they called *Supremus.* This periodical was never published, falling victim to the war and finally to the February Revolution, but a section on applied Suprematism was planned for it, and here the women intended to publish designs featuring embroidered Suprematist logos.

In winter 1917, Davydova organized the *Second Exhibition of Decorative Arts* of the Verbovka group. It opened at the Mikhailova Art Salon in central Moscow on December 6 in the midst of massive strikes and demonstrations and stringent rationing of bread. The artists from the earlier Verbovka show were now joined by the new Suprematists Pestel, Popova, Rozanova, and Udaltsova. The sewing was done by the village women. Of the four hundred items shown, many of the fabric designs were based on the visual vocabulary developed in the Supremus Society, being translated from painting or collage. This exhibition was followed by the *Contemporary Art* show, which opened before the end of the year with an entire section of embroidery, and by the *Decorative-Industrial Exhibition*, which included porcelain and embroidered items. The Verbovka group made another appearance in Moscow in 1919 at a joint exhibition of the Free Art Workshops (Svomas) and several other applied-art organizations, showing avant-garde fabric decorations, pillows, scarves, and handbags.

During World War I the Russian theater was a malleable refuge from the real world, which, as the German offensive intensified, became increasingly depressing and deadly. In the progressive theater, two great directors, Alexander Tairov and Vsevolod Meierkhold, supplied competing aesthetics and objectives, and in 1915 and 1916 — the darkest years of the war — the work of Exter, Goncharova, Mukhina, and Popova contributed much to Tairov's brilliant new Chamber Theater

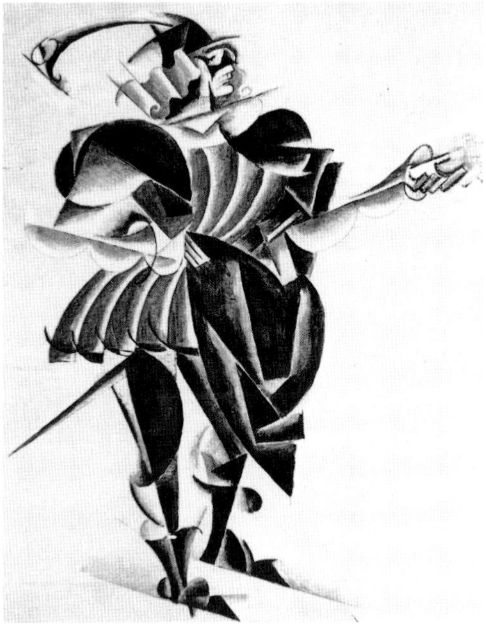

figure 9. LIUBOV POPOVA
Romeo in a Mask, costume design for
Romeo and Juliet, ca. 1920
Gouache on paper, 38.5 x 31.5 cm
Private collection, Moscow

in Moscow. Though relatively small, the theater offered an opportunity to create environments out of costumes, sets, and lighting; and at a time when war and revolution were creating great privation, it gave major scope to the artists' vision.

Theater continued to be a major site of artistic innovation into the 1920s. At a time when the avant-garde no longer saw painting alone as a viable artistic option, theater afforded a way to communicate directly with a new "democratic" audience on topics of immediate social relevance. At the same time, it offered artists a wide scope for invention. Between 1917 and 1924, Exter, Goncharova, Popova, Mukhina, and Stepanova produced hundreds of designs for theatrical costumes and sets. Not all the projects were realized, of course, and when a production was proposed, it was not always clear from the beginning who would be the chosen artist. Both Exter and Popova worked extensively on *Romeo and Juliet* for the Chamber Theater; and while Stepanova designed *The Death of Tarelkin* for Meierkhold's studio, Exter designed the same play for the studio of the Moscow Art Theater. The artists worked in close partnership with singers, actors, dancers, and directors, and in the resulting productions the visual element assumed a prominent, often primary role.

Exter returned to Moscow from a year-and-a-half-long interlude in Kiev during fall 1920, and to the shock of many she married again. Georgii Nekrasov was a minor actor four years her senior; old friends considered him beneath her station in life, and added responsibility for her in a difficult time. But Nekrasov proved a faithful mate, supportive of her art, and helpful in practical ways. For the Chamber Theater, Exter took up a project she had dropped three years earlier: decor for *Romeo and Juliet*, which she had last worked on in the less complicated days of the summer of 1917. Popova too began to develop ideas for the play, both women responding to Tairov's interpretation of Shakespeare's tragedy in purely theatrical terms, as the clash of ancient elemental forces, rather than as a historically based psychological drama. Indeed, Tairov had cautioned against too much verisimilitude. The characters don't have to be young or old, he said; "women can substitute for men, and vice versa." [30] The two sets of designs, though very different from one another, suggest that the two women were well aware of each other's sketches and developed ideas back and forth in competition.

It was Exter's designs that were produced. On May 17, 1921, the curtain rose on *Romeo and Juliet* to reveal an elaborate Italianate decor (see fig. 8); while making no detailed reference to any specific period or place, the artist hoped to convey a feeling she remembered from her visits to Venice and Florence. Popova's watercolors for *Romeo and Juliet* show similar scrolling, but the space is more clearly articulated; where Exter's designs are colorful and exuberant, Popova's are precise and restrained. Exter's figures are the result of her work on rhythm and motion with Bronislava Nijinska and Tairov, Popova's are reminiscent of her Cubo-Futurist painting of 1915 and 1916 (see fig. 9). Exter's set became an active player in the plot of the play, as Popova's schematic and revolving construction would be the next year for Meierkhold's production of Fernand Crommelynck's *The Magnanimous Cuckold* in 1922.

Stepanova too would work in the theater. The youngest of the six women, she was also unlike most of them in that she came from a working-class background; while she was growing up, her mother had worked as a maid. After marrying Dmitrii Fedorov, a young architect, Stepanova had spent three years at the very reputable Kazan art school. Here she began to write poetry, work as an artist, and exhibit. In the spring of 1914 she returned to Moscow, without finishing her art education, and began to support herself by working as a seamstress, typist, and bookkeeper in a hardware store. At the same time, she continued to study art, at the Yuon/Dudin school and at the school of Mikhail Leblan. In 1916, having left her husband, she began to live with Alexander Rodchenko, a similarly impoverished young artist with whom she had fallen in love at the Kazan art school. They would remain a couple for the rest of their lives.

Even after moving to Moscow, Stepanova drew and wrote in an Art Nouveau style influenced by English artist Aubrey Beardsley. She was introduced to avant-garde art only in 1916, but she progressed quickly; her works on paper from 1917 and 1918 might be considered a last bright spark of Russian Cubo-Futurism. She also began to write "transrational" or "non-objective" poetry, and to produce some of the most delightful and successful, and at the same time radical and abstract, artist's books. Her move into book graphics followed the path of Sonia Delaunay and Rozanova, but her work is distinctive in its own right.

The October Revolution did away with the private shops and offices in which

Stepanova had made her living, but the various art institutions established by the Soviet government provided her with a new means of livelihood. Soon after the Revolution, she took on administrative duties as a deputy director of the Literature and Art Subsection of IZO Narkompros. At the same time, she served on the Presidium for the Visual Arts of the artists' professional union, Rabis. Between 1920 and 1925 her position on the arts faculty at the Academy for Social Education gave her an opportunity to work out her artistic ideas with students. When Inkhuk was formed, in 1920, she was one of its founding members, and served as academic secretary during its organizational phase.

Popova, Stepanova, and Udaltsova took leading roles in the Inkhuk discussions of the social significance, purpose, and "laws" of art. The two-part *5 x 5 = 25* exhibition in September and October 1921 demonstrated their conclusions. The exhibition's title was indicative: on one level it meant that five artists — Exter, Popova, Stepanova, Alexander Vesnin, and Rodchenko — contributed five works for each show, but the mathematical equation also gave notice of practical aims. These shows were to be the artists' concluding statements in painting and graphics; they were meant to be mined for their utilitarian ideas.

Udaltsova did not take part; she had given birth to a son just weeks earlier.[31] There was also another reason, however: she strongly disagreed with the Constructivists' resolution to abandon easel painting in favor of more practical art forms. In fact, Udaltsova and artist Andrei Drevin left Inkhuk and spent the next years painting in a productive new style, in search of a way out of the formal and theoretical dead end that seemed to them inherent in Constructivism.

After the defining *5 x 5 = 25* exhibitions, Exter, Popova, and Stepanova began to expand Constructivist principles onto the stage. This move coincided with the culmination of the avant-garde's withdrawal from psychologically oriented theater influenced by the introduction, by Meierkhold and others, of techniques borrowed from the circus, vaudeville, popular reviews, and film. Meierkhold and sympathetic critics defended the new theater as a move away from the elitism of the pre-Revolutionary stage, an appeal to the public through genuinely democratic forms.

The close relationship between Popova and Stepanova was cemented by the work both did for Meierkhold's theater. Their productions played in close proximity. Popova's set for *The Magnanimous Cuckold*, with its slides and ladders, revolving doors and large rotating wheels, made its debut at Meierkhold's Free Studio at the State Higher Theatrical Workshops on April 25, 1922. The collapsing furniture and turning human "meat grinder" that Stepanova invented for *The Death of Tarelkin* appeared on November 24, at the GITIS Theater; and from November 28 to December 3, 1922, the two productions played alternate evenings in a double bill. Both Popova and Stepanova were listed as "constructors" of their respective creations.

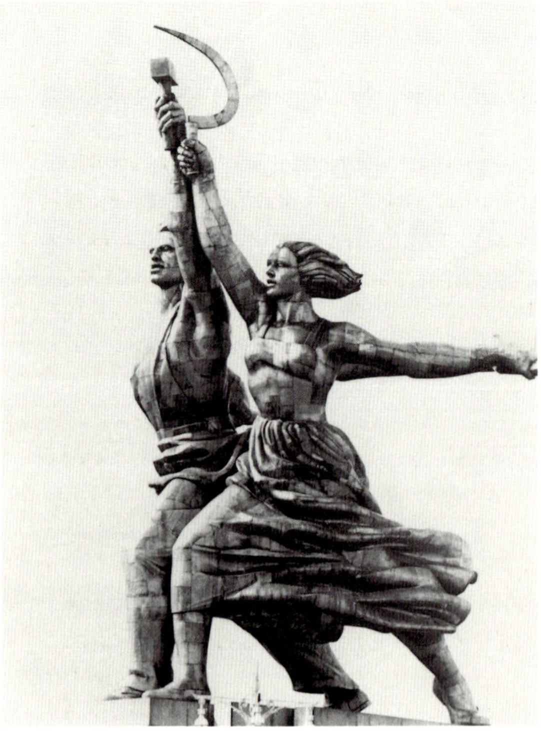

figure 10. VERA IGNATIEVNA MUKHINA
The Worker and the Collective Farm Woman, 1937
Stainless steel, 24 meters high

Goncharova had left Russia during the war, well before the Revolution, and did not return when she might have. Exter remained in Russia while her mother was still alive, and while she could eke out a living; she prudently left for Paris in 1924, when the nature of the Soviet regime, her art, and her origins put her in jeopardy. In Western Europe the careers of both women ultimately foundered. Karetnikova, Pestel, Popova, Rozanova, Stepanova, Udaltsova at first threw themselves into artistic work under the stringent conditions of the Revolution and the Russian Civil War, but with varying results. Rozanova and Popova died in 1918 and 1924 respectively, of diseases brought on by war, revolution, and the collapse of the country's infrastructure. Udaltsova survived, but her father did not; he was shot by revolutionary functionaries in September 1918. Her sister, Liudmila, died three weeks later, the result of her long illness; and Udaltsova's husband, Drevin was executed in 1938 as an "enemy of the people."

As the 1920s proceeded, the post-Revolutionary avant-garde gradually lost its ascendancy, first falling victim to the political fundamentalism of younger artists and their own ready abandonment of fine art. By the late 1920s and early 1930s, economic and political pressures and physical threat did away with almost all innovation in the arts. In the end, women were exposed to the same random and harsh fates of so many at the time. In the late 1920s and early '30s Stepanova did photomontage for books and journals extolling the state. During the Stalinist terror she turned to painting landscapes and still lifes. She and Udaltsova lived quietly in

Russia, publicly playing down their involvement with the avant-garde and keeping their thoughts to themselves and their intimates. Of the other women mentioned in this essay, Mukhina was recognized by the regime for her sculpture *The Worker and Collective Farm Woman*, which stood atop the U.S.S.R. Pavilion at the Paris World's Fair in 1937, but she and her son were briefly arrested, and her husband, Alexei Zamkov, a physician, was imprisoned and exiled. Karetnikova was arrested in the 1930s and sent to Siberia; her husband and son were also arrested and died in captivity. When she heard about the death of her son, Karetnikova committed suicide.

Is Russian art history, as seen from the point of view suggested by the lives and practices of these women artists, sharply different from the male experience? Not very. They participated in the same historic exhibitions, sought the same kinds of success. Perhaps greater weight should be given to their work in stage design: Exter, Goncharova, Popova, and Stepanova are all responsible for notable innovations in the theater. And textile design plays a greater role in their artistic profiles than in the male paradigm. Collectively, they had more experience in Western Europe than the men in the movement, although it is clear that their greatest opportunities came at home, during World War I and the Russian Civil War. While friendly with one another to varying degrees, they could also be bitterly competitive — a circumstance in which they are also no different from their male counterparts. In fact, if we now see these women as belonging to a different category from the men, it is because we are accustomed to seeing male artists as the norm, and women as somehow deviant from it. There is some evidence that the same attitude initially held true in regard to the women themselves, but such comments became rarer with time, as society was inundated by war and revolution. Perhaps, as they wished, we should simply consider them superb artists.

1. The letters and diaries of various Russian women artists have now been published, usually by their families. Most of the published versions have omissions and ellipses, however, and are generally not forthright about the basis of such exclusions. After 1991, there was little reason to omit the artists' expressions of their political sentiments, but Russians are still apt to be reticent about publishing anything of a personal or sexual nature, or political views that might be embarrassing to families or living persons.
2. After the Russian Revolution, Evgenia Pribylskaia would organize the crafts section of the 1925 *Exposition Internationale des Arts Décoratifs et Industriels Modernes*, in Paris.
3. On embroidery and the Russian avant-garde, see Charlotte Douglas, "Suprematist Embroidered Ornament," *Art Journal* (New York) 34, no. 1 (April 1995), pp. 42–45.
4. Alisa Koonen, *Stranitsy zhizni* (Moscow: Iskusstvo, 1975), p. 225.
5. The show included a number of other women, among them Mariia Chembers, Elizaveta Kruglikova, Anna Ostrumova-Lebedeva, and Marianne Werefkin. Non-Russian women included Marie Laurencin, Gabriele Münter, and Maroussia (Lentovska).

6. Elena Genrikhovna Guro (1877–1913) was a writer, poet, and painter; she died at an early age, of leukemia. Anna Zelmanova exhibited extensively in Russia before the Revolution, then later lived in the United States. She died in 1948.
7. G. G. Pospelov, "Stranitsa istorii 'Moskovskii zhivopisi,'" *Iz istorii russkogo iskusstva vtoroi poloviny XIX–nachalo XX veka* (Moscow: Iskusstvo, 1978), p. 92.
8. David Burliuk spoke on "Cubism and Other New Directions in Painting," and Nikolai Kulbin on "Free Art as the Basis of Life."
9. Benedikt Livshits, *Polutoraglazyi strelets: stikhotvoreniia, perevody, vospominaniia* (Leningrad: Sovetskii pisatel, 1989), p. 363.
10. Mikhail Larionov himself did not inspire confidence about his work. Composer Igor Stravinsky, who knew the couple well, said of Larionov, "He made a vocation of laziness, like Oblomov, and we always believed that his wife did his work for him." Igor Stravinsky and Robert Craft, *Conversations with Igor Stravinsky* (Berkeley and Los Angeles: University of California Press, 1980), p. 99.
11. The exhibition was held in the Art Salon at 11 Bolshaia Dmitrovka, Moscow.
12. Sergei Diaghilev, quoted in M. Chamot, "The Early Work of Goncharova and Larionov," *Burlington Magazine* (London), June 1955, p. 172.
13. Goncharova sent three major works to the "Second Post-Impressionist Exhibition": *The Evangelists*, *A Street in Moscow*, and *The Grape Harvest*.
14. Vera Mukhina also worked in the studio run by the sculptor Nina Sinitsyna. Konstantin Yuon was a member of the Union of Russian Artists and active in the Society of Free Aesthetics. He and Ivan Dudin opened their studio for classes in 1900.
15. The women were at Yuon's in the following years: Nadezhda Udaltsova 1905–08, Vera Pestel 1906–07, Liubov Popova and Liudmila Prudkovskaia 1908–09, Mukhina 1908–11.
16. Károly Kiss was born in Arad (now Romania) on October 24, 1883; he died in Nagybnya (now Baia Mare, Romania) on May 30, 1953. He studied at Nagybnya, Munich, and Budapest, and his name is listed among students at the Nagybnya free school for 1902 and 1903. In 1904 he was among Hollósy's students in Munich. During World War I, Kiss was interned in Moscow for four years as an enemy alien. After returning home, he withdrew to Vilgos, near Arad, and in 1931 he settled at the artist's colony in Nagybnya. See Jenö Muradin, *Nagybnya: A festötelep müveszei* (Miskolc, Hungary, 1994). The author thanks Katalin Keseru and Oliver Botar for pointing out this information.
17. Sergei Shchukin, a Moscow industrialist, was collector of an extraordinary number of works by Gauguin, Matisse, and Picasso, among others, before World War I. His collection now forms the core of the Post-Impressionist holdings of the Hermitage in St. Petersburg and the Pushkin Museum of Fine Arts in Moscow. He opened his mansion to local artists and students for study on Sundays.
18. Mukhina, quoted in N. Voronov, "Umolchaniia, iskazheniia, oshibki. K biografii V. I. Mukhinoi," *Iskusstvo* (Moscow), no. 11 (1989), p. 20.
19. Madame Jeanne catered to her Russian clientele by serving Russian food.
20. Udaltsova had been married in October 1908, to Alexander Udaltsov.
21. Udaltsova, "Moi vospominaniia. Moia khudozhestvennia zhizn," in Ekaterina Drevina and Vasilii Rakitin, *Nadezhda Udaltsova: Zhizn russkoi kubistki. Dnevniki, stati, vospominaniia* (Moscow: RA, 1994), p. 10.
22. Other young women from Moscow at Émile-Antoine Bourdelle's school included Iza Burmeister, Sofia Rozental, and Nadezhda Krandievskaia. On the many Russian students at Bourdelle's see

Alexandra Shatskikh, "Russkie ucheniki Burdelia," in *Sovetskaia skulptura* (Moscow), no. 10 (1986): 211–34.

23. Mukhina, quoted in Voronov, "Umolchaniia, iskazheniia, oshibki: K biografii V. I. Mukhinoi," p. 19.
24. The trip was made in May. Boris Ternovets was a young sculptor from Moscow; after the Revolution he became the director of the Museum of the New Western Art. He had moved to Paris in February, from Munich, where he had been a student of Simon Hollósy. See L. Aleshina and N. Yavorkaia, eds., *B. N. Ternovets: Pisma. Dnevniki. Stati* (Moscow: Sovetskii khudozhnik, 1977), p. 58.
25. Iza Burmeister, also from Moscow, was a sculptor and friend of Mukhina at Bourdelle's. They remained in Paris after Udaltsova and Popova returned to Moscow.
26. *Le Coq d'Or* premiered on May 24, 1914. The exhibition was open from June 17 – 30.
27. Guillaume Apollinaire, quoted in Leroy C. Bruenig, ed., *Apollinaire on Art 1902–1918* (New York: Viking, 1972), p. 413.
28. The premiere was on 15 June, 1914.
29. Other women in *The Store* show were Sofia Tolstaia (later Dymshits-Tolstaia) and Marie Vassilieff (Vasileva).
30. Alexander Tairov, quoted in Georgii Kovalenko, *Alexandra Exter* (Moscow: Galart, 1993), from Pavel Markov, ed., *A. Tairov, Zapiski rezhissera: Stati. Besedy. Rechi. Pisma* (Moscow: VTO, 1970), pp. 287–88.
31. Udaltsova's and Alexander Drevin's son Andrei was born on August 26, 1921.

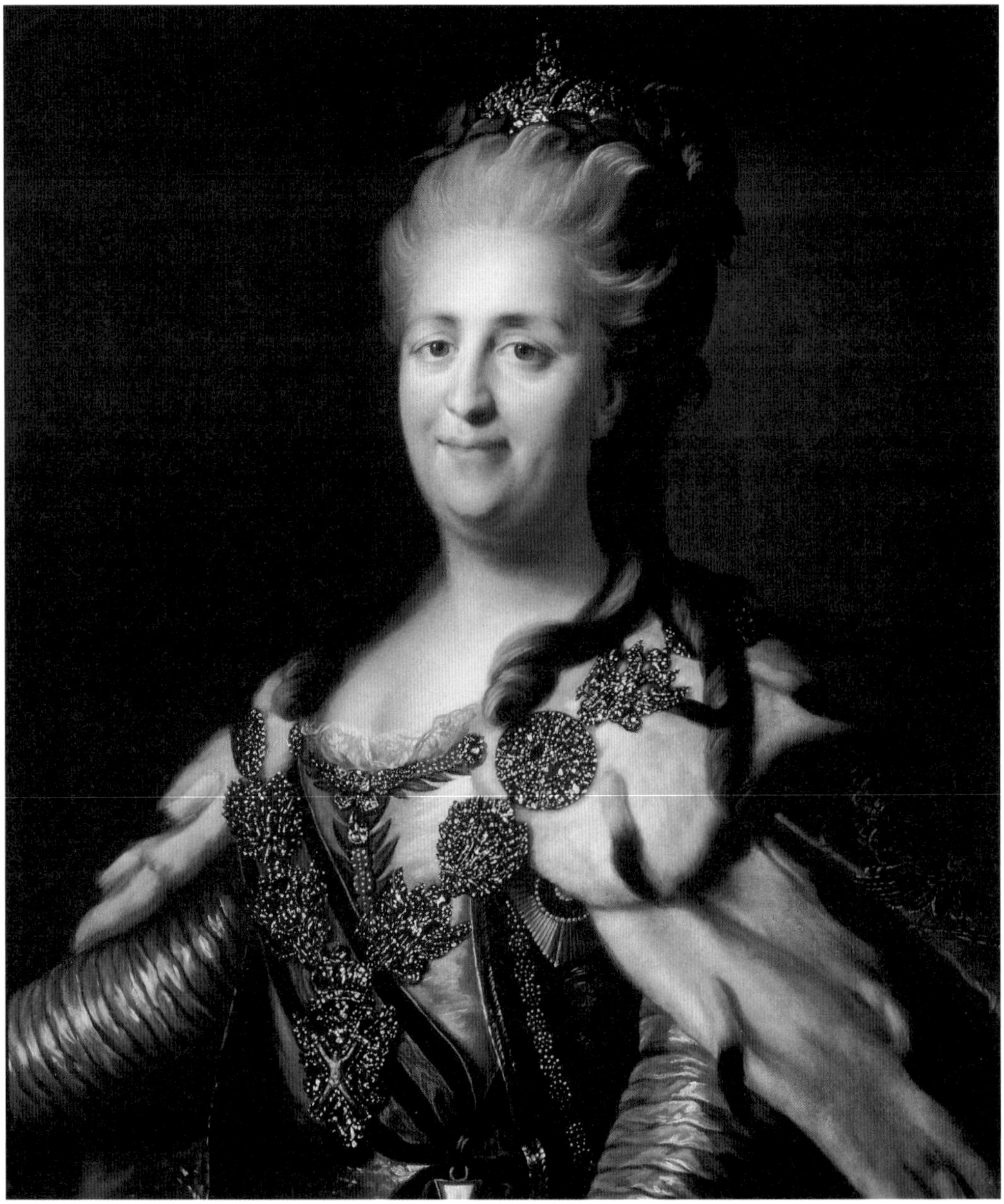

figure 11. Anonymous artist, *Empress Catherine II of Russia*, 1729
Oil on canvas, 85.8 x 68 cm
Portraitgalerie, Schloss Ambras, Innsbruck, Austria

Between Old and New: Russia's Modern Women

Laura Engelstein

The artists featured in this exhibition came of age in turn-of-the-century imperial Russia. When, in 1917, the autocracy collapsed under the strain of war and social unrest, they had already launched important artistic careers. How surprising, it would seem, for an old regime that clung to the values and public institutions of a preindustrial time, inhibiting both the free expression of ideas and the free activity of its subjects, to have presided over the emergence of a vital modernist culture. Even more surprising, perhaps, that women, in such circumstances, should have played so prominent a role in the production of artistic modernity. Yet Russian women in some ways benefited from the mixture of traditionalism and innovation that characterized the old order in its encounter with the modern world.

Peter the Great (r. 1682–1725) was not the first Russian ruler to appropriate elements of European culture and statecraft to enhance the power and welfare of the realm. Yet Russians came to associate his dramatic program of state-driven cultural change with the onset of the modern age. When Peter "opened the window to Europe," in Alexander Pushkin's phrase, the emperor inaugurated a new era for women as well. Court ladies, he declared, were to begin appearing in public alongside their men.[1] Rejecting tradition, even in the matter of succession, Peter had his wife Catherine crowned empress. Whether he intended her to rule in her own right was unclear, but after his death she occupied the throne for two years, and female monarchs ruled Russia for most of the rest of the eighteenth century, culminating in the reign of Catherine the Great (r. 1762–1796), who rose to power by conniving in the murder of her husband, Peter III (r. 1762). Among her other notable actions, she appointed a woman as president of the Russian Academy of Sciences and was herself the first patron of the St. Petersburg Academy of Arts after its official incorporation in 1764.

Paul I (r. 1796–1801), Catherine's resentful son, changed the law of succession to exclude women. The monarchs who followed him invented a new traditionalism, asserting their masculinity on the parade ground and advertising their devotion to family life.[2] High-born ladies continued, however, to play a role in court politics. The Tver salon of Ekaterina Pavlovna (1788–1818), the sister of Alexander I (r. 1801–1825), attracted the leading conservatives of the period. In the opposite political direction, the forward-looking bureaucrats who shaped the Emancipation and Great Reforms of the 1860s discussed their plans in the drawing room of Grand Duchess Elena Pavlovna (1807–1873), a woman of culture, intellect, and wide-ranging interests, who used her fortune to sponsor artists, scholars, and intellectuals, as well as contributing to policy debates.[3] Such figures were an exceptional handful even within the country's tiny educated elite, which comprised less than 3 percent of a population of 125 million at century's end. Ordinary women were restricted in their public roles by convention, limited education, and exclusion from civil service.

At the beginning of the twentieth century, the vast majority of Russians still lived in the countryside, where patriarchy was the backbone of communal life. Households and villages were run by senior males. Compared to peasant wives and daughters, husbands and sons had greater mobility and wider access to urban life, schools, and other avenues of cultural improvement. Among the peasantry, 29 percent of men could read, against a mere 10 percent of women. By 1913, only 21 percent of the somewhat better-off female factory workers were literate.[4] It is not surprising, then, that critics of the regime cited the peasant woman's lot as the emblem of all that was unjust and outmoded about the traditional social order.

The theme of women's oppression had a pedigree dating back to the generation of the 1840s, when philosopher Alexander Herzen (1812–1870) wrote eloquently of the damage inflicted on the privileged as well as the dispossessed by the operation of absolute power. He, and later Nikolai Chernyshevskii (1828–1889), used the theme of women's subordination to symbolize the problem of hierarchy and domination in the polity at large. Rejecting patriarchal mores and bourgeois moralism alike, they advocated equality of the sexes and freedom of sexual expression as intrinsic to the project of social transformation. In the 1860s, the generation that came of age after the Great Reforms proudly rejected established values in the name of science and social change. Young women cropped their hair, wore dark clothing, and spent their time reading — preferably philosophical tomes. Some followed the lead of Vera Pavlovna, the heroine of Chernyshevskii's novel *What Is to*

Be Done? (1863), entering marriages of intellectual convenience or ménages à trois and running workshops for lower-class women. Advocacy of women's rights became a hallmark of the emergent intelligentsia.[5]

These attitudes evolved into the fervent Populism of the 1870s, as educated young people, including numerous women, dispersed to the villages, preaching popular self-liberation. When the resolutely patriarchal common folk spurned all talk of revolution, the radicals resorted to violent means. Vera Zasulich (1849–1919) achieved celebrity by shooting a public official for having mistreated a political prisoner. Acquitted by a jury in 1878, Zasulich was applauded as a symbol of resistance to oppression. Among those involved in the assassination of Alexander II (r. 1855–1881), Sofia Perovskaia (1853–1881), a general's daughter, became the first woman executed for a political crime.[6]

As the Populists tried unsuccessfully to mobilize a popular following, the village life they wanted to preserve was increasingly threatened by industrial development, the growth of cities, and cultural change. Market forces created new opportunities for peasant women but also eroded their moral stature. While some found work in textile mills or as domestic servants, others trafficked in abandoned babies or in their own bodies, to the distress of Populists and moral reformers alike.[7] By the 1890s an exploited working class had joined the impoverished peasantry at the bottom of the social pyramid. In this context, nostalgic agrarianism seemed increasingly out-of-date. Embracing capitalism as a necessary stage on the way to socialist revolution, Marxists displaced Populists in the ideological ranks. The campaign for class justice now left little room for the cause of sexual equality.

The woman's issue had never been the monopoly of radicals and young people, however. Calls for women's education, professional opportunity, and civil rights came from a range of figures in state service, high society, and the cultural elite. In the wake of the Crimean War (1854–1856), the educator and physician Nikolai Pirogov (1810–1881) endorsed the training of women as nurses. In the 1870s, the Ministry of War, under Dmitrii Miliutin (1816–1912), admitted women to its medical academy. Post-Reform doctors and lawyers went to the countryside not to stir revolt but to serve in the newly instituted local courts or work for the newly created organs of rural self-administration (the *zemstvos*). They bemoaned the abuse of peasant wives at their husbands' hands and decried the laws that made divorce and even legal separation difficult to obtain. Eager to transform the autocracy into a modern regime through incremental change, jurists pressed for the liberalization of divorce and women's inheritance rights.[8]

Yet for all the public's litany of complaints, and despite the turbulent forces unleashed by the regime's own program of economic advancement, the tsars remained staunchly conservative. Both Alexander III (r. 1881–1894) and Nicholas II (r. 1894–1917) turned to the pre-Petrine age for myths of old-style autocratic

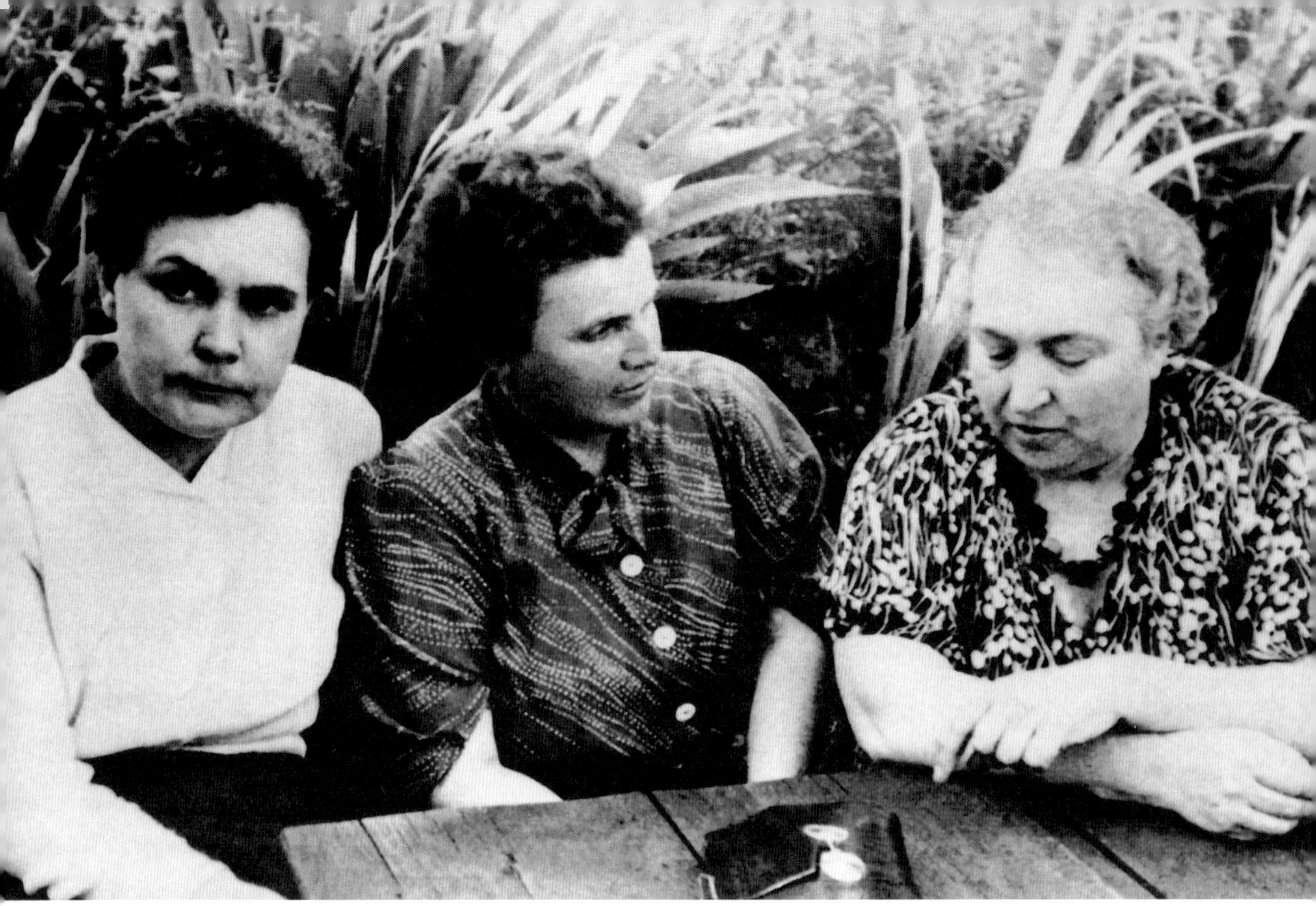

figure 12. Zinaida Ivanova, Vera Mukhina, and
Alexandra Exter at Fontenay-aux-Roses, France, 1937.

rule, while the use of domestic life as an emblem of public virtue reached its incongruous apogee in the Victorian idyll of Nicholas and Alexandra (1872–1918), even as the autocracy entered its final decline.[9] Yet while the monarchs clung to symbols of tradition and resisted political change, preferring, for example, to sponsor the canonization of saints than grant religious toleration, the cultural atmosphere was alive with innovation — in music, theater, poetry, prose, the applied and fine arts, and the new technology of cinema.

The six artists in this exhibition are products of this contradictory time. They represent a single generation and belong to roughly the same social milieu. Five (save Varvara Stepanova) were born in the 1880s, none into impoverished families. The girls all started life in the provinces and, having learned their craft in the art schools of Moscow, St. Petersburg, Kiev, and Kazan, pursued their careers in Moscow. Alexandra Exter, Liubov Popova, Nadezhda Udaltsova, and Natalia Goncharova had been to Europe before 1914. Three of the six women married fellow artists, with whom they sometimes collaborated. For all of them, the crucial years were those that spanned the revolutions of 1905 and 1917. The group's fate neatly illustrates the possible consequences of the Bolshevik victory. Exter and Goncharova emigrated; the others remained — Rozanova and Popova quickly succumbing to illness, and Stepanova and Udaltsova surviving into the Khrushchev years.

For purposes of framing this generation, then, we must investigate their formative experiences both culturally and in terms of their career opportunities as women. What were women doing on behalf of their sex? What were they, simply, doing? What models of self-fashioning did they encounter? If the "new people" of the 1860s created a style for the radical bluestocking of mid-century, what was the prototype for the so-called New Woman of the 1910s, a figure as noticeable on Russian city streets as she was in Berlin or London?

In nineteenth-century Europe and the United States women were excluded from political life. In Russia before the 1905 revolution, the only elections were local; the few qualified women voted by male proxy. After 1905, the czar created a national assembly (the Duma) based on a restricted male franchise. But despite the limited role for women in public affairs, they managed to exercise their social, intellectual, and creative ingenuity. Their activities can be divided into three spheres: social causes; education and the professions; and culture.

Women were prominent in philanthropy, not because charity was seen as a peculiarly feminine concern, but because Orthodox Christian values infused public life, and despite its firm patriarchalism, the Church allowed considerable latitude for female spiritual initiative. With its sanction, women had begun founding their own religious communities in the late eighteenth century, and by 1917 there were more than two hundred, with members from every social rank. Founders of high station used their wealth and contacts in pursuing spiritual goals, but some of humbler stock rose to leadership on the strength of moral dedication. Typically, the communities performed a number of charitable services, such as sheltering orphans, caring for elderly women, running schools for girls, hospitals, and handicraft workshops. Their leaders were venerated for their devotion to spiritual ideals, but they were also resourceful entrepreneurs, skilled in the politics of patronage.[10]

Private charity remained an important sphere of public activity, because the state did not assume the burden of poor relief or social welfare. The imperial womenfolk set the example. To aid the victims of the war against Napoleon, Alexander I's wife Elizabeth (1779–1826) founded the Women's Patriotic Society, which went on to provide schooling for girls. Even Nicholas I (r. 1825–1855), suspicious of any independent social activity, tolerated philanthropic enterprises, to which his own mother, Maria Fedorovna, lent her support. "Founding a charitable association," writes historian Adele Lindenmeyr, "became virtually part of the job description for the wives of high-ranking state officials."[11] Even after the

Great Reforms, elite women continued to focus on charity and social improvement. Grand Duchess Elena Pavlovna, for example, founded a semireligious nursing community during the Crimean War. After her husband was assassinated in 1905, Grand Duchess Elizaveta Fedorovna (1864–1918), the tsarina's sister (later murdered along with the imperial family), devoted herself to religious life and founded a charitable order for women. Less exalted women helped establish lying-in hospitals and sponsored the training of midwives. The Church had always promoted almsgiving, but industrial poverty demanded a more systematic response, such as the guardianships of the poor that flourished in the 1890s. But even when philanthropy became relatively depersonalized, women continued to participate in charitable projects and institutions.[12]

It was one thing for society matrons and industrialists' wives to volunteer their time and efforts; to enter the professions, however, women needed access to higher education. In the 1860s, liberals such as Konstantin Kavelin (1818–1885) and Mikhail Stasiulevich (1826–1911) urged admitting women to the universities, but the Ministry of Education kept them out. Women seeking specialized medical training went to Europe instead. Sofia Kovalevskaia (1850–1891), the first woman to receive a doctorate in mathematics, studied abroad. In the 1870s, Russian medical institutes began admitting women; though excluded again from 1882 to 1897, women continued to flock to the profession.[13]

Although women were allowed only briefly, between 1906 and 1908, to attend university on an equal basis with men, they were able to study in special advanced courses first offered to women in the 1870s, on the urging of the feminist Nadezhda Stasova (1822–1897) and others, by distinguished professors in Moscow and St. Petersburg.[14] By 1910, similar courses had been created in ten other cities, and in 1911 female graduates in St. Petersburg, Moscow, Kiev, and Kazan were allowed to sit for state examinations. By 1914, women constituted 30 percent of students in institutions of higher learning, which, however, enrolled well under 1 percent of the population. In these rarefied ranks, women made considerable progress. In 1894, the Russian Academy of Sciences elected Countess Praskovia Uvarova (1840–1924), an archaeologist, as its first woman member. About 40 percent of the very small number of people (4 percent of the urban labor force) listed as professionals and semiprofessionals in the 1902 Moscow city census were women. By 1910, they constituted about 7 percent of physicians and 10 percent of pharmacists. By 1906, St. Petersburg could boast two female-owned pharmacies, one sponsored by the Society for the Preservation of Women's Health. The intersection of social concern, women's rights, and professional self-assertion is evident in the career of Maria Pokrovskaia (1852–?), a public-health physician who became an outspoken opponent of regulated prostitution and the founder of a feminist journal, *Zhenskii vestnik* (*Women's Herald*), and a political association, the

Women's Progressive Party. By 1912, women constituted a majority of school teachers. Directly connected to affairs of state, the legal profession was the least hospitable to women's ambitions. Only after 1906 was it possible for women to study law in Russia, but they were not authorized to plead in court.[15]

The revolution of 1905 had unleashed some of these changes as part of a general widening of the public sphere and of opportunities for political and civic engagement. Although peasants and laborers had joined the social movement, the protest had gotten its start among landowners, professors, physicians, lawyers, bankers, industrialists, and self-proclaimed feminists, pressing for involvement in political life, protection of the law, and a social policy designed to smooth the transition to modernity. The concessions wrested from the regime achieved some of these goals. Women did not win the vote and were disappointed in their bid for equal rights, but they continued to mobilize in support of social causes (poverty, prostitution, public health, temperance). They linked up with international women's associations and organized a massive congress (1908), which included many professionals and a vocal delegation of socialists; in 1912, feminists held a conference on the subject of women's education.[16]

Even though in these years women's professional gains were significant and their political gains few, the condition of women continued to impress contemporaries as a bellwether of the nation's cultural achievement. As mid-century moderates and radicals had measured social injustice by the intensity of women's oppression — burdened by poverty, patriarchy, and the moral double standard — so at century's end conservatives saw the nation's decline (or impending doom) in the measure of women's emancipation. The archreactionary Duma deputy Vladimir Purishkevich (1870–1920) inveighed against Jews and educated women, whose presence in public life he feared would open the floodgates to social and moral chaos.[17]

Purishkevich's anxiety only reflected the temper of the times. Indeed, the sober business of women's rights was a good deal less fascinating than the erotic glitter of the so-called sexual question that captivated public opinion in the 1890s and survived the upheaval of 1905. Throughout the period, newspapers, magazines, professional congresses, and bourgeois drawing rooms buzzed with the hot topics of the day: divorce, abortion, and regulated prostitution; syphilis, masturbation, and white slavery. Those of a scholarly bent could find cause for alarm in the thick volumes published by physician and criminologist Praskovia Tarnovskaia (1848–1910), adapting fashionable theories of criminal anthropology to the study of Russian prostitutes and female thieves. Tarnovskaia belonged to the Society for the Protection of Women, founded in 1901 on the British model to combat the international prostitution trade. Two thirds of the three hundred delegates to the Society's 1910 congress were female, including two dozen physicians. This organization demonstrated how women's charitable impulses had converged with their professional goals, both mobilized in the interests of civic amelioration.[18]

This kind of feminism, as its radical critics pointed out, did not intend to remake the social order. It was, however, committed to the common good, not merely to personal self-improvement. It was able to combine the religious impulse behind philanthropy with a secular concern for cultural uplift (education, public health, vocational training). The same tension between self-realization and self-sacrifice, so central to the intelligentsia ethos of mid-century, found classic expression in the writings of Lev Tolstoy (1828–1910). Public debate on the sexual question can reasonably be said to have opened with the appearance of Tolstoy's novella *The Kreutzer Sonata* (1889–91), which castigated male lust, female sensuality, and the ideal of the liberated woman in equally fervid terms. Even when sanctified by the marital bond, Tolstoy declared, sexual indulgence signified the partners' capitulation to their lowest animal urges. The wife in *The Kreutzer Sonata* is murdered by a husband driven mad, readers were led to believe, by her treacherous sexual charms. (Both the novella and the novel *Anna Karenina* [1877] were adapted to the screen in 1914, bringing their highly charged plots to a broad urban audience.) Reassured perhaps by Tolstoy's moralizing, while excited by his hot-blooded description of the passions he denounced, female readers flooded him with letters recounting their personal desires and torments.[19]

Christian philosopher Vasilii Rozanov (1856–1919), for his part, contributed to the sexual debate with fervent advocacy of divorce reform (which would have allowed him to obtain one), while celebrating sexual intimacy and procreation as spiritual gifts. Rozanov joined Tolstoy in scorning the modern bluestocking as a distortion of true womanhood, yet he extolled the charms of old-style patriarchal domesticity, all the while embracing the modern opportunity to discourse about sex. Like Tolstoy, he too received letters from readers testifying to the public's hunger for self-reflection and self-revelation.

For the same reason, theatergoers — male and female — flocked to watch Henrik Ibsen's frustrated heroines writhe in the tentacles of Victorian morality.[20] In Ibsen's dramas of thwarted female selfhood, the characters on stage represented the New Woman's conflict between devotion to others and to herself. The actresses who portrayed them, by contrast, embodied the New Woman's bold ideal of the creative personality. Vera Komissarszhevskaia (1864–1910), who played Hedda, was the most charismatic of a string of prominent actresses who made their mark in these years. A few of them also went backstage to run the show. In close-ups on the silent screen, Vera Kholodnaia (1893–1919) radiated pathos and glamour.[21]

For all its distance from classical literature and serious theater, commercial culture also focused on the cultivation of the self, particularly for women. If dreams of stardom did not come true, readers could empathize with the fictional heroines depicted in novels such as the wildly successful *Keys to Happiness* (1911–13), a six-volume potboiler written and marketed with commercial savvy by Anastasia Verbitskaia (1861–1928), who also wrote the scenario for the film version that appeared in 1913. Verbitskaia made a career not only as the author of boulevard prose but as a literary entrepreneur. Her stories dramatized the dilemmas of modern womanhood, torn between the desire for love and the urge to self-expression. Alexandra Kollontai (1872–1952), the Social Democratic feminist, writing in 1913, hailed these boulevard heroines as portraits of the actual "new women" who populated the workplaces, lecture halls, and shops of the prewar cities: Gainfully employed, self-confident, ambitious, they were the center of their own dramas, not the object of men's.[22]

Laws and conventions may have impeded a young woman's path to independence, but the times encouraged creative ambition. Verbitskaia's readers might have honed their girlhood fantasies by devouring the eighty or so serialized tales published by Lidiia Charskaia (1875–1937) between 1902 and 1918. These stories depicted girls of boarding-school age in familiar settings (dormitories and classrooms) and exotic locales (Siberia, the Caucasus). Passionate fans sent Charskaia endless letters, expressing their sense of identification with both characters and author.[23] Another popular work, the diary of Marie Bashkirtseff (1858–1884), recorded the brief life of a young Russian woman who, living in Paris, dreamt as much of art as of love. Translated in 1889 from the original French, its inwardness and self-involvement earned it a wide readership, especially among women.[24]

Women were not excluded from the best training in the fine arts, but their opportunities for recognition expanded only after a new generation of painters had challenged the authority of the imperial academies and private patronage offered an alternative to official sources of support.[25] Some female artists, like the six exhibited here, were able to develop their talents and pursue distinctive careers. Others took their first steps not as solo practitioners but as sponsors and shapers of socially oriented production. Like the charity matrons with whom they worked, they used acceptable forms of female activity to propel themselves into the public and creative domains.

Such opportunities often evolved, as in philanthropy, as an outgrowth of family-centered life. The tight-knit clans of the merchant elite, in which Popova, for example, was raised, were active in social and cultural affairs. Their proverbial patriarchalism seems not to have prevented their daughters from being educated at home and exercising their talents. For example, textile magnate Pavel Tretiakov (1832–1898), who used his considerable art collection as the core of the national picture gallery that still bears his name, was married to a woman from the Mamontov clan, which also devoted itself to patronage of the arts. Two of the Tretiakov daughters married sons of the Botkin family, whose fortunes derived

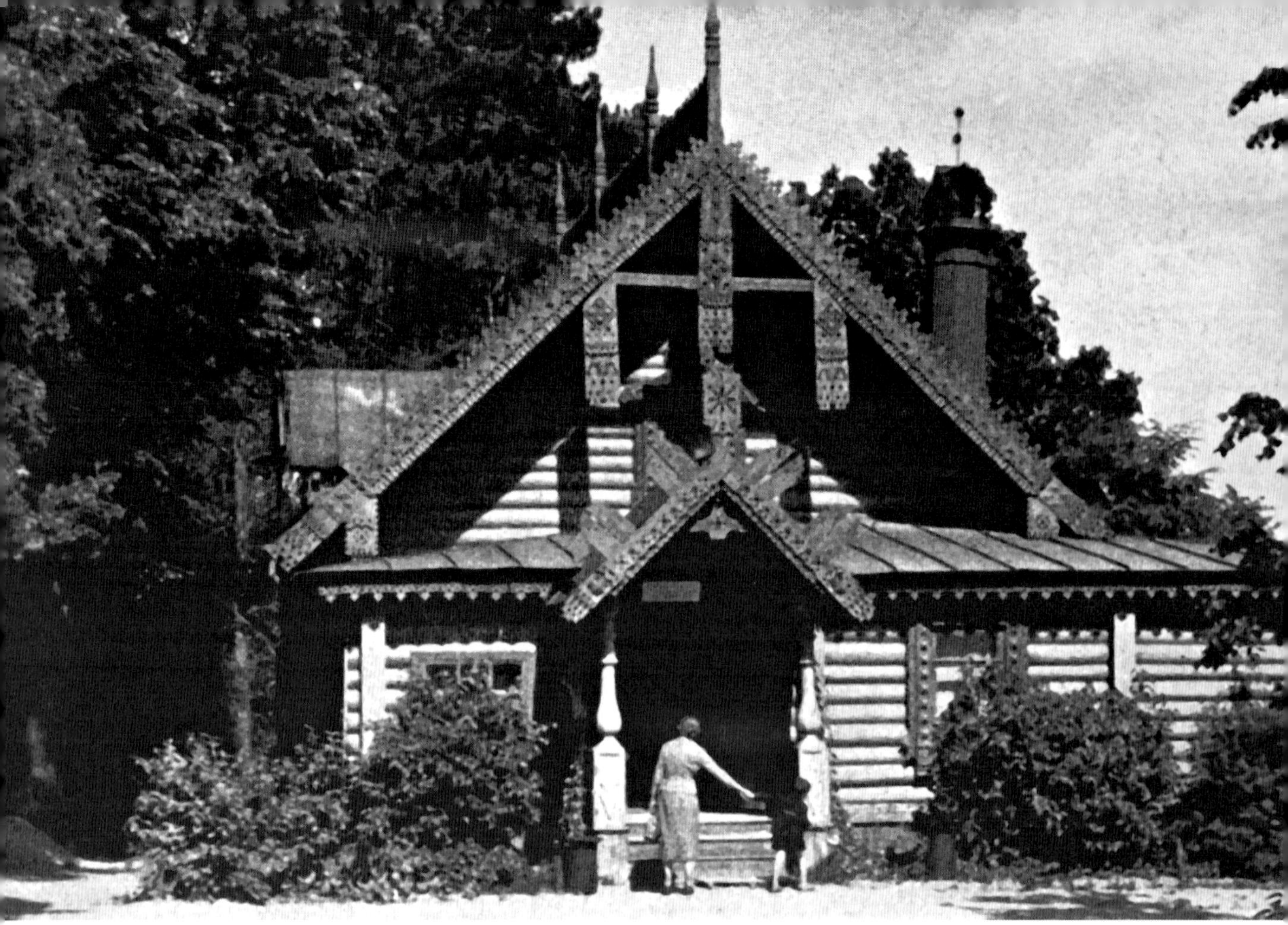

figure 13. The Abramtsevo Museum.

from the tea trade. The brothers became physicians and art connoisseurs, demonstrating the convergence of commercial, cultural, and professional interests in the urban elites of the day. Alexandra Botkina (1867–1959), Tretiakov's older daughter, was an amateur photographer and salon hostess, who sat on the gallery's board of directors and welcomed celebrated artists and performers, including ballerina Tamara Karsavina (1885–1978) and poet Zinaida Gippius (1869–1945), into her drawing room.[26]

The arts-and-crafts movement is where women came into their own, both as entrepreneurs and artists. As a symbol, in historian Wendy R. Salmond's words, "of tradition reconciled to progress, of vernacular Russian forms integrated . . . with the dominant Western style," the new aestheticized folk art perfectly represents women's own position between tradition and change. It also provided the conduit to women artists' engagement with Modernism, an outcome, as Salmond notes, "of this long tradition of women's work in the *kustar* [handicraft] arts."[27]

It is in this context that we encounter some of the artists featured in this exhibition. The vernacular revival had its roots in the 1870s, in the aftermath of serfdom, when peasants were struggling with the economic hardship created by the terms of emancipation and beginning to suffer the impact of social change. Populists, labor economists, agronomists, and philanthropists worried about the human and cultural damage that might ensue. One of the strategies devised for cushioning the villages against the effects of industrial growth and urban culture was to reinforce the declining tradition of peasant crafts.[28]

The various rescue missions launched in pursuit of this goal also depended on familial, professional, and commercial ties. In this context, women were instrumental in reshaping the image of the folk tradition, preserving its primitivist cachet, while adapting it to a demanding market. The first folk-revival workshop was created by Elizaveta Mamontova (1847–1908), daughter of a silk manufacturer and the wife of Savva Mamontov (1841–1918), who made a fortune in railroads and devoted his life to supporting the arts. After founding a school and a hospital on their Abramtsevo estate, Elizaveta opened a joinery workshop in 1876. To train the artisans in the lost art of peasant crafts and to improve the quality of their products, she enlisted the services of Elena Polenova (1850–1898), who left her personal signature on the modernized handicrafts that were sold in Moscow shops (often run by merchants' wives and society matrons) and achieved wide popularity in America and Europe.[29]

Polenova's background demonstrates the classic combination of the themes sounded here. Her father was a distinguished archaeologist, her mother wrote and illustrated children's books, and her brother was an accomplished painter. After volunteering as a nurse during the war with Turkey (1877–78), Polenova attended medical courses, then taught drawing in a charitable school for girls, before taking classes in watercolor and ceramics. As director of the Abramtsevo workshop from 1885 to 1890, she forged a decorative style from folk motifs that, in Salmond's words, attempted "to mend the thread connecting Russia's past and present." She was praised by Vladimir Stasov (1824–1906) as part of "that generation of new Russian women who . . . have a keen sense of our national character." In reconciling continuity and innovation, women of the commercial classes behaved in much the spirit of their culture-minded husbands and fathers, who invested the profits from enterprises that were reshaping the face of Russia in the production and preservation of cultural goods meant to honor tradition and further progress at the same time. This was the case of Maria Iakunchikova (1864–1952), born a Mamontov, who married a textile magnate and created the Solomenko workshop, which specialized in designer embroidery. The outlook also typifies Princess Maria Tenisheva (1867–1928), the wife of a gentry industrialist, who joined with Savva Mamontov in bankrolling Sergei Diaghilev's (1872–1929) journal, *Mir iskusstva (The World of Art)*, which first appeared in 1898. She also created her own craft workshop at her Talashkino estate.[30]

The artists who designed for the handicraft workshops took the basic vocabulary of folk art and fashioned a design grammar legible to the urban consumer. A similar combination of primitive and modern was at work in the painting by Mikhail Larionov (1881–1964) and Goncharova during this period and in the stylistic eclecticism of the European-oriented World of Art school. For all its contribution to developing a modern decorative aesthetic, however, the handicraft movement never abandoned its social goals. During World War I, Alexandra Exter, on behalf of the Kiev Handicraft Society, convinced her St. Petersburg colleagues (including Popova, Rozanova, and Udaltsova) to help produce useful decorated goods. The three were by then associated with the Supremus group of Kazimir Malevich (1878–1935); Exter dubbed them the "folk futurists."[31] They continued into the Soviet future, when the relation between old and new was inverted. Whereas old-regime traditionalism had left room for cultural innovation, the ideology of progress would enforce artistic conformity and create a traditionalism of its own, but not before the Modern had ushered in the new age and its New Women.

1. See Lindsey Hughes, "Peter the Great's Two Weddings: Changing Images of Women in a Transitional Age," in *Women in Russia and Ukraine*, ed. and tr. Rosalind Marsh (Cambridge: Cambridge University Press, 1996), pp. 31–44. Quote from Pushkin's poem "The Bronze Horseman."
2. See Richard S. Wortman, *Scenarios of Power: Myth and Ceremony in Russian Monarchy* (Princeton: Princeton University Press, 1995), vol 1, pp. 62–66; idem, "Images of Rule and Problems of Gender in the Upbringing of Paul I and Alexander I," in *Imperial Russia 1700–1917*, ed. Ezra Mendelsohn and Marshall S. Shatz (DeKalb, IL: Northern Illinois University Press, 1988), pp. 58–75.
3. See Alexander M. Martin, *Romantics, Reformers, Reactionaries: Russian Conservative Thought and Politics in the Reign of Alexander I* (DeKalb, IL: Northern Illinois University Press, 1997), pp. 91–109; W. Bruce Lincoln, *In the Vanguard of Reform: Russia's Enlightened Bureaucrats 1825–1861* (DeKalb, IL: Northern Illinois University Press, 1982), pp. 148–62; Lina Bernstein, "Women on the Verge of a New Language: Russian Salon Hostesses in the First Half of the Nineteenth Century," in *Russia, Women, Culture*, ed. Helena Goscilo and Beth Holmgren (Bloomington: Indiana University Press, 1996), pp. 209–24.
4. See Jane McDermid and Anna Hillyar, *Women and Work in Russia 1880–1930: A Study in Continuity through Change* (London and New York: Longman, 1998), pp. 35, 68; *Rossiia 1913 god: Statistiko-dokumental'nyi spravochnik*, ed. A. P. Korelin (St. Petersburg: Rossiiskaia akademiia nauk, Institut Rossiiskoi istorii, 1995), pp. 17, 23, 219, 221, 223, 327.
5. The classic account is Richard Stites, *The Women's Liberation Movement in Russia: Feminism, Nihilism, and Bolshevism, 1860–1930* (Princeton: Princeton University Press, 1978); see also Barbara Alpern Engel, *Mothers and Daughters: Women of the Intelligentsia in Nineteenth-Century Russia* (Cambridge: Cambridge University Press, 1983).

6. See *Five Sisters: Women Against the Tsar*, ed. and tr. Barbara Alpern Engel and Clifford N. Rosenthal (New York: Knopf, 1975); Vera Broido, *Apostles into Terrorists: Women and the Revolutionary Movement in the Russia of Alexander II* (New York: Viking, 1977); Stites, *Women's Liberation*, pp. 138–54; Jay Bergman, *Vera Zasulich: A Biography* (Stanford: Stanford University Press, 1983); Vera Figner, *Memoirs of a Revolutionist*, intro. Richard Stites (DeKalb, IL: Northern Illinois University Press, 1991).
7. See Barbara Alpern Engel, *Between the Fields and the City: Women, Work, and Family in Russia, 1861–1914* (Cambridge: Cambridge University Press, 1994); Rose L. Glickman, *Russian Factory Women: Workplace and Society, 1880–1914* (Berkeley: University of California Press, 1984); David L. Ransel, *Mothers of Misery: Child Abandonment in Russia* (Princeton: Princeton University Press, 1988); Laurie Bernstein, *Sonia's Daughters: Prostitutes and Their Regulation in Imperial Russia* (Berkeley: University of California Press, 1995).
8. For an overview, see Stites, *Women's Liberation*; also Laura Engelstein, *The Keys to Happiness: Sex and the Search for Modernity in Fin-de-Siècle Russia* (Ithaca: Cornell University Press, 1992); William G. Wagner, *Marriage, Property and Law in Late Imperial Russia* (Oxford: Oxford University Press, 1994); idem, "The Trojan Mare: Women's Rights and Civil Rights in Late Imperial Russia," in *Civil Rights in Russia*, ed. Olga Crisp and Linda Edmondson (Oxford: Clarendon Press, 1989), pp. 65–84.
9. See Wortman, *Scenarios*, vol. 1, pp. 149–51; idem, "Moscow and Petersburg: The Problem of Political Center in Tsarist Russia, 1881–1914," in *Rites of Power: Symbolism, Ritual, and Politics Since the Middle Ages*, ed. Sean Wilentz (Philadelphia: University of Pennsylvania Press, 1985), pp. 244–71; idem, "Nikolai i obraz samoderzhaviia," in *Reformy ili revoliutsiia? Rossiia 1861–1917* (St. Petersburg: Nauka, 1992), pp. 18–30; and idem, "Publicizing Nicholas II in 1913," in *Self and Story in Russian History*, ed. Laura Engelstein and Stephanie Sandler (Ithaca: Cornell University Press, 2000).
10. See Adele Lindenmeyr, *Poverty Is Not a Vice: Charity, Society, and the State in Imperial Russia* (Princeton: Princeton University Press, 1996), p. 15; Brenda Meehan, *Holy Women of Russia: The Lives of Five Orthodox Women Offer Spiritual Guidance for Today* (San Francisco: Harper, 1993), pp. 13–14, and passim; Gregory L. Freeze, "Bringing Order to the Russian Family: Marriage and Divorce in Imperial Russia, 1760–1860," *Journal of Modern History* 62 (1990), pp. 709–46.
11. Lindenmeyr, *Poverty*, p. 116.
12. See ibid., pp. 97, 125–26, 151; Catriona Kelly, "Teacups and Coffins: The Culture of Russian Merchant Women, 1850–1917," in *Women in Russia and Ukraine*, pp. 55–77.
13. See Stites, *Women's Liberation*, pp. 85–86, 166–76; Natalia Pushkareva, *Women in Russian History: From the Tenth to the Twentieth Century*, tr. and ed. Eve Levin (Armonk: M. E. Sharpe, 1997), pp. 209–12; Sofya Kovalevskaya, *A Russian Childhood*, tr. and ed. Beatrice Stillman (New York: Springer, 1978); Ann Hibner Koblitz, *A Convergence of Lives: Sofia Kovalevskaia, Scientist, Writer, Revolutionary* (Boston: Birkhäuser, 1983).
14. See Christine Johanson, *Women's Struggle for Higher Education in Russia, 1855–1900* (Kingston and Montreal: McGill-Queen's University Press, 1987).
15. See *Rossiia 1913 god*, pp. 346–47; James McClelland, "Diversification in Russian-Soviet Education," in *The Transformation of Higher Learning, 1860–1930: Expansion, Diversification, Social Opening, and Professionalization in England, Germany, Russia, and the United States*, ed. Konrad H. Jarausch (Chicago: University of Chicago Press, 1983), pp. 184, 187; Joseph Bradley, "Moscow: From Big Village to Metropolis," in *The City in Late Imperial Russia*, ed. Michael F. Hamm (Bloomington: Indiana University Press, 1986), p. 21; Nancy Mandelker Frieden, *Russian*

Physicians in an Era of Reform and Revolution, 1856–1905 (Princeton: Princeton University Press, 1981), p. 323; Linda Edmondson, *Feminism in Russia, 1900–1917* (Stanford: Stanford University Press, 1984), p. 147; Mary Schaeffer Conroy, "Women Pharmacists in Russia before World War I: Women's Emancipation, Feminism, Professionalization, Nationalism, and Class Conflict," in *Women and Society in Russia and the Soviet Union*, ed. Linda Edmondson (Cambridge: Cambridge University Press, 1992), p. 48; Engelstein, *Keys to Happiness*, pp. 192–93, 223–25; Stites, *Women's Liberation*, pp. 202–3, 225–26; Pushkareva, *Women in Russian History*, 211; McDermid and Hillyar, *Women and Work*, 71–76; Christine Ruane, *Gender, Class, and the Professionalization of Russian City Teachers, 1860–1914* (Pittsburgh: University of Pittsburgh Press, 1994).

16. See Edmondson, *Feminism*, pp. 139–50; idem, "Women's Rights, Civil Rights, and the Debate Over Citizenship in the 1905 Revolution," in *Women and Society*, pp. 77–100; *Constructing Russian Culture in the Age of Revolution: 1881–1940*, ed. Catriona Kelly and David Sheperd (Oxford: Oxford University Press, 1998), pp. 193–211.
17. See Engelstein, *Keys to Happiness*, p. 313.
18. See ibid., pp. 69–70, 137–54, 281.
19. See ibid., pp. 218–21, 373–74; Engelstein, "'Kreitserova sonata' L'va Tolstogo, russkii fin-de-s'ekl' i voprosy seksa," in *Kul'turologicheskie zapiski*, vol. 3: *Eros v ku'ture* (Moscow: Gosudarstvennyi institut iskusstvoznaniia,1997), pp. 30–44; Peter Ulf Møller, *Postlude to "The Kreutzer Sonata": Tolstoj and the Debate on Sexual Morality in Russian Literature in the 1890s*, tr. John Kendal (Leiden: E. J. Brill, 1988).
20. See Engelstein, *Keys to Happiness*, pp. 299–333.
21. See Osip Mandelstam, "The Noise of Time," in *The Prose of Osip Mandelstam*, tr. and intro. Clarence Brown (Princeton: Princeton University Press, 1965), p. 123 (and in general for the mood of the period); Catherine A. Schuler, *Women in Russian Theater: The Actress in the Silver Age* (London and New York: Routledge, 1996); Louise McReynolds, "The Silent Movie Melodrama: Evgenii Bauer Fashions the Hero(in)ic Self," in *Self and Story*.
22. See Engelstein, *Keys to Happiness*, pp. 399–404; Jeffrey Brooks, *When Russia Learned to Read: Literacy and Popular Literature, 1861–1917* (Princeton: Princeton University Press, 1985), pp. 153–60; Beth Holmgren, "Gendering the Icon: Marketing Women Writers in Fin-de-Siècle Russia," in *Russia, Women, Culture*, pp. 321–46. See also *Constructing Russian Culture*, pp. 113–25.
23. See Susan Larsen, "Girl Talk: Lidiia Charskaia and Her Readers," in *Self and Story*; Beth Holmgren, "Why Russian Girls Loved Charskaia," *Russian Review* 54:1 (1995), pp. 91–106.
24. See Charlotte Rosenthal, "The Silver Age: Highpoint for Women?," in *Women and Society*, pp. 34–36, 44–45; *Russia Through Women's Eyes: Autobiographies from Tsarist Russia*, ed. Toby W. Clyman and Judith Vowles (New Haven: Yale University Press, 1996), p. 41; also Catriona Kelly, *A History of Russian Women's Writing, 1820–1992* (Oxford: Oxford University Press, 1994), pp. 155–56 (dates slightly off). Eve Le Gallienne wrote about the character Hedda Gabler, that "there is a lot of Marie Bashkirtseff in her": Henrik Ibsen, *Hedda Gabler*, preface by Eve Le Gallienne (New York: New York University Press, 1955), p. 8.
25. See Alison Hilton, "Domestic Crafts and Creative Freedom: Russian Women's Art," in *Russia, Women, Culture*, pp. 347–76.
26. Muriel Joffe and Adele Lindenmeyr, "Daughters, Wives, and Partners: Women of the Moscow Merchant Elite," in *Merchant Moscow: Images of Russia's Vanished Bourgeoisie*, ed. James L. West and Iurii A. Petrov (Princeton: Princeton University Press, 1998), pp. 95–108. Also, more generally, John O. Norman, "Pavel Tretiakov and Merchant Art Patronage, 1850–1900" and John E. Bowlt, "The Moscow Art Market," in *Between Tsar and People: Educated Society and the Quest for*

Public Identity in Late Imperial Russia, ed. Edith W. Clowes, Samuel D. Kassow, and James L. West (Princeton: Princeton University Press, 1991), pp. 93–128; Jo Ann Ruckman, *The Moscow Business Elite: A Social and Cultural Portrait of Two Generations, 1840–1905* (DeKalb, IL: Northern Illinois University Press, 1984); *Serebrianyi vek v fotografiiakh A. P. Botkinoi*, ed. E. S. Khokhlova (Moscow: Nashe nasledie, 1998) (thanks to Stephen Kotkin for this source).

27. Wendy R. Salmond, *Arts and Crafts in Late Imperial Russia* (Cambridge: Cambridge University Press, 1996), pp. 3, 13.
28. Lewis H. Siegelbaum, "Exhibiting *Kustar* Industry in Late Imperial Russia/Exhibiting Late Imperial Russia in *Kustar* Industry," in *Transforming Peasants: Society, State, and the Peasantry, 1861–1930*, ed. Judith Pallot (Basingstoke: Macmillan, 1998), pp. 37–63.
29. Salmond, *Arts and Crafts*, chapter 1; John E. Bowlt, *The Silver Age, Russian Art of the Early Twentieth Century, and the "World of Art" Group* (Newtonville, MA: Oriental Research Partners, 1979), pp. 30–39.
30. Salmond, *Arts and Crafts*, pp. 53, 48 (quotes); Bowlt, *Silver Age*, pp. 39–46.
31. Salmond, *Arts and Crafts*, p. 184.

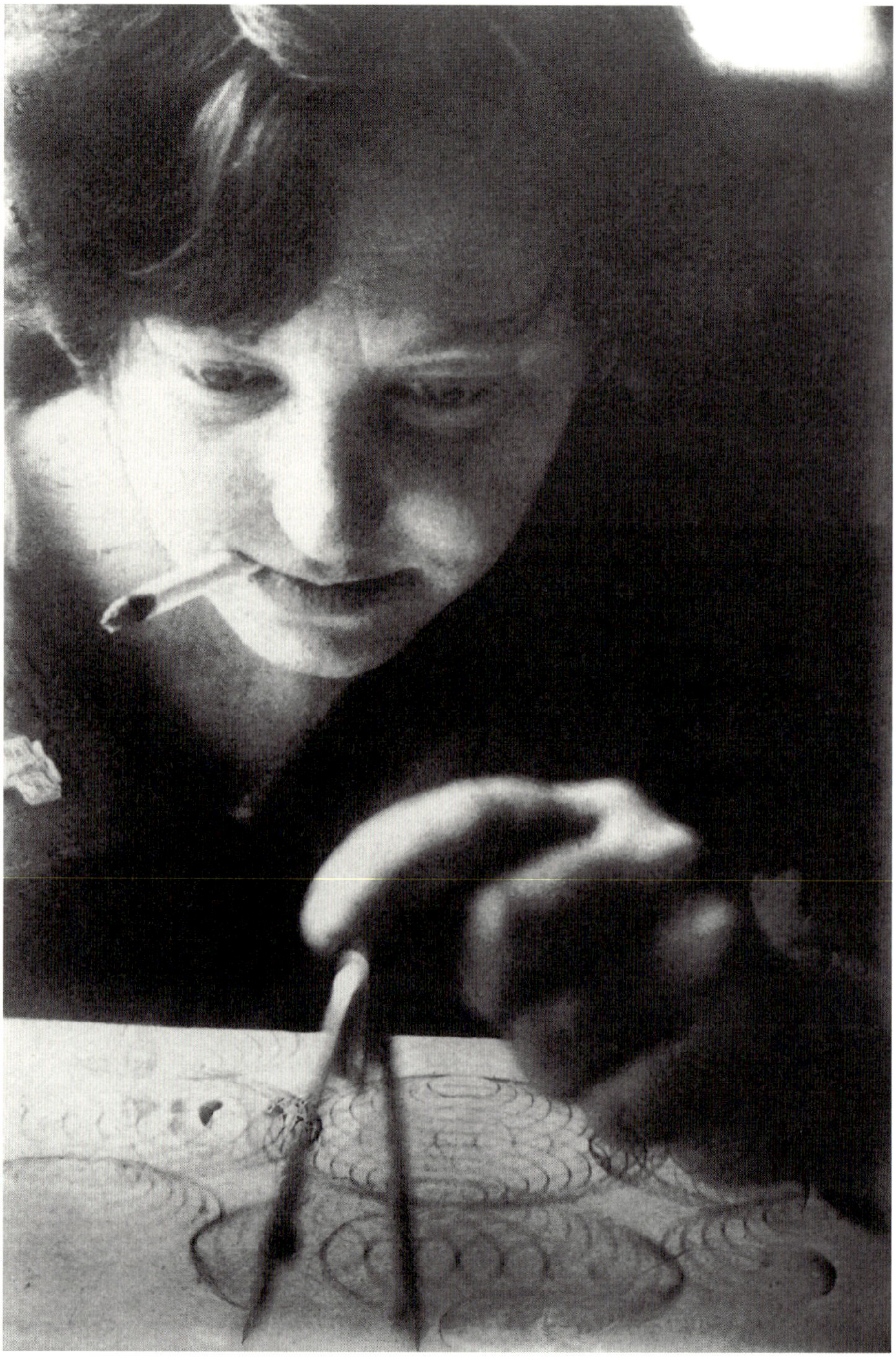

figure 14. Varvara Stepanova drawing textile designs, photographed by Alexander Rodchenko, 1924.

Gender Trouble in the Amazonian Kingdom: Turn-of-the-Century Representations of Women in Russia

Olga Matich

Questions of sex and gender informed, if not pervaded, European culture of the late-nineteenth and early twentieth centuries. The destabilization of gender in an age obsessed with female power and its threat to men characterized the lives and work of many artists and writers. The desire to veil what became known as the "phallic woman" existed alongside the wish to unveil her "phallic power." Those obsessed with society's physical health pathologized the ambiguities of female sexuality. The demonization of women posed a challenge to the strongest among them, resulting in an eruption of female creativity, based in part on women's phantasmic power. This liberating burst of energy exposed female desire and gender ambiguity, reflecting what Elaine Showalter calls fin-de-siècle "sexual anarchy."[1]

In Russia, women poets and artists were also experimenting with gender at the turn of the twentieth century. Cross-voicing in poetry and cross-dressing in public characterized the (self-)representation of some of the more radical creative women of the time. The destabilization of gender typified not only their art, but also the way they exhibited their bodies, and it informed their subjectivity in a totalizing way. This essay focuses on the visual and poetic representations of "sexual anarchy" embodied by three Russian women — Zinaida Nikolaevna Gippius (1869–1945), Ida Lvovna Rubinstein (1885–1960), and Elizaveta Sergeevna Kruglikova (1865–1941) — who invested their creativity in the act of unveiling their gender ambiguity. Their literary, performative, and artistic strategies reflected the desire to cross gender boundaries by challenging the presumed impermeability of male difference. Although some of the visual representations discussed in this essay were crafted by men, my claim is that these powerful women imposed their self-image on these male artists. Such a relationship between artist and female model may have been normalized by the "feminization" of fin-de-siècle artistic sensibility. This feminization contributed directly to the cultural ambience out of which the subsequent, even more radical, generation of women emerged.

The six avant-garde artists featured in this exhibition also treated the human figure in terms that blurred gender boundaries. But unlike their older sisters, they tended not to invest themselves personally in a gender-bending subjectivity; accordingly, references here will be almost exclusively to their artistic output, not to their public personas and personal lives. The connotations of gender ambiguity were quite different for the women of the avant-garde. Their goal was the representation of the new "man" (*chelovek* in Russian, a noun referring to both men and women), who was an androgyne of sorts. Instead of referring to gender trouble, the avant-garde androgyne was frequently modeled on the African mask, which had also inspired the representation of the human face in the European avant-garde. This unisex figure was stylized, not pathologized or sexualized, a condition that may well be associated with Natalia Goncharova's Neo-Primitivist works.

A common term for gender destabilization in the European fin de siècle was androgyny, which had a variety of connotations: it represented an aesthetic ideal, but it also served as a euphemistic substitute for lesbianism and homosexuality. The figure of the androgyne reflected castration anxiety, a key trope of Western European Decadence. This figure of indeterminate gender was considered "degenerate" (a term popularized by Max Nordau's book *Degeneration* [1892][2]) or pathological, because it undermined reproductive health and the continuity of the race.

By contrast, the androgyne of Russian Symbolism of the 1890s to 1910s, as defined by the idealist philosopher Vladimir Soloviev, was a Platonic spiritual hybrid that heralded the desired transfiguration of the body. It transcended gender difference by reference to Platonic androgyny, a philosophical, not an aesthetic or pathological, concept. Instead of fixating on the androgyne as a figure of castration anxiety, some Russians focused on its apocalyptic, or utopian, antiprocreationism, resulting — according to Soloviev and his followers — in an immortalized body. The utopian goal was the transcendence of the death-dealing natural cycle, in which birth inevitably leads to death. The Platonic utopian androgyne prefigured the end of time exalted by the early Russian Modernists of the Symbolist generation. It marked the beginning of the awaited collective utopia, which would include bodily, not just social, change. The ideology of utopian Symbolists and the subsequent utopian avant-garde focused not on castration, an individual fear, but on the collective transfiguration of life.[3] This is a broad generalization regarding the Russian view of the coming end and naturally has many exceptions, such as Goncharova's apocalyptic *Maiden on the Beast*, 1911 (see fig. 89 for the later woodcut version). The image invokes the whore of Babylon, a phallic woman, even though Goncharova emphasized the maternal stomach and breasts, underscoring the role of the female as procreatrix.

The most celebrated gender-bending woman of the Symbolist generation was Zinaida Gippius, who preached Soloviev's vision of utopian androgyny. A major poet, prose writer, critic, religious thinker, and salon hostess, she remains nearly unknown in the West.[4] Gippius's cross-gendered literary persona revealed itself in her metaphysical poetry, whose lyrical "I" was grammatically masculine when expressing itself in the past tense and in personal adjectives. (Russian grammar has three genders: masculine, feminine, and neuter.) In the desire to scramble her gender, Gippius wrote much of her poetry in the male voice, yet signed it as a woman; as a critic, she appeared under the male pseudonym Anton the Extreme.

Just as provocative and more flamboyant than Gippius's refined poetry and prose was her self-representation in life and in the arena of Symbolist "life-creation" (*zhiznetvorchestvo*), which had among its goals the redefinition of gender, even of physiology. Despite her utopian agenda, however, her public persona was that of a phallic woman. The verbal portraits of Gippius by contemporaries describe her in Decadent terms. They emphasize her flat-chested, narrow-hipped body, green mermaid eyes, serpentine sting, and bright red mouth, which is associated with La Gioconda's ambiguous smile as well as the phallic woman's bloodthirstiness. Andrei Bely[5] wrote a stylized, grotesque portrait of Gippius, invoking the name of the misogynistic English artist Aubrey Beardsley in describing her seductively demonic emaciated figure:

> *Z. Gippius is just like a human-sized wasp, if she is not the skeleton of a "seductress" (the pen of Aubrey Beardsley); a lump of distended red hair . . . ; powder and luster from a lorgnette . . . ; the flame of a lip . . . ; from her forehead, like a beaming eye, dangled a stone; on a black cord, a black cross rattled from her breastless bosom . . . ; legs crossed; she tossed back the train of her close-fitting dress; the charm of her bony, hip-less skeleton recalled a communicant deftly captivating Satan.*[6]

White was Gippius's favorite color. Symbolist poet Valerii Briusov noted in his diary that she asked him once whether white could be worn in Moscow for all occasions, claiming that her skin was allergic to other colors.[7] Gippius posed for photographers dressed in white and declaimed her poetry in public wearing white gowns with gauze wings at the shoulders. A full-length, frontal photograph of the beautiful young Gippius presents her in a demure long white dress with a train carefully draped in front, in the conventional style of the time; on a long chain hangs her ever-present lorgnette (the female dandy's monocle), which she would bring to her haughty, nearsighted eyes in conversation (fig. 15). Gippius appar-

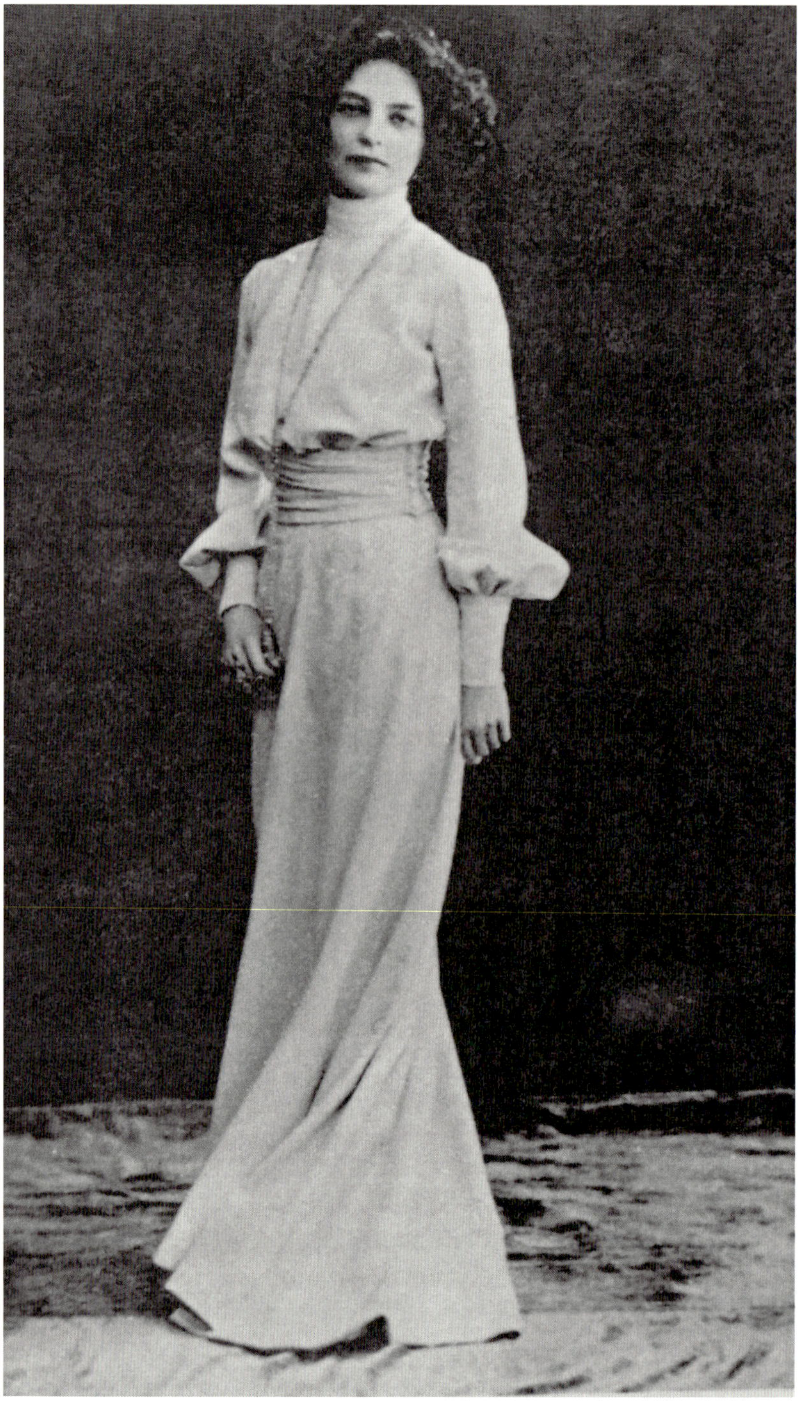

figure 15. Zinaida Gippius, photographed by Otto Renar, Moscow, ca. 1900.

ently lived a celibate life, and the white dresses were symbolic of her virginity. During the first ten years of her marriage to Dmitrii Merezhkovsky, she sometimes sported a single braid as an emblem of her chastity. In considering Gippius as a seductress of the Russian fin de siècle, we have to bear in mind this paradoxical sexuality, informed as it was by self-conscious chastity and spiritual androgyny. (How different was this behavior from the no-nonsense sexuality of the Amazons!)

Another facet of Gippius's public image was that of a self-styled Cleopatra, a prototype of the modern femme fatale. A forehead pendant was one of the accouterments of Gippius's Cleopatrine costume, and, staging herself as St. Petersburg's Egyptian queen, she would sometimes receive guests, especially young male acolytes, reclining on a sofa in her apartment. Olga Rozanova's *Portrait of a Lady in Pink (Portrait of Anna Rozanova, the Artist's Sister)*, 1911–12 (plate 42) comes to mind here, for it also displays a seductive woman reposing on a sofa.[8]

Gippius's Cleopatrine image included a cigarette holder and perfumed cigarettes, which modernized the figure of the ancient queen. The visual representation of women smoking was rare at the time, for not only was it emblematic of mannishness, but it was also considered a sign of lesbian sexuality. Havelock Ellis wrote in 1895 that the "pronounced tendency to adopt male attire" and the "pronounced taste for smoking" characterized sexually inverted women.[9] Anna Akhmatova, who was soon to become the reigning queen of the Russian Silver Age, was a smoker, but this fact did not enter her public portrait. The habit was also downplayed in descriptions of Alexandra Exter, a heavy smoker. Some years later, photographic portraits of Varvara Stepanova — many of them taken by her husband, Alexander Rodchenko, Russia's leading avant-garde photographer — typically featured a cigarette between her lips or fingers (see fig. 14). In this case, however, smoking was not a signpost of gender, but of affiliation with the working class.[10]

In a 1907 caricature, Gippius is represented in profile, sheathed in a tight-fitting white dress with a fashionable train forming a flared bottom and a pocket containing a pack of cigarettes (fig. 16). A cigarette between her lips, she holds a lorgnette in one hand, while from the other, like a pendant, hangs a sinister spider. Her face is dwarfed by her large coiffure, and she casts a small black shadow behind her. She is phallic, but not mannish — an image projected not only by the cigarette she holds in her mouth, but also from the profile view. According to philosopher and mathematician Pavel Florensky, the profile signifies power in contrast to the frontal view; it is a destabilizing facial angle that connotes forward movement.[11] While Florensky does not address the question of gender, his interpretation explains why the profile might have held appeal for women like Gippius.

Léon Bakst's famous 1906 full-length portrait of Gippius displays a tall figure reclining in a chair, presenting herself as a dandy. She wears tight knee-length

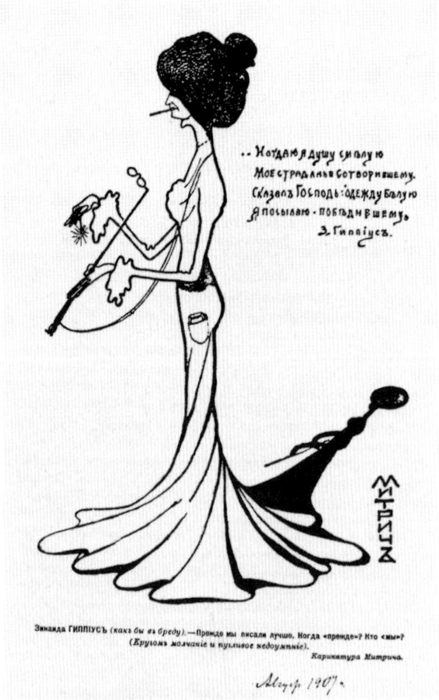

figure 16. MITRICH
[Dmitrii Dmitrievich Togolsky]
Caricature of Zinaida Gippius, 1907

pants (Gippius was known to sport culottes as well). Her long legs are artfully crossed and her hands are in her pockets, gestures marked as male. Her face, framed by a head of thick red hair and a filmy white jabot, is appropriately pale; languid eyes are disdainfully averted from the viewer's curious gaze; a sensuous mouth displays an ironic, Gioconda-like smile.[12] According to John Bowlt, "The remarkable portrait (which [Gippius] did not like) reveals at once the contradictions of this extraordinary personality — her refinement and her affectation, her maliciousness and her frailty." [13] Most important, the image reveals a Wildean dandy, a turn-of-the-century aristocratic transvestite who subverts the binary system of gender. According to Charles Baudelaire, the dandy was the most privileged of the male gender because he was artfully self-constructed; thus the appropriation of the dandy look by women reveals a desire to outdo men in the act of self-presentation.[14]

Gippius undoubtedly participated in the construction of her own image in this portrait by Bakst. She was not a passive female model, but the cocreator of the representation, thus blurring the relation between model and artist. Since the dandy by definition chooses his or her visual embodiment, the power relation between model and artist in this case had to be fluid. Moreover, one simply cannot imagine the willful and capricious Gippius submitting to Bakst's personal vision.[15]

Gippius's sex life and sexual preferences corresponded to the discursive fluidity of her gender boundaries, a fluidity that was not only a matter of dress but also of psychology. Like so many fin-de-siècle men and women, Gippius had difficulty inhabiting her body, and this difficulty was perhaps due to her gender indeterminacy. In a passage from her diary of love affairs, we can see that this blurring of genders was not only a strategy to destabilize social convention and transform life, but it was also a source of deep personal anxiety:

> *I do not desire exclusive femininity, just as I do not desire exclusive masculinity. Each time someone is insulted and dissatisfied within me; with women, my femininity is active, with men — my masculinity. In my thoughts, my desires, in my spirit — I am more a man; in my body — I am more a woman. Yet they are so fused together that I know nothing.*[16]

Gippius lived in a celibate marriage with Merezhkovsky for fifty-four years. He was sexually attracted to women, but not to his wife. Meanwhile, Gippius had multiple triangulated "love affairs" with both men and women, which in all likelihood — at least in the case of the men — were sexually unconsummated. She clearly privileged the male gender, however, and her favorite men were homosexual. In 1898, Gippius and Merezhkovsky stayed in Taormina at the villa of Franz von Gloeden, the well-known homosexual artist and photographer. She wrote in her diary about one of the other guests, "I like the illusion of possibility — as if there were a tinge of bisexuality; he seems to be both woman and man."[17] It was at Von Gloeden's villa that Gippius met a musician, Elizabeth von Overbeck, with whom she was reputed to have had a lesbian relationship, although she never referred to it herself. Gippius flaunted her attraction to homosexual men, but not to women. The great love of her life was Dmitrii Filosofov, Diaghilev's cousin and lover and cofounder of the first Modernist art journal in Russia, *Mir iskusstva* (*World of Art*). After parting from Diaghilev, Filosofov lived with Gippius and Merezhkovsky in a chaste ménage à trois for fifteen difficult years.[18] The supposed function of this arrangement was a utopian transfiguration of life based on a nonprocreative triple union.

Gippius masterminded her erotic life on both the phantasmic and real-life levels. Even though her public persona resembled the figure of the Decadent androgyne, her poetry and philosophical essays focused on spiritual androgyny and its function in the awaited transfiguration of life. In other words, Gippius's persona revealed a fundamental split between the imaginary utopian androgyne and the one that resembled the Decadent phallic woman. While this split, which was rooted in her sexuality and her body (there were persistent rumors that Gippius was a hermaphrodite), was the source of a deep anguish, it was also the source of Gippius's creativity and subversive experimentation with gender.

If Cleopatra was a prominent prototype of the femme fatale in Russia, the reigning queen of European Decadence was Salomé. In the words of Carl Schorske, "Salomé [was] the fin de siècle's favorite phallic woman."[19] Her dance of the veils liberated the female performer, while it both liberated and threatened her audience. The destabilization of traditional gender roles that this dance represented empowered women and those men whose self-identity departed from the image of the conventional phallic male. Exposing female desire — which included decapitation, or castration, of the male — Salomé's unveiling reflected male fear of women's sexuality and of the uncertainties of gender difference. Salomé was the symbol of both the epoch's "sexual anarchy" and the castrating female. In Russia, the Salomé craze was initiated by the publication in Russian of Oscar Wilde's eponymous play in 1904 by the Symbolist poet Konstantin Balmont; it was reprinted five times in the following four years. In 1907, Konstantin Stanislavsky's Moscow Art Theater applied to the theatrical censor for permission to stage *Salomé*, without success. Several theaters, including provincial ones, did manage to perform abbreviated versions of the play in that and the following year, but none of these productions made theatrical history.

The Russian-born Ida Lvovna Rubinstein, who became a notorious Salomé on the European stage, put together her own *Salomé* production in St. Petersburg in 1908. The daughter of a rich banker, she commissioned some of the most exciting Russian theatrical talent of the time: Vsevolod Meierkhold as director, Bakst as set and costume designer, Alexander Glazunov as composer, and Michel Fokine as choreographer. However, the performance apparently never reached the public, as it was banned shortly before opening night. But Salomé's costume and dance of the veils migrated into Diaghilev's 1909 production of *Cléopatre*, which was one of the biggest hits of the Ballets Russes's first Paris season (see fig. 17).[20] Salomé became Cleopatra in this production, as if the two were fundamentally the same. Describing Rubinstein's appearance onstage, Jean Cocteau gave a compelling Orientalist depiction of Cleopatra unwinding her veils. Using Art Nouveau images, he rendered the unveiling of Cleopatra's corpse from layers of history and nature; his description contrasts her sepulchral image with the living veils, which gradually unwound to reveal the destabilizing femme fatale of the European Decadence:

> *From within [the casket] emerged a kind of glorified mummy, swathed in veils. . . . The first veil . . . was red wrought with lotuses and silver crocodiles, the second was green with all the history of the dynasties in gold filigree upon it, the third was orange shot with a hundred prismatic hues, . . . the twelfth [veil], was of indigo, and under [it] the outline of a woman could be discerned. Each of the veils unwound itself in a fashion of its own: one [resembled] the peeling of a walnut, [another] the airy detachment of petals from a rose, and the eleventh . . . came away all in one piece like the bark of the eucalyptus tree. The twelfth veil . . . released Madame Rubinstein, who let it fall herself with a sweeping circular gesture.*[21]

The performance launched Rubinstein's reputation, not at home but in Paris, where she was considered an exotic figure who spoke French with a heavy Russian accent.

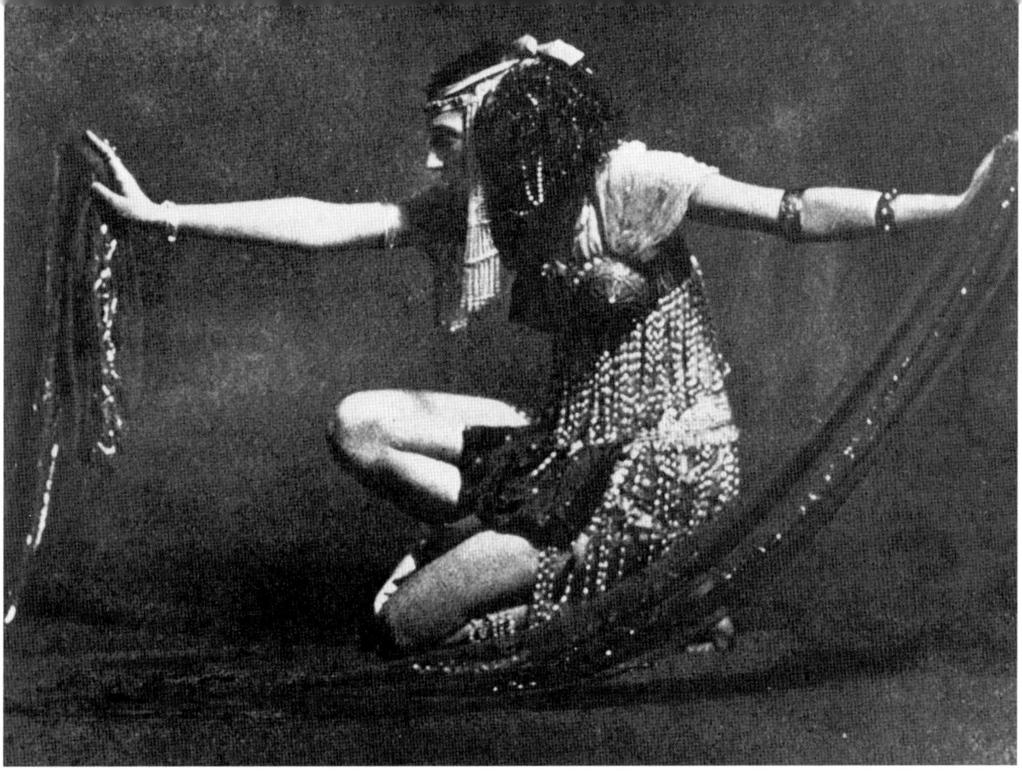

figure 17. Ida Rubinstein, wearing costume designed by Léon Bakst, in *Cléopatre*, Paris, 1909.

The best-known production of *Salomé* in Russia appeared in 1908 in the Theater of Vera Kommissarzhevskaia, who was herself a famous actress. Rubinstein — then still an aspiring actress and dancer — had tried hard to get the lead in the production, but had failed. The play's director, Nikolai Evreinov, an experimental, androgynous figure of the Russian theater (and a friend of Exter, Goncharova, and Rozanova), received permission to stage the play, but he also failed to bring *Salomé* to a major Russian stage. In a preemptive attempt to avoid the outrage of Russian Orthodox institutions, Evreinov removed the biblical names from the play and replaced them with generic ones. He also excised the play's most provocative scene, which fetishizes the phallus, in which Salomé addresses the head of the Baptist in an erotic monologue; instead, she spoke her words into the opening of a cistern, at the bottom of which lay the saint's corpse.

The play's dress rehearsal, on October 27, became legend. St. Petersburg's governing and cultural élite attended the event, including the vice-mayor, members of the State Council and State Duma (among them the reactionary anti-Semite Vladimir Purishkevich), and writers such as Fedor Sologub, Leonid Andreev, and Alexander Blok, the premier poet of Russian Symbolism, whose poetry was inspired by the figure of the veiled woman.[22] (Evreinov's Salomé was Natalia Volokhova, Blok's dark muse.) The day after the dress rehearsal, several hours before opening night, Evreinov's production was banned, creating a furor in the Russian press.

Audience members at the play's dress rehearsal had witnessed Nikolai Kalmakov's stylized set and costume designs, which, like Evreinov's production as a whole, were self-consciously erotic. A costume design for Salomé (signed with Kalmakov's trademark stylized phallus) depicts a female figure who appears to be naked, but turns out to be wearing a body stocking with red nipples on her small androgynous breasts to symbolize her nudity. In the performance itself, Salomé was draped in white veils of innocence, slipping out of them during the dance.

The dance in Evreinov's production was suggestively seductive but not explicit, with nakedness rendered symbolically, and the removal of Salomé's final layer took place on a darkened stage.[23] Kalmakov's sets had been influenced by Beardsley[24]; echoing Beardsley's image of Wilde in the "Woman in the Moon," the huge moon on the set contained the imprint of a woman's naked body. "Look closely at [the moon]," wrote a reviewer in *Birzhevye vedomosti* (*Stock-Exchange News*), "and you will discern in it the silhouette of a naked woman."[25] According to some sources, the main set for the first act was in the shape of female genitalia.[26] If this is true, the female genitals would have invoked, at least in some members of the audience, the image of the vagina dentata, a fantasy image that had inspired fear as well as desire in the fin-de-siècle male imagination, especially in Europe.

The theatrical ban of Wilde's *Salomé* in Russia was lifted in 1917, shortly after the February Revolution. But by then the new society was no longer so interested in the hothouse gender-bending and sexual experimentation that had fascinated Rubinstein and Evreinov. Times had changed; politics and social revolution were the dominant concerns. Still, the famous production of *Salomé* directed by Tairov and performed at the Chamber Theater in Petrograd the year the ban was lifted was reminiscent of the ill-fated earlier productions. This was especially true of the set and costume designs by Exter. Despite its dynamism, her architectonic set, which prefigured Constructivist decor, was reminiscent of Kalmakov's spectacle, as was her angular yet billowing costume for Salomé; her Amazonian Salomé was still modeled on the Decadent phallic woman. Exter's stage design of the 1910s in general had an affinity with Evreinov's Symbolist *Salomé* production and also with Bakst's *Salomé* and *Cléopatre.*

Rubinstein, the best-known Russian Salomé abroad, turned not only to Salomé but also to the ancient cultures of Egypt, Greece, and Rome for artistic inspiration. Of Russian-Jewish origin, she was a mime more than a dancer. After she left Diaghilev's company, she formed her own in 1911, and was its star. Tall, very thin, exotically beautiful, eccentric, expensively and flamboyantly dressed, Rubinstein had a chiseled aquiline profile (evident in her archly posed photographs and portraits) that evoked Egyptian wall painting or Greek bas-reliefs and vases. Describing her as Cleopatra in 1909, Prince Peter Lieven refers to Rubinstein's "marvellous Eastern profile . . . that seemed to have descended from an Egyptian bas-relief."[27]

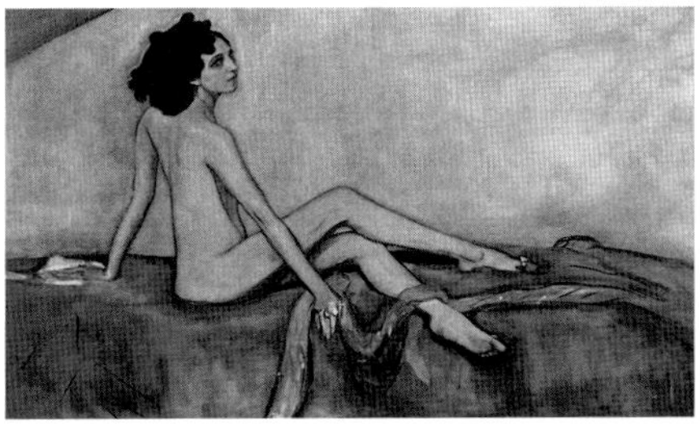

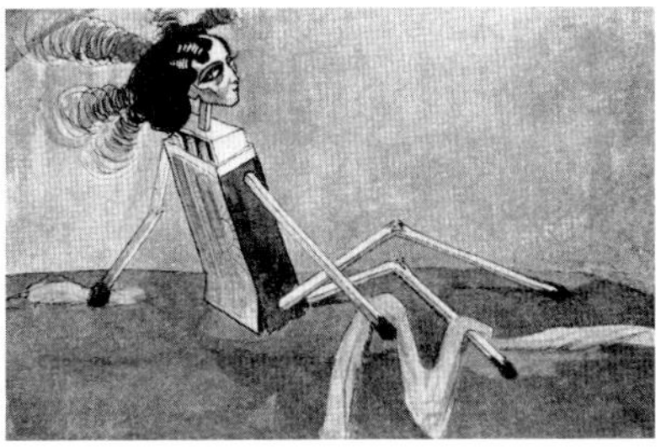

left:
figure 18. VALENTIN SEROV
Portrait of Ida Rubinstein, 1910
Tempera on canvas, 147 x 233 cm
State Russian Museum, St. Petersburg

figure 19. ALEXEI RADAKOV
Caricature of Ida Rubinstein, 1912

In an age that revived Orientalism and popularized Decadent emaciation, Rubinstein cultivated a look that was both Oriental and corpselike. She was an independent, liberated woman whose tastes were bisexual. Her affairs with Italian poet Gabriele D'Annunzio and Romaine Brooks, a lesbian American artist who lived in Paris, were common knowledge. She inspired several famous homosexual artists, including Baron Robert de Montesquiou, Vaslav Nijinsky, and Cocteau.

The removal of exotic layers of clothing to reveal the naked body characterized the performative, as well as the phantasmic, image of Europe's femme fatale, and according to Alexandre Benois, artistic designer for the Ballets Russes, Rubinstein would sometimes strip naked in public to create a special artistic effect.[28] In fact, there exist several paintings and photographs of Rubinstein in the nude. Valentin Serov, Russia's leading portrait artist of the turn of the century and a professor at the Moscow Institute of Painting, Sculpture, and Architecture, cradle of Moscow's avant-garde, painted her in the nude in 1910 (fig. 18). The portrait—intended as a poster for the Ballets Russes's 1910 Paris season—was controversial, despite Serov's concealment of the genital area by the angle. Rubinstein's anorexic sepulchral figure, the blue draping, the green veil that covers her left leg, and the rings on her fingers and toes correspond to the vision of Cleopatra as an unveiled mummy in Diaghilev's ballet.

Serov's portrait was parodied by Alexei Radakov in 1912 (fig. 19). The pose and veils in Radakov's version remain the same, but the body is highly stylized; Radakov reduced the already limited lines in Serov's portrait even further, so that Rubinstein appears as no more than a stick figure. The representation suggests the image of a match girl: Rubinstein's torso is a matchbox slightly open at the top, her limbs are burnt matches breaking at the joints, and her Medusa-like head is impaled on a lit match, with funnels of smoke in the shape of giant spiraling curls. Viewed in reference to Salomé, the figure suggests self-immolation. Though

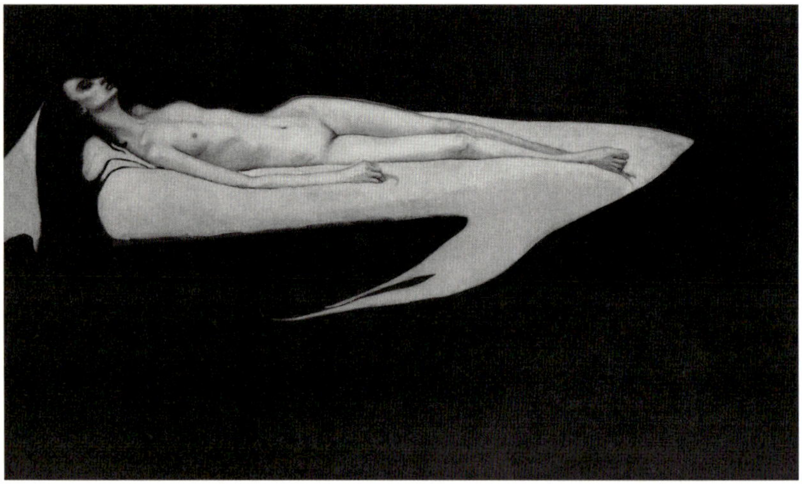

figure 20. ROMAINE BROOKS
Le Trajet (The Voyage), ca. 1911
Oil on canvas, 115.2 x 191.4 cm
National Museum of American Art, Smithsonian Institution, Washington, D.C., Gift of the artist.

intended as a caricature, the representation evokes contemporaneous abstract human forms in which lines have been reduced to a minimum, such as Stepanova's unisex, degendered stick figures. True, Stepanova's reductionism derived from the avant-garde's quest for a universal common denominator — the human machine in motion — but there is still a bond between her stick figures and Radakov's depiction of Rubinstein.

There are also two nude portraits of Rubinstein by Brooks. The better-known one, entitled *Le Trajet (The Voyage)*, ca. 1911 (fig. 20), depicts an emaciated white female corpse lying prone on what appears to be a bed, against a black backdrop. It is an androgynous and almost abstract representation of the Decadent dead woman, a figure whose power was fetishized during the fin de siècle. Even though women are sometimes "deformed" in Cubist representations, the female corpse as an emblem of power was not the subtext of these works.

Rubinstein's charisma was based not only on her sepulchral image and her androgynous roles.[29] She was also a woman of high fashion who displayed and advertised leading couturiers' dresses. In 1913, for example, she appeared on the cover of the French theater and fashion magazine *Comoedia Illustré* wearing a beautiful Worth gown (fig. 21). According to the Russian-born couturier Erté [Roman de Tirtoff], Rubinstein launched the 1913 vogue for "walking slinkily à la leopard" after her appearance in D'Annunzio's *La Pisanella*, in which she "walked a leopard on a long chain."[30] Writers and artists at the turn of the century perceived women's fascination with wild cats as an expression of the femme-fatale's beastliness.

Even though the incarnation of Rubinstein as a cross-gendered exotic figure was accomplished primarily by male stage and fashion designers, the impetus for these representations came from her. She selected the artists with whom she worked, and financed productions with the ultimate goal of staging her provocative androgynous persona. She was an artiste fashioning her own success. Her image of an exotic, elegantly dressed femme fatale was an emblematic female construction

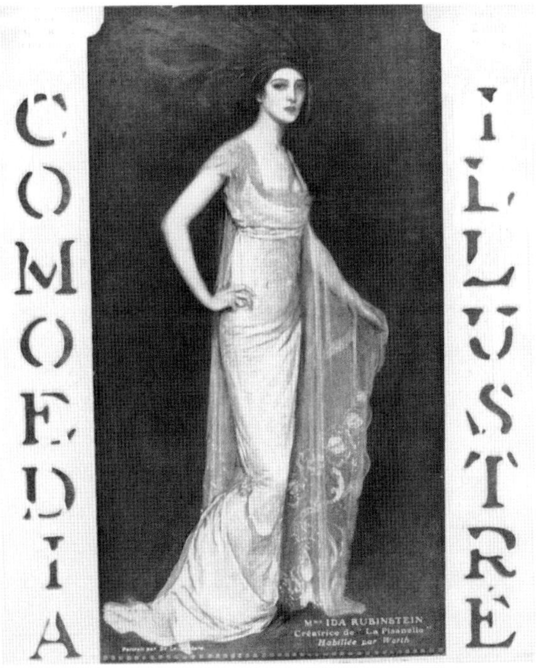

figure 21. De la Gandara's portrait of Ida Rubinstein, reproduced on the front cover of *Comoedia Illustré* (Paris), no. 18 (June 20, 1913).

of the time, and her liberating figure could not have gone unnoticed by women artists such as Goncharova and Rozanova.

Graphic artist Elizaveta Sergeevna Kruglikova is considerably less known than Gippius or Rubinstein. Her self-representation in art and in life was androgynous as well, but in contrast to these other two women's seductive, albeit phallic, personas, hers was self-consciously mannish.[31] A professional New Woman, Kruglikova represented a different aspect of female sexual anarchy. Cross-dressing in her case lacked a spiritual or titillating subtext; rather, it was a sign of lesbianism and followed the conventions of a "butch" code, which included smoking. Anna Petrovna Ostroumova-Lebedeva (1871–1944), an important member of the World of Art group as a painter and graphic artist,[32] painted Kruglikova in 1925, showing her dressed in work clothes and holding a cigarette. True, the portrait was painted after the Revolution, at a time when Stepanova and other women were represented at work and smoking. We can conclude that Kruglikova's sexual identity was less slippery than Gippius's or Rubinstein's; furthermore, unlike Gippius, she did not hide her lesbian orientation, and, unlike Rubinstein, she was not an exhibitionist. Kruglikova's masculine style included participation in male sports, such as long-distance cycling and mountain climbing. Benois described the artist and her girlfriend, Mademoiselle Sellier, cycling from Paris to Brittany around 1905, wearing special cyclist trousers that were still considered to be rather shocking in provincial France.[33]

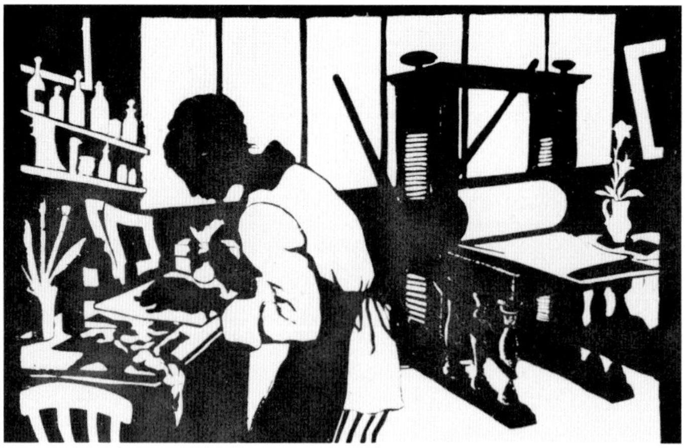

figure 22.
ELIZAVETA KRUGLIKOVA
Printing an Etching. Self-Portrait, 1915
Linocut, 9.6 x 16 cm
State Russian Museum,
St. Petersburg

Kruglikova went to Paris to study, as did many of her contemporaries (including younger avant-garde women artists such as Liubov Popova and Nadezhda Udaltsova, who went in 1912). Kruglikova arrived in Paris in 1895 and had her first solo exhibition there only seven years later. She shared a studio with another Russian artist, Alexandra Davidenko, in Montparnasse, which was an important gathering place for Russian and French bohemian artists. The creator of masterful monotype engravings and silhouettes,[34] Kruglikova made many self-portraits, the best of which — executed in profile — display the process of work. Like her younger avant-garde sisters Popova and Stepanova, Kruglikova worked in the sphere of mass culture at the newspaper *Novoe vremia* (*New Time*), which was widely read at the turn of the century. In a painted self-portrait of 1906, Kruglikova represents herself bent over a machine tool, wearing the large masculine gloves used by workers during the printing process. A 1915 engraving shows her printing an etching (fig. 22), an image of female physical labor that would serve as a prototype for the Soviet redefinition of women's work. (Kruglikova's 1923 propaganda poster for women's literacy was a well-known example of early Soviet agitprop.)[35] Similarly, Popova and Stepanova designed working clothes in a unisexual, Constructivist mode in the early 1920s (see fig. 75). Stepanova was known for her unisex sports costumes that transformed the body by means of the dynamic use of geometric design, while her self-caricature *The Constructor Stepanova*, 1922, represents a strong, mannish figure wearing a dress. Goncharova also portrayed women (and men) at work, although these tend to be peasants, not industrial workers.

Kruglikova made portraits of other new women. For example, around 1915, she made a silhouette of Nadezhda Dobychina, owner of the celebrated St. Petersburg Art Bureau and sponsor of avant-garde exhibitions, including Goncharova's one-woman exhibition of 1914 and *0.10* the following year. Thus many works by Exter, Goncharova, Popova, Rozanova, and Udaltsova passed through her hands.

Kruglikova's image of Dobychina shows her scrutinizing a painting on an easel, hands in her pockets with a cigarette between her lips. It is a masculinized image focusing on the subject's professional life, which is typically rendered by means of conventional male props.

Kruglikova's strongest artworks are her black silhouettes against white backgrounds. Her self-portraits in this mode evoke the fin-de-siècle figure of the Wildean dandy. She presented herself dressed in a frock coat, elaborate dress shirt, and bow tie; her hair is bobbed, and the profile masks her gender. Unlike the engravings that picture her at work, the self-representations as a dandy aestheticize her mannishness. In a silhouette of 1921, which seems late in its allusion to the figure of the dandy, Kruglikova depicted herself cutting out a silhouette surrounded by the tools of her trade, a long-established convention of artists' self-representation that was appropriated widely by both male and female artists.[36] Udaltsova's Cubist *Self-Portrait with Palette*, 1915 (plate 80), for example, also represents the artist with her professional tools.

The form of the silhouette revived at the turn of the century differs from its late-eighteenth-century model in that it features men and women in profile instead of the conventional realist *en face.* The emphasis on the profile — and the silhouette — had historical forebears in ancient Egyptian, Greek, and Roman art. *Mir iskusstva*, which was launched in 1898, not only featured silhouettes, but also Egyptomania and a fascination with ancient Greek beauty. The preference for profile or frontal representation in any era depends on the conception of individual character that predominates at that time. The art of stylization typically has little interest in the more intimate individualized frontal portrait. For example, Pisanello's and Boticelli's fifteenth-century profile portraits of young women, with their unusually long necks and tautly pulled-back hair, express a distant stylized beauty, reflecting the profile's inherent remoteness and affinity to abstract figurative design. With the increase of psychological portraiture during the High Renaissance, artists began to paint their models in three-quarter view and later in full face.[37] In full-length female nudes painted *en face*, the subjects assumed the power of the gaze, staring provocatively at the viewer. Frontal representations of women were characteristic also of the second half of the nineteenth century, and the powerful female gaze left traces in works produced by the avant-garde, including Goncharova's *Self-Portrait with Yellow Lilies*, 1907 (plate 13). Although the androgynous face in Stepanova's Neo-Primitivist *Self-Portrait,* 1920 (plate 71), looks angrily at the viewer, its source is not the fin-de-siècle image of female power, but rather the African mask.

After the prevalence of frontal views in the nineteenth century, the profile reemerged at the end of the century in stylized, rather than psychological, portraits in both painting and photography. In the context of an age that liberated women and emphasized nonprocreative sexual indeterminacy, the facial profile offered women more possibilities of crossing the strictures of gender boundaries. This was especially true if the subject had what is called a strong profile, and Rubinstein, Gippius, and Kruglikova all did. Avant-garde artists continued the fashion for profile views, especially in Cubist representations, such as Popova's *Lady with Guitar*, 1915 (plate 32).

While the avant-garde's break with Symbolism was radical, marking a point of rupture, the production of the six women artists in this exhibition does not necessarily reflect a total break with the past. Several of them, including Rozanova, began as Symbolists, before quickly turning to Cubism and geometric abstraction; even Stepanova, the most "un-Decadent" of the six artists, was known to express herself in a Beardsleyian or Decadent style.[39] Exter, Popova, and Stepanova all designed stylish dresses and hats for women, not just unisexual workers' garments and sports clothes, and Goncharova designed gowns for Nadezhda Lamanova, Moscow's queen of haute couture, and lavish sets for the Ballets Russes. Although these examples represent only fragments of their work, they reflect the fact that these radical Amazons also expressed themselves in the fashionable artistic mode of the turn of the century. Yet while the figurative paintings of these six artists can certainly be considered androgynous, they are not gender-bending; they do not reveal the same kind of gender destabilization as do the lives and works of the three women discussed in this essay. Furthermore, the work of Exter, Goncharova, Popova, Rozanova, Stepanova, and Udaltsova does not display the characteristic fin-de-siècle ambivalence toward the problematized female body.

1. Elaine Showalter, *Sexual Anarchy: Gender and Culture at the Fin de Siècle* (New York: Viking, 1990).
2. Max Nordau, *Degeneration* (New York: Howard Fertig, 1968). The German original, *Entartung*, appeared in 1892; it was first translated into English in 1895.
3. For the Russian notion of the androgynous ideal, see Olga Matich, "Androgyny and the Russian Religious Renaissance," in Anthony Mklikotin, ed., *Western Philosophical Systems in Russian Literature* (Los Angeles: University of Southern California, n.d.), pp. 165–76.
4. The novels of her husband, Dmitrii Merezhkovsky, especially *The Romance of Leonardo da Vinci* (1901), were very popular throughout Europe. Merezhkovsky's *Leonardo* was the main source of Sigmund Freud's psychoanalytic essay on the artist.
5. Andrei Bely wrote *Petersburg* (1915), considered the most important novel of early Russian Modernism.
6. Alexander Lavrov, ed., *Andrei Bely: "Nachalo veka"* (Moscow: Khudozhestvennaia literatura, 1990), p. 194.
7. I. Briusova and N. Ashukin, eds., *Valerii Briusov. "Dnevniki 1891–1910"* (Moscow: Sytnikov, 1927), p. 109.
8. For a discussion of the Cleopatra myth in Russian culture, especially as embodied by Gippius, see Olga Matich, "Zinaida Gippius' Personal Myth," in Boris Gasparov, Robert P. Hughes, and Irina Paperno, eds., *Cultural Mythologies of Russian Modernism: From the Golden Age to the Silver Age*

(Berkeley: University of California Press, 1992), pp. 52–72. There is a curious parallel here with a photograph of the poet Anna Akhmatova in which, adopting a "Cleopatra" pose, she lies serpent-like on a divan; for a reproduction, see Krystyna Rubinger, ed., *Künsterlerinnen der russischen Avantgarde, 1910–1930* (Cologne: Galerie Gmuszynsk, 1979), p. 15.

9. Havelock Ellis, "Sexual Inversion in Women," in *Alienist and Neurologist* (St. Louis: 1895), vol. 18, no. 2, pp. 152–54; as quoted in Marjorie Garber, *Vested Interests: Cross-Dressing and Cultural Anxiety* (New York: Routledge, 1992), p. 155.
10. In a late-nineteenth-century photographic self-portrait, the American Frances Benjamin Johnston "posed herself in a 'male' manner. [Sitting in profile,] elbow out, mannish cap on her head, tankard in one hand and cigarette in the other, she leans forward with the calf of one leg resting on the thigh of the other" (Frances Borzello, *Seeing Ourselves: Women's Self-Portraits* [London: Abrams, 1998], p. 115). A cigarette figures prominently in a photograph by Paul Nadar of the elegantly dressed, liberated Lucie Delarue-Mardus, lover of Natalie Barbey and member of the prewar sisterhood of Europe's gender-benders. (See William Howard Adams, *A Proust Souvenir: Period Photographs by Paul Nadar* [New York: The Vendome Press, 1984], p. 121.)
11. Igumen Andronik and M. Trubachev, eds., *Pavel Florensky. "Analiz prostranstvennosti i vremeni v khudozhestvenno-izobrazitelnykh proizvedeniiakh"* (Moscow: Progress, 1993), pp. 146–71.
12. Bakst's portrait of Gippius, which was commissioned by Nikolai Riabushinsky, publisher of the Symbolist journal *Zolotoe runo (Golden Fleece)* and one of the first collectors of the early avant-garde, was displayed in Paris and London and at a controversial exhibition of women's portraits sponsored by the journal *Apollon (Apollo)* that was held in St. Petersburg in 1910.
13. John E. Bowlt, *The Silver Age: Russian Art of the Early Twentieth Century and the "World of Art" Group* (Newtonville, Mass.: Oriental Research Partners, 1982), pp. 223–24.
14. Within the lesbian *beau monde* of Paris, such well-known artists and writers as the Marquise de Belbeuf, Romaine Brooks, Radclyffe Hall, and Una Troubridge dressed in high transvestite (or dandy) style; the latter two even sported a monocle. In London, Vita Sackville-West also fashioned herself as a dandy.
15. A self-styled dandy who loved artifice, Bakst was infatuated with Gippius and her heady theology of sex. As a teacher or as a colleague, he was in touch with many of the members of the avant-garde, and his sensual designs for Sergei Diaghilev's production of *Cléopatre*, performed by the Ballets Russes in Paris in 1909, surely informed Exter's sets and costumes for Alexander Tairov's production of *Salomé* in Petrograd in 1917.
16. Zinaida Gippius, "Contes d'amour," in Temira Pachmuss, ed., *Between Paris and St. Petersburg: Selected Diaries of Zinaida Hippius* (Urbana: University of Illinois Press, 1975), p. 77.
17. Ibid., p. 74.
18. Like Gippius, Romaine Brooks did not consummate her marriage. She entered into a "white" marriage with John Ellingham Brooks, a homosexual dilettante pianist. During the 1910s, she developed an amorous relationship with American artist Natalie Clifford Barney, which lasted until Brooks's death. Similar marital arrangements characterized the personal lives of the Bloomsbury group.
19. Carl Schorske, *Fin-de-Siècle Vienna: Politics and Culture* (New York: Vintage Books, 1981), p. 224.
20. Diaghilev's ballet was first performed in St. Petersburg in 1908. It was revised and renamed for the Paris performance, although there is some debate over the original title. Some scholars believe that it was titled *Une Nuit d'Egypte* and was based on an 1845 story of the same name by Théophile Gautier, while others claim that it was titled *Egyptian Nights* and was based on Pushkin's unfinished eponymous society tale of the 1830s. Emblematic of the Cleopatra myth in

Russian culture, in both stories the Egyptian queen offers to exchange a night of love for a young man's life. Both texts were revived at the turn of the century; they fascinated not only ballet artists but also Russian Symbolist poet Valerii Briusov, who completed Pushkin's *Egyptian Nights* by rendering the tale in verse. For a discussion of *Cléopatre* in the context of the Ballets Russes and its history, see Deborah Jowitt, "The Veils of Salomé," in *Time and Dancing Image* (New York: William Morrow, 1988), pp. 105–15.

21. Jean Cocteau, "Cléopatre," in Arséne Alexandre, ed., *The Decorative Art of Leon Bakst* (New York: Dover, 1972), pp. 29–30. This is a reprint of an exhibition catalogue originally published by the Fine Art Society of London in 1913, which features Bakst's ballet designs and commentary by Cocteau.
22. "Na generalnoi repetitsii," *Birzhevye vedomosti* (St. Petersburg), October 28, 1906, p. 3 ("Okolo rampy" [title of newspaper column]).
23. M. Veikone, "Teatr Komissarzhevskoi," *Teatr i iskusstvo* (St. Petersburg), no. 44 (1908), p. 764.
24. Evreinov published a monograph on Beardsley in 1912.
25. Vasilii R., "Na gneral'noi repetitsii 'Tsarevny,'" *Birzhevye vedomosti*, October 28, 1908, p. 3 ("Okolo rampy").
26. Nina Lobanov-Rostovsky, "A Bargain on Marché aux Puces: The Pictures of Nicolai Kalmakov," in A. Flegon, *Eroticism in Russian Art* (London: Flegon Press, 1976), p. 306. (Lobanov-Rostovsky is a major collector of Russian stage design [1900–1930].)
27. Prince Peter Lieven, *The Birth of Ballets-Russes* (London: Allen and Urwin: 1936, p. 97). Rozanova's Amazonian *Queen of Spades*, from her *Playing Cards* series, is similarly evocative of representations of women in Egyptian art; the Queen's head appears in profile, while her body is portrayed frontally. The queen of spades as the female symbol of demonic evil power in Russian cultural mythology dates to Pushkin's eponymous novella of 1833.
28. N. Alexandrova, ed., *Alexandr Benua: Moi vospominaniia* (Moscow: Nauka, 1990), vol. 2, p. 471.
29. Rubinstein's most overtly androgynous role was that of St. Sebastian in D'Annunzio's *The Martyrdom of Saint Sebastian* (1911).
30. Quoted in Michael de Cossart, *Ida Rubinstein (1885–1960): A Theatrical Life* (Liverpool: Liverpool University Press, 1987), p. 57.
31. There were also more conventional models of femininity at the turn of the century. For example, Olga Glebova-Sudeikina, a charming and graceful actress, artist, and poet, performed unambiguously feminine/female roles on the stage and in St. Petersburg cabarets, where she is reputed to have danced provocatively on tables. She also made beautiful embroideries, Art Nouveau puppets, and fine ceramic statuettes. Glebova married artist Sergei Sudeikin, who designed the sets and costumes for Diaghilev's production of *The Tragedy of Salomé* in Paris in 1913. Sudeikin was bisexual; his most important homosexual affair was with poet Mikhail Kuzmin, who styled himself as a dandy and wore makeup. Later Glebova participated in another homoerotic triangle, with Kuzmin and Vsevolod Kniazev. It was also rumored that she had an amorous relationship with Akhmatova. This kind of overlapping bisexual triangulation was characteristic of erotic life in the Petersburg hothouse at the turn of the century. On Glebova-Sudeikina, Sudeikin, and their friends, see John E. Bowlt, ed., *The Salon Album of Vera Sudeikin-Stravinsky* (Princeton: Princeton University Press, 1990).
32. In her time, Ostroumova-Lebedeva was the most important female member of the World of Art association. She was close to the group's journal, *Mir iskusstva*. She was one of its retrospectivists that reappropriated the images of eighteenth-century St. Petersburg. For information on Ostroumova-Lebedeva, see M. Kiselev, *Grafika A. P. Ostroumovoi-Lebedevoi* (Moscow: Iskusstvo,

1984), and E. Poliakova, *Gorod Ostroumovoi-Lebedevoi* (Moscow: Sovetskii khudozhnik, 1983).

33. See Alexandrova, ed., *Alexandr Benua*, vol. 2, p. 433.
34. See Alexandre Benois, introduction in *Parizh nakanune voiny v monotipiiakh E. S. Kruglkovoi* (Petrograd: Union, 1918). The book includes poems about Paris by Viacheslav Ivanov, Feodor Sologub, and Kruglikova's close friends Konstantin Balmont and Maximilian Voloshin. It was rumored that at one time Kruglikova was in love with the androgynous Voloshin. On Kruglikova, see P. Kornilov, comp., *Elizaveta Sergeevna Kruglikova. Zhizn i tvorchestvo. Sbornik* (Leningrad: Khudozhnik RSFSR, 1969), and E. Grishina, *E. S. Kruglikova* (Leningrad: Khudozhnik RSFSR, 1989).
35. On female images in Soviet poster art, see Victoria Bonnell, *Iconography of Power: Soviet Political Posters under Lenin and Stalin* (Berkeley: University of California Press, 1997), pp. 65–135.
36. See, for example, the self-portraits by Marie Bashkirtseva. Born in Russia, Bashkirtseva studied and worked in France; she died in 1884 at the age of twenty-six. See Colette Cosnier, *Marie Bashkirtseff. Un portrait sans retouches* (Paris: Horay, 1985), and *Journal de Marie Bashkirtseff* (Paris: Mazarine, 1980).
37. A technical explanation for the early Renaissance preference for the profile is also possible, which suggests that painting naturalistic representations of the frontal view, especially of the model looking out at the viewer, was simply too difficult at the time.
38. S. Stepanova, "The Poetics of Creativity," in Alexander Lavrentiev and John E. Bowlt, *Varvara Stepanova: The Complete Work* (Cambridge, Mass.: MIT Press, 1988), pp. 14–17.

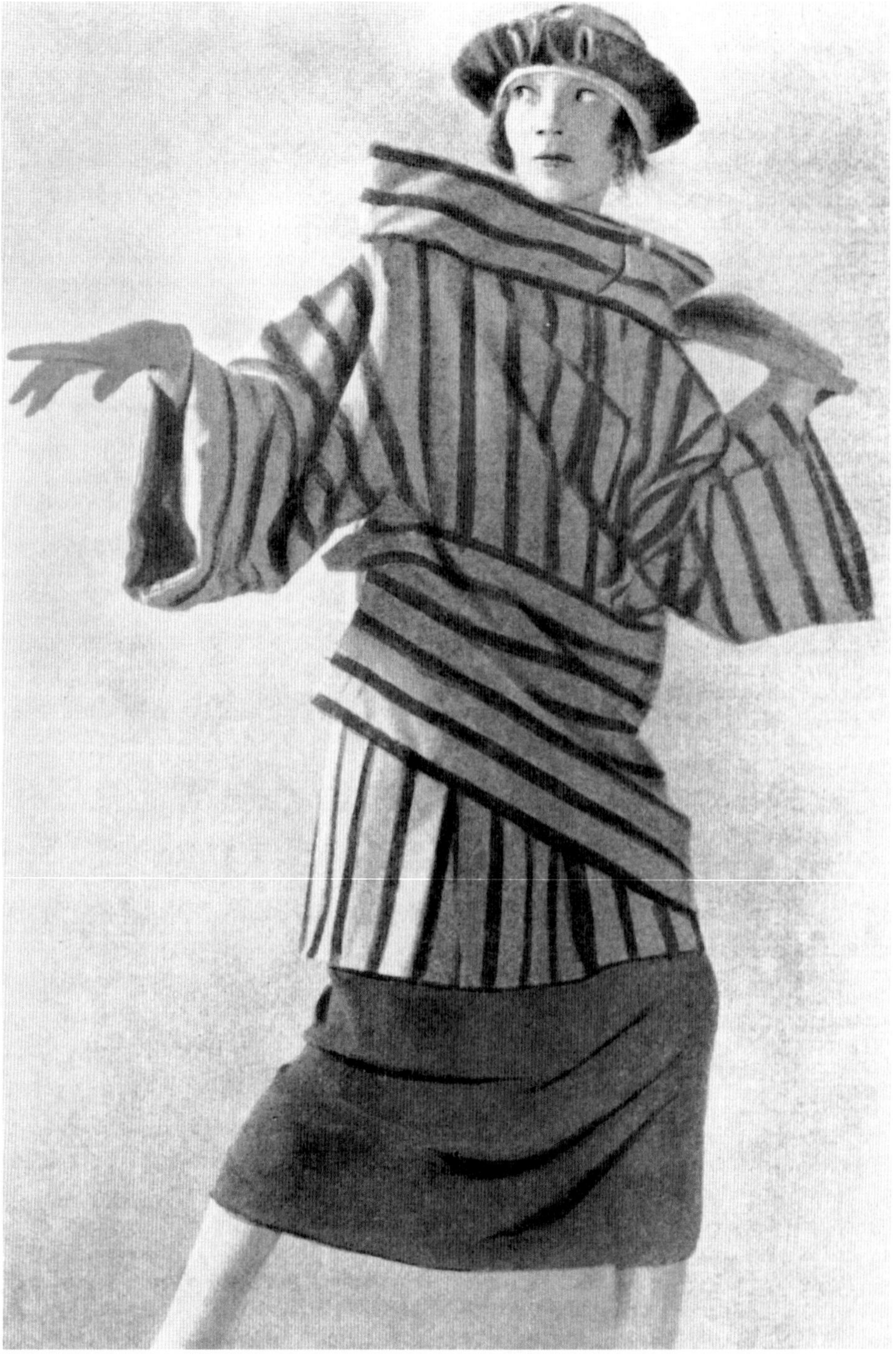

figure 23. Alexandra Khokhlova modeling a dress designed by Nadezhda Lamanova, ca. 1924.

Dressing Up and Dressing Down: The Body of the Avant-Garde

Nicoletta Misler

The paintings of the Russian avant-garde's women artists include numerous images of objects and tools. While these images may be strategically masked in Cubist disassembling and dislocation or in the alogical fragmentation and dissociation of *zaum* (transrational language), they remind us that these protagonists did not completely renounce their female occupations or the particularly female creativity that such occupations entail.

For example, the hated/beloved sewing machine is the emphatic presence in Nadezhda Udaltsova's Cubist work *Seamstress*, 1912–13 (plate 74), while the spools of thread, fabric remnants, lace, and trinkets that a good housewife would never throw away grace Olga Rozanova's near-Suprematist *Work Box,* 1915 (fig. 66). The loom figures prominently in Natalia Goncharova's *The Weaver (Loom + Woman)*, 1912–13 (plate 21), although in this case it indicates an escape from the four walls of domesticity, toward a Futurist machine. According to Alexander Lavrentiev, Varvara Stepanova, despite her loud statements in support of industrial garments, loved to sew her own clothes and would occasionally assume the classic female role, sewing the revolutionary overalls designed by her husband, Alexander Rodchenko. The same Stepanova who filled her canvases with severe robotic mannequins plays coyly with a string of pearls (the quintessence of the bourgeois lady) in photographs taken by Rodchenko in 1928 (see fig. 24).

These Amazons — so revolutionary in their art and politics — did not with to give up embroideries or purses and evening bags (the most feminine of objects).

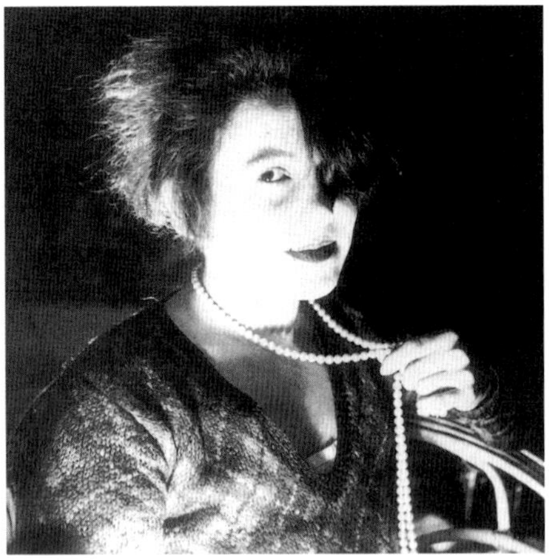

figure 24. Varvara Stepanova, photographed by Alexander Rodchenko, 1928.

In fact, some of Stepanova's handbags, along with many of her other personal items, have been kept religiously by her family. At least one of Alexandra Exter's handbags has also survived, despite the vicissitudes of revolution and emigration. Rozanova made several designs for Futurist handbags, as did Udaltsova and Ksenia Boguslavskaia, wife of Ivan Puni (see fig. 25).[1] In the collage entitled *Toilette*, 1914–15 (fig. 26), Boguslavskaia assembled dressing-table objects, including a powder compact, cuttings from fashion magazines, and a medicine bottle, rather as Rozanova did in the interior of *Work Box*. Although Liubov Popova does not seem to have fallen into the temptation of creating a Suprematist evening bag for herself, she did have a weakness for female bric-a-brac; this is manifest in the colored feathers and gloves of *Subject from a Dyer's Shop*, 1914 (fig. 27). Popova also carved out her own modest feminine territory with the Suprematist embroidery designs that she made for the Verbovka women's enterprise.[2] But male avant-garde artists, from Malevich to Puni, also designed or made handbags and embroideries.[3] Malevich said: "My mother used to do different kinds of embroidery and lace-making. I learned that art from her and also did embroidery and crochet."[4]

Handbags are not only symbolic autonomous objects but are also accessories, and nearly all the women artists who concern us here designed fashionable costumes and clothing. For example, in her 1913 Moscow retrospective, Goncharova showed numerous contemporary costume and embroidery designs, some of which couturier Nadezhda Lamanova acquired for her fashion salon. Exter theorized about the significance of contemporary dress,[5] and Popova and Stepanova tried to explain the meaning and purpose of the *prozodezhda* (overalls for specific activities such as sports or the theater).[6] But, again, costume theory and design were not restricted to women, for even the philosopher Pavel Florensky hastened to emphasize the importance of women's fashion: "Ladies' fashions are one of the most subtle regents of any culture. It is enough just to glance at a woman's dress, to understand the dominant spirit and tone of the entire culture in which such a fashion is permissible."[7]

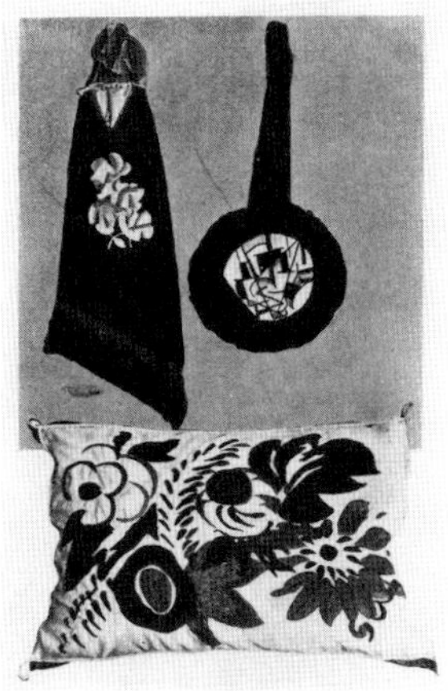

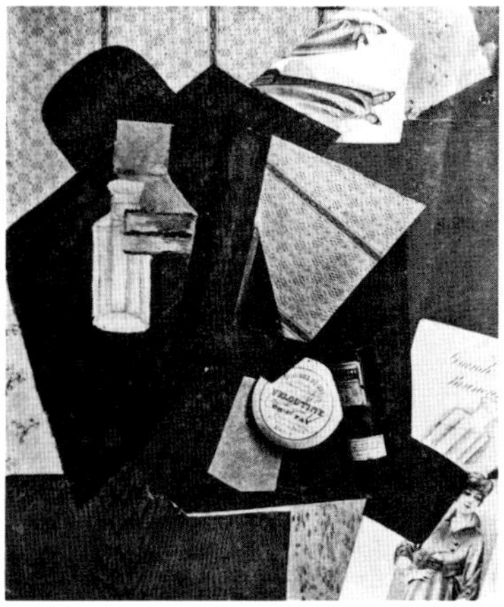

far left:
figure 25. Scarf, handbag (?), and pillow designed by Ksenia Boguslavskaia at the *World of Art* exhibition, Petrograd, 1916.

figure 26. KSENIA BOGUSLAVSKAIA
Toilette, 1914–15 (destroyed)
Oil and collage on canvas, 42 x 33 cm

From a practical point of view, male avant-garde artists also had something to say about the new clothing — from Vladimir Tatlin's mass-produced garments[8] to Rodchenko's overalls. Ippolit Sokolov, radical advocate of the Constructivist movement and its clothing, declared unambiguously that the "style of the U.S.S.R. is the straight line!" Emil Mindlin observed that the new style was an arrangement of horizontal and vertical lines, like the architecture of the Parthenon, and thus the collarless peasant shirt (*tolstovka*) promoted by Constructivist designers could, in fact, be regarded as a new Parthenon.[9] This reductionist statement, a broader indication of the puritanism and asceticism that pervaded post-Revolutionary avant-garde ideology, was the extreme result of the obvious repression of the body and its physiological functions, which can be identified with the later avant-garde.[10] Strangely enough, this was even more evident in the female contingent of the avant-garde. Certainly, they did not reject their everyday female identity, as we can sense from their cult of the evening bag and the dressing table, but the very essence of female identity — the recognition and depiction of the female body — engendered ambiguous and by no means homogeneous interpretations. In fact, the female body seemed to disappear within the spacious, if clumsy, geometric volumes of the new style, at least in the case of Exter, Popova, and Stepanova.

Awareness of the body is awareness of one's own body, and if we look at our six Amazons, we see that at least four of them (excluding the tall, thin Goncharova and the petite Rozanova) could hardly have been reduced to the movement of a single line. Rather, their solid, squarish bodies were compatible with the radical simplification of the *prozodezhda*, designs that almost banished sexuality and eroticism. In Popova's *Composition with Figures*, 1913 (plate 28), the solid, tubular figures resemble Popova herself, whose female form seemed to presage the ideal Soviet female body, in opposition to the androgynous silhouette of the Symbolist heroines. Popova's *Portrait of a Lady (Plastic Design)*, 1915, presents an image so scarcely female that it seems to be a direct extension of the jug in her *Jug on Table. Plastic Painting* of the same year (plate 34).

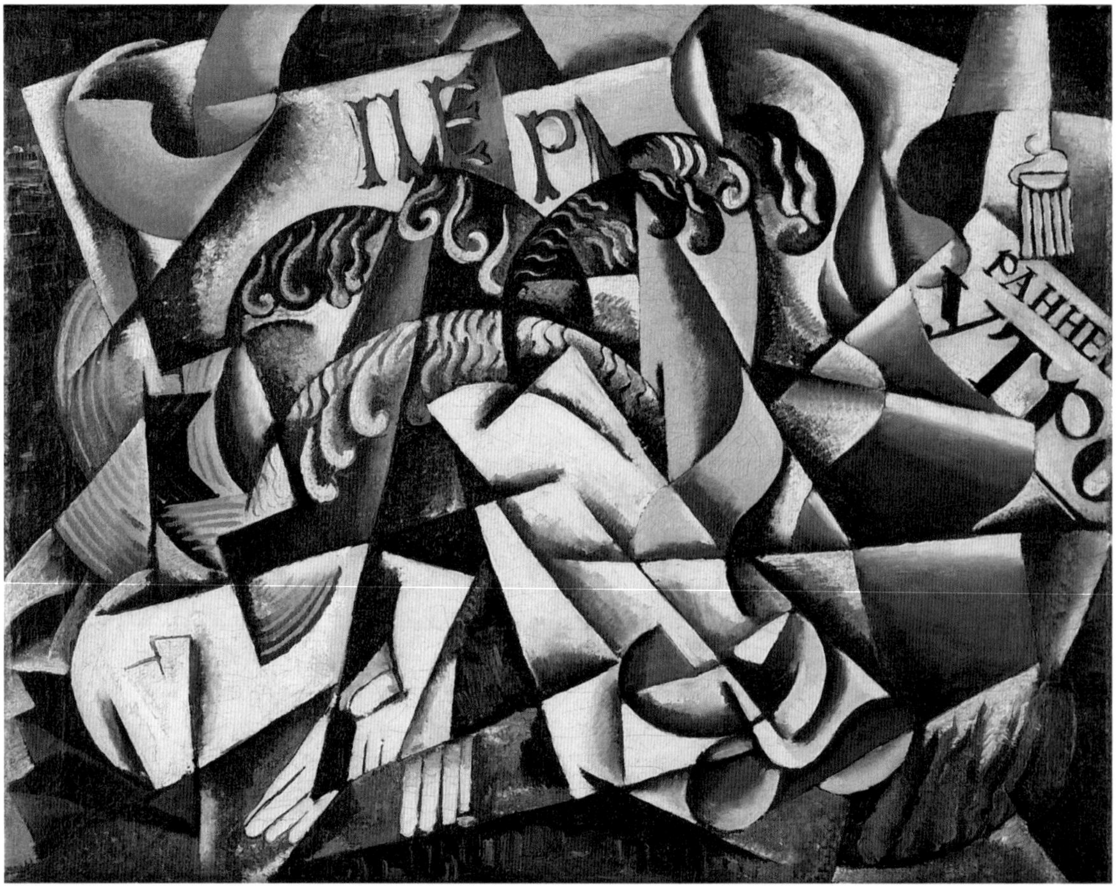

figure 27. LIUBOV POPOVA
Subject from a Dyer's Shop, 1914
Oil on canvas, 71 x 89 cm
The Museum of Modern Art, New York,
The Riklis Collection of McCrory Corporation

The parenthetical denotation of "plastic" in the title of Popova's work brings to mind the plastic dance (*plastika*) so popular in Moscow at that time, a form of dance that, through its promotion of the liberation of the body, elicited a positive response among the female population. What was the relationship between this kind of artistic expression — plastic dance — which is female in essence, and the painters in our exhibition, whose oeuvres, incidentally, contain many references to dance and who often worked as set and costume designers for the performing arts? Good Amazons all, they removed this feminine plasticity from their discourse in order to concentrate on the more austere battle for new form; and if they did concern themselves with dance and movement, it was a robotic or eccentric dance to which they turned. The spare mannequins in Stepanova's *Dancing Figures on White*, 1920 (plate 65) and *Five Figures on a White Background*, 1920 (plate 66) are the antithesis of soft or acrobatic, nude plastic dancing, which achieved its widest popularity just after the Revolution, and they were painted just before the cult of nudity onstage and in dance that took place in Moscow in 1922. This was the year in which the demonstrations *Evenings of the Denuded Body*, directed by Yurii Ars,[11] and *Evenings of the Liberated Body*, directed by Lev Lukin, were performed. It was also the year of Kasian Goleizovsky's manifesto of the naked body onstage[12] and his production of *The Faun*, in which Boris Erdman reduced the costumes to short skirts and loincloths with fringes.[13]

But the Amazonian reaction to Goleizovsky's presentation was prudish, if not restrained. Popova, for example, avoided the hot issue of *The Faun*'s nudity altogether: "After all, how truer is the equipment and deckwork of the crew of a warship. . . . Why do the Pierrots gesticulate and pose under red lamps (as in Goleizovsky's set)?"[14] In contrast, the critical reactions for and against these manifestations of performance nudity were more explicit: "Eroticism or Pornography?" and "This Pornography Must Stop!" are among the titles of such articles. Indeed, the body that seemed to epitomize sensuality in early Soviet dance was not the female body, but, above all, the abstractly elegant male body of the dancer and mime Alexander Rumnev, in all its provocative homosexual beauty.[15] Rumnev's elongated lines, emphasized by the muscular stretching of his angular poses, also became the preferred subject of the celebrated photographers of the time, including Nikolai Svishchev-Paolo, who forced his model into statuary poses and excruciating contortions (see figs. 28, 29).[16] The vociferous complaints in the Soviet press about pornography and the free dance of naked bodies replicated criticisms directed at Goncharova a decade before. In her primitive nudes, such as *Pillars of Salt*, 1908 (plate 15), Goncharova expelled the eroticism of the fin-de-siècle plastic dancers with their Dionysian ecstasies, but the censors now saw an exposition of the darkest, most disturbing and aesthetically disagreeable aspects of femininity: procreation and the female power that this expresses.[17]

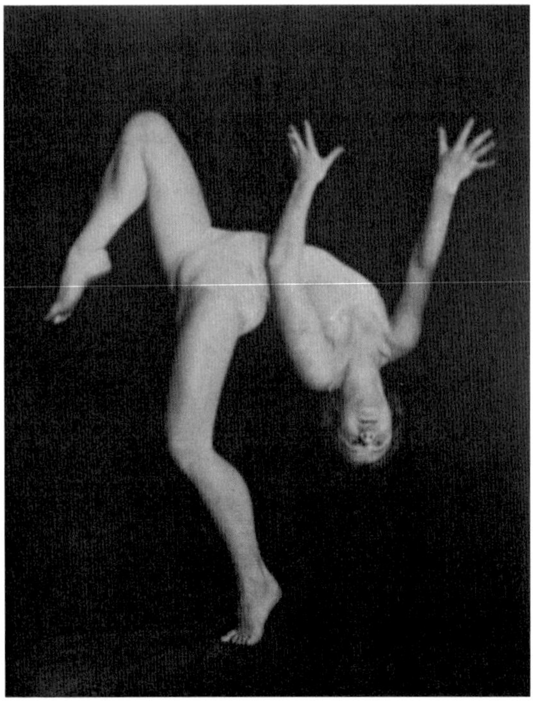

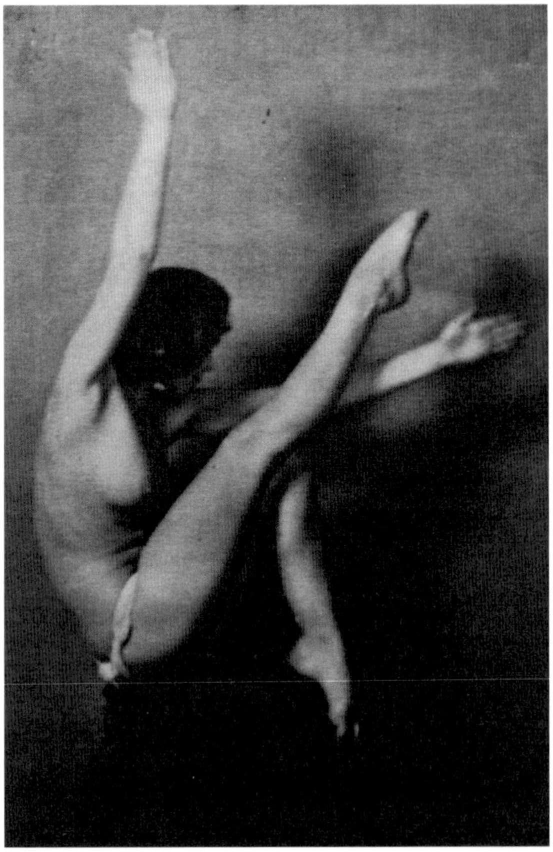

left:
figure 28. Dancer, photographed by Nikolai Svishchev-Paolo(?).

above:
figure 29. Nude dancer, photographed by Nikolai Svishchev-Paolo.

Curiously enough, the feminine-homosexual body that the Free Dance of the 1920s manifested onstage was in sharp contrast to the image of the new, maternal Soviet woman that coalesced in monumental forms in painting, sculpture, and costume design. This contrast was reflected in the avant-garde's puritanical negation of the body as an erotic instrument, so different from the explicit exhibitionism of the nude dancers of the 1920s. The latter flaunted a decadence that derived from the Symbolist era, summarized in Valentin Serov's nude portrait of the hermaphroditic Ida Rubinstein (fig. 18).[18] Florensky, in his interpretation of the archaeological statuette of the Knossos Snake Charmer as a Symbolist femme fatale, seems to have had in mind the icon of the naked Rubinstein with green cloth coiling like a serpent around her slender ankle: "On the dancer's neck is a collar. . . . Two intertwined snakes form her belt, the head of one in front of her body and its tail around her right ear. The head of a third snake rises above the tiara. But fear not, these are imaginary terrors, no more terrifying than ladies' boas, muffs, and winter hats trimmed with the snarling jaws of polecats and other wild beasts. . . . I fancy the snakes of our bayadères are equally harmless."[19] In the same essay, Florensky juxtaposed the snake charmer with another archaeological image, the pagan Russian stone maiden (*kamennaia baba*), which Goncharova had accepted as an artistic and ideological model of femininity for her primitive "pornographic" paintings.[20] For Goncharova, the square, three-dimensional stone maidens were images of female fertility, engrossed in their lapidary bodies and deprived of any appeal (sex appeal, in particular) toward the external world.[21] The naked bodies of these statues carry a clear physical charge, but it is the physicality of procreation, not of eroticism and seduction.

Rubinstein was not the only woman in fin-de-siècle Russia, of both the bourgeoisie and the intelligentsia, who wished to free herself from her clothing and reappropriate her body. Isadora Duncan's early performances in Moscow and St. Petersburg, beginning in 1904, had a lasting effect on this movement, particularly after the opening of her school in Moscow in October 1921. Duncan not only freed the feet of dancers from the constrictions of ballet shoes (resulting in the Russian name for her young followers, *bosonozhki*—literally, barefoot ones), but she also loosened their corsets and their female forms. The dancer Olga Desmond also introduced the concept of total nudity in her *Evenings of Beauty* in 1908,[22] albeit without the artistic legitimacy of Duncan's references to the classical world. In 1911, playwright and theater director Nikolai Evreinov defended the importance of artistic nudity in an illustrated book, *Nagota na stsene* (*Nudity on Stage*), and in 1923 advocated the feminine game of fashion in the magazine *Atelie* (*Atelier*), praising the significance of chic, which he claimed distinguished a Parisienne from a lady of Berlin or Petrograd.[23]

Duncan surrounded herself with young girls dressed in short tunics, seeking in their childlike spontaneity a primitive, inner expressiveness. Her interest coincided with analogous research being conducted immediately after the Revolution, not in the field of dance, but in the area of infantile sexuality.[24] These studies took place in the Nursery Laboratory, established in May 1921 within the Department of Psychology of the State Psycho-Neurological Institute in Moscow (where art historian Alexei Sidorov directed a Department of Experimental Aesthetics).[25] The Institute became the nucleus of Ivan Ermakov's Psychoanalytic Institute, founded the following year. Indeed, the birth of psychoanalysis in Russia is closely linked with the new approach to the visual arts encompassing experimental dance — and thus corporeal expression and communication — as well as the philosophy of art and "pure visibility." Vasily Kandinsky was one of the promoters of this new aesthetic, which took into account the "inexpressible" disturbances of the psyche. Stepanova seems to have been acknowledging Kandinsky's notion of the spiritual in art when she stated, "As yet non-objective creativity is just the dawning of a great new epoch, of a time of great creativity hitherto unseen, destined to open the doors to mysteries more profound than science and technology." [26]

On the basis of these different but converging fields of interest, the body in its psychophysical entirety became the subject of a complex interdisciplinary line of research undertaken by Kandinsky before he emigrated from Russia in 1921. He approached the body as an entity capable of communicating or expressing inner emotions, like a living artifact, in all its beauty, male and female. A primary advocate of this approach was Sidorov, who studied both dance and the graphic work of German Expressionism, an art movement with which he wished to associate the work of Exter and Rozanova.[27] He wrote: "In painting — our eye; in music — our ear; in architecture — our perception of space; in dance — the body is the material of art. Precisely the body in and of itself. . . . Because it is in the body that analysis must be rooted, at least starting with the problem of the role of costume and nudity in the art of dance." [28]

The complex dialectic of dressed/undressed left a deep imprint on current ideas about Russian costume, both for the stage and for everyday, and the subject was a favorite topic of discussion, particularly among critics of a more Symbolist persuasion. Sidorov, who considered the "naked body to be the static principle of dance," [29] concluded that "we are for nudity on stage," because nudity allowed the public to decodify a living mechanism in the movement of even the slightest muscle, which is why he felt that the costume ought to be reduced to body makeup.[30] Still, the erotic "body as such" is absent from the work of the six women artists in this exhibition, both before and after the Revolution, even if they did have something to say about body makeup. Goncharova gave an audacious performance in the movie *Drama in the Futurists' Cabaret No. 13*, 1913, appearing with her breasts and face painted, and Exter decorated the bodies of the dancers in a 1925 ballet in

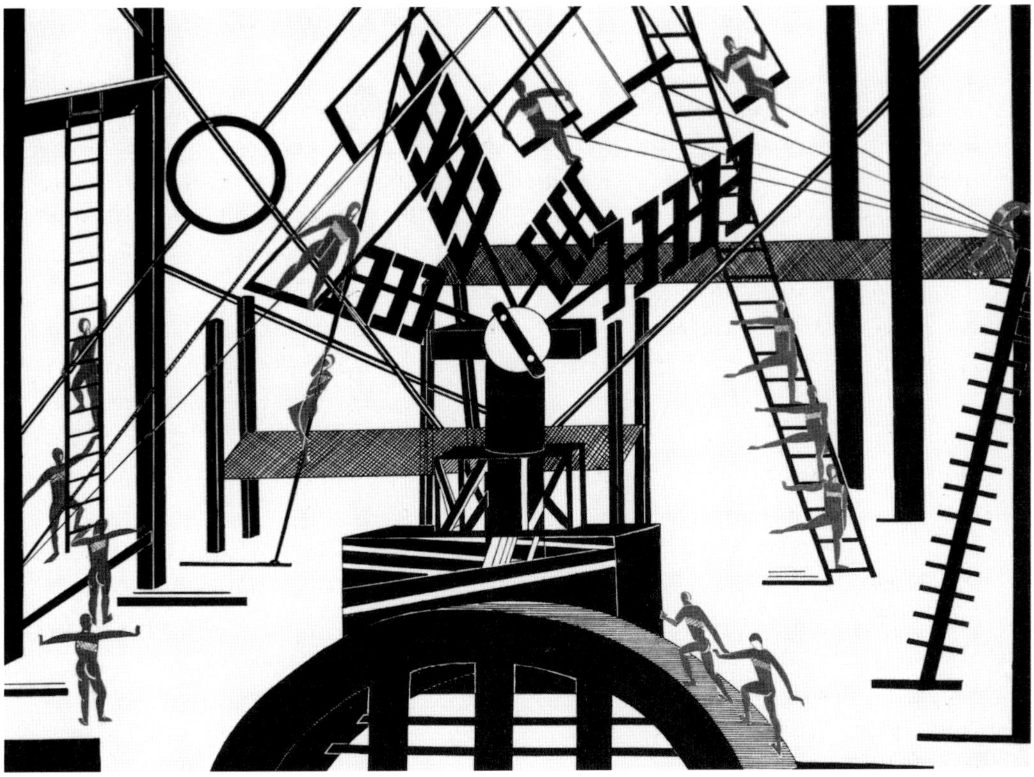

figure 30. ALEXANDRA EXTER
Set design for Dramballet Studio's unrealized production of Alexander Skriabin's *Ballet Satanique*, 1922
Gouache and pencil on paper, 48.7 x 55.1 cm
Bakhrushin State Theater Museum, Moscow

"epidermic costumes." "Strip away the colored rags that are called costumes from the dancer, rags that until now have had only aesthetic significance," urged one critic. "Rejecting aestheticism, we also reject costumes of this type. We must dress the dancer in overalls, which allow the body to move freely."[31] Alternative standards of dress were also represented by Stepanova's functional and unsexy sports tunics (*sportodezhda*), Popova's very proper summer dresses and autumn coats, and the uniform bodysuits that Exter designed for the unrealized *Ballet Satanique* in 1922 (fig. 30).

Exter was very concerned with the body and its costume, whether for dance, theater, or informal wear. Disregarding the erotic aspect of clothing, she was always mindful of rhythm and movement: "Materials that give, for example, any type of silk . . . make it possible to create garments for movements (i.e., for dance) and to devise more complicated shapes (circles, polygons). This type of costume 'constructed' on the dynamic movement of the body, must itself be 'mobile' in its components."[32] Exter applied her theory to the sets and costumes she designed for

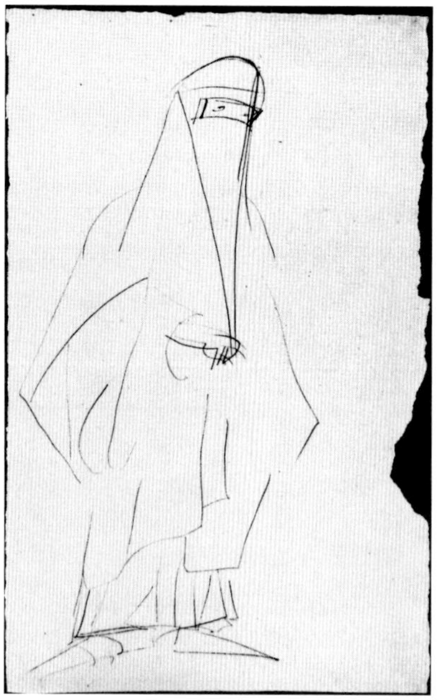

figure 31. LIUBOV POPOVA
Woman in a Yashmak, 1922
Costume design for Vsevolod Meierkhold's unrealized production of S. Polivanov's *The Priest of Tarquinia*, 1922
Pencil on paper, 35.1 x 22 cm
Private collection, Moscow

the Chamber Theater in Moscow, especially for the 1921 production of *Romeo and Juliet* (see fig. 8). The form of the body, male or female, vanished in the "Cubo-Baroque" volutes of her costumes.[33] This was also true of Popova's sets and costumes for her own *Romeo and Juliet* project in 1920, and even more so for the unstaged *Priest of Tarquinia* the following year, where the female figures were swallowed up by the dynamic folds of their veils (fig. 31).

Exter, Popova, and Stepanova, in particular, all favored a neutral approach to the body, which is linked to Constructivism and to their support of biomechanics, whereby the human body is a tool to be disciplined on the basis of rhythmic-mechanical criteria. For Constructivist theoretician Alexei Gan, husband of film-maker Esfir Shub, the human body had to become a total technological tool.[34] The primary model chosen to interpret his Constructivist movements was the actress Alexandra Khokhlova, whose long, thin body gave her top model status (Lamanova hired her to model clothes) (see fig. 23) and fascinated Rodchenko, who captured her image in the 1926 film *The Journalist*.[35] Gan's biomechanical interpretation of the body was supported by Petr Galadzhev — an artist who had studied with Rozanova at the Moscow Stroganov Institute in the 1910s — who illustrated how to rationalize and standardize actions (such as a telephone conversation) onstage or in everyday life (see fig. 32). His projects for Gan and for Popova's and Stepanova's *prozodezhda* eliminated gender identity. Stepanova approached the same theme — the analysis of the gesture/rhythm and all its possible variations — in her *Figures*, which Lavrentiev rightly advised to "read" not separately, but as a sequence.

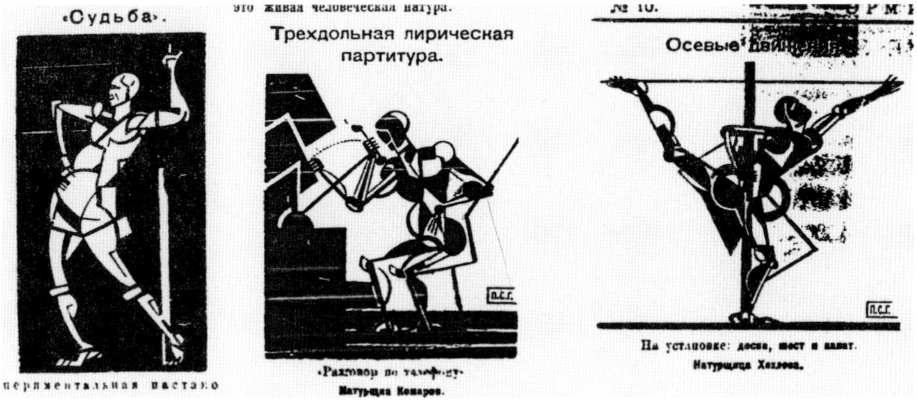

figure 32. PETR GALADZHEV
Three renderings of dancers illustrating Alexei Gan's article "Kino-tekhnikum" in *Zrelishcha* (Moscow), no. 10 (1922), pp. 10–11. Left to right: *Destiny. An Experimental Production. Khokhlova Posing; Tripartite Lyrical Score. Phone Conversation. Komarov Posing; and Axial Movements. Board, Stick and Rope. Khokhlova Posing.*

Exter, along with Lamanova, Evgeniia Pribylskaia, and sculptor Vera Mukhina, was a moving spirit behind the periodical *Atelie*, which published a single issue, in 1923. Mouthpiece of the Moscow Atelier of Fashions, it contained discussions of haute couture and elegant color plates, implying that high fashion was now for everyone. (The Atelier even indulged in private commissions, a far cry from the egalitarian spirit of the Revolution.) Soon enough, however, the theme of the standardized female body was taken up by Soviet fashion, which went on to develop the precocious ideas of Popova and Stepanova. Popova often designed her textiles in relation to the shape of the clothes, utilizing the principles of optical illusion in order to facilitate the passage from the two-dimensional surface of the material to the three-dimensional volume of the human figure.[36] But it was precisely the extreme desire to rationalize the figure of the new Soviet woman that led to a negation of the body as an expression of concrete, psychological, and sexual individuality — a process that had begun with the artists of the avant-garde.

1. Handbag designs by Rozanova and Udaltsova are illustrated in Larisa Zhadova, *Malevich and Suprematism in Russian Art 1910–1930* (London: Thames and Hudson, 1982), p. 37. Others by Rozanova are reproduced in Vera Terekhina et al., *Olga Rozanova 1886–1918*, exh. cat. (Helsinki: Helsinki City Museum, 1992), nos. 111 and 112. Some of Boguslavskaia's embroideries, including a Suprematist piece, were included in the *World of Art* exhibition in Petrograd in 1916; they are reproduced in *Stolitsa i usadba* (Petrograd), no. 56 (April 15, 1916), p. 23.
2. See Dimitrii Sarabianov and Natalia Adaskina, *Liubov Popova* (New York: Abrams, 1990), pp. 272,

294–97. See also Charlotte Douglas, "Six (and a Few More) Russian Women of the Avant-Garde," in this publication.

3. See Douglas, "Six (and a Few More) Russian Women of the Avant-Garde."
4. Kazimir Malevich, "Glavy iz avtobiografii khudozhnika," Vasilii Rakitin and Andrei Sarabianov, eds., *N. I. Khardzhiev. Stati ob svangarde* (Moscow: RA, 1997), vol. 1, p. 114.
5. Alexandra Exter, "On the Structure of Dress" (1923), Lydia Zaletova et al., *Revolutionary Costume: Soviet Clothing and Textiles of the 1920s* (New York: Rizzoli, 1989), p. 171; "Sovremennaia odezhda," *Krasnaia niva* (Moscow), no. 21 (May 27, 1923), p. 31.
6. See Varvara Stepanova, "Today's Fashion is the Worker's Overall" (1923), Zaletova et al., *Revolutionary Costume*, pp. 173–74.
7. Pavel Florensky, "The Stratification of Aegean Culture," Nicoletta Misler, ed., *Pavel Florensky: Writings on Art* (Philadelphia: Pennsylvania State University, forthcoming); originally published in *Bogosloovskii vestnik* (Moscow) 2, no. 6 (1913).
8. See, for example, Anatolii Strigalev and Jurgen Harten, eds., *Vladimir Tatlin*, exh. cat. (Cologne: Du Mont, 1993), p. 131, figs. 103–06.
9. Evgenii Mindlin, "O priamoi, ob evoliutsii pidzhaka i o stile v RSFSR," *Zrelishcha* (Moscow), no. 8 (1922), p. 10.
10. On the subject of the body, sexuality, and Russian women, see J. Costlow, ed., *Sexuality and the Body in Russian Culture* (Stanford, Calif.: Stanford University Press, 1993).
11. See Evgenii Kan, "Telo i odezhda," *Zrelishcha* (Moscow), no. 7 (1922), p. 16.
12. Kasian Goleizovsky, "Obnozhennoe telo na stsene," *Teatr i studia* (Moscow), nos. 1–2 (1922), pp. 36–38.
13. See Elizaveta Souritz, *Soviet Choreographers* (Durham, N.C.: Duke University Press, 1990), pp. 173–75.
14. Liubov Popova, "On a Precise Criterion," Sarabianov and Adaskina, *Liubov Popova*, pp. 380–81.
15. See Militsa Ullitskaia, "Po khoreograficheskim kontsertam," *Sovetskoe Iskusstvo* (Moscow), nos. 8–9 (1926), pp. 59–60.
16. See Anatolii Fomin, *Svetopis N. I. Svishchova-Paola* (Moscow: Iskusstvo, 1964).
17. See Nicoletta Misler, "Apocalypse and the Russian Peasantry: The Great War in Natalia Goncharova's Primitivist Paintings," *Experiment* (Los Angeles), no. 4 (1997), pp. 62–76.
18. See Olga Matich's "Gender Trouble in the Amazonian Kingdom: Turn-of-the-Century Representations of Women in Russia" in this publication.
19. Pavel Florensky, "The Stratification of Aegean Culture."
20. For example, *Stone Maiden*, *Still-Life (Packages and Stone Maiden)*, and *Still-life (Stone Maiden and Pineapple)* (all works, 1908); see *Vystavka kartin Natalii Sergevny Goncharovoi*, exh. cat. (Moscow: Art Salon, 1913), nos. 67, 155, and 245.
21. Florensky, "The Stratification of Aegean Culture."
22. See Nicolai Evreinov, *Nagota na stsene* (St. Petersburg: Typography of the Maritime Ministry, 1911).
23. Nicolai Evreinov, "Oblik parizhanki 1923 g," *Atelie* (Moscow), no. 1 (1923), pp. 7–8.
24. See Alexander Etkind, *Eros nevozmozhnogo. Istoriia psikhoanaliza v Rossii* (St. Petersburg: Meduza, 1993); and N. Penezhko et al., *Shekhtel, Riabushnsky, Gorky* (Moscow: Nalsedie, 1997).
25. See Alexei Sidorov, "Lichnoe delo," in RGALI [Rossiiskii Gosudarstvennyi arkhiv literatury i iskusstva] (inv. no. f.941, op. 10, ed. khr. 189,1.1).
26. Varvara Stepanova, "Non-Objective Creativity" (1919), in Alexander Lavrentiev and John E. Bowlt, eds. *Varvara Stepanova: The Complete Work* (Cambridge: MIT Press, 1988), p. 169.

27. See Alexei Sidorov, *Russkaia grafika za gody revoliutsii, 1917–1922* (Moscow: Dom pechati, 1923); reprinted in Alexei Sidorov, *O masterakh zarubezhnogo, russkogo i sovetskogo iskusstva. Izbrannye trudy* (Moscow: Sovetskii khudozhnik, 1985), p. 278.
28. Alexei Sidorov, "Ocherednye zadachi iskusstva tantsa," *Teatr i studiia*, nos. 1–2 (1922), p. 16.
29. Inna Chernetskaia, "Plastika i analiz zhesta (Diskussiia. Protokol No. 6 Zasedaniia. Khoreograficheskaia sektsiia RAKhN 10/12/1923)," in RGALI [Rossiskii gosudarstvennyi arkhiv literatury i iskusstva] (inv. no. 941, op. 17, ed. khr. 2, 1. 14).
30. Alexei Sidorov, "Boris Erdman, khudozhnik kostiuma," *Zrelishcha* (Moscow), no. 43 (1923), pp. 4–5.
31. Frank [Vladimir Fedorov], "Ektsentricheskii balet (v poriadke diskussii). Mysli o tantse v postanovke Lukina," *Ermitazh* (Moscow), no. 9 (1922), p. 7.
32. Exter, "On the Structure of Dress," p. 171.
33. Yakov Tugendkhold, *Alexandra Exter* (Berlin: Zaria, 1922), p. 26.
34. See Alexei Gan, "Kino-tekhnikum," *Ermitazh* (Moscow), no. 10 (1922), pp. 10–11.
35. See Daniel Girardin et al., *La Femme enjeu: Alexandr Rodtchenko* (Annecy: La Petite Ecole, 1998), pp. 128.
36. See Elena Murina, "Tkani Liubovi Popovoi," *Dekorativnoe Iskusstvo SSSR* (Moscow), no. 8 (1967), pp. 24–27.

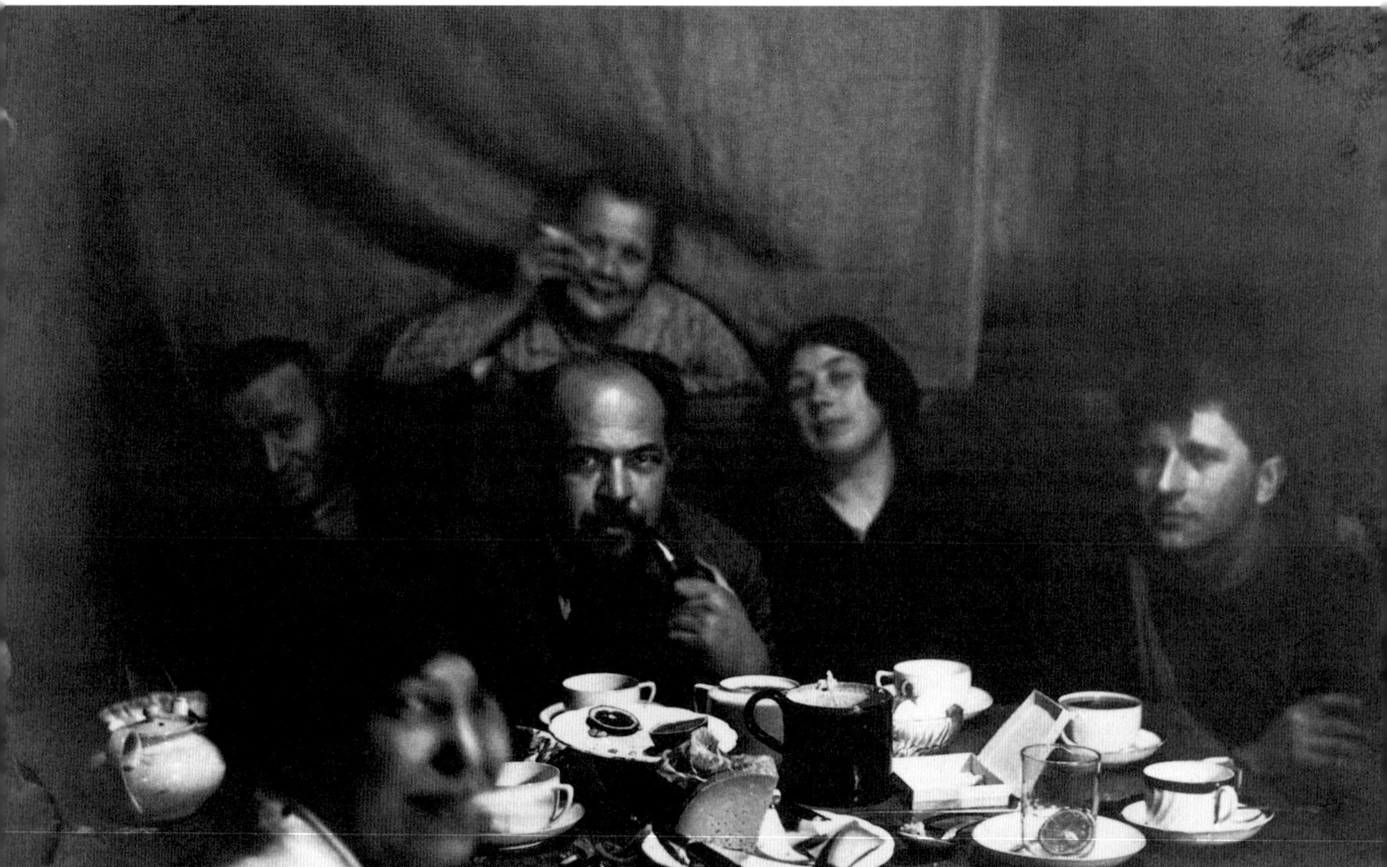

figure 33. Left to right: Anton Lavinsky, Olga Rodchenko (Alexander Rodchenko's mother), Alexander Vesnin, Liubov Popova, Nikolai Sobolev, and Varvara Stepanova (in foreground), photographed by Alexander Rodchenko, Moscow, 1924.

Creative Women, Creative Men, and Paradigms of Creativity: Why Have There Been Great Women Artists?

Ekaterina Dyogot

Why *have* there been great women artists? Thus we might rephrase the classic question posed by Linda Nochlin in 1971[1] when considering the Russian avant-garde. Although French Surrealism was one of the most tolerant twentieth-century cultural movements in its attitude toward female artists, women artists signed none of the Surrealists' declarations, were absent from group portraits, and created their major works outside the movement. Yet the situation was quite different in Russia. Within the avant-garde, men welcomed their women colleagues as allies and accomplices, perhaps also at times as rivals, but always as equals; women artists were held in high regard. (Even before the October Revolution, Alexandra Exter and Natalia Goncharova achieved notoriety in Russia, while Liubov Popova and Nadezhda Udaltsova emerged as Cubists in Paris [fig. 34], an accomplishment unattained by the men of their circle.) The avant-garde in Russia was in dire need of bolstering its ranks, and women took advantage of this opportunity. Women artists even wrote and published theoretical texts, violating the final taboo of logocentrism.

For the past twenty years, feminist criticism has been expanding the history of twentieth-century art. Certain women artists — among them Hannah Höch, Frida Kahlo, Kate Sage, and Sophie Täuber-Arp — have been removed from the familial and sexual biographies of their male partners, while the traditionally female roles of "muse," "silent partner," and portrait object have been elevated to the status of artistic contributions.[2] Yet within the Russian avant-garde, the women artists

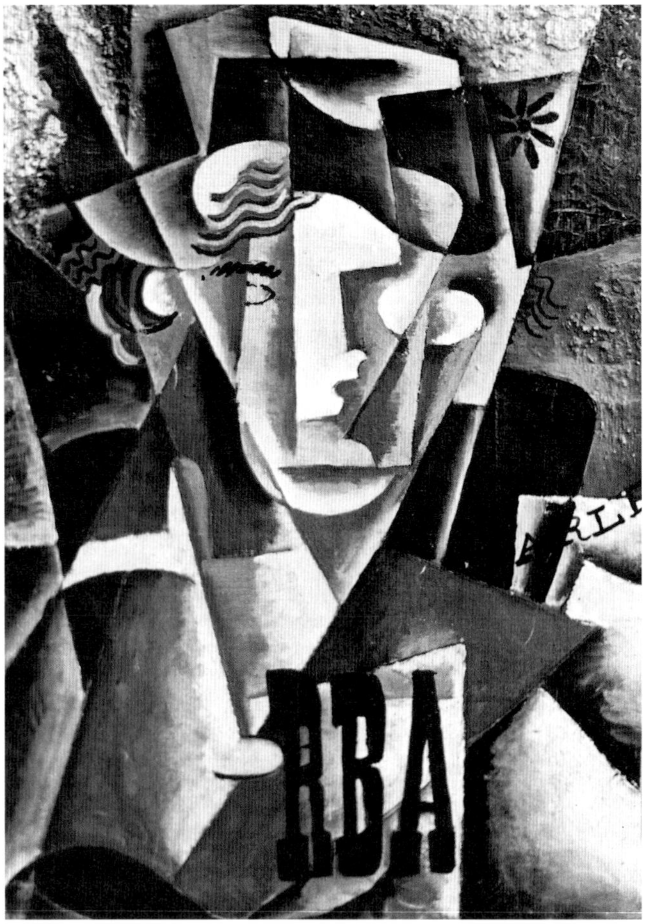

figure 34. LIUBOV POPOVA
Portrait of a Philosopher, 1915
Oil on canvas, 35.5 x 26.7 cm
Private collection, Moscow

erased the gendered aspects of creativity, partly because they saw themselves as artists "in general." (Although the women of French Surrealism also saw themselves this way, no one doubts that their art is explicitly gendered.)[3] At the same time, Russian women artists felt a common identity and solidarity with one another; Goncharova served not only as a stylistic source for Olga Rozanova, but also as a role model, while Rozanova, in turn, served as a model for Varvara Stepanova.

The first women to take their place in the history of Russian art were connected to male artists by blood: Elena Polenova was the sister of Vasilii Polenov and Maria Yakunchikova was the sister of his wife, while Zinaida Serebriakova was the daughter of sculptor Evgenii A. Lancéray, the sister of painter Evgenii E. Lancéray, and the niece of Alexandre Benois. The women artists of the next generation, however, were almost all involved in artistic and sexual relationships with male artists. Yet there is not a single study that analyzes the partnerships of Goncharova and Mikhail Larionov, Elena Guro and Mikhail Matiushin, Stepanova and Alexander Rodchenko, or Udaltsova and Alexander Drevin, and one usually finds only passing remarks that Rozanova was the wife of poet and theorist Alexei Kruchenykh (although they were never officially married), that Exter is rumored to have been the lover of Ardengo Soffici, or that more than professional concerns and a common studio at Vkhutemas connected Popova and Alexander Vesnin. These partnerships were often formed after or during a woman's first marriage when her husband was less than her intellectual equal.[4] The ideology of an equal marriage, became common in educated circles in Russia in the 1860s, and this peculiarity should be considered — along with institutional, sociological, historical, artistic, and biographical factors[5] — in any attempt to explain the presence of "great Russian women artists" in the 1910s and 1920s.

How did these unions between great artists function? What kinds of cultural and aesthetic constructions of masculine/feminine creativity were established? The Modernist drama of binarity, in which the Other is encoded automatically as unconscious, natural, and feminine, now unfolds.

Even if twentieth-century Russian women artists were more visible than their Western counterparts, we should not ignore issues of exclusion and exploitation. But gender-oriented criticism is not an exposé of, or a defense against, sexual harassment in art history, and it should not be used to police an artist's life or aesthetic system. In attempting to reverse one of the alleged repressions of Modernism, are we not concurring that the repressed Other is feminine? Would it not be more beneficial to question the codification of whatever is repressed as "natural" (although nature itself is also repressive) and, consequently, as feminine? Should Modernism really be "refashioned around such figures as Sonia Delaunay"[6] (who created more forms than ideas), as many feminist critics demand? More to the point, to what extent can we reject a dominant paradigm? Is there an advantage to taking an anthropological approach to art? Wouldn't women become banners for anti-Modernist revenge, as they did in Soviet criticism, which extolled women for their "emotionality" (that is, their failure to grasp art as an idea), "subtlety" (incapacity for radical innovation), and "wise aspiration to overcome destructive excesses"?

Goncharova and Larionov: The Career of the Other

To be a woman artist at the beginning of the twentieth century was no easy task. The catastrophic overproduction of nudes in the preceding decades (though fewer were produced in Russia than in Europe) had caused women to be equated with the art object, and since Modernism despised the object's passivity and understood innovation in terms of medium and "device" (to use the Russian formalists' term) — both of which were associated with the phallus and logos) — it simply could not favor the feminine. In the 1913 manifesto *Slovo kak takovoe* (*The Word as Such*), Kruchenykh spoke with irony of "feminine" criteria applied to language ("clear, melodious, pleasant," and so on), while observing that "first and foremost lan-

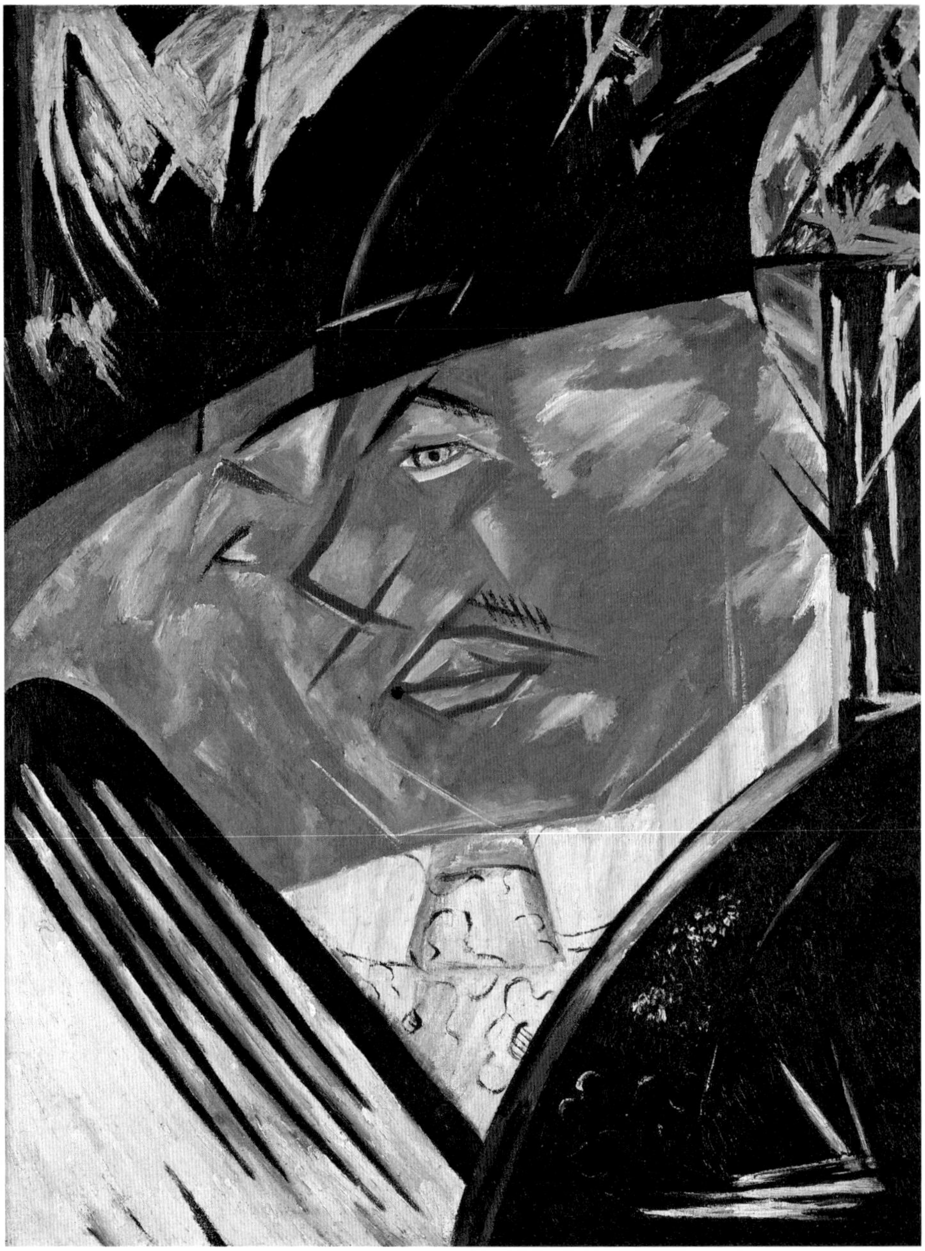

figure 35. NATALIA GONCHAROVA
Portrait of Mikhail Larionov, 1913
Oil on canvas, 105 x 78 cm
Museum Ludwig, Cologne

guage must be language and if it has to remind us of something, then better the saw or the poisoned arrow of the savage."[7] The saw, as a symbol of a violent (and virile) intervention in nature, appears in both Kazimir Malevich's Cubo-Futurist paintings and Vasily Kandinsky's theoretical writings. Describing the painting process, the latter observed in 1913: "At first, it stands there like a pure, chaste maiden, with clear gaze and heavenly joy — this pure canvas that is itself as beautiful as a picture. And then comes the imperial brush, conquering it gradually, first here, then there, employing all its native energy, like a European colonist, who with axe, spade, hammer, and saw penetrated the virgin jungle where no human foot had trod, bending it to conform to its will."[8]

But while any fin-de-siècle Russian artist would have perceived the Freudian aspect of Kandinsky's tirade with the joy of an accomplice, the second, "Eurocentric" aspect would have been received differently. Living in a country whose intellectuals often engaged in discussion about its tragic (or perhaps fortunate) dissimilarity to rational Europe, the Russian artist would have tended to identify with Kandinsky's "virgin jungle." Russian Futurism was, indeed, fervently nationalistic. Consequently, if the Modernist identification of women with objects might have made Russian women artists uneasy, then the association of women with the Other (the mysterious, the unconscious, the archaic) was likely to have been a comfortable position, since Russian philosophy favored the Other. To early twentieth-century Russian audiences, women embodied Russian art, and for a while Goncharova filled this role with her peasant Primitivism.[9]

Due to her economic independence and higher social status (she belonged to the old nobility), Goncharova was able to develop her relationship with Larionov (who had a much humbler background) on an equal footing. They met in 1900 as students at the Moscow Institute of Painting, Sculpture, and Architecture, and from then on their creative partnership never faltered. It was Larionov who oriented Goncharova toward painting (when they met she was still studying sculpture); he pointed out — in accordance with the stereotype of the "feminine" — that her strength lay in subtle coloring and not in powerful form. But while Larionov ceded first place to Goncharova in everything, as memoirists unanimously contend, she once slapped someone for calling her "Madame Larionova."[10] Her participation in artistic debates, the many references to her in newspapers, as well as her ready social adaptability and personal independence during their years as emigrés in France (their familial relationship ended — apparently on the initiative of Goncharova — although they remained a creative tandem) enhanced her image as an Amazon.

The roles in Goncharova's and Larionov's artistic union were well defined. Larionov was a legend among Russian artistic circles, but Goncharova enjoyed greater media and commercial success.[11] She was an indefatigable "picture-

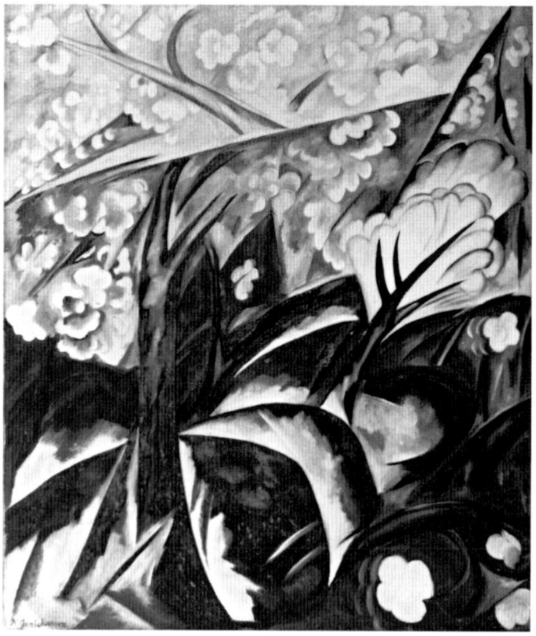

figure 36. natalia goncharova
Apple Trees in Bloom, 1913
Oil on canvas, 105 x 84.5 cm

maker," contributing almost eight hundred works to her Moscow retrospective in 1913, but Larionov nonetheless reproached her for not working hard enough.[12] Larionov's commitment to painting was less absolute, for he also assumed other key roles, which Goncharova never took upon herself: institutional organizer, theoretician (with the support of Ilia Zdanevich), and inventor of radical ideas (including Rayism, Rayist theater, and face painting). The imperative of theory compelled Larionov to act not only as the pioneer of a new movement with diligent students such as Mikhail Le-Dantiu, but also as the discoverer of objectively existing tendencies who saw his insights confirmed in the work of naïve artists such as Georgian painter Niko Pirosmanashvili. Goncharova's fiery individualism placed her in the company of these naïve artists, as an unconscious ally of Larionov rather than a student of his theories.

For Goncharova's 1913 retrospective, Zdanevich delivered a special lecture entitled "Natalia Goncharova and Everythingism," repeating more or less what Larionov had declared at *The Target* exhibition a few months before. Everythingism, as he defined it, lay not in the eclectic diversity of appropriation, but in the principle of positive and uncritical acknowledgment, as opposed to the criticism of Western Modernism. Marina Tsvetaeva associates Goncharova with the "Russian genius who appropriates everything" and with the ethics of nature, since "Goncharova embraced the machine as nature does."[13] A parallel to Everythingism is found in the views of poet Benedikt Livshits, a member of the same circle, who debated Filippo Tommaso Marinetti during the Italian's visit to St. Petersburg at the beginning of 1914. Livshits believed that Russia's anti-Western essence lay in "our inner proximity to material, our exceptional sensation of it, our inborn ability to transubstantiate, which removes all intermediary links between material and creator."[14] If the sense of national identity in Russia was based on the notion of "unconditional unification" as opposed to European individualism, this opposition paralleled the social construction of the "feminine" and the "masculine."[15] Indeed, the gender aspects of this dichotomy did not escape the attention of the Russian Futurists. Livshits, for example, spoke ironically of Marinetti's "one hundred horse-power phallic pathos."[16]

The Russian avant-garde's xenophobic campaign helped elaborate a strategy whereby the East as Other was not only rehabilitated, but also promoted as the "grand narrative" out of which European Modernism had grown. The East, in this view, already contained the West. The "feminine" also had to demonstrate its universality and self-sufficiency. Goncharova synthesized both ideas, asserting that the "Scythian stone maidens, the Russian painted wooden dolls . . . are made in the manner of Cubism."[17] Like the painted dolls, the "stone maidens" to which Goncharova referred — effigies created by the nomads of the Russian steppes — are not representations specifically of women, but anthropomorphic representations in general. Thus Goncharova's picture of the world was distinctly matriarchal, as her painting *Boys Bathing (Direct Perception)*, 1911, (Leonard Hutton Galleries, New York), with its gender reversal, suggests. Larionov's *Soldier Cycle* and *Venuses*, which he began after Goncharova had staked out her matriarchal territory, might be seen as an attempt at an ironic construction of a "masculine" world.

Guro and Matiushin: The Mother Refeminized

Elena Guro had not only an earthly destiny awaiting her, but also a fantastic posthumous one. Through the efforts of Mikhail Matiushin (her husband), many artists came to identify Guro with nature as a source of creative power. Matiushin's attitude toward Guro included a very strong element of spiritual fetishism. "In toto she is perhaps a sign," he wrote in *Troe* (*The Three*, 1913), an anthology dedicated to her memory.[18] During Guro's lifetime, Matiushin published her books, translated and annotated esoteric literature, and composed music for her plays. He began to emerge as an outstanding artist and inventor of original spatial theories only after her death. (The day after she died, on April 23, 1913, he resigned from the orchestra in which he had played violin for thirty years to devote himself to art.)[19] At the beginning of the 1920s, he established the Elena Guro Commune, whose participants, mainly the Ender family, not only staged performances of her plays, but also communicated with her through spiritualist séances.[20] In other words, Guro participated in the construction of a collective body, in which Matiushin perceived the creative subject of the future.

Matiushin first saw Guro in Yan Tsioglinsky's St. Petersburg studio in 1900. He recalled: "Elena Guro was drawing the spirit of 'genius' (from plaster). I have never seen such unity between the creator and the subject under observation."[21] Without question, Matiushin was implying in this passage that Guro herself was a genius. He expressed the cultural construct of the unity between subject and object not as "feminine" or as "Russian," but as a definition of creativity itself — something that the Symbolists, especially poet and philosopher Vladimir Soloviev, identified with "love."[22] Guro's pronouncement that the "poet is the one that gives life, not the one that takes it away"[23] is crucial; she opposed her art to the reductionist line of Modernism (which by that time was moving rapidly toward Malevich's *Black Square*, 1915), and was among those who were searching for an alternative. For that reason, she approached abstraction not through analysis but through an absence of violence, a weakening of energy. As Matiushin noted, Guro made her ink drawings with a brush, never with a pen so that she would not scratch or dig into the object.[24] Her favorite color was green, which both Kandinsky and Malevich despised, not so much for its "natural" quality as for its mediocre, nonradical character (due to its reconciliation of yellow and blue).

Guro's timid abstractions would not be as noteworthy as they are were it not for the gendered narration of the move from Symbolism to abstraction that appears in her prose, in which the central mythologem is the incorporeal son. In her main work, the poem "Bednyi rytsar" (Poor knight), the youth appears before the heroine, who recognizes him as her own son; she experiences his incorporeality and independence of logos (she cannot recall his name) as both tragedy and grace.[25] This many-sided motif can be read in the context of Symbolism and the biological procreativeness in "life-creation," which Futurism transformed, in Marinetti's novel *Mafarka-Futurist* (1910), into a myth about the birth of a "mechanical son" by a human being. Whereas Guro, whose work carries a moral and aesthetic prohibition on negation, spoke of a son who is disembodied, this motif appears in Malevich's work as the gaping absence of a "living, regal infant" (as Malevich called his *Black Square*).[26]

Guro's work inspired not only the "pantheistic" Matiushin, but also people who were much more distant from the ideal of nature. These included Kruchenykh, whom Guro impressed with her thoughts on linguistics. Speaking of the mechanisms of repression she sensed so keenly, Guro wrote in a chapter entitled "Offended Words" in her literary diary: "I am aware that I avoid these words faintheartedly and feel like a criminal, because it is precisely I who should work to liberate them. What am I to do? There are words that receive no affection and glory through belief in their heroism. In literature, it seems to me, such is the entire feminine gender, which has been deprived by its lack of independence, and which proved unable to value the purity of loneliness. . . . What can be done so that they cease to be words of insignificance?"[27] Kruchenykh's "transrationality" provided an answer to this question: destroy the hierarchical system. His projected structure for a transrational language allowed for a "lack of agreement in case, number, tense and gender between subject and predicate, adjective and noun."[28] A case in point is the subtitle *Tsvetnaia klei* (*Colored Glue*) for Kruchenykh's *Vselenskaia voina* (*Universal War*), an album of collages made under the influence of Rozanova.[29] (An outstanding monument to the Russian avant-garde, it was published in January 1916, coinciding with the *0.10* exhibition, at which Malevich's *Black Square* was shown.) The lack of grammatical agreement between the Russian words for "colored" and "glue" ("colored" takes the feminine form, while "glue" is masculine) served to create not only an absurd semantic unity, but also an atmosphere of total freedom in the selection of gender identities. One manifestation of this entropic democratism was the "shifting" identity of Kruchenykh himself. In his Cubo-Futurist opera *Victory Over the Sun*, he declared, "Everything became masculine," and a number of words lose their feminine ending. Kruchenykh devised the feminine word "euy" from the vowels of his surname to replace "lily," which he felt had been "raped" through overuse,[30] and used it as the mark of his publishing enterprise.

ROZANOVA AND KRUCHENYKH: UNCONDITIONAL FREEDOM

It appears that Kruchenykh tried to develop his collaboration with Rozanova on a similarly androgynous basis. They met in 1912 (Kruchenykh formulated the concept of "transrationality" in the context of their romance), and, soon after, Rozanova began to illustrate nearly all of Kruchenykh's books, including *Utinoe gnezdyshko durnykh slov* (*Duck's Nest of Bad Words*, 1913)(fig. 37), *Te Li Le* (1914) (fig. 67), and others. Their collaborative works, which are striking for their complete synthesis of representation and text, led Rozanova to take up "transrational" poetry and Kruchenykh to take up collage.

In the preface to *Vselenskaia voina*, which Kruchenykh composed independently of Rozanova, he accorded her primacy in non-objectivity, remarking that "now several other artists are developing [this], including Malevich, Puni and others, who have given it the non-expressive appellation 'Suprematism.'"[31]

In summer 1915, Russia witnessed the creation of not one, but two equally influential versions of non-objective aesthetics. One (Suprematism) was developed by Malevich, the other (*The Word as Such*) by Kruchenykh. Working at Malevich's dacha in Kuntsevo, Kruchenykh presumably would have passed along information about Malevich's activities to Rozanova. Malevich was busy with the problem of the "zero of forms" as a radical "conflagration" of the visible world, and the shift to a qualitatively new level ("beyond zero"). "I think that Suprematism is the most appropriate [title]," Malevich wrote to Matiushin while searching for a

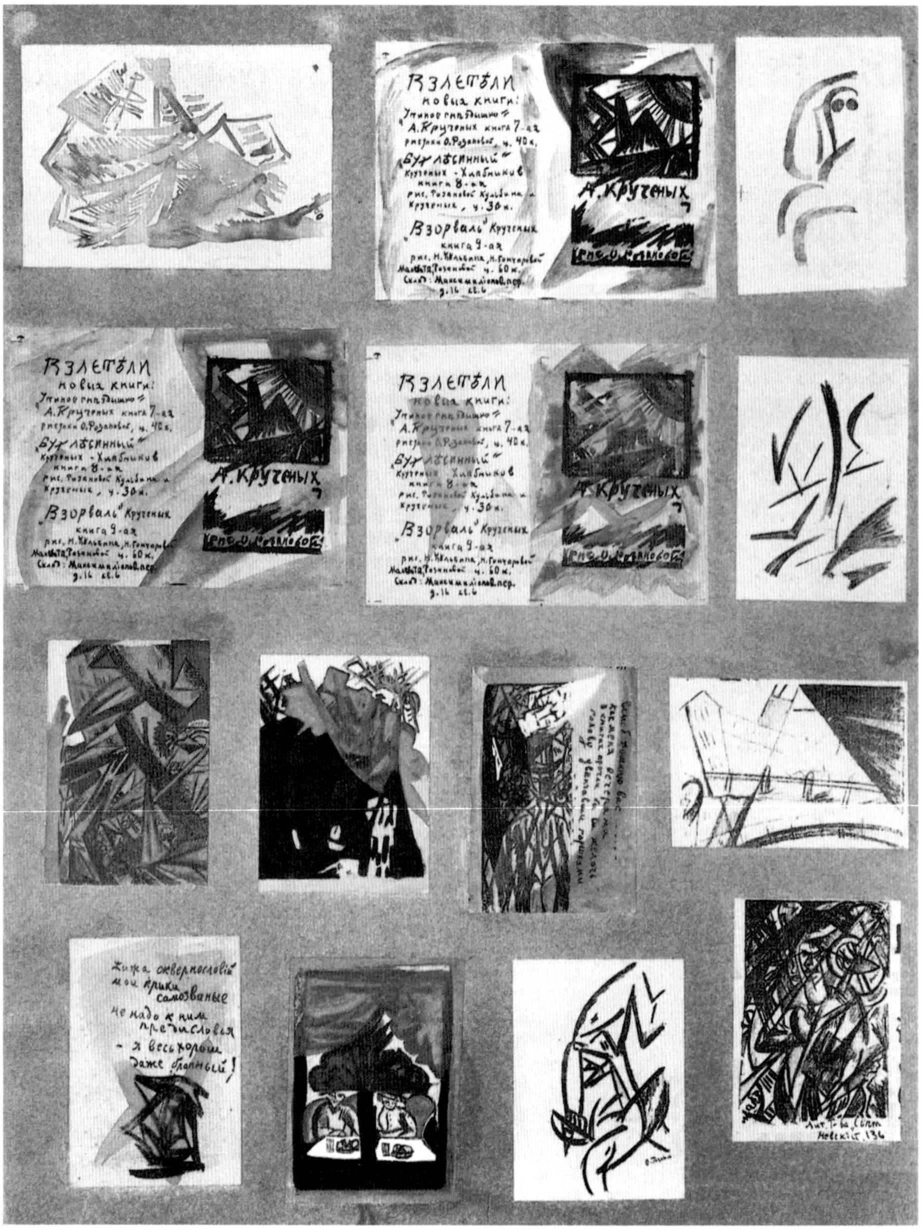

figure 37. OLGA ROZANOVA
Illustrations for Alexei Kruchenykh's
Utinoe gnezdyshko . . . durnykh slov, St. Petersburg, 1913
Watercolor and lithograph, 91 x 67 cm
Collection of Luce Marinetti, Rome

name for the new art, "since it designates dominion."[32] In Kruchenykh's theory of "the word as such," the motif of liberation and "loosening up" — in contrast to Malevich's tense, commanding "grasp" — plays a substantial role.

Kruchenykh's theory and its manifestation in Rozanova's work grew out of a concern shared by many artists and theoreticians of the Russian avant-garde: the question of how to reduce form without placing it under the drastic and repressive submission of the artist's conscious will (for which French Cubism and Italian Futurism were criticized). While Malevich brought this latent Cubist violence to its extreme conclusion in his *Black Square*, Guro, Matiushin, and Pavel Filonov chose an intrinsic prohibition of Minimalism and reduction (which is sometimes compulsive in Filonov's overcrowded paintings). Rozanova was the only artist who simplified forms in a radical way without emphasizing the means of doing violence to them. In her 1917 essay "Cubism, Futurism, Suprematism," she wrote: "Figurative art has been born of a love for color."[33] Unlike Malevich, Rozanova preferred the word "color" to the word "paint,"[34] favoring the end over the means and surpassing the violence of the latter in the notion of "love," a concept that Malevich often excised.[35] Rozanova appears to have followed Platonic, Romantic, and Symbolist traditions by using this term to refer to the blending of the subject with the object, of the means with the end. She wrote, "Futurism provided art with a unique expression, the fusion of two worlds, the subjective and the objective."[36]

In her extraordinary late paintings of 1917–18 (fig. 38), Rozanova blurred the boundaries between figure and ground, eventually removing them altogether, along with representation as the demonstration of power (which is still evident in Malevich's *Black Square*). She was the only artist who proved able to develop Suprematism (even to create an alternative to it) without staining its aesthetic purity with too much emotion, lyricism, or intimacy, and her contribution to the Russian avant-garde was truly unique. But her late paintings also derive from her understanding of Kruchenykh's theories of 1913–15, which were oriented toward the radical deconstruction of binary pairs. ("We started seeing 'here' and 'there,'" he wrote.)[37] Kruchenykh and Rozanova searched for "transrational" areas where these binaries could be challenged and then effaced, not in the silence of Malevich's eternal "nothing," but in unstable syntheses. (This is reminiscent of objectives later articulated by André Breton in the Surrealist manifestos.) One such area was male/female erotic relationships; another was collaborative ventures. The book, with its simultaneity of image and word, served as the place for the "transrational" meeting of representation and text. Many enthusiastic lines have been written about the brilliant publications of Kruchenykh and Rozanova, for whom the book appeared to be less a form of collaboration between poet and artist than an artistic form with a completely new structure of subject-object relations. It served as a replacement for the picture, in which the woman was always the object

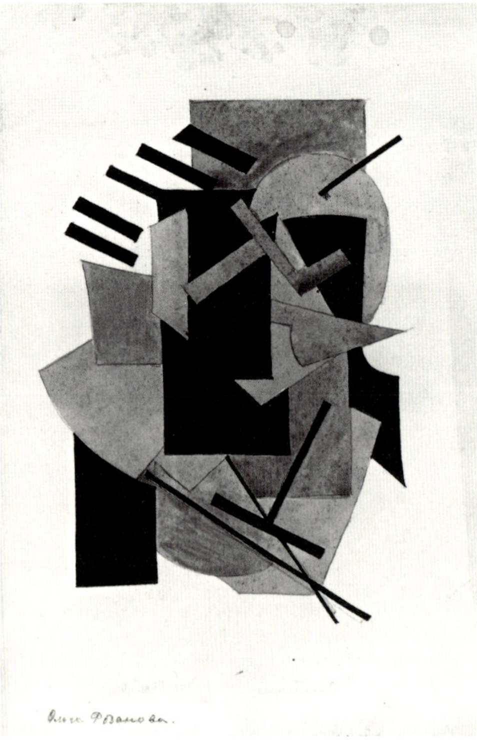

figure 38. OLGA ROZANOVA
Decorative Motif, 1917
Watercolor, pencil, and india ink, 24.8 x 17 cm
The Judith Rothschild Foundation

and the man the subject (or the object was always a woman and the subject a man); rather, it proved to be a field of "dual subjectivity."

Neither Rozanova and Kruchenykh's collaborative partnership nor their personal relationship was free of problems, it seems. "I have been asked how much you pay me for my illustrations of your books and why I keep silent about it," Rozanova wrote to Kruchenykh in 1914. "I am told you are exploiting me, making me illustrate prints and stitch your books. . . . A notary has a secretary who is usually his mistress. You think I can be both your mistress and illustrator of your books."[38] In his memoirs, Kruchenykh acknowledged that he handwrote his own texts in his early lithographic books extremely unwillingly, and that he did so only because he was short of cash to pay an artist to do it;[39] after 1913, it was Rozanova who undertook this task. Kruchenykh also asserted, moreover, that he handwrote the texts for *Starinnaia liubov* (Old-time love) himself, although according to the text of his and Velimir Khlebnikov's manifesto *Bukva Kak Takovaja* (*The Letter as Such*, 1913), it was Larionov who did so.[40] While *Bukva kak takovaia* ascribes the utmost significance to handwriting as an expression of the poet's emotional state and is emphatic that the text should not be typeset, it expresses a curious indifference toward the question of who should handwrite the text in a collaborative book—the author or the artist. In the books themselves the artist is always credited, but they do not indicate who handwrote the text. Perhaps coauthorship in this case can be understood not as collaboration, but as a kind of musical performance by the artist, who unconsciously identified with the poet in illustrating the text. Kruchenykh's remark that Rozanova "was helpless in practical affairs . . . a sensitive child-like woman. This is both a great merit and a shortcoming"[41] brings to mind the Surrealists' notion of the "femme-enfant," the more so since the Russian transrationalists also hoped to enter the space of the unconscious through contact (of a nonsexual kind) with naïve little girls.[42] Apparently, Kruchenykh was not free from perceptions of women as doors into the unconscious.

As Nina Gurianova has pointed out, Kruchenykh often finished Rozanova's verses, and sometimes signed them with two signatures.[43] While he was in Tbilisi publishing his "autographic" books in 1917–18, he sent her the sketch of a visual poem, which she colored before he made more changes, and he occasionally used such works in his books with no reference to her. What does this mean? Exploitation? A radical attitude to the problem of authorship? Is it a peculiarity of the creative personality of Rozanova herself? Or does it point to the irreducibility of the power relations between word and representation, in which privilege always belongs to the text?

Stepanova and Rodchenko: People and Things

From the 1920s on, Stepanova and Rodchenko were considered an artists' couple who represented the egalitarian ideals of independence, comradeship, and joint professional success. The reality was less idyllic. Among the many roles that Stepanova filled in the artistic sphere — artist, author of declarations, creator of new artistic structures, agitator for the new art — her function as a recording device for Rodchenko's numerous ideas was especially important. Without her diary notes, in which the pronoun "I" refers sometimes to her, sometimes to him, the ideas of 1919–21 (at least) would have been lost. Later on, Stepanova assumed yet another role — as "manager" of their book designs, prompting her daughter, Varvara, to compare her to "a 'robot' secretary."[44] In a strange way, this image recalls Stepanova's paintings from 1919–21, with their representations of "mechanized" men.

In 1915, Rodchenko recorded in his diary a prophecy of his creative path: "I shall make things live like souls and souls like things."[45] In the late 1910s and early 1920s, he devoted himself mainly to "things," working on "non-objective subjects" full of vitalistic Romanticism, such as luminescent abstractions and architectural and mobile constructions. Stepanova devoted herself to the opposite task of making things from souls, a more radical but less rewarding task. In 1919, she abandoned her brilliant visual poetry in order to draw miniature figures, as if to fulfill a duty of dehumanizing the body. In their first joint photograph, *Street Musicians*, 1920, Rodchenko and Stepanova appear against a background of these drawings. Although the photograph was made in the style of her art — their poses

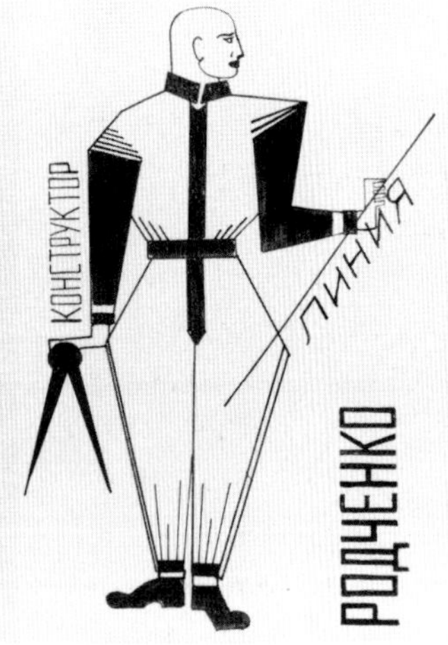

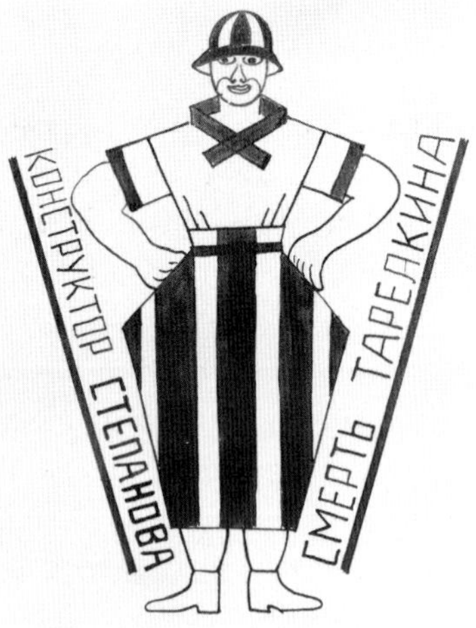

far left:
figure 39. Varvara Stepanova
Caricature of Alexander Rodchenko, 1922
India ink on paper,
23.5 x 18 cm
Private collection

figure 40. Varvara Stepanova
Self-Caricature, 1922
India ink on paper,
23.5 x 17.5 cm
Private collection

are reminiscent of her figures — Stepanova nonetheless appears to be passive and dependent in the photograph. She is different in later photographs made by Rodchenko on his own, but she still seems to submit to the idea of answering to him with great enthusiasm: she appears as a woman laborer in a kerchief (one of her designs), a saleswoman at the State Publishing House store, or a living advertisement for one of Rodchenko's logo designs. Stepanova's pseudonym, "Varst," is striking not so much for its lack of a feminine ending, but rather because it allowed her to speak of herself in the third person ("Varst's works").

The demand for both independence and dependence that defined Stepanova's work in the context of her relationship with Rodchenko derived from a variety of sources, among them social reality, personal characteristics, and feelings (Stepanova's letters and diaries demonstrate her boundless devotion to her husband). But what is most interesting in terms of her work is the role played by the duality of the Constructivist aesthetic program. The key problem in Constructivism concerned the object, which supplanted the obsolete conception of the painting. Invariably, the painting became associated with a woman, and frequently a prostitute. (Malevich referred to it as a "plump Venus.") To the Constructivists, the picture was always pornographic: regardless of what it represented; it appealed shamelessly to the sexuality of the viewer and thirsted to be purchased. In one of his first photographs, made in 1924, Rodchenko depicted Lef member Anton Lavinsky with a small photograph of a nude model in the background. Having Lavinsky turn away from the nude, Rodchenko opposed the objectified body with the face of a new creator, a new subject. Woman had to cease to be a thing, a commodity, the object of a picture. Visiting Paris in 1925, Rodchenko found the cult of woman as thing and the invincibility of the picture distasteful. (Among the first things that he saw were dirty postcards.) He wrote from there: "Light from the East bears a new attitude toward man, toward woman, and toward things. Things in our hands should also be equal, should also be our comrades."[46]

According to this line of thought, thing and woman should be creators themselves. The border between subject and object is removed not so much by the strength of love for the subject (as in Symbolism, which lay at the foundation of aesthetic resolutions of the 1900s and 1910s) as by the strength of the object's positive response. Constructivist design was also devoted to the production of a certain substance of a positive nature, a certain functional readiness to act. This was embodied in Stepanova's studies for athletic costumes; the figures in these studies are usually shown with legs spread wide apart, and the costumes often have diamond-shaped patches in the area of the knees so that the closing and opening of the legs would constitute the outfit's main visual effect. There was something erotic, of course, in this demonstration of independence and sexual openness, but Constructivism did not so much deny this quality as fail to recognize it, since this eroticism was virtually a side effect of the primary goal, which was to abolish alienation in the structure of the thing-commodity, picture-commodity, body-commodity. This was intended to create a new space of total freedom and comradeship, a "new way of life," a goal that Sergei Tretiakov — a member, with Rodchenko, of the Lef group, which advocated Constructivism — proclaimed as the primary task of the new art.[47]

There was a problem that the Lef group did not fully understand, however: the lack of distinction between the aesthetic product and the role played in the "new way of life" by personal relations. In 1927, an essay in *Novyi Lef* (*New Left*) stated that "like true lovers, Lef and reality preserve the inventive freshness of their relationship,"[48] meaning that the group had still not broken with its former lover, aesthetics. On exactly which territory the new lovers could meet, however, was not clear. Many of the works created by the Lef group at that time (including exhibition designs and book covers) became standard fare, just a way of making ends meet. It is characteristic that it was mostly women, including Stepanova, who pursued this kind of activity as a job, remaining loyal to the single medium they chose. The elements of the erotic and the accidental in forms of the "new way of life" (often recalling the Surrealist circle) took the place of the anarchic creative substance of 1918 to 1921. During the 1920s, the gatherings of the Lef group proceeded like séances or maniacal games of Chinese *Ma-Jong*. Stepanova's neighbor and colleague Elizaveta Lavinskaia asserted that the circle made a practical study of the possibilities of freedom from property relations: "Varvara Stepanova pretended to be a saint, she picked out mistresses for Rodchenko herself, and then fell into hysterics. . . . Of course, all of them [the Lef circle] removed themselves from art, profaned and defiled the very concept of love!"[49]

In her memoirs, written in 1948, Lavinskaia connected the "new way of life" as practiced by the Brik-Mayakovsky family (Osip Brik, Lilya Brik, and Vladimir Mayakovsky) to the destruction of art, primarily of the studio painting. After all, the painting opposed aesthetic and sexual promiscuity with its own uniqueness — which the Lef group censured as the basis of fetishism — and with the exclusive character of its own subjective-objective relations. Despite this, Constructivism was not at all free from fetishism: in studying Rodchenko's letters from Paris as well as the socialist object theory of Lef theoretician Alexander Bogdanov, Christina Kiaer writes of the deeply fetishistic character of the Constructivist theory of the object.[50] If the Constructivists were slow to realize that their projects for the objects of the "new way of life" were not so functional, but rather carried an enormous potential of desire, then their work on advertisements in the mid-1920s soon confirmed it. The mark of desire within Constructivism is apparent in Stepanova's work for the motion picture *Alienation* (1926), in which the walls of the bizarre, expensive hairdresser's shop where the villains spend their time are decorated with her designs for the Young Communist League.[51] In his 1928 photographs of Stepanova, in which she appears on a bed in a tightly fitting sweater, Rodchenko embellishes her image with an erotic fetish: one of the most striking photographs shows her with closed eyes, caressing her face with a long string of beads.

In 1927–28, Rodchenko launched a photographic experiment to study and re-eroticize the passive object, evident in his still lifes with glass objects reproduced in the eleventh issue of *Novyi Lef*, in 1928. Aesthetically, he was prepared for the dramatic love story that he lived out at the beginning of the 1930s with Evgeniia Lemberg, the long-unidentified figure in Rodchenko's *Young Woman with a "Leica" Camera*, 1934.[52] The nude photographs he took of Lemberg while they were staying together in the Crimea (which until recently remained unknown) change our impression of him. The assumption that an object is always an object of desire — and one that pays with the distortion of its image — led Rodchenko to his dramatic photographs of human bodies on the beach (taken during the same trip to the Crimea), his circus photographs during the 1930s, and his Surrealist abstractions made in 1934. The personal is always the aesthetic after all.

1. Linda Nochlin, "Why Have There Been No Great Women Artists?" (1971), in Nochlin, *Women, Art, and Power and Other Essays* (New York: Harper & Row, 1988), pp. 145–78.
2. See, for example, Whitney Chadwick, *Women Artists and the Surrealist Movement* (Boston: Little, Brown, 1985); Whitney Chadwick and Isabelle de Courtivron, eds., *Significant Others: Creativity and Intimate Partnership* (London: Thames & Hudson, 1993); and Renee Riese Hubert, *Magnifying Mirrors: Women, Surrealism, and Partnership* (Lincoln: University of Nebraska Press, 1994).
3. See Hubert, *Magnifying Mirrors*, p. 23.
4. Popova's husband, Boris von Eding, died in 1918, a year after they were married. In 1903, Exter married the lawyer Nikolai Exter, who did not hinder his wife's lengthy trips to Paris, Moscow, and St. Petersburg, or her friendship with members of the avant-garde; in sum, he "did not interfere in her life." (A. Koonen, quoted in Georgii Kovalenko, *Alexandra Exter* [Moscow: Galart, 1993], p. 180.) Udaltsova, who married in 1908, wrote ten years later that her husband "did not

assist at all . . . in . . . [her] hard and difficult life." (Ekaterina Drevina and Vasilii Rakitin, eds., *Nadezhda Udaltsova: Zhizn russkoi kubistki. Dnevniki, stati, vospominaniia* [Moscow: RA, 1994], p. 49.) Stepanova married architect Dmitrii Fedorov in 1913, split with him in 1915, but still carried his surname in 1925. She entered into official marriage with Rodchenko during World War II.

5. Access to accurate biographical information is often difficult in these cases, as the children of these couples — having lived to see the acknowledgment of their parents' work after many years of persecution and oblivion in the U.S.S.R. — tend to be extremely selective in choosing the facts from their personal lives with which to acquaint the reader. Any approach to the present topic requires a thorough familiarity with the archives.
6. Chadwick and Courtivron, eds., *Significant Others*, p. 33.
7. Herbert Eagle and Anna Lawton, eds., *Russian Futurism through its Manifestoes, 1912–1928* (Ithaca: Cornell University Press, 1988), p. 61.
8. Vasily Kandinsky, "Reminiscences/Three Pictures" (1913), in Kenneth C. Lindsay and Peter Vergo, eds., *Kandinsky: Complete Writings on Art* (New York: De Capo Press, 1994), pp. 372–73.
9. Marina Tsvetaeva referred to Goncharova as "Old Russia" in "Natalia Goncharova (Zhizn i tvorchestvo)," in Georgii Kovalenko, ed., *Natalia Goncharova, Mikhail Larionov. Vospominaniia sovremennikov* (Moscow: Galart, 1995), p. 53.
10. A. Krusanov, *Russkii avangard: 1907–1932. Istoricheskii obzor v trekh tomakh. Tom 1: Boevoe desiatiletie* (St. Petersburg: Novoe literaturnoe obozrenie, 1996), p. 133.
11. Ballet master Michel Fokine, who was distant from new-art circles, referred to them as "Goncharova and her co-worker M. F. Larionov." "Protiv techenia," in Kovalenko, ed., *Natalia Goncharova, Mikhail Larionov,* p. 119. On the commercial success of Goncharova's 1913 Moscow retrospective (Larionov never had a solo show in Russia), see Krusanov, *Russkii avangard, 1907–1932*, pp. 126–27.
12. See "A Conversation with Alexandra Korsakova (1904–1990)," *Heresies* (New York), no. 26 (1992), p. 93.
13. Tsvetaeva, "Natalia Goncharova (Zhizn i tvorchestvo)," in Kovalenko, ed., *Natalia Goncharova, Mikhail Larionov*, pp. 34, 81.
14. Benedikt Livshits, *The One and a Half-Eyed Archer*, trans. John E. Bowlt (Newtonville, Mass.: Oriental Research Partners, 1977), p. 208.
15. See Nancy Chodorow, *The Reproduction of Mothering: Psychoanalysis and the Sociology of Gender* (Berkeley: University of California Press, 1978).
16. Livshits, *The One and a Half-Eyed Archer*, p. 197.
17. Krusanov, *Ruskii avangard: 1907–1932*, p. 64.
18. Quoted in Alexander Ocheretiansky, Dzherald Yanechek, and Vadim Kreid, *Zabytyi avangard: Rossiia. Pervaia tret XX stoletiia. Sbornik spravochnykh i teoreticheskikh materialov* (New York and St. Petersburg: n.p., 1993), p. 46.
19. Vasilii Rakitin and Andrei Sarabianov, eds., *N. I. Khardzhiev. Stati ob avangarde* (Moscow: RA, 1997), p. 168.
20. *Elena Guro: Poet i khudozhnik. 1877–1913*, exh. cat. (St. Petersburg: Mifril, 1994), p. 52.
21. Quoted in Rakitin and Sarabianov, eds., *N. I. Khardzhiev*, p. 152.
22. See Olga Matich, "The Symbolist Meaning of Love: Theory and Practice," Irina Paperno and Joan Delaney Grossman, eds., *Creating Life: The Aesthetic Utopia of Russian Modernism* (Stanford: Stanford University Press, 1994), pp. 24–50. The relationship between Guro and Matiushin has much in common with the Symbolists' notion of "spiritual marriage."

23. Elena Guro, *Nebesnye verbliuzhata* (Rostov-na-Donu: Rostov University, 1993), p. 53.
24. Rakitin and Sarabianov, eds., *N. I. Khardzhiev*, p. 155.
25. Guro, *Nebesnye verbliuzhata*, p. 189.
26. Jean-Claude Marcadé demonstrates the iconographic similarity between a 1930 self-portrait by Malevich and Mother-and-Child icons, apart from the significant absence of the child in Malevich's work. Jean-Claude Marcadé, *Malévitch* (Paris: Nouvelles Éditions Françaises, 1990), p. 266.
27. Guro, *Nebesnye verbliuzhata*, p. 31.
28. Alexei Kruchenykh, "New Ways of the Word," in Lawton and Eagle, eds., *Russian Futurism through Its Manifestoes*, p. 73.
29. From the standpoint of gender, *Vselenskaia voina* is a unique monument in the history of world art, since it was long attributed to a woman on the basis that a man was thought to be incapable of creating such a work. On the authorship, see Gerald Janacek, *The Look of Russian Literature: Avant-garde Visual Experiments 1900–1930* (Princeton: Princeton University Press, 1984), pp. 100–102; and Juliette R. Stapanian, "Universal War and the Development of 'Zaum': Abstraction Toward a New Pictorial and Literary Realism," *Slavic and East European Journal* 29, no. 1 (1985), pp. 34–35, n. 2.
30. Alexei Kruchenykh, "Declaration of the Word as Such," in Lawton and Eagle, eds., *Russian Futurism*, p. 67.
31. Quoted in Nina Gurianova, "Suprematism and Transrational Poetry," *Elementa* (Yverton, Switzerland) 1 (1994), p. 369. Gurianova has demonstrated that Kruchenykh was referring here to Rozanova's abstract collages.
32. "Pisma K. S. Malevicha k M. V. Matiushinu," in Evgeneii Kovtun et al., *Ezhegodnik Rukopisnogo otdela Pushkinskogo doma na 1974 g* (Leningrad: Nauka, 1976), p. 187.
33. Olga Rozanova, "Cubism, Futurism, Suprematism," in *From Painting to Design: Russian Constructivist Art of the Twenties*, exh. cat. (Cologne: Galerie Gmurzynska, 1981), p. 100.
34. See Nina Gurianova, "Suprematism i tsvetopis,'" in V. Ivanov, ed., *Avangard v krugu evropeiskoi kultury* (Moscow: RADIKS, 1993), pp. 142–58.
35. Kazimir Malevich, "Izgnanie prirody, liubvi i iskrennosti iz predelov tvorchestva," in Alexandra Shatskikh, ed., *Kazimir Malevich. Sobranie sochinenii v 5 tt. (Tom 1: Stati, manifesty, teoreticheskie sochineniia i drugie raboty. 1913–1929)* (Moscow: Gileia, 1995), p. 82.
36. Rozanova, "Cubism, Futurism, Suprematism," p. 103.
37. Kruchenykh, "New Ways of the Word," in Lawton and Eagle, eds., *Russian Futurism*, p. 75.
38. Quoted in *Olga Rozanova, 1886–1918*, exh. cat. (Helsinki: Helsinki City Museum, 1992), p. 37.
39. Alexei Kruchenykh, *Our Arrival: From the History of Russian Futurism* (Moscow: RA, 1995), p. 46.
40. See *Russian Futurism*, p. 64.
41. Quoted in *Olga Rozanova, 1886–1918*, p. 117.
42. See John E. Bowlt, "Esoteric Culture and Russian Society," Maurice Tuchman, ed., *The Spiritual in Art: Abstract Painting, 1890–1985* (Los Angeles: Los Angeles County Museum of Art; New York: Abbeville Press, 1986), p. 178.
43. Gurianova, "Suprematism and Transrational Poetry," p. 377.
44. Quoted in Varvara Rodchenko, "Life and Art," in Lavrentiev and Bowlt, eds., *Varvara Stepanova*, p. 162.
45. Varvara Rodchenko, ed., *Alexander Rodchenko: Opyty dlia budushchego* (Moscow: Grant, 1996), p. 41.
46. Ibid., p. 151.

47. Sergei Tretiakov, "Otkuda i kuda?" *Lef* (Moscow), no. 16 (1924), pp. 192–203.
48. Viktor Pertsov, "Grafik sovremennogo LEFa," *Novyi Lef* (Moscow), no. 1 (1927), p. 17.
49. Elizaveta Lavinskaia, "Vospominaniia o vstrechakh s Maiakovskim," in *Maiakovskii v vospominaniakh rodnykh i druzei* (Moscow: Moskovskii rabochii, 1968), p. 353.
50. Christina Kiaer, "Rodchenko in Paris," *October* (New York), no. 75 (winter 1996), pp. 3–35, and "Boris Arvatov's Socialist Objects," *October*, no. 81 (summer 1997), pp. 105–18.
51. See the photograph illustrated in Lavrentiev and Bowlt, eds., *Varvara Stepanova*, p. 100.
52. Judging from Rodchenko's diaries and letters (see V. Rodchenko, ed., *Alexander Rodchenko*), he was deeply in love with Lemberg and was considering leaving Stepanova for her, but Lemberg died in a train accident in the summer of 1934.

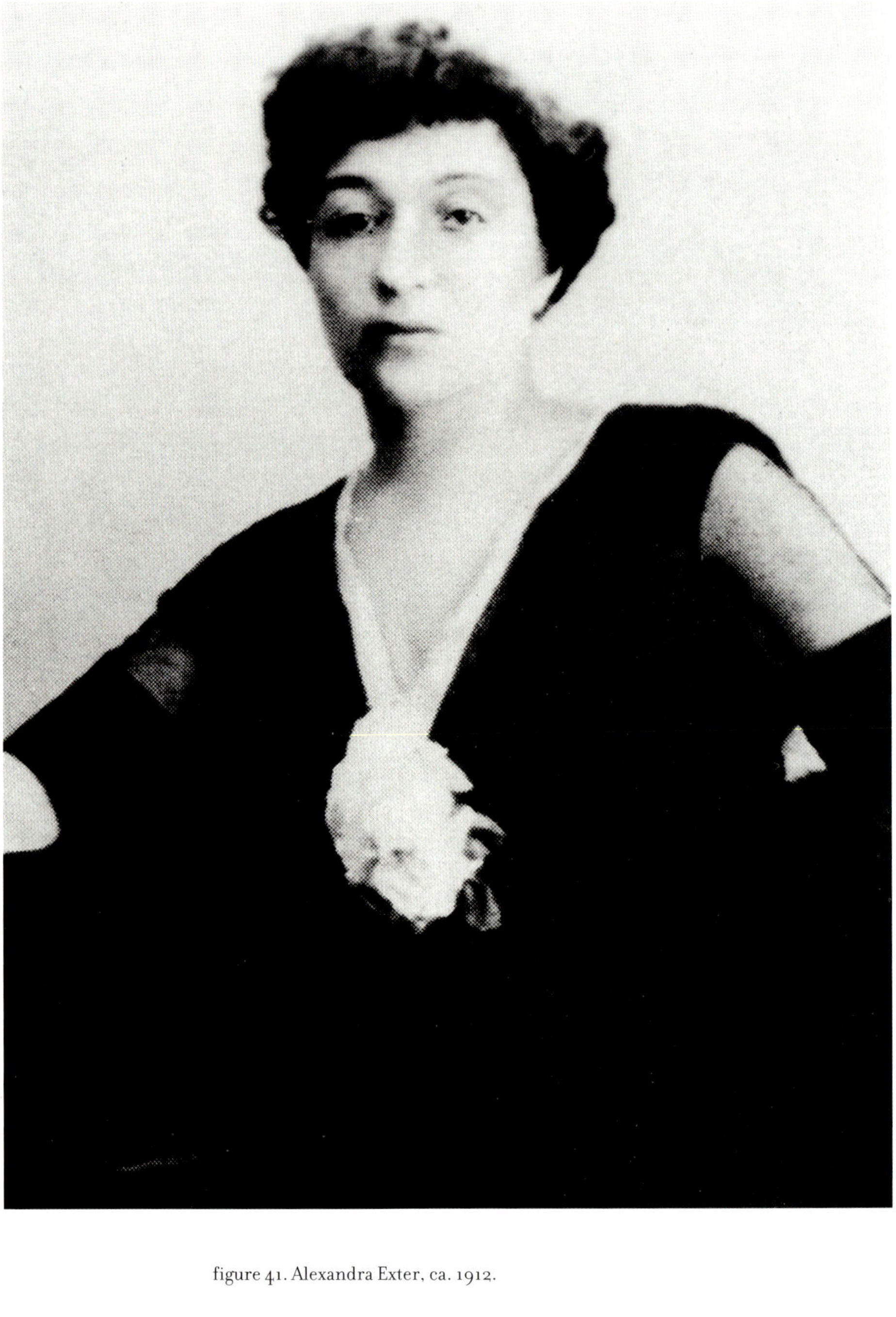

figure 41. Alexandra Exter, ca. 1912.

Alexandra Exter

Georgii Kovalenko

Alexandra Alexandrovna Exter (1882–1949) is one of the brightest stars in the firmament of the Russian — or perhaps we should say, Ukrainian — avant-garde. Born in Ukraine, Exter grew up in Kiev, attended art school there, and developed a strong interest in national Ukrainian culture.[1] Although in the early 1900s Exter moved frequently between St. Petersburg, Moscow, Venice, and Paris, she always returned to Kiev — to her studio, her family, and her home, at least until she left for good in 1920. The city of Kiev was an important motif in her paintings; and in her conversations and correspondence as an émigré toward the end of her life, she continued to evoke the memory of the city of her youth.[2]

In the late nineteenth and early twentieth centuries, the Ukrainian city of Kiev was very different from Russia's Moscow and St. Petersburg. Kiev was distant and insulated from the cultural mainstream of Russia and the West, although Exter, at least, did all she could to transplant new and experimental ideas directly onto Ukrainian soil. Thanks in no small degree to her advocacy, artists and intellectuals in Kiev were able to discover and appreciate trends such as Neo-Primitivism and Cubism. For example, Exter helped organize two avant-garde exhibitions in Kiev, *The Link* (1908) and *The Ring* (1914). There was also Vladimir Izdebsky's first international *Salon*, which traveled from Odessa to Kiev in 1910 and in which Exter played an important organizational role.[3] Here the Ukrainian public saw, for the first time, examples of the latest trends in French, German, Russian, and Ukrainian art — including David Burliuk's and Mikhail Larionov's Neo-Primitivist

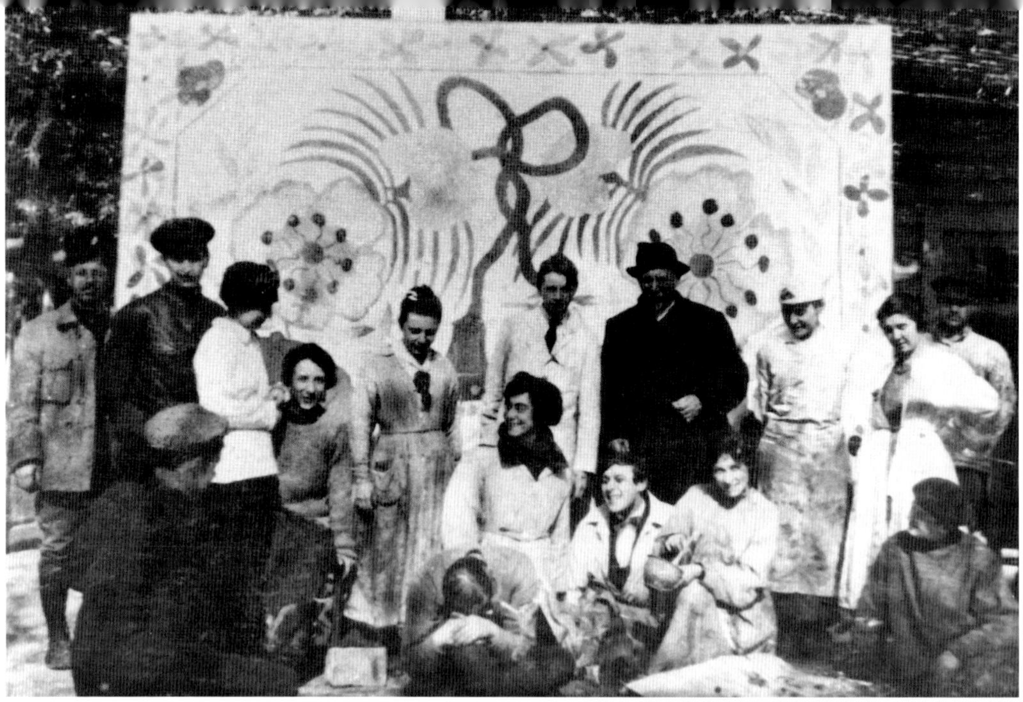

figure 42. Exter (seated in center) and her students in Kiev, 1918–19, in front of a panel painting by Pavel Tchelitchew, who is seated next to Exter.

compositions, Vasily Kandinsky's *Improvisations*, and Exter's first response to French Cubism. The *Salon* was a major artistic event, bringing the art of Giacomo Balla, Maurice Denis, Albert Gleizes, Alfred Kubin, Marie Laurencin, Henri Le Fauconnier, Henri Matisse, Jean Metzinger, Gabriele Münter, and many other European artists to the attention of the Kiev public.

In the early 1910s Kiev emerged rapidly as a center of intense intellectual and literary exploration. Not surprisingly, the Exter household welcomed many well-known and accomplished men and women of the time, including artists; Exter was especially close to the painter Alexander Bogomazov[4] and the sculptor Alexander Archipenko.[5] However, she discovered even deeper intellectual common ground with philosophers such as Nikolai Berdiaev and Lev Shestov, poets such as Anna Akhmatova, Ivan Aksenov, Benedikt Livshits, and Vladimir Mayakovsky, musicians such as Pavel Kokhansky, Genrikh Neigauz, and Karol Szymanovsky, and patrons and cognoscenti such as the Khanenko and Tereshchenko families. It was in Kiev also that Exter cultivated an abiding interest in Ukrainian folk culture, which she studied, promoted, and exhibited, often incorporating indigenous iconographic references into her own studio work.

Between 1918 and 1920, in the wake of war and insurrection, Kiev became a city of violence and devastation. Stranded in Kiev and thus isolated from Europe, Moscow, and St. Petersburg, Exter worked harder than ever before, and, despite the chaos and confusion of the ever-shifting conditions produced by revolution and counterrevolution, Exter helped maintain Kiev as a major center for artistic experiment. Her studio there brought together not only artists and writers, but also theater directors and choreographers such as Les Kurbas, Konstantin Mardzhanov, and Bronislava Nijinska. Above all, Exter nurtured an entire generation of aspiring painters who came to her for lessons and advice — some of whom, such as Alexander Khvostenko-Khvostov, Vadim Meller, and Anatolii Petritsky, would achieve solid reputations as designers for the Soviet stage.

Exter first went to Paris in the fall of 1907, just as Cubism was evolving into a distinct and sophisticated style, and she was quick to understand its potential. However, Exter did not study Cubism in formal classes, as her Russian colleagues Liubov Popova and Nadezhda Udaltsova did under Jean Metzinger and Henri Le Fauconnier. Instead, she learned about Cubism through personal contact with its inventors, for by the end of 1907, poet and critic Guillaume Apollinaire and painter Serge Férat had introduced her to Picasso, Braque, and poet Max Jacob, and shortly thereafter she met both Fernand Léger and Ardengo Soffici. In the clear, lucid principles of the Cubism of Braque and Picasso, Exter found partial answers to the problems of the correlation of volume and surface, texture and form, composition and rhythm. But she found it difficult to accept what the Cubists were saying about color or how they were applying it (or not applying it), because to Exter color was everything — it was the alpha and omega of the art of painting. In Braque's and Picasso's still lifes of 1911–12, the object and its environment are interdependent, whereas in Exter's they are clearly separate and almost autonomous, active and energetic in their own right. Decorative surfaces approach the objects, surrounding and dominating them. Exter removes figuration, while retaining a definite order. The result is the construction of a Cubist style that touches every object and every form, but it is a Cubist style distinguished by a remarkable vitality of color, deriving more from the rich traditions of the Ukrainian decorative arts than from the sober conventions of Braque and Picasso.

There is reason to believe that Exter was responsible for introducing the term "Cubo-Futurism" into the Russian lexicon, for she happened to be in Paris in October 1912, just as Marcel Boulanger was coining and promoting the term.[6] At any rate, Exter employed "Cubo-Futurism" on many occasions, trying to adapt it to the exigencies of the Russian artistic environment which until that point had preferred the impetus of Gleizes, Metzinger, and Le Fauconnier. Aware of both Cubism and Futurism from her trips to Paris and Milan, Exter tried to combine both tendencies in a stylistic amalgam that she tailored to Russian and Ukrainian subject matter. Thus, she could render an Italian city in a Cubist and even Simultanist manner (she was acquainted with the Delaunays in Paris), while also including references to the colorful patterns of Ukrainian Easter eggs.

In the mid 1910s, Exter painted many cityscapes, often nocturnal, such as *City at Night*, 1915 (fig. 43) and *Florence*, 1914–15 (fig. 44). These are not mere renderings of urban scenes, but fleeting experiments in bold and dynamic color compositions charged with the energy of movement. In *City at Night*, for example, luminous surfaces pile up, slide off, collide, and combine to form fantastic constructions. The light, which moves from the concrete to the conditional, from the cohesion of forms to their individual elements, is intensified by dazzling colors and fast movement, a combination that brings to mind the concurrent experiments of Giacomo Balla and Umberto Boccioni. However, Exter did not fully embrace the doctrine of Italian Futurism, even if the first Futurist manifestos and exhibitions (such as those in Paris in 1912) coincided with her own aesthetic ideas during the 1910s, and often the Italian statements could have been her own: "It is essential to impart a dynamic feeling, that is, the special rhythm of every object, its inclination, its movement, or, shall we say, its inner force. . . . Our bodies enter the couches we sit on, and the couches enter us. The bus rushes toward the buildings it passes and, in its turn, the buildings rush toward the bus and merge with it."[7]

Although Exter acknowledged the value of Italian Futurism, she did not follow blindly and was not especially interested in the vehicle hurtling through space that so fascinated Boccioni and his colleagues. Of course, movement — both its anticipation and actuality — was very important to Exter's pictorial philosophy, and, like the Italians, she tended to equate movement and rhythm. It is in the rhythmic structures of her painting that the potential for movement resides; and for Exter — as for Boccioni — rhythm was a primary component of movement. Her ideas about rhythm were also similar to those of radical Moscow critic Nikolai Tarabukhin, who wrote in 1916 (just as Exter was developing her theories): "As an element of movement, rhythm is an illustration. . . . Rhythm presumes stability, on the basis of which its free impulse unfolds."[8]

Yakov Tugendkhold, a strong advocate of Exter's oeuvre, wrote in his biography of her in 1922: "[Exter's] 'non-objective' works produce a strange and unsettling impression. The gaze of the viewer . . . searches first of all for human content, analogies, and suggestions of various kinds of customary concrete images — and is about to turn away in futile disappointment. . . . However, it is impossible to turn away, for you begin to sense the enchantment, cold and pure, like music, of these suspensions and declivities of multi-colored forms amidst the endless space of the white canvas. . . . This is no portrait, landscape, or still life; this is some kind of 'world in the clouds,' in which abide only pure concepts of painting, concepts of space and depth, balance and movement."[9] These "pure concepts of painting" inform all of Exter's art, including the studio paintings and the stage designs, especially in her treatment and manipulation of color.

Explosions of color are a characteristic feature of Exter's painting. If, in Picasso's painting, form often absorbs color, Exter's colors overflow, transcending the laws and conventions of composition, as if to emphasize that the intrinsic laws

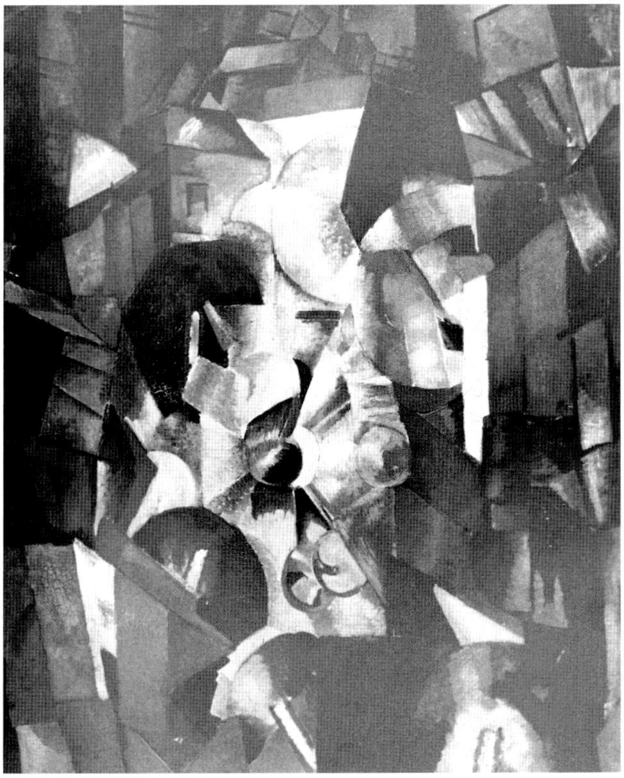

left:
figure 43. ALEXANDRA EXTER
City at Night, 1915
Oil on canvas, 88 x 71 cm
State Russian Museum, St. Petersburg

below:
figure 44. ALEXANDRA EXTER
Florence, 1914–15
Oil on canvas, 91 x 78 cm
State Tretiakov Gallery, Moscow

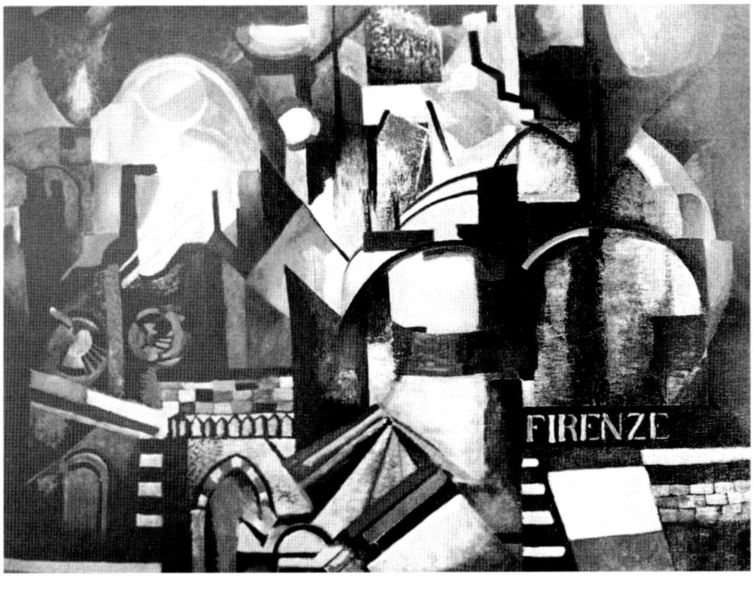

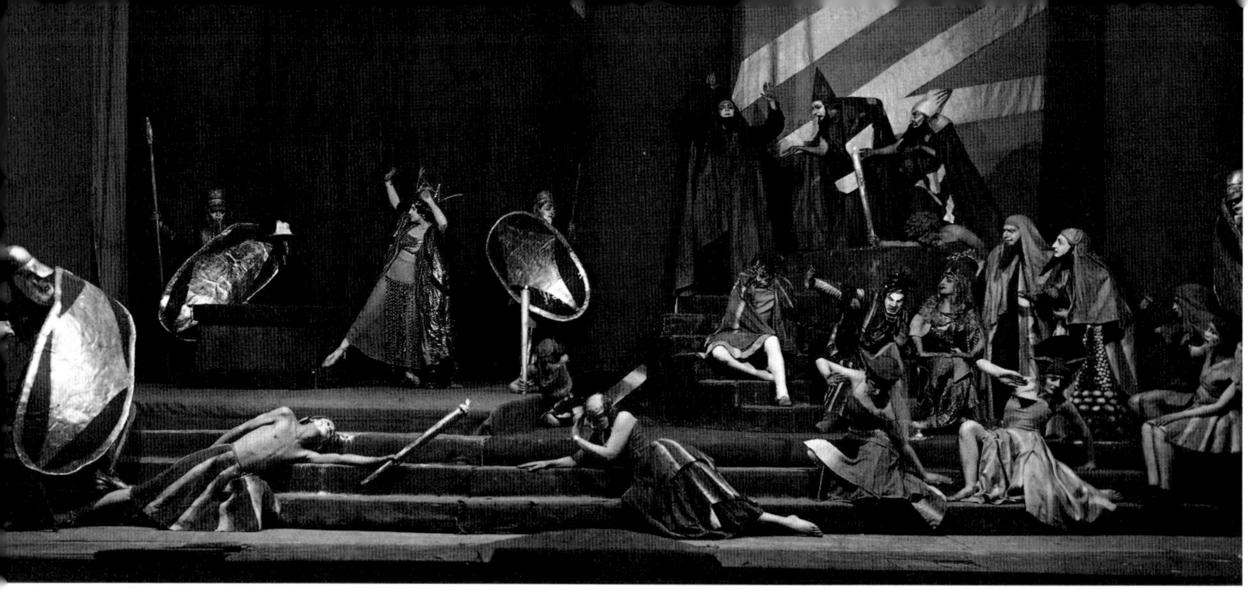

of color are just as essential as those of any other entity. Exter's colors tend to "explode" beyond the boundaries of a given form, producing liberated and almost independent zones of color, which, however, serve as reflections of, or commentaries on, the formal shapes within the painting.

Exter came to nonobjective painting gradually and consistently, with the Cubo-Futurist phase already containing the basic elements of the more advanced, abstract experiments (as in, for example, *Cityscape (Composition)*, ca. 1916 [plate 8]). She gave straightforward names to her non-objective paintings, such as *Composition: Movement of Planes*, 1917–18 (plate 10), *Non-Objective Composition*, 1917 (plate 9), and *Construction of Color Planes*, 1921 (plate 11). Such paintings give the impression of being cool, calculated arrangements of forms and colors, determined by the logic of carefully worked out aesthetic principles — but Exter's temperament and individuality could never be tamed and tempered by the sobriety of mere logic or calculation. True, Exter often described her non-objective compositions using terms from physics such as speed and acceleration, vector and mass, energy and direction; and, as in the world of physics, her non-objective compositions are never static, creating an almost hypnotic impression of constant change and evolution. Yet for all their sophistication, Exter's abstract paintings seem also to derive from a more local, domestic source, for the angularities of these works bring to mind the zigzag lines of flowers in Ukrainian peasant paintings: certainly, her triangles, trapezoids, and rhomboids suggest an immediate affinity with Ukrainian ornament.

Exter's Cubo-Futurist and non-objective experiments marked the high point of her artistic career — and she applied them to many of her concurrent activities, especially her work for Alexander Tairov's productions at the Moscow Chamber Theater: Innokentii Annensky's *Thamira Khytharedes* (1916), Oscar Wilde's *Salomé* (1917), and William Shakespeare's *Romeo and Juliet* (1921). Critic Abram Efros described Exter's sets for *Thamira Khytharedes* as a "festive parade of Cubism"[10] — an apt description, inasmuch as Exter was the first to bring Cubism

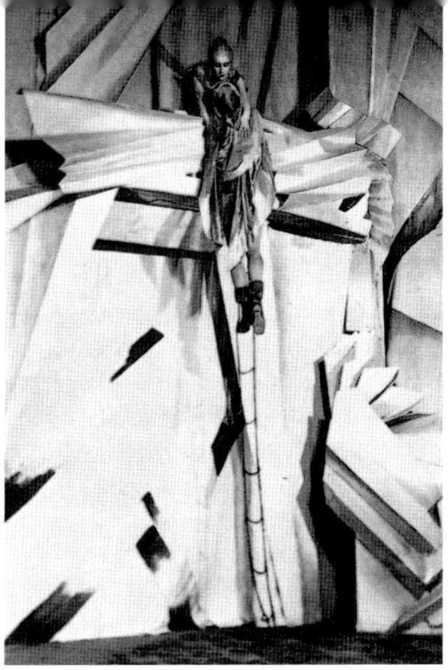

facing page:
figure 45. Oscar Wilde's *Salomé*, produced at the Chamber Theater, Moscow, with set and costume designs by Exter, 1917.

left:
figure 46. The balcony scene in William Shakespeare's *Romeo and Juliet*, produced at the Chamber Theater, Moscow, with set and costume designs by Exter, 1921.

to the Russian stage and to demonstrate how Cubist painting could respond to the discipline of theater. In fact, Exter's stage designs opened a new era, for she no longer subordinated the set and costume to a purely utilitarian function but exposed the active or kinetic element so as to complement and extend the action of the plot.

With its vitality of color, the Tairov/Exter *Salomé* production was also "festive," although it was the evocation of colored, volumetrical space and the extension of that space beyond the proscenium that surprised and delighted. Her designs for *Romeo and Juliet* were even more dynamic: unpredictable in their physical contrast, interaction of mass, and convergence and divergence of line, with a constant interplay of forms, colors, light, and shade in which the space itself became a principle "character." The sets were integrated with the intricate system of curtains, which fell from above and moved apart diagonally, parallel to the footlights, dividing or reducing or expanding the space of the stage. The curtains were also used to introduce each episode with a particular color, be it lemon, violet, orange, or crimson. We can understand why Efros referred to this *Romeo and Juliet* as a "most Cubist Cubism in a most Baroque Baroque."[11] Here and elsewhere, Exter's ideas about costumes were no less radical, for she insisted on the need for the costumes to interact organically with the sets or backdrops, so that their planar divisions and volumetrical interrelationships would correspond to the equivalent plastic relationships established within the broader space of the stage.

The Tairov productions brought Exter widespread recognition as a stage designer, and thenceforth the performing arts continued to play a major role in her career. For example, she collaborated with dancer Elza Kriuger and choreographer Bronislava Nijinska in Berlin and Paris; the focus of her exhibitions in Berlin, London, Paris, and Prague in the 1920s was on her work for the theater, the ballet, the movies, and marionettes; and in the 1920s she taught stage design at Léger's art school in Paris, the Academie Moderne. In 1930 she published a set of experimental projects for the stage in *Alexandra Exter: Décors de Théâtre*, an anthology of

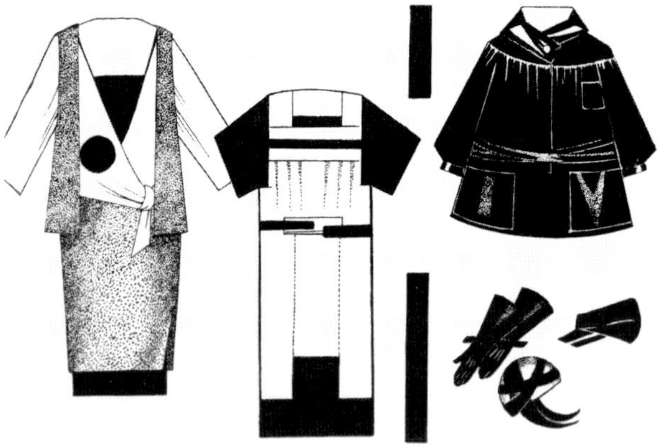

figure 47. ALEXANDRA EXTER
Clothing designs, 1923
Illustration accompanying Exter's article "Prostota i praktichnost v odezhde," in *Krasnaia niva* (Moscow), no. 21 (May 27, 1923), p. 31

designs and proposals for the circus, operettas and revues, and drama (with an introduction by Tairov). Well after she emigrated, Exter found solace in the theater, creating designs for costumes and sets for plays by Aeschylus and Sophocles, though without any specific commission or production in mind. During the 1930s Exter also returned to the theme of the commedia dell'arte, the personages of her paintings and drawings becoming ballerinas and acrobats. Even her ceramic designs and the several maquettes that she made for editions in the 1930s (most of them, unfortunately, not published) carry references to the theater.

Exter was an important member of the international avant-garde. She participated in the major Russian exhibitions such as *Tramway V* (1915) and *The Store* (1916); was a colleague of Natalia Goncharova, Liubov Popova, Olga Rozanova, and Nadezha Udaltsova; and constantly traveled in the 1910s, serving as an important link between Russia and France and Italy.

Remembered also as a teacher, Exter molded an entire school of younger Ukrainian and Russian artists, some of whom became well known in Europe and the United States, such as Simon Lissim and Pavel Tchelitchew. Her talent as an artist overflowed into many related fields, including interior design (as in the Kriuger apartment in Berlin in the 1920s), exhibition design (the *All-Union Agricultural Exhibition* in Moscow in 1923), clothing design (for the Atelier fashion house in Moscow in 1923), book design (Ivan Aksenov's poetry), and movie-set design (for the Martian sequence in Yakov Protazanov's film *Aelita* in 1924). An inspiration to many, the strangely proper Exter was regarded as the ultimate arbiter of improper taste, praising the great cathedrals of France, yet fascinated by a single flower on a Ukrainian costume, championing the complex schemes of Cubism and yet welcoming the fresh and savage art of the Russian avant-garde.

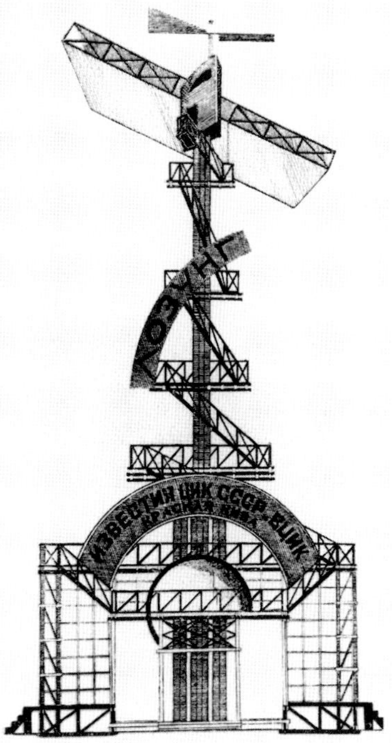

figure 48. ALEXANDRA EXTER WITH BORIS GLADKOV AND VERA MUKHINA
Design for the Izvestiia Pavilion at the All-Union Agricultural Exhibition, Moscow, 1923

1. Exter was born in Belostok (now Poland); she moved with her parents to Kiev when she was sixteen.
2. See, for example, Exter's letters to Vera Mukhina in RGALI (inv. no. 2326, op. 1).
3. It was Exter's idea to organize the two *Salons* that Izdebsky financed and toured in 1910 and 1911. For information on these two *Salons*, including the Kiev venue, see Dimitrii Severiukhin, "Vladimir Izdebsky and His *Salons*," *Experiment* (Los Angeles), no. 1 (1995), pp. 57–71.
4. The Kiev artist Alexander Konstantinovich Bogomazov (1880–1930) was one of the most original members of the Cubo-Futurist movement. Of particular interest is his treatise *Painting and Its Elements*. For information on Bogomazov, see André B. Nakov, *Alexandre Bogomazov*, exh. cat. (Toulouse: Musée d'Art Moderne, 1991); and Dimitrii Gorbachev's Introduction in Alexander Bogomazov, *Zhivopis ta elementi* [*Painting and Its Elements*] (Kiev: Popova, 1996).
5. Exter made the acquaintance of Archipenko while they were both students at the Kiev Art Institute. She also attended Archipenko's first exhibition in Kiev in 1906.
6. See Giovanni Lista, "Futurisme et cubofuturisme," *Cahiers du Musée national d'art moderne* (Paris), no. 5 (1980), p. 459.
7. Filippo Tommaso Marinetti, "Futurizm," in Genrikh Tasteven, ed., *Futurizm* (Moscow: Iris, 1914), pp. 143–44.
8. Nikolai Tarabukin, *Opyt teorii zhivopisi* (Moscow: Vserossiiskii proletkult, 1923), p. 39.
9. Yakov Tugendkhold, *Alexandra Exter kak zhivopisets i khudozhnik stseny* (Berlin: Zaria 1922), p. 10.
10. Abram Efros, *Khudozhniki Kamernogo teatra* (Moscow: VTO, 1934), p. xxiv.
11. Ibid., pp. xxxii–xxxiii.

ALEXANDRA ALEXANDROVNA EXTER
(née Grigorovich)
(1882–1949)

1882	Born January 6, Belestok, near Kiev.
1892–99	Attends the St. Olga Women's Gymnasium in Kiev.
1901–03	Attends the Kiev Art Institute.
1904	Marries her cousin, Nikolai Exter, a lawyer.
1906–08	Reenrolls in the Kiev Art Institute.
1907	Begins visiting Paris and other European cities.
1908	Takes part in several Kiev exhibitions, including the avant-garde show *The Link*. Produces her first book illustrations.
1909–14	Travels and lives abroad frequently. Becomes acquainted with Apollinaire, Braque, Picasso, Soffici, and many other members of the international avant-garde.
1910	Contributes to *The Triangle* and *Union of Youth* exhibitions in St. Petersburg.
1910–11	Contributes to the first *Jack of Diamonds* exhibition in Moscow.
1912–13	Moves to St. Petersburg. Continues to contribute to major exhibitions.
1913–14	Lives mainly in France.
1915	Influenced by Malevich and Tatlin, begins to investigate non-objective painting.
1915–16	Contributes to the exhibitions *Tramway V* and *The Store*.
1916–17	Begins her professional theater work with designs for *Thamira Khytharedes* in 1916 and *Salomé* in 1917, both produced by Alexander Tairov at the Chamber Theater, Moscow.
1918	Nikolai Exter dies.
1918–19	Opens her own studio in Kiev; among her students are many artists who later achieve success, such as Isaak Rabinovich, Pavel Tchelitchew, and Alexander Tyshler.
1918–20	Works intermittently in Odessa as a teacher and stage designer.
1920	Moves to Moscow. Marries Georgii Nekrasov, an actor. Works at the Theater of the People's House.
1921	Contributes to the exhibition *5 x 5 = 25* in Moscow.
1921–22	Teaches at Vkhutemas.
1923	Turns to textile and fashion design for the Atelier of Fashions in Moscow. Is a member of the design team for the *Izvestiia* Pavilion at

the *All-Union Agricultural Exhibition* in Moscow. Begins work on the costumes for Yakov Protozanov's movie *Aelita*.

1924 Emigrates to Paris. Contributes to the Venice *Biennale*. Works for the Ballets Russes, with Léon Zack and Pavel Tchelitchew. Teaches at Fernand Léger's Académie Moderne.

1925 Contributes to the *Exposition Internationale des Arts Décoratifs et Industriels Modernes* in Paris. Continues to work on stage design and interior design (which she will do throughout the 1920s and 1930s); designs costumes for seven ballets performed by Bronislava Nijinska's Théâtre Choréographique.

1927 Exhibition at Der Sturm, Berlin.

1929 Exhibition at Galerie des Quatre Chemins, Paris.

1936 Illustrates several elegant children's books, beginning with her own *Mon Jardin* (1936).

1937 Exhibition at the Musée des Arts et Métiers, Paris.

1949 Dies March 17, in Paris.

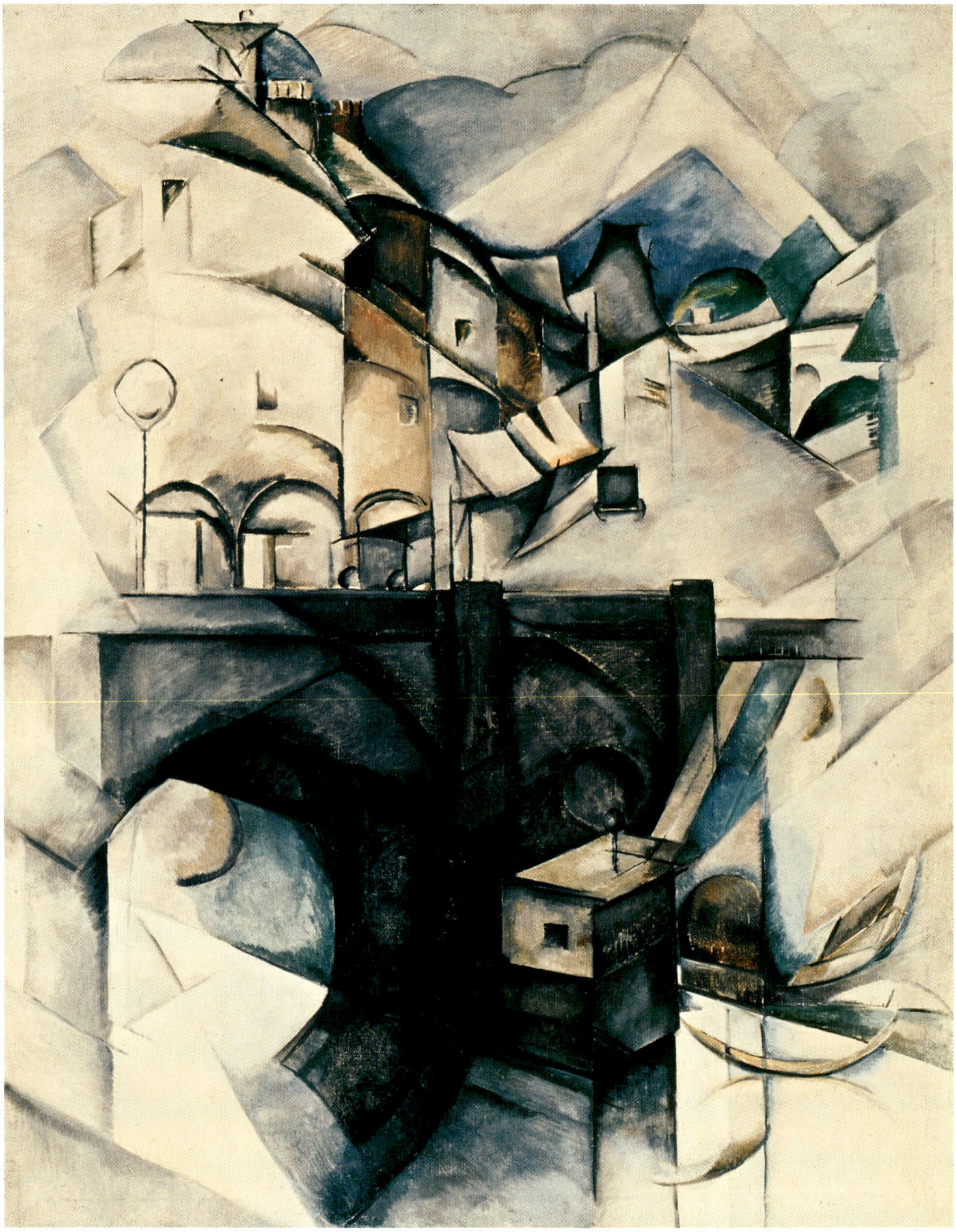

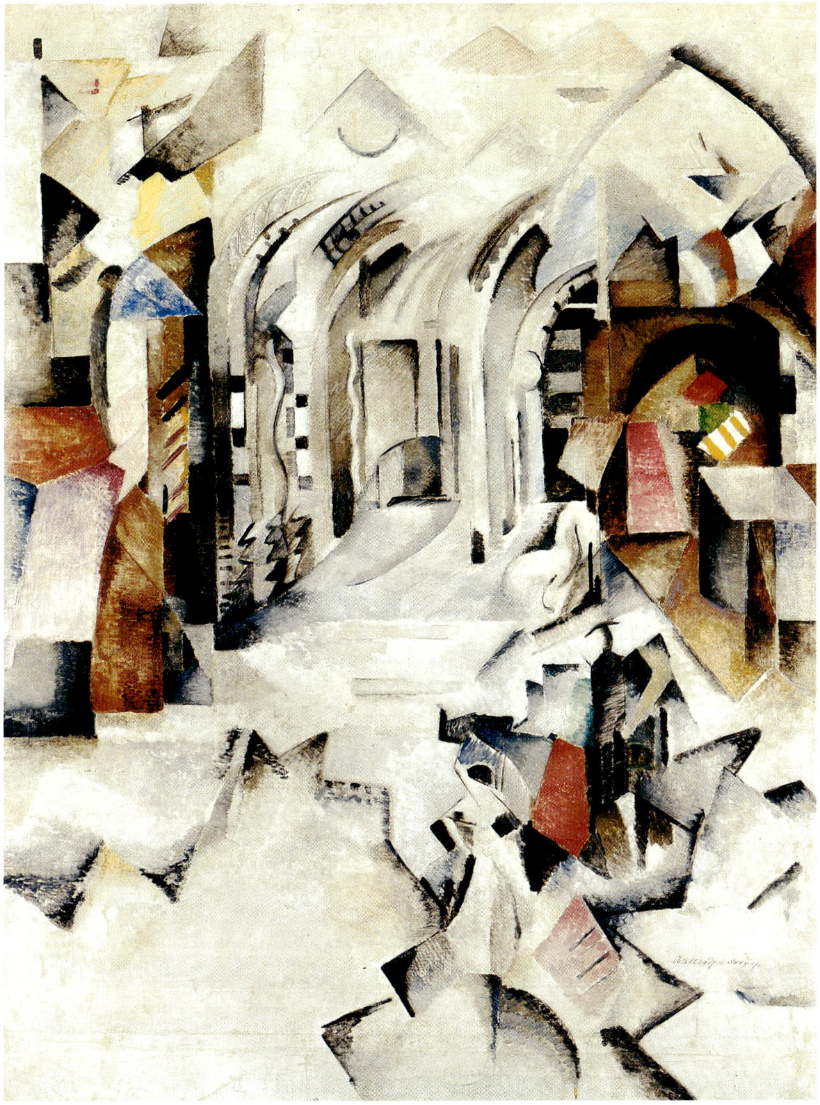

facing page:
plate 1. ALEXANDRA EXTER
The Bridge (Sèvres), 1912
Oil on canvas, 145 x 115 cm
National Art Museum of Ukraine, Kiev

above:
plate 2. ALEXANDRA EXTER
Composition (Genoa), 1912–14
Oil on canvas, 115.5 x 86.5 cm
Museum Ludwig, Cologne

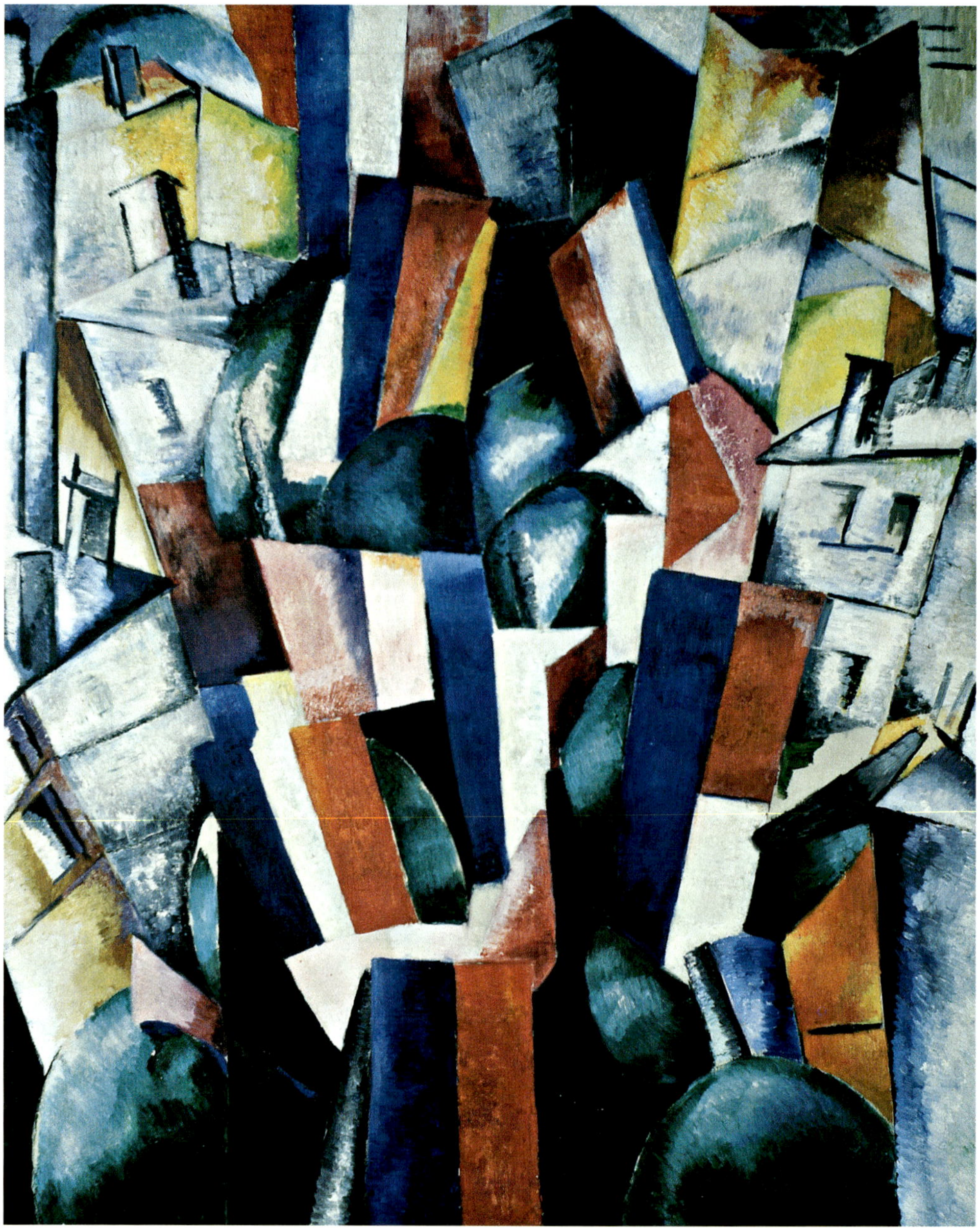

plate 3. ALEXANDRA EXTER
City, 1913
Oil on canvas, 88.5 x 70.5 cm
Regional Picture Gallery, Vologda

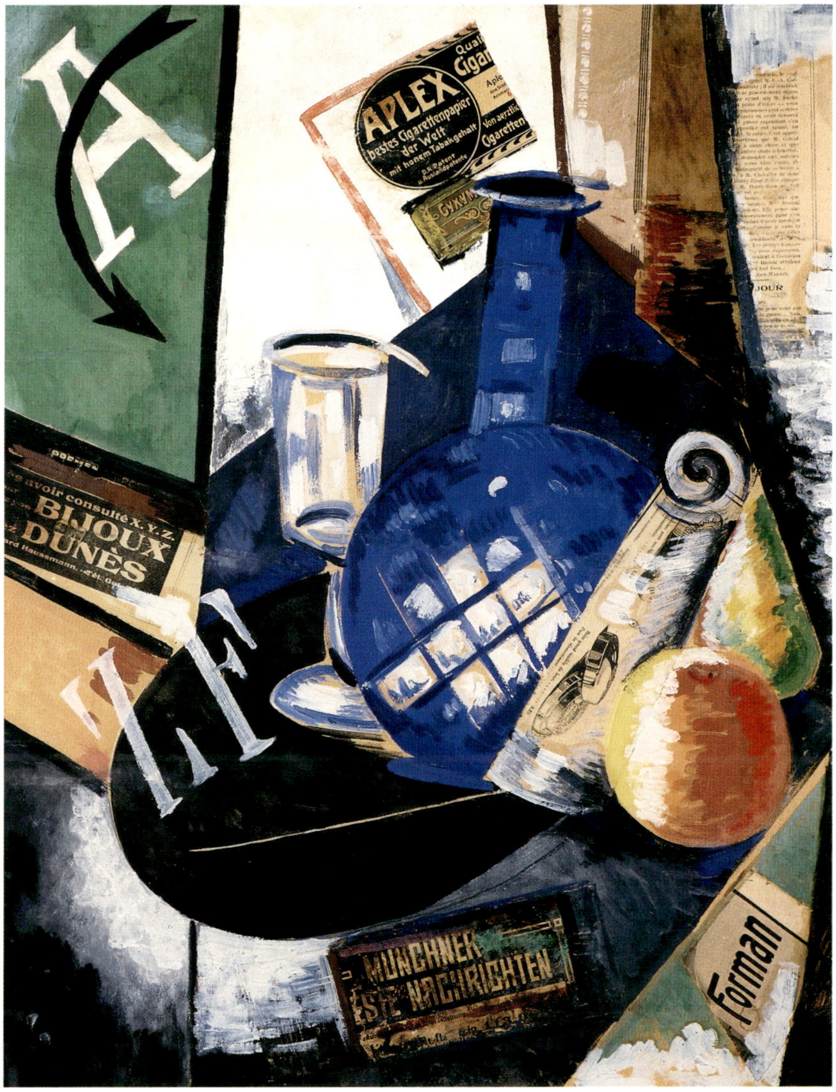

plate 4. ALEXANDRA EXTER
Still Life, ca. 1913
Oil on canvas, 68 x 53 cm
Museo Thyssen-Bornemisza, Madrid

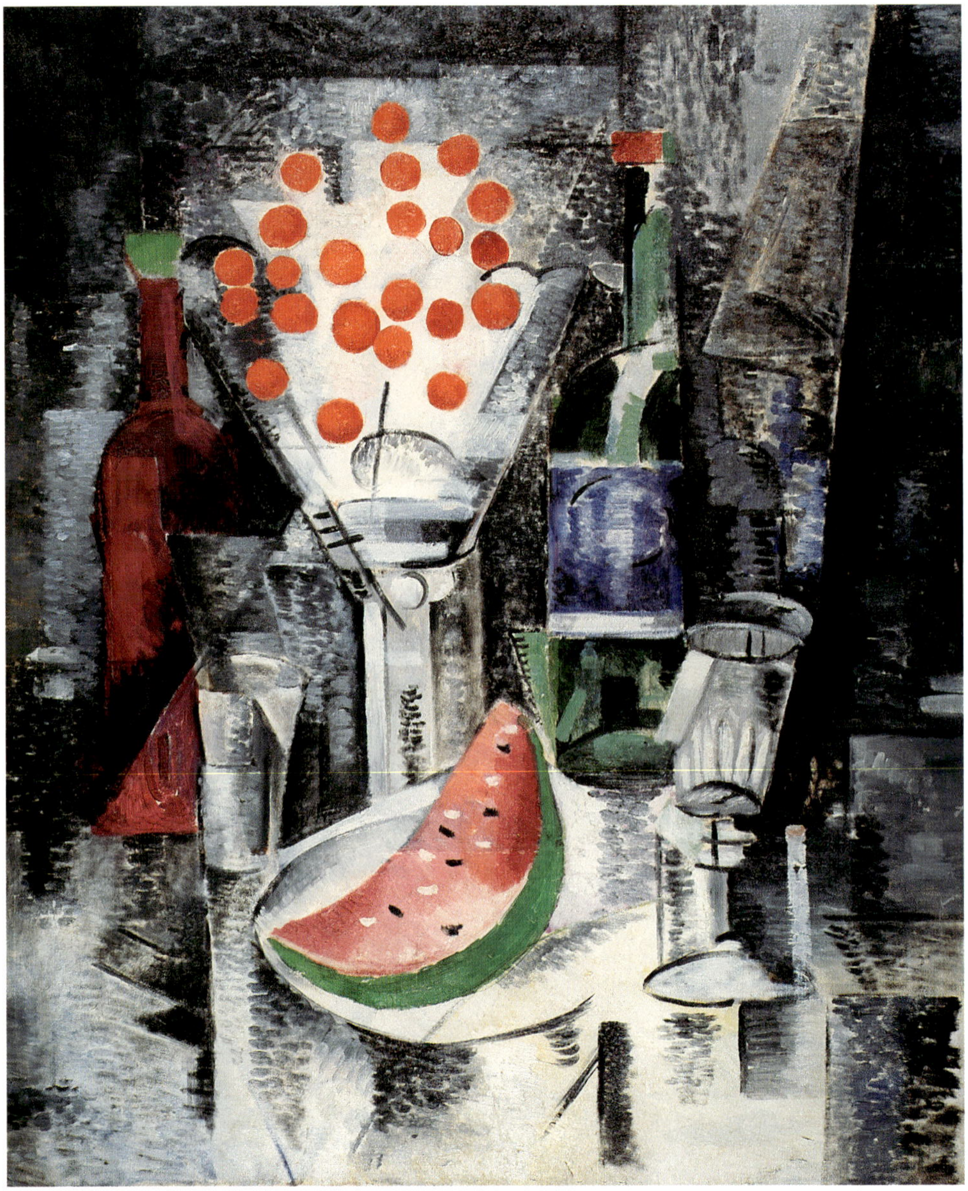

plate 5. ALEXANDRA EXTER
Still Life. Bowl of Cherries, 1914
Oil on canvas, 89 x 72 cm
Rostov Kremlin State Museum Preserve

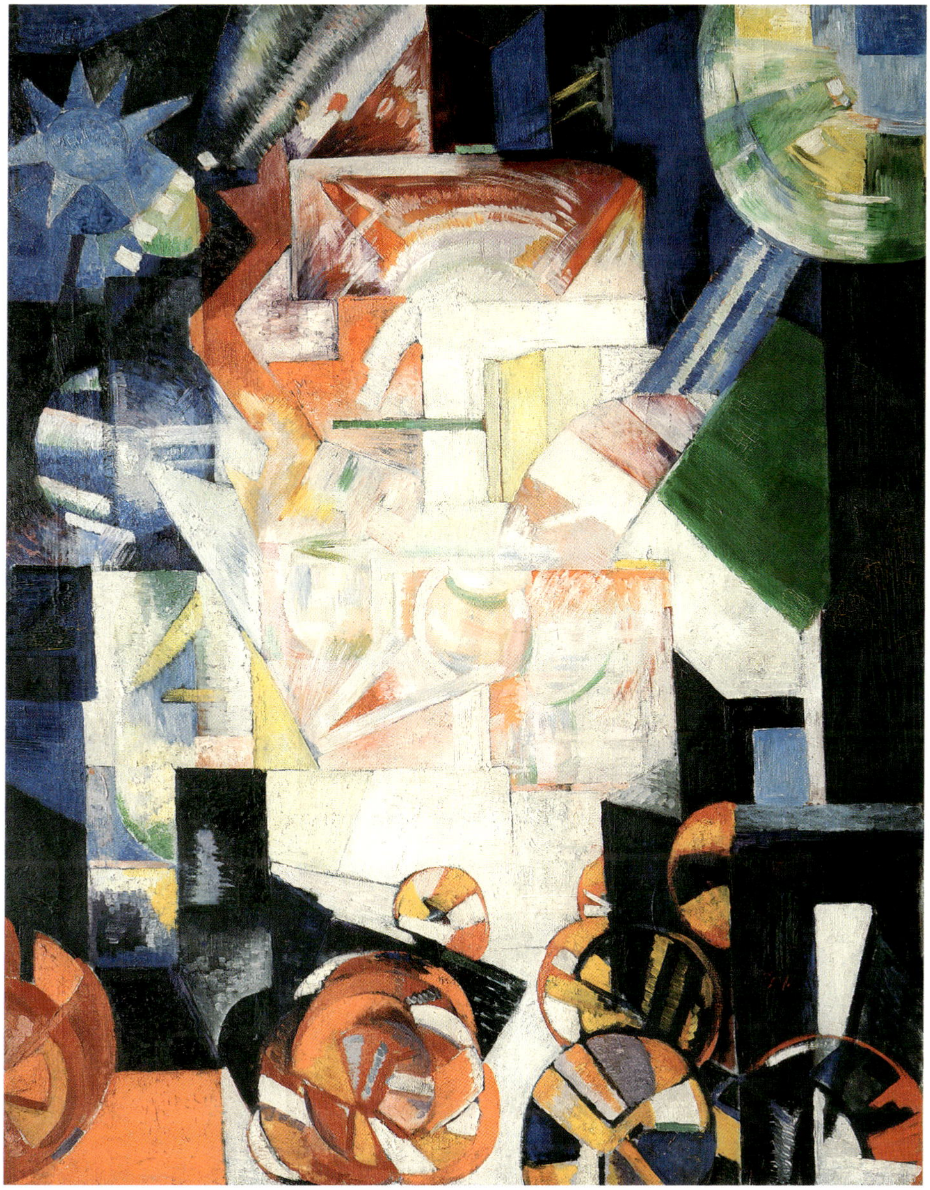

plate 6. ALEXANDRA EXTER
Composition, 1914
Oil on canvas, 90.7 x 72.5 cm
State Tretiakov Gallery, Moscow

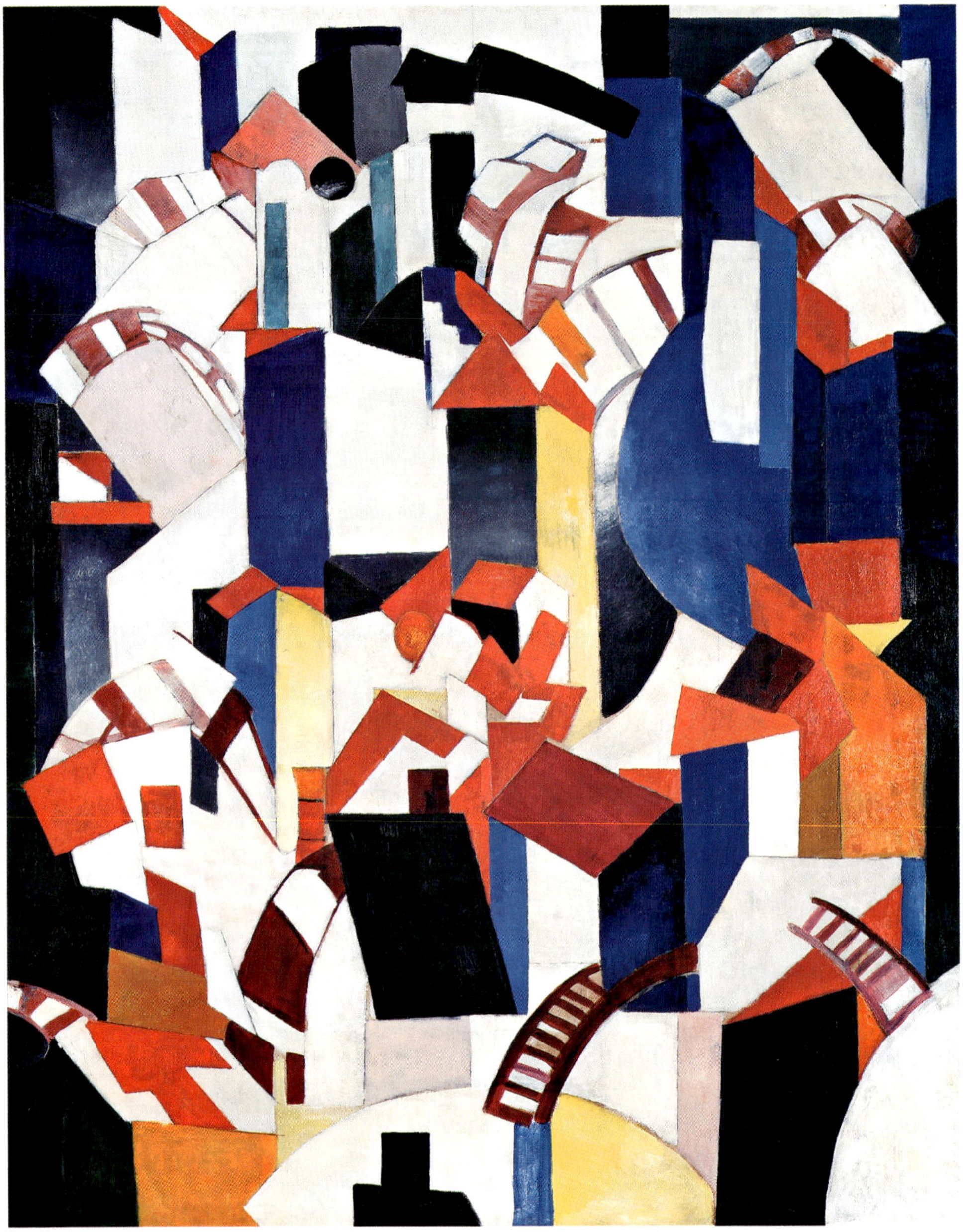

plate 7. ALEXANDRA EXTER
Venice, 1915
Oil on canvas, 123 x 97 cm
Moderna Museet, Stockholm

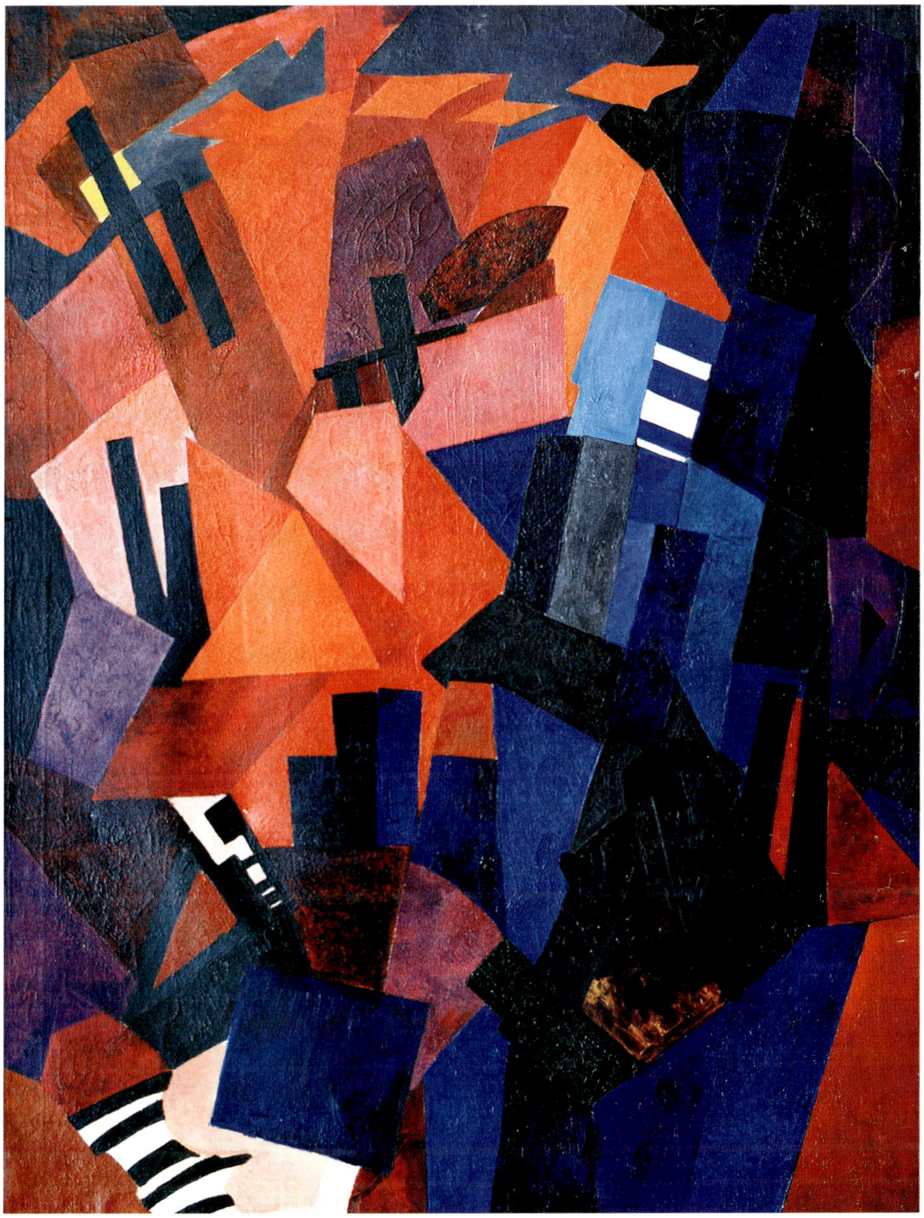

plate 8. ALEXANDRA EXTER
Cityscape (Composition), ca. 1916
Oil on canvas, 117 x 88 cm
Slobodskoi Museum and Exhibition Center

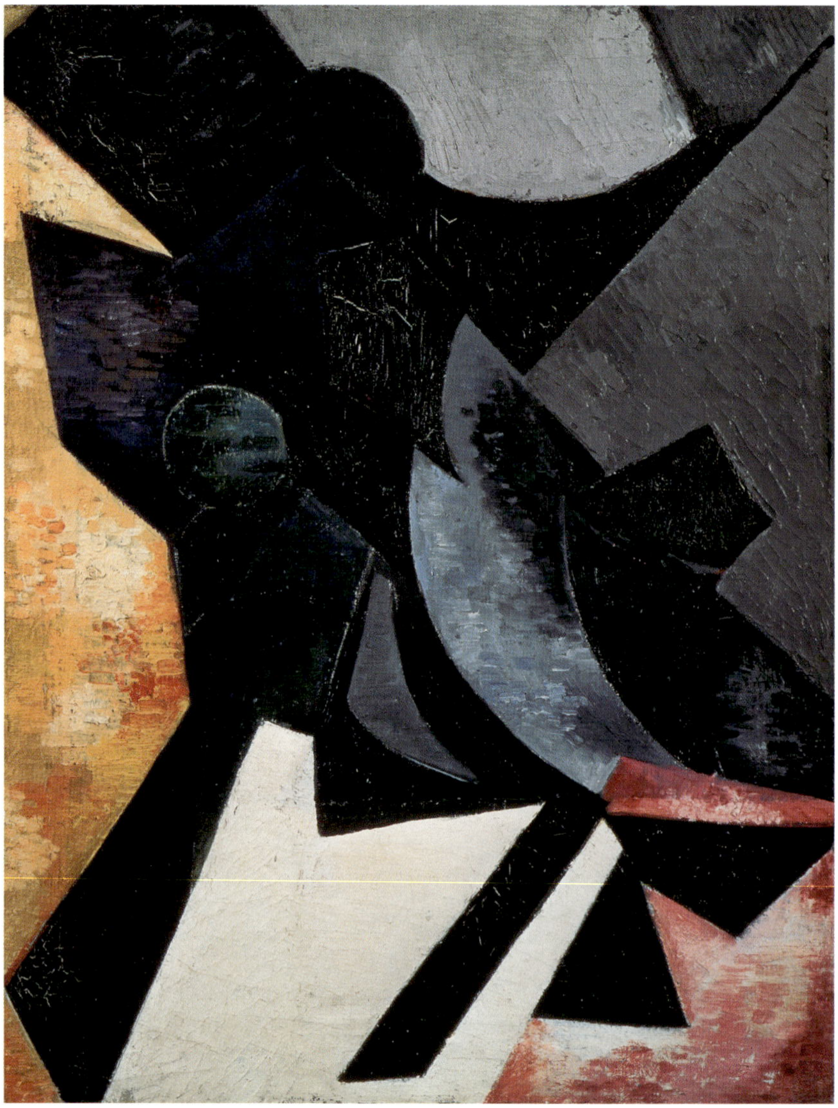

above:
plate 9. ALEXANDRA EXTER
Non-Objective Composition, 1917
Oil on canvas, 71 x 53 cm
Krasnodar District Kovalenko Art Museum

facing page:
plate 10. ALEXANDRA EXTER
Composition. Movement of Planes, 1917–18
Oil on canvas, 92.5 x 76.9 cm
State Museum of Visual Arts, Nizhnii Tagil

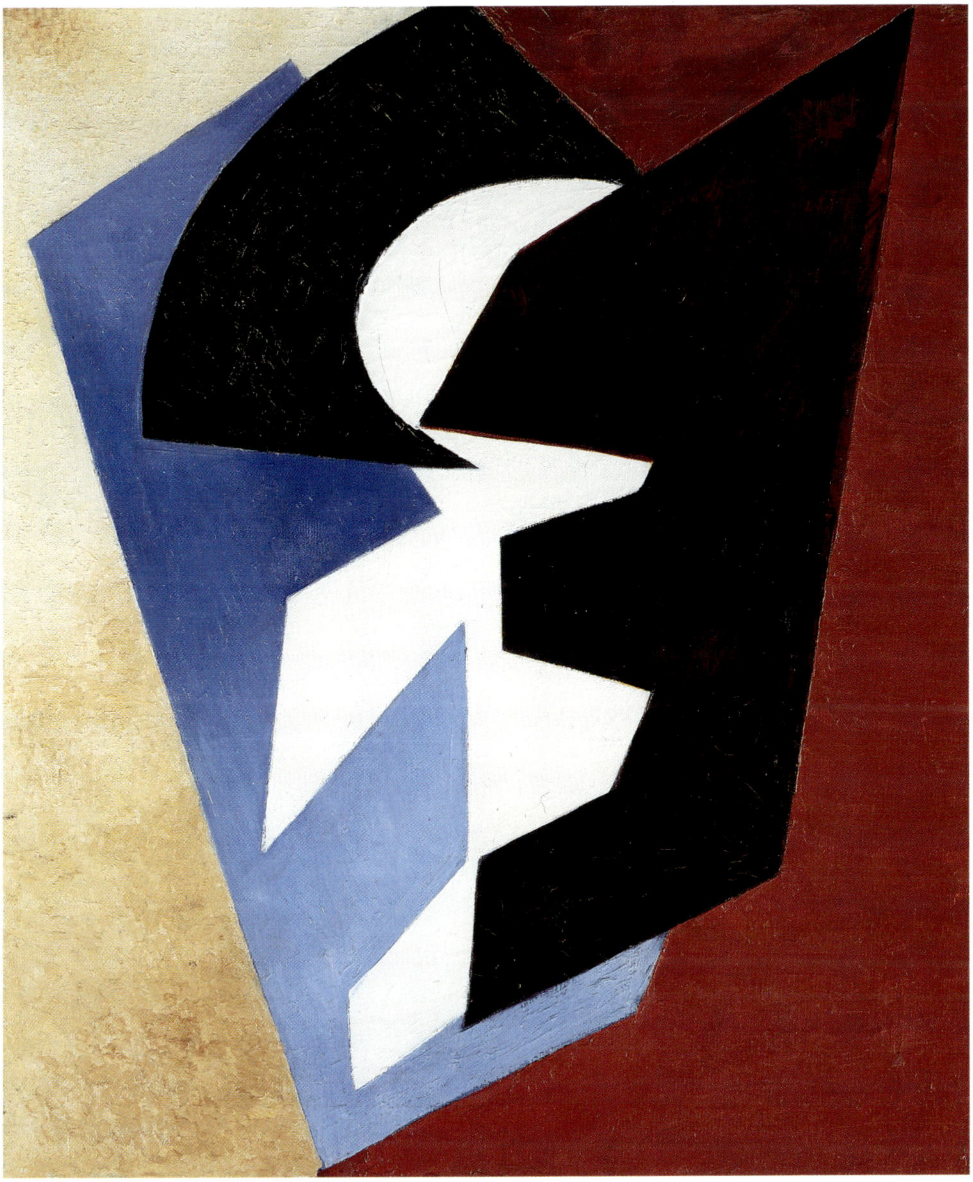

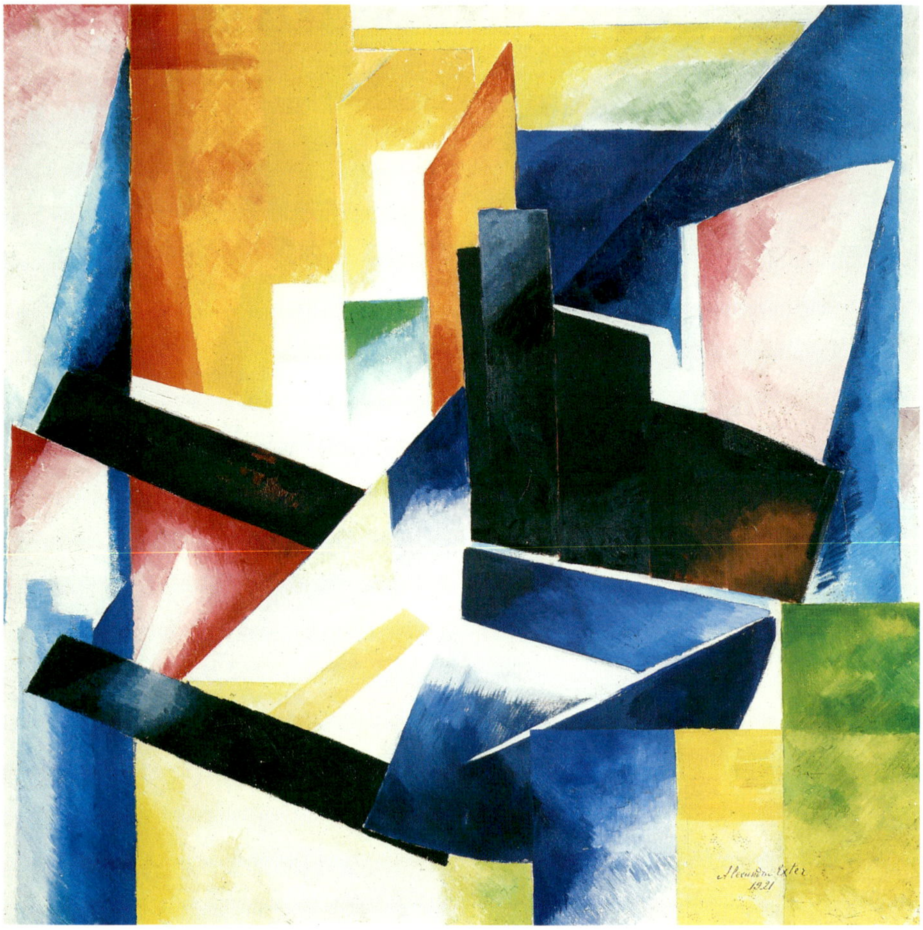

plate 11. ALEXANDRA EXTER
Construction of Color Planes, 1921
Oil on canvas, 89 x 89 cm
State Radischev Art Museum, Saratov

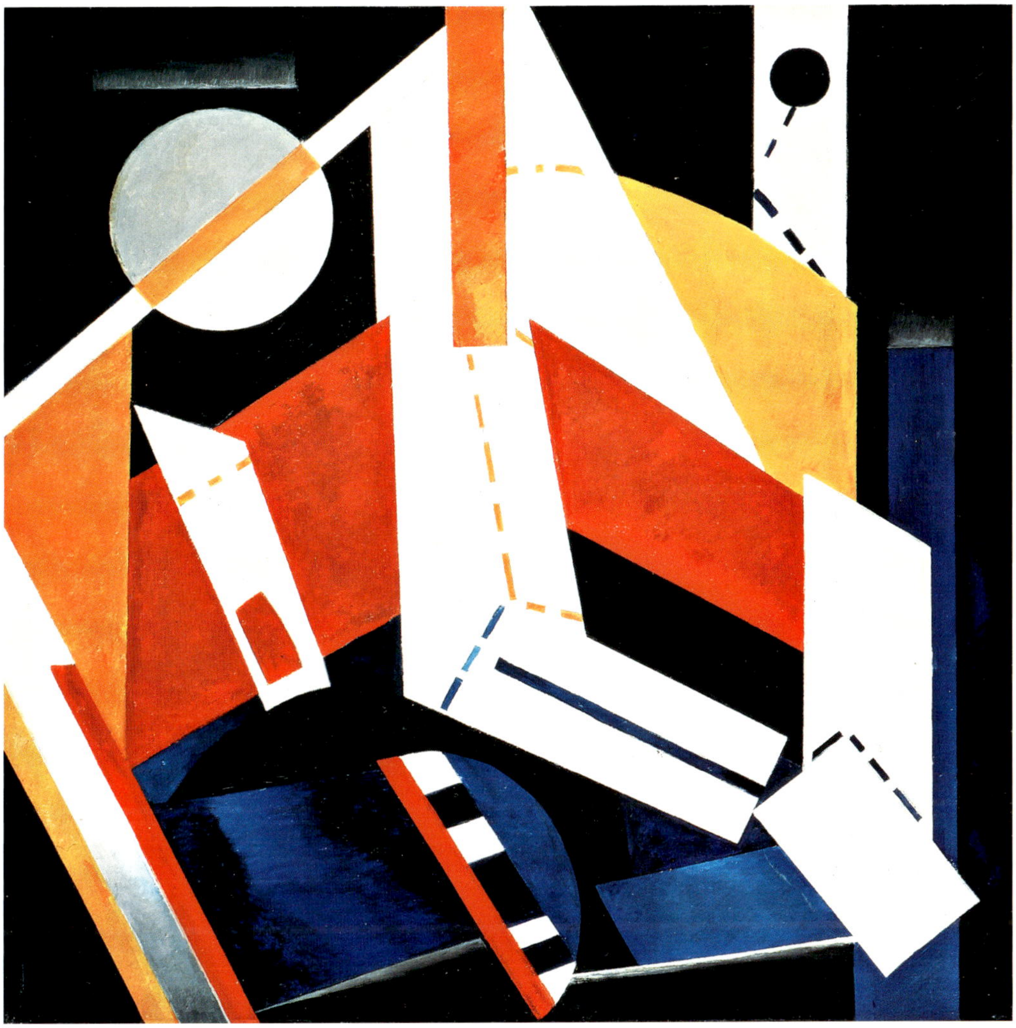

plate 12. ALEXANDRA EXTER
Construction, 1922–23
Oil on canvas, 89.8 x 89.2 cm
The Museum of Modern Art, New York.
The Riklis Collection of McCrory Corporation (partial gift).

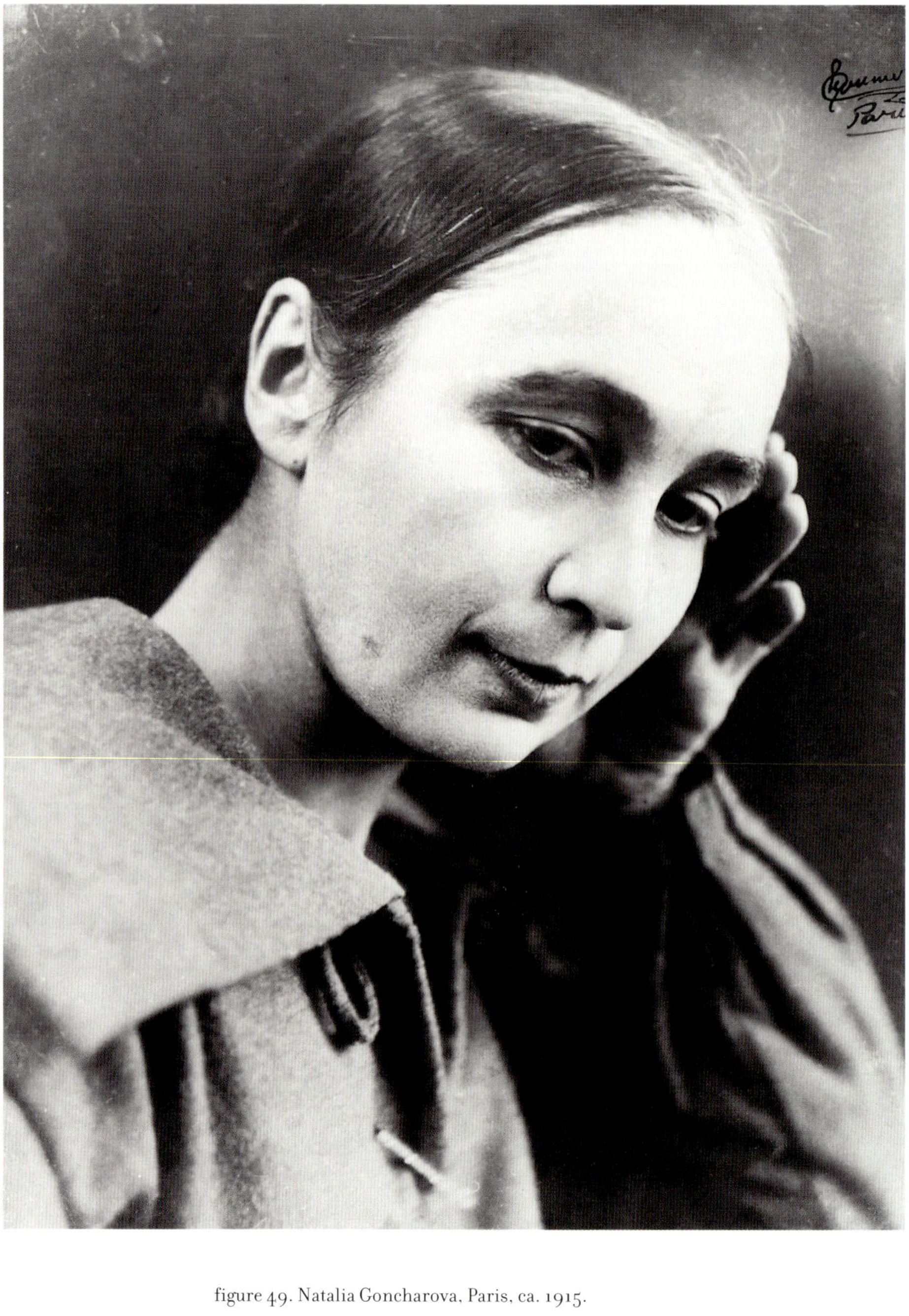

figure 49. Natalia Goncharova, Paris, ca. 1915.

Natalia Goncharova

Jane A. Sharp

Natalia Goncharova: Lives of the Artist

In an essay that remains the best study on Goncharova to date, poet Marina Tsvetaeva distinguishes Goncharova's biography, her "outer life," from her creative work and persona. This "inner life" cannot be distilled into a narrative of historical and personal events, for it is shaped through the agency that the painter demonstrates in her art. Goncharova transcends rather than succumbs to "daily life" (*byt*, in Russian).[1] Today it is less difficult to argue that Goncharova requires biographical, historical representation. We now know that she viewed her own creative practices as repetitive, exhausting work, and that her art directly engaged the conditions and prejudices of everyday life, particularly insofar as they determined her experiences as a woman. Indeed, Tsvetaeva's approach is somewhat contradictory. Goncharova's identity as an artist is framed by two poles within her biography, i.e., her life in Russia and her life as an émigré, "after Russia" — the point at which the poet reconnected with the painter, former neighbors who met each other first in Moscow but became friends only as expatriates in Paris.[2]

Natalia Sergeevna Goncharova was born on June 21, 1881 (the same year as Larionov, Picasso, and Léger) in the village of Nagaevo, in the Chern district of Tula province.[3] Goncharova's immediate family were politically liberal and well-educated members of the rural gentry. Her father, Sergei, an architect (graduate of the Moscow Institute of Painting, Sculpture, and Architecture), designed and built their Moscow home on Trekhprudnyi Lane. Goncharova and her younger brother, Afanasii, were raised and educated primarily by their mother and paternal grandmother in family homes in the Orlov and Tula provinces. Goncharova moved to Moscow in 1892 to attend the Fourth Women's Gymnasium, from which she graduated in 1898. After several false starts in history, zoology, botany, and medicine, Goncharova finally decided on a career as a sculptor and entered the Moscow Institute of Painting, Sculpture, and Architecture in the fall of 1901.

Goncharova experienced the contradictions between city and country as a crisis in her life — one that places her work within the continuum of European (and Russian) Modernism. Bridges between workaday, urban Moscow and summer retreats to the country are everywhere apparent in her art. Photographs of the family estate show her playing peasant, dressed in local clothing, but wearing city shoes. A group of three early self-portraits reveal her interest in elite masquerades as well; in one, she depicts herself as an 1840s gentlewoman relaxing at home in her morning dress; the others focus on her identity as a painter (see *Self-Portrait with Yellow Lilies*, 1907, plate 13). In these paintings, we see the continuity of "outer" and "inner" lives mapped out in the congruence of images and realities. Rural Russia emerges complete from the painter's Moscow studio. *Self-Portrait with Yellow Lilies*, one painted frame abuts and is contained within the actual picture frame — underscoring the self-conscious mastery of the artist and to experiences both lived and imagined.

russia: polotnianyi zavod

Goncharova's early pastels and paintings draw on her rural environs, particularly the family's main estate in Kaluga province, named Polotnianyi Zavod in reference to the paper (formerly textile) factory that occupied the same grounds as the palatial dwelling.[4] Descriptions of life on the estate suggest a blurring of boundaries of class, work, leisure, and culture that may be associated with liberal reform efforts in late-nineteenth- and early-twentieth-century Russia. The estate's owner, Dmitrii Dmitrievich Goncharov, himself a talented amateur singer, maintained a "worker's" theater on the grounds and was married to a star in Sergei Zimin's Moscow opera company. Both of them performed and invited others to participate in evenings of music and drama. Among the more celebrated visitors during Goncharova's era was theater critic Anatolii Lunacharsky (later Lenin's Commissar of Enlightenment).[5]

Given the frequent travel between family homes, it is likely that Goncharova witnessed some of the theatrical performances at Polotnianyi Zavod, although she does not mention them in any of her autobiographical sketches. Instead, what impressed her most were the daily activities of the servants and peasants who lived

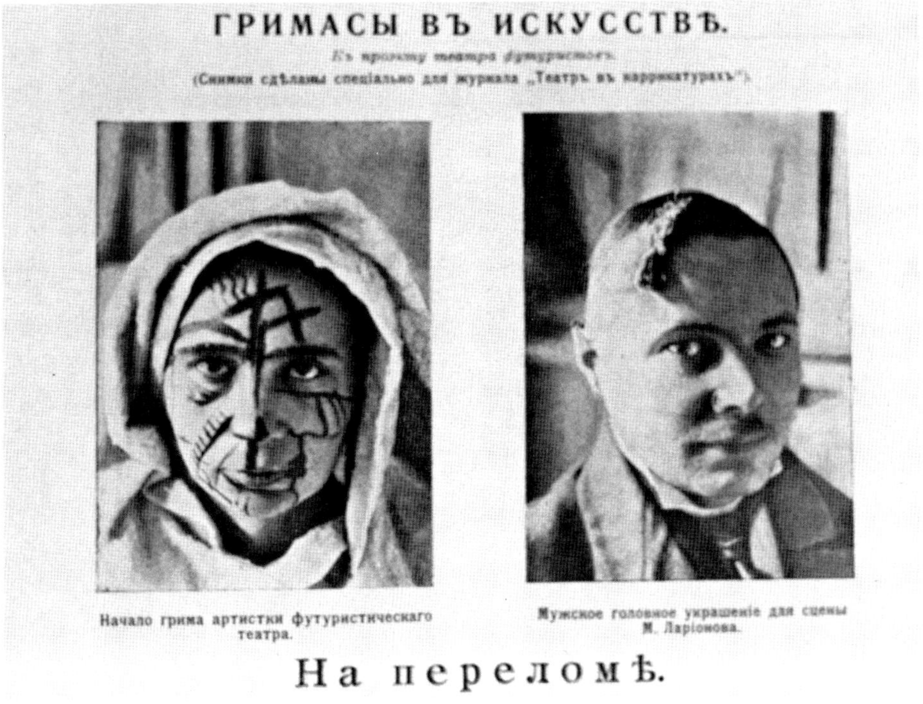

figure 50. "Grimaces in Art. In Connection with the Project for a Theater of the Futurists." Photograph of Natalia Goncharova (captioned "Initial makeup for an actress of the Futurist theater") and Mikhail Larionov (captioned "Male head ornament for the stage by M. Larionov") (1913). Reproduced in *Teatr v karrikaturakh* (Moscow), no. 3 (September 21, 1913), p. 9.

on the property.[6] Views and reconstructed maps of the estate give some indication of the proximity of the factory, farming, and the peasant dwellings that stretch just beyond the Sukhodrev river that runs through the estate. A series of interconnected ponds, artificially maintained with supplies of fish for the benefit of the local population, are depicted in Goncharova's fishing cycle. Her farming cycle and a number of gardening images can also be identified with specific landscapes at Polotnianyi Zavod during the years 1906–09 when she regularly returned there to paint.[7]

LIFE INTO ART: THE MOSCOW INSTITUTE AND THE INDEPENDENT EXHIBITION

Goncharova's training in the visual arts reflects both the limits of official art institutions — which at the turn of the century no longer segregated male and female students, but denied women equal rights upon completion of the degree — and the importance of independent studios. Goncharova's claim that she had little training

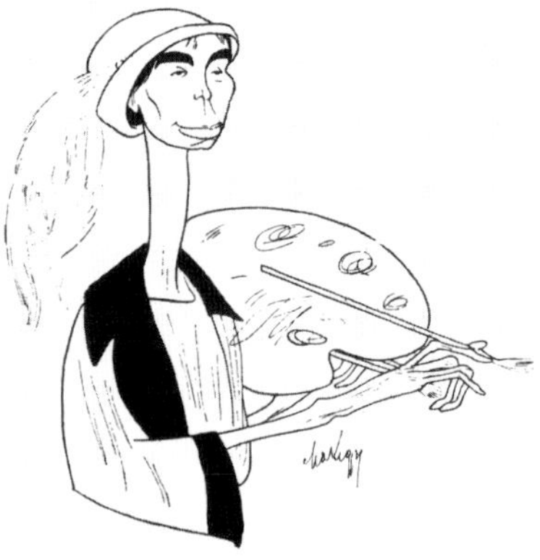

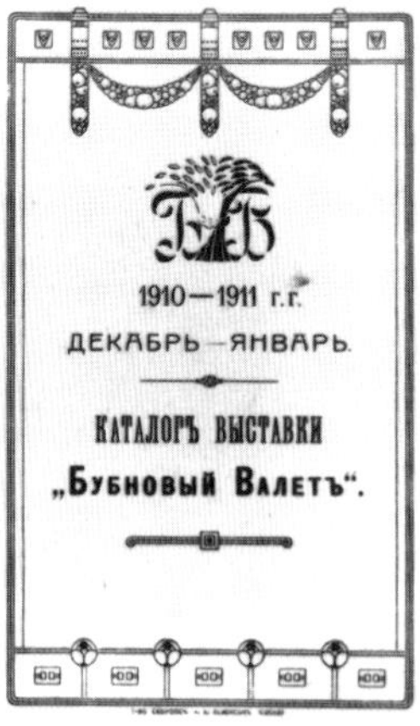

far left:
figure 51. mak [Pavel Petrovich Ivanov]
Natalia Goncharova, 1914
Ink on paper, 15 x 12.5 cm
Courtesy of Dimitri Dourdine-Mak, Brussels

left:
figure 52. natalia goncharova
(attributed to)
Cover of the *Jack of Diamonds*
exhibition catalogue, Moscow, 1910

as a painter is belied by numerous sources. She attended the Moscow Institute infrequently following her receipt of a small silver medal for sculpture (1903–04), yet she did not officially withdraw until 1909.[8] From at least 1908, she both taught and attended classes given at Ilia Mashkov's and Alexander Mikhailovsky's studio on Malyi Kharitonevskii Lane in Moscow.[9] It was here that she studied and made numerous sketches of the male and female nude, completing the studio exercises that would have concluded her course of study at the Moscow Institute. While at the Moscow Institute, Goncharova had met Larionov; soon after he moved into the Goncharov house, where together they maintained a studio and living quarters.[10] Clearly, he was her most important instructor, at times repainting or correcting her work.[11] Memoirs of colleagues and friends underscore the reciprocity of their relationship and the central place it occupied in Moscow's bohemian circles.[12]

The Moscow Institute studios, Larionov's in particular, provided Goncharova with her immediate milieu: the cast of ever shifting participants in the avant-garde exhibitions organized in Moscow. Following the January 1910 mass expulsion of students from Konstantin Korovin's portrait-genre class for their imitation of contemporary European Modernist painting, a group consisting of Larionov, Robert Falk, Petr Konchalovsky, Alexander Kuprin, Mashkov (expelled the year earlier), and others formed the first radical Muscovite independent exhibiting group, which Larionov named the Jack of Diamonds — a provocative title that evoked associations with boulevard literature and the identifying pattern on prison uniforms. Goncharova exhibited her Primitivist and Cubist paintings in that group's first show, which took place in December 1910–1911, and was prominently reviewed in the press. She dominated a subsequent exhibition, *The Donkey's Tail*, organized by Larionov and held in March–April 1912, with more than fifty-five of her paintings in the first hall of the gallery space. The other major Moscow shows in which she participated were *The Target* (March–April 1913), and *No. 4* (March–April 1914). Larionov may be credited with

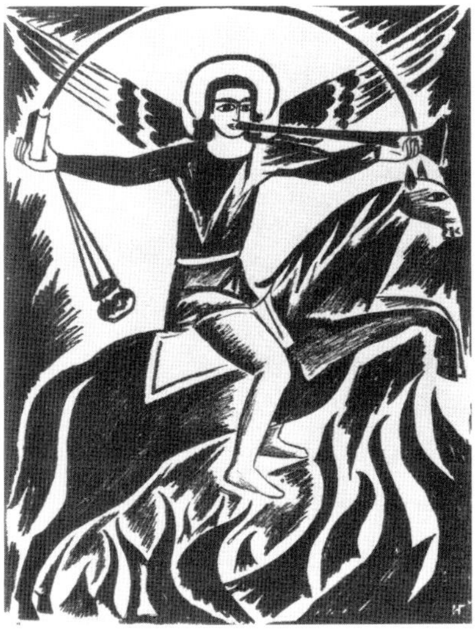

figure 53. NATALIA GONCHAROVA
Archistrategus Michael, 1914
Sheet no. 7 in Natalia Goncharova's
album of lithographs, *Misticheskie obrazy voiny*;
32.5 x 24.8 cm
Private collection.

promoting her career over his own in these exhibitions and with arranging her retrospectives in 1913 (Moscow) and 1914 (St. Petersburg).[13]

Quite apart from Larionov's efforts on her behalf, Goncharova played a unique role among the Russian, specifically Muscovite, avant-garde. She put into practice many of the aesthetic programs advanced by him and others. Moreover, her oeuvre in its wide-ranging dialogue with both Eastern and Western traditions served as a catalyst for several movements and manifestos, and she pioneered both Cubo-Futurism (see *Airplane over a Train*, 1913, plate 22) and Rayism (see *Yellow and Green Forest*, 1913, plate 24) in paintings, publications, and exhibitions.

Although dating Goncharova's shifts in her pre–World War I style remains problematic, her participation in the exhibitions mentioned above and her statements, including the catalogue essay for her Moscow retrospective (co-authored by Larionov and Ilia Zdanevich), charted the course for the Moscow avant-garde's orientation toward both Western European Modernism and the visual traditions of the East. She declared in a press interview of April 1910 to be inspired by the "sculptural clarity" of Le Fauconnier, Picasso, and Braque, but her first "Cubist" works are dated to at least the year before. By 1912 she claimed to be deriving her Cubist style from the forms of Scythian stone statues (*kamennye baby*) (see *Peasants Gathering Grapes*, 1912, plate 19) and Russia's popular arts — the latter familiar to the artist from childhood.[14] In an account of *The Donkey's Tail* and *The Target* exhibitions, author Varsanofii Parkin (possibly a pseudonym for Larionov) attributes to Goncharova the decision to "fight against Cézanne and Picasso and not Repin and Raphael," a policy that was perhaps more significant as a polemical tool than as actual practice.[15]

Undoubtedly, Goncharova's oeuvre inspired the theory and nationalist rhetoric of Neo-Primitivism as it was publicized by Larionov, Alexander Shevchenko, and Zdanevich in 1913. Drawing on the formal tradition of French avant-garde

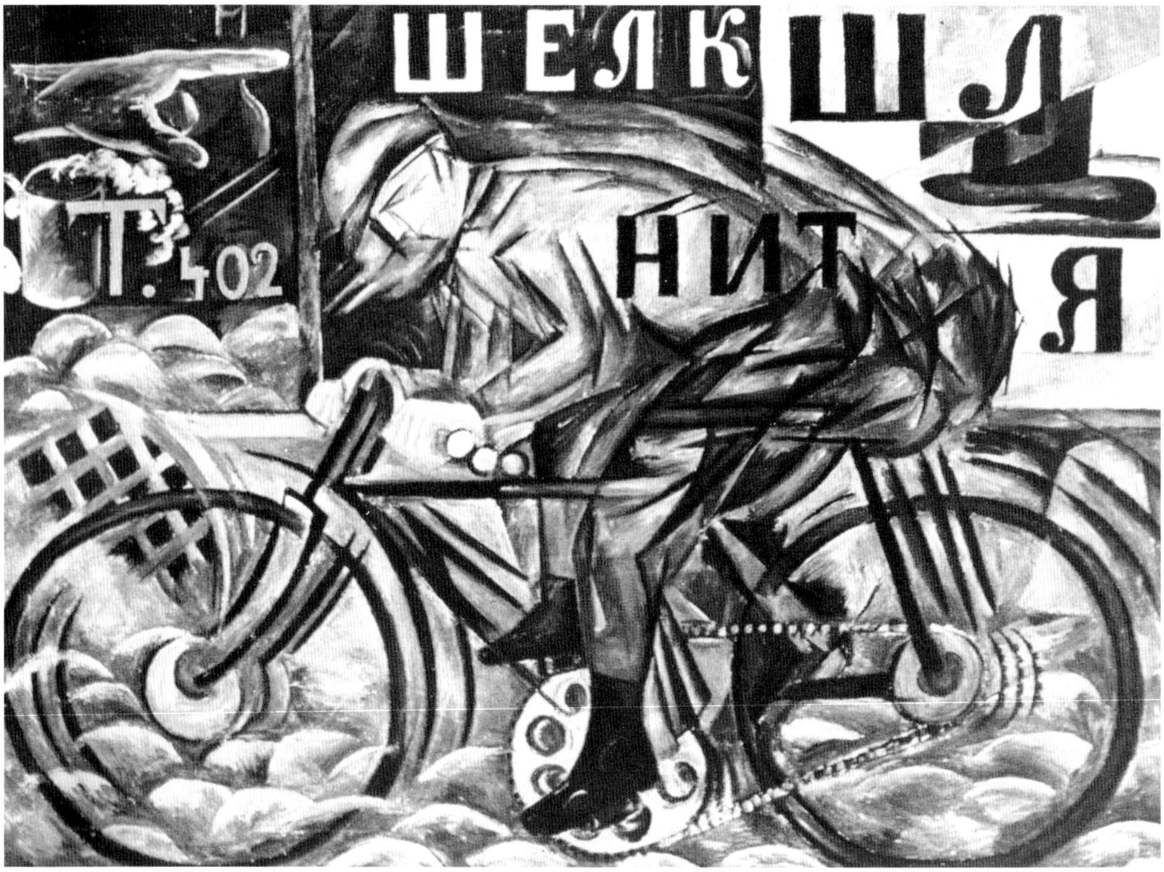

figure 54. Natalia Goncharova
The Bicyclist, 1912–13
Oil on canvas, 78 x 105 cm
State Russian Museum, St. Petersburg

painting and Russian decorative and Byzantine models, this theory promoted dual readings of images and the assimilative (rather than exclusionistic) character of Russian national identity. The hybrid nature of Russian Modernism was manifested most dramatically in Goncharova's religious images. Works such as *The Evangelists*, 1911 (plate 17) model their formal effects on the icon, the broadsheet, and the Western European Modernists Cézanne and Matisse. The fact that such eclectic sources within her work can be traced back to images painted and exhibited much earlier (in the *Golden Fleece* exhibitions of 1908–09, for example) has been one of the justifications for antedating Neo-Primitivism as a movement and a style to those years.[16]

The last avant-garde movement with which Goncharova may be identified in Russia — *vsechestvo* (everythingism) — was an extension of Neo-Primitivism. Zdanevich, the author of Goncharova's first biography (as the pseudonymious Eli Eganbiuri), gave two lectures on her, the first in Moscow on November 5, 1913 (the closing day of Goncharova's Moscow retrospective) and the second in St. Petersburg on March 17, 1914, a few days after the opening of her retrospective in that city.[17] Both of Zdanevich's lectures focused on her deliberate multiplicity as an artist as a way of countering the hegemony of European Modernist movements and art criticism. He argues that it is futile for a Russian artist to seek stable referents within Modernist art while basing one's art on Russian examples. New art should aspire to heterogeneity: diverse cultural traditions (East and West) and period styles (Cubism and Futurism) may be assimilated together. In *vsechestvo*, decorative and ornamental practices that are continuous in Russia and the East are promoted with a view to erasing boundaries between origin and copy — Goncharova's modus operandi.

Goncharova's voice is arguably present in Zdanevich's writings. Among her last Russian polemical writings (written in the same period as Zdanevich's lectures) is a letter she drafted in 1914 to the head of the Italian Futurist movement, Filippo Tomasso Marinetti, which accused the Italians of generating a new academy — and echoes the priorities of *vsechestvo* to be free and untrammeled by preordained artistic laws. The notion of European Modernist movements becoming canonical and losing their radical force would be a recurring motif in Larionov's writings from the 1930s to the 1950s on the history of Cubism as the new academy. As émigrés, all three — Goncharova, Larionov, and Zdanevich — would continue to represent their activities in Moscow as a decentering of Russia's European legacy.

Goncharova's solo exhibitions of 1910, 1913, and 1914 were landmarks in the history of avant-garde public provocations, polarizing an already partisan critical press. Her first solo exhibition — held for only a single evening, on March 24, 1910, by the Society of Free Aesthetics in Moscow — made her uniquely visible as an artist; it led to her trial (with several members of the Society) for pornography on December 22, 1910.[18] Her religious paintings were physically removed by the police from several exhibitions, including *The Donkey's Tail* of 1912, and again at the St. Petersburg retrospective in March 1914. Denounced as the work of an "anti-artist,"[19] a blasphemous counterpart to the "Antichrist," her religious paintings were temporarily banned by the Ecclesiastical Censorship Committee of the Holy Synod.[20]

Goncharova's notoriety as a radical painter was paired with public and critical acclaim. In 1913 the acquisitions committee for the Tretiakov Gallery bought their first painting by Goncharova after the extraordinary success of her Moscow retrospective.[21] The first full-scale retrospective in the capital to show the work of an avant-garde artist, it was also the first for a woman artist (sponsored by one of Moscow's first art dealers, also a woman, Klavdiia Mikhailova) and contained more than 760 works. If she was an "anti-artist" and the "suffragist of Russian painting" she was also, as one critic put it, an "overnight sensation." Nowhere in the history of Russian Modernism was there a more striking collusion of the disruptive promotion of "new" painting and its assimilation. During these years, Goncharova designed textiles, clothing, and wallpaper, and she planned to publish her own broadsheets. She thus initiated an interchange between fine and popular arts that became the focus of post-Revolutionary avant-garde projects. When Larionov and Goncharova left Moscow for Paris to mount their set designs for the ballet *Le Coq d'Or* (fig. 6; with music by Rimsky-Korsakov and choreography by Michel Fokine) for Diaghilev's Ballets Russes, Goncharova was at the peak of her Russian career. A model for her generation, and particularly for women artists such as Sofiia Dymshits-Tolstaia and Nadezhda Udaltsova (both of whom wrote about the positive impact that Goncharova's studio visits had on them), she had demonstrated for the first time in the history of Russian art what each still hoped to achieve.[22]

"after russia": diaghilev's commissions and life in emigration

Goncharova and Larionov left Moscow for Paris on April 29, 1914, although with the last phase of Larionov's service in the Russian Imperial army falling due, both returned to Moscow shortly thereafter.[23] Her first sets for *Le Coq d'Or* (painted by both Larionov and Goncharova) were spectacular displays of color and simplified form that Parisian viewers appreciated as exotic and as properly Russian. Based on its success, the productions that followed, including several unrealized ones, such as *Liturgie* (1915), continued to draw on Russia's Byzantine and folk heritage. These sets and costumes established a new key in Russian Orientalist self-fashioning, which forever marked Goncharova as a Russian artist rather than a transnational avant-garde artist of the time.

Their life as émigrés was consumed by theater, writing, traveling, as well as installing (Larionov), painting (Goncharova), and waiting. Letters to friends over the course of the 1920s and memoirs written in the Stalinist era underscore how much both artists longed to return to Russia. Occasionally finances are blamed, at other times they recognize the potential dangers that awaited them as former leaders of the pre-Revolutionary avant-garde. In 1917–18 Goncharova spoke of her excitement over the Revolution and the urgent need for news of political events, just as in the 1930s she lamented its diabolical about-face. Her level of political engagement is not clear during the pre-Revolutionary period. But numerous illustrations for the Socialist journal *Le populaire* in Paris (edited by Oreste Rosenfeld and Léon Blum), suggest that Goncharova was sympathetic to leftist politics in Europe.[24]

In Paris, Goncharova was a more productive painter than Larionov, working in cycles (as she did before emigrating), beginning with the Spanish women in the 1910s and 1920s and ending with her exploration of space motifs: images with planet- and meteor-shaped forms inspired by the first Russian Sputnik launch in the 1950s. Her shifts in style correspond loosely to shifts in the School of Paris — her paintings in the 1910s and 1920s move from a Cubist idiom to a more neoclassical treatment of the figure. It is clear, too, that Goncharova was engaged in repainting earlier images either by adding decorative elements to the surfaces of pre-Revolutionary works or by repainting whole portions of the canvas. Obviously, this has further compromised the historical reconstruction of her career, a project that will require years of comparative, collaborative work among scholars.

On June 2, 1955, after decades of living together and following Larionov's stroke (in 1951), the two artists married in Paris so as to ensure each the benefits of any inheritance following their death. Nearly paralyzed with rhumatoid arthritis, Goncharova died first, on October 17, 1962.

1. Marina Tsvetaeva, "Natalia Goncharova (zhizn i tvorchestvo)," *Volia Rossii* (Prague), nos. V–VI, VII, VIII–IX (1929); republished with notes and introduction by Dimitrii Sarabianov in *Prometei* (Moscow), no. 7 (1969), pp. 144–201 (all further citations to this essay by Tsvetaeva refer to this last publication). Unless otherwise noted, all translations from the Russian and French are my own.
2. The artist and the poet were raised in Moscow in the Tverskaia district, in houses Nos. 7 and 8, Trekhprudnyi Lane, and first met when Goncharova was asked to escort Tsvetaeva home from the school that they attended together (in different classes); Tsvetaeva, "Natalia Goncharova (zhizn i tvorchestvo)," p. 154.
3. There is still some confusion over her exact birthplace: her certificate of christening (Staryi Roskovets, June 26, 1881), indicates that her father was "landowner in the village of Nagaevo." However, Tsvetaeva's essay gives Goncharova's birthplace as Lodyzhino, also in Tula province (Tsvetaeva, p. 154). Family members record several moves, from Lodyzhino to Luzhino (where Goncharova lived for seven years), and then to Akatovo, all villages on the border of Orlov and

Tula provinces. A copy of the certificate is in the archives of the Moscow Institute of Painting, Sculpture, and Architecture (RGALI; inv. no. f. 680, op. 2, ed. khr. 1638, p. 9).

4. The estate is not far from Lev Tolstoi's Yasnaia Poliana estate, and it is less than an hour from the city of Kaluga. During the Soviet era, much of the interior contents were deposited in the city museum, and the estate itself with its parks and ponds was transformed into a sanatorium. Damaged severely during World War II, it is now a shell of a structure and has recently been sold to a private investor. I am grateful to various members of the Goncharov family who have provided much of the information published here, particularly Igor Glebovich Goncharov and Valentina Alexandrovna Zhilina, a restoration architect (and Goncharova's cousin) who was involved with plans to restore Polotnianyi Zavod.
5. Igor Goncharov has stated that his grandfather was a social democrat, who expressed his political sympathies for leftist causes by supplying Lunacharsky with free paper for party publications. He introduced an eight-hour work day at Polotnianyi Zavod (in the 1890s?); Igor Goncharov, in interviews with the author in June 1997. The theater was described as a "worker's theater" during this time; see *Pushkiniana kaluzhskoi gubernii* (Tula: Kommunar, 1990), no. 2, p. 26.
6. Ilia Zdanevich, Goncharova's first biographer, underscored the significance of the artist's rural experiences on the estate; Eli Eganbiuri (pseudonym for Ilia Zdanevich) *Natalia Goncharova, Mikhail Larionov* (Moscow: Miunster, 1913), p. 13.
7. Jane A. Sharp, "L'exercice de la répétition: les cycles et les composition sérielles de Nathalie Gontcharova de 1907–1911," in Jessica Boissel, *Nathalie Gontcharova. Michel Larionov*, pp. 178–87.
8. The Moscow Institute of Painting, Sculpture, and Architecture, registration form for Natalia Sergeevna Goncharova, RGALI inv. no. f. 680, op. 2, ed. khr. 1638, p. 12. She is registered from the fall of 1901 (entering as an auditor in the "head class") through 1909 when she was expelled for non-payment of tuition. In 1908–09 she was registered in the "drawing from nature class," and the "sculpture studio," having been advanced to both in 1906–07. In 1903–04 she was awarded the "small silver medal for sculpture," but because she was only an auditor, she was not able to claim it. She also passed a course in perspective. Her correspondence with the school indicates that for health reasons she did not plan to attend classes in 1903–04 (letter from Goncharova to the Director of the School, dated August 25, 1903, p. 13). Her registration form also indicates her class status (*soslovie*) as "daughter of a member of the gentry."
9. Gleb Pospelov, *Bubnovyi valet: primitiv i gorodskoi folklor v moskovskoi zhivopisi 1910-x godov* (Moscow: Sovetskii khudozhnik, 1990), p. 27. For Goncharova's participation in the studio, see Jane A. Sharp, "Redrawing the Margins of Russian Vanguard Art: Natalia Goncharova's Trial for Pornography in 1910," in Jane T. Costlow, Stephanie Sandler, and Judith Vowles, eds., *Sexuality and the Body in Russian Culture* (Stanford: Stanford University Press, 1993), pp. 104–06.
10. Eganbiuri, *Natalia Goncharova, Mikhail Larionov*, p. 14.
11. Elena Ovsiannikova, "Iz istorii odnoi illiustratsii," *Panorama iskusstv* (Moscow), no. 11 (1988), p. 248.
12. Georgii Kovalenko, ed., *Zhizn khudozhnikov, Natalia Goncharova, Mikhail Larionov* (Moscow: Galart, 1995), pp. 103–16, 122–28.
13. *Vystavka kartin Natalii Sergeevny Goncharovoi, 1900–1913*, Khudozhestvennyi salon, 11 Bolshaia Dmitrovka, Moscow, September 30–November 5, 1913; *Natalia Goncharova, 1900–1913*, Art Bureau, 63 Moika, St. Petersburg, March 15 –April 20, 1914.
14. See "Beseda s N. S. Goncharovoi," *Stolichnaia molva* (Moscow), no. 115, April 5, 1910, p. 3; and "Pismo N. Goncharovoi," *Protiv techeniia* (St. Petersburg), March 3, 1912, p. 3.
15. Varsanofii Parkin, "Oslinyi khvost i Mishen," in Mikhail Larionov et al., *Oslinyi khvost i Mishen*

(Moscow: Miunster, 1913), p. 82.

16. Although the dating of this movement has varied from scholar to scholar, use of the term in Russian can be dated to 1913; see Jane Ashton Sharp, "Primitivism, 'Neoprimitivism' and the Art of Natalia Goncharova" (Ph.D. diss., Yale University, 1992), pp. 1–7, 203–07.
17. Several variants of these lectures exist in draft form in the Russian Museum, Manuscript Division, inv. no. f. 177, op. 14, ed. khr. 24: see Elena Basner, "Nataliia Goncharova i Ilia Zdanevich, o proiskhozhdenii Vsechestva," in *Iskusstvo Avangarda: Yazyk mirovogo obshcheniia, materialy mezhdunarodnoi konferentsii*, December 10–11, 1992 (Ufa, 1993), pp. 68–80. A manifesto written by Mikhail Le Dantiu also mentions Goncharova: "Zhivopis vsekov," (signed manuscript, dated 1914), RGALI, inv. no. f. 792, op. 1, ed. khr. 1, ll. 17–35, 35–36; a variant was published by John E. Bowlt in *Minuvshee* (Paris), no. 5 (1988), pp. 183–202 (see n. 1, p. 183, for publication and draft details).
18. Sharp, "Redrawing the Margins," pp. 97–123.
19. Valentin Songaillo, *O vystave kartin Natalii Goncharovoi* (Moscow: Sablin, 1913), p. 6.
20. See Sharp (1992), pp. 383–98.
21. *Bouquet and a Bottle of Paints* (*Buket i flakon krasok*), 1909, oil on canvas (101 x 71.5 cm), inv. no. 3861. For details on the reception of the exhibition, see Sharp (1992), pp. 370–83.
22. Sofiia Dymshits-Tolstaia, "Vospominaniia khudozhnitsy," typescript with hand-written notations by the artist, dated 1950s, located with the artist's family, pp. 27, 32; Ekaterina Drevina and Vasilii Rakitin, eds., *N. Udaltsova, Zhizn russkoi kubistki: dnevniki, stat'i, vospominaniia*, Moscow: RA, 1994, pp. 31–32.
23. In an undated letter to Le Dantiu, Larionov explains: "Natalia Sergeevna and I finally left on the 29th. I was held up a bit on account of the costumes." State Russian Museum, Manuscript Division, inv. no. f. 135, op. 7, p. 2.
24. Jessica Boissel, "Catalogue des oeuvres"; Viviane Tarenne, "Le populaire," in *Nathalie Gontcharova, Michel Larionov* (1995), pp. 138–39.

NATALIA SERGEEVNA GONCHAROVA
(1881–1962)

1881	Born June 21, in the village of Nagaevo, in Tula province.
1892–98	Moves to Moscow to attend school there.
1900	Meets Mikhail Larionov, a fellow student, who encourages her to paint, and he becomes her lifelong companion.
1901	Enrolls at the Moscow Institute of Painting, Sculpture, and Architecture to study sculpture.
1906	Contributes to the Russian Section at the *Salon d'Automne* in Paris, but does not accompany Larionov to Paris.
1906–07	Begins to work in Primitivist style.
1908–10	Begins to work in Cubist style. Contributes to the three exhibitions organized by Nikolai Riabushinsky, editor of the journal *Zolotoe runo* (*The Golden Fleece*) in Moscow.
1910	With Larionov and others, co-founds the Jack of Diamonds group and participates in the group's first exhibition, December 1910–January 1911.
1910	One-day exhibition of Goncharova's work is held March 24 at the Society for Free Aesthetics in Moscow. Consequently, she was tried and acquitted on charges of pornography for exhibiting nude life studies.
1912	Contributes to the *Der Blaue Reiter* exhibition in Munich, and the *Second Post-Impressionist Exhibition*, London, organized by Roger Fry.
1912–14	The Jack of Diamonds group splits up in February 1912, when she and Larionov dissociate themselves from David Burliuk and the others. She participates in rival exhibitions organized by Larionov: *The Donkey's Tail* (1912), *The Target* (1913), and *No. 4* (1914).
1912–13	Works in Cubo-Futurist and Rayist styles.
1913	Contributes to Herwarth Walden's *First German Autumn Exhibition*, Berlin.
1913–14	Major retrospective exhibitions of Goncharova's work, in Moscow (1913) and St. Petersburg (1914).
1914	Leaves for Paris on April 29 with Larionov to mount their set designs for Sergei Diaghilev's ballet production of *Le Coq d'Or.* Galerie Paul Guillaume holds a joint exhibition of both artists' work.

1915	Returns briefly to Moscow, where she designs Alexander Tairov's production of Carlo Goldoni's *Il Ventaglio* at the Chamber Theater, Moscow.
1917	Travels with Diaghilev's company to Spain and Italy. Settles in Paris with Larionov.
1920s	She and Larionov collaborate on numerous designs for Diaghilev and other impresarios.
1920–21	Contributes to the *Exposition Internationale d'Art Moderne* in Geneva (which also includes work by Larionov).
1922	Exhibits at the Kingore Gallery, New York (which also includes work by Larionov).
1920s–30s	Continues to paint, teach, illustrate books, and design ballet and theater productions, including Boris Romanov's *A Romantic Adventure of an Italian Ballerina and a Marquis* for the Chauve-Souris, New York (1931).
1940s–50s	Except for occasional contributions to exhibitions, Larionov and Goncharova live unrecognized and impoverished. However, through the efforts of Mary Chamot, author of Goncharova's first major monograph, a number of their works enter museum collections, including the Tate Gallery in London, the National Gallery of Modern Art in Edinburgh, and the National Art Gallery in Wellington, New Zealand.
1954	Goncharova and Larionov's work is resurrected at Richard Buckle's *Diaghilev* exhibition in Edinburgh and London.
1955	Goncharova and Larionov are married.
1961	Art Council of Great Britain organizes a major retrospective of Goncharova's and Larionov's works.
1962	Dies October 17, in Paris.

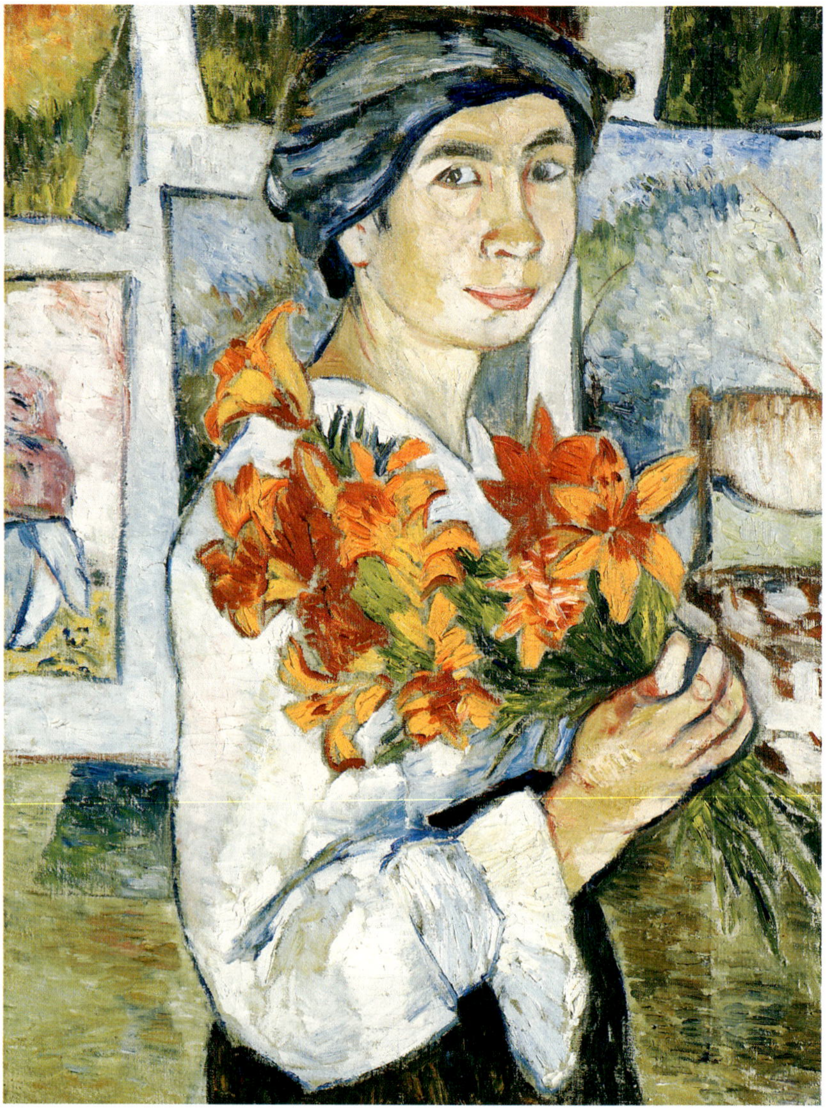

plate 13. NATALIA GONCHAROVA
Self-Portrait with Yellow Lilies, 1907
Oil on canvas, 77 x 58.2 cm
State Tretiakov Gallery, Moscow

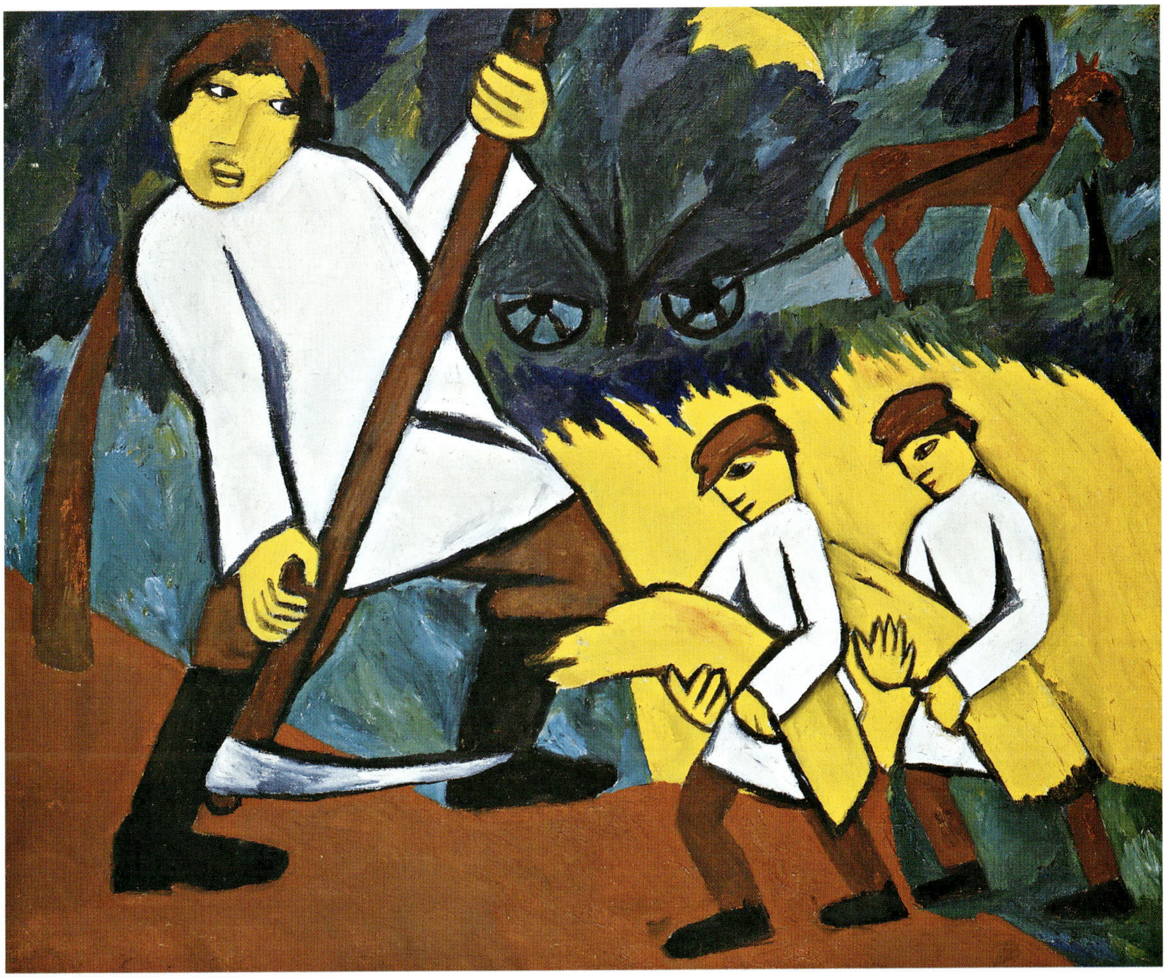

plate 14. NATALIA GONCHAROVA
Mowers, 1907–08
Oil on canvas, 98 x 118 cm
Private Collection, Courtesy Gallery Gmurzynska, Cologne

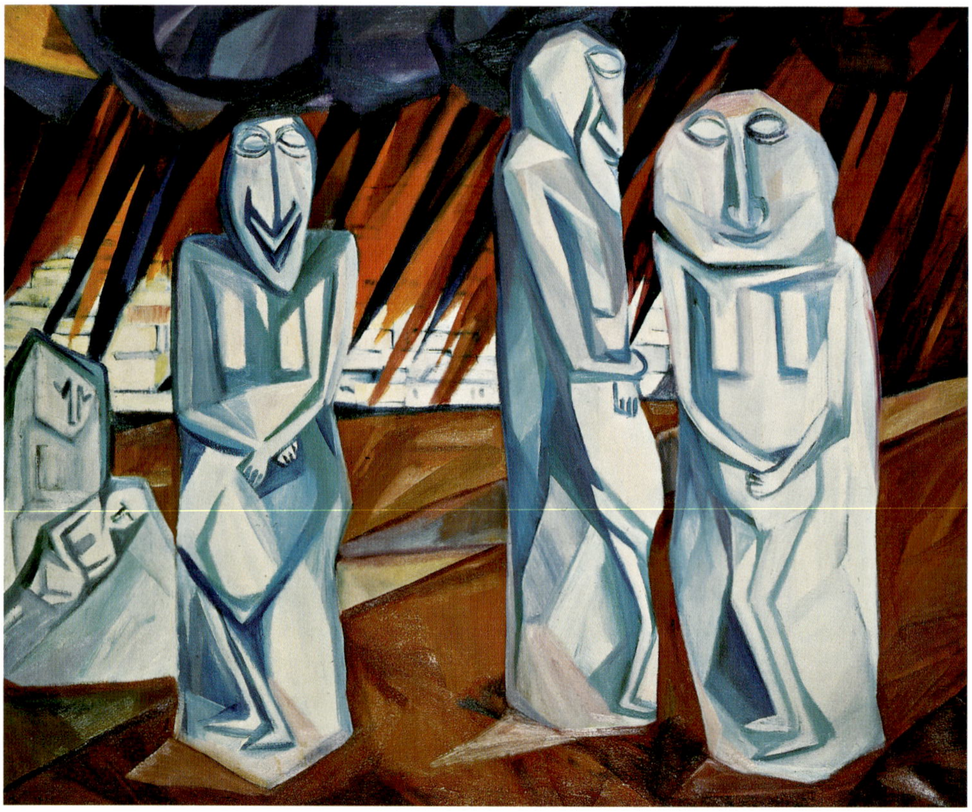

plate 15. NATALIA GONCHAROVA
Pillars of Salt, 1908
Oil on canvas, 80.5 x 96 cm
State Tretiakov Gallery, Moscow

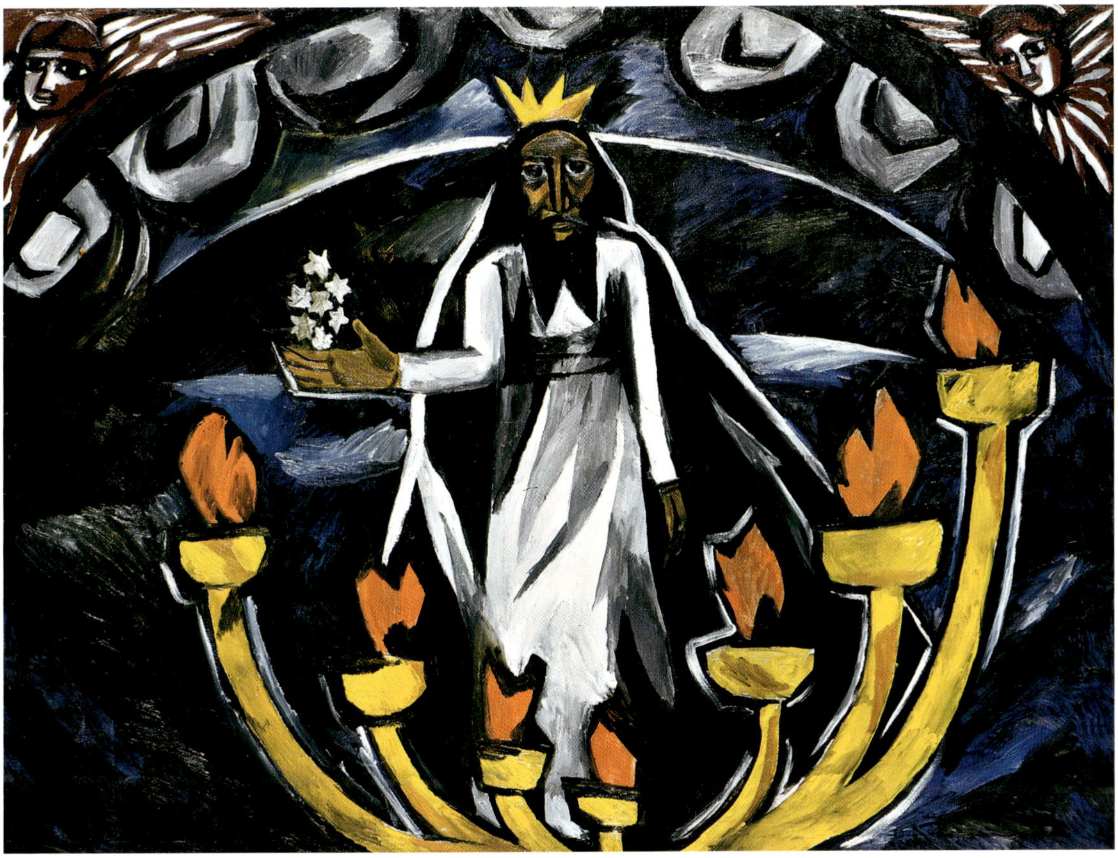

plate 16. NATALIA GONCHAROVA
Apocalypse (Elder with Seven Stars), ca. 1910–11
Oil on canvas, 147 x 188 cm
State Tretiakov Gallery, Moscow

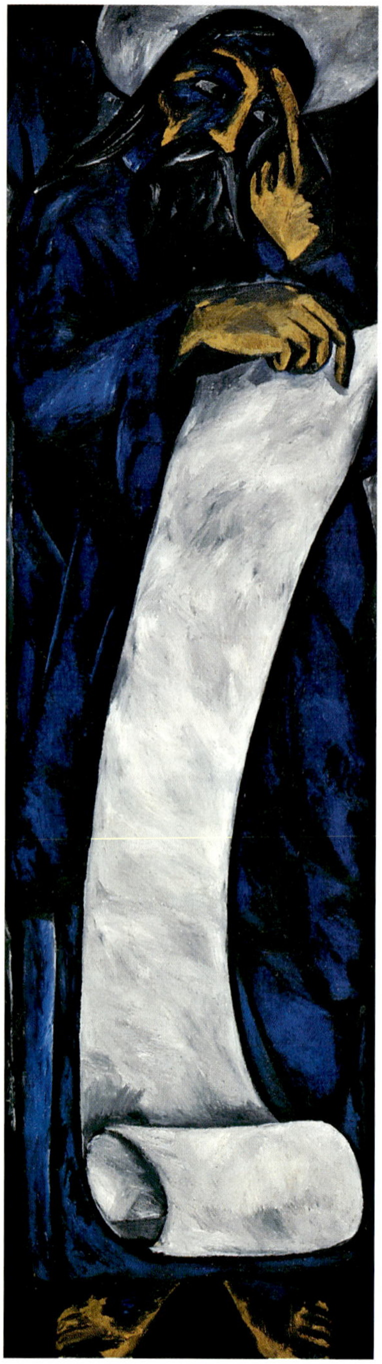

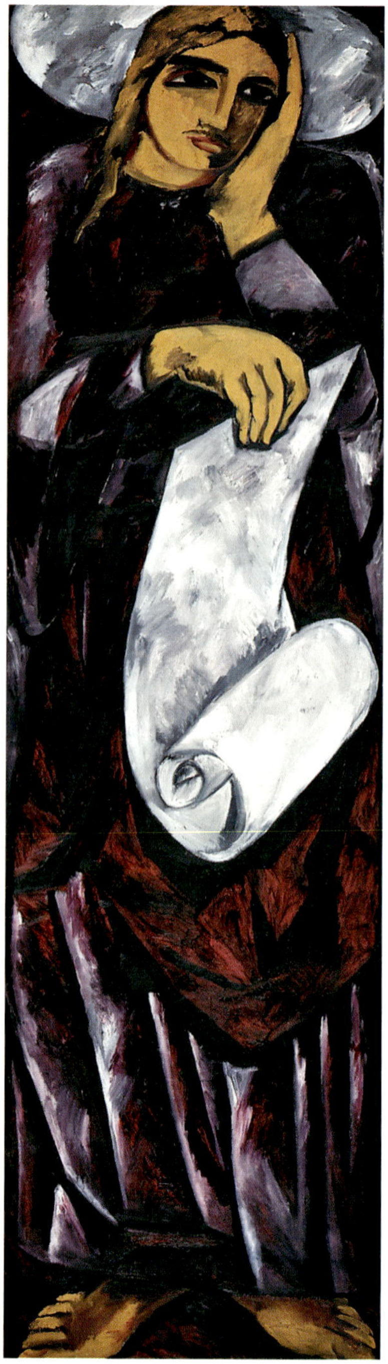

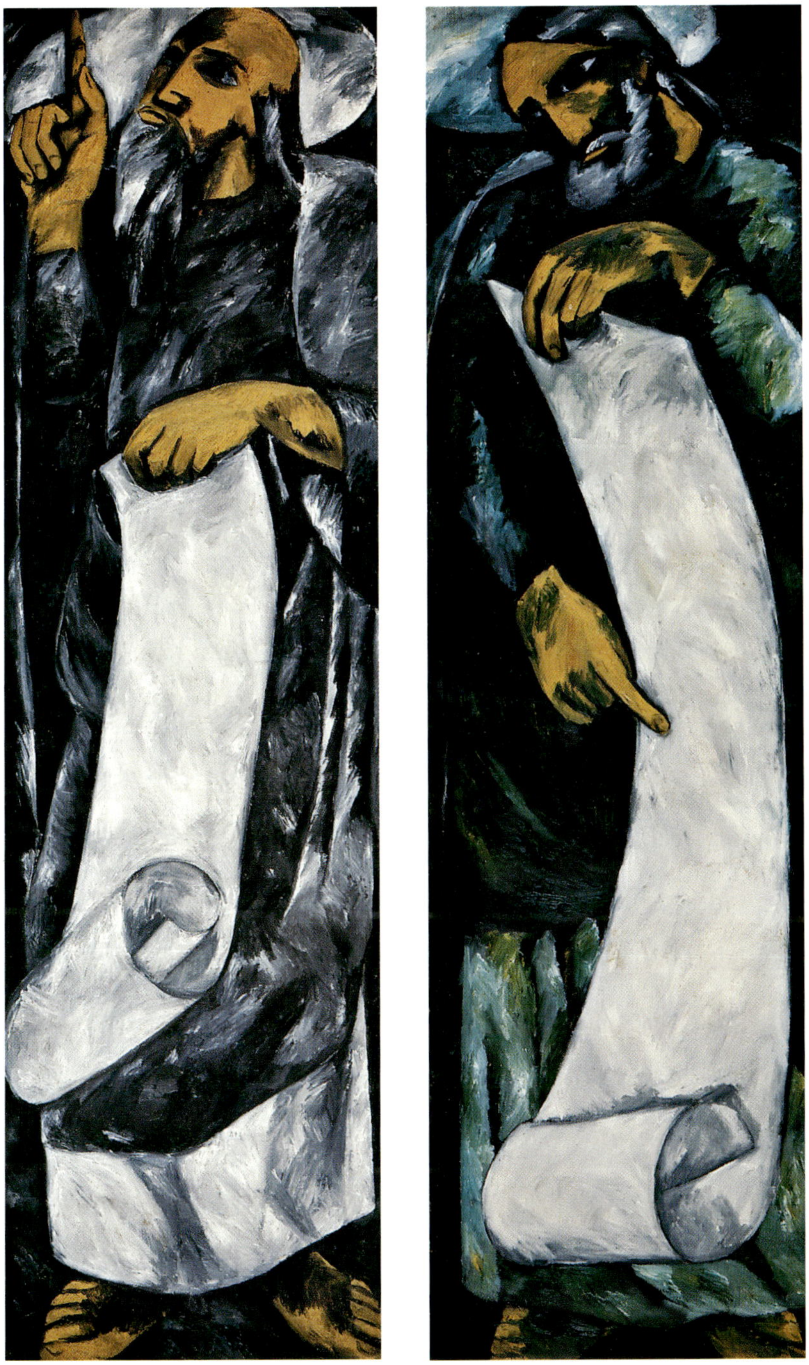

plate 17. NATALIA GONCHAROVA
The Evangelists (in Four Parts), 1911
1) *In Blue*; 2) *In Red*; 3) *In Gray*; 4) *In Green*
Oil on canvas, 204 x 58 cm each
State Russian Museum, St. Petersburg

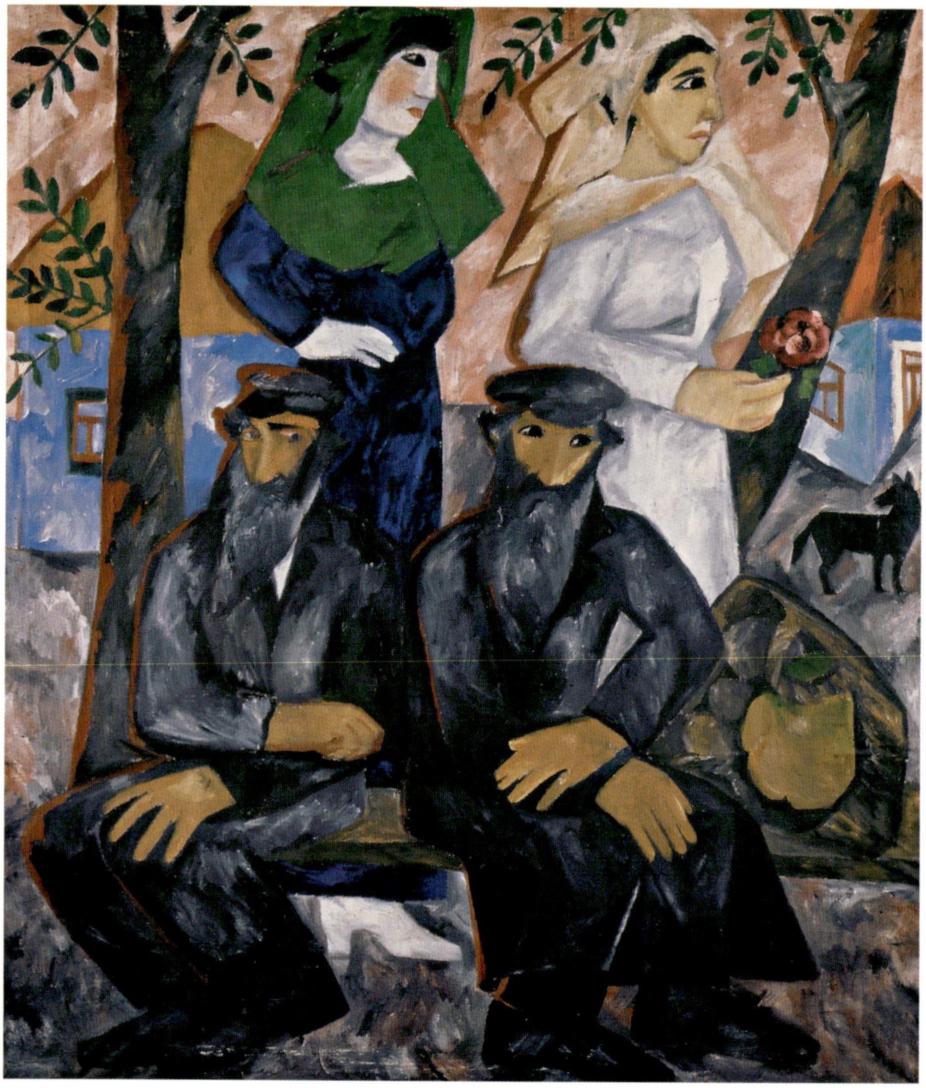

plate 18. NATALIA GONCHAROVA
Sabbath, 1912
Oil on canvas, 137.5 x 118 cm
State Museum of the Visual Arts of Tatarstan, Kazan

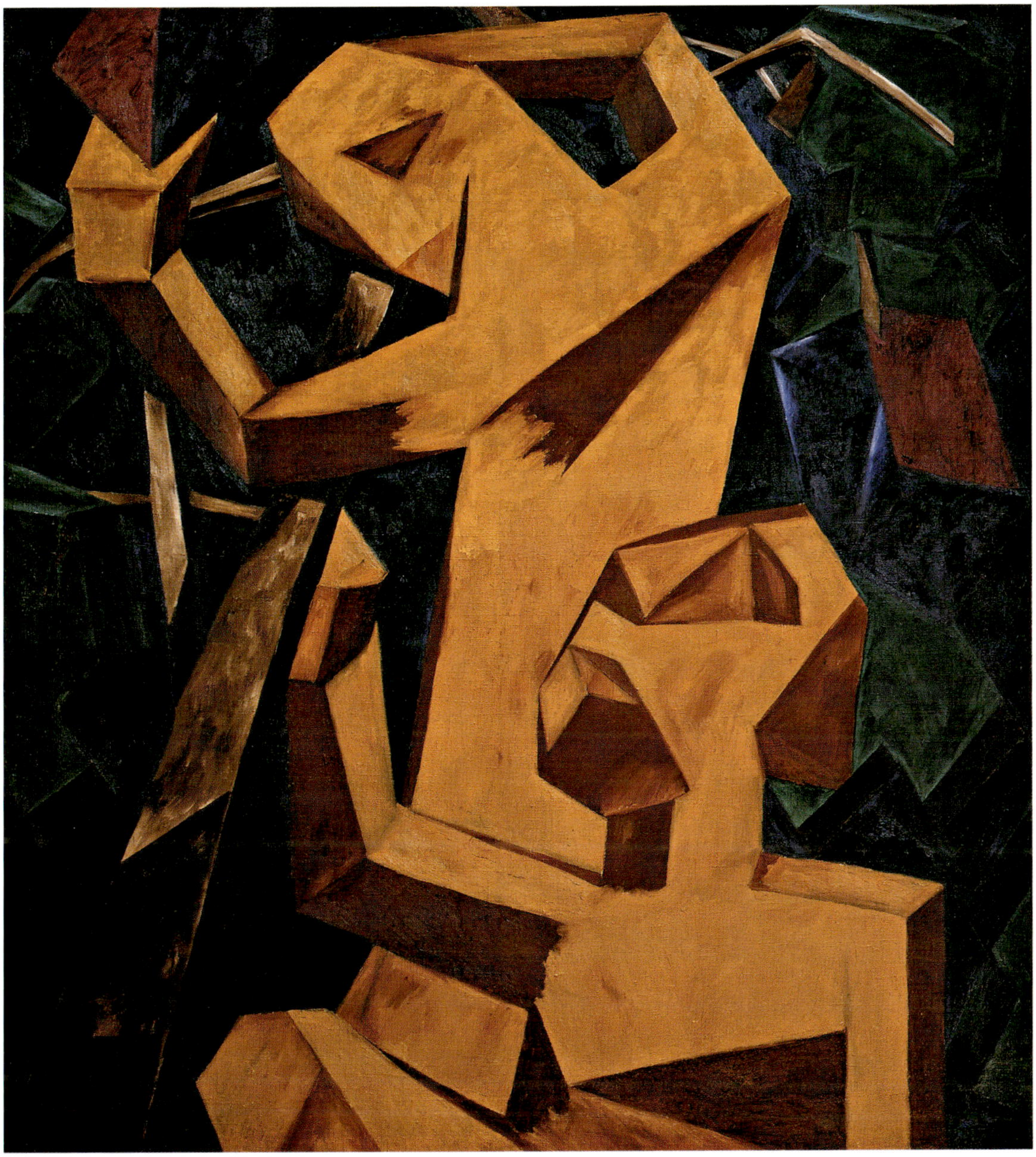

plate 19. NATALIA GONCHAROVA
Peasants Gathering Grapes, 1912
Oil on canvas, 145 x 130 cm
State Art Museum of Bashkkortostan, Ufa

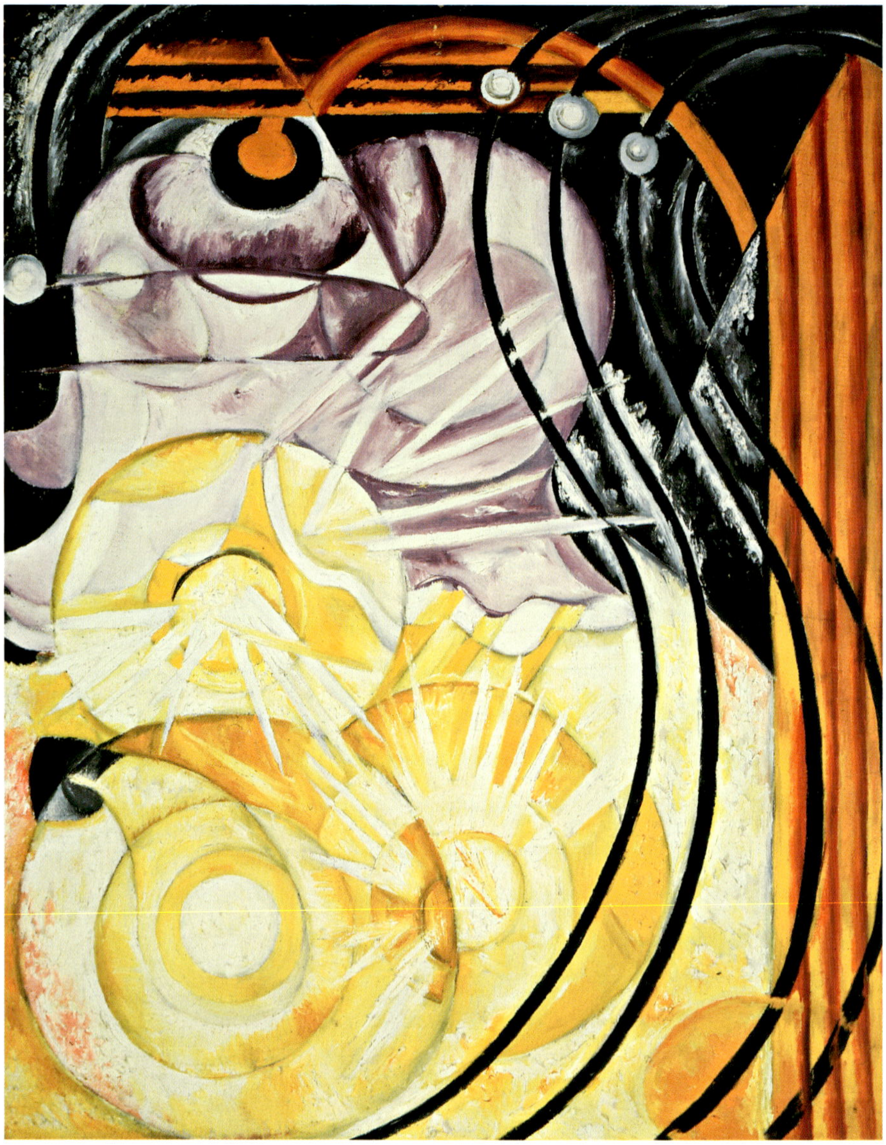

above:
plate 20. NATALIA GONCHAROVA
Electric Lamp, 1913
Oil on canvas, 125 x 81.5 cm
Centre Georges Pompidou,
Musée national d'art moderne, Paris

facing page:
plate 21. NATALIA GONCHAROVA
The Weaver (Loom + Woman), 1912–13
Oil on canvas, 153.3 x 99 cm
National Museum and Gallery, Cardiff

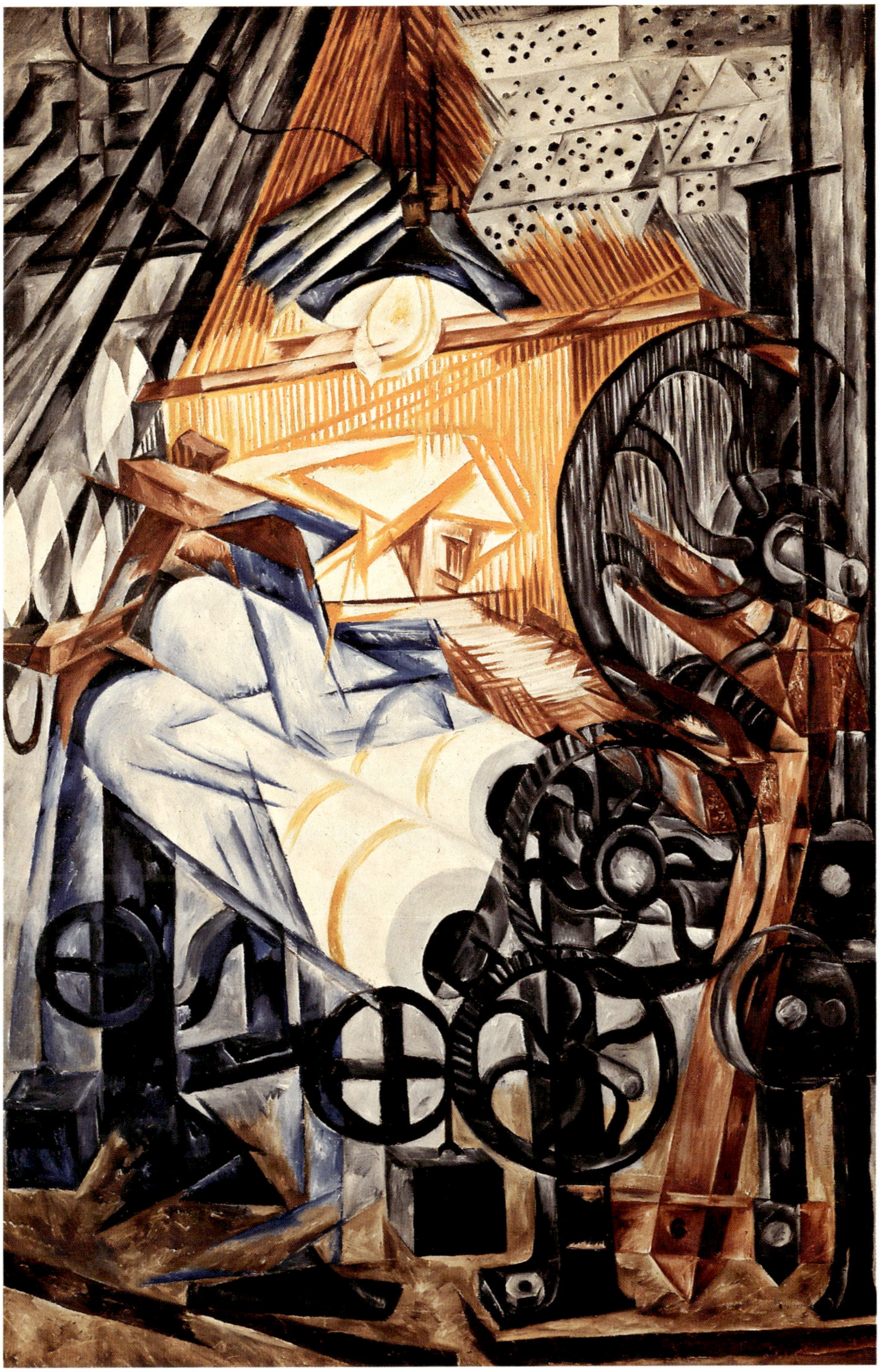

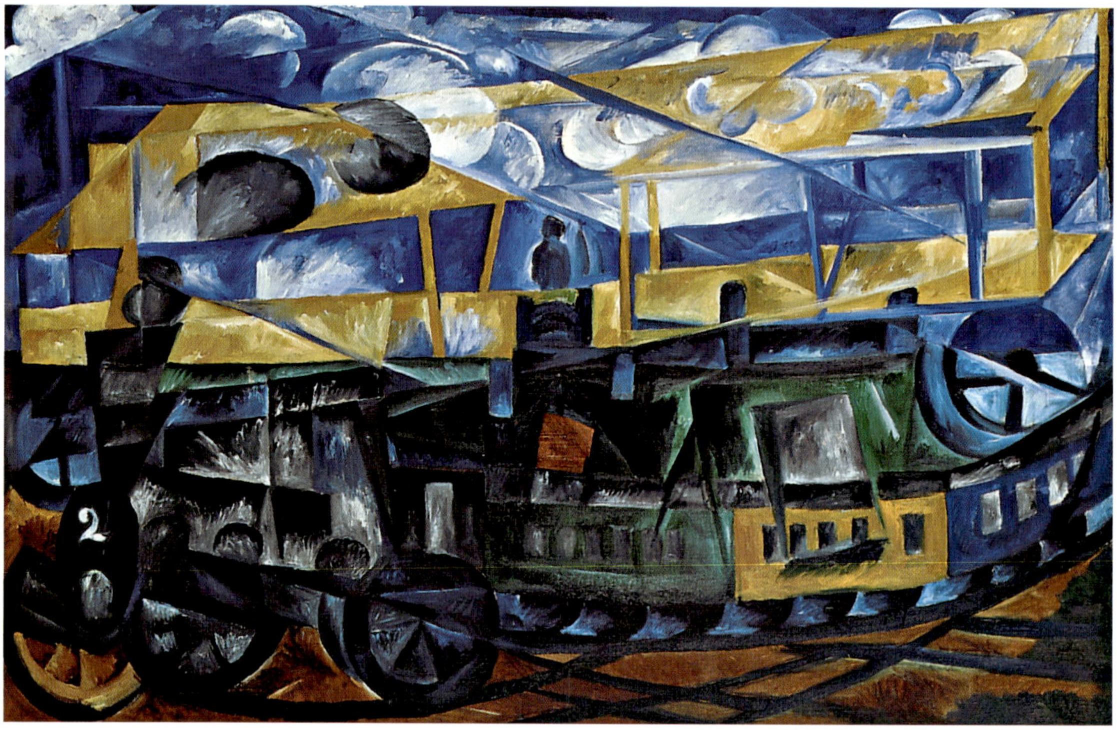

plate 22. NATALIA GONCHAROVA
Airplane over a Train, 1913
Oil on canvas, 55 x 83.5 cm
State Museum of the Visual Arts of Tatarstan, Kazan

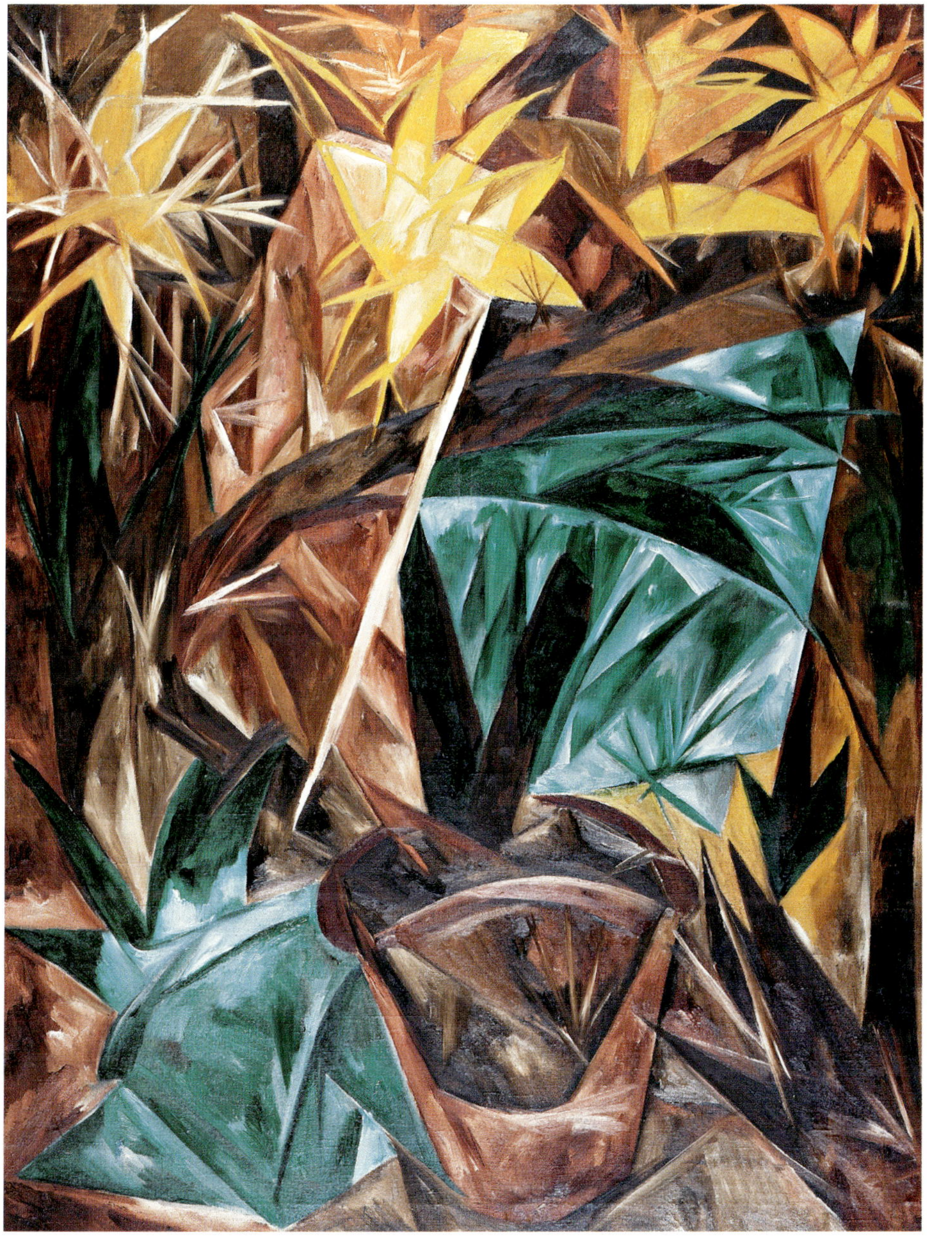

plate 23. NATALIA GONCHAROVA
Rayist Lilies, 1913
Oil on canvas, 91 x 75.4 cm
State Picture Gallery, Perm

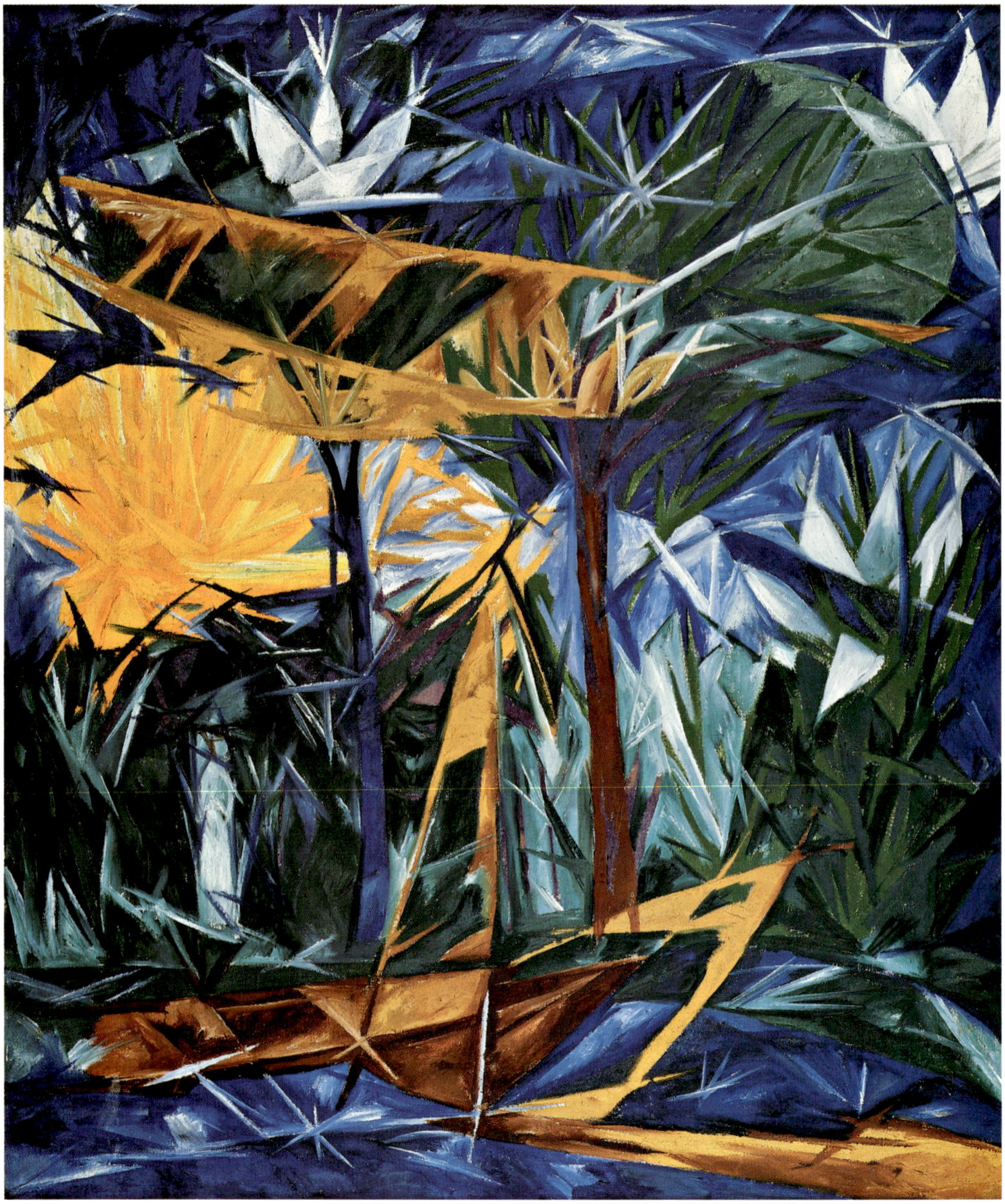

plate 24. NATALIA GONCHAROVA
Yellow and Green Forest, 1913
Oil on canvas, 102 x 85 cm
Staatsgalerie, Stuttgart

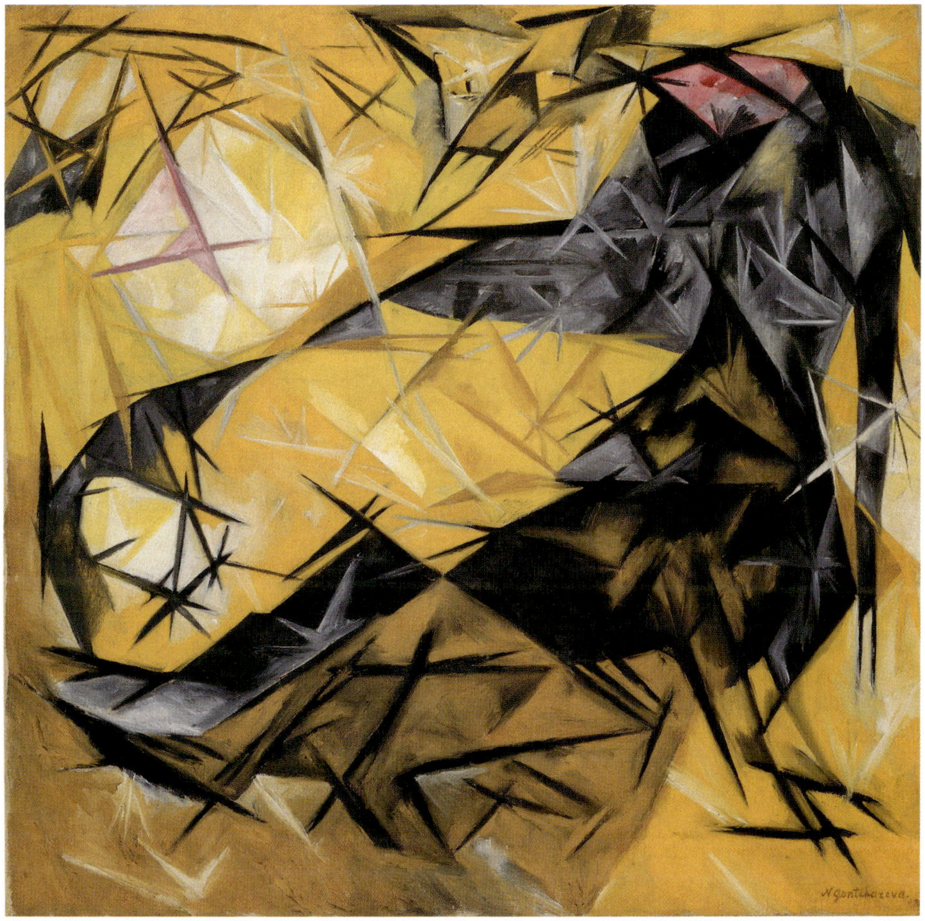

plate 25. NATALIA GONCHAROVA
Cats (rayist percep.[tion] in rose, black, and yellow), 1913
Oil on canvas, 84.5 x 83.8 cm
Solomon R. Guggenheim Museum, New York 57.1484

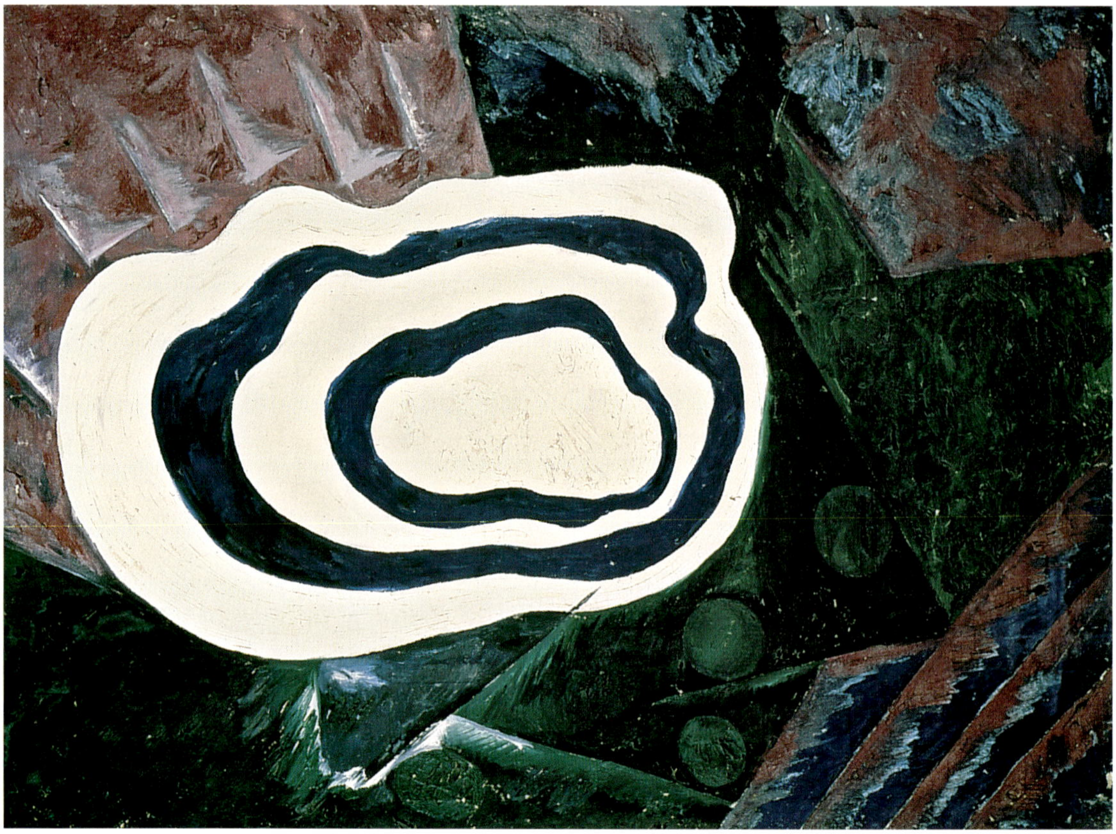

plate 26. NATALIA GONCHAROVA
Emptiness, 1913
Mixed media on canvas, 80 x 106 cm
State Tretiakov Gallery, Moscow

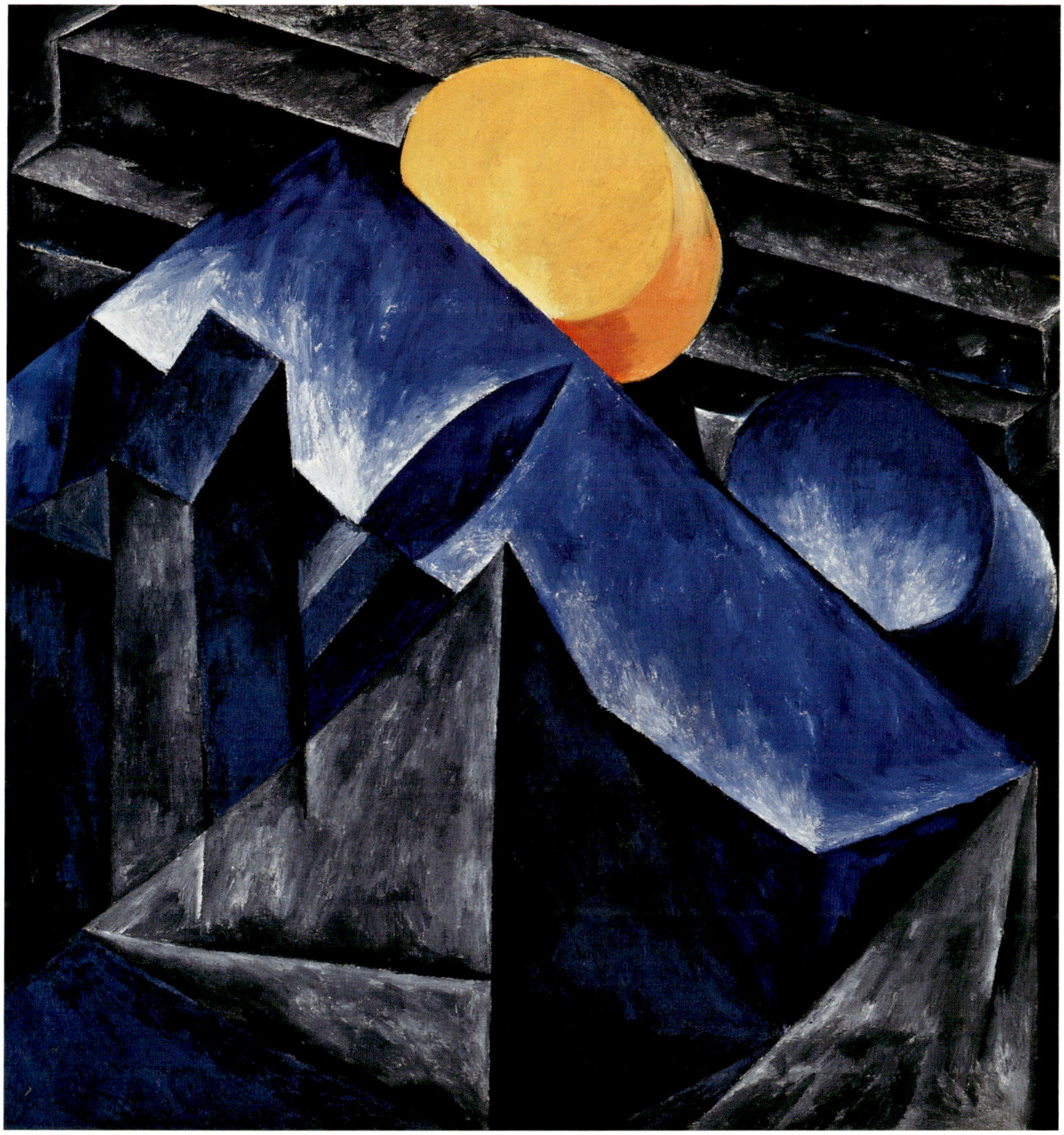

plate 27. NATALIA GONCHAROVA
Composition, 1913–14
Oil on canvas, 103.5 x 97.2 cm
Centre Georges Pompidou,
Musée national d'art moderne, Paris

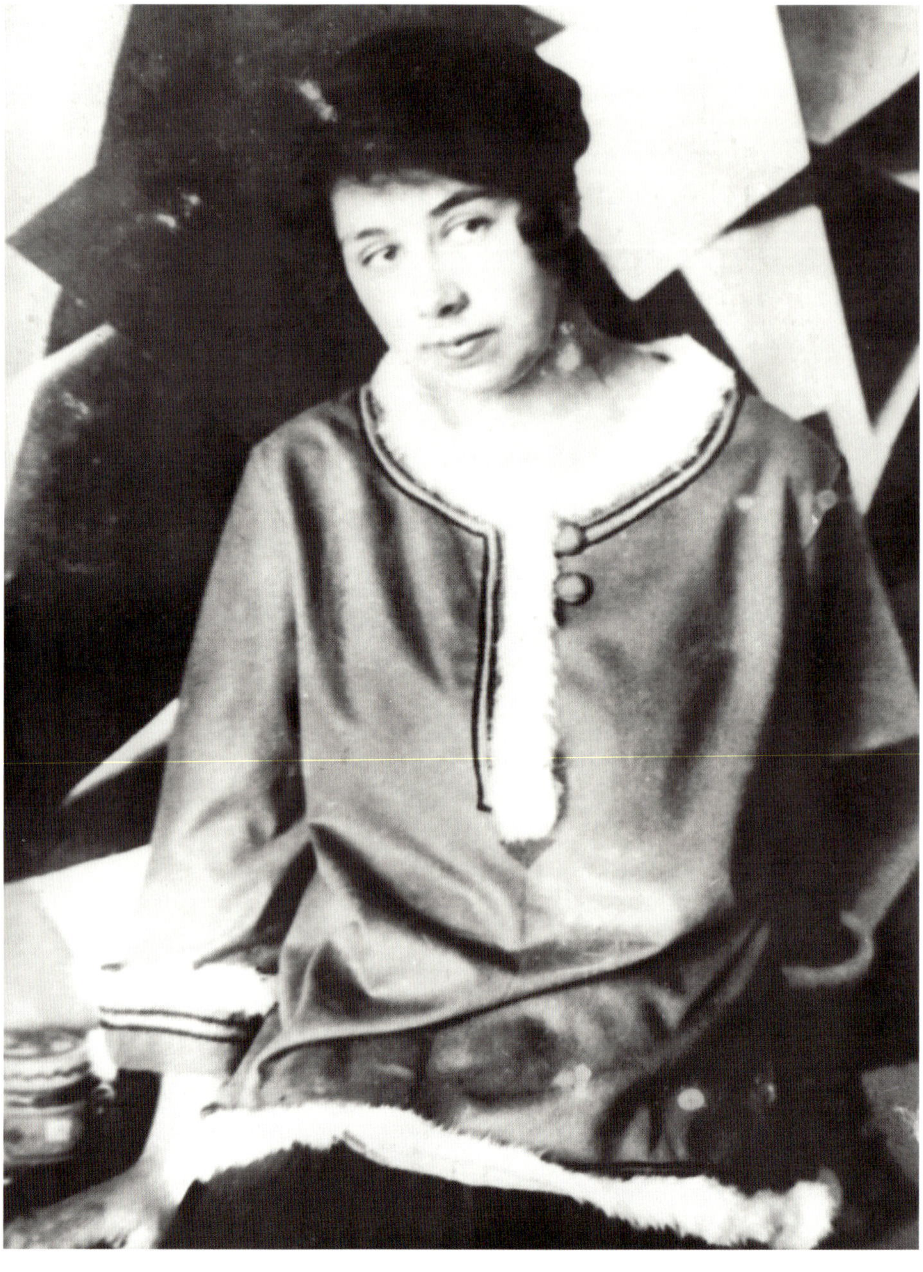

figure 55. Liubov Popova in her studio, Moscow, 1919.

LIUBOV POPOVA

NATALIA ADASKINA AND DMITRII SARABIANOV

LIUBOV POPOVA AND HER CONTEMPORARIES

NATALIA ADASKINA

"Man is a really remarkable creature. He has only to quit working and all life comes to a halt, cities die out. But as soon as people get down to work, however, the city lives. What a terrible force is human labor!" So Popova wrote in a letter to her mother from Italy on the eve of World War I.[1]

The image of Popova that we are attempting to recapture here would not have been obvious to contemporaries of the young Popova. Before them stood a smart, elegant, independent young woman of a high station and with the right upbringing, a status that distinguished her from many artists with whom she worked at La Palette in Paris (also known as the Académie de la Palette) or at the Tower in Moscow. Alexander Rodchenko, for example, recalled that "Popova, an artist from a wealthy background, regarded us with condescension and contempt, since she considered us unsuitable company. . . . Later on, during the Revolution, she changed greatly and became a true comrade. . . . At the *Store* exhibition she left behind a fragrance of expensive perfume and a trace of beautiful apparel."[2]

Vera Mukhina, who became well known as a sculptor, met Popova in Moscow at the art school of Konstantin Yuon and Ivan Dudin, and described her as "tall, well-proportioned, with wonderful eyes and luxuriant hair. For all her femininity, she perceived art and life with incredible acuity. She embraced Gauguin, van Gogh,

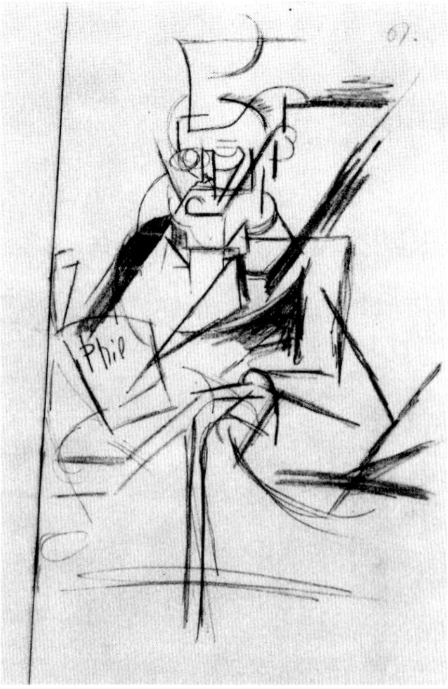

figure 56. LIUBOV POPOVA
Preliminary drawing for *Portrait of a Philosopher*, 1915
Pencil on paper,
35.5 x 21 cm
Private collection, Moscow

and Cézanne one after the other. Once interested in them, she began to study them and to work like van Gogh, etc. She had a marvelous sense of color and, in general, a great talent."[3]

In the Yuon/Dudin studio, Popova also befriended Liudmila Prudkovskaia and her sister, Nadezhda Prudkovskaia (the future Udaltsova), and Alexander Vesnin; Alexei Grishchenko and Vera Pestel also studied there at one time.

For Popova the period between Yuon's studio and La Palette was a very difficult one, not only artistically, but also psychologically. She felt pulled in different directions: her enthusiasm for the work of Mikhail Vrubel (1856–1910),[4] which was natural for a romantically inclined painter such as Popova, encouraged her artistic evolution along the path of Cubism and analysis. Popova not only became interested in the artistic ideas of the Symbolists, but also attempted to assimilate the lessons of contemporary philosophers, both Russian and European. No doubt, her younger brother Pavel exerted a certain influence here, for he was a professional philosopher and very close to Mikhail Bulgakov. Still, reconciling the mysticism of Symbolism and the tense spirituality of "Gothic" forms was a difficult task. For Popova, according to Ivan Aksenov, this stage "nearly drove her out of her mind" and "nearly cost her her life."[5] One may presume that the mental illness of her best friend at that time, Liudmila Prudkovskaia, also left a deep imprint upon her, although, fortunately, new circumstances facilitated her escape from depression — not least, her Paris apprenticeship with Henri Le Fauconnier and Jean Metzinger and her enthusiastic embrace of Cubism.

To all appearances, Popova possessed a strong organizational talent and enjoyed authority among her colleagues. Our knowledge of the Paris season of 1912–13, when Popova was working under Le Fauconnier, Metzinger, and André Dunoyer de Segonzac at La Palette, comes mainly from the diaries of Udaltsova, the letters of Boris Ternovets, and the memoirs of Mukhina. A stern Udaltsova remarks that Popova's "sketches are not bad, except that all her figures are distended. [December 15, 1912]. . . . L.S. is much bolder than I am. Metzinger has already praised her [January 2, 1913]."[6] In photographs of that time we see a happy, smiling Popova in the company of friends. Probably through Mukhina, Popova entered the circle of young sculptors — students of Bourdelle — such as Iza Burmeister, Nadezhda Krandievskaia (wife of writer Alexei Tolstoi), Sofia Rozental, Ternovets, and Alexander Vertepov.

Popova first visited Italy in 1910 with her family. During that short vacation she became interested in the fifteenth- and sixteenth-century masters, but by 1914, on her second trip, alongside the monuments of Classical art and architecture, she acquainted herself with contemporary Italian Futurism, to which some of her paintings of that time, not least *Italian Still Life*, 1914 [1917–18] (plate 29), bear witness. From the old classical models, Popova extrapolated formal structures and, as Mukhina recalled, "interpreted Italy very passionately. . . . At that time she was studying the interrelation of colors in an attempt to determine the power of color and its weight."[7] Nearly a decade later, this knowledge of the laws of painting became the foundation of Popova's work as a teacher at Vkhutemas, on which she elaborated in her papers for Inkhuk. Popova's trip through Italy — including stops in Rome, Florence, Venice, Genoa, Naples, Capri, Livorno, Pisa, Bologna, and Padua — left vivid impressions. By 1913–14, Popova was beginning her professional career and, in February 1914, made her debut in the *Jack of Diamonds* exhibition in Moscow. Both before her trip to Paris (in 1912–13) and after, she worked in various independent Moscow studios such as the Tower on Kuznetskii Most and in the studio at 37 Ostozhenka, whose strongest supporter was Vladimir Tatlin.

Although Popova was undoubtedly much influenced by Kazimir Malevich, the evolution of her painting reveals a personal independence and a lack of concern with conventions. Popova participated in the artistic life of the avant-garde, and many of her associates have left recollections of the "weekly gatherings on art" in her apartment on Novinskii Boulevard during the winter of 1914–15. The circle included Popova's old friends from the Yuon school and Paris such as Grishchenko, Pestel, Ternovets, Udaltsova, and Alexander Vesnin; and, according to Grishchenko, even Malevich attended the meetings. Art historians such as Boris von Eding (a specialist in ancient Russian architecture, and later Popova's husband) and Boris Vipper, philosopher Pavel Florensky, and others also joined in the discussions. In 1915–16 Popova took an eager part in the organization of the Supremus group; and at the gatherings at Udaltsova's apartment, Popova mixed

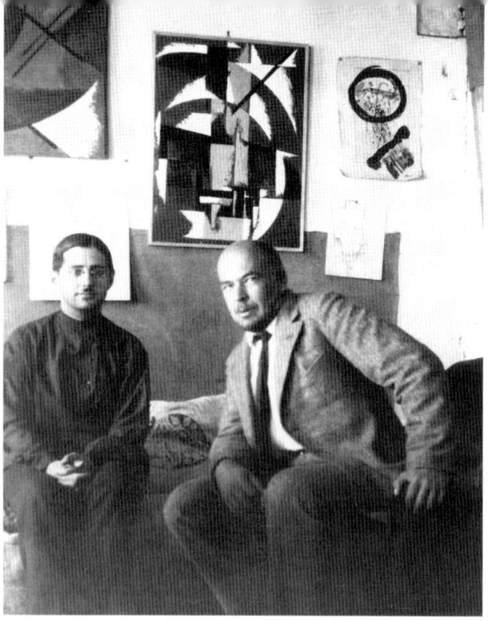

left:
figure 57. Pavel Popov (Liubov Popova's brother and the sitter for her painting *Portrait of a Philosopher*) and Alexander Vesnin, photographed by Alexander Rodchenko in Popova's studio, Moscow, 1924.

facing page:
figure 58. Posthumous exhibition of Popova's work, Moscow, 1924.

with many other participants of the avant-garde movement, including Alexandra Exter, Kliun, and Rozanova; poet Alexei Kruchenykh and critic Aliagrov (Roman Jakobson) were also there. In addition, avant-garde exhibitions brought Popova closer to the left in Petrograd, too. For example, she was a frequent visitor to the what was known as Apartment No. 5, the home of the artist Lev Bruni and a regular meeting place of the Petrograd bohemia in 1914–15.

After the October Revolution, professional artists attached to IZO Narkompros took over the task of organizing numerous exhibitions, helped acquire works of art for the state depositories, and commissioned new work. In March 1918, in the midst of all these activities, Popova married von Eding, and in November she gave birth to a son. To save themselves from starvation during the summer of 1919, Popova, Eding, their son, and her governess and friend, Adelaida Dege, moved to Rostov-on-Don. But there Eding Nikolaevich contracted typhoid fever and died, while Popova herself became seriously ill with typhoid, which caused a serious heart complication. In November, Popova returned to cold and hungry Moscow. Evidently, her leftist friends helped her to withstand the rigors of that time, for she managed to sell works to the State Purchasing Commission and, at the end of 1920 was hired by Vkhutemas, where she was given a studio in the Painting Department to share with her good friend Alexander Vesnin (fig. 57). During the last three years of her life, Popova investigated new genres such as stage, poster, and book design, and it is thanks especially to her efforts that the Constructivist approach began to be applied to sets and costumes for the theater. Not only did she now become a professional teacher, but she also managed to coordinate the loose curricula of the Painting Department at Vkhutemas into a methodical introductory course. Moreover, Popova now put the theory of the Productionists into practice, quickly emerging as a master of textile design.

Friends and students recall Popova at the beginning of the 1920s as young, beautiful, full of joie de vivre. Boris Rybchenkov, for example, then a student at

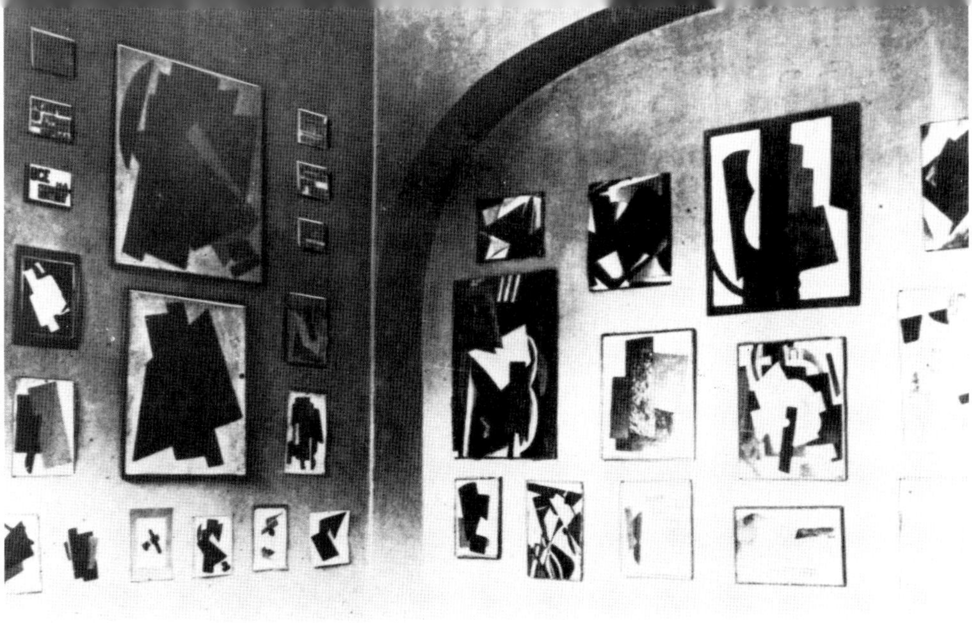

Vkhutemas, wrote that the "young, amazingly beautiful, ever cordial, festively dressed Liubov Sergeevna seemed to glow. . . . She believed that the highest form of the new art was abstraction. . . . Liubov Sergeevna tried to make us understand the supreme principles of constructing something beautiful, free from the reality of the surrounding material world. . . . This, it appears, also prompted Liubov Sergeevna to tame her own, to some extent, feminine . . . form of Suprematism."[8] The transition from studio painting to production art was symptomatic of a crisis in the arts, but Popova's ideas provided some solutions. Another reason for Popova's optimism and tenacity was the unflagging support of those around her, their friendship, and love. Sergei Bobrov dedicated poetry to her, while Aksenov's articles convey a deep veneration, tinged perhaps by a more amorous sentiment. Popova was in close contact with both writers within the publishing-house and bohemian circle called Centrifuge.

But Popova's closest, most important friend was Alexander Vesnin, and everyone knew of their intimate relationship. Natalia Vesnina, the wife of his brother Viktor, writes in her memoirs that the "younger Vesnin fell in love with this gifted, beautiful woman as a young man and preserved his feeling for her throughout his life, even though she married another man."[9] In the summer of 1923 Popova traveled with Vesnin to the Caucasus. Since their youth, they had been tied by the close bonds of friendship as well as by a common artistic mission, sharing a studio at Vkhutemas, and collaborating, for example, on the production of *Romeo and Juliet* that the Chamber Theater prepared (but did not produce) and on an agitprop event.

In the catalogue of her posthumous exhibition, Popova's brother, Pavel, wrote: "Impetuous and passionate, never satisfied with what had been achieved and forever aspiring forward, from a young age Popova displayed an enthusiasm for revolutionary forms and movements both in art in particular and in the basic orientations of life. This revolutionary spirit was characteristic of her steadfast leftism in all spheres of activity."[10] Aksenov even asserted that in her last years Popova regarded her artistic work as a "duty and a social obligation."[11] Although Popova did not emphasize the theme of social service in her own theoretical texts, she did underscore the need to unite the two revolutions — the artistic and the social. Without addressing the question of why the Russian avant-garde embraced the ideology of production art (and unconditional acceptance of the social revolution was part of that), we should remember that Popova responded enthusiastically to the demands of the new reality, and that is how her colleagues at Inkhuk, those associated with the journal *Lef* (*Left Front of the Arts*), and those in Vsevolod Meierkhold's theater perceived her and her work (fig. 61).

1. Quoted from Pavel Popov in *Posmertinaia vystavka khudozhnika-konstruktora L. S. Popova*, catalogue of posthumous exhibition, Museum of Painterly Culture, Moscow, 1924, p. 5.
2. Varvara Rodchenko, comp., *A. M. Rodchenko: Stati. Vospominaniia. Avtobiograficheskie zapiski. Pisma* (Moscow: Sovetskii khudozhnik), 1982, p. 85.
3. Quoted in Petr Suzdalev, *Vera Mukhina* (Moscow: Iskusstvo, 1981), p. 41.
4. Mikhail Alexandrovich Vrubel (1856–1910), Russia's primary artist of the fin de siècle, shared the Symbolists' premise that the world of appearances was but a mere shadow of the higher, cosmic truth. Correspondingly, he displaced and distorted outward forms in order to express the intensity of his inner vision. Artists of the avant-garde held Vrubel in high esteem, even regarding him as the first "Cubist."
5. Ivan Aksenov, "Posmertnaia vystavka L.S. Popovoi," *Zhizn iskusstva* (Leningrad), no. 5 (1925), p. 5.
6. Diary entries by Nadezhda Udaltsova for December 15, 1912 and January 2, 1913, in Ekaterina Drevin and Vasilii Rakitin, eds., *N. A. Udaltsova Zhizn russkoi kubistki* (Moscow: RA, 1994), pp. 19–21.
7. Quoted in Suzdalev, *Vera Mukhina*, p. 85.
8. Boris Rybchenkov, "Rasskazy B. F. Rybchenkova," in Natalia Tamruchi, comp., *Prostranstvo kartiny: Sbornik statei* (Moscow: Sovetskii khudozhnik, 1989), pp. 293–94.
9. Natalia Vesnina, "Moi vospominaniia ob arkhitektorakh bratiakh Vesninykh," *Panorama iskusstv* (Moscow), no. 8 (1985), p. 169.
10. Pavel Popov, *L. S. Popova*, p. 5.
11. Ivan Aksenov, "Posmertnaia vystavka," p. 5.

LIUBOV POPOVA AND ARTISTIC SYNTHESIS

DMITRII SARABIANOV

During her brief life, Popova moved rapidly from realism and decorative Impressionism through Cubo-Futurism and Suprematism to Constructivism. She did so by first absorbing the general principles of modern European art and then embracing the inventions of the Russian avant-garde. But Popova's mature work of the late 1910s and early 1920s is an even broader synthesis, for it reflects the most disparate tendencies — an interest in the classical art of the West (particularly the Italian Renaissance), Russian icons, French Cubism (which she studied in Paris, under Henri Le Fauconnier and Jean Metzinger at La Palette in 1912 and 1913), Italian Futurism (to which she was especially drawn during her 1914 stay in Italy), and, finally, the composite, if antithetical, influences of the two pillars of the Russian avant-garde — Kazimir Malevich and Vladimir Tatlin.

Perhaps the most surprising component of this synthesis is that of classical Italian art. As a rule, Russian artists of the avant-garde rejected the Italian tradition as an archaic, pernicious convention, either implicitly or explicitly. Popova, though, while still an art student, traveled to St. Petersburg to study Italian painting in the Hermitage. From the paintings that she observed there, she made drawings — both skillful copies and free interpretations — that included biblical figures in Renaissance rendering, figure compositions with strong equilibrium, and the motif of the arch within a semi-tondo frame. Later, when planning her Italian itinerary (by which time she was an avant-gardist), she selected cities that were celebrated for their collections of classical art. As Popova noted in her diaries, Nadezhda Udaltsova, her traveling companion in the 1910s, also cultivated a deep interest in classical painting.

Popova grew up in an enlightened merchant family with a strong interest in art, especially Italian Renaissance painting, and her understanding of the structural underpinnings of Renaissance form infuses her abstract paintings and drawings from 1916 and 1917. Distinctive characteristics of these works include a precise sense of up and down, a frontality in the construction of form, and a strong awareness of foreground or surface. Often the center of the composition is fixed and proportions define relationships, whether simple or multiple. These proportions are based on a numerical correlation that seems to have been calculated consciously and deliberately as a lucid, plastic expression of the logic of intersecting parts; there is nothing of the enigma or mystery of Piet Mondrian's geometric compositions here. All of Popova's works express the anthropomorphic spirit, not because the forms recall human figures, but because the creative principles themselves are human, natural, and simple.

How does this affinity for Renaissance form relate to Popova's parallel interest in ancient Russian art — two completely different and seemingly incompatible styles? Just as she visited St. Petersburg to study Italian Renaissance painting, she traveled to the ancient cities of Kiev, Novgorod, Pskov, Yaroslavl, Rostov, and Suzdal and studied the icon paintings there. Using her distinct sensibility and her own inner logic as a guide, Popova discovered the roots of Byzantine and Russian art, and, through simple color comparisons and numerical correlations, found a classical logic in the traditions of both the Renaissance and Old Russia. A similar effect can be seen in the reduced space of Popova's *Painterly Architectonics*, 1918 (plate 37), for example, in which flat, geometric forms are arranged to create an impression of overlapping layers, thus negating the conventional linear perspective without destroying it entirely.

For Popova, Russian icon painting and Italian Renaissance painting shared certain principles, though on an abstract level. She was interested not only in the holy images, but also in the wooden board on which the icon was painted, which she connected with Tatlin's interest in the icon and which prompted her — and Vladimir Baranov-Rossiné, Ivan Kliun, Ivan Puni, and Olga Rozanova, as well as Tatlin — to turn to the painted relief as a new medium. From 1915 on, Popova incorporated "icon boards" in her series of *Painterly Architectonics*; the posthumous list of works compiled by her close associates Ivan Aksenov and Alexander Vesnin includes examples of *Painterly Architectonics* subtitled *With Yellow Icon Board*, *With Black Icon Board*, and *With Gray Board*, and some of her Cubo-Futurist works also bear traces of the texture of the icon board.

Popova also found inspiration in nature and in the human figure, which underwent complex transformations in her work — especially the motif of trees (compare Popova's treatment of trees to Mondrian's concurrent work featuring this motif) and that of the female nude. The latter works demonstrate her particular affinity for Cubist principles and practice, which she assimilated rapidly in Paris. Her *Composition with Figures*, 1913 (plate 28), painted after her return to Moscow — and which was first on the list of works that she compiled herself — shows the influence not only of Le Fauconnier and Metzinger, but also of Tatlin.

Popova's approach changed after she saw such prototypical Cubo-Futurist paintings as Malevich's *The Knife-Grinder*, 1912, and Goncharova's *The Bicyclist*, 1912–13 (fig. 54), in which two opposing forms of energy clash, restraining and at the same time encouraging the perception of the object and its environment as merging together. Popova began to experiment with this emphasis on abstract rhythms and patterns, creating her own Cubo-Futurist works such as *The Pianist*, ca. 1914–15 (plate 31), *Man + Air + Space, Portrait of a Philosopher*, 1915, and the two versions of the *Traveling Woman*, 1915 (plate 33), in which Popova achieved an effective balance between the centrifugal and the centripetal. Such paintings also demonstrate an equivalence of body, object, and empty space, and pinpoint an

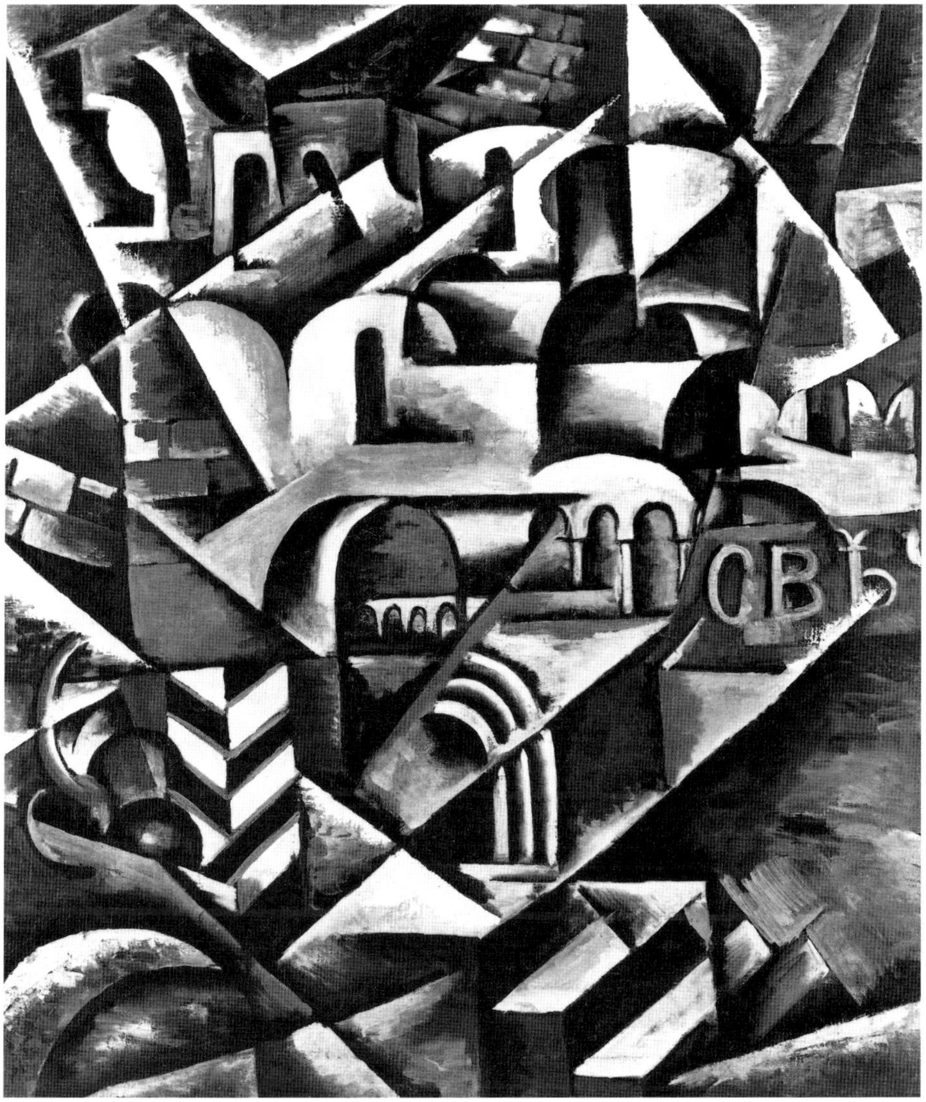

figure 59. LIUBOV POPOVA
Cubist Cityscape, ca. 1914
Oil on canvas, 137.1 x 91.4 cm.
Private collection

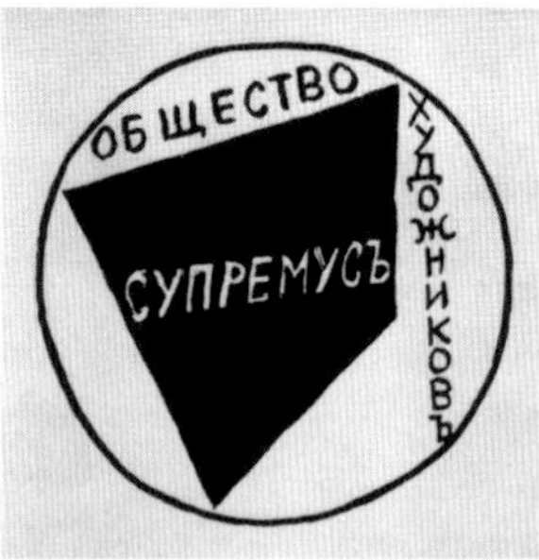

figure 60. LIUBOV POPOVA
Design for the logo of the Supremus Society of Artists, 1916–17
India ink on paper, 9 x 11 cm
Courtesy of Krystyna Gmurzynska, Cologne

important divergence from French Cubism. Albert Gleizes, Metzinger, and Picasso (who in his Cubist works of 1913–14 often depicted a female figure in a chair, with a mandolin or a guitar) always separated the figure from the ground by giving it an emphatic plasticity. This was not a hard-and-fast principle for the French (Fernand Léger tended to ignore it), whereas the Russian artists (Kliun, Malevich, Popova) sometimes carried it to an extreme. In this respect, Malevich's *Knife-Grinder* must have been an ideal model for Popova; her two versions of the *Traveling Woman* (a.k.a. *The Traveler*) show a similar dissolution of legibility within the complex rhythm of the intricate lines and forms, with the fragments of both the figure and its surrounding environment almost losing their connection with reality. The result is a kind of alogical rebus, so that the mimetic purpose becomes secondary and the painting itself verges on non-objectivity.

A comparison of Gleizes's *Woman at a Piano*, 1914 and Popova's *The Pianist*, ca. 1914–15 (plate 31), demonstrates the differences between the French and Russian interpretations of Cubist form and space. Gleizes observes fundamental rules in his representation of the scene, reducing his foreshortening to a nearly absolute flatness (as, for example, in the triangle of the keyboard). Popova, however, gives us a mostly frontal view of the face, while showing the hand from the side, in profile, and the keyboard from above, with a layered array of sheet music floating in the middle. Within a year she would be making completely non-objective paintings similar to this.

Around 1914, after painting in a Cubo-Futurist manner for about two years, Malevich began to work in a completely abstract style using geometric forms, which he called Suprematism, and a group of like-minded artists formed around him (which included Kliun, Alexander Rodchenko, Rozanova, and Nadezhda Udaltsova). Supremus anticipated the goals of the Parisian groups Cercle et Carré (1929) and Abstraction (1931). Not surprisingly, in 1916 Popova became a member of Malevich's Supremus group, and embraced Suprematism in her synthetic system that, in turn, prepared her for the next phase, Constructivism, which was closely related to Suprematism. In the late 1910s, Popova was discovering new forms: just as Cubism had once looked for construction in the human figure and the object, so now Popova subjected

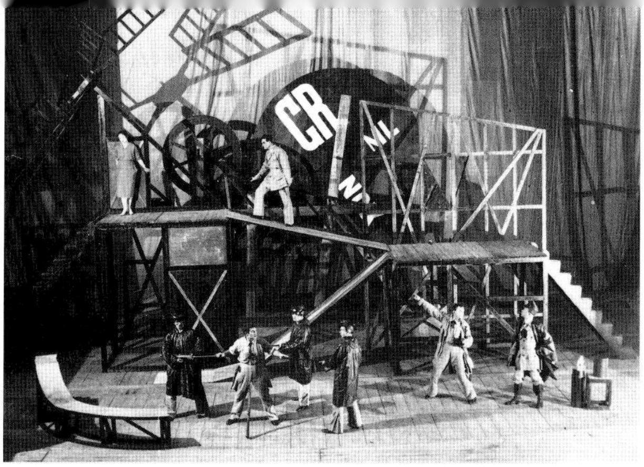

figure 61. Vsevolod Meierkhold's production of Fernand Crommelynck's *The Magnanimous Cuckold*, Moscow, 1922.

abstract forms to reductive analysis by revealing their constructive foundations as geometric, plastic units. Instead of trapezoids or triangles, which once comprised the living matter of the painting, there the edge of the painting assumes major importance, becoming virtually the foundation of the composition, replacing the surface as the principal focal element. The planes have become stripes, totally disconnected from reality, and now simply suspended in the immense space of the universe.

A dual process is occurring here. As Popova undermines the Suprematist totality with Constructivist analysis, she also renews the synthesis: her *Spatial-Force Constructions*, 1921 (see plates 39–41) which succeeded the *Painterly Architectonics*, produce the impression of consonance and stability, thanks to the interactive energy of different forms, directions, and forces. Now, movement unfolds not in real space, but in a new, unearthly dimension that rejects Constructivism in favor of Suprematism. Nevertheless, the same interactions of centrifugal and centripetal still lead to their harmonious union, rather like the unity of static and dynamic that is characteristic of Cubo-Futurism.

To a considerable extent, Popova's abstract paintings constituted a laboratory of forms that prepared her for the richer compounds of Constructivism and Production art that she investigated with such alacrity after the October Revolution. The radical accomplishments that we associate with Popova's stage, fashion, and book designs of the early 1920s, while public, utilitarian, and often ideologically inspired, are organic extensions of her studio painting of several years earlier. Indeed, without the rigorous formal explorations that Popova pursued in the architectonic and spatial-force compositions, her spectacular works of the early 1920s — such as her scenography for Vsevolod Meierkhold's interpretation of *The Magnanimous Cuckold* in 1922 (fig. 61) — would have been impossible.

LIUBOV SERGEEVNA POPOVA
(1889–1924)

1889 Born April 24, 1889, near Moscow.

1899 Receives art lessons at home. Graduates from the Arseniev Gymnasium.

1907 Studies under Stanislav Zhukovsky at his studio.

1908–09 Attends the art school of Konstantin Yuon and Ivan Dudin. Meets Alexander Vesnin there.

1909 Travels to Kiev in autumn.

1910 Travels to Italy with her family, and is especially impressed by the work of Giotto and the 15th- and 16th-century masters. That summer, travels to Pskov and Novgorod to study icons.

1911 Makes several trips to ancient Russian cities.

1912 Works in the Moscow studio known as the Tower, with Ivan Aksenov, Viktor Bart, Alexei Grishchenko, Vladimir Tatlin, and Kirill Zdanevich. Visits Sergei Shchukin's collection of modern French art.

1912–13 Goes with Nadezhda Udaltsova to Paris, where they study under Henri Le Fauconnier, Jean Metzinger, and André Dunoyer de Segonzac at La Palette.

1913 Meets Alexander Archipenko and Ossip Zadkine. After spending May in Brittany with Vera Mukhina and Boris Ternovets, returns to Russia and again works closely with Tatlin, Udaltsova, and Alexander Vesnin.

1914 Travels to France and Italy again, accompanied by Vera Mukhina.

1914–15 Her Moscow home becomes a regular meeting place for artists (including Grishchenko, Vera Pestel, Ternovets, Udaltsova, Alexander Vesnin) and writers (including art historian Boris von Eding).

1914–16 Contributes to several exhibitions, notably the two *Jack of Diamonds* exhibitions in Moscow (1914—making her professional debut—and 1916), *Tramway V* and *0.10*, (both in Petrograd), and *The Store* in Moscow.

1915 Begins to paint in a non-objective style, most notably with her series of *Painterly Architectonics*.

1916 Joins the Supremus group.

1917 Continues her series of *Painterly Architectonics* and makes textile designs for Natalia Davydova's enterprise in Verbovka.

1918	Marries von Eding. Works on designs for Soviet agitprop. Gives birth to a son in November.
1919	Contributes to the *Tenth State Exhibition: Non-Objective Creativity and Suprematism*. Her husband dies from typhoid fever.
1919–21	Paints more advanced non-objective works.
1920	Makes stage designs for Alexander Tairov's production of *Romeo and Juliet* at the Chamber Theater, Moscow. Teaches at Vkhutemas, where she organizes a program on "color discipline." Joins Inkhuk.
1921	Contributes to the exhibition *5 x 5 = 25* in Moscow. Becomes active as a Constructivist, designing book covers, porcelain, stage sets, and textiles. Makes series of *Spatial-Force Constructions*. Teaches at the State Higher Theater Studios.
1921–24	Designs book and sheet-music covers.
1922	Creates the sets and costumes for Vsevolod Meierkhold's production of *The Magnanimous Cuckold.* Contributes to the *Erste russische Kunstausstellung* in Berlin.
1923	Designs Meierkhold's production of *Earth on End.* Moves away from painting and sculpture and becomes completely involved with production art.
1923–24	Works on textile and dress designs for the First State Textile Factory.
1924	Dies May 25, in Moscow. A large posthumous exhibition of her work opens in Moscow (December 21).

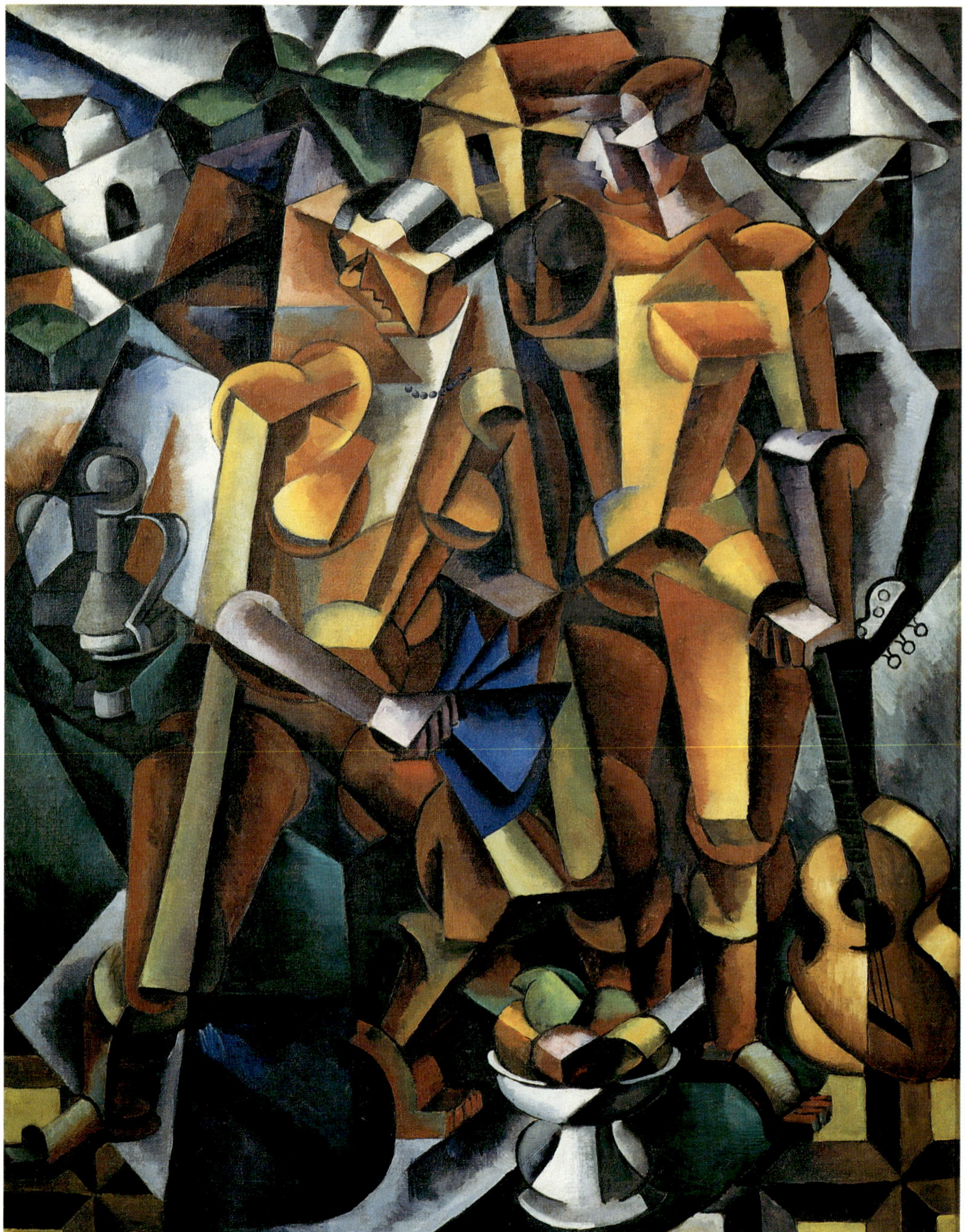

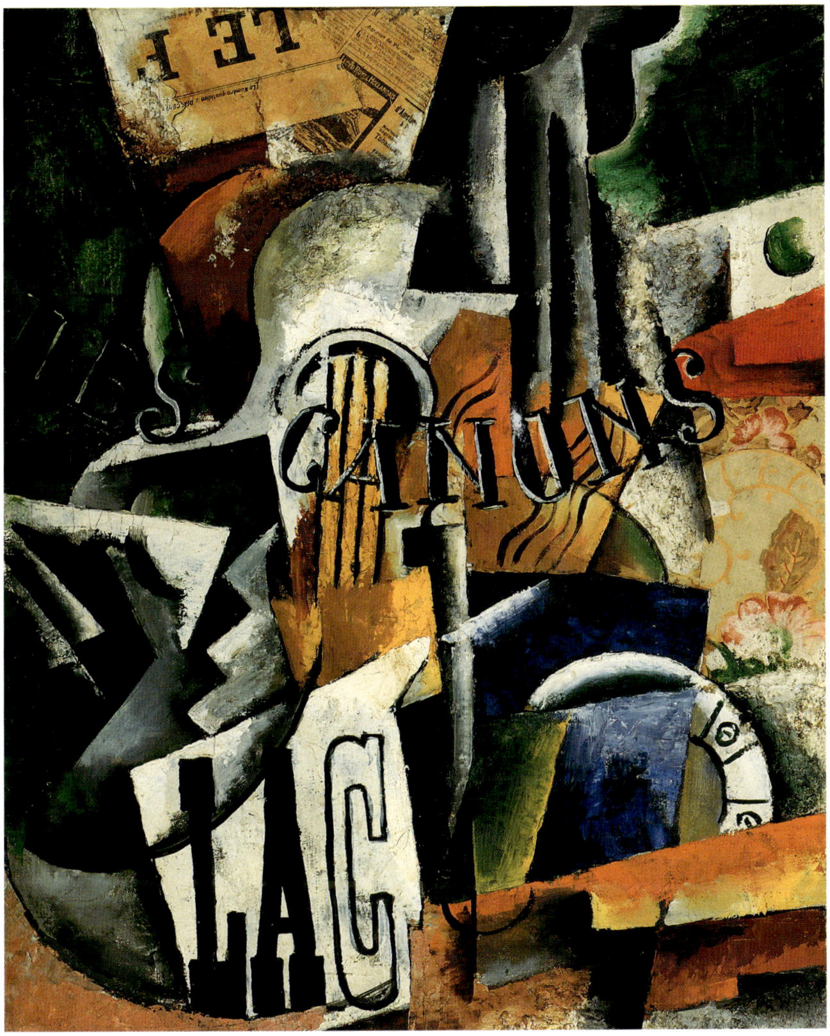

facing page:
plate 28. LIUBOV POPOVA
Composition with Figures, 1913
Oil on canvas, 160 x 124.3 cm
State Tretiakov Gallery, Moscow

above:
plate 29. LIUBOV POPOVA
Italian Still Life, 1914 [1917–18]
Oil, plaster, and paper collage on canvas,
61.5 x 48 cm
State Tretiakov Gallery, Moscow

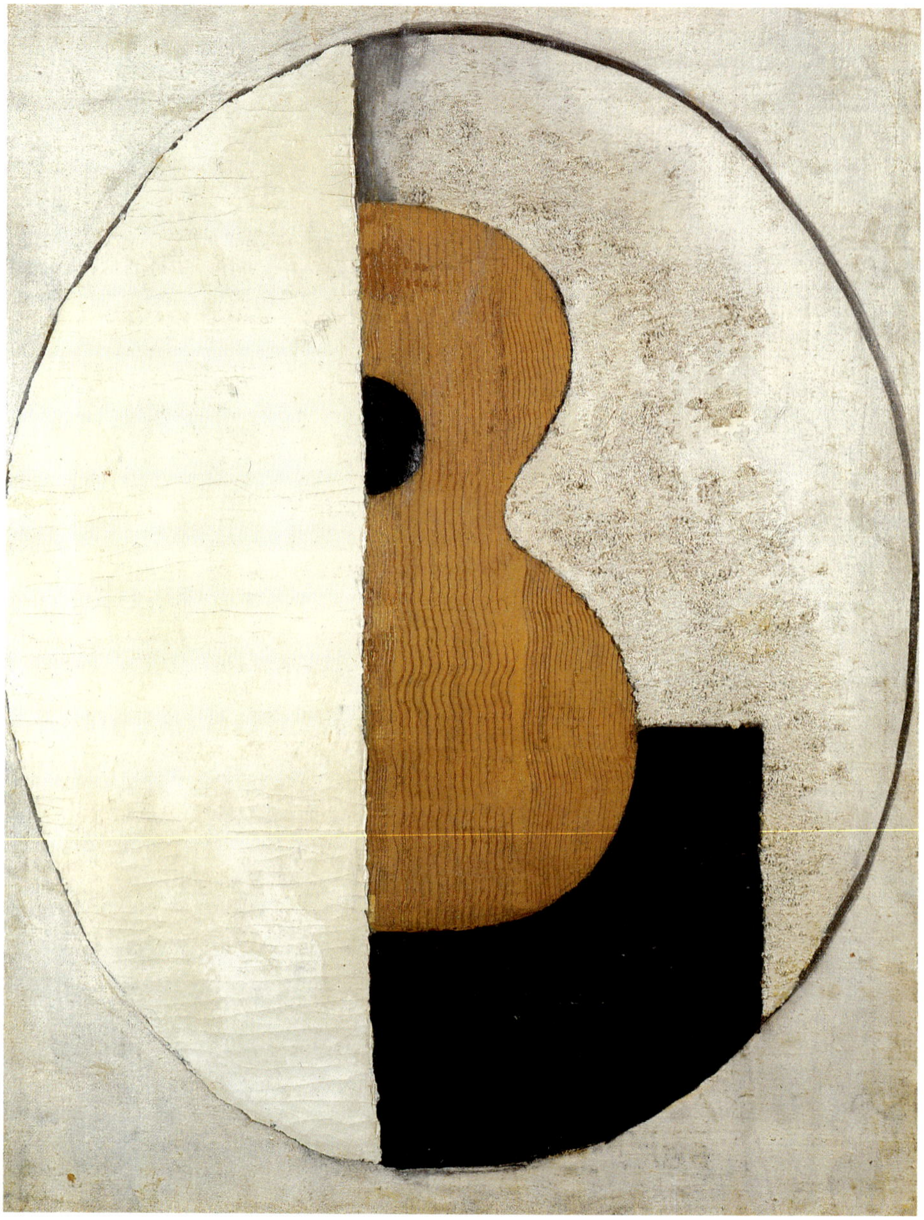

plate 30. LIUBOV POPOVA
Guitar, 1914
Oil on canvas, 83.5 x 71 cm
Collection of Elena Murina and
Dmitrii Sarabianov, Moscow

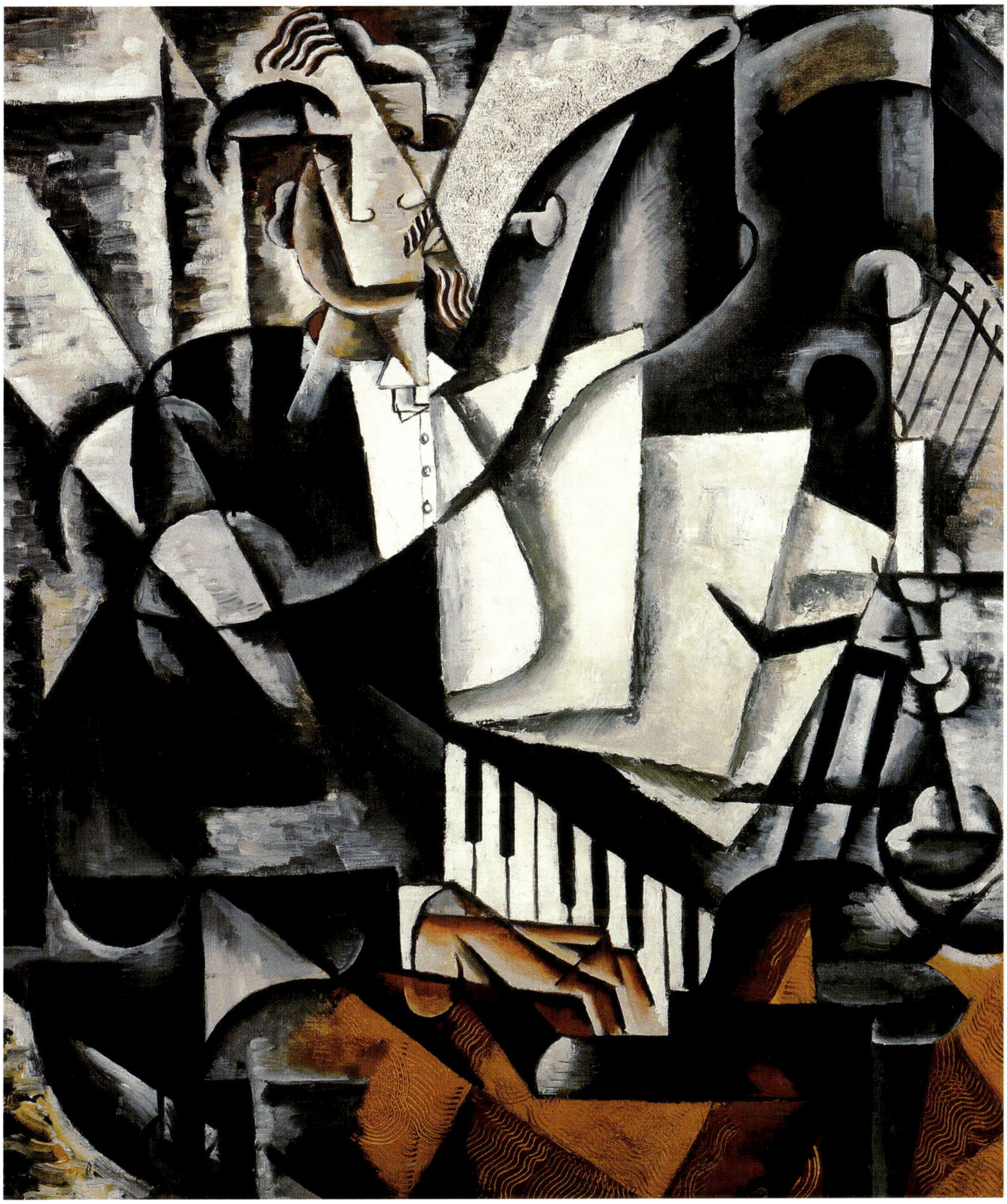

plate 31. LIUBOV POPOVA
The Pianist, ca. 1914–15
Oil on canvas, 106.5 x 88.7 cm
National Gallery of Canada, Ottawa

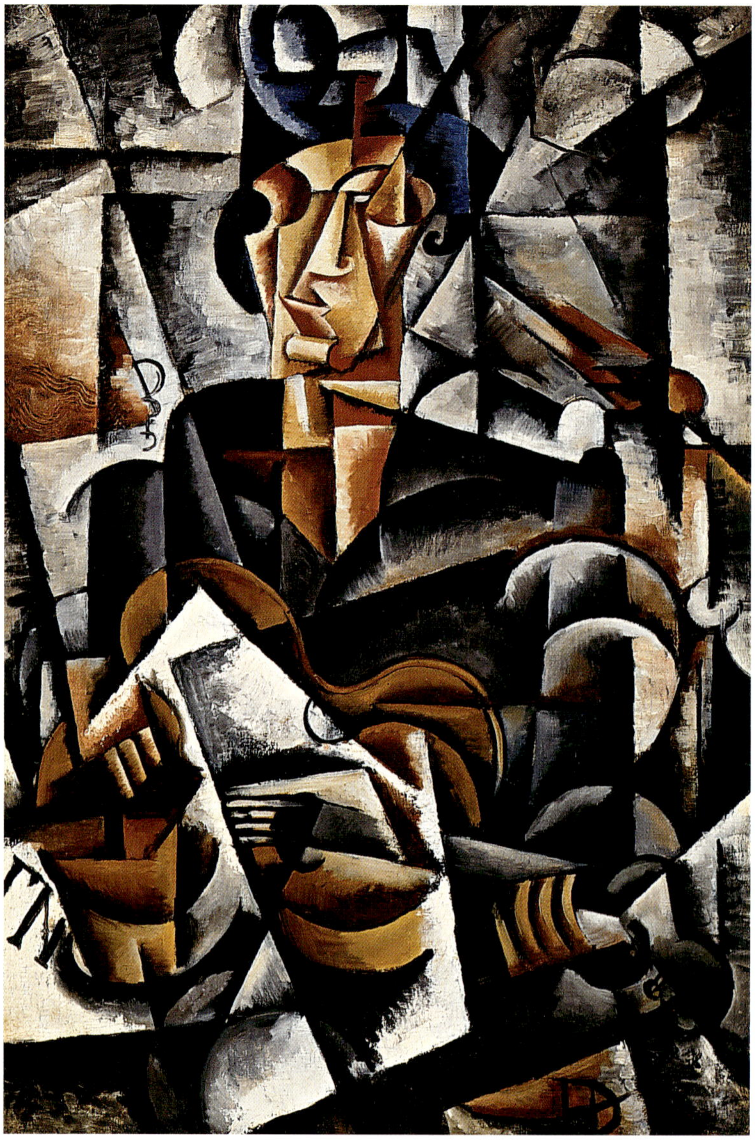

above:
plate 32. LIUBOV POPOVA
Lady with a Guitar, 1915
Oil on canvas, 107 x 71.5 cm
State Museum of History, Architecture, and Art, Smolensk

facing page:
plate 33. LIUBOV POPOVA
Traveling Woman, 1915
Oil on canvas, 158.5 x 123 cm
Art Co. Ltd. (George Costakis Collection)

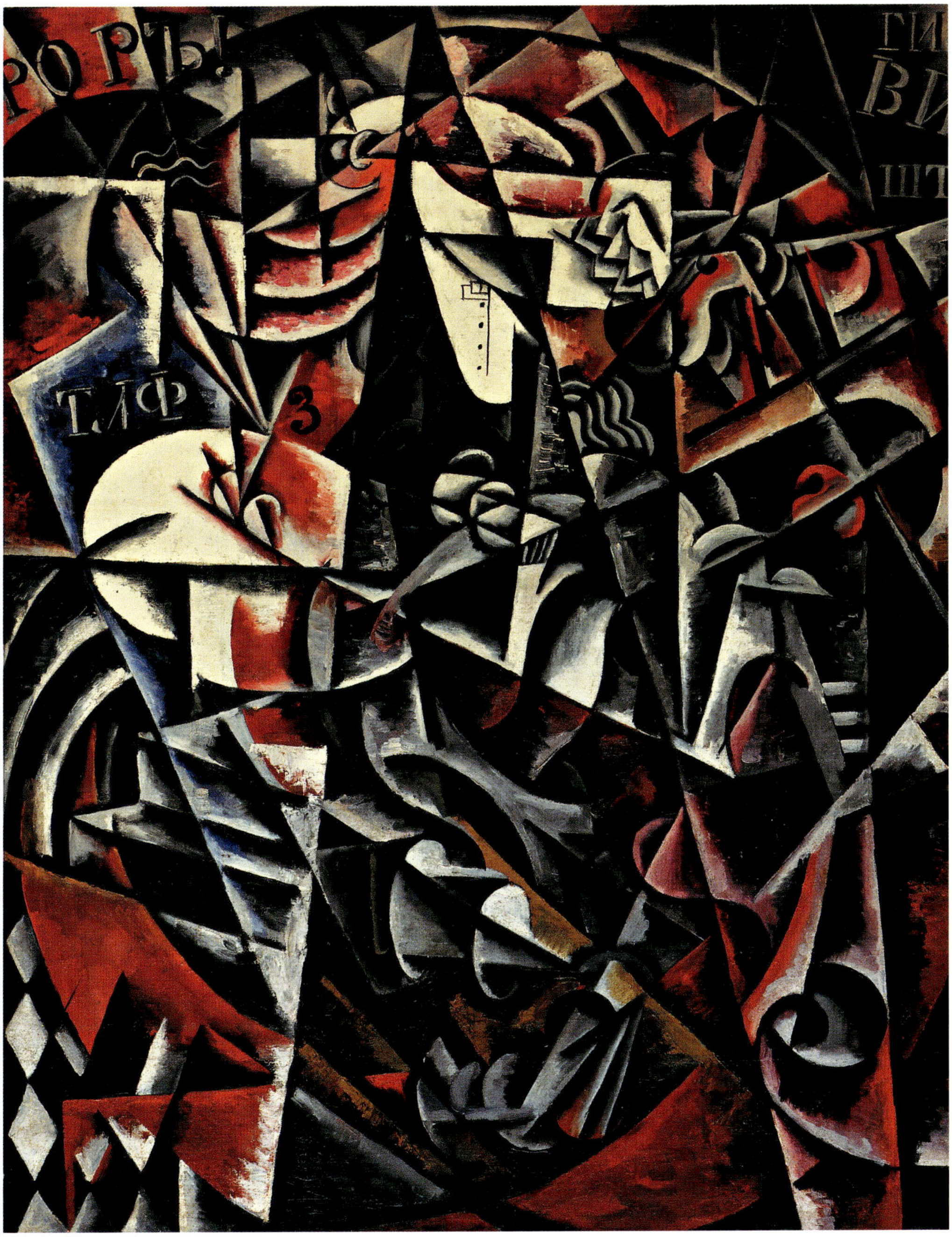
РО РЪ!
Т.ЛФ
3
ГИ
ВИ
ШТ

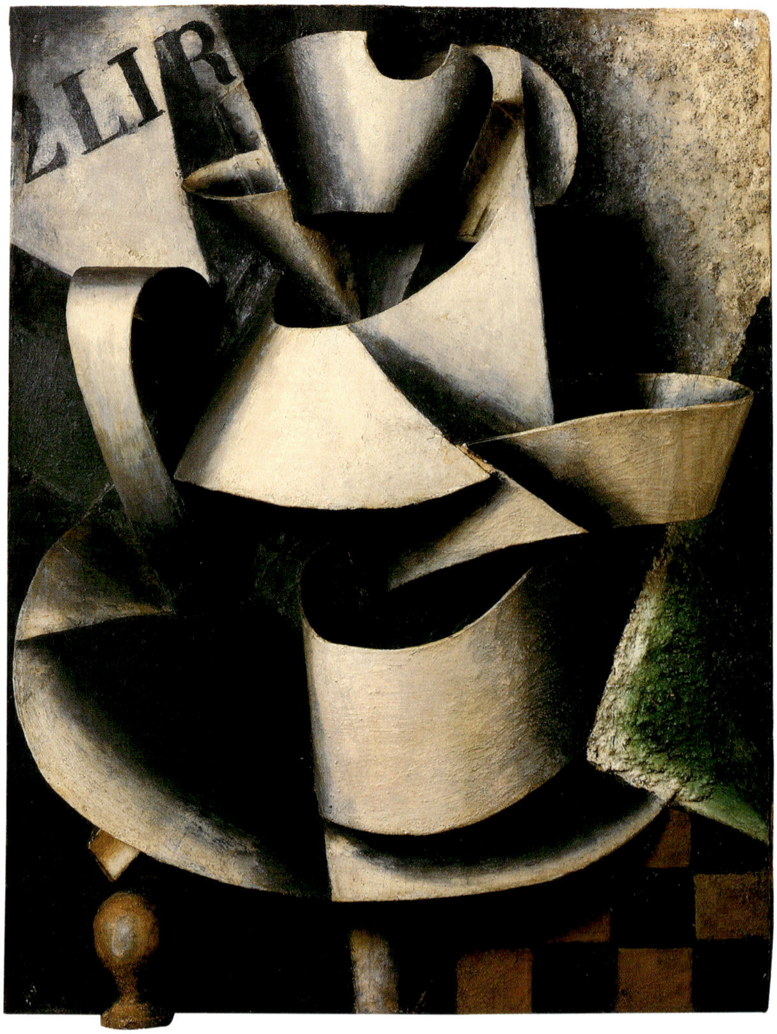

above:
plate 34. LIUBOV POPOVA
Jug on Table. Plastic Painting, 1915
Oil on cardboard, mounted on panel,
59.1 x 45.3 cm
State Tretiakov Gallery, Moscow,
Gift, George Costakis

facing page:
plate 35. LIUBOV POPOVA
Birsk, 1916
Oil on canvas, 106 x 69.5 cm
Solomon R. Guggenheim Museum, New York,
Gift, George Costakis 81.2822.1

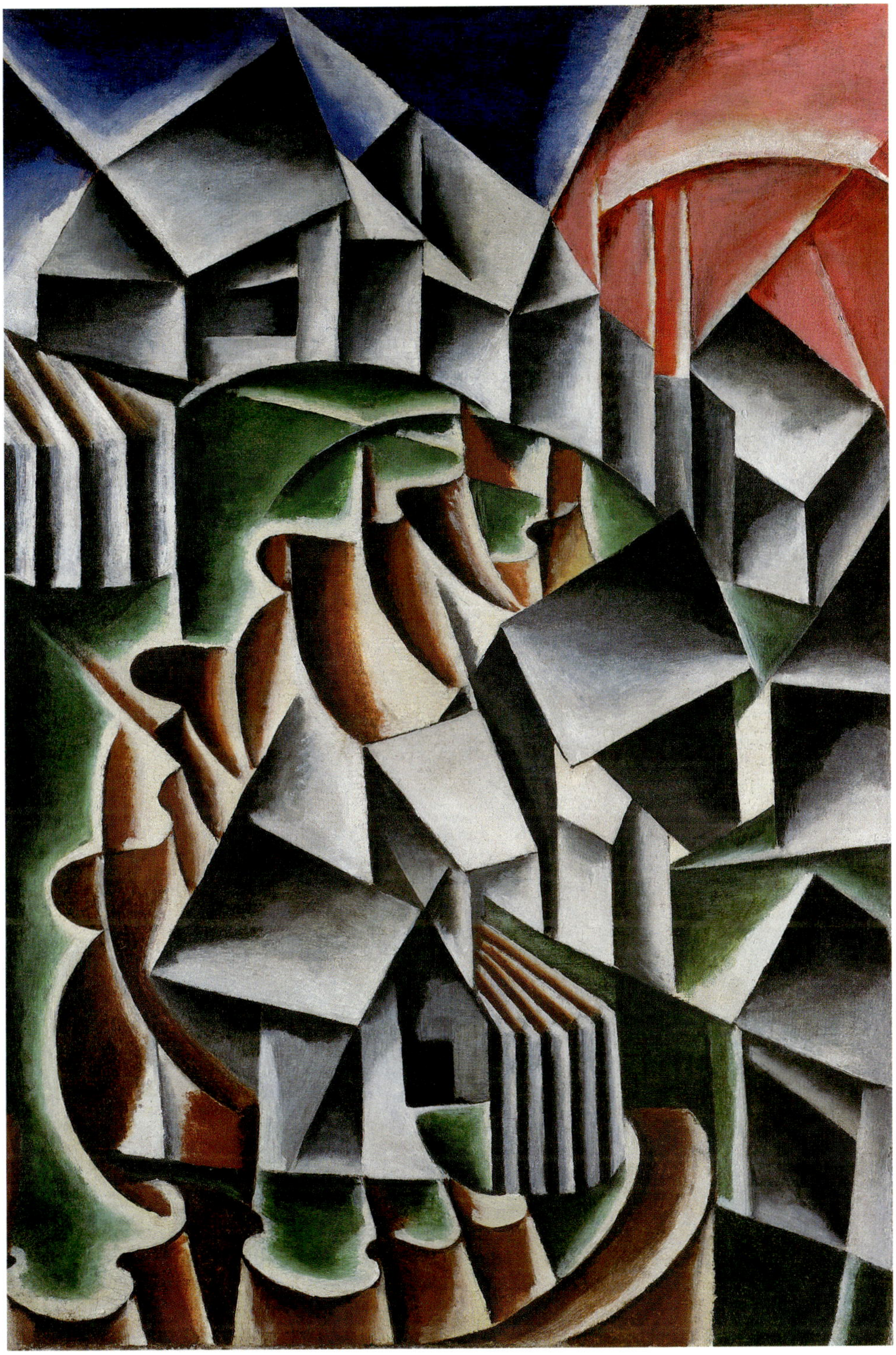

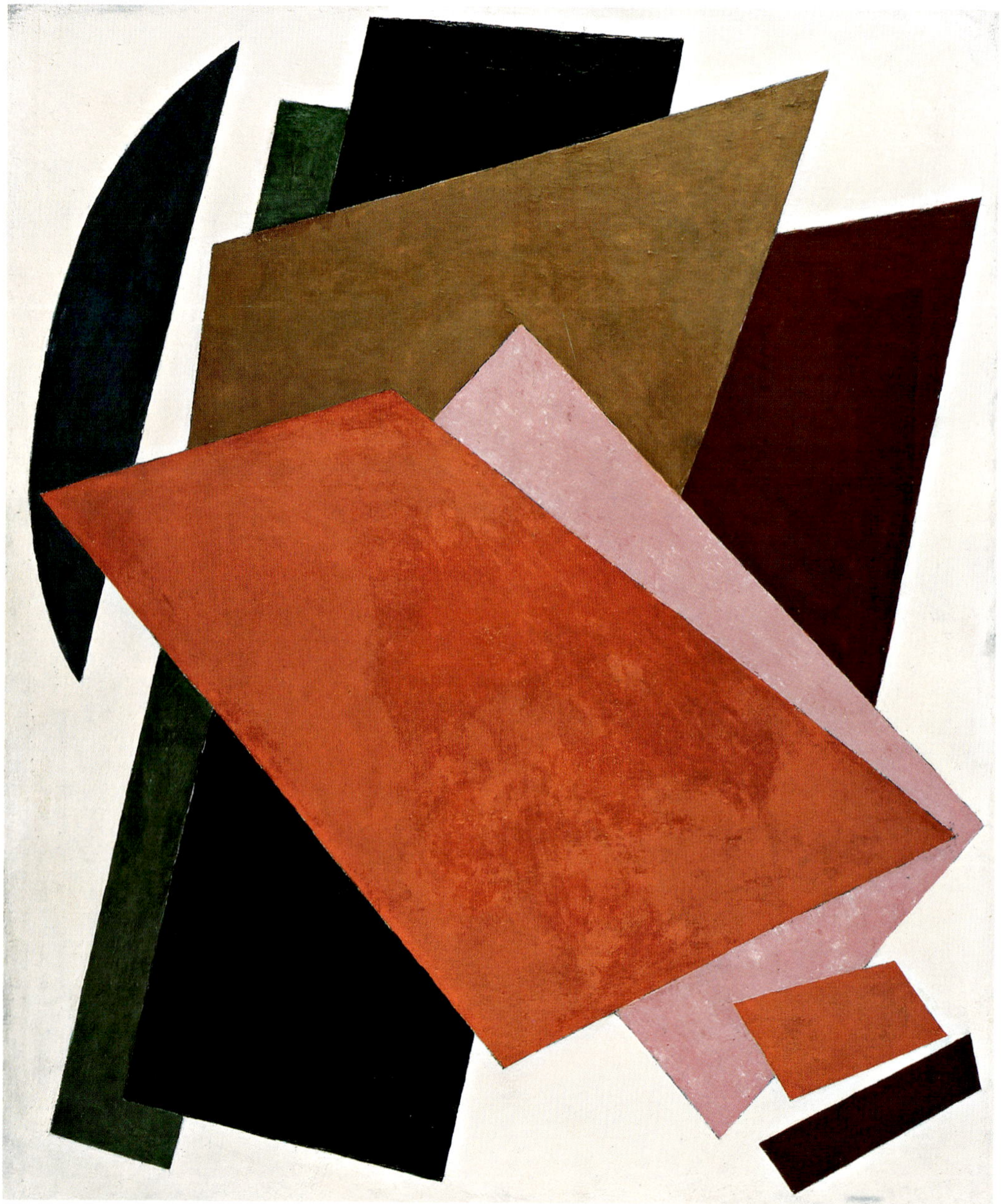

plate 36. LIUBOV POPOVA
Painterly Architectonics, 1917
Oil on canvas, 107 x 88 cm
Krasnodar District Kovalenko Art Museum

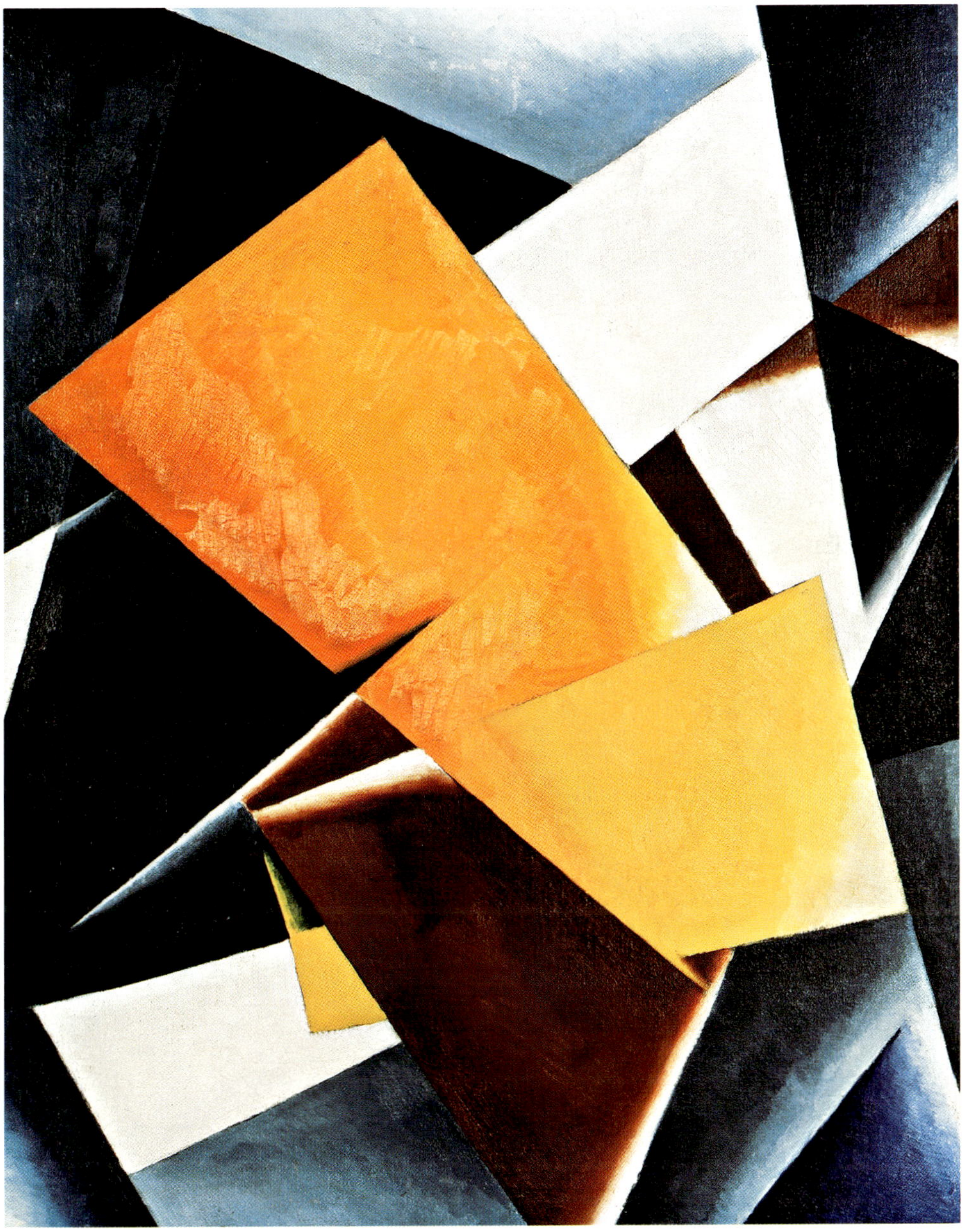

plate 37. LIUBOV POPOVA
Painterly Architectonics, 1918
Oil on canvas, 105 x 80 cm
Slobodskoi Museum and Exhibition Center

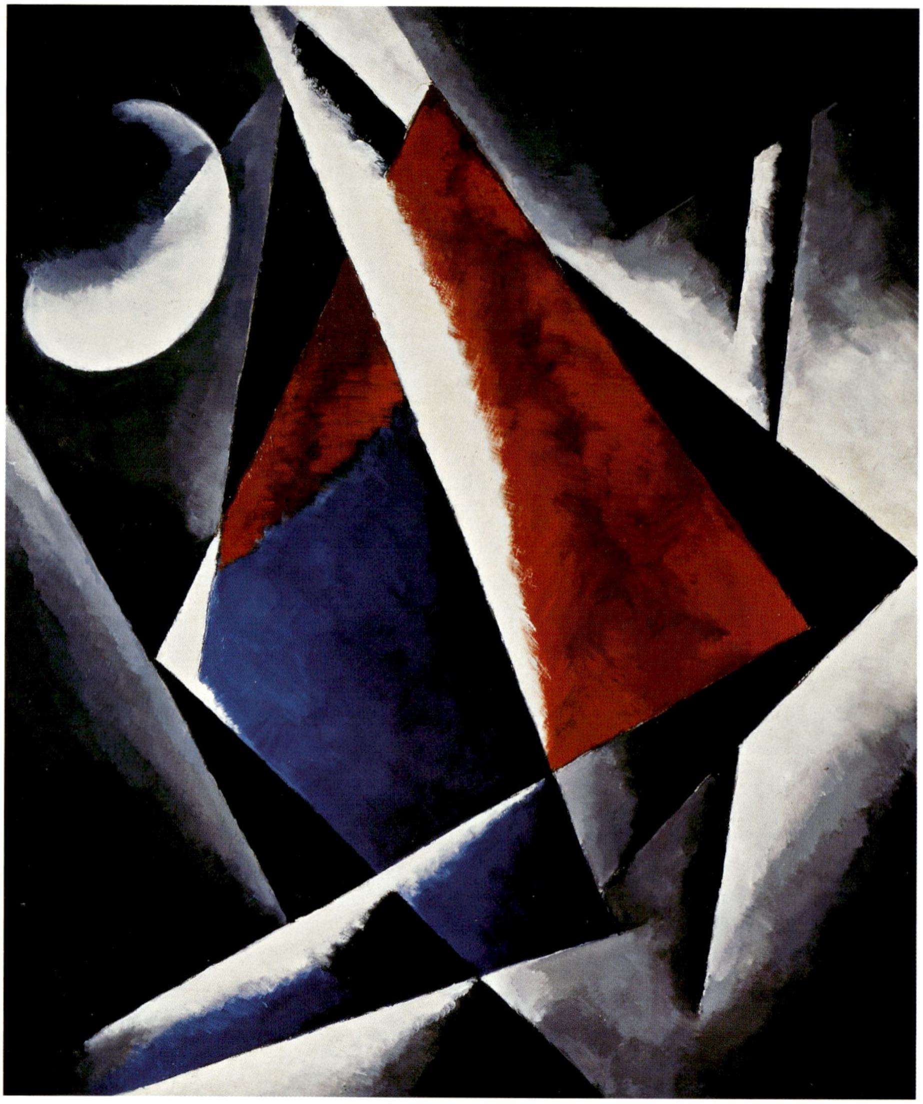

plate 38. LIUBOV POPOVA
Construction, 1920
Oil on canvas, 106.8 x 88.7 cm
State Tretiakov Gallery, Moscow

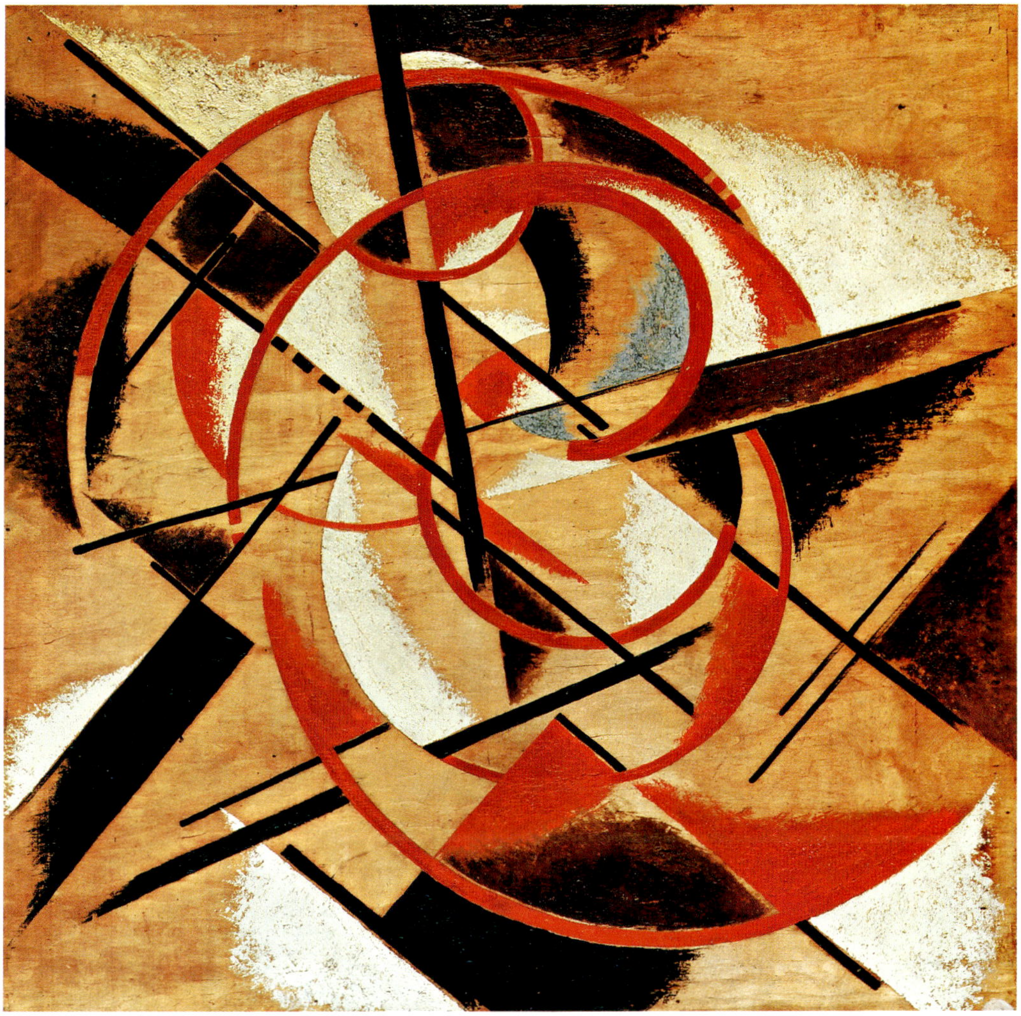

plate 39. LIUBOV POPOVA
Spatial-Force Construction, 1921
Oil with marble dust on plywood, 112.7 x 112.7 cm
Art Co. Ltd. (George Costakis Collection)

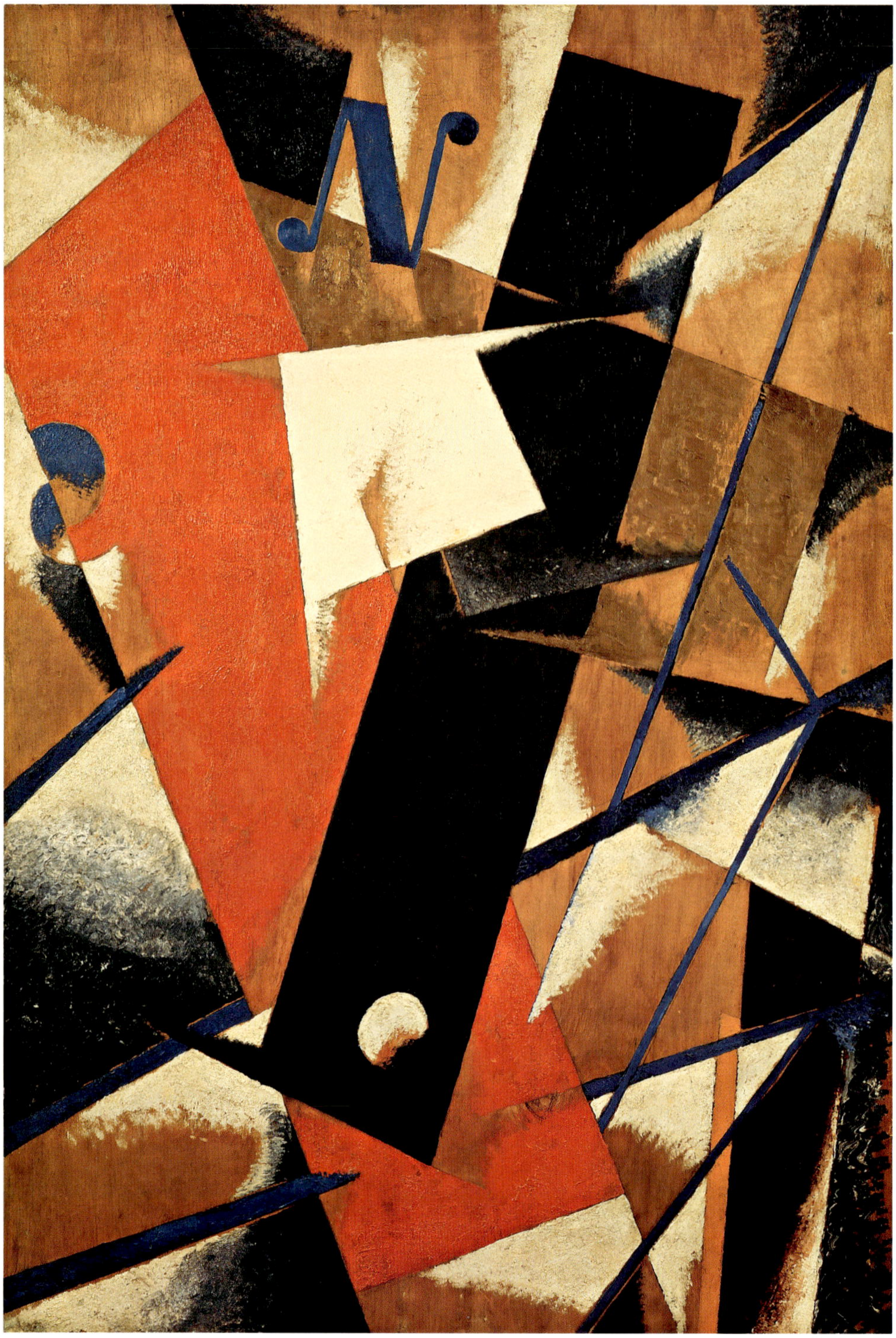

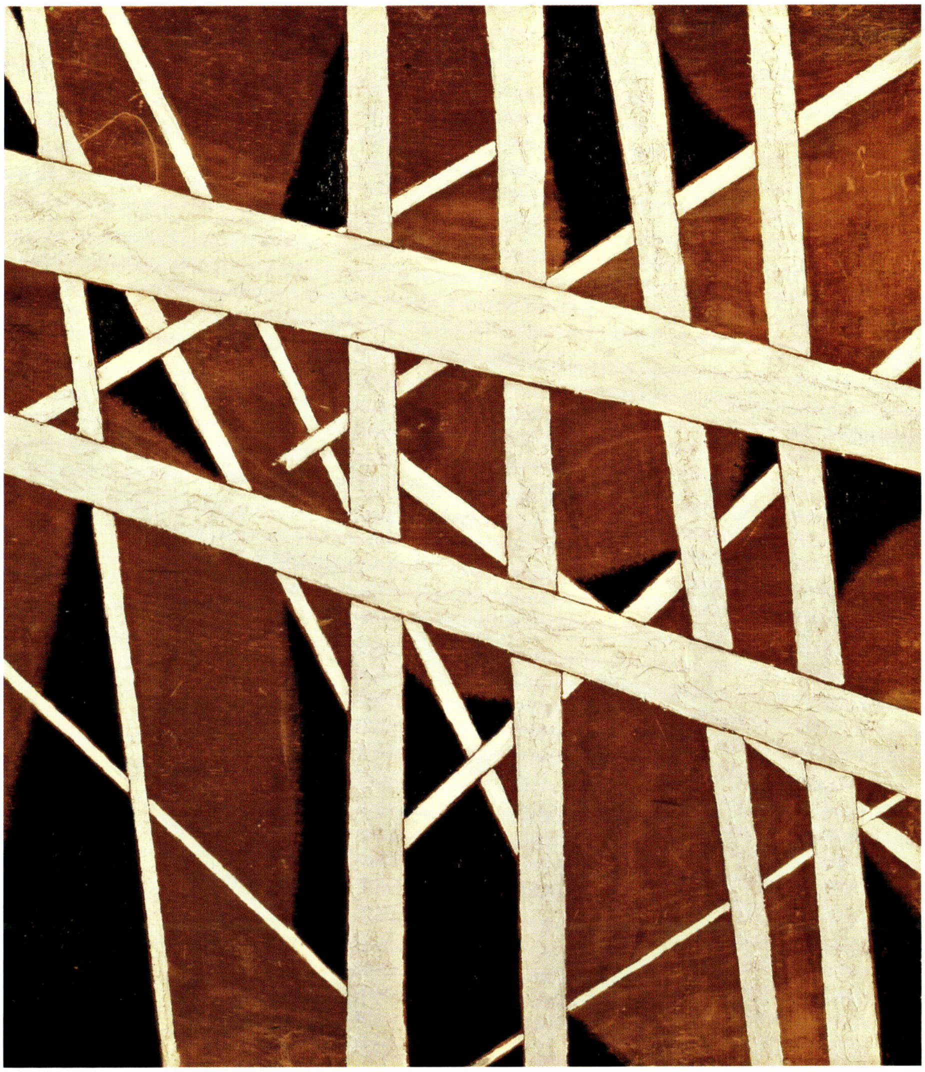

facing page:
plate 40. LIUBOV POPOVA
Spatial-Force Construction, 1921
Oil over pencil on plywood, 124 x 82.3 cm
State Tretiakov Gallery, Moscow,
Gift, George Costakis

above:
plate 41. LIUBOV POPOVA
Spatial-Force Construction, 1921
Oil with marble dust on plywood, 71 x 64 cm
Art Co. Ltd. (George Costakis Collection)

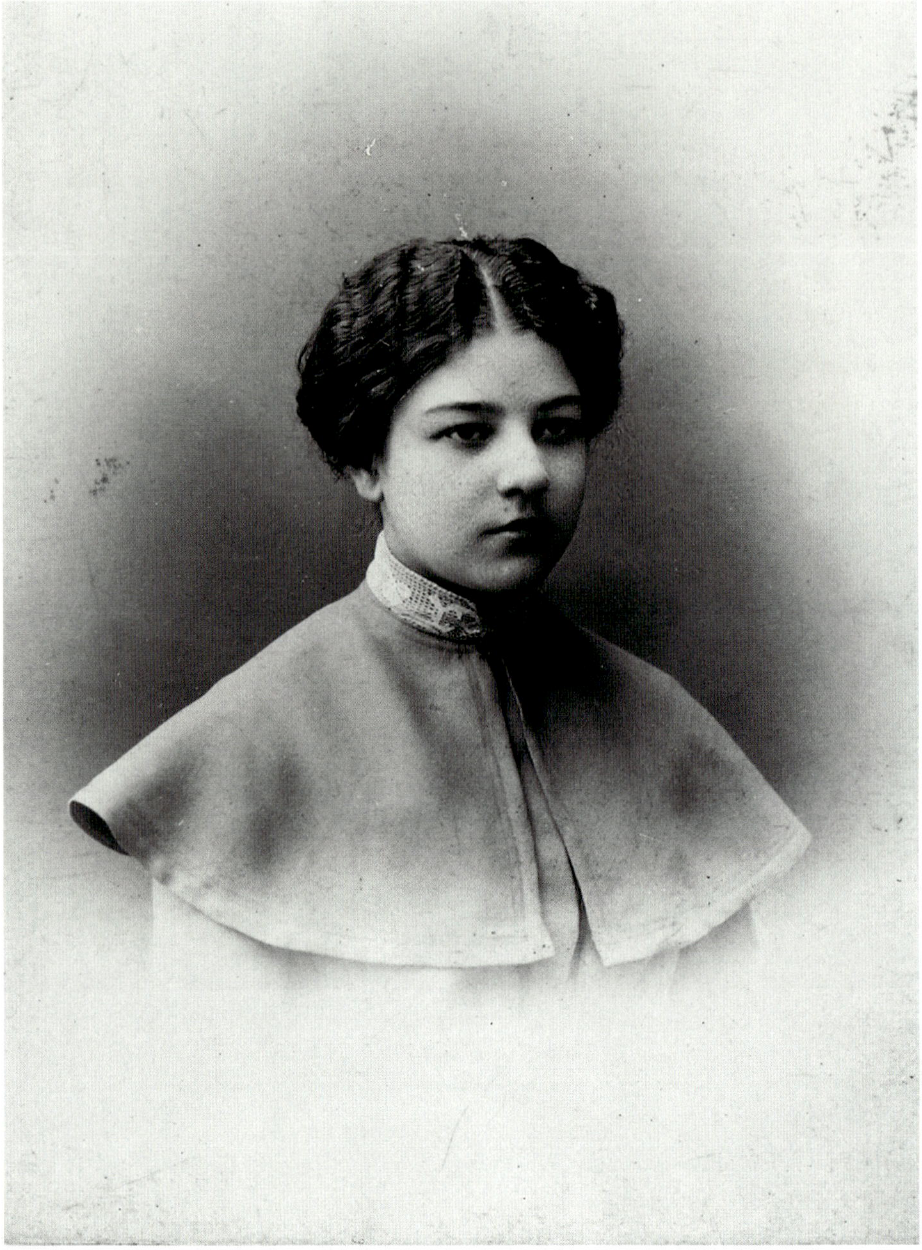

figure 62. Olga Rozanova, photographed by M. P. Koreneva in Vladimir, ca. 1900.

OLGA ROZANOVA

NINA GURIANOVA

OLGA ROZANOVA: EXPLORING COLOR

While working in the most diverse directions and styles, Olga Rozanova always retained her artistic individuality. Consequently, her oeuvre cannot be accommodated easily within the sole categories of Cubo-Futurism or Suprematism, for her paintings, drawings, and designs contain a strength and originality that pushes them far beyond conventional conceptual boundaries. Rozanova's work seems to exist within a compressed time, to exist as a single, compact entity; and this is no more manifest than in her conscious reliance upon color correlations as being the fundamental element in composition. Such was her method in creating her early paintings, when she worked more by intuition, and also in her later art, which she based on a rigorous theory of color interrelationships. In turn, exploration of color became the distinguishing feature of her entire artistic process, something that today — both in theory and in practice — helps us understand more clearly the development of color theory in twentieth-century abstract painting.

From the very beginning of her artistic career, Rozanova tended mostly toward abstract composition based on dynamics, interaction of color, and discordant linear rhythm. She passed quickly from early Neo-Primitivist still lifes and portraits, for example, *Portrait of a Lady in Pink (Portrait of Anna Rozanova, the Artist's Sister)*, 1911 (plate 42), toward a new Futurist rhythmic displacement that she identified with the dissonance of the industrial city — manifest in the paintings that she con-

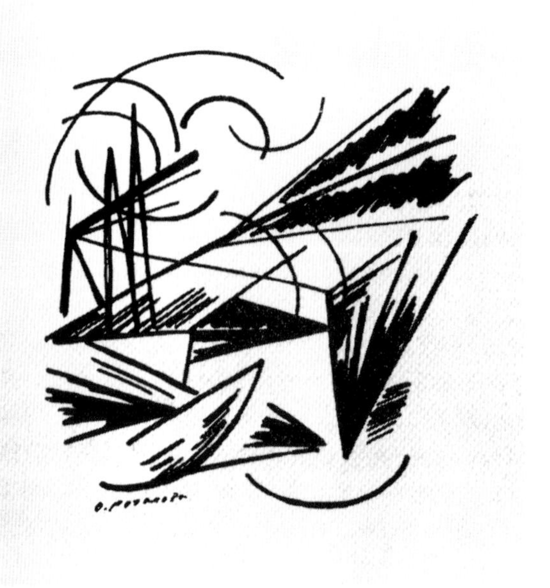

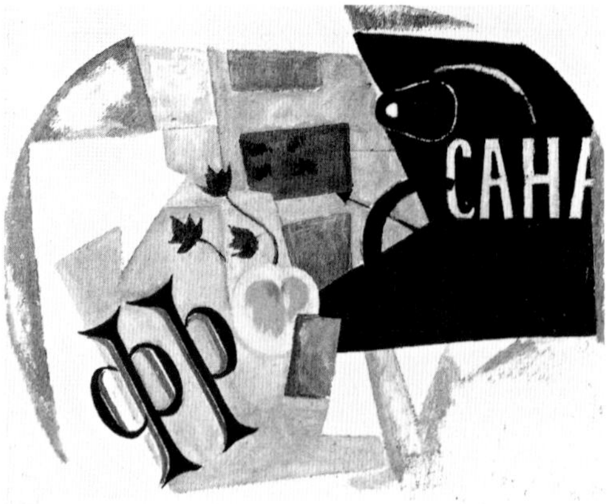

left:
figure 63. OLGA ROZANOVA
Illustration for *Soiuz molodezhi* (St. Petersburg), no. 3 (1913). Lithograph.
Institute of Modern Russian Culture.

above:
figure 64. OLGA ROZANOVA
Non-Objective Composition, 1914–15
Oil on canvas, 56 x 65 cm
State Russian Museum, St. Petersburg.

tributed to the last *Union of Youth* exhibition in November 1913 (*Landscape-Inertia*, 1913, *Dissonance*, 1913, and *Trajectoglyphs of Movements of the Soul*, 1913). Indeed, the latter bears a strong resemblance to images within Boccioni's series of *Stati d'animo*, 1911, and indicates that Rozanova's primary artistic purpose was to convey movement — if not the external and the visible, then the internal and the spiritual.

Rozanova's strongest compositions in this genre, including *City (Industrial Landscape)*, 1913 (Slobodskoi Museum and Exhibition Center, Slobodskoi), *The Factory and the Bridge*, 1913 (Museum of Modern Art, New York), *Man on the Street (Analysis of Volumes)*, 1913 (Museo Thyssen-Bornemisza, Madrid), and *Fire in the City (Cityscape)*, 1914 (plate 43) are characterized by rich surface treatment and the striking application of black lines and contours, something that produces the impression of a shimmering, quivering texture; in turn, this takes on an autonomous painterly quality. In *Man on the Street (Analysis of Volumes)* the figures seem to expand arbitrarily and the composition to yield to a dynamic rhythm that pulsates throughout the work. Rozanova treats the theme of the city in which disparate elements, objects, and forms are transformed into an autonomous organism. Still, unlike the Italian Futurists, Rozanova approaches the city and the machine with caution, but she endows them with a sense of mystery and danger. In her Futurist urban landscapes of 1913–14, the "actors" or "characters" are the buildings, streetlights, and factory chimneys in which human figures, if they are present, dissipate and dissolve.

By 1915 the Russian avant-garde was developing rapidly, assimilating many sytlistic and philosophical concepts and forcing reason to "burst the boundaries of the known."[1] Rozanova's paintings at the *0.10* exhibition were no exception, representing a fusion of Cubo-Futurism and a new impetus toward abstraction (which not only forced her to search for a new painterly style, but also, as she herself might have said, to subordinate this style to a new aesthetic psychology). This duality lends a special attraction to the novel and unpredictable quality of her 1915 works, which hover on the boundary between objective and non-objective. In any case, in following Rozanova's works through the exhibitions of 1915, we cannot help but notice a metamorphosis as she advances from the Cubo-Futurist portraits of 1913–14 or the dramatic *Fire in the City* (*Cityscape*) to the unprecedented abstract reliefs *Automobile*, 1915, and *Bicyclist*, 1915, shown at *0.10*.[2] The Futurist notions of rhythm and dynamism are here transformed into tight Suprematist shapes (semi-sphere, triangle, rectangle) enhanced by a three-dimensional solidity of form.

In this respect, the *Playing Cards* series of 1912(?)–15 (see plates 45–47), which Rozanova linked with her color linocuts and first showed in April 1915 at the *Exhibition of Painting of Leftist Trends* (Dobychina Art Bureau, Petrograd), may seem to be a glance back to the Neo-Primitivism of Natalia Goncharova and Mikhail Larionov.[3] At first, the Neo-Primitivists, too, had been attracted by playing cards as a requisite component of contemporary urban folklore: the signs and symbols of playing cards continued to grace dream books, picture postcards, and the latest fortune-telling books. Larionov was drawing upon all these connotations when he organized the controversial *Jack of Diamonds* exhibition in 1910.[4]

Thus, Rozanova was observing a precedent when she introduced the theme of playing cards into the cycle of eleven compositions, perhaps her most fanciful creation.[5] Here she creates a formal portrait gallery of playing-card queens, kings, and jacks in the spirit of Malevich's "alogism" (Malevich's own term, meaning "non-sense realism" or "transrational realism"[6]) or Lewis Carroll's paradoxes from *Beyond the Looking Glass*. These faces and figures strike us by the sharp contrast of bright colors, with the black-gray grisaille of the faces and hands of the half-alive characters. The irony of the subject is underscored by the rough, even crude method of execution that brings to mind a hand-painted photograph or a brightly colored postcard sold at some provincial fair. The very idea of composing such a group and the very manner of execution go well beyond the conventions of both Neo-Primitivism and Cubo-Futurism, and to some extent anticipate the aesthetics of Pop art. The process whereby playing cards turn into people counterbalances the reverse transformation, which occurs when real-life, historical personages are equated with playing-card figures as, for example, in the special "historical" decks of cards popular in Russia, Europe, and America in the nineteenth century.

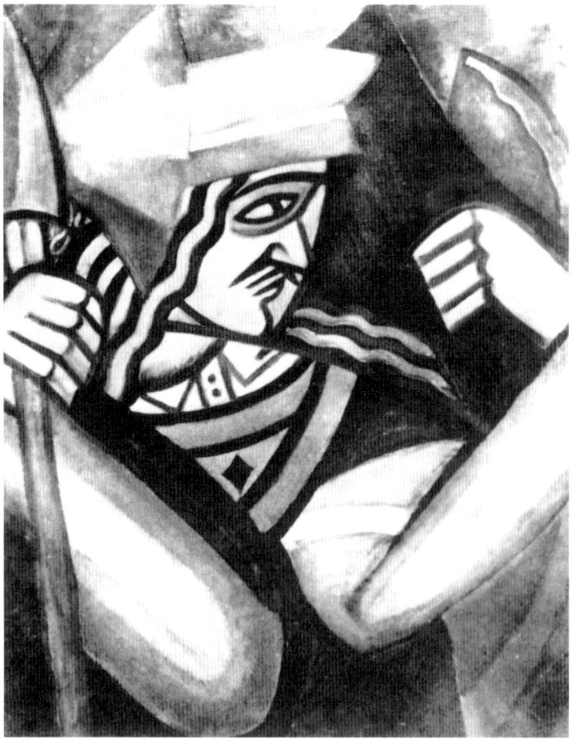

figure 65. OLGA ROZANOVA
Jack of Diamonds, 1915
Oil on canvas, 80 x 69 cm
Present whereabouts unknown

What one might refer to as Rozanova's local color and lapidary application, her fragmentation of complex forms into basic geometrical shapes, their autonomy emphasized by black contour, and the neutrality or virtual absence of background have much in common with Malevich's proto-Suprematist sketches. *Four Aces: Simultaneous Representation*, for example, contains only the geometrized "primal element" of the card sign — the rhombus, circle, and cross. Indeed, Rozanova's canvases of 1914–15 anticipate the abstraction of Suprematism, as in *Metronome*, 1915 (Tretiakov Gallery, Moscow), *Workbox*, 1915 (fig. 66), *Writing Desk*, 1915 (Russian Museum, St. Petersburg), *Pub (Auction)*, 1914 (plate 44), or *The "Moderne" Movie Theater (In the Street)*, 1915 (plate 48). The last anticipates her later style of color-painting, manifest in the attention to translucent, semi-transparent planes and in the fragments of light-rays against a colored rainbow spectrum. Entirely absent here, however, are the Futurist intonations of dynamism and simultaneity; compositions such as *The "Moderne" Movie Theater (In the Street)* bring to mind the "alogical" phase of Malevich's Cubo-Futurism in *Lady at an Advertisement Column*, 1914 (Stedelijk Museum, Amsterdam). Rozanova's compositions, however, can be seen as a kind of hypothetical "picture" or rebus. The isolated sign or object, divorced from its usual context, becomes a requisite attribute of such compositions; the irrational laws of construction of such painterly texts are identical in many ways to the those governing the Russians' *zaum* (transrational poetry).

Indeed, one of Rozanova's strongest talents was her ability to improvise — and the malleability of her graphic art suited itself perfectly to the poetry of Alexei Kruchenykh, inventor and theoretician of *zaum*. In 1913, he and Khlebnikov published his manifesto *Slovo kak takovoe (The Word as Such)*, proclaiming a new verbal form in a language lacking a determinate rational meaning. The close personal relationship between Kruchenykh and Rozanova resulted in a fruitful collaboration and in the unique style of the Russian Cubo-Futurist book: in 1913–14, for example, they published *Te li le*, an early virtuoso example of visual poetry in which line is coequal with word, and color with sound.

In 1915–16 Rozanova and Kruchenykh created a new version of the avant-garde book by using collages made from colored paper. Rozanova employed this technique to particular advantage in her designs for *Zaumnaia gniga (Transrational Book)*, 1915, by Kruchenykh and Aliagrov (pseudonym of Roman Jakobson) and *Voina (War)*, 1916 (designed in the summer of 1915), which contained color linocuts, collages, and a collection of poetry by Kruchenykh.

The cover of *Voina* is the first Suprematist experiment in book design. The majestic simplicity of the colors (white, blue, and black) and of the shapes (rectangle, square, circle, and triangle) suggests comparison with Malevich's works shown at *0.10*, although there was not a single painting by Rozanova at this exhibition that could be called Suprematist.[7] This apparent incongruity, however, can be explained by the fact that she came to Suprematism by way of collage, a path that was predetermined by the previous evolution of her art. Rozanova was so enthusiastic about transrational poetry that she began to compose verse herself, albeit under the influence of Kruchenykh. In turn, Kruchenykh applied himself to the visual arts and under Rozanova's guidance created a set of abstract collages for his album *Vselenskaia voina (Universal War)*, 1916. In the preface to this edition he declared transrational (i.e., abstract) painting to be supreme, affirming that the original idea had been Rozanova's.

Throughout Rozanova's artistic career, color remained her chief concern. In such sophisticated abstract paintings as *Non-Objective Composition (Flight of an Airplane)*, 1916 (plate 49), and two works titled *Non-Objective Composition (Suprematism)*, 1916 (plates 50, 51), she reveals a "discordant concordance" of interactive colored planes to create her own variant of Suprematism based on the dominant role of color. Malevich appreciated Rozanova's painting of this period, once even calling her the "only true Suprematist."[8] Nonetheless, in her article "Cubism, Futurism, Suprematism" — much of which was devoted to color in abstract art — Rozanova entered into a dialogue with Malevich: whereas for Malevich "*paint* is the main thing,"[9] for Rozanova all abstract art is born of a "love of *color*."[10]

The two words "paint" and "color" are in no way synonyms, for each carries the essence of Malevich's and Rozanova's respective approaches to abstract art. When

Malevich speaks of paint as the most important element in Suprematism, he has in mind the concrete materiality of pigment as the primary means of expression, the principal instrument. Even when he uses the word "color" in his writings (the "self-sufficient components in painting are color and texture"),[11] he still means "paint," with all its materiality and the texture it produces when applied to canvas. In contrast, Rozanova sees the essence of color to lie in its "non-materiality."[12] Color is no longer an instrument, but a universal goal that the artist strives to reach by all the means of expression at his or her disposal. According to Rozanova, the task of Suprematism is "to create quality of form in connection with quality of color,"[13] not vice versa, for she considered form as merely deriving from color. Later, in 1917–18, she conceived of the notion of the destruction of form — which is yet another important distinction between her and Malevich, who acknowledged the dominant role of the painterly form as such.

This significant difference between Malevich and Rozanova becomes clear when we compare two analogous paintings, such as Malevich's *Suprematist Composition: Airplane Flying*, 1915 (Museum of Modern Art, New York), and *Non-Objective Composition (Flight of an Airplane)*. Three colors figure in this work by Malevich — red, yellow, and black on a white background, symbolizing the nothingness of metaphysical space — and three "floating" forms correspond to these colors: a rectangle, a square, and a narrow strip stretched almost into a line. But seventeen colors — the three primary colors, their complimentary colors, and eleven mixed colors — resound in Rozanova's composition. Color variety is justified by a corresponding variety of painterly forms. The texture of the painted surfaces is variegated, so that the brushstrokes and thinning layers of paint sometimes come through. Numerous geometrized shapes consisting of interconnected parts of triangles, circles, rectangles, and other segments intersect in a rhythmic dissonance that seems to have exploded and distributed them with enormous centrifugal force. Three large colored planes loom in the background — blue, light blue, and yellow — united into a single static figure (a structure reminiscent of Liubov Popova's *Painterly Architectonics* [plate 36]); and they seem to have crowded out the white background, which remains only as a narrow strip along the edges of the canvas. The foreground is in sharp contrast to this static element of the painting, and the dissonant energy here is the principal difference between her works and Popova's *Architectonics*, which, in their utopian equilibrium, appear to overcome the chaos of reality and to restore harmony.[14]

Unlike Popova, in whose works color emerges with the plastic, almost sculpted form of her *Architectonics*, and unlike Malevich, who subordinates color to the new dimension of the dominating space, Rozanova achieves a spe-

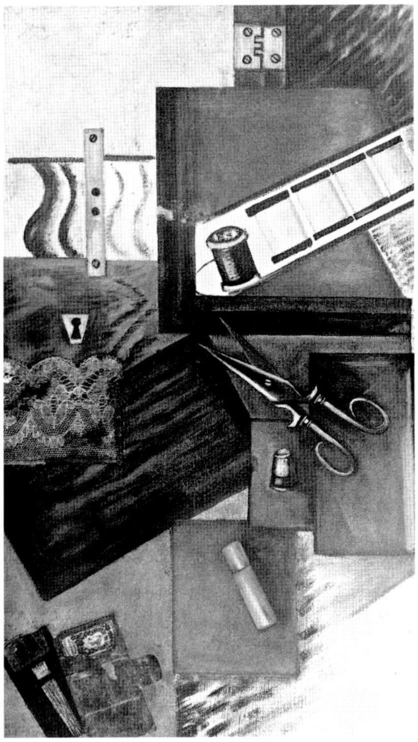

figure 66. OLGA ROZANOVA
Workbox, 1915
Oil on canvas with collage, 53 x 33 cm
State Tretiakov Gallery, Moscow

cial painterly effect through contrast, dissonance, and the chance harmony of various color combinations determined by rhythm, dynamics, and emotion (as in a musical composition). By means of hyperbolic color and a metaphoric combination of light and dark, Rozanova introduced a new quality into the geometry of Suprematism. The result embodies her idea that "it is the properties of color that create dynamism, engender style, and justify the construction."[15]

The leitmotif of Rozanova's Suprematist compositions is the rebirth of color, much as in her poetry it is the rebirth of sound in the dissonant, contrasting combinations of light and dark, heavy and light, warm and cold, harmonious and atonal. Her Suprematist works have the same compositional completeness and uniform rhythm: the basic color combinations are reflected endlessly in supplemental, fragmentary forms that fill the surrounding space. Her *Non-Objective Composition (Suprematism)*, 1916 (plate 50), for example, has only six colors (black, white, yellow, blue, and two shades of gray), but they are complementary opposites, the white triangle against the gray background embodying the fullness and completeness of absolute silence. The contrast of black and white makes for the strongest dissonance, which may be read as the archetype in our consciousness. With its yellow-gold equivalent of lightning scattered over the cool fragments of blue, the color composition bends to a displacement, an almost Gothic sweep. This composition, one of the most atectonic in construction and rhythmically tense and expressive, might be called an example of "Romantic" Suprematism.

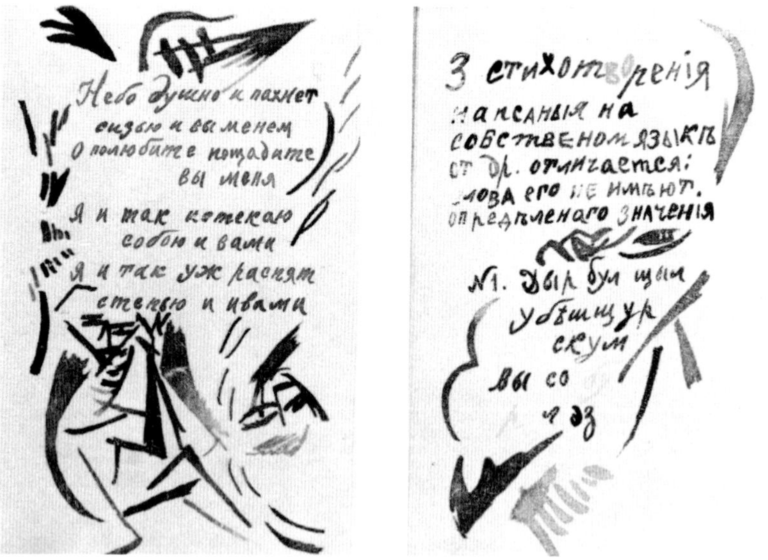

figure 67. Olga Rozanova
Illustrations for Alexei Kruchenykh and Velimir Khlebnikov, *Te li le* (St. Petersburg: 1914) Institute of Modern Russian Culture, Los Angeles

Rozanova created a number of expressive abstract works that were rather different from the initial stage of Suprematism, employing simple forms (usually rectangles) or broad, rich planes of color with rough outlines that seem to stick to the surface of the canvas. These paintings give the impression of a solid, heavy mass of color. Such is the spare, abstract composition in the State Russian Museum, which consists of a dissonant arrangement of red, black, and yellow pastoge. In 1917 Rozanova wrote: "I have found a new way of investigating color; if it is not at variance with the 'transfigured' method then it can be used in Suprematist painting as well."[16]

Rozanova concluded her own color theory — in which she distanced herself from Malevich's Suprematism — with the concept of color-painting (*tsvetopis*). Several of her paintings carried this denotation at her posthumous exhibition within the *First State Exhibition*, held in December 1918–January 1919.[17] *The Tenth State Exhibition: Non-Objective Creativity and Suprematism* a few months later also demonstrated a clear boundary between generic Suprematism and Rozanova's color-painting, the exhibition featured color compositions by Ivan Kliun, Mikhail Menkov, Alexander Rodchenko, and Alexander Vesnin, as well as several by Rozanova. In the catalogue, Malevich remarked on the problem of color, repeating some of the principles he had formulated in his 1917 essay on color-painting.

Rozanova's article "Cubism, Futurism, Suprematism" expresses her ideas on the nature of color and its function in abstract art. Referring to the materialization of the "immaterial essence of the color," she emphasizes that the "texture of the material hinders the pure nature of color."[18] This passage indicates why she turned to collages of materials possessing minimal texture, such as transparent colored paper. After experimenting with various transformations, she reached her ideal — to convey the immaterial essence of color, its inner energy, and luminosity in

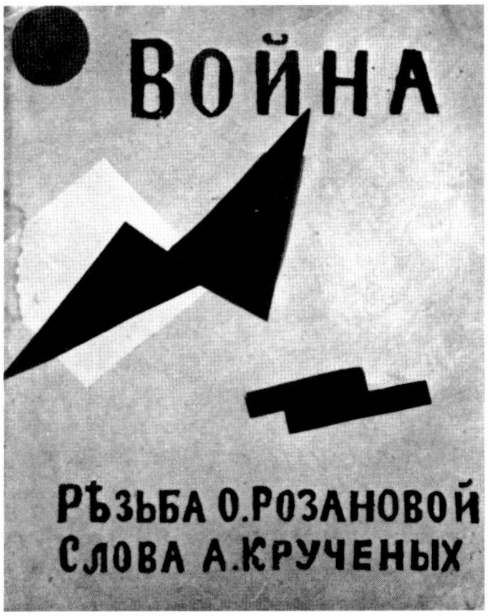

figure 68. OLGA ROZANOVA
Cover for Alexei Kruchenykh, *Voina*
(Petrograd: 1916)
Linocut, 40 x 31 cm
Courtesy Galerie Gmurzynska, Cologne

painting. Here, the emphasis switched from form and painterly texture to the spiritual, mystical qualities of color and its interconnection with light. In the 1916 *Non-Objective Composition (Suprematism)* (plate 50), *Green Stripe (Color Painting)*, 1917 (plate 54), and a number of other concurrent paintings, the transparency is so great that the effect is of a colored ray of light projected on the white background of the primed canvas. In the 1917 compositions, Rozanova achieves a maximum luminosity of texture through a transparent color glazing applied to the strongly reflective white ground.

Green Stripe is surely among the most interesting pieces of twentieth-century abstract painting, above all for the radiance of the elusive, palpitating light that envelops the translucent green column. Moreover, there is evidence to assume that this composition was part of a triptych that also included *Yellow Stripe* (location unknown) and *Purple Stripe*.[19] The effect brings to mind a phototransparency projected onto a wall or the experimental painted films of German avant-gardists Hans Richter and Viking Eggeling in the 1920s. In his "Posthumous Word" on Rozanova, Rodchenko wrote: "Was it not you who wanted to light up the world in cascades of color? Was it not you who proposed projecting color compositions into the ether. . . . You thought of creating color through light."[20]

Suprematism became a laboratory whose experiments led Rozanova to put her innovative ideas into seemingly contrary practices — by creating "color-painting" or, as she put it, a "painting of transfigured color far from utilitarian goals" — and by attempting to transform the everyday into a "living environment" for art, as was the case with the Suprematist designs for women's fashions, handbags, and embroideries.[21] Perhaps, after all, Rozanova was the only Suprematist able to combine a "cosmic" disharmony with the human dimension, and the spiritual, mystical and mental with the emotional, intuitive, and sensual. In her last works she found — consciously or intuitively — a way out from the Suprematist impasse. If Malevich perceived a new religion imbued with the poetics of dehumanization in the uncompromising, totalitarian stance of his innovation, Rozanova spoke of a new humanized beauty: "Nevertheless, we do believe that the time will come when for many our art will become an esthetic necessity, an art justified by a selfless aspiration to present a new beauty to the world."[22] With a natural elegance, Rozanova combined the universality and severe grandeur of theoretical Suprematism with a more local dimension of beauty; she tinged the spiritual and the mystical with emotion and irony and transmuted the "*nonobjectness*" of Suprematism into *objects* of art.

1. Vasilii Katanian, ed., *V.V. Mayakovsky: Polnoe sobranie sochinenii* (Moscow: GIKhL, 1955), vol. 1, p. 397.
2. The present location of these works is unknown, and they are presumed lost. For a black-and-white reproduction of both, see *Ogonek* (Petrograd), January 3, 1916, p. 11. The George Costakis collection (Art Co. Ltd.) contains sketches for these paintings.
3. That Rozanova made this series of linocuts in 1914 (which she then incorporated into *Zaumnaia gniga*) is evident from a letter that she wrote to Andrei Shemshurin in the summer of 1915 (Manuscript Department, Russian National Library, Moscow [inv. no. f. 339, op. 5, ed. khr. 14]). In other words, the linocuts supposedly preceded the paintings on the same theme.
4. John Bowlt has explained this semantic provocation not so much as a publicity device for generating mockery and confusion as a method for transcending the contrived borders between "high" and "low." See John Bowlt, "A Brazen Can-Can in the Temple of Art: The Russian Avant-Garde and Popular Culture," in Kirk Varnedoe and Adam Gopnik, eds., *Modern Art and Popular Culture: Readings in High and Low* (New York: Abrams, 1990), pp. 135–58. For the historical derivation of the name "Jack of Diamonds," including its connection with Poncon du Terrail's adventure novel *Rocambole, le club des valets de coeur* (which everybody — "from servants to artists" — was reading), see Gleb Pospelov, *Bubnovyi valet* (Moscow: Sovetskii khudozhnik, 1990), pp. 99–100.
5. This series includes *Simultaneous Representation of Four Aces* (State Russian Museum, St. Petersburg), *Simultaneous Representation of the Queen of Spades and the Queen of Hearts* (location unknown), *Simultaneous Representation of the King of Hearts and the King of Diamonds* (Kustodiev Picture Gallery, Astrakhan), *King of Spades* (location unknown), *King of Clubs* (plate 46), *Queen of Spades* (plate 47), *Queen of Hearts* (location unknown), *Queen of Diamonds* (Nizhnii-Novgorod Art Museum), *Jack of Hearts* (plate 45), *Jack of Diamonds* (location unknown), and *Jack of Clubs* (Ivanovo-Voznesensk Art Museum). Rozanova replaced the *Queen of Hearts* and *Jack of Spades* in the linocut series by a new card — the *Jack of Hearts* — in the painting series.
6. Camilla Gray, *The Russian Experiment in Art, 1863–1922* (London: Thames and Hudson, 1962), pp. 291–92 n. 223.
7. See the letters from Rozanova to Alexei Kruchenykh [December 1915; see Documents section].
8. Kazimir Malevich, "Vystavka profsoiuza khudozhnikov-zhivopistsev: Levaia federatsiia (molodaia fraktsiia)," in *Anarkhiia* (Moscow), no. 89, 1918, unpaginated.
9. Kazimir Malevich, "Ot kubizma i futurizma k suprematizmu: Novyi zhivopisnyi realizm" (1916), in Alexandra Shatskikh and Andrei Sarabianov, eds., *Kazimir Malevich: Sobranie sochinenii*, 5 vols. (Moscow: Gileia, 1995), vol. 1, p. 50.

10. Olga Rozanova, "Cubism, Futurism, Suprematism," [see Documents section].
11. Kazimir Malevich, "Ot kubizma i futurizma k suprematizmu," p. 41.
12. Olga Rozanova, "Cubism, Futurism, Suprematism," [see Documents section].
13. Ibid.
14. Dmitrii Sarabianov, "Stankovaia zhivopis i grafik L. S. Popovoi," in *L. S. Popova*, catalogue of exhibition at the State Tretiakov Gallery, Moscow, 1990, pp. 56–57.
15. Olga Rozanova, "Cubism, Futurism, Suprematism," [see Documents section].
16. Olga Rozanova, letter to Andrei Shemshurin dated February 18, 1917. Manuscript Department, Russian National Library, Moscow (inv. no. f. 339, op. 5, ed. khr. 14).
17. Literally translated, "color-painting." It is difficult to say whether Rozanova coined the term "color-painting" or not. *Tsvetopis* (and also the word *svetopis* — "light painting," or photography) occurs in Khlebnikov's manuscripts of the 1910s.
18. Olga Rozanova, "Cubism, Futurism. Suprematism," [see Documents section].
19. *Purple Stripe*, which consisted of a diagonal purple stripe on a white background, was in the collection of the Museum of Architecture and Art, Rostovo-Yaroslavskii, in the early 1920s. However, inventory records indicate that the painting was later removed from the collection as "a work of no artistic value," and its present whereabouts is unknown.
20. Alexander Rodchenko, untitled manuscript on Rozanova in the Rodchenko-Stepanova Archive, Moscow. I would like to thank Alexander Lavrentiev for granting me access to this document.
21. See Charlotte Douglas, "Suprematist Embroidered Ornament," *Art Journal* (New York) 54, no. 1 (Spring 1995), p. 42.
22. Olga Rozanova, "Cubism, Futurism, Suprematism," [see Documents section].

OLGA VLADIMIROVNA ROZANOVA
(1886–1918)

1886	Born June 22 in Melenki, Vladimir Province, Russia.
1896–1904	Attends school in Vladimir-on-Kliazma.
1904–10	Studies at the art school of Konstantin Yuon and Ivan Dudin.
1907	Audits classes at the Bolshakov Painting and Sculpture Institute and at the Central Stroganov Industrial Art Institute, both in Moscow.
1911–13	Moves to St. Petersburg in 1911. Attends the Zvantseva Art School. In 1912, makes the acquaintance of Russian Futurist poet Alexei Kruchenykh, inventor and theoretician of *zaum* ("transrational," or nonsense realism). Maintains close association with the Union of Youth, contributing to first *Union of Youth* exhibition in St. Petersburg (1912–13) and its journal in 1913.
1913–15	Begins to illustrate a series of Cubo-Futurist books, including *Te li le* (1914) and *Zaumnaia gniga* (*Transrational Book*; 1915). In 1914, meets Marinetti in St. Petersburg, and contributes to the *Prima Esposizione Libera Futurista Internationale* in Rome.
1915	Creates fashion and textile designs, some of which she contributes to *Women Artists for the Victims of War* in Moscow. Contributes to *Tramway V* exhibition in March, to *Exhibition of Painting of Leftist Trends* in April, and to *0.10* in December, all Petrograd. Works with Kruchenykh on the album *Voina* (*War*; 1916). Moves to Moscow.
1916–17	With Kazimir Malevich, Mikhail Matiushin, Liubov Popova, Nikolai Roslavets, and others, becomes a member of the Supremus group and secretary of its journal (which was not published). Contributes to the last *Jack of Diamonds* exhibition (the fifth), which opens in Moscow in November 1916. Contributes poems to Kruchenykh's *Balos* (1917).
1918	Helps decorate the Moscow streets and squares for May Day. Becomes a member of IZO Narkompros, with Alexander Rodchenko in charge of the Art-Industry Sub-Section of IZO. Helps organize Svomas in several provincial towns. Publishes in the newspaper *Anarkhiia* (*Anarchy*). Acts as secretary of the Leftist Federation of the Professional Union of Artists and Painters and contributes to its first exhibition. Contributes to Kruchenykh's *Exhibition of Moscow Futurists* in Tiflis. Dies November 7, in Moscow. Posthumous exhibition opens

as the *First State Exhibition* in Moscow, with more than 250 pieces.

1919 Represented at the *Tenth State Exhibition: Non-Objective Creativity and Suprematism*.

1922 Represented at the *Erste russische Kunstaustellung* in Berlin.

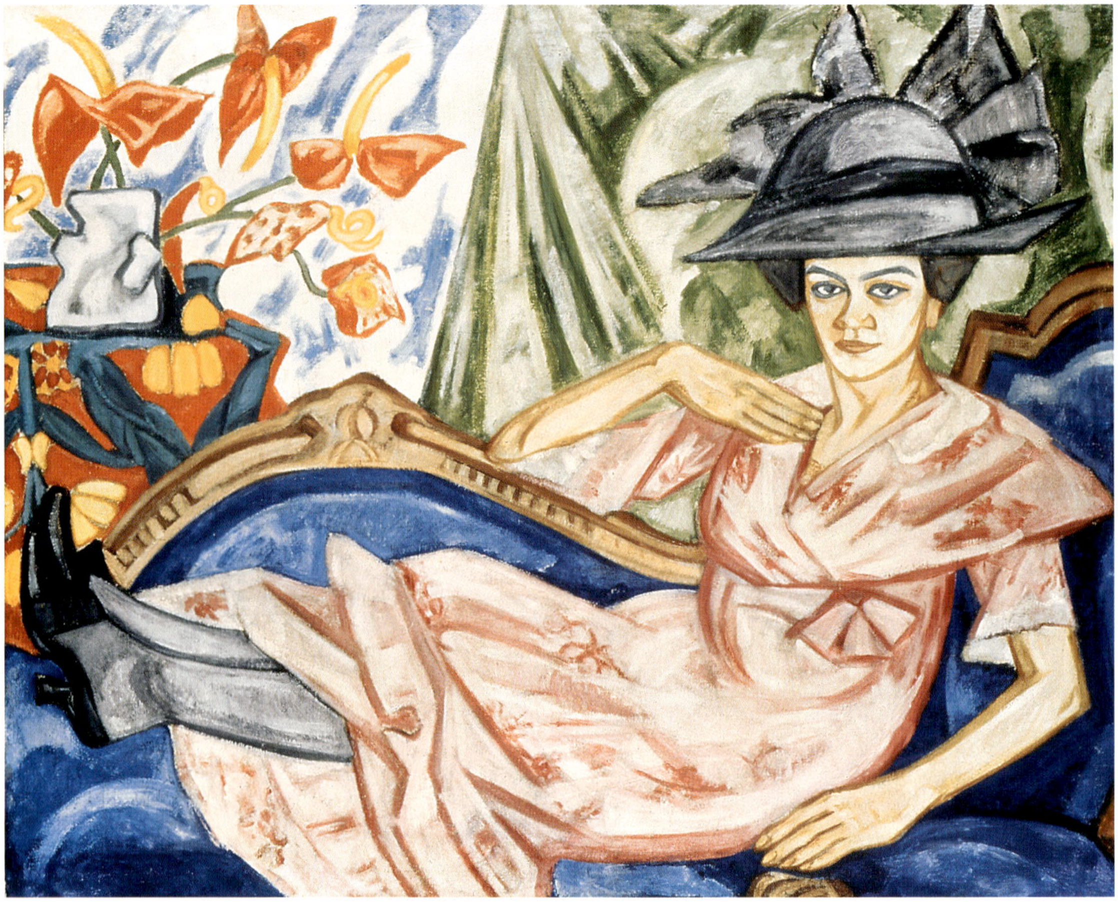

plate 42. OLGA ROZANOVA
Portrait of a Lady in Pink (Portrait of Anna Rozanova, the Artist's Sister), 1911
Oil on canvas, 113 x 139 cm
Museum of Visual Arts, Ekaterinburg

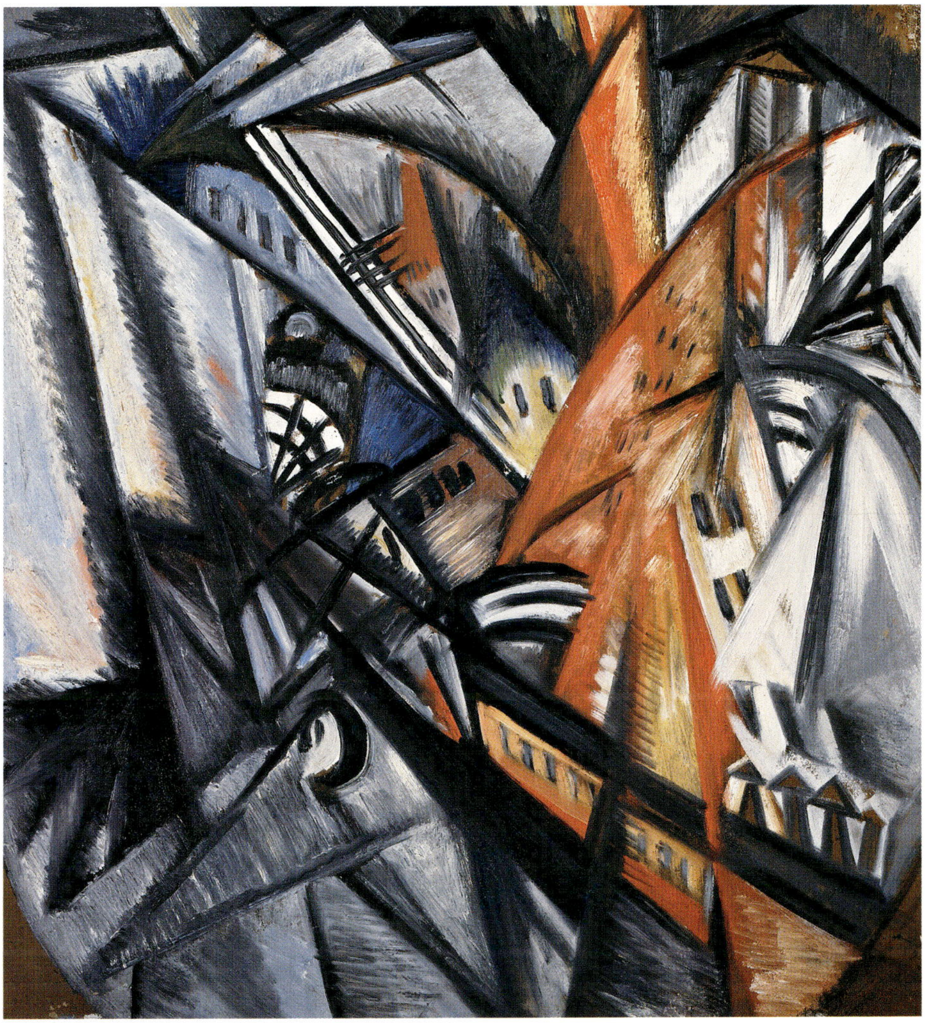

plate 43. OLGA ROZANOVA
Fire in the City (Cityscape), 1914
Oil on metal, 71 x 71 cm
Art Museum, Samara

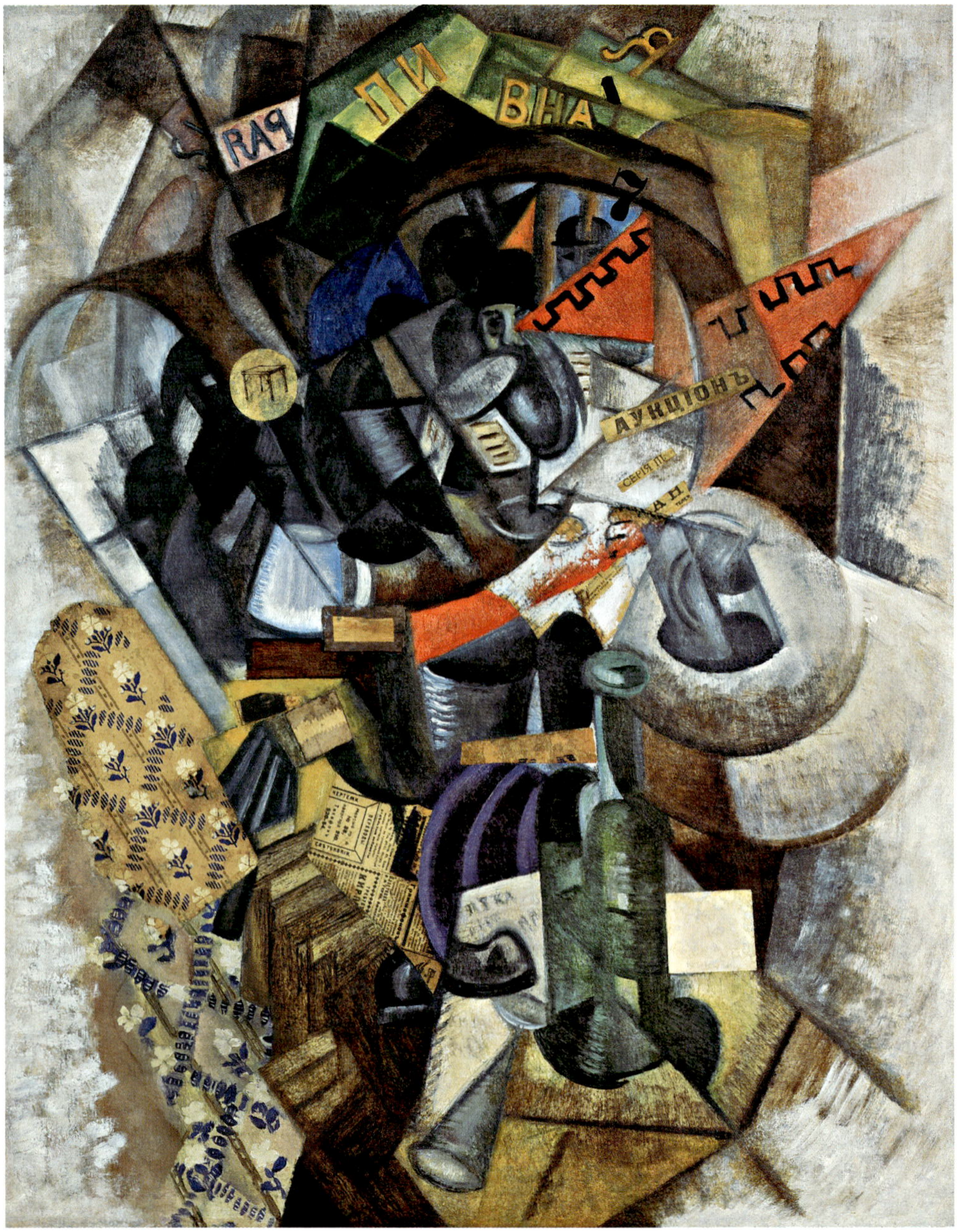

plate 44. OLGA ROZANOVA
Pub (Auction), 1914
Oil on canvas, 84 x 66 cm
State Unified Art Museum, Kostroma

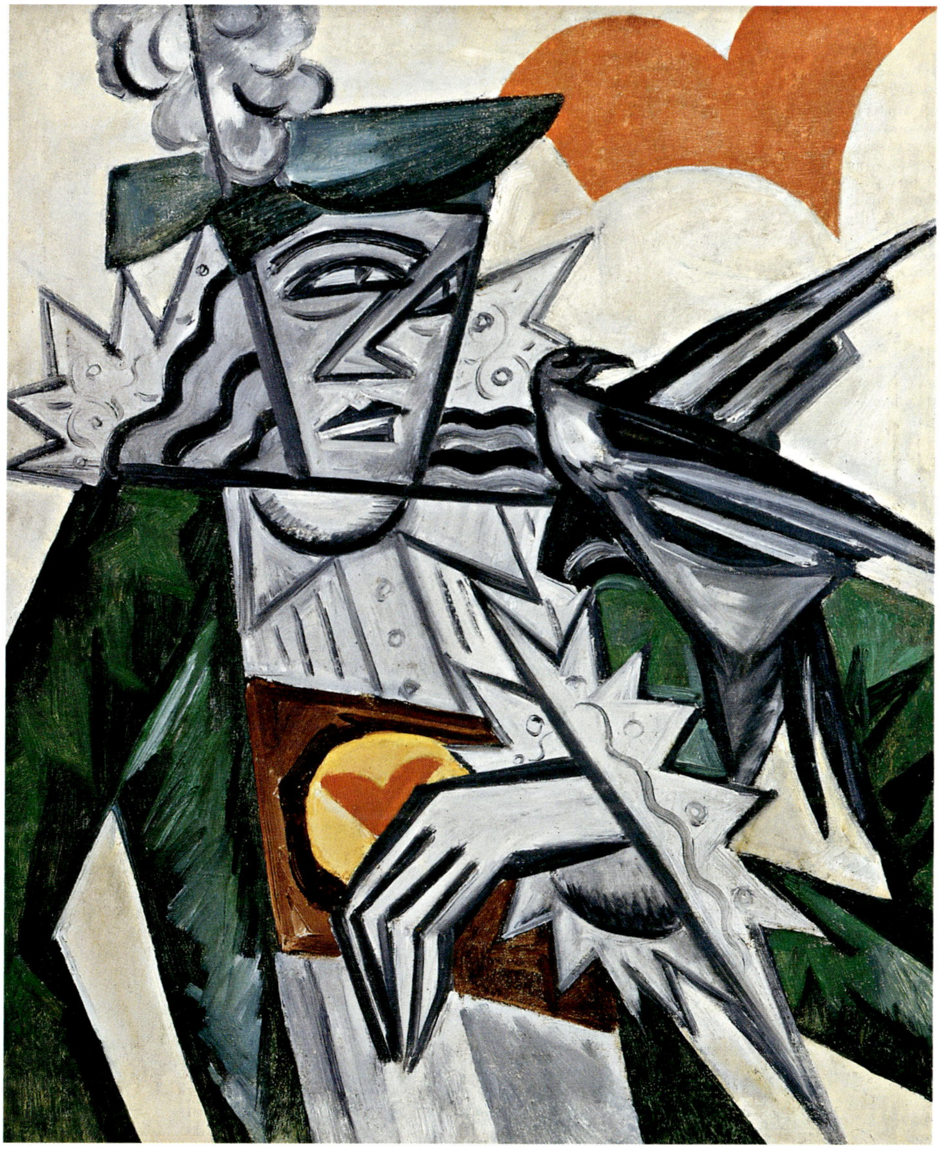

plate 45. OLGA ROZANOVA
Jack of Hearts, 1912(?)–15, from the series *Playing Cards*
Oil on canvas, 80 x 65 cm
Slobodskoi Museum and Exhibition Center

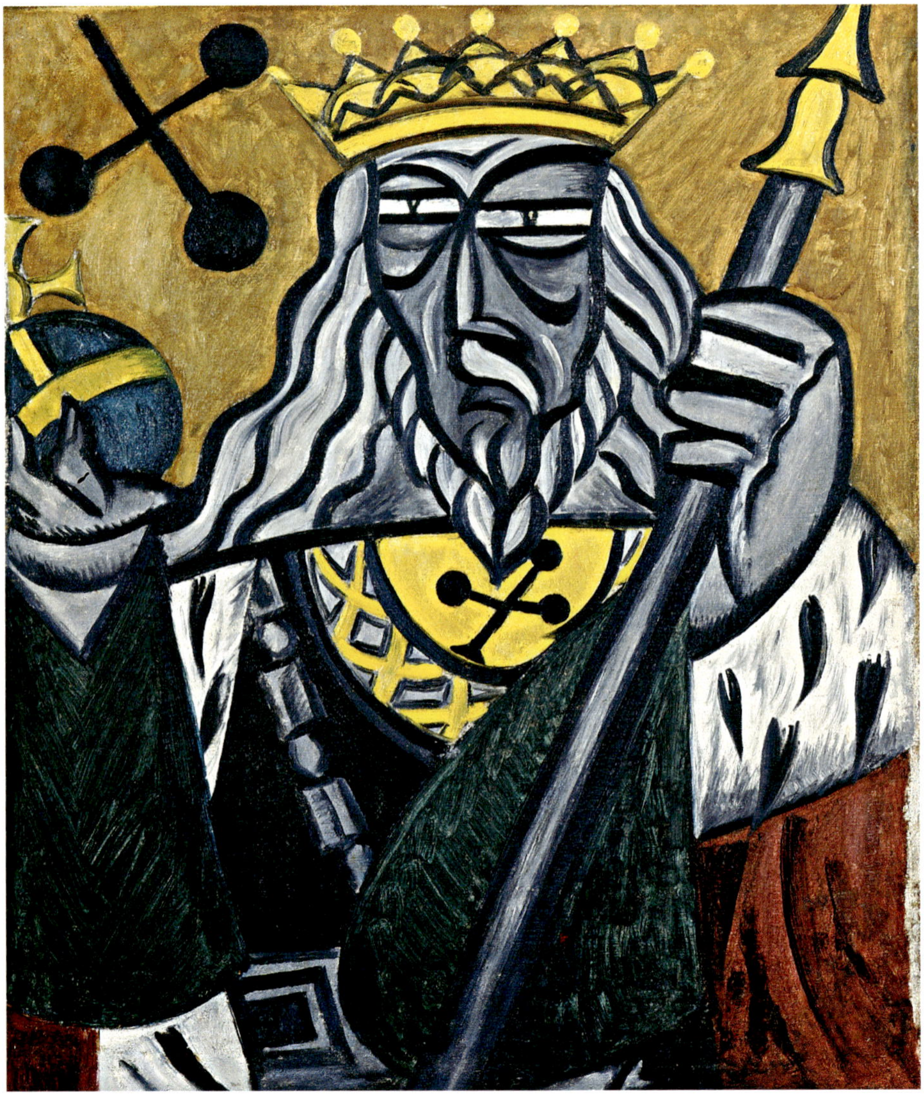

plate 46. OLGA ROZANOVA
King of Clubs, 1915, from the series *Playing Cards*
Oil on canvas, 72 x 60 cm
Slobodskoi Museum and Exhibition Center

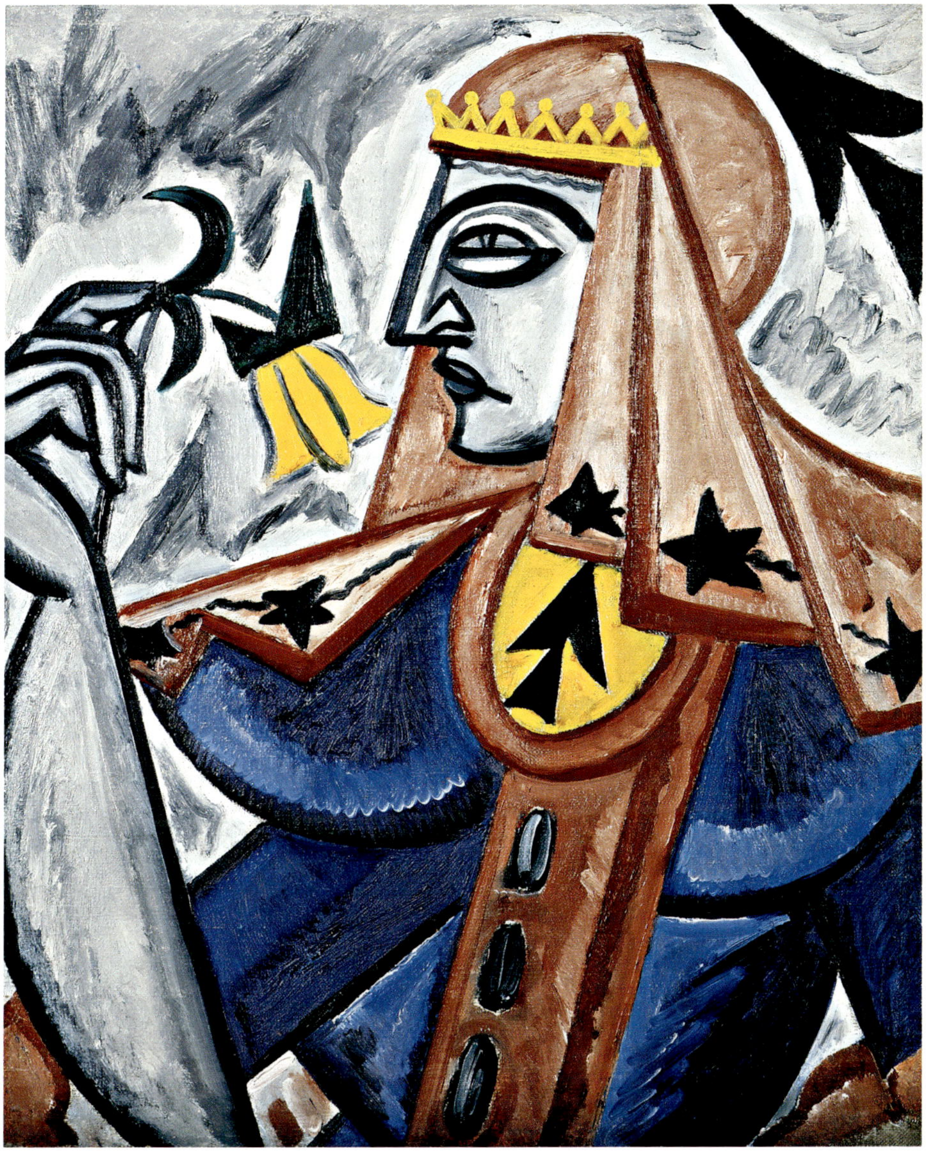

plate 47. OLGA ROZANOVA
Queen of Spades, ca. 1916, from the series *Playing Cards*
Oil on canvas, 77.5 x 61.5 cm
Art Museum, Ulyanovsk

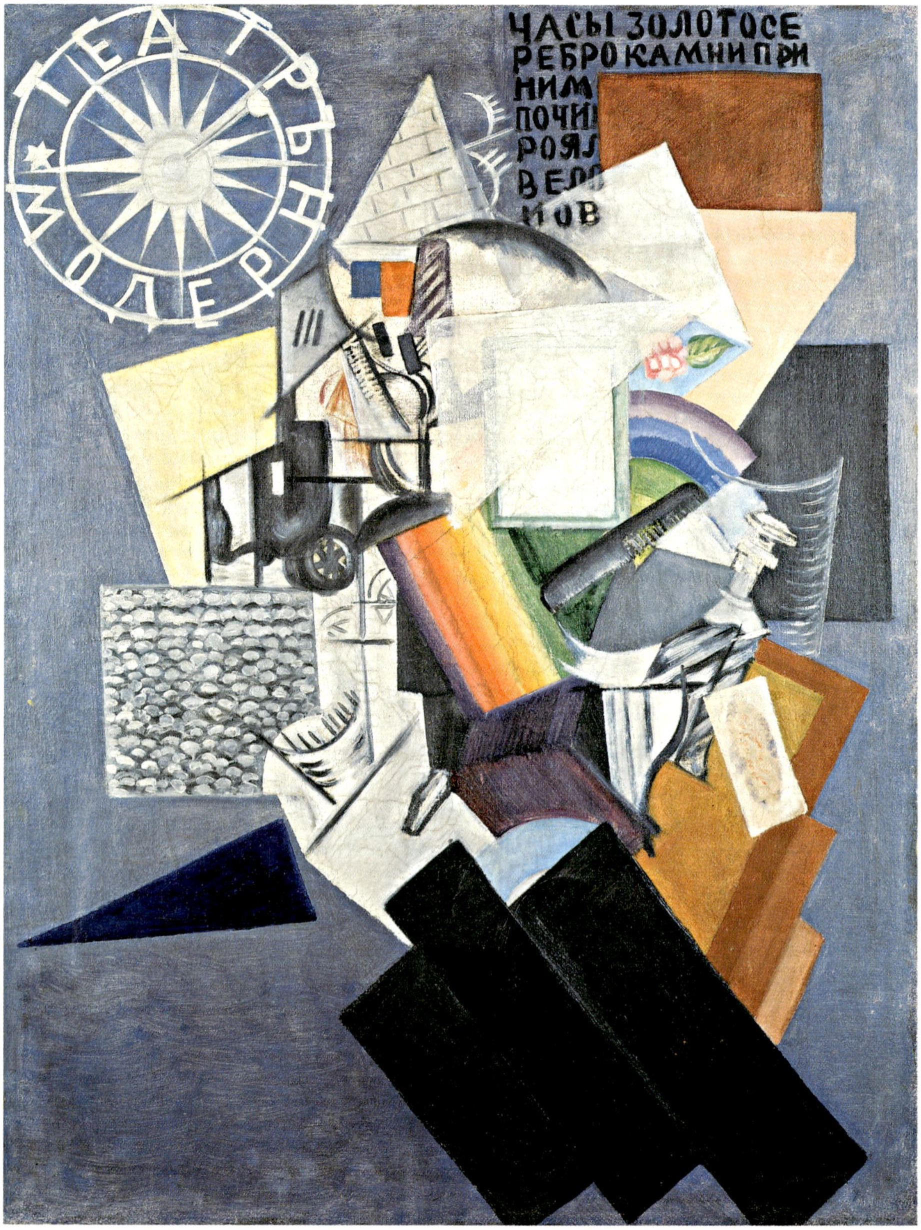

plate 48. OLGA ROZANOVA
The "Moderne" Movie Theater (In the Street), 1915
Oil on canvas, 101 x 77 cm
Slobodskoi Museum and Exhibition Center

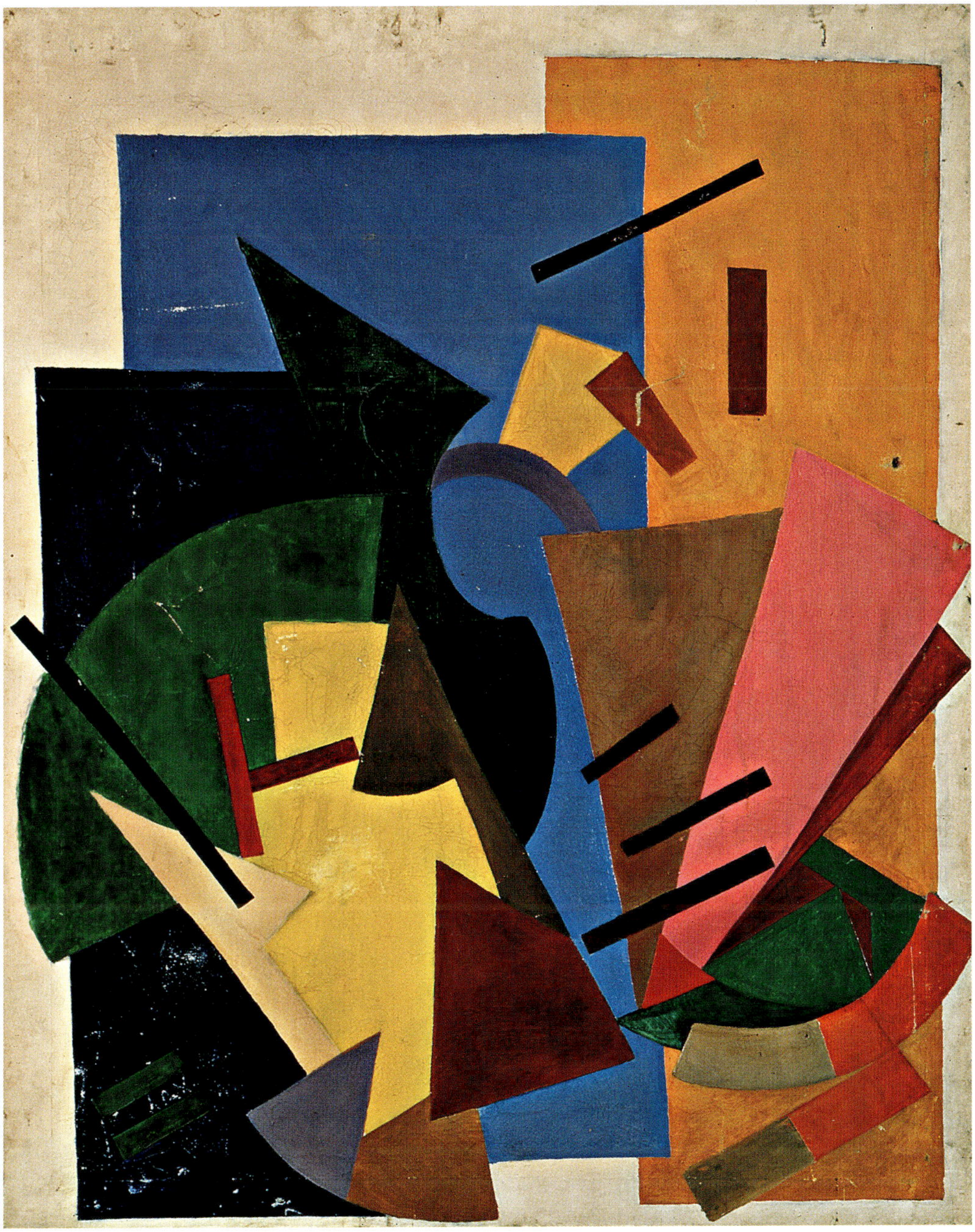

plate 49. OLGA ROZANOVA
Non-Objective Composition (Flight of an Airplane), 1916
Oil on canvas, 118 x 101 cm
Art Museum, Samara

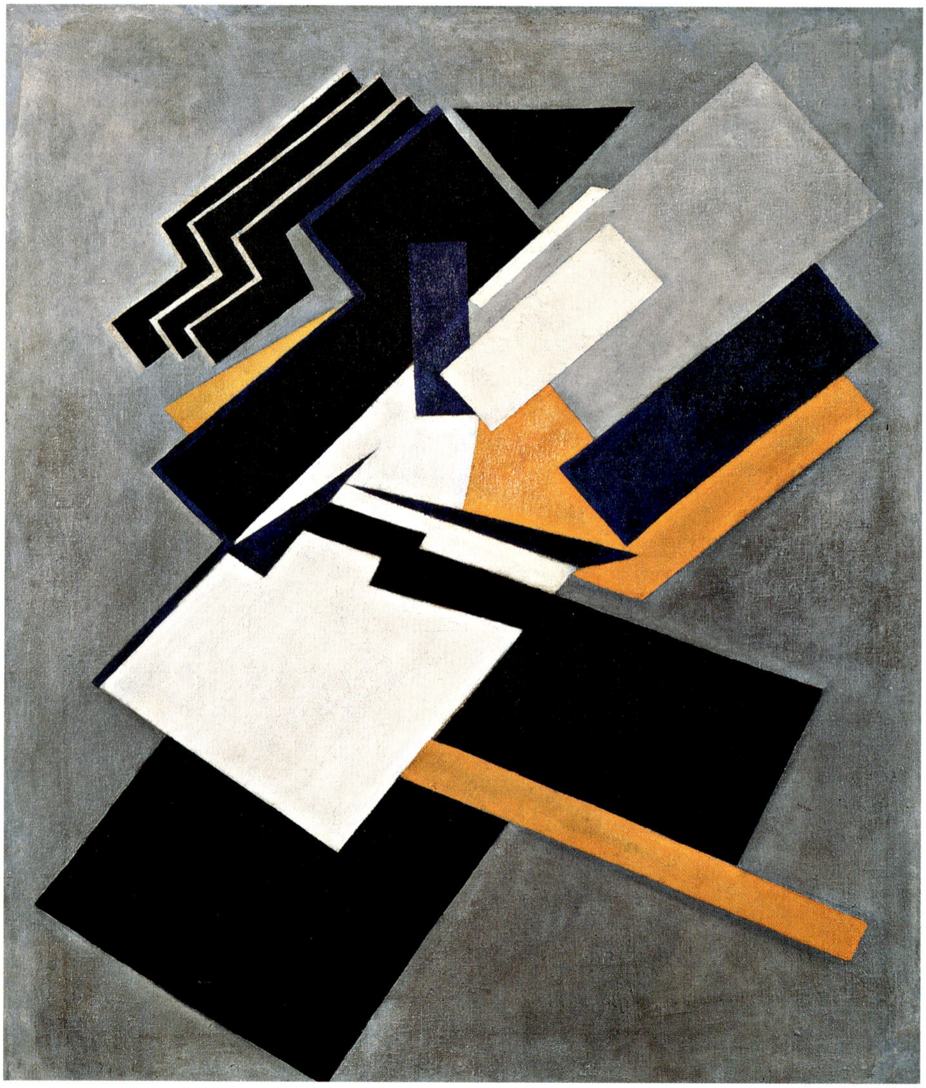

plate 50. OLGA ROZANOVA
Non-Objective Composition (Suprematism), 1916
Oil on canvas, 90 x 74 cm
Museum of Visual Arts, Ekaterinburg

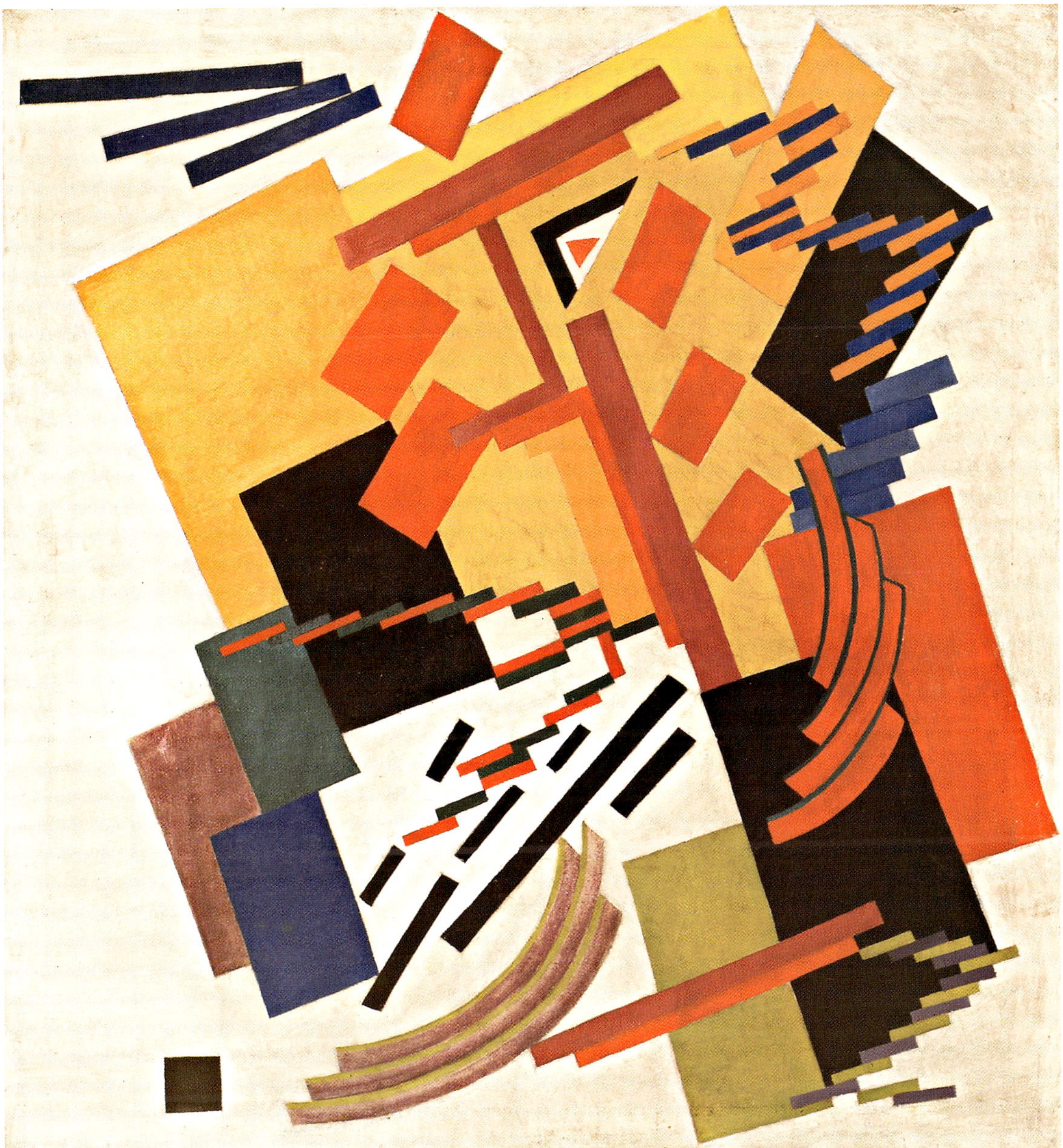

plate 51. OLGA ROZANOVA
Non-Objective Composition (Suprematism), 1916
Oil on canvas, 102 x 94 cm
Museum of Visual Arts, Ekaterinburg

plate 52. OLGA ROZANOVA
Color Painting (Non-Objective Composition), 1917
Oil on canvas, 62.5 x 40.5 cm
State Russian Museum, St. Petersburg

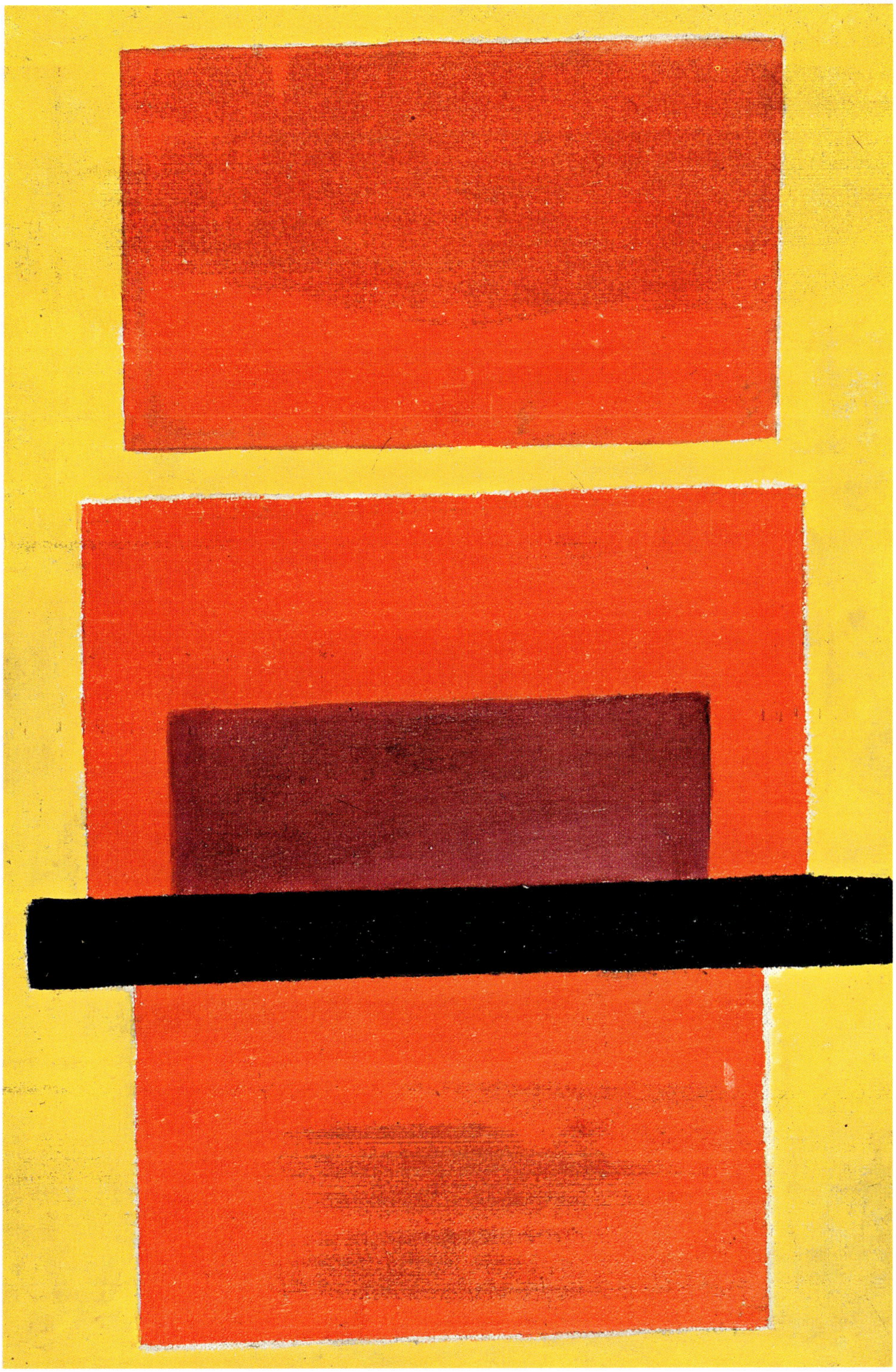

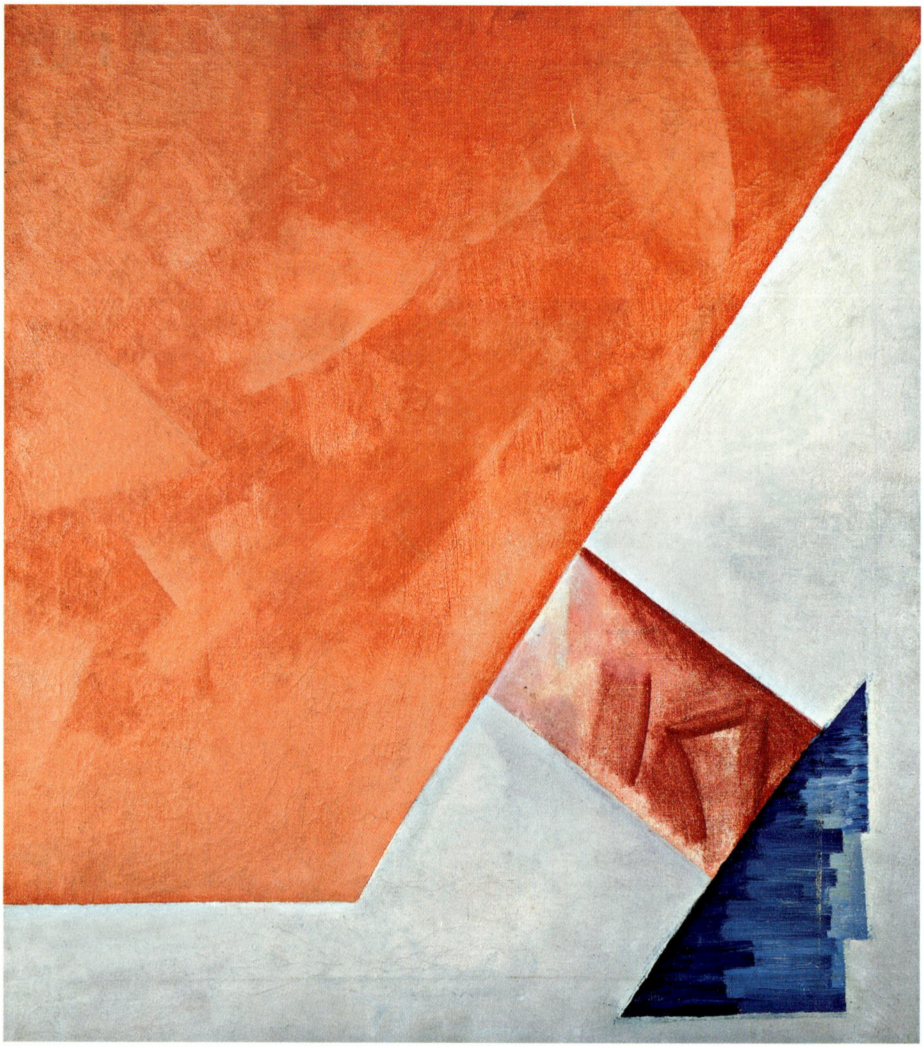

above:
plate 53. OLGA ROZANOVA
Non-Objective Composition (Color Composition), 1917
Oil on canvas, 71 x 64 cm
Regional Art Museum, Ulyanovsk

facing page:
plate 54. OLGA ROZANOVA
Green Stripe (Color Painting), 1917
Oil on canvas, 71.5 x 49 cm
Rostov Kremlin State Museum Preserve

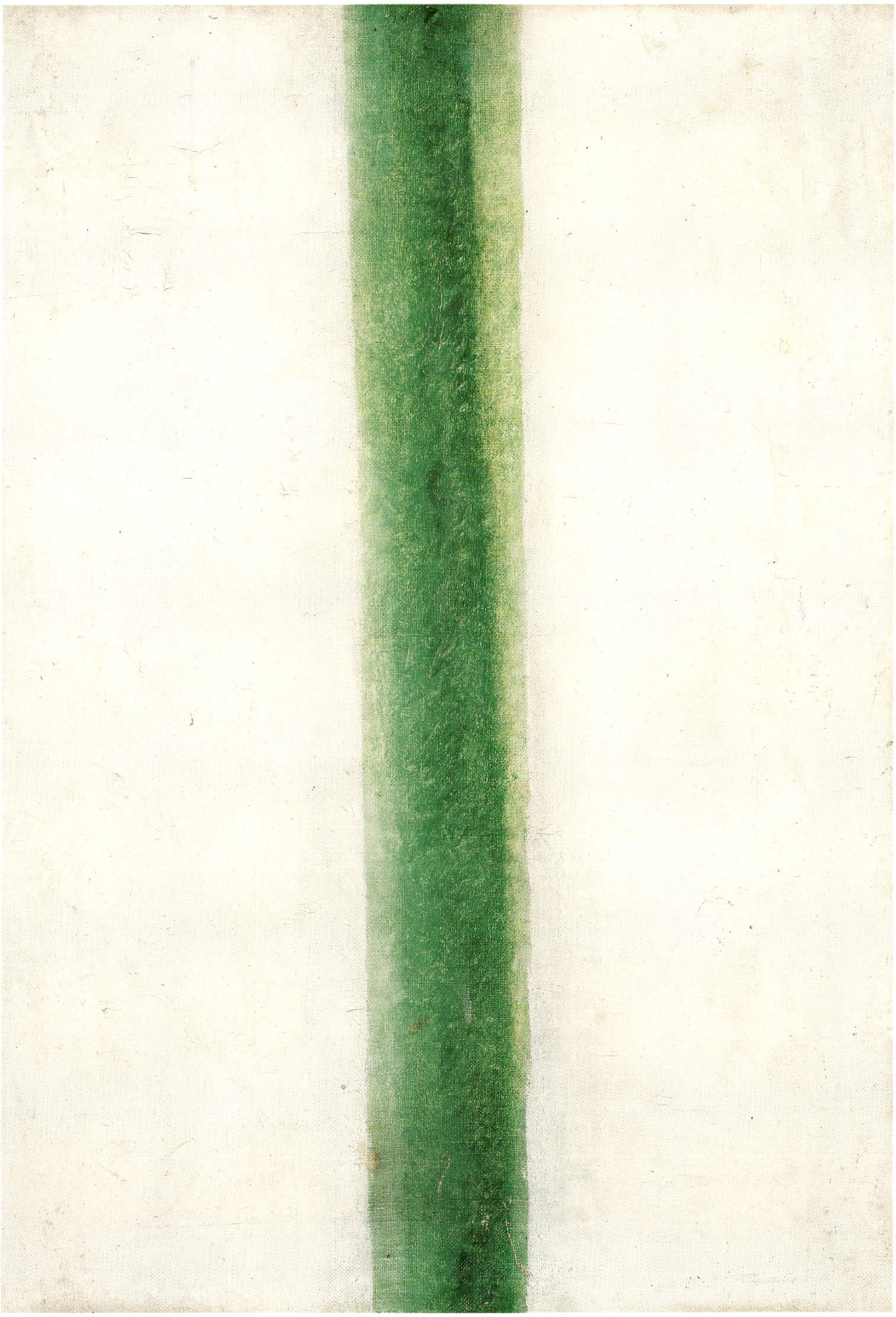

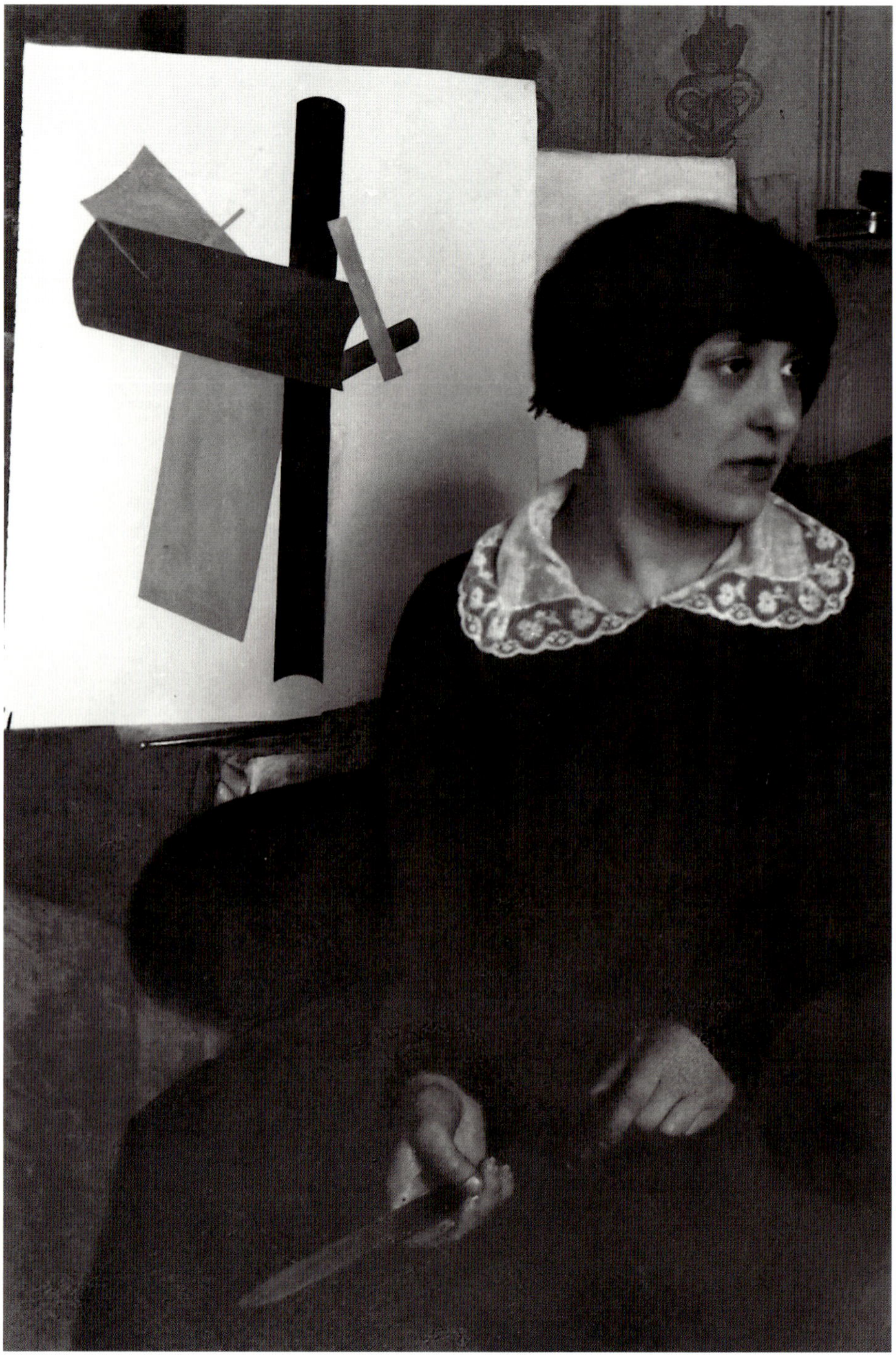

figure 69. Varvara Stepanova, Moscow, 1916.

Varvara Stepanova

Alexander Lavrentiev

The "Frenzied" Stepanova: Between Analysis and Synthesis

Convinced that inventive (analytical) and synthetic (combinatory) capabilities reflected different kinds of creative thought, Alexander Rodchenko, Varvara Stepanova's husband, used to divide artists into two groups, analysts and synthesists.[1] Rodchenko classified the work of Kazimir Malevich, Olga Rozanova, and his own as analytical, and regarded that of Alexander Drevin and Ivan Kliun, for example, as synthetic. "Synthesists" know how to take the aesthetic components and potentially useful ideas discovered by other inventors and apply them to specific fields of creativity such as the theater, the printing arts, and design. They can assemble a new style out of the many possibilities discovered in the course of their own experiments, although, of course, any artist is bound to resolve both analytic and synthetic issues — and Stepanova was no exception.

Born in 1894, Stepanova, who was of a generation later than the pioneers of the avant-garde, moved rapidly from Impressionism and Cézannism to Neo-Primitivism, Cubism, Futurism, and, finally, abstract art. That is one reason why Stepanova was able to synthesize easily — for example, she integrated non-objective graphic art and transrational poetry, geometric abstraction and figures, and combined many systems in her work for the theater, printing, and design. In the late 1910s and early 1920s, Stepanova worked closely with the non-objective

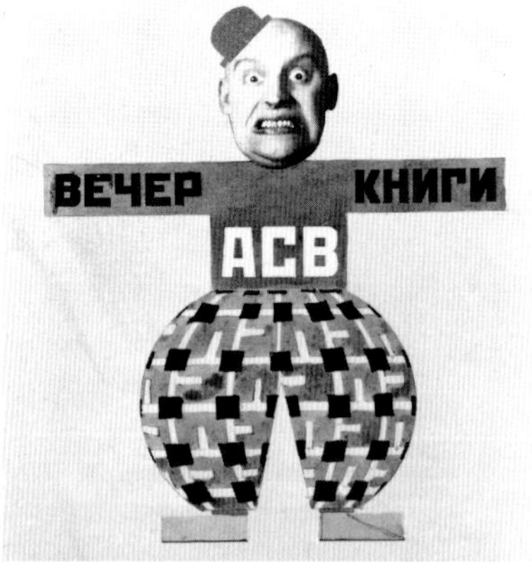

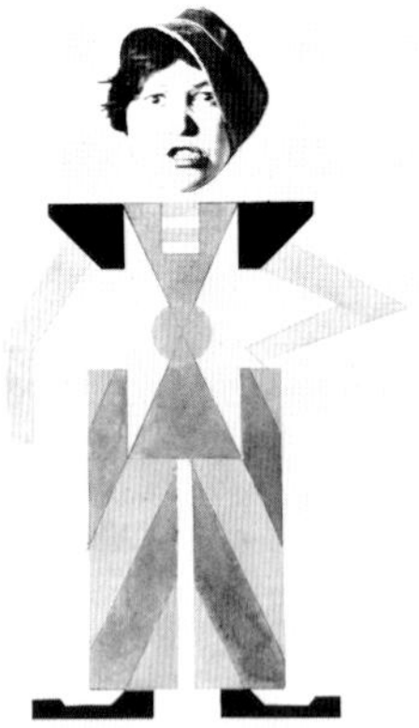

far left:
figure 70. varvara stepanova
Caricature of Alexander Rodchenko as a Clown, 1923
Watercolor, pencil, and photographic collage, 27.5 x 27.5 cm
Private collection

left:
figure 71. varvara stepanova
Self-Caricature as a Clown, 1923
Watercolor, pencil, and photographic collage, 34.5 x 25.5 cm
Private collection

painters, even though she had had no real Cubist or Futurist training,[2] and in 1917–18 she experimented with non-objective art herself; a year later, however, she turned back to the human figure, though in a spare, geometric style. Among the earliest artworks by Stepanova that have come down to us is a printed silk book marker (1909), a tempera study of a rose. Another composition, a fragment of a canvas dated 1912 (when she was studying at the Kazan Art Institute), depicts two female figures in luxurious dresses with bright stripes of colored fabric and decorative sequins.

Stepanova cannot be understood without Rodchenko, and vice versa. They were a creative team, and although Stepanova may be considered Rodchenko's student, she guarded her independence jealously (figs. 70, 71). Turning to the past seemed pointless to her, for during the 1920s the artists of the left followed only one vector — the future. Rodchenko wrote: "Innovators of all times and countries, inventors, constructors of the new, the eternally new, we rush into the infinity of conquests."[3] Rodchenko and Stepanova met in Kazan in 1914, but at first they expressed their sentiments only in intimate poems and letters. The inscription in one of her albums of verses and drawings reads: "King of my reveries and dreams . . . Verses of V.S., 23 November, 1914." The "king" is Rodchenko. This album includes an elegant portrait of Rodchenko and of the queen herself, surrounded by flowers and two moons. The style is that of Aubrey Beardsley, whose work Rodchenko and Stepanova knew from Russian publications.

The Russian Cubo-Futurists (David Burliuk, Vasilii Kamensky, Velimir Khlebnikov, Alexei Kruchenykh, Vladimir Mayakovsky, and others) tried to combine words and images in many different ways. They experimented with various typefaces and with automatic writing, assumed the double role of artist and writer, and investigated phonetic experiments with alliteration of voiceless and voiced consonants. Rozanova was especially interested in stress variation and rhythmic repetition, as demonstrated by this example:

Zbrzhest zdeban
zhbzmets etta
zhmuts dekhkha
umerets
ittera.[4]

Stepanova, however, tried to unite the phonetic texture of a text with its written texture. In her non-objective poetry you sometimes sense a coarse phonic texture as in "Shukh taz khkon," and other times a delicate melodic texture, as in "Fianta chiol":

Afta iur inka
nair prazi
Taveniu lirka
taiuz fai
O male totti
O le maiaft
izva leiatti
Ifta liiard.[5]

As Stepanova affirmed: "I am connecting the new movement of non-objective verse as sound and letter with painterly perception and this infuses a new living, visual impression into the sound of verse. . . . I am approaching a new form of creation. However, in reproducing the painterly and graphic non-objective poetry of [my] two books — *Zigra Ar* and *Rtny Khomle* [both 1918], I introduce sound as a new quality into the painting of the graphic element and thereby increase the latter's possibilities quantitatively."[6]

The variable scale of the letters and their free distribution and orientation — all this deliberately hindered the reading of the text, as Kruchenykh and Khlebnikov explained in their 1913 brochure, *The Word as Such*.[7] In Stepanova's compositions, color plays an analogous role: some letters seem to be close, others far; some are warm, others cold; the color of the letters and forms, on the one hand, and the timbre and type of sound, on the other, make for a complex aural and visual interaction. When the elements of color, form, sound, and sign all appear together, the result is equivalent to densely layered orchestration, with all the components perceived simultaneously[8] (see plates 59–64), rather as Blaise Cendrars and the Delaunays were doing with their Simultanism.

Stepanova contributed eight works to the *Fifth State Exhibition* in 1918–19: four illustrations to Kruchenykh's *Gly-Gly* (fig. 72) and a composition of letters and abstract forms on pages pasted into her handwritten book *Rtny Kholme*. She signed these works "Varst" (i.e., Varvara Stepanova). At the *Tenth State Exhibition: Non-Objective Creativity and Suprematism* in 1919, Stepanova contributed more than thirty illustrations to *Gly-Gly* and two series of color prints, also from *Zigra Ar* and

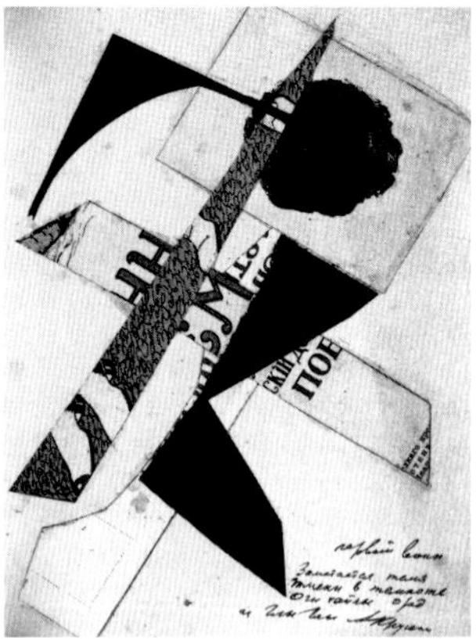

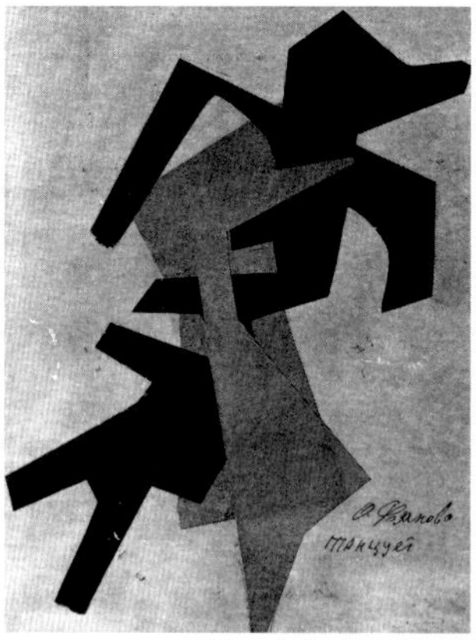

far left:
figure 72. VARVARA STEPANOVA
Illustration for Alexei Kruchenykh's *Gly-Gly*, 1918
Collage and india ink on paper, 15.5 x 11 cm
Private collection

left:
figure 73. VARVARA STEPANOVA
Rozanova Dancing, 1918–19
Collage, 15.5 x 11 cm
Private collection

Rtny Khomle. The *Gly-Gly* illustrations are visual parodies of many representatives of the Russian avant-garde arranged on medium-size sheets of thin white cardboard and carrying references to Malevich's *Black Square*, Kliun's Suprematism, a musical imitation of Mikhail Matiushin, the painterly planes of Popova, and a very unstable composition called *Rozanova Dancing* (fig. 73). But the same year Stepanova went even further by creating a completely new book object — titled *Gaust chaba* — in a press run of fifty copies. She wrote the verses by hand on sheets of newspaper in large black letters running across the newsprint and made non-objective collages on some of the pages.

During the first post-Revolutionary years, Rodchenko and Stepanova had no permanent apartment. They either rented a room, or lived in the Kandinsky family house or at the Museum of Painterly Culture, where in 1920 Rodchenko had been appointed curator of the collection of contemporary art, assisted by Stepanova (the Museum was in the courtyard of 14 Volkhonka Street, now the Museum of Private Collections, which includes the paintings and graphic works by Rodchenko and Stepanova). The *Tenth State Exhibition* was a watershed in the artistic careers of Stepanova and her colleagues Drevin, Popova, Rodchenko, and Nadezhda Udaltsova.

By the summer of 1919, Stepanova was emphasizing a formal tendency that, in 1921, would be called Contructivist. She had moved from synthesis to analysis. In her linocuts of 1919, Stepanova explored the expressive possibilities of line and combinations of geometric forms. From the fall of 1919 through 1921, she produced a figural series of paintings and graphic compositions using a stencil and outlining contours with a ruler or a compass. The head is always a circle, while the torso, arms, and legs are rectangles. In her compositions of the 1920s, Stepanova, like Rodchenko, also used the technique of the semi-dry brush, something that generated a homogeneous color texture as if from a sprayer. Unlike a spray texture, however, this technique was more malleable and allowed the artist to model large and small forms. In several drawings, Stepanova employed another tool — the toothed wheel dipped in paint which left a repeating pattern of points on the

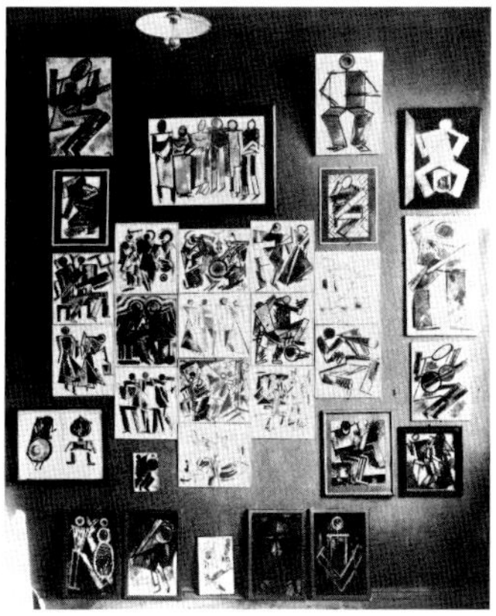

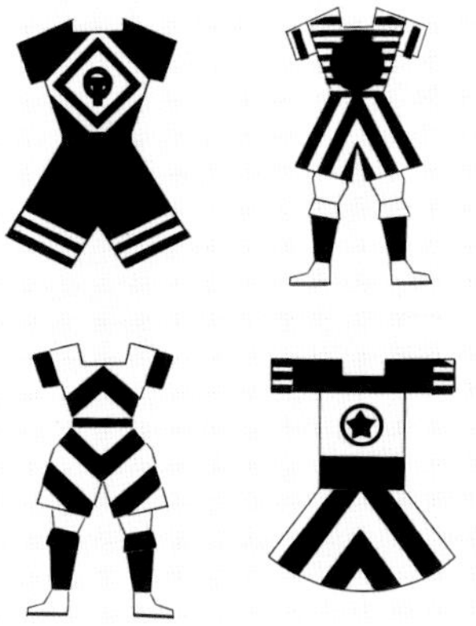

far left:
figure 74. Works by Stepanova in the studio she shared with Alexander Rodchenko, Moscow, 1921.

left:
figure 75. VARVARA STEPANOVA
Design for Sports Clothing, 1924
Gouache and india ink,
30.2 x 21.7 cm
Private collection

paper. This little wheel was nothing more than a standard tailor's tool for pressing, which she utilized to press a design onto fabric. Stepanova, who knew how to cut fabric, sewed dresses for herself and for Rodchenko's mother, and put together the Rodchenko production outfit. Stepanova regarded any medium or set of tools as possessing a potential for some creative use, whether her Corona typewriter (at one time Stepanova earned her living as a factory accountant), her Singer sewing machine (which to this day still works), or a tailor's instruments.

In her paintings, Stepanova presented a universal type of human figure with a logical, mechanized structure that recalls a child's Lego constructions or her own cardboard dolls for the cartoon booklets that she made in 1926 for Sergei Tretiakov's verses for children, i.e., *Auto-Animals* (*Samozveri*). She first showed the *Figures* series at the *Nineteenth State Exhibition* in Moscow (at the end of 1920), where Rodchenko and Stepanova filled an entire hall with their paintings and graphics. The catalogue for that show includes twenty-one oils and fifty-three graphic pieces by Stepanova, the subjects being music, sports, and even the ballet. The exhibition proved to be an important one for Stepanova. Vasilii Kandinsky, playing with the words "Varvara" and "varvarism," coined the term "varvaric art" for some of the works she was making at that time. Some observers found that Stepanova's paintings were more "masculine" than those of Rodchenko.

By 1921, many Russian artists were becoming increasingly interested in the notion of construction. Karel Ioganson, Konstantin Medunetsky, Rodchenko, and Georgii and Vladimir Stenberg made their first free-standing sculptures, and Stepanova, too, demonstrated her own understanding of the Constructivist idea. She no longer simply searched for schematic, anatomical principles, but tried to convey the structural nature of the head, the torso, and the figure as a whole. Collector and commentator George Costakis aptly called these works "robots."[9]

Together with Rodchenko and the other three participants in the *5 x 5 = 25* exhibition, Stepanova announced her decisive move from easel painting to production art in September 1921. Terms such as "construction," "production," "engineering," "technology," and "object" predominated in their discussions

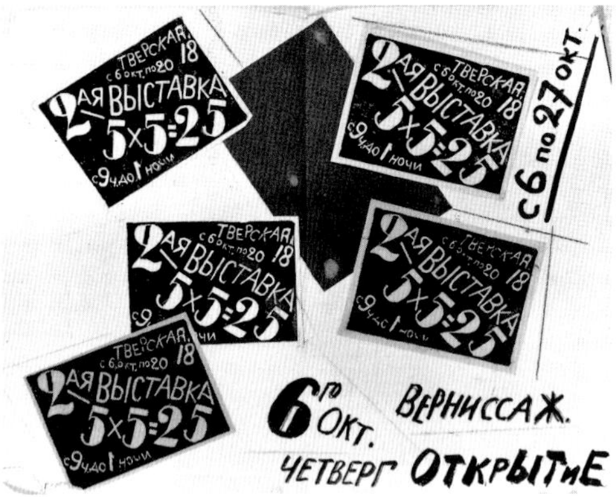

figure 76. varvara stepanova
Poster for the second part of the
5 x 5 = 25 exhibition, Moscow, 1921
Collage, india ink, and pencil on paper,
36 x 44.5 cm
Private collection

during this period. The first part of *5 x 5 = 25* consisted of painting, while the second part (which opened two weeks later) consisted mainly of graphic works. Rodchenko contributed his construction projects and, as an example of practical fabrication, several designs for lamps, Popova designs for constructions, and Stepanova her last *Figures* (plates 72, 73). At that time, Stepanova was teaching art at the Krupskaia Academy of Social (Communist) Education[10] and was a member of its Institute of Aesthetic Education, where she gave particular attention to children's art. As a result, Stepanova moved from the geometric construction of form to the primitive and the spontaneous. Indeed, some of her figures resemble totems, although once during an Inkhuk discussion, Vladimir Stenberg called them "tadpoles."[11]

After *5 x 5 = 25*, Popova and then Stepanova joined Vsevolod Meierkhold's Theater of the Revolution as stage designers. Constructivism as a theory, a practical application, and a utopian project was just asserting itself. Rodchenko and Stepanova also became members of Inkhuk, where one of her duties was to record the protocols of the meetings and discussions, and they also took part in the debates around the journal *Lef* (*Left Front of the Arts*). What Mayakovsky once said of her is very suggestive: in a copy of his book *Liubliu* (*I Love*) which he presented to Stepanova, the poet wrote: "To the 'Frenzied' Stepanova with heartfelt feelings."[12]

1. Stepanova recorded Rodchenko's thoughts about "synthesists" and "analysts" in an entry in her diary in 1919. See Vladimir Rodchenko and Alexander Lavrentiev, eds., *Varvara Stepanova: Chelovek ne mozhet zhit bez chuda. Pisma. Poeticheskie opyty. Zapiski khudozhnitsy* (Moscow: Sfera, 1994), pp. 77–78, 89.
2. One point of view holds that together with the Non-Objectivist circle of artists (Popova, Rodchenko, Rozanova, and Udaltsova), Stepanova followed Malevich in her researches; see Evgenii Kovtun, "Put Malevicha," in *Malevich*, catalogue of exhibition at the State Russian Museum, Leningrad [St. Petersburg], 1989, p. 16. This assertion needs serious qualification: the Non-Objectivists were united with Malevich in their refusal to imitate nature, but they did not adhere to the system of Suprematism.
3. Alexander Rodchenko, "Iz manifesta suprematistov i bespredmetnikov" (1919), in

O. V. Melnikov and V. I. Shchenikov, eds., *Alexander Rodchenko: Opyty dlia budushchego* (Moscow: Grant, 1996), p. 67.

4. Olga Rozanova, untitled poem dated June 8, 1916. Manuscript in the Rodchenko-Stepanova Archive, Moscow.
5. Varvara Stepanova, "Bespredmetnye stikhi, 1918–1919," in Rodchenko and Lavrentiev, eds., *Varvara Stepanova*, pp. 41–47.
6. V. Agrarykh [a one-time pseudonym of Stepanova, invented as a kind of "non-objective" word], "O vystavlennykh grafikakh," in *X Gosudarstvennaia vystavka*, catalogue of exhibition, Moscow, 1919.
7. Quoted in N. Khardzhiev, "Mayakovsky i zhivopis," in N. Khardzhiev and T. Grits, *Mayakovsky: Materialy i issledovaniia* (Moscow: Giz, 1950), p. 380.
8. Ibid.
9. Angelica Zander Rudenstine, ed., *Russian Avant-Garde Art: The George Costakis Collection* (New York: Abrams, 1981).
10. In 1931 the Krupskaia Academy of Social (Communist) Education was renamed the Krupskaia Moscow Regional Pedagogical Institute.
11. Unpublished typescript. Rodchenko-Stepanova Archive, Moscow.
12. Mayakovsky also gave Stepanova a copy of his book *Voina i mir* (*War and Peace*), in which he wrote the following dedication: "To Comrade Stepanova in memory of the attack on Friche. V. Mayakovsky." Vladimir Maximovich Friche (1870–1929) was a Marxist historian of literature and art.

varvara fedorovna stepanova
(1894–1958)

1894	Born November 5, in Kovno (Kaunas), Lithuania.
1910–14	Studies at the Kazan Art Institute, where she meets Alexander Rodchenko. Moves to Moscow. Studies under Mikhail Leblan, Ilia Mashkov, and Konstantin Yuon.
1914	Attends the Stroganov Art Institute, Moscow. Gives private art lessons. Exhibits at the Moscow Salon.
1915–17	Works as an accountant and secretary in a factory. Resumes studies with Leblan and Yuon. Begins living with Rodchenko in Moscow (1916).
1917	Experiments with non-objective art and begins to create experimental non-objective visual poetry.
1918	Produces non-objective graphic poems such as *Zigra Ar* and *Rtny Khomle*. Contributes to the *First Exhibition of Paintings of the Young Leftist Federation of the Professional Union of Artists and Painters* and the *Fifth State Exhibition*. Becomes involved with IZO NKP (Visual Arts Section of the People's Commissariat for Enlightenment).
1919	Contributes to the *Tenth State Exhibition: Non-Objective Creativity and Suprematism*. Illustrates Alexei Kruchenykh's book *Gly-Gly*. Begins making works in a style that by 1921 came to be known as Constructivism.
1920–23	Participates in discussions and activities of Inkhuk, in Moscow, as a member and, in 1920–21, as research secretary.
1921	Contributes to the exhibition *5 x 5 = 25*.
1920–25	Teaches at the Krupskaia Academy of Social (Communist) Education.
1922	Makes collages for the journal *Kino-fot*. Designs sets and costumes for Vsevolod Meierkhold's production of *The Death of Tarelkin* at the Theater of the Revolution. Makes a series of linocuts on the subject of Charlie Chaplin.
1923–28	Closely involved with the journals *Lef* (*Left Front of the Arts*) and *Novyi lef* (*New Left Front of the Arts*).
1924–25	Works for the First State Textile Factory in Moscow as a designer, and teaches in the Textile Department of Vkhutemas.

1925	Contributes to the *Exposition Internationale des Arts Décoratifs et Industriels Modernes* in Paris.
1926–32	Works predominantly as a book and journal designer, fulfilling major government commissions.
1930s–50s	Continues to paint, design, and exhibit.
1941–42	Lives in Perm.
1958	Dies May 20, in Moscow.

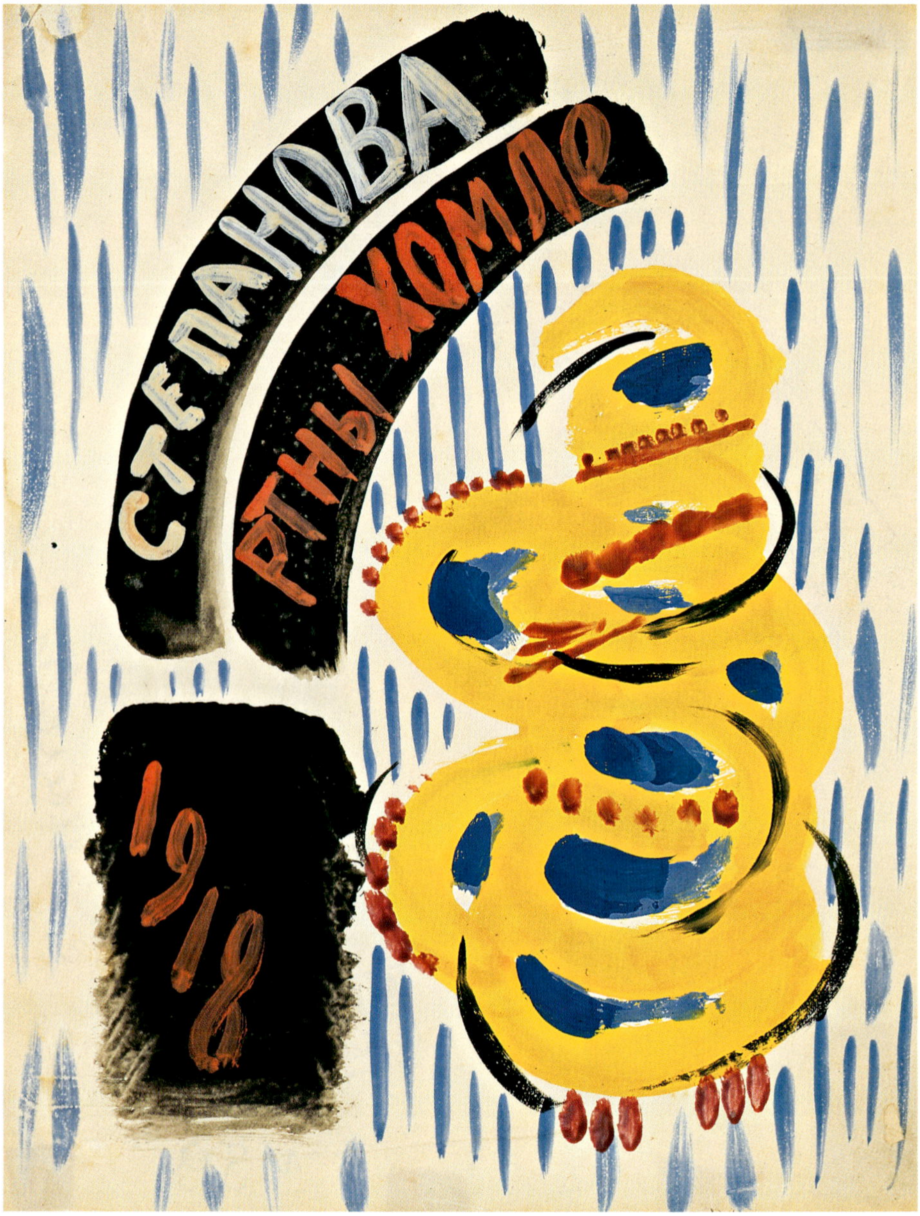

plate 55. VARVARA STEPANOVA
Illustration for the poem "Rtny Khomle," 1918
Watercolor on paper, 23.3 x 17.7 cm
Private collection

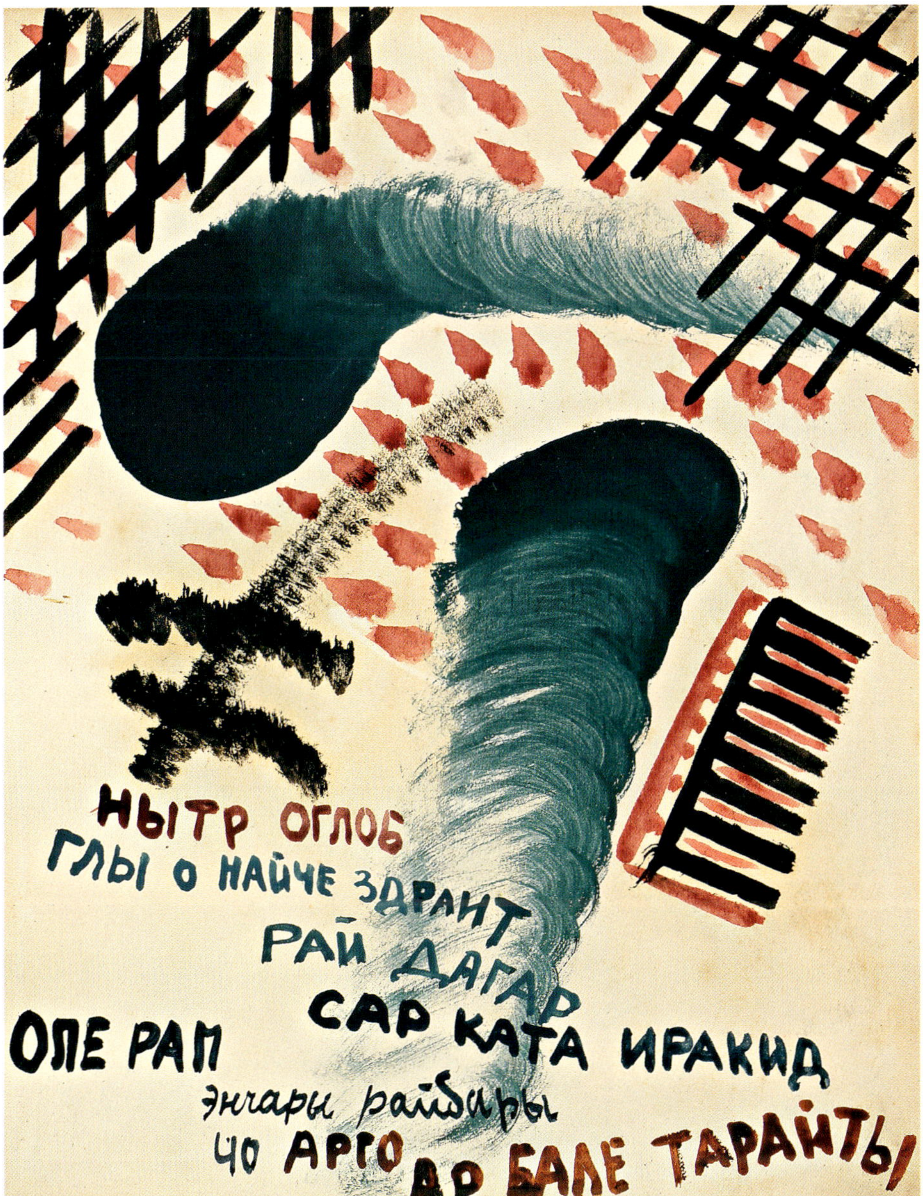

plate 56. varvara stepanova
Illustration for the poem "Rtny Khomle," 1918
Watercolor on paper, 23.3 x 17.7 cm
Private collection

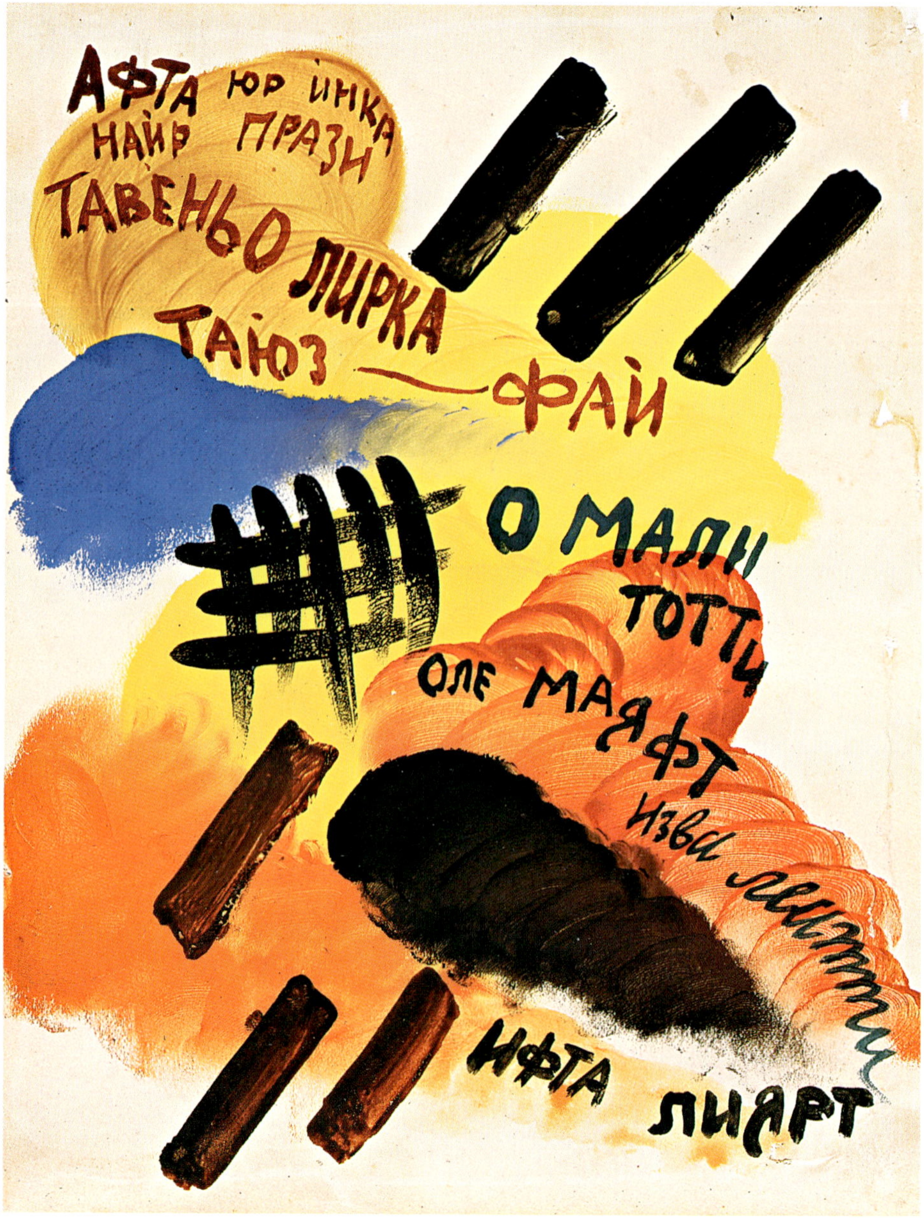

plate 57. VARVARA STEPANOVA
Illustration for the poem "Rtny Khomle," 1918
Watercolor on paper, 23.3 x 17.7 cm
Private collection

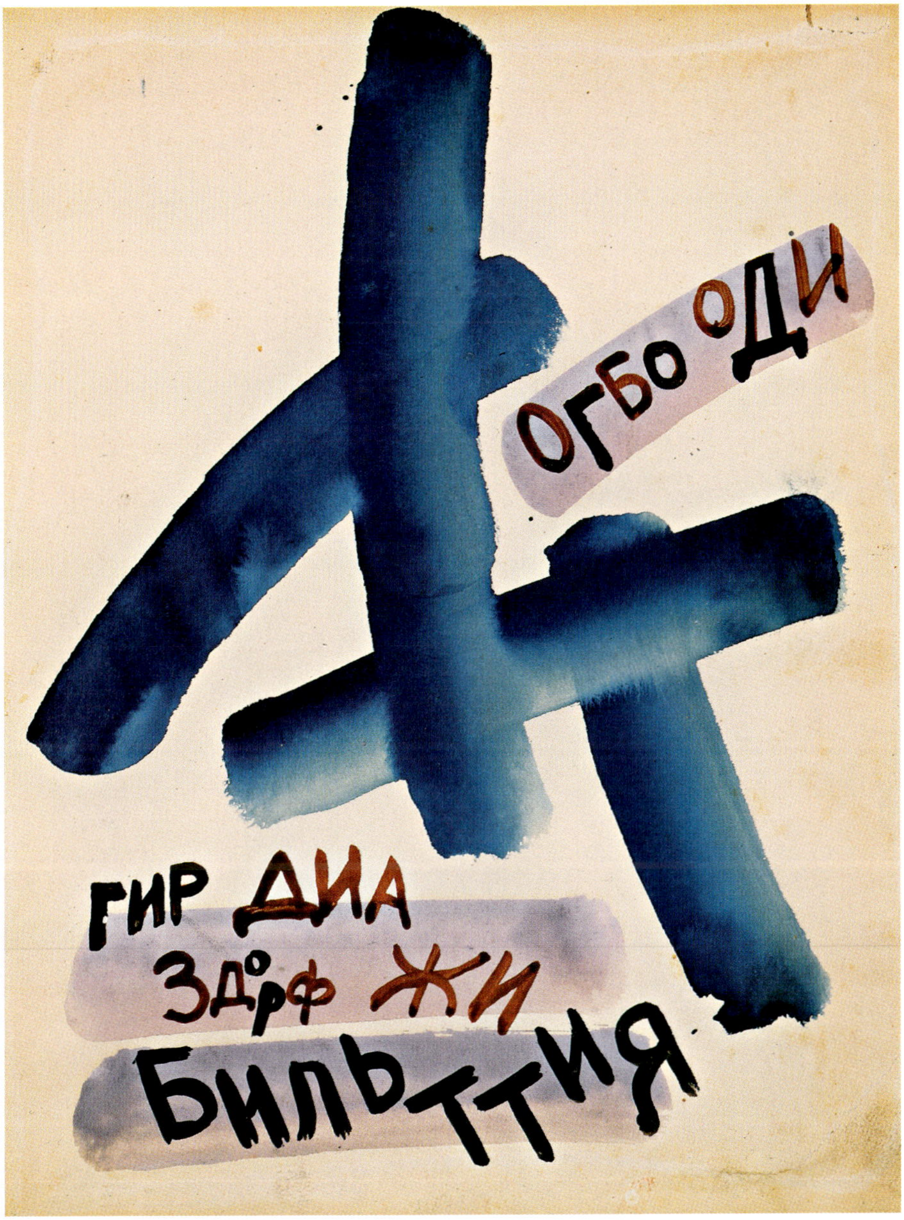

plate 58. varvara stepanova
Illustration for the poem "Rtny Khomle," 1918
Watercolor on paper, 23.3 x 17.7 cm
Private collection

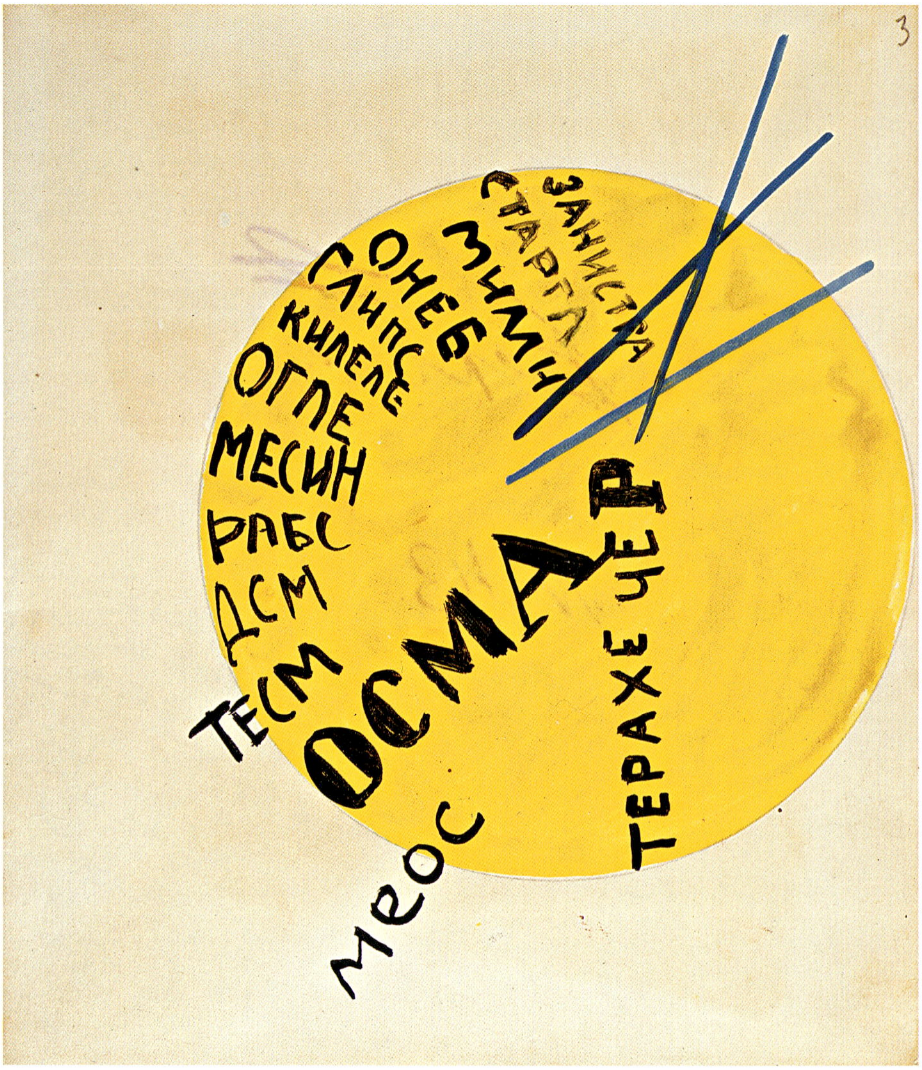

plate 59. VARVARA STEPANOVA
Illustration for the poem "Zigra Ar," 1918
Watercolor on paper, 18.8 x 16 cm
Private collection

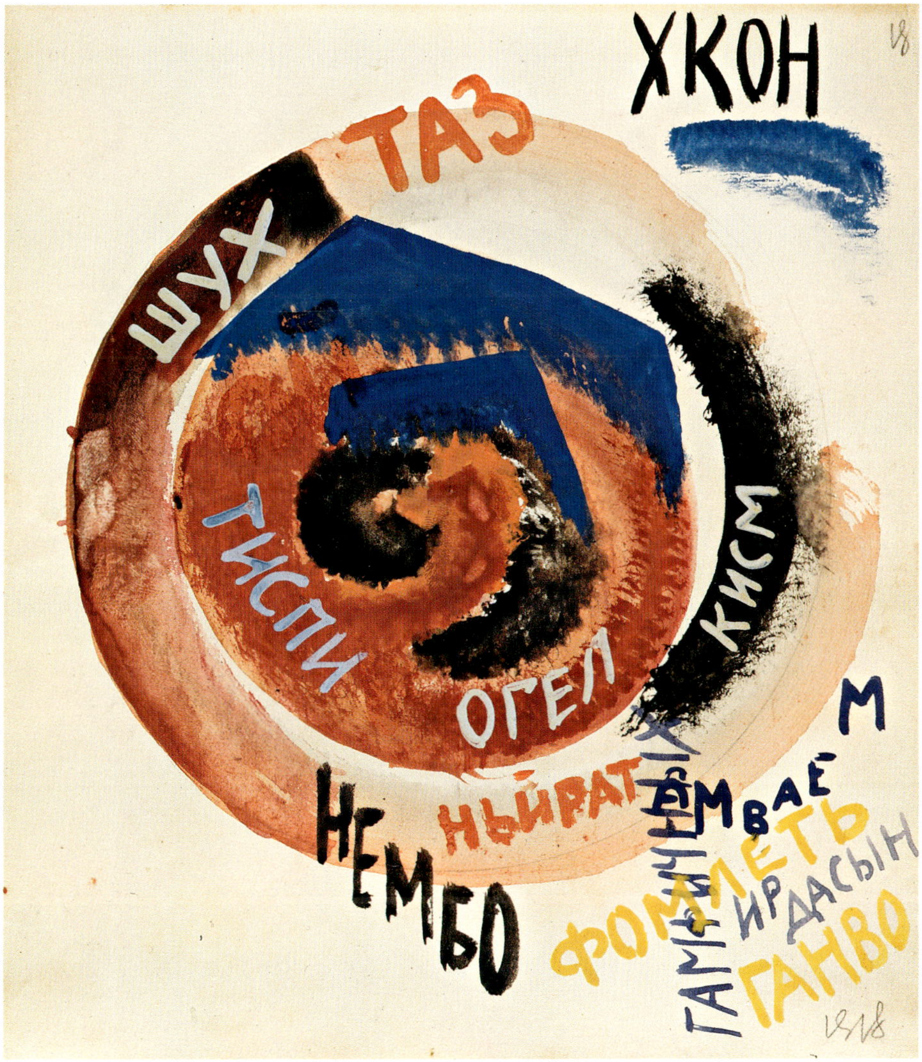

plate 60. VARVARA STEPANOVA
Illustration for the poem "Zigra Ar," 1918
Watercolor on paper, 18.8 x 16 cm
Private collection

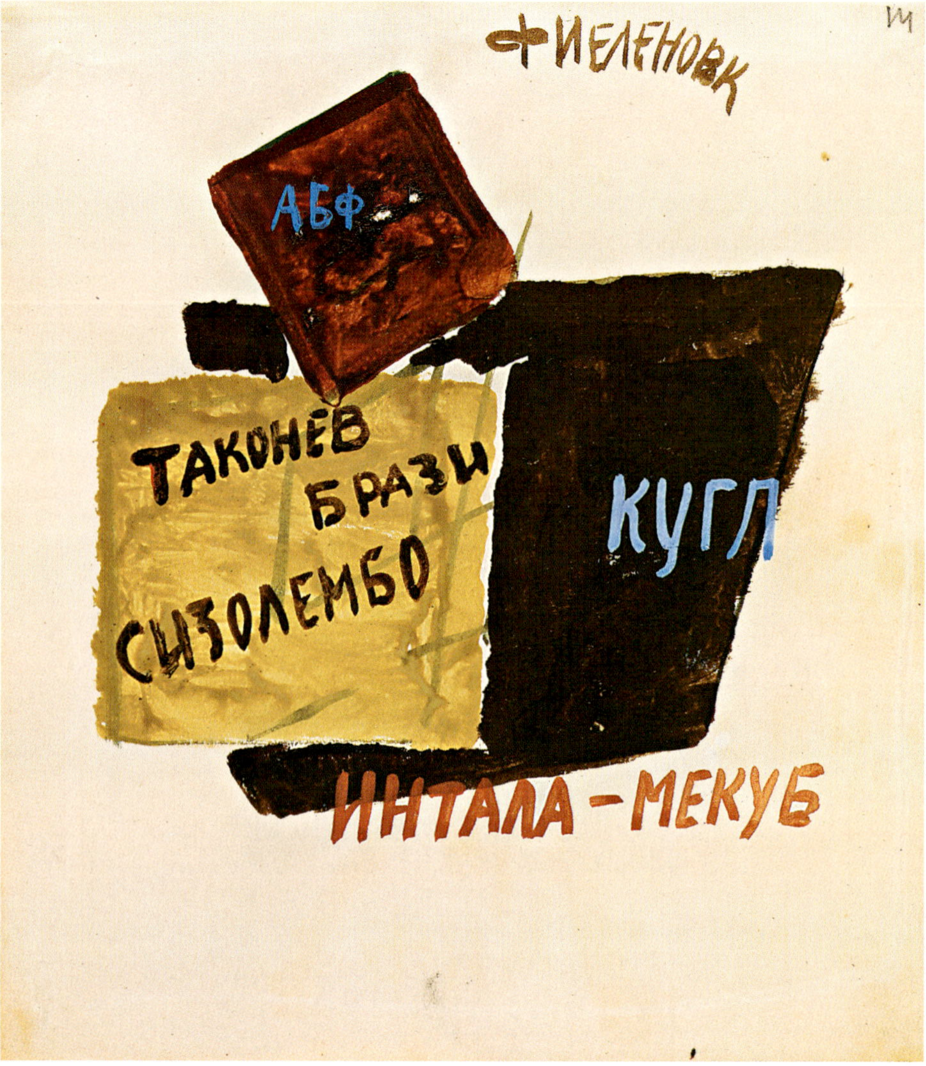

plate 61. VARVARA STEPANOVA
Illustration for the poem "Zigra Ar," 1918
Watercolor on paper, 18.8 x 16 cm
Private collection

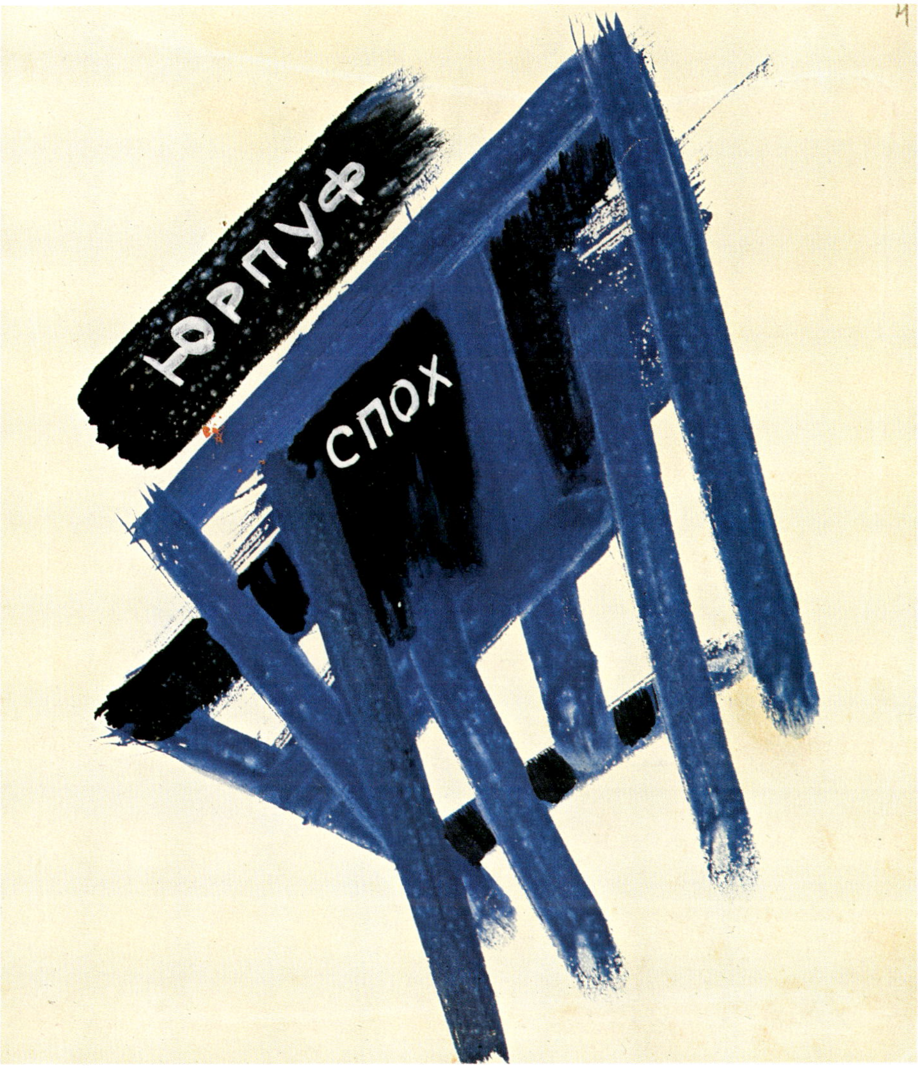

plate 62. VARVARA STEPANOVA
Illustration for the poem "Zigra Ar," 1918
Watercolor on paper, 18.8 x 16 cm
Private collection

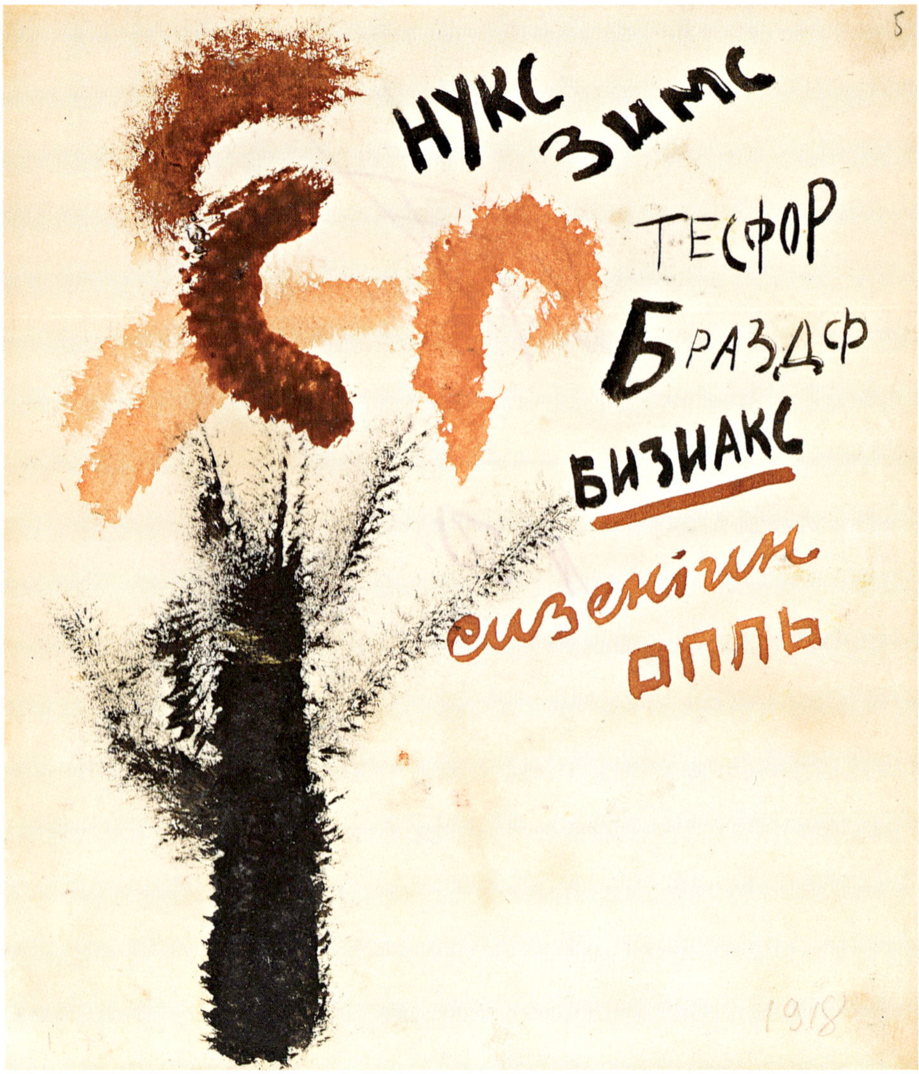

plate 63. VARVARA STEPANOVA
Illustration for the poem "Zigra Ar," 1918
Watercolor on paper, 18.8 x 16 cm
Private collection

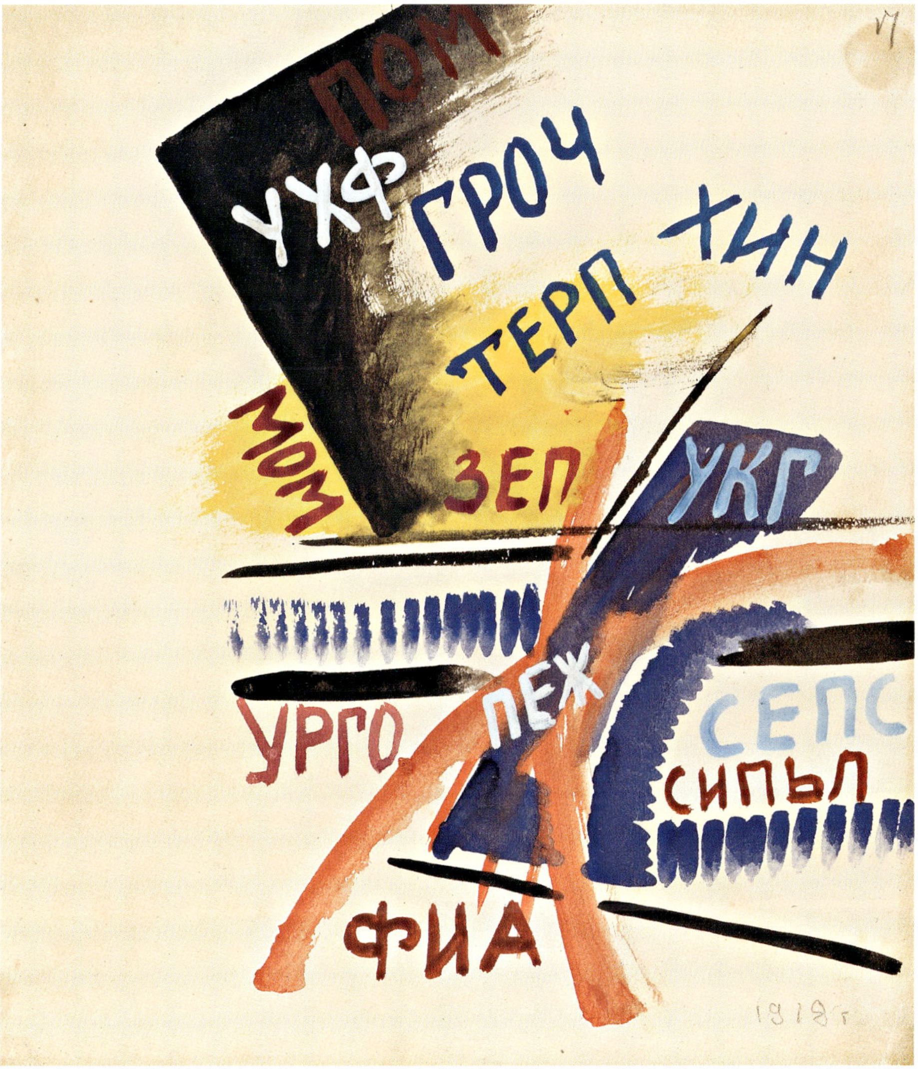

plate 64. varvara stepanova
Illustration for the poem "Zigra Ar," 1918
Watercolor on paper, 18.8 x 16 cm
Private collection

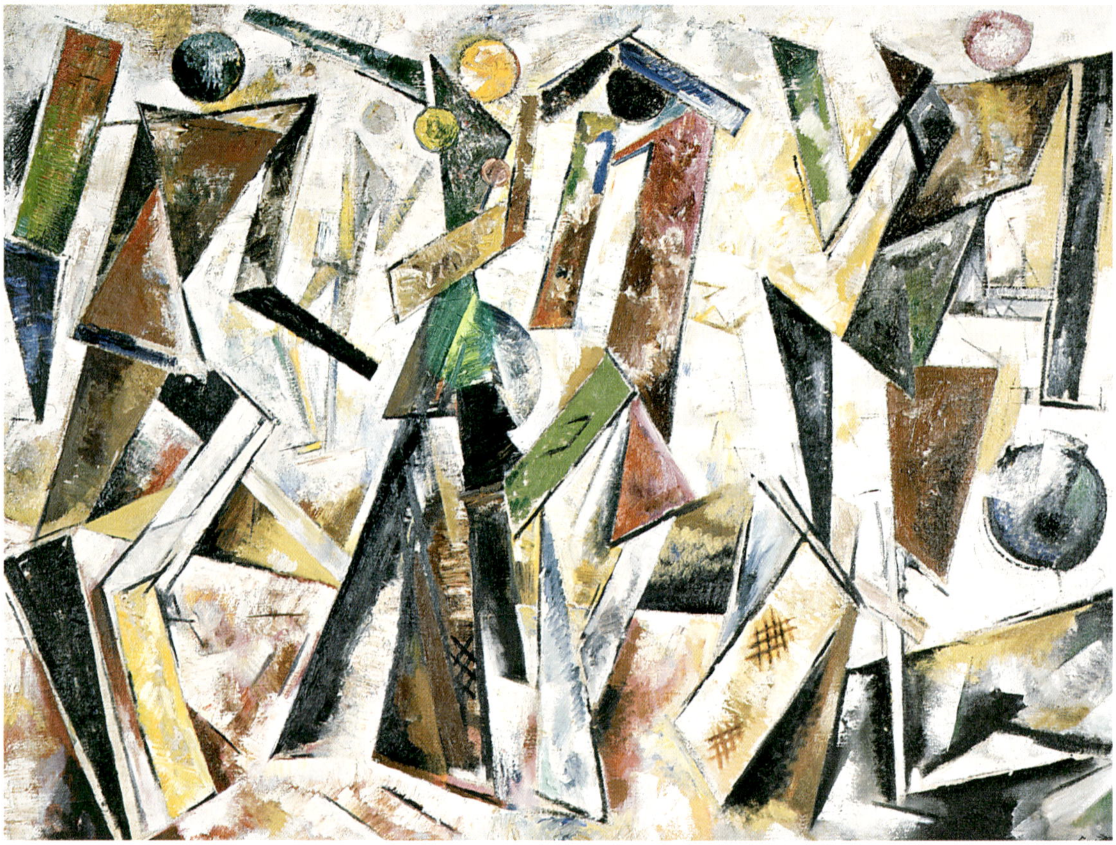

plate 65. VARVARA STEPANOVA
Dancing Figures on White, 1920
Oil on canvas, 107.5 x 143.5 cm
State Tretiakov Gallery, Moscow

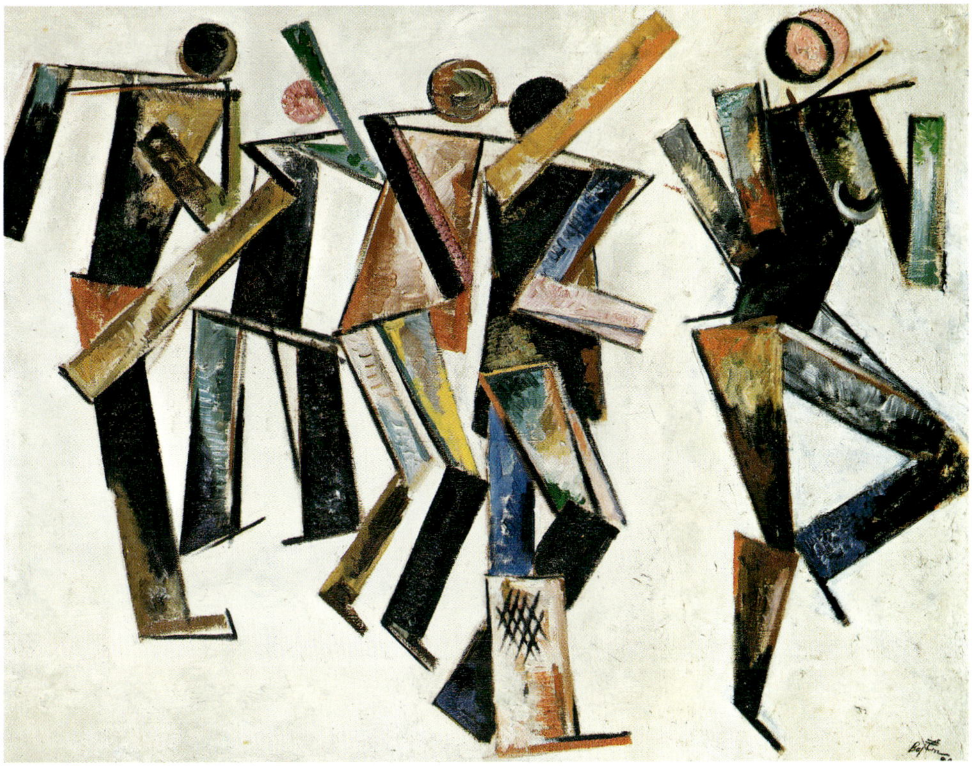

plate 66. VARVARA STEPANOVA
Five Figures on a White Background, 1920
Oil on canvas, 80 x 98 cm
Private collection

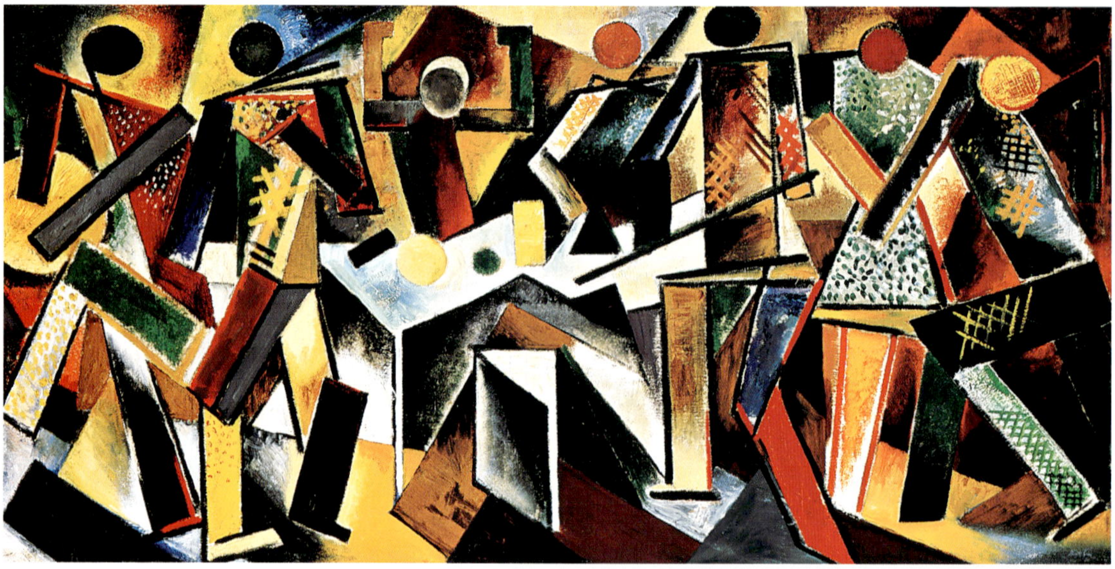

plate 67. VARVARA STEPANOVA
Billiard Players, 1920
Oil on canvas, 68 x 129 cm
Carmen Thyssen-Bornemisza Collection

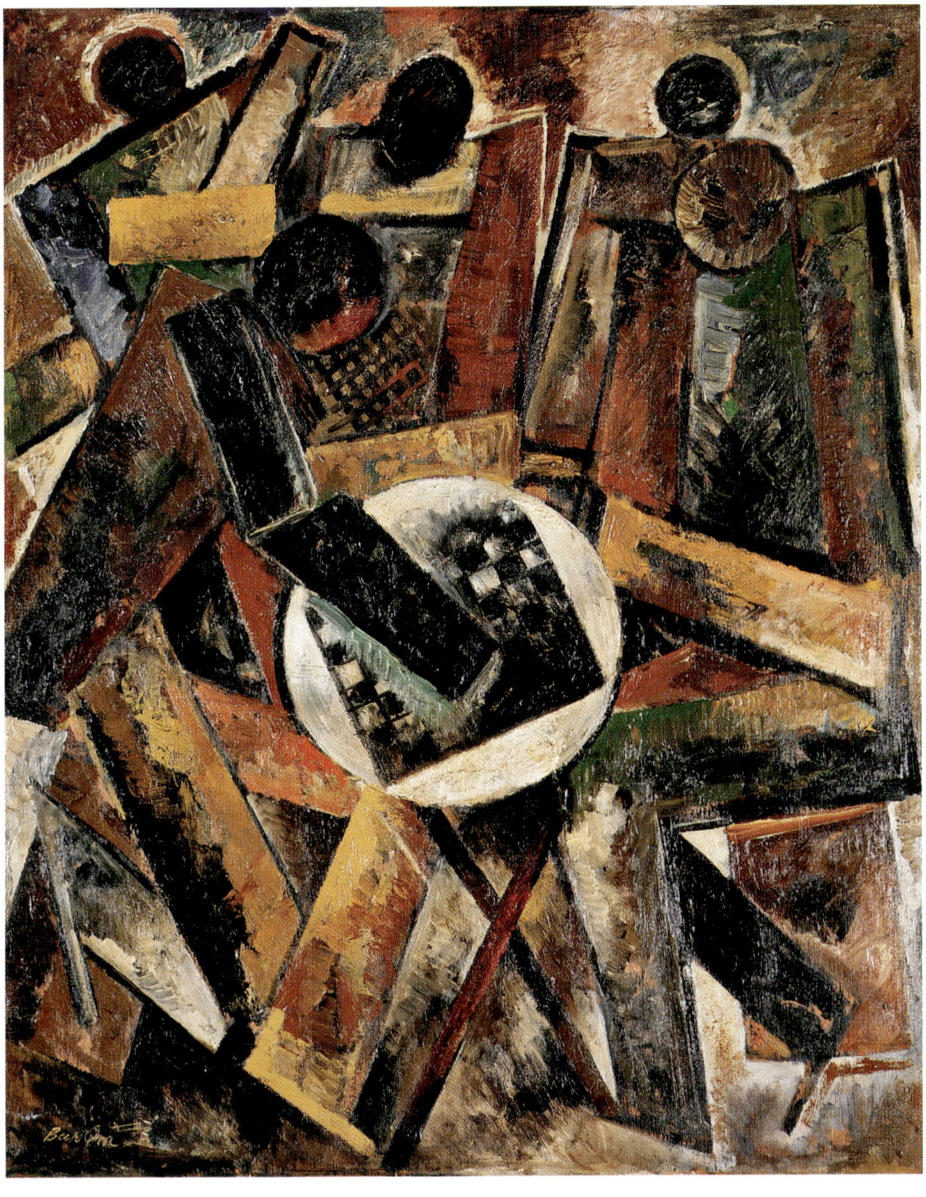

plate 68. VARVARA STEPANOVA
Playing Draughts, 1920
Oil on plywood, 78 x 62 cm
Private collection

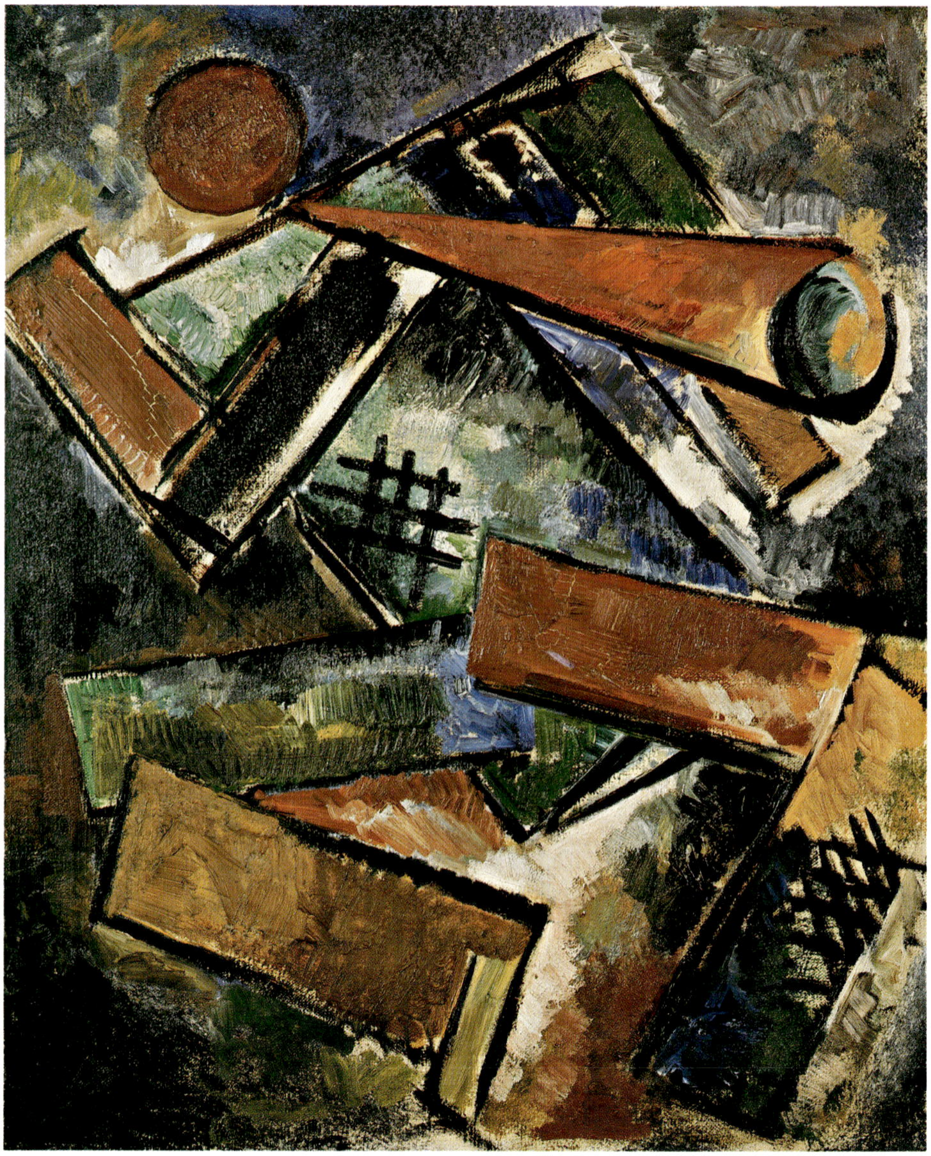

plate 69. VARVARA STEPANOVA
Trumpet Player, 1920
Oil on canvas, 70 x 57 cm
Private collection

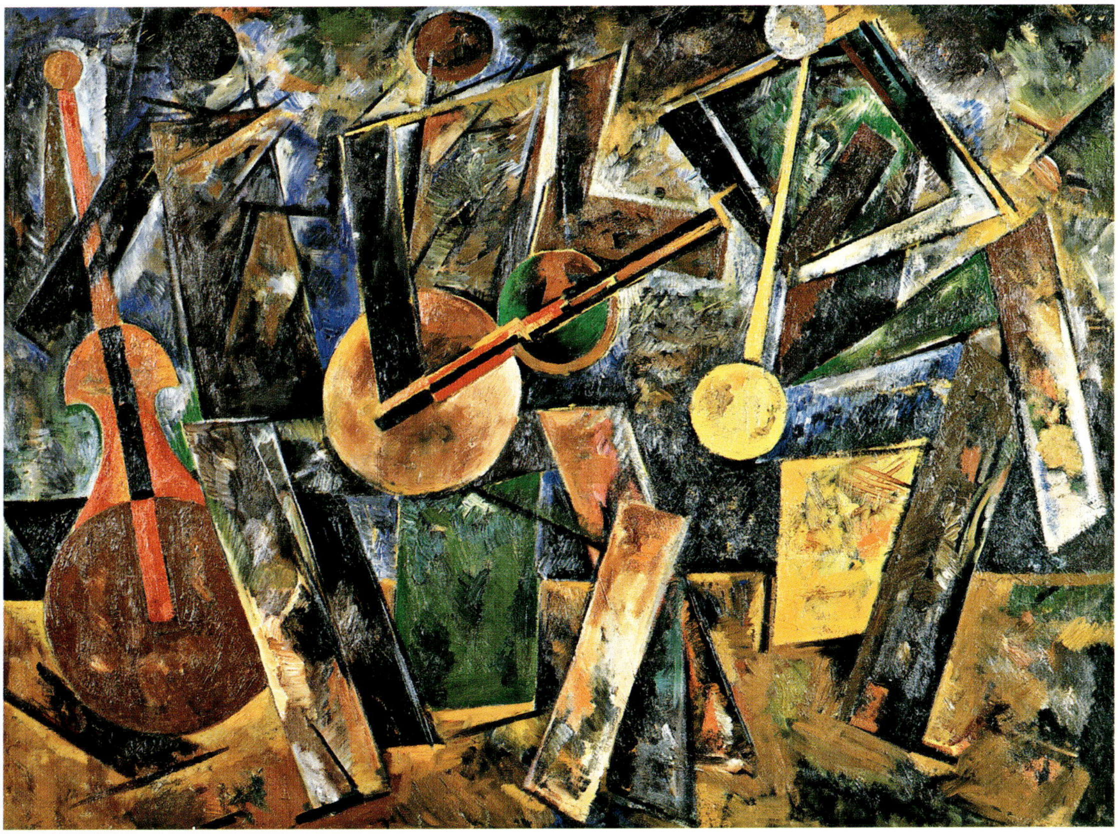

plate 70. VARVARA STEPANOVA
Musicians, 1920
Oil on canvas, 106 x 142 cm
Museum of Private Collections,
Pushkin Museum of Fine Arts, Moscow

plate 71. VARVARA STEPANOVA
Self-Portrait, 1920
Oil on plywood, 71 x 52.5 cm
Museum of Private Collections,
Pushkin Museum of Fine Arts, Moscow

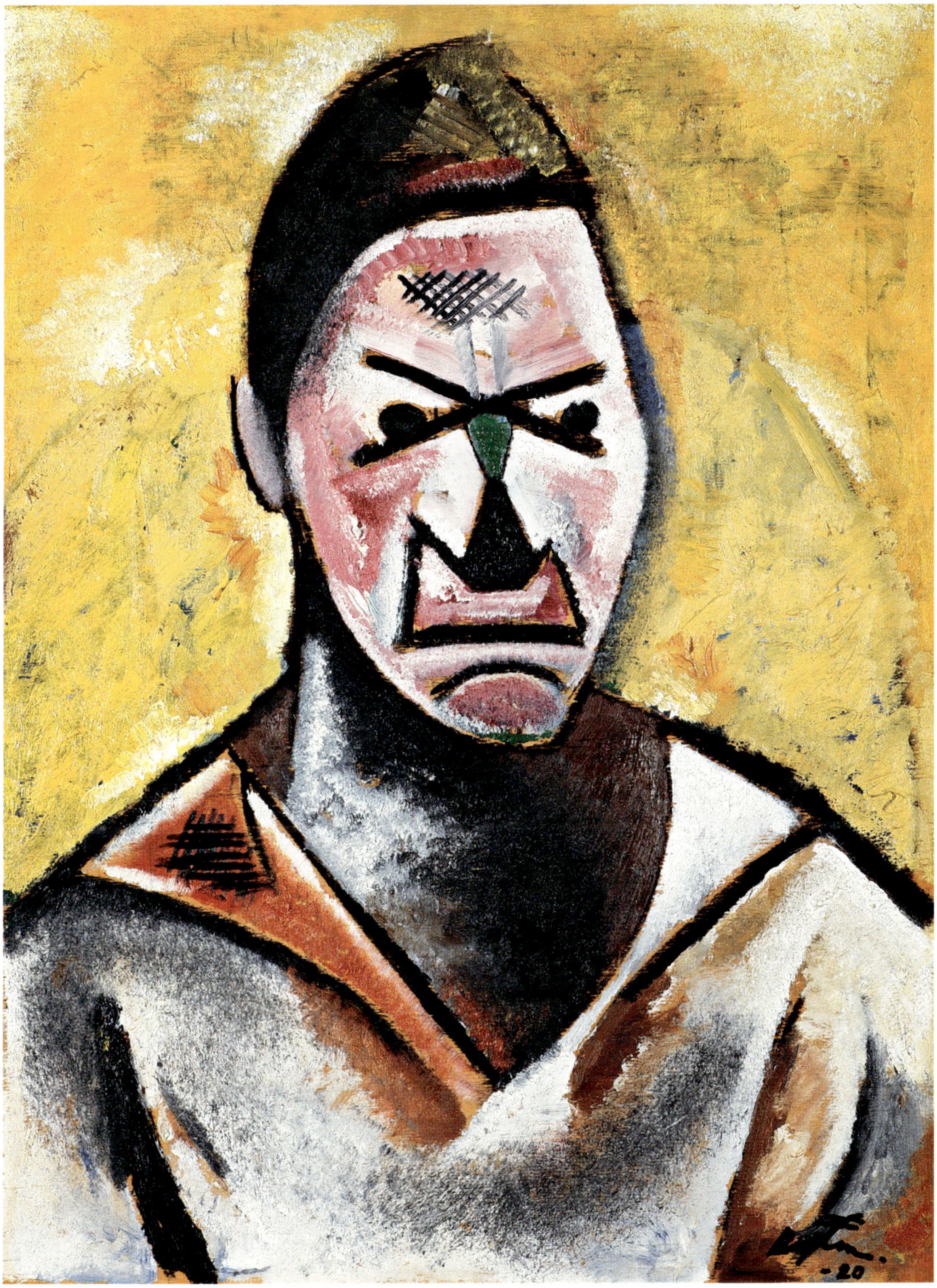

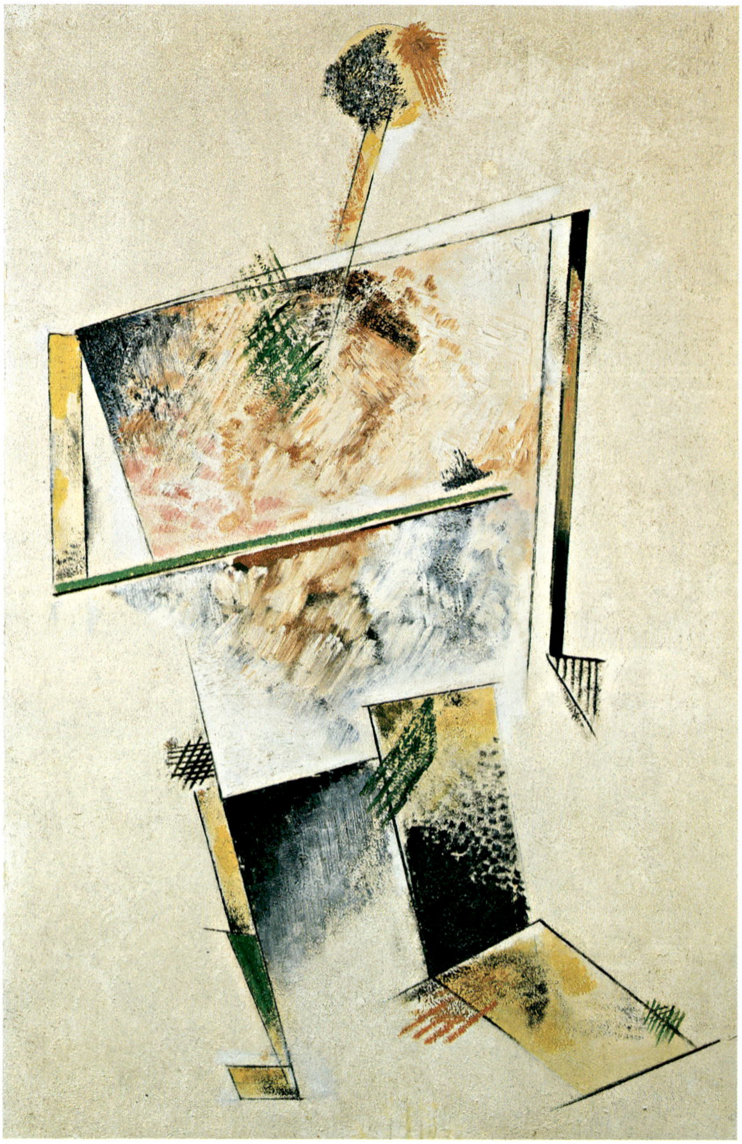

above:
plate 72. VARVARA STEPANOVA
Figure (Peasant), 1921
Oil on canvas, 99.5 x 65.5 cm
Private collection

facing page:
plate 73. VARVARA STEPANOVA
Figure, 1921
Oil on canvas, 125 x 71.5 cm
Private collection

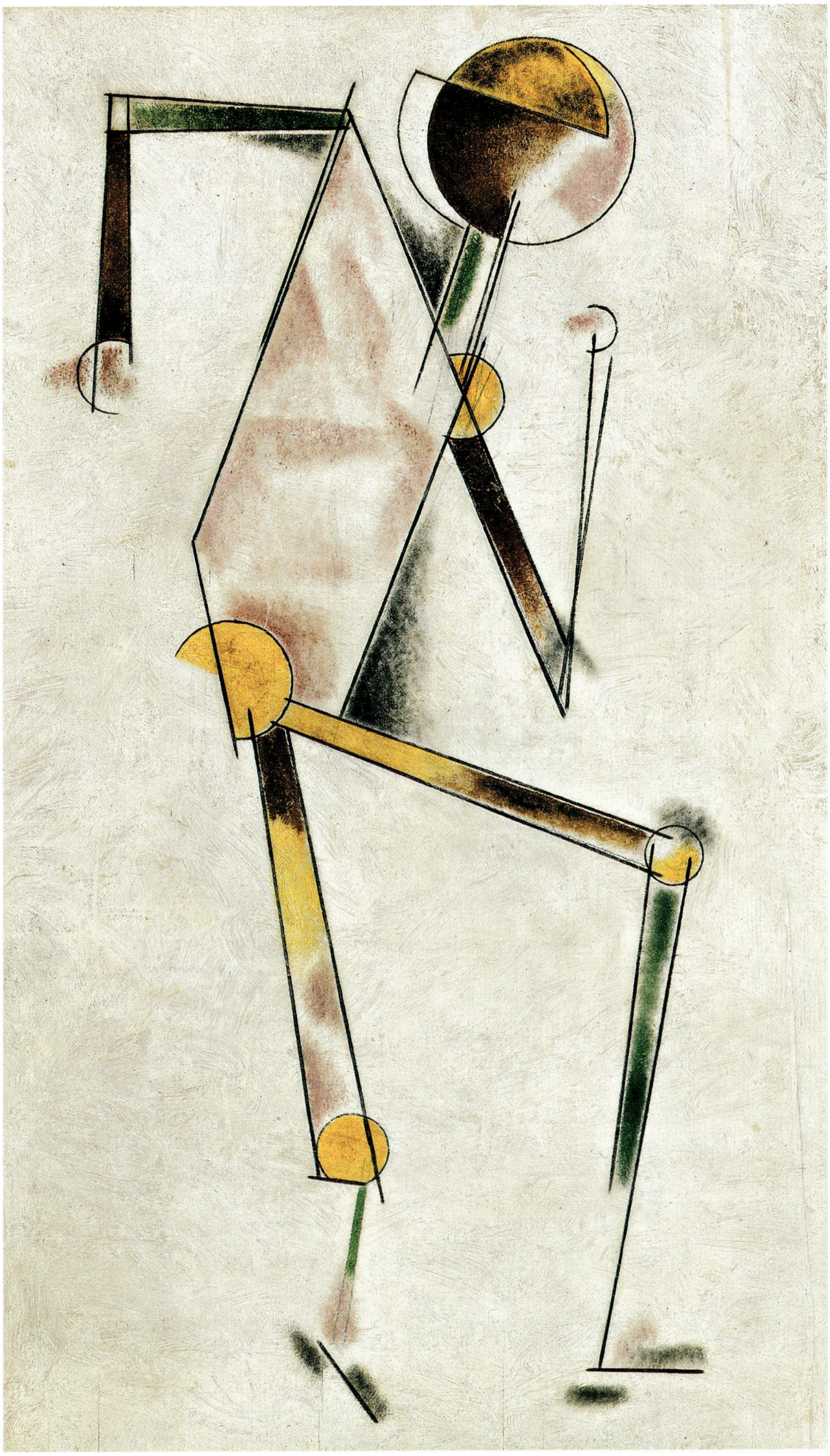

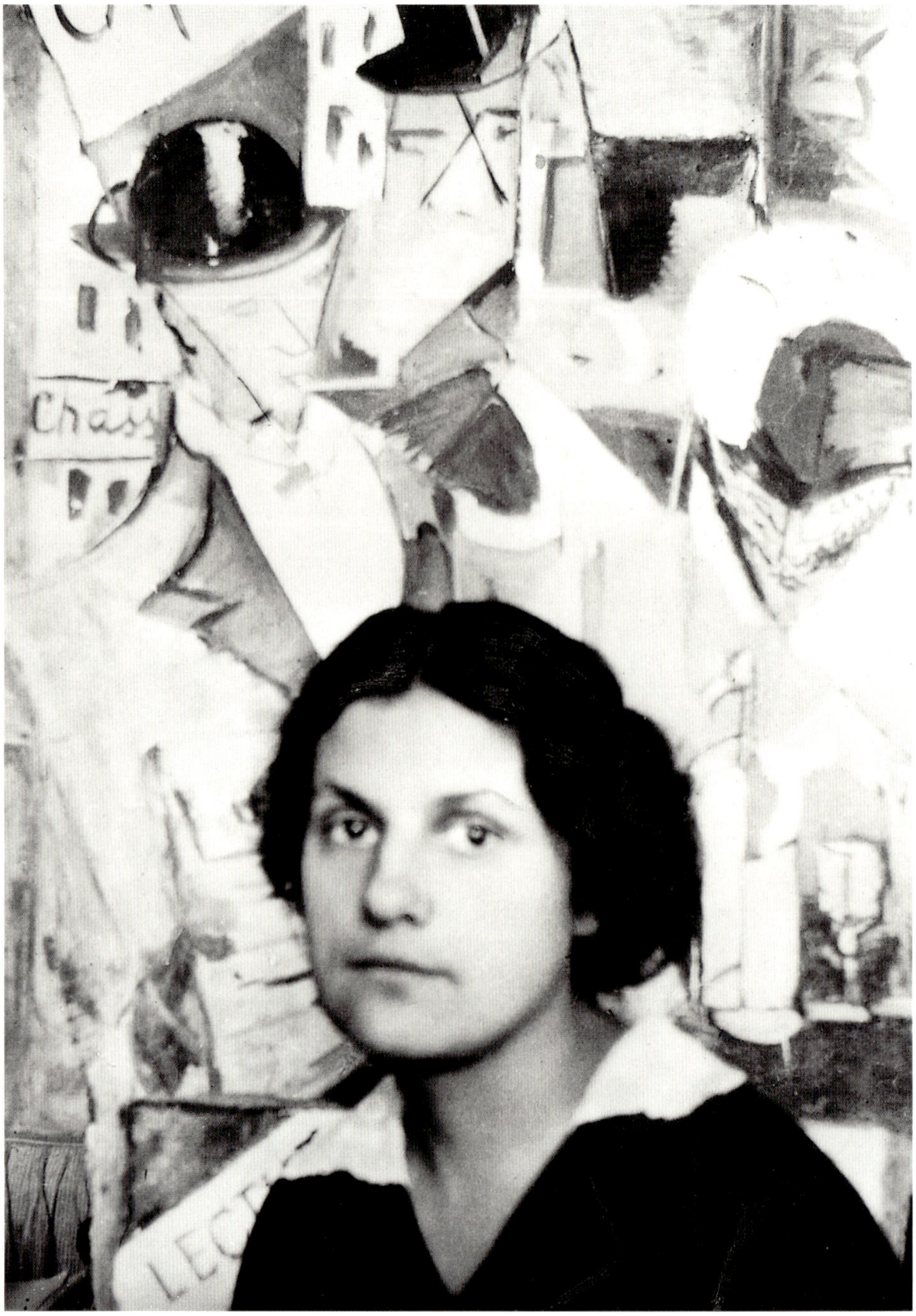

figure 77. Nadezhda Udaltsova in front of her painting
Restaurant (plate 83), 1915, Moscow.

Nadezhda Udaltsova

Vasilii Rakitin

A Professional Painter

The life of Nadezhda Udaltsova is a tragic one. Her mother died when she was twenty-seven years old; she suffered from a psychological breakdown following the painful death of one of her younger sisters, Liudmila Prudkovskaia, who was also an artist; her father, a retired general, was shot by the Bolsheviks; and her husband, fellow artist Alexander Drevin, was arrested and shot in 1938, although she fostered the hope that by some miracle he was still alive. But Udaltsova's saving grace was art. It was her passion and her guiding light.

Udaltsova made her debut as a professional artist at the *Jack of Diamonds* exhibition in Moscow in the winter of 1914, together with her friend Liubov Popova (fig. 78). But only one reviewer, Alexei Grishchenko, an artist whom they knew from various Moscow studios, noted their contribution, mentioning that while almost the entire exhibition moved under the banner of Picasso, these two young women showed an enthusiasm for another French artist — Jean Metzinger — and his painting *Oiseau bleu* (*Blue Bird*).[1]

That Udaltsova and Popova were exhibiting alongside Henri Le Fauconnier, who had sent ten works to Moscow, was not mere chance. Through Le Fauconnier, Albert Gleizes, and Metzinger, they had studied the grammar of Cubism at La Palette in Paris (also known under the more respectable name Académie de la Palette). At this point, the two women's drawing styles were very similar and

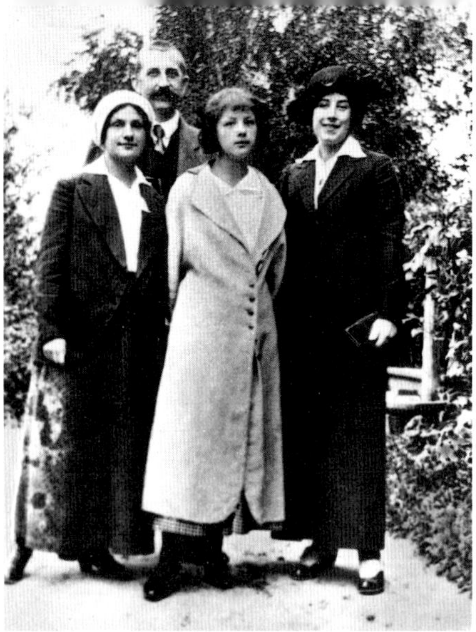

figure 78. Group photograph taken in the summer of 1915 at Vlakhernskaia Station, near Moscow. Left to right: Udaltsova, unidentified man, Varvara Prudkovskaia (Udaltsova's sister), and Liubov Popova.

demonstrated that they had assimilated their Cubist lessons well, even though their paintings relied on a broader and more universal application of Parisian Cubism (fig. 79).

Cubism, of course, was not just another "ism" — it marked an entirely new era as well as a totally new way of making and perceiving art. However, the canon of Cubism did not hinder the expression of individuality. Udaltsova, for example, accepted Cubism as a legitimate phenomenon that was linked organically to the history of European art — with Leonardo da Vinci, the Middle Ages, Poussin — and with the environment of Paris itself. When one looked at the "cubes of its houses and the interweavings of its viaducts, with its locomotive smoke trails, airborne planes and dirigibles, [the city] seemed to be a fantastic and picturesque display of original art. The architecture of the houses with their ocher and silver tones found their embodiment in the Cubist constructions of Picasso."[2] Of course, Picasso drew on many other traditions and sources of inspiration, but this lyrical interpretation of Cubist painting tells us much about the sensibility and character of Udaltsova herself.

Udaltsova's rendering of space in the paintings of 1914–15 often resembles beehives with a multitude of honeycombs, a reticulation however, that does not represent a mere accumulation of forms and divisions (see *At the Piano*, plate 76; *Guitar Fugue*, plate 77, and *New*, plate 79). As a rule, her Cubist and post-Cubist pictorial "constructions" are transparent and light; unfortunately, comparatively little of her work from the 1910s has survived, although she made later versions of several early pieces.

During the 1920s, the Tretiakov Gallery, the Russian Museum, and the various Museums of Artistic Culture displayed the works of Udaltsova as examples of Cubism — and justifiably so. Indeed, Udaltsova's paintings are perhaps the most organic manifestation of Russian Cubism or of what we refer to conditionally as Russian Cubism, the history of which has yet to be written.[3] Skillfully made, Udaltsova's paintings function by understatement and through a precise expression of her intent, and are characterized by a pictorial serenity, a Cubist *sfumato* (see *The Blue Jug*, 1915, fig. 81). Malevich declared that the absence of talent among the Cubist painters "testifies to its complex essence,"[4] but gradually Udaltsova fathomed the laws of Cubism, moving from analytical compositions toward a more plastic synthesis.

For Udaltsova, the path to the new painting culminated in the non-objective. She compared what she was doing with the work of colleagues, and wondered who was right. There was the subtle Vladimir Tatlin, for example, who abandoned painting, even though creating a work out of iron and wood might not be much different from "painting a sunny landscape or the portrait of a girl."[5] Udaltsova, while in Paris in her mid-twenties, and sensing the Romantic nature of Tatlin's reliefs, understood perfectly well that he was not a Russian Picasso. Tatlin recognized the value of her insight into his work, and, in fact, the text in the promotional booklet that he distributed at the *0.10* exhibition in December 1915 was by Udaltsova.[6] Although Udaltsova herself did not construct reliefs, some of her paintings have much in common with the plastic works of Tatlin — for example, her *Self-Portrait with Palette*, 1915 (plate 80), and the spiral form of his *Monument to the Third International*, 1919. Although each of them followed a distinct path, the ultimate destiny of the new art was of mutual concern to them, and they formed a united bloc at *Tramway V*, *0.10*, and *The Store*, disturbing still further the delicate balance between Malevich and Tatlin.

Udaltsova adhered closely to her aesthetic principles, even though she was not an advocate of cool and rational calculation. The various versions of the painting *Restaurant*, 1915, for example (plates 82, 83; fig. 80), demonstrate her skill in undertaking a sophisticated game of form and lettering, light and shade, relief and plane, while remaining firmly committed to the triumph of painting. In other words, the culture of painting as such and the tradition of European painting in particular were of extreme importance to Udaltsova, even if she did reexamine and interpret the Russian icon.

War and revolution disrupted the common course and ready interchange of the new art, although for the Russians the isolation proved to be beneficial. What happened to their painting after Cubism? Certainly, Udaltsova was among the first to appreciate Popova's architectonic paintings (plates 36, 37), and, even if she was interested in the plasticity of Suprematism as viewed from the standpoint of Cubism and Tatlin, she was also drawn both to its pure color and to its decorative potential. When Natalia Davydova asked her to make textile designs for the Verbovka peasant art cooperative, the results showed the influence of the charismatic Malevich — indeed, Suprematism seemed an ideal style for the applied arts.

In the winter of 1916–17, Udaltsova and her colleagues began referring to themselves not as Futurists but as Suprematists, and started to work on a new

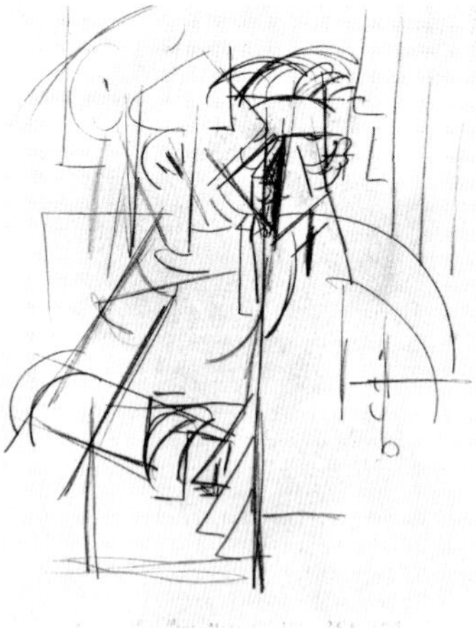

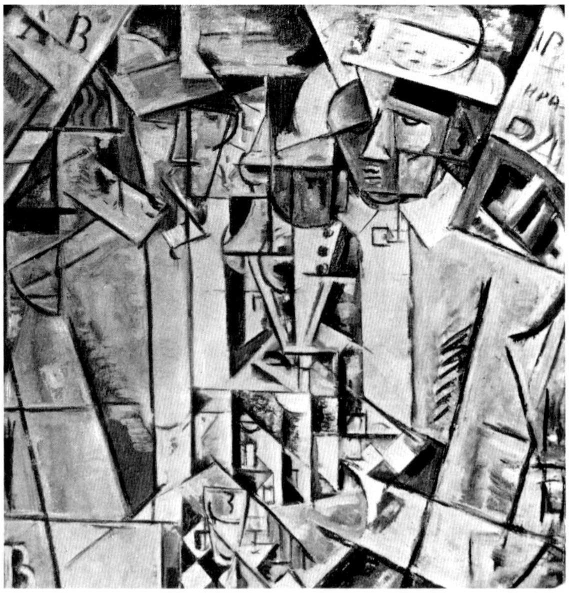

journal, *Supremus* (which never appeared). Udaltsova, Vera Pestel, and Popova also applied their Suprematist ideas to their decoration for the Club of the Young Leftist Federation of the Professional Union of Artists and Painters. However, Malevich, a born leader, could not reconcile himself to the wide range of opinions within the Supremus circle, even if he did welcome Udaltsova's works, inviting her to co-direct a studio at Svomas.[7] They had every intention of continuing with textile designs and, subsequently, Udaltsova did teach textile design at Vkhutemas-Vkhutein and the Textile Institute in Moscow. But as with Suprematist painting, decorative art never became her primary interest. After all, Udaltsova thought in terms of rigorous, abstract, monumental compositions; Varvara Stepanova even referred to three large canvases by Udaltsova called *Tectonic Temples*.[8] Yet at exhibitions, Udaltsova continued to include her earlier works from 1914–15, because she recognized a strong link between her present and her past.

With fellow artist Alexander Drevin (whom she married in 1919), she tried to unite with Vesnin, Stepanova, and Rodchenko within the Association of Extreme Innovators (Askranov). The attempt failed, but she continued to nurture the idea of a united front for the new art, and in 1920 tried again with the Objectivists at Inkhuk.[9] However, during one of the many debates in that group, an extreme faction declared that painting was not consistent with the goals of modernity and should be abandoned, in response to which Drevin, Kandinsky, Ivan Kliun, Boris Korolev, and Udaltsova all resigned. But unlike many of her avant-garde colleagues, Udaltsova could appreciate the work of artists with temperaments contrary to her own — Rodchenko, for example — although, in general, Constructivism was not her cup of tea. For her, painting was primary, and only once, with Drevin and their students, did she build a model for a large spatial construction.[10] This had

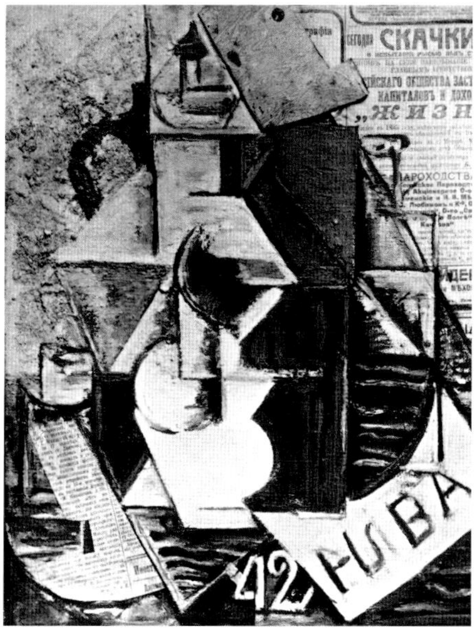

facing page, left:
figure 79. Nadezhda Udaltsova
Seated Figure, Paris, 1913
Pencil on paper, 26.6 x 20.5 cm
Private collection

facing page, right:
figure 80. Nadezhda Udaltsova
Restaurant, 1915 (first version; destroyed)
Oil on canvas

left:
figure 81. Nadezhda Udaltsova
The Blue Jug, 1915 (first version; destroyed)
Oil on canvas

been patently clear at the exhibition *The Store*, where she and Popova had put up a handmade poster in their section, reading, "Room for Professional Painters" — clearly a polemical challenge to Tatlin.

Udaltsova's experimental paintings attracted attention at the *Erste russische Kunstausstellung* in Berlin in 1922, but within months she and Drevin were moving away from abstract art. Udaltsova began to paint intense Fauvist landscapes and portraits, which she showed at the Vkhutemas *Exhibition of Paintings* in 1923 and then at the Venice *Biennale* the following year. She appeared to be moving "back to nature," and finding Constable and Corot more exciting than Modernism. But appearances are deceptive. If the Jack of Diamonds artists turned toward a more trivial kind of Realism, Udaltsova and Drevin (who left a strong imprint on her work) presented nature as a grand non-objective painting, as a vital exercise in plastic values. Painterly intuition became both subject and object, while painterly expression and inner contemplation formed a new unity; so it is not surprising that their art failed to concur with the schematic canons of the new Realism during the 1920s and early 1930s. When the struggle against experimental art began in earnest, Udaltsova and Drevin were labeled "formalists" and "cosmopolitanists," a stigma that persisted until well after World War II.

Udaltsova did not accept the aesthetic of Socialist Realism, instead continuing to adhere to her nonconformist principles. She showed her best works — portraits, trees, still lifes — not at public exhibitions, of course, but in the privacy of her studio and to close friends (fig. 82), such as Alexander Osmerkin and Robert Falk, and on one occasion to the celebrated writer Ilya Ehrenburg, who had not forgotten his own passion for the avant-garde and for Picasso in particular. But how criteria change! Rodchenko, one of the leaders of the Constructivists — with whom

Udaltsova used to wrangle so furiously over the destiny of painting — once wrote to Stepanova, the champion of production art: "I was at Udaltsova's and she showed me this painting. What a shame you haven't seen it. A really great piece."[11]

1. A. Grishchenko, "Bubnovyi valet'. Vpechatleniia s vystavki," in *Nov* (Moscow), no. 22, 1914, pp. 9–10. Metzinger's *Oiseau bleu* is now in the collection of the Musée d'Art Moderne de la Ville de Paris.
2. Nadezhda Udaltsova, "Avtobiografiia," in V. Starodubova and E. Drevina, eds., *Alexander Drevin. Nadezhda Udaltsova.* Catalogue of exhibition at the Union of Artists of the U.S.S.R. (Moscow: Sovetskii khudozhnik, 1991), p. 91.
3. Artist and administrator David Shterenberg wrote in his preface to the catalogue of the *Erste russische Kunstausstellung* in 1922: "Russian Cubism developed independently. Hence the impression that our Cubist artists did not follow a common scheme" (Shterenberg, "Zur Einführung," in *Erste russische Kunstausstellung* [Berlin: Galerie Van Diemen, 1922], p. 12). Critic Nikolai Punin agreed: "Cubism in Russia and Cubism in Paris are such different entities that they may even defy comparison" (1929; quoted in I Karasik, comp., *Muzei v muzee. Russkii avangard iz kollektsii Muzeia khudozhestvennoi kultury v sobranii Gosudarstvennogo Russkogo muzeia* [St. Petersburg: Palace Editions, 1998], p. 397).
4. Kazimir Malevich, "Vystavka professionalnogo soiuza khudozhnikov-zhivopistsev. Levaia federatsiia (molodaia fraktsiia)" (1918); quoted in A. Shatskikh, ed., *Kazimir Malevich. Sobranie sochinenii*, 2 vols. (Moscow: Gileia, 1995), vol. 1, p. 119.
5. Nadezhda Udaltsova, Letter to Olga Rozanova (1917). See below.
6. Nadezhda Udaltsova, "Vladimir Evgrafovich Tatlin," in [anon.], *Vladimir Evgrafovich Tatlin* (Petrograd: Zhurnal dlia vsekh, 1915), unpaginated.
7. Characteristic of Malevich, pioneer and polemicist of Suprematism, is the fact that he listed "Malevich, Kliun, Davydova, Rozanova, Menkov, Yurkevich, Udaltsova, Popova, et al." as representatives of Suprematism (i.e., the Supremus circle), but "forgot" about Rodchenko and Alexander Vesnin, who were not members of his group.
8. A. Lavrentiev and V. Rodchenko, eds., *Varvara Stepanova: Chelovek ne mozhet zhit bez chuda. Pisma. Poeticheskie opyty. Zapiski khudozhnitsy* (Moscow: Sfera, 1994), p. 75.
9. See the Popova essay in this catalogue, n. 4.
10. The spatial model for a rostrum is reproduced in S. Luchishkin, *Ya ochen liubliu zhizn* (Moscow: Sovetskii khudozhnik, 1988), p. 58.
11. Vladimir Rodchenko, ed., *A. M. Rodchenko: Stati. Vospominaniia. Avtobiograficheskie zapiski* (Moscow: Sovetskii khudozhnik, 1982), p. 122.

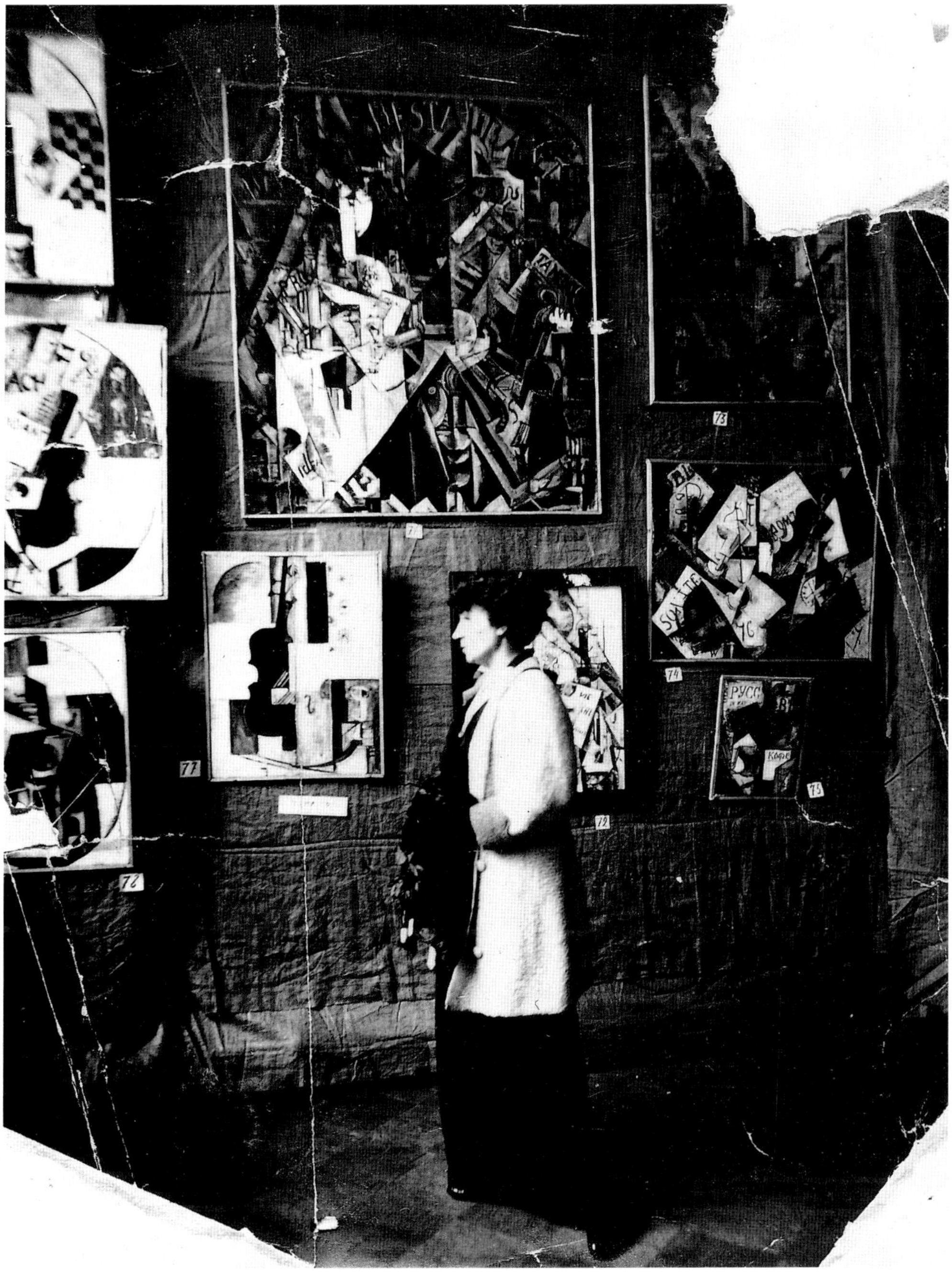

figure 82. Alexandra Exter in front of Udaltsova's paintings at the exhibition *The Store*, Moscow, 1916. Among the works visible are *Restaurant* (plate 83) and *Violin* (State Tretiakov Gallery, Moscow).

NADEZHDA ANDREEVNA UDALTSOVA
(1886–1961)

1886	Born December 29, in the village of Orel, to Vera Nikolaevna Udaltsova (née Choglakova) and Andrei Timofeevich Prudkovsky.
1892	The Udaltsova family moves to Moscow.
1905	Graduates from a women's school, and enrolls in the art school of Konstantin Yuon and Ivan Dudin in September.
1907	Meets Vera Mukhina, Liubov Popova, and Alexander Vesnin at the Yuon/Dudin school.
1908	Visits the Shchukin collection. Travels to Berlin and Dresden in May–June. Fails entrance exam for the Institute of Painting, Sculpture, and Architecture.
1910–11	Studies at various private studios, including the Tower (1911).
1912–13	With Popova, studies under Henri Le Fauconnier, Jean Metzinger, and André Dunoyer de Segonzac at La Palette in Paris.
1913	Returns to Moscow, and works in Tatlin's studio on Ostozhenka Street, with Alexei Grishchenko, Popova, Vesnin, and other artists.
1914	Makes her debut as a professional artist at the fourth *Jack of Diamonds* exhibition in Moscow, together with Popova.
1915–16	Contributes works to the Futurist exhibition *Tramway V* in Petrograd,to the *0.10* exhibition in Petrograd, and to the exhibition *The Store* (1916) in Moscow.
1916	Breaks with Tatlin. Is commissioned by Natalia Davydova to design textiles. Shows works at an exhibition at the Unicorn Art Salon.
1916–17	Contributes to the last *Jack of Diamonds* exhibition. That winter, she and her colleagues begin referring to themselves as Suprematists and work on preparations for publishing a new journal, *Supremus*, which never appears.
1917	Is elected to the Club of the Young Leftist Federation of the Professional Union of Artists and Painters. Collaborates on the decoration of the Café Pittoresque. Contributes to the *Second Exhibition of Contemporary Decorative Art*.
1918	Collaborates with Alexei Gan, Alexei Morgunov, Malevich, and Alexander Rodchenko on the newspaper *Anarkhiia* (*Anarchy*). Works in various institutions, including the Moscow Proletcult with Rozanova.

1918–20	Teaches at Svomas, co-directing a studio at Malevich's invitation.
1919	Contributes eleven pieces from 1914–15 to the *Fifth State Exhibition*. Marries Alexander Drevin.
1920–21	Member of Inkhuk.
1920–30	Teaches textile design at Vkhutemas-Vkhutein, and at the Textile Institute in Moscow.
1922	Contributes to the *Erste russische Kunstausstellung* at the Galerie Van Diemen in Berlin, which travels to the Stedelijk Museum in Amsterdam the following spring.
1923–24	Begins to paint Fauvist landscapes and portraits, some of which she shows at the Vkhutemas *Exhibition of Paintings* in 1923, and then at the Venice *Biennale* in 1924.
1927–35	Contributes to many international exhibitions, including joint exhibitions with Drevin at the Russian Museum in Leningrad in 1928 and in Erevan in 1934.
1932–33	Contributes to *Artists of the RSFSR Over the Last Fifteen Years* in Leningrad and Moscow, and is criticized for formalist tendencies.
1938	Drevin is arrested during the night of January 16–17.
1945	Solo exhibition at the Moscow Union of Soviet Artists.
1958	Contributes to a group exhibition at the House of the Artist in Moscow in October.
1961	Dies January 25, in Moscow.

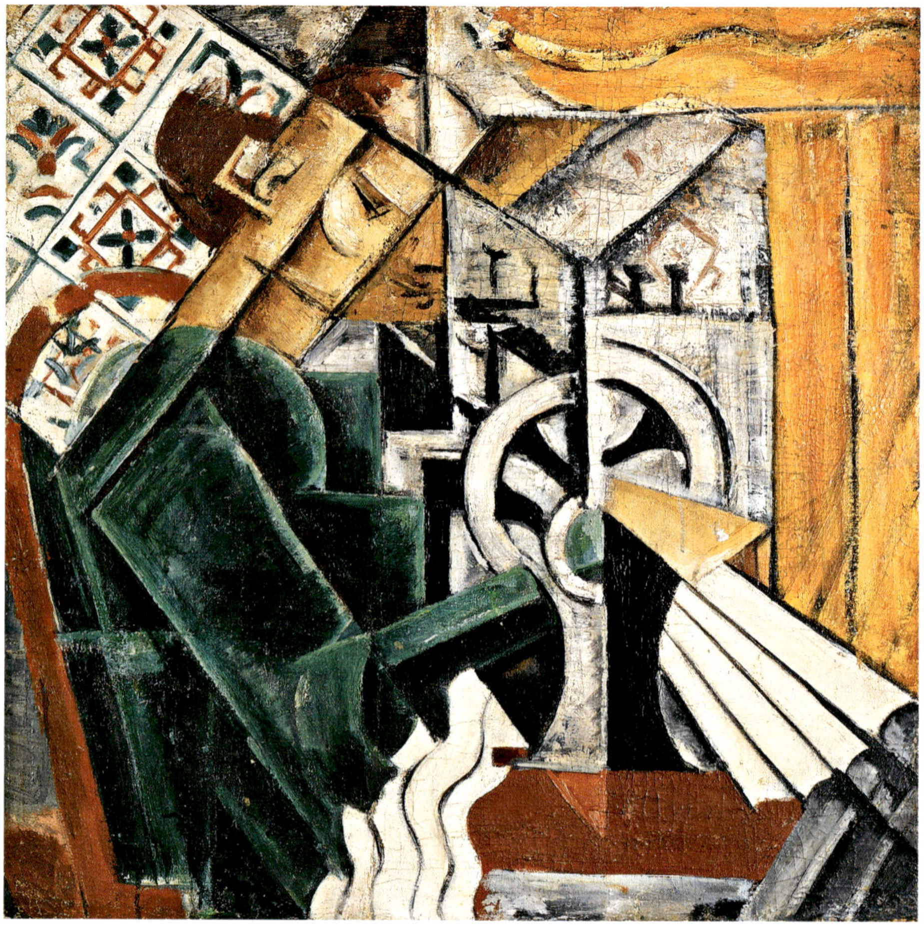

plate 74. NADEZHDA UDALTSOVA
Seamstress, 1912–13
Oil on canvas, 71.5 x 70.5 cm
State Tretiakov Gallery, Moscow

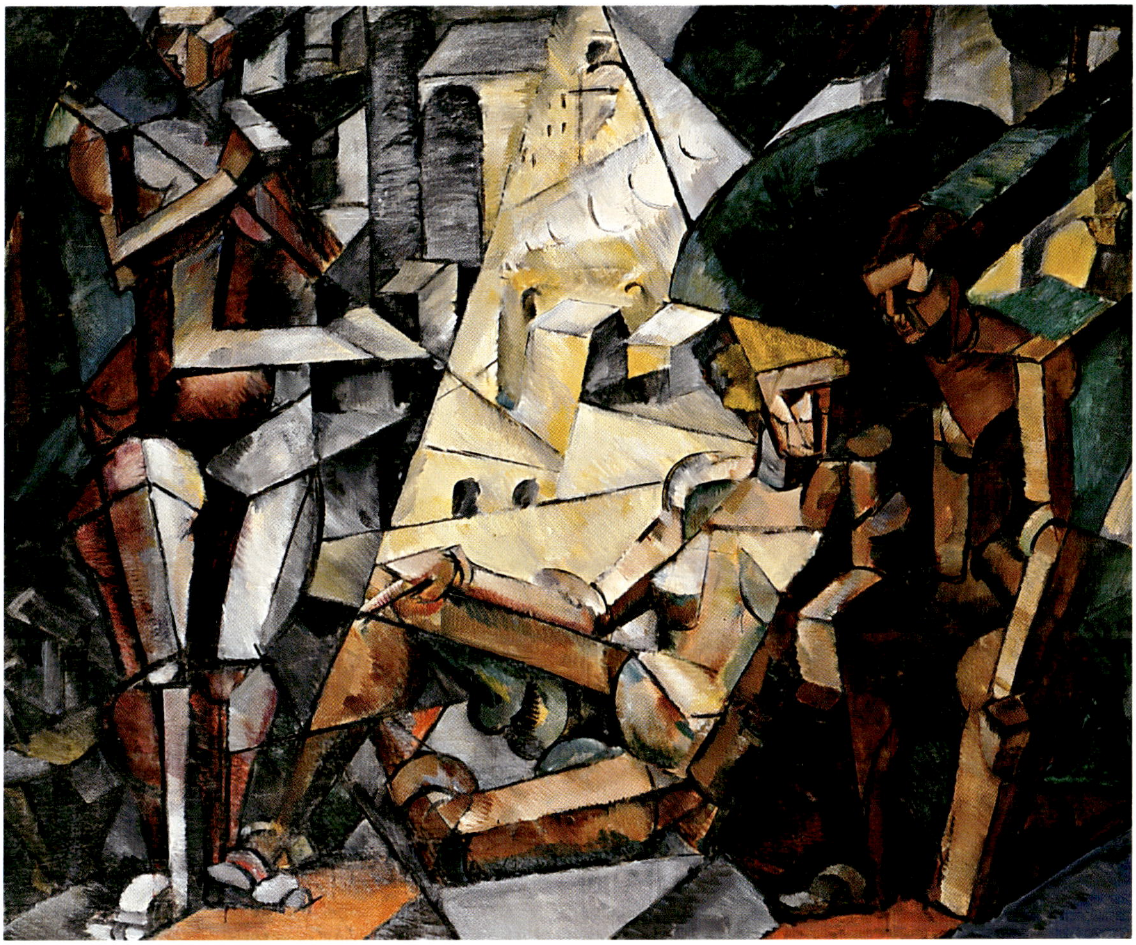

plate 75. NADEZHDA UDALTSOVA
Composition, 1913
Oil on canvas, 111.5 x 133 cm
Museum of History and Architecture,
Pereslavl-Zalesskii

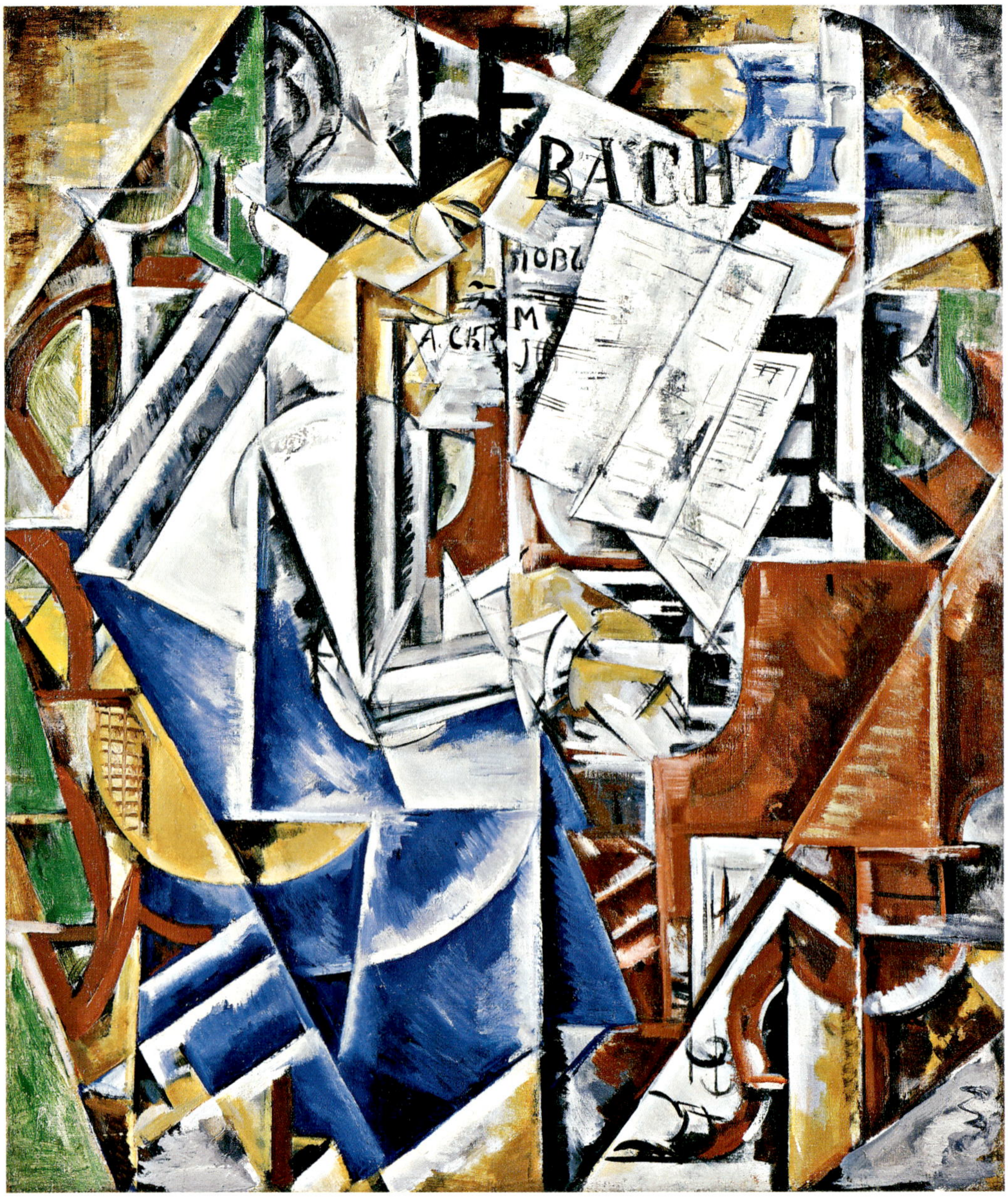

plate 76. NADEZHDA UDALTSOVA
At the Piano, 1915
Oil on canvas, 107 x 89 cm
Yale University Art Gallery,
Gift of Collection Société Anonyme

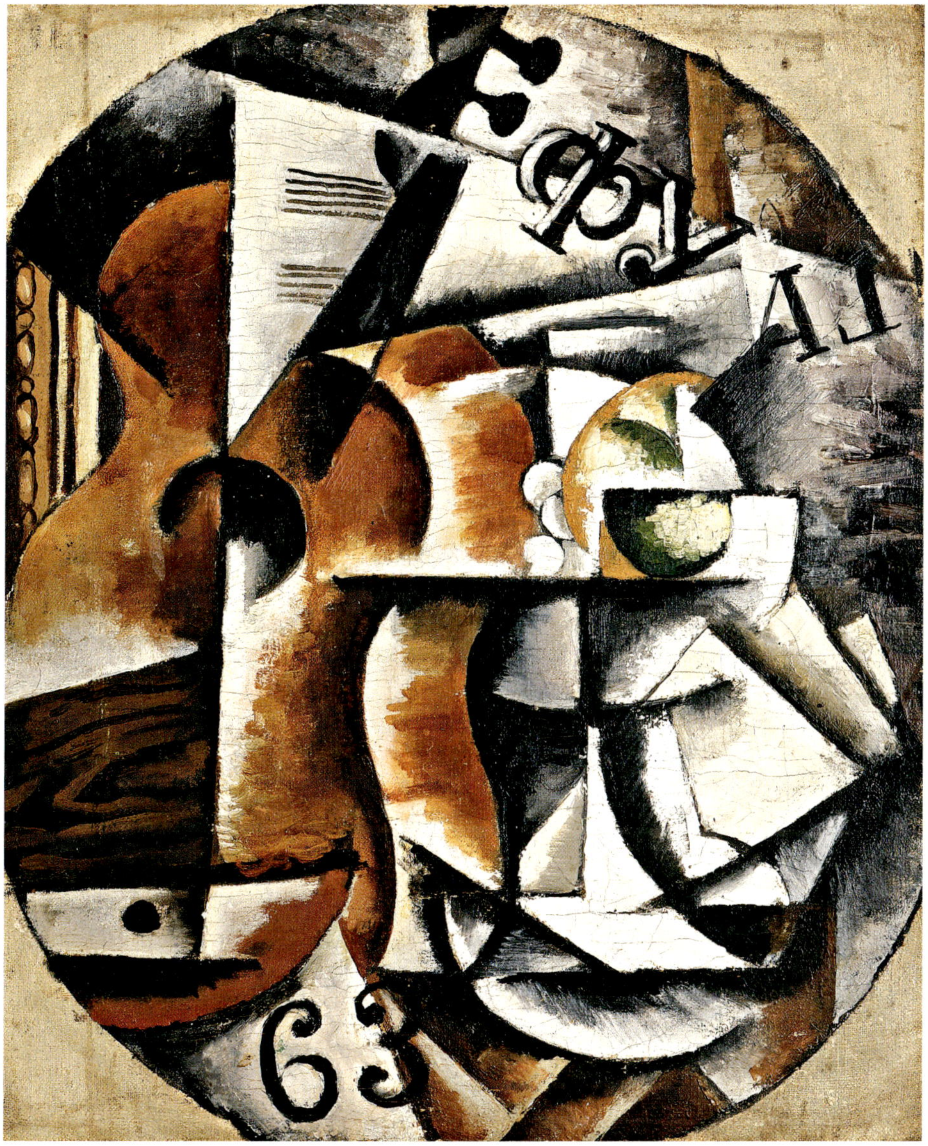

plate 77. NADEZHDA UDALTSOVA
Guitar Fugue, 1914–15
Oil on canvas, 106 x 71 cm
State Tretiakov Gallery, Moscow,
Gift, George Costakis

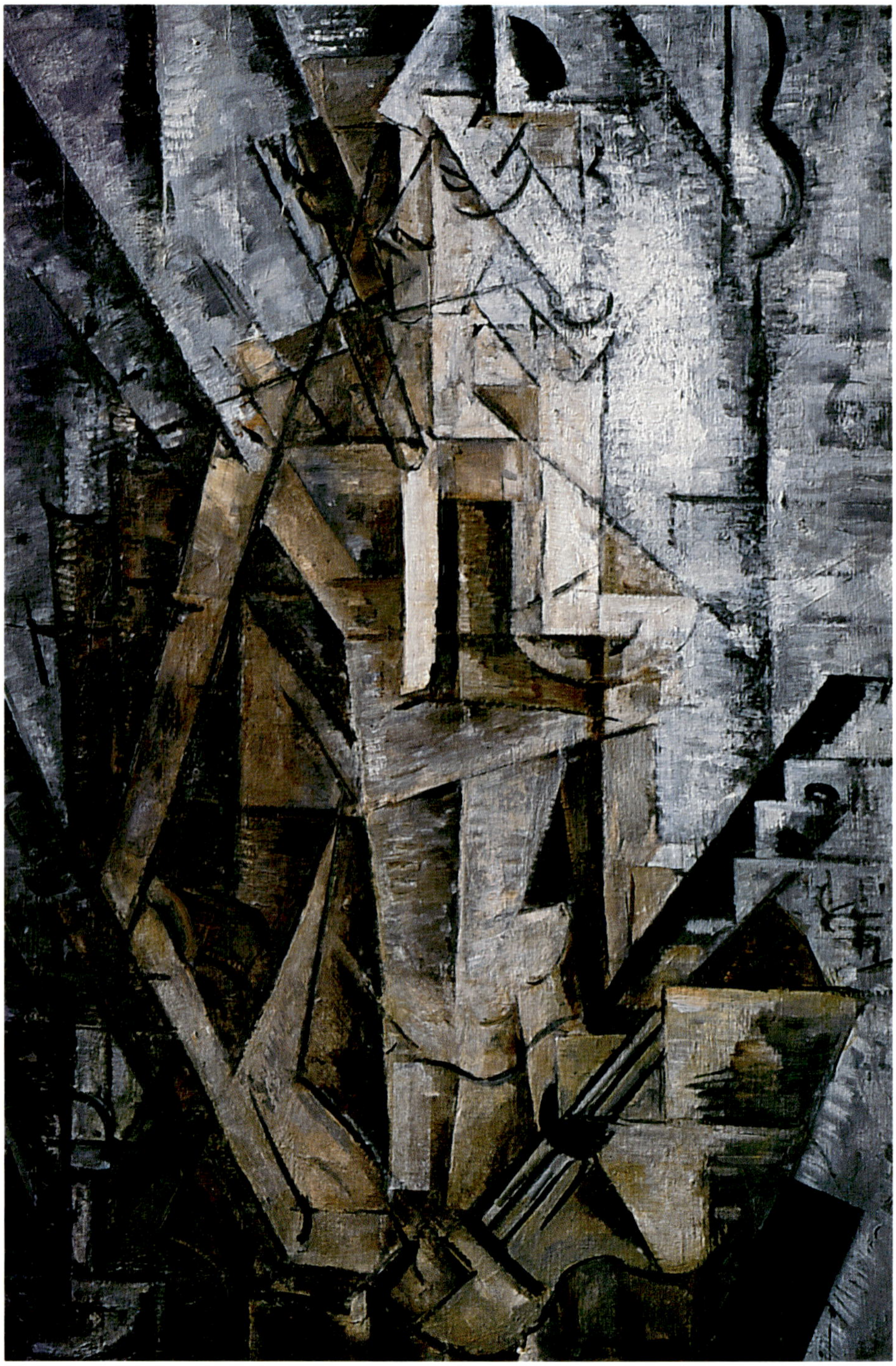

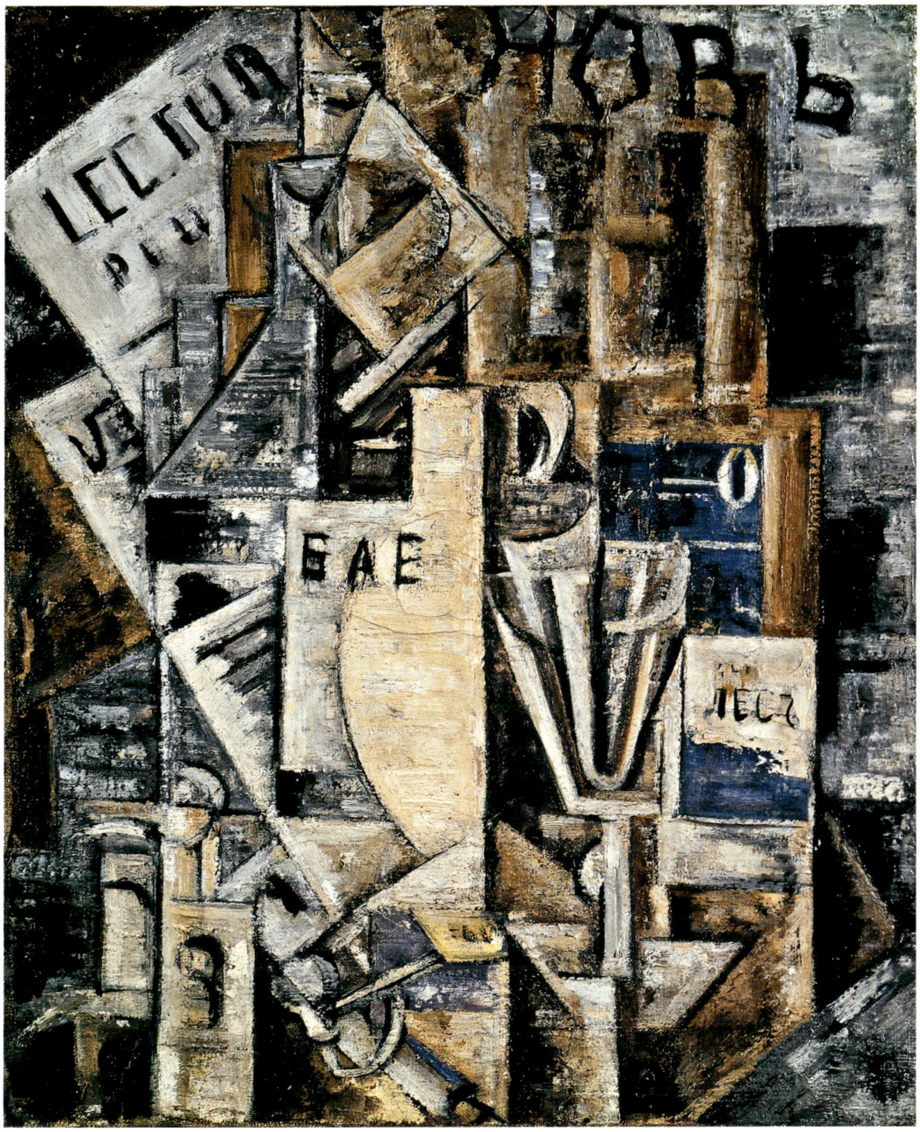

facing page:
plate 78. NADEZHDA UDALTSOVA
Artist's Model, 1914
Oil on canvas, 106 x 71 cm
State Russian Museum, St. Petersburg

above:
plate 79. NADEZHDA UDALTSOVA
New, 1914–15
Oil on canvas, 60 x 48 cm
Vastenov Regional Art Museum, Kirov

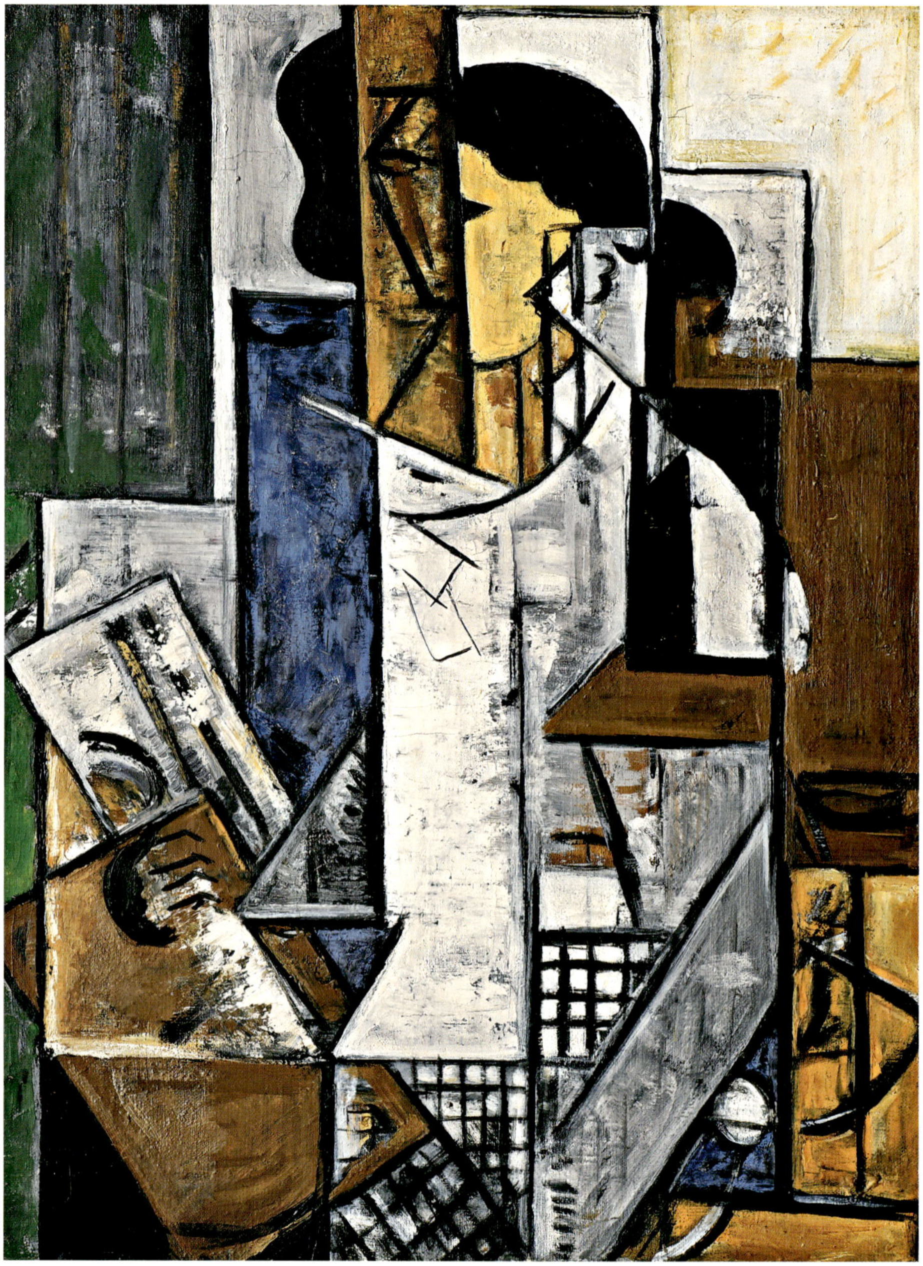

plate 80. NADEZHDA UDALTSOVA
Self-Portrait with Palette, 1915
Oil on canvas, 72 x 53 cm
State Tretiakov Gallery, Moscow

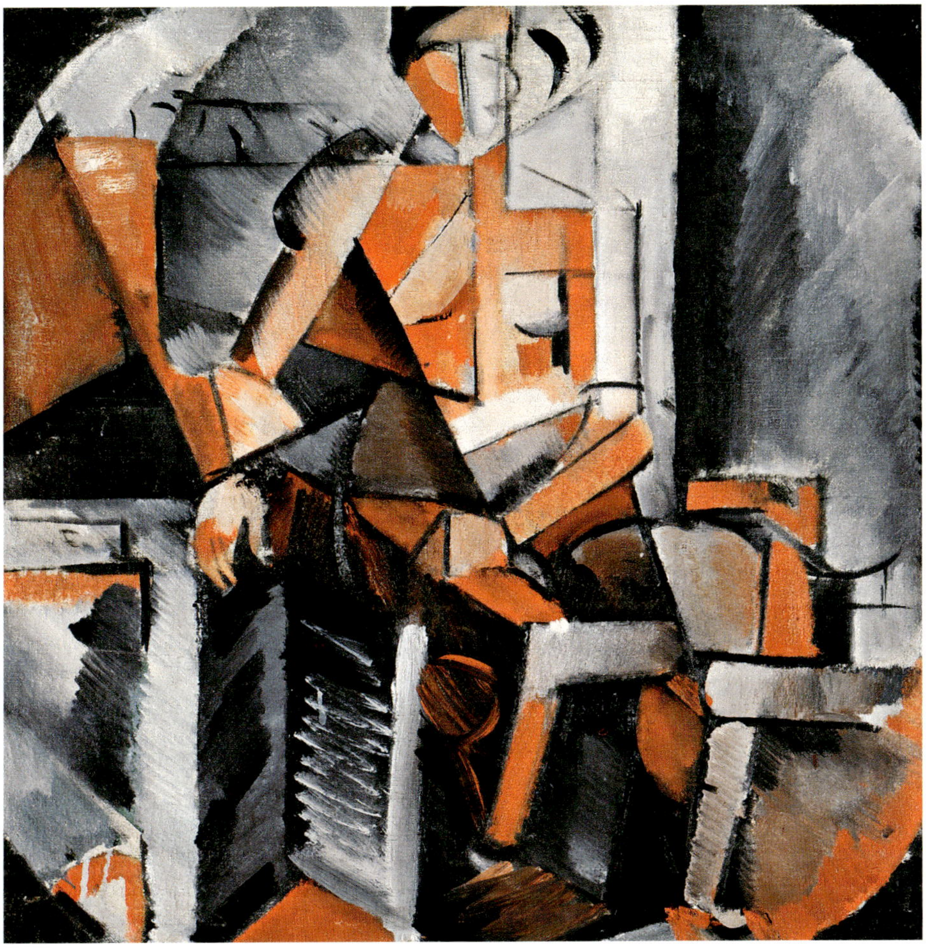

plate 81. NADEZHDA UDALTSOVA
Red Figure, 1915
Oil on canvas, 70 x 70 cm
Rostov Kremlin State Museum Preserve

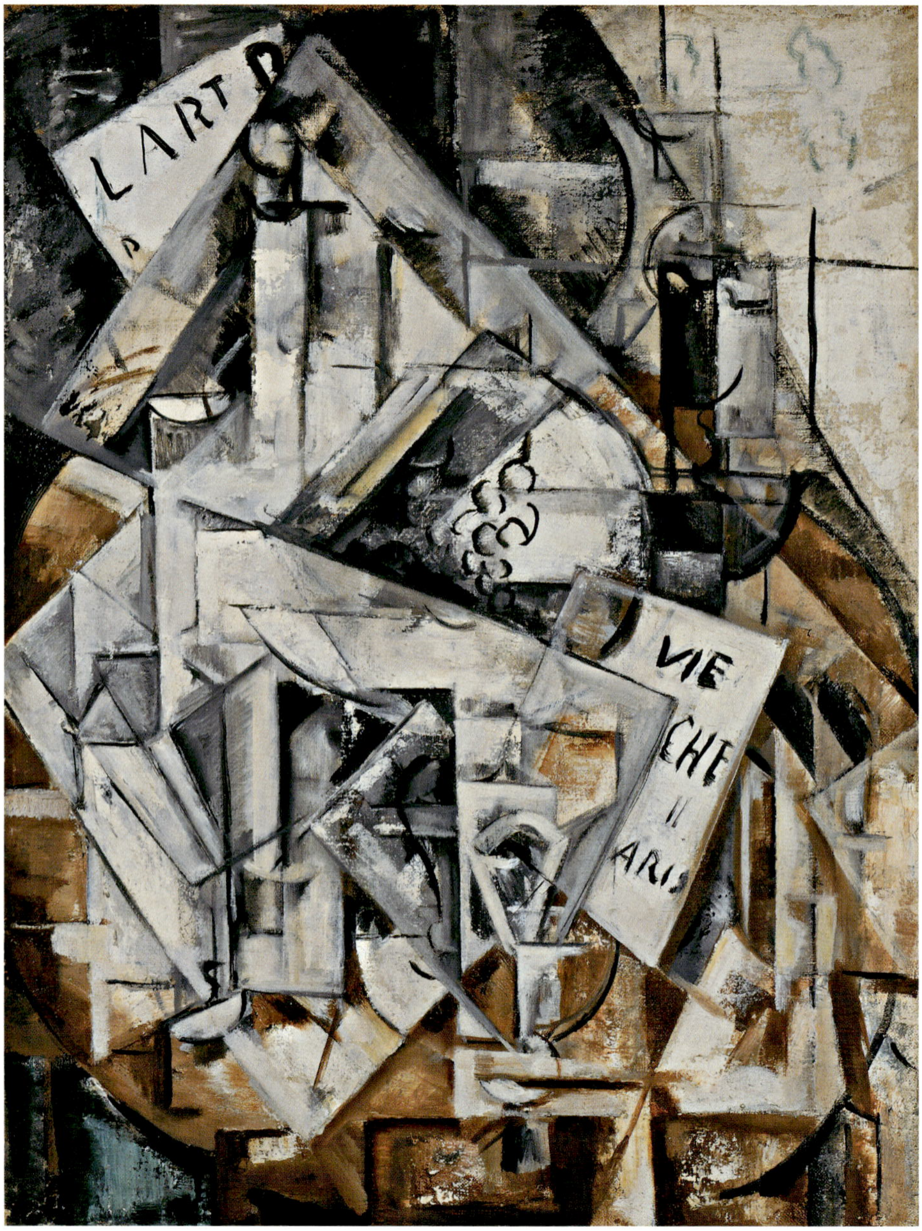

plate 82. NADEZHDA UDALTSOVA
Study for *Restaurant*, 1915
Oil on canvas, 71 x 53 cm
State Tretiakov Gallery, Moscow

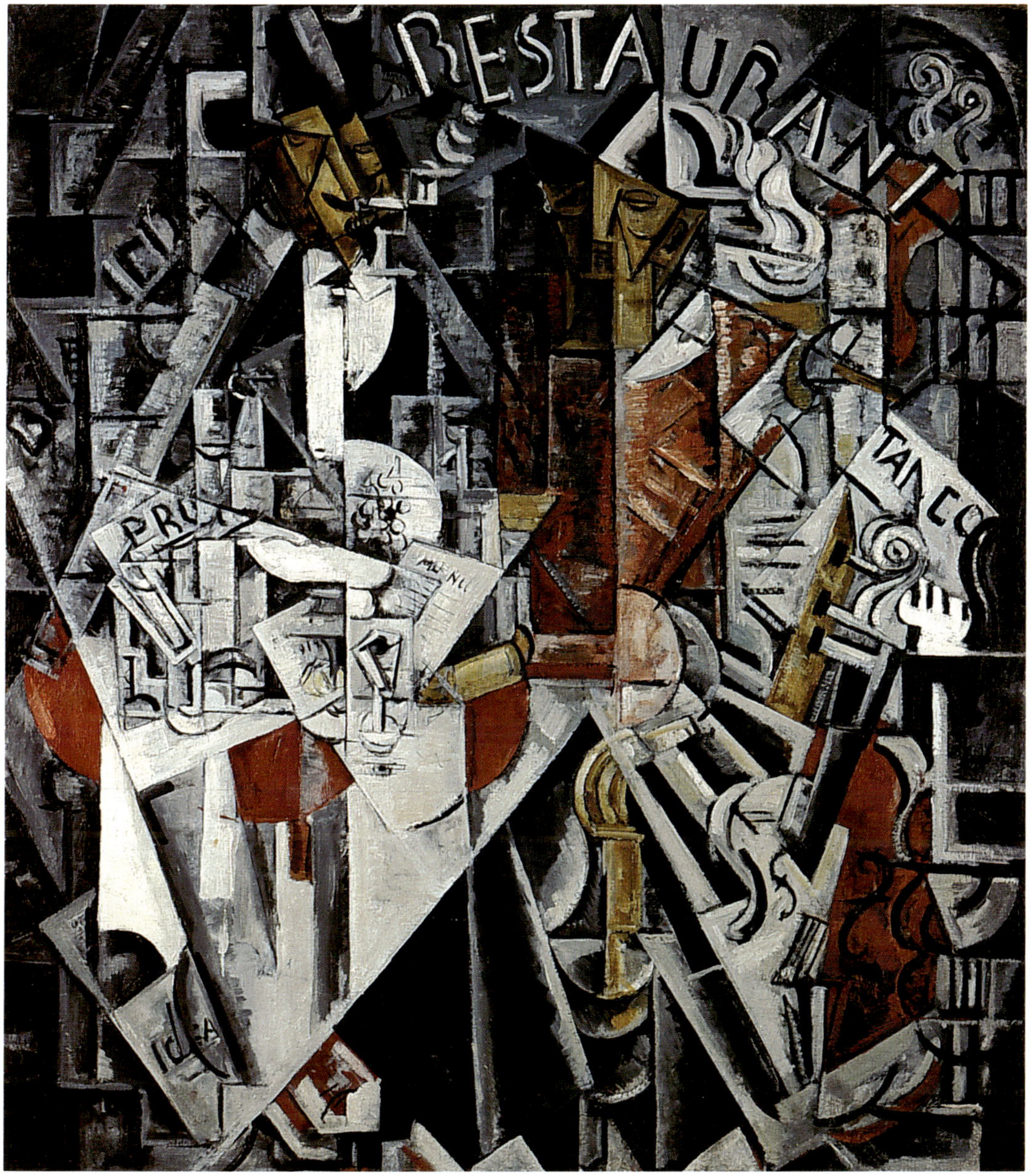

plate 83. NADEZHDA UDALTSOVA
Restaurant, 1915
Oil on canvas, 134 x 116 cm
State Russian Museum, St. Petersburg

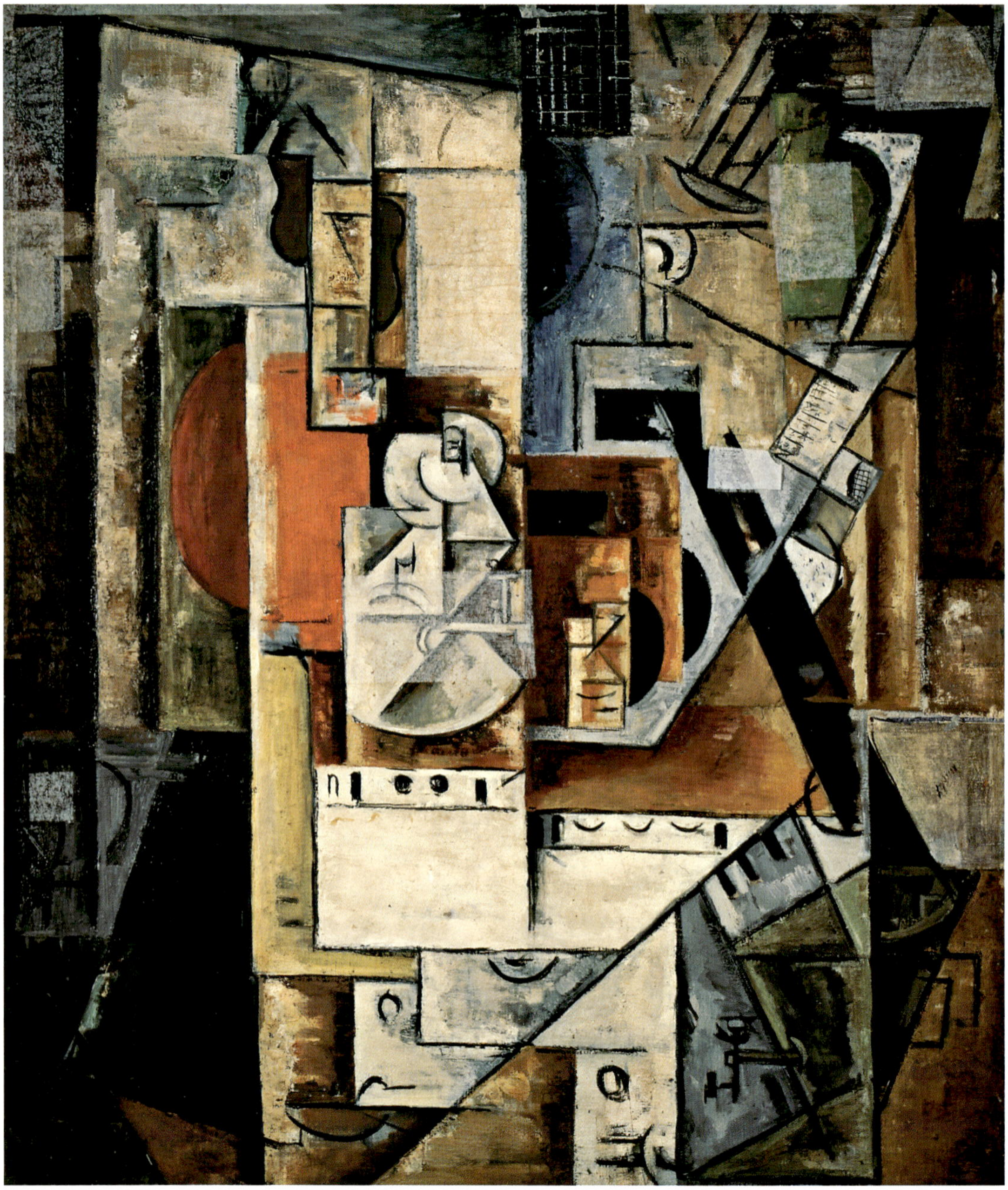

plate 84. NADEZHDA UDALTSOVA
Kitchen, 1915
Oil on canvas, 161 x 165 cm
Museum of Visual Arts, Ekaterinburg

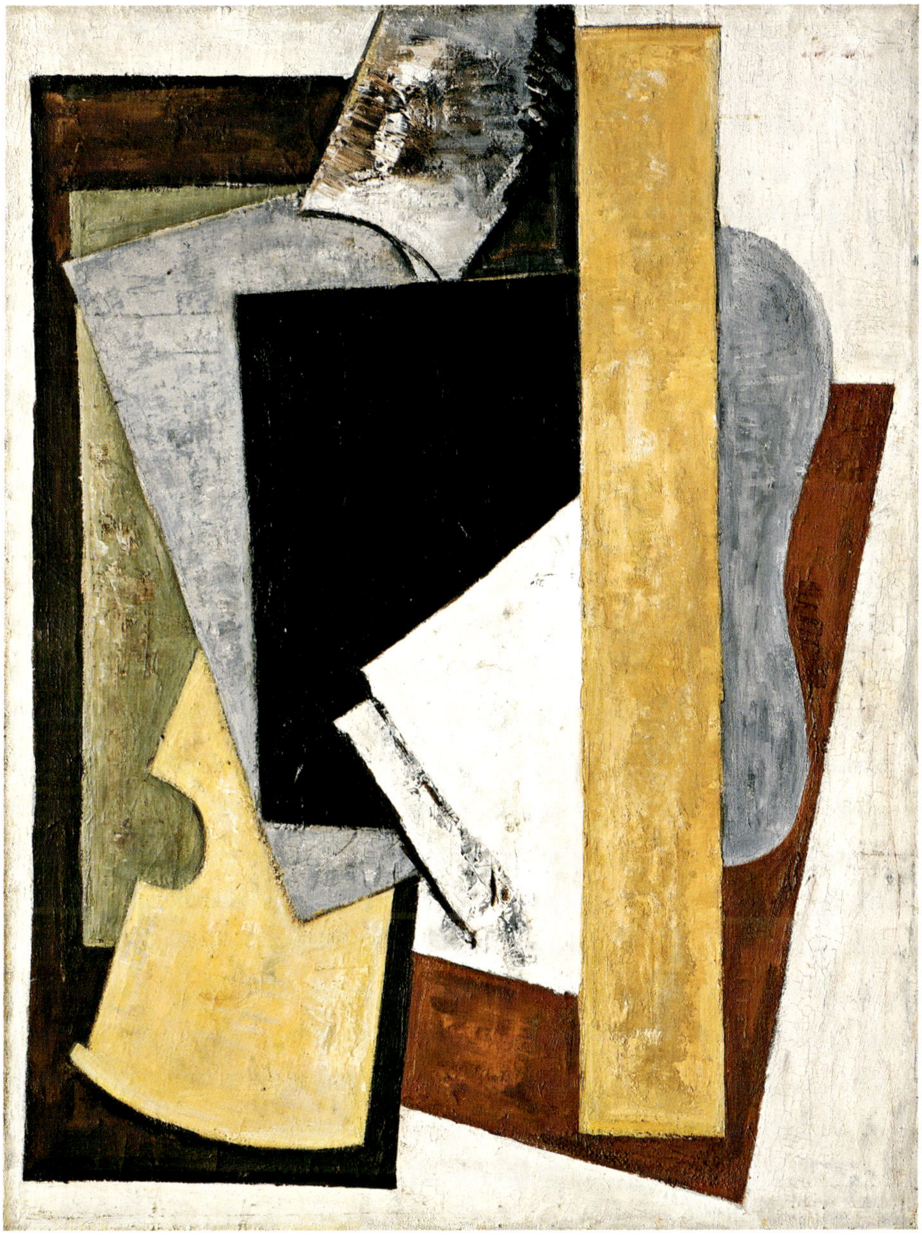

plate 85. NADEZHDA UDALTSOVA
Painterly Construction, 1916
Oil on canvas, 109 x 79 cm
State Tretiakov Gallery, Moscow

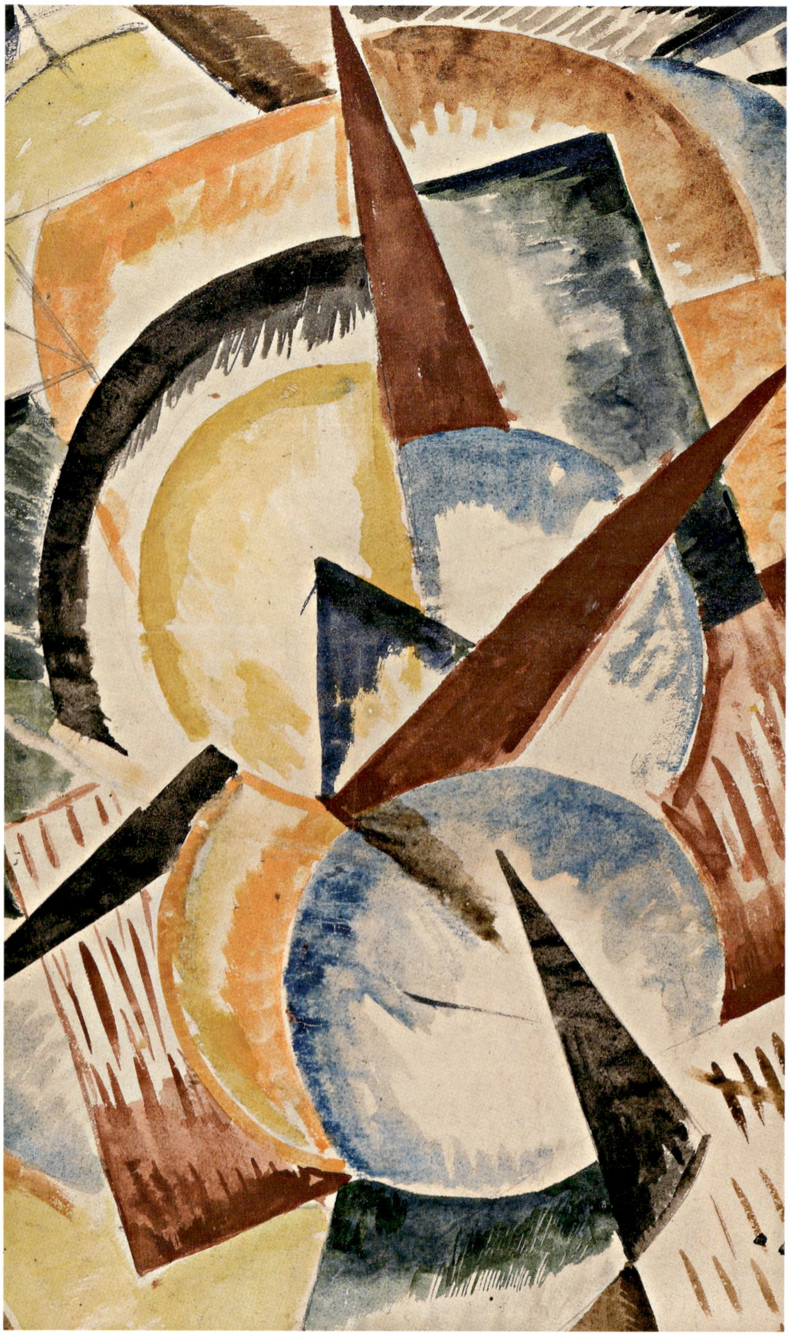

plate 86. NADEZHDA UDALTSOVA
Untitled, ca. 1918
Watercolor on paper, 48 x 40 cm
Art Co. Ltd. (George Costakis Collection)

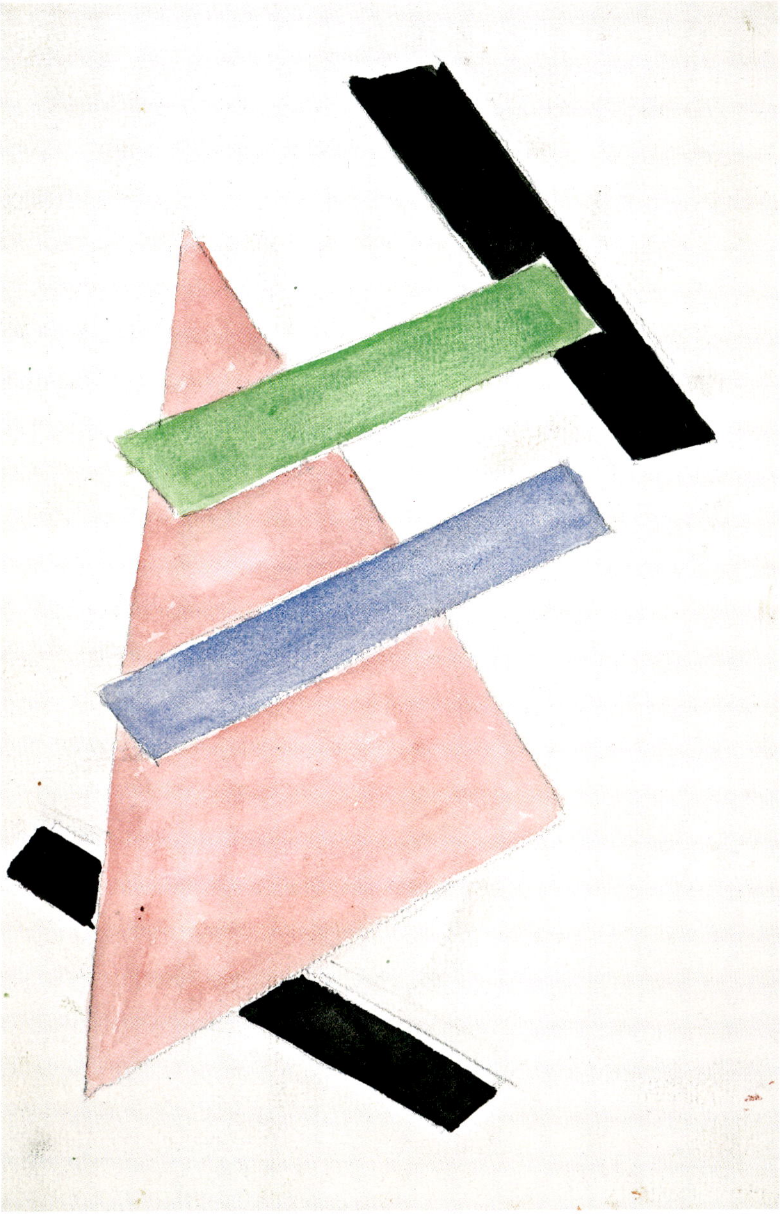

plate 87. NADEZHDA UDALTSOVA
Untitled, ca. 1918–20
Gouache and pencil on paper, 24.6 x 15.9 cm
Art Co. Ltd. (George Costakis Collection)

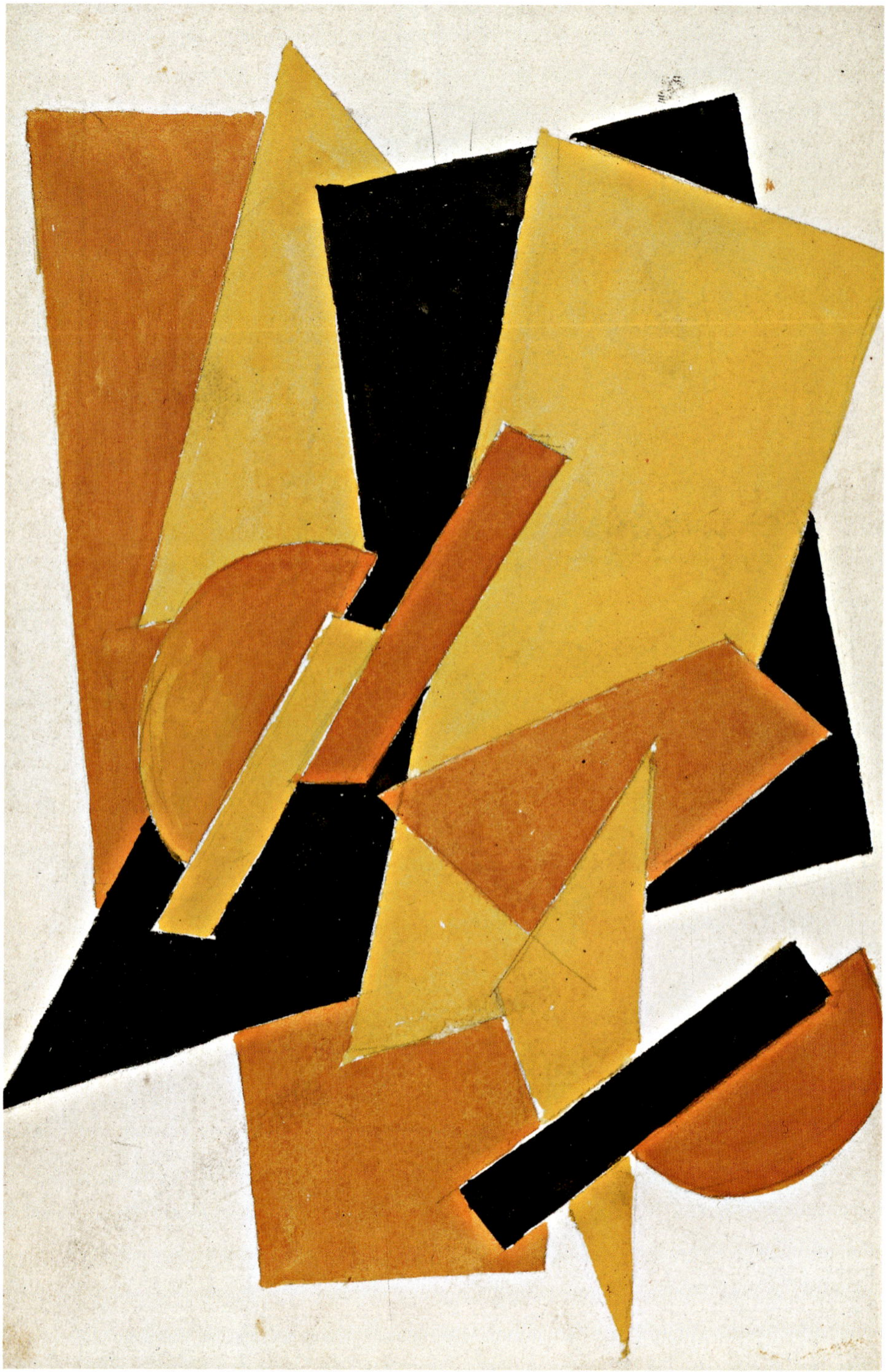

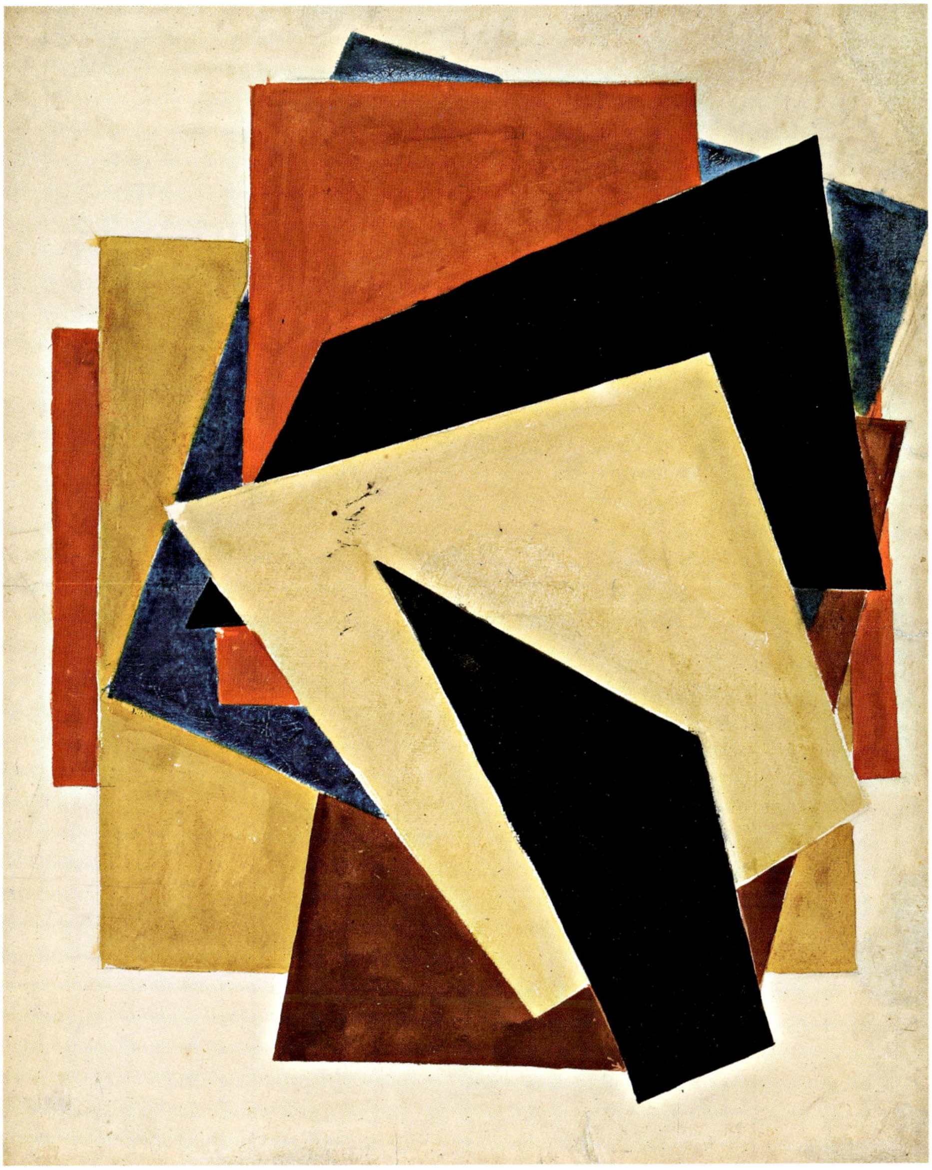

facing page:
plate 88. NADEZHDA UDALTSOVA
Untitled, ca. 1920
Gouache on paper, 48 x 38.5
Art Co. Ltd. (George Costakis Collection)

above:
plate 89. NADEZHDA UDALTSOVA
Untitled, ca. 1920
Gouache on paper, 64 x 44.5 cm
Art Co. Ltd. (George Costakis Collection)

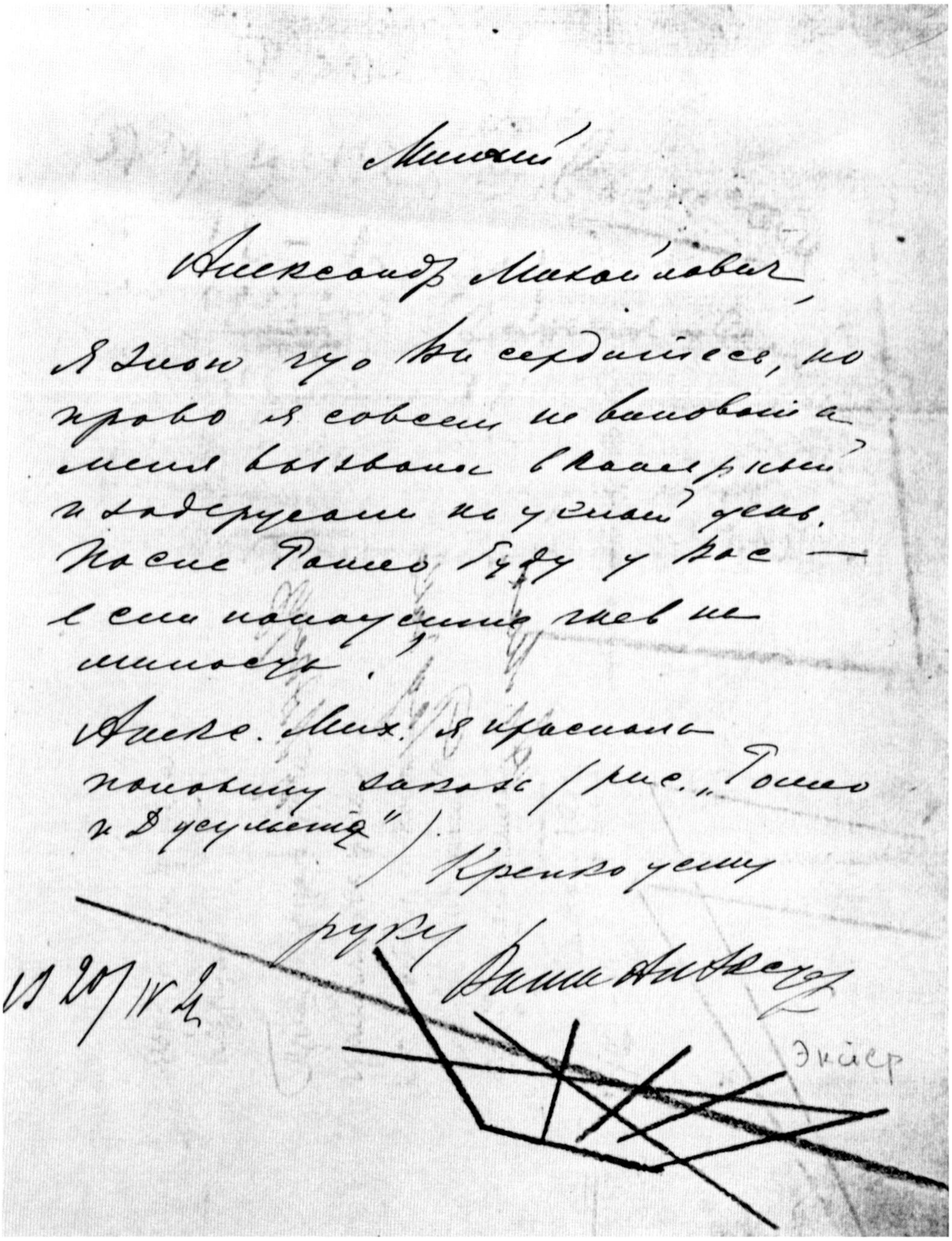

Милый

Александр Михайлович,

Я знаю что Вы сердитесь, но право я совсем не виновата а меня вызвали в Камерный и задержали на целый день. После Ромео буду у Вас — смените гнев на милость.

Алекс. Мих. я прислала половину заказа (рис. „Ромео и Джульетта").

Крепко жму руку Ваша А. Экстер

1920/IV 21

Экстер

figure 83. Handwritten letter from Exter to Alexander Rodchenko, dated April, 21, 1920. Private collection. (Translation on page 306.)

Alexandra Exter

Letter to Nikolai Kulbin (1913–14)[1]

. . . I am now rather close to Archipenko and I'd like to help him. Not only is he the only sculptor that Russia has, but he's the best here, too, even if he's not known in Russia. He really should be talked about, an article really ought to be placed. . . . Judging by the mood here, I feel that people are expecting [a lot] from us Russians, so that's why we should try to attract somebody like Archipenko."

An Exhibition of Decorative Designs by Elena Pribylskaia and Ganna Sobachko (1918)[2]

Types of decorative art include, among others, designs for the weaving, sewing, and printing of fabric and rugs. An essential characteristic of this kind of art is the planar resolution of forms in vegetable, animal, and architectural ornament. A decorative composition itself differs from a painterly composition in that it is conditioned by the fundamental requirements of rhythm — that is, by the repetitiveness of colored, silhouetted forms in designs, for example, for fabrics in which rhythm may be freer and more complicated. A symmetrical representation, which we often observe in primitive compositions, could also be mentioned as a simpler kind of rhythm.

Decorative designs must submit to the technical demands of their future execution and, therefore, only designs for the embroidery and weaving of rugs may be resolved more freely in lines and colors.

When we turn to popular art and study it or a composition deriving from it, we see that the traditional approach had been purely external. Wary of losing "style," artists feared to go beyond the conventional form and also chose that particular color which the period in question had created. Intensity of color, characteristic of more recent ethnic groups, particularly the Slavs, was replaced by the patina of the time, which seemed correct and appealing since it recalled the good old days.

However, this kind of approach may certainly not be regarded as work in the popular style, since its basis includes no investigation into the roots and laws of color and line composition.

For laws governing the composition of coloring in folk art we may point to ancient icons, whose initial coloring achieves maximum tension and whose composition possesses an inner rhythm and balance. Examples of contemporary folk creations in Slavic art also reveal a purity and intensity of color.

In decorative folk art, we perceive the development of the laws of composition, from primitive rhythm (the rug, clay) to dynamic rhythm (the painted Easter egg).

In Search of New Clothing (1923)[3]

Clothing design has always depended on both climactic conditions and social structures and the way of life that this may generate. Although during the early stage of human history clothing design was also the product of a collective, unconscious creativity, nonetheless, at the foundation of this creativity always lay the elements of a certain conformity and expediency. In the sphere of clothing, a conscious and individual kind of art appeared only much later.

That is why historical shifts themselves have always occasioned change and sometimes a total negation of earlier clothing designs that failed to meet the conditions of life. [The Great] War of 1914 and its laws, without any kind of ideological aspirations, greatly transformed the form and color of army uniforms. Clothing evolved from ostentatious conventionality to designs dictated by expedient necessity, both in active military service and in passive defense. The demands of war forced the change from an originally cold, gray color to a defensive camouflage color that blended with the earth. Various colored stripes and conventional insignia were replaced, and the design [of the uniform] itself was simplified. This was expedient and, therefore, legitimate. Only the civilian segment, which visited the front occasionally, degenerated and distorted this simple working military uniform by carrying its characteristic features to the blatantly absurd. Thus, for example, the uniform of the Russian "land hussar" consisted of foreign jodhpurs and service jacket, which look naturally right onto the body of the athletic European — but now transferred onto the stocky figure of the Russian, who lacks any sort of physical training.

During the Civil War, a diversity and indeterminateness of color dominated clothes — which is quite understandable from a psychological standpoint inasmuch as life had developed so rapidly and the forms of existence had been destroyed so swiftly that there could be no thought of creating a new kind of clothing. The very idea seemed inessential in the broader context of those grand elemental events. Only now, after emerging victorious from the struggle, Russian life is entering the path of conscious work leading toward the ideological elaboration of questions in everyday life and toward the external look of the human being — his clothing. Where tailoring was once dominated by a single "fashion," serious investigations and scientific and artistic research into new forms have begun.

The most important achievement in this area has been the outfitting of the Red Army. . . .

Clothing white-collar workers,

however, has proved less successful. The design remains quite unresolved, while all our institutions abound in the most ill-assorted kinds of clothing. This is a problem that still confronts artists and specialists alike. Expediency, practicality, conformity to each special field — these are the foundations upon which professional and Soviet clothing should be created. Form, material, and color — these are the elements from which this should be created. In the interests of utility in both warm and cold periods, this clothing should be constructed from materials of different thickness, that is, parts should be able to be removed from the outfit without violating its general meaning and logic. The color of the clothes worn by a given number of people in a particular space should be, convention notwithstanding, not neutral, but a dark, primary color — no more bureaucratic coldness and anonymity.

Experiments for specific "production clothing" have also been undertaken in the sphere of theatrical costume. Here, however, there is still a confusion of conceptions between the costume of the theatrical performer and the outfit of workers in other areas of production. The actor [could be] dressed in a worker's outfit, whether of a mason or of a carpenter, which had no real connection with the performer. Onstage, we saw workers of some kind of unprecedented "guild" who had never existed and workers who, in spite of their proletarian aprons, did

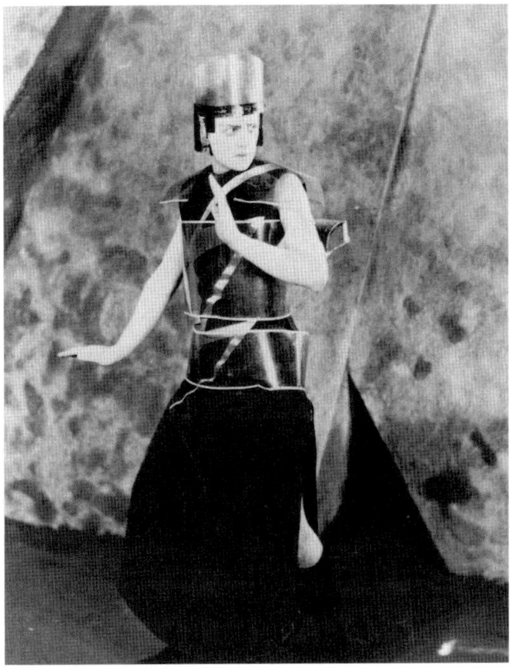

figure 84. Frame from the movie *Aelita*, 1924, produced by Yakov Protozanov with costumes by Exter and sets by Isaak Rabinovich.

not honestly labor, but rather played and jumped without soiling their outfit or just utilizing their apron as needed. In other theaters, the confusion reached such a point that we saw the conventional, painted, theatrical costume, production clothing, and modifiable costume of the heroine. It has to be said that the contemporary specialized costume for stage performers has still not been discovered. However, this kind of production clothing has existed for centuries: the "tutu," i.e., a costume constructed according to the movement of the body during a classical dance. Ballet shoes, leg tights, lightness of the skirt, flexibility of the torso — all these are logically connected with the dance and make the "tutu" the production clothing of clas-

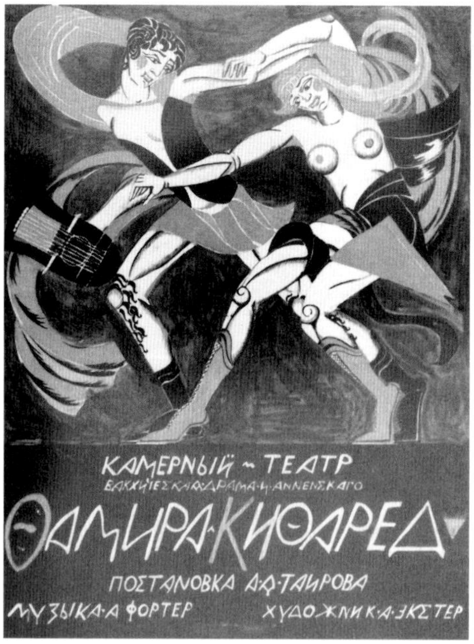

figure 85. Poster for Alexander Tairov's production of Innokentii Annensky's *Thamira Khytharedes*, Chamber Theater, Moscow, 1916. Bakhrushin State Theater Museum.

sical ballet. Right now, when the theater is studying every possible kind of movement (physical, emotional, tightrope walking, etc.), the theater should base its production clothing on the movement of the actor's body. Fundamental laws of the costume should be found that, of course, would allow for variations and changes of one kind or another. . . .

The fundamental condition of contemporary aesthetics should also be observed: respect for material. In this case, the material is fabric and we should not constrain this material for the sake of the caprices of fashion, but proceed from it. That is the condition of the new costume. It should be incorporated into distinct geometric forms, one or two, rarely three. Color should emerge from the design itself. The vivid colors so characteristic of folk costume, particularly of the Slavs, cannot be preserved completely under urban conditions; but to reject it out of hand would mean to follow the path of European civilization, with its homogenizing spirit. The very environment of Russia demands color—rich, primary colors, moreover, and not mere tones, as, for example, with the diffused color of France (Germany dresses more brightly and more sharply than France does).

Simplicity of designs and respect for material are dictated not only by the new aesthetics, but also by the demands of life itself. . . .

The Artist in the Theater (1919)[4]

. . . In preserving the flat painted decoration, designers who worked in the style of Bakst were unable to resolve the most crucial problems of stage design. The ordinary stage with its backdrop and curtains was fraught with two problems of plastic discordance. First, the painted perspective and volume of flat decorations could not work together with the concrete volume of the actor's figure. Second, the motionless, painted background could not enter into rhythmic unity with the figures moving out in front. Consequently, the designers, despite their fanfare of colors, never achieved the desired harmony and wholeness of a single and common impression. The architectural decorations of [Gordon] Craig and [Adolphe] Appia came much closer to resolving the fundamental plastic problems of the theater.

Free movement is the fundamental element of the theatrical act. The bland contemporary stage must be enriched above all with movement. As a consequence, the artist's mission is to give as much space on the stage to the dynamic powers of drama as possible while at the same time keeping them under control. The artist may achieve this mastery over the dynamic action [only] through architectonic constructions. It is essential to make a clean break with the painted decoration and to replace it with three-dimensional forms in different combinations. The fundamental guidelines of these combinations should be calculated so that the essential dramatic movement can develop freely with them in accordance with the inner rhythm of the drama. The action can be moved to a greater height by uniting the floor of the stage with the upper edge of the stage box by means of platforms, ladders, and bridges. This will give the actors a chance to display the maximum degree of dynamic action. On these bridges and ladders, [they] can perform short, individual dramatic scenes, quick in tempo, as in some of Shakespeare's dramas.[5]

Dramas that differ in their rhythm demand different methods of stage construction. Thus in Innokentii Annensky's *Thamira Khytharedes*, simplified volumetric forms of rocks and cypresses arranged in a semicircular line guided the movement of the Bacchic translations.[6] Only architectonic constructions assisted by volumetric forms may blend into a harmonious, plastic whole with freely moving figures. Amidst sets that are painted, even if brilliantly so, such a confluence in unthinkable.

In dramas more reserved and concentrated, with minimal external movement, such as Oscar Wilde's *Salomé*,[7] one can apply the method of animating certain elements of the set, in this case consisting of colored planes that move by means of an electric current.

Their dynamism should conform strictly to the action in the drama. The effect of moving colored planes follows from the emotional power of the harmony of the colors. It is also possible to modulate light. With this method, the light in the auditorium and onstage increases, weakens, and modulates in color and intensity according to the course of the drama. At the same time, the auditorium and stage join together as if in one common atmosphere, which strengthens the effect of the drama significantly. In general, all these methods serve a single goal: to allow the inner rhythm of the drama to manifest itself within the movement onstage.

As for the representational side of the sets, a general allusion to the nature of the environment in which the action takes place should suffice, so that the actor may direct all the attention of the audience to the dynamic action, to the performance of his body.

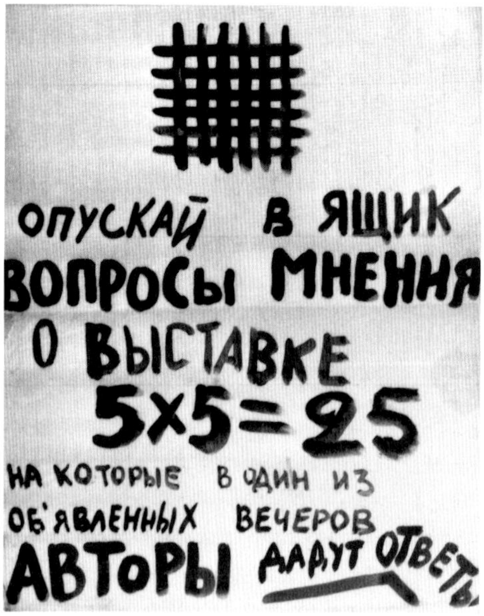

figure 86. Varvara Stepanova, Poster for the *5 x 5 = 25* exhibition, 1921, collage, 36 x 44.5 cm. Private collection. The poster reads: "Put questions and opinions about the exhibition *5 x 5 = 25* in the box, and the artists will respond at one of the scheduled evenings."

For the artistic reproduction of a particular period onstage, all you need to do is to capture the fundamental plastic idea of its style, which can be embodied quite freely, without resorting to the copying of museum specimens. One can observe this fundamental idea most easily in the architecture and ornamental design of a given period. Thus, for example, having utilized a pointed arch characteristic of the Medieval Gothic, you can echo it in the costumes and stage constructions. In this way, the artist can endow style with a totally new, unexpected interpretation while preserving a general faithfulness to the very spirit of the period in question.

For the costumes, it is essential to employ the same principles as in stage construction: principles of dynamic action. The composition of the costume, its form and color, should conform strictly to the character of the bearer's movements. This is fully attainable, since the various combinations of form and color may either strengthen or weaken the effects of the movement by imparting this or that tone to them. When studying the stage and the actor as a plastic whole, moreover, it is difficult to agree with the use of costumes made of "real" material alongside simplified, conventional three-dimensional sets. Costumes should be painted by the artist: the folds may be suggested by the paintbrush, [and] ornaments may be presented as individual fragments and in greatly exaggerated proportions, so that accidental folds and intricate needlework will not disrupt the clarity and integrity of the overall impression. Only under such conditions may the will of the artist be observed completely and the necessary unity achieved. The actor in a "real" costume on the conventional stage creates a crude dissonance. . . .

Artist's Statement in the Catalogue of the Exhibition *5 x 5 = 25* (1921)[8]

These works form part of a general plan of experiments on color which, in part, helps to resolve the issues of the interrelationship of color, its mutual tension, rhythmic development, and transition to color construction based on the laws of color itself.

Letter to Vera Mukhina, (March 3, 1929)[9]

Dearest Vera,

. . . I am now preparing an exhibition at the Quatre Chemins for May 15.[10] I don't know what will happen after that! As always after every exhibition, I shall begin to paint in earnest, because I really want to, and anyway I do want to present myself as an active painter. Morally I've grown stronger over the past year and I'm no longer in the confused state that you found me in last summer. Some mornings I even feel a new strength, and I feel that once again I can believe in my powers. I think that your visit exerted a profound influence on me. . . .

I suppose that the heroes of the season are de Chirico and Rouault. Diaghilev has invited both of them to design new sets, a characteristic nod to the latest fashion. I understand that de Chirico might do something interesting, but I can't imagine what Rouault can do for the stage. Nothing, obviously.

However, Utrillo and Modigliani have vanished from gallery windows. Hidden away. Concealed.

Of [current] exhibitions, I'm impressed by the show of a certain German, Helmut Kolle . . . Made a deep impression on me and I, too, had this desperate desire to paint people, but without psychological [interpretation]. Our discussions last summer convinced me and made it clear that with every fiber of my being I protest against psychology, however much it might be the thing right now. You know, Vera, there's something very stubborn in me, and on principle I always protest energetically whatever's "in," as one of my old friends says. No doubt, I've left behind the present, but from my point of view that's better than trying to pursue what's fashionable, and you can understand that like nobody else. After all, you, too, have always protested against "fashion." Maybe now is the only time when you and your tastes have coincided with the times, but Vera, believe me, this is a moment only. It will pass, and once again you will be alone in art. I've been through it all and am going through it again now in the deep sense of losing stylistic "collegiality," because what I believed in has gone. Turning toward individuality is what's left.

A propos of individuality — I looked at the first issue of the *Cahiers d'art*, which has photographs of the contemporary Moscow sculpture by the Vesnin brothers and others.[11] Well, with documents in hand I can show you what's been borrowed, and from where, or downright stolen both in the idea and in its parts. Nothing, nothing original. . . .

I'd like to see Russians above everyone else, for I'm convinced that Russians are the strongest and most talented people. They're strongest in the theater, but in the other plastic arts we are pathetic and clumsy imitators, always have been, but maybe one day we won't be like that.

Letter to Vera Mukhina (December 4, 1945)[12]

My dear,
Late last night I found out that I might have news of you. I got so worked up that my heart began to ache. In general, my health's not good . . . Pain in my heart, cramps in my hand, very weak, have to lie down. I lie around the whole day just by myself and see nothing but the inside of my apartment. . . .

I work away quietly, but joylessly, with no feelings. Just can't finish the commissions. . . . I feel really bad, hopeless. . . . Loneliness, sickness, lack of will power and energy, work that brings no joy — that's all I have left. Occasionally there are days when I feel more serene, but then I again fall into a depression. Events have really broken me and I no longer want to live."[13]

Translation of figure 83: I know that you're angry, but really it's not entirely my fault. I was asked to go by the Chamber [Theater] and had to stay there the whole day. I'll drop by after *Romeo [and Juliet]* — if you'll replace your anger with kindliness. Alexander Mikhailovich, I've sent in half the commission (sketch for *Romeo and Juliet*). Best wishes, Alexandra Exter

1. This extract was published in Kolesnikov, "Alexandra Exter i Vera Mukhina" (1989), p. 105; translated from the Russian by John E. Bowlt. Exter sent this letter from Paris (where she was living in 1913–14) to Nikolai Ivanovich Kulbin (1868–1917), an artist and "Doctor of Russian Futurism." Kulbin was a a leading light among the St. Petersburg Cubo-Futurists, writing, lecturing, and organizing innovative exhibitions such as *The Triangle* (St. Petersburg, 1910), to which Exter contributed. The letter is in the Department of Manuscripts, Russian State Museum, St. Petersburg (inv. no. f. 134, ed. khr. 62).
2. This extract was published in Alexandra Exter, "Vystavka dekorativnykh risunkov E. I. Pribylskoi i Ganny Sobachko," *Teatralnaia zhizn* (Kiev), no. 9 (1918), p. 18. Exter was personally acquainted with Evgeniia Ivanovna Pribylskaia (1877–1948) and Ganna Sobachko (1883–1965), two Ukrainian artists.
3. A. E-r [Exter], "V poiskakh novoi odezhdy," *Vserossiiskaia vystavka* (Moscow), no. 2 (1923), pp. 16–18.
4. Exter's thoughts about the theater were noted down by her student, Filipp Goziason, and published as "Khudozhnik v teatre. Iz besedy s Alexandroi Exter," in *Odesskii listok* (Odessa), no. 130, September 28, 1919, p. 4. Filipp Osipovich Goziason (1898–1978) was a stage and book designer who spent most of his life in France.
5. Exter designed productions of several Shakespeare plays, such as *Othello* and *Merchant of Venice*, in this way. Her album of pochoirs, *Alexandra Exter: Décors pour Théâtre* (Paris: Quatre Chemins, 1930; with a Preface by Alexander Tairov) includes designs for some of these.
6. Exter designed the sets and costumes for Alexander Tairov's production of *Thamira Khytharedes* at the Chamber Theater, Moscow, in 1916.
7. Exter designed the sets and costumes for Alexander Tairov's production of *Salomé* at the Chamber Theater, Moscow, in 1917.
8. Alexandra Exter, untitled statement in the catalogue (unpaginated) of the exhibition *5 x 5 = 25*, held at the All-Russian Writers' Club, Moscow, in September 1921. Exter contributed five works to the exhibition: *Problem of Color Contrasts*, *Color Tension*, and three *Color Rhythms*, under the general title "Planar-Color Construction." A second

5 x 5 = 25, with the same artists also represented by five works each (Exter, Liubov Popova, Alexander Rodchenko, Varvara Stepanova, and Alexander Vesnin), followed in October.

9. This extract was published in Kolesnikov, "Alexandra Exter i Vera Mukhina," (1989), p. 108; translated from the Russian by John E. Bowlt. Living as an émigré in Paris, Exter maintained a regular correspondence with her Soviet friend and colleague Vera Ignatievna Mukhina (1889–1953). Mukhina was a sculptor who in 1937 achieved instant fame with her enormous stainless-steel statue of a worker on top of the Soviet pavilion at the *Exposition Internationale des Arts et Techniques dans la Vie Moderne in Paris*. In spite of her official status as an official Soviet artist, Mukhina still went to see Exter during her visits to Paris in 1928, 1937, and 1945. Exter and Mukhina had first collaborated as designers for Alexander Tairov's Chamber Theater in Moscow before the 1917 Revolution and, until Exter's departure in 1924, continued to work on joint projects such as dress designs for the Moscow Atelier of Fashions; Mukhina even helped Exter with the costumes for Yakov Protozanov's movie *Aelita*. The letter is in the Russian State Archive of Literature and Art, Moscow (inv. no. f. 2326, op. 1, d. kh r. 254).
10. Exter's exhibition at the Quatre Chemins gallery in Paris consisted of fifty stage designs and maquettes.
11. There were three Vesnin brothers, all of them architects: Alexander Alexandrovich (1883–1959), Leonid Alexandrovich (1880–1933), and Viktor Alexandrovich (1882–1950).
12. This extract was published in Kolesnikov, "Alexandra Exter i Vera Mukhina," (1989), p. 108; translated from the Russian by John E. Bowlt. The letter is in the Russian State Archive of Literature and Art, Moscow (inv. no. f. 2326, op. 1, d. kh r. 254).
13. Exter was in ill health (she had a serious heart condition), and had just lost her second husband, Georgii Georgievich Nekrasov (1878–1945).

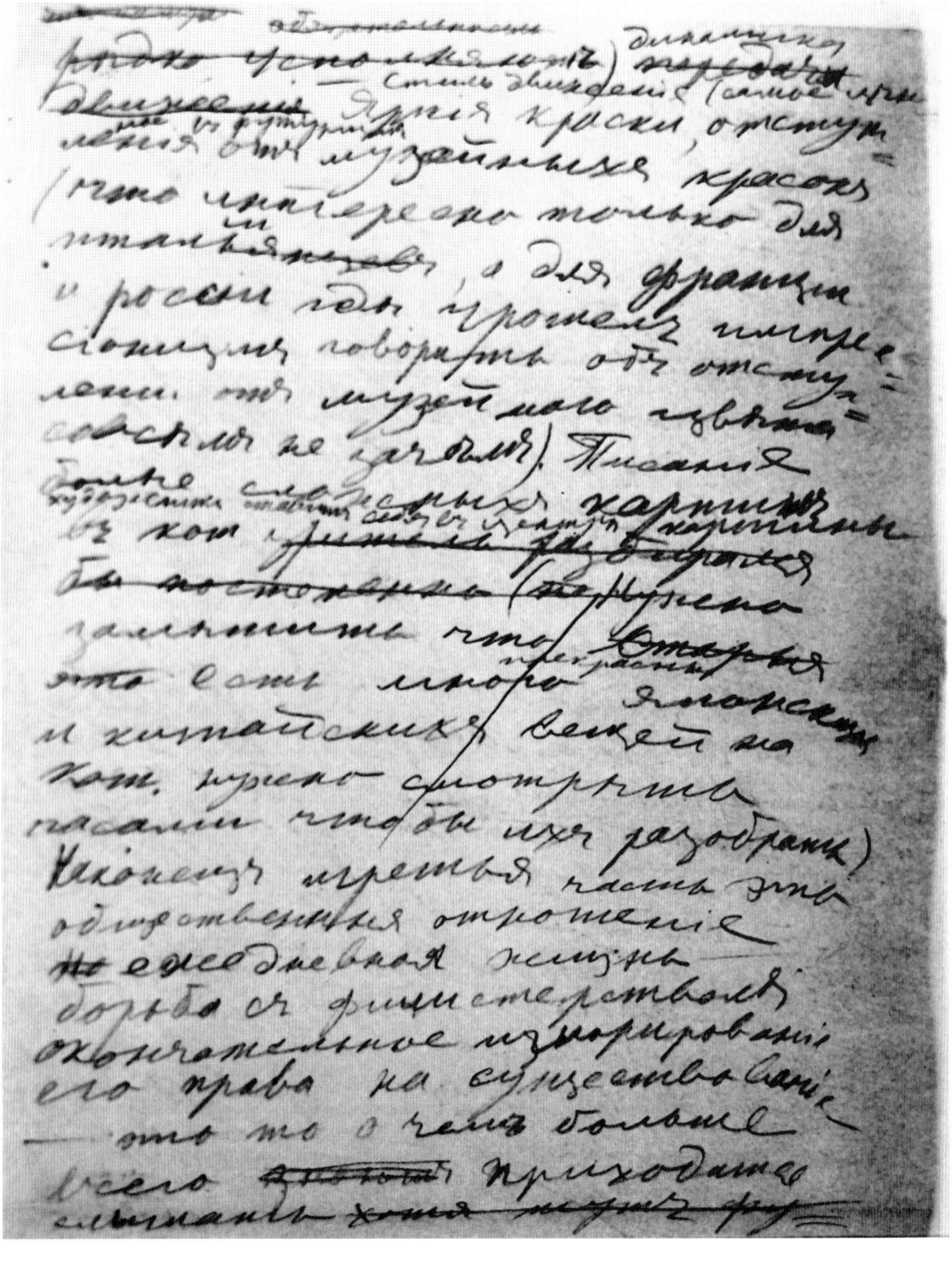

figure 87. Part of manuscript by Goncharova on art movements, ca. 1914.
Collection of the Khardzhiev-Chaga Cultural Foundation, Amsterdam (Box 78).

Natalia Goncharova

Album (1911?)[1]

When I follow the path of Cézanne, my works satisfy me less than those that derive from totally different artifacts such as icons, the Gothic style, and so on. Perhaps this is because of a lack of talent or of a kinship with other souls, and this terrifies me sometimes. But I am taking the path I want. Cézanne and icons are of equal value, but the works that I have made under the influence of Cézanne and those that I've made under the influence of icons are not. Corot is outstanding, but I just can't work under his influence. I'm not European at all. Eureka.

A church mural motif. An ocher background, light with chrome. In the background, pale green, yellowish branches weave together around the whole cupola. Many of the branches hold tiny leaves, like those of a dahlia (in three shades of green). The branches have flowers, pink (scarlet and cinnabar) with white lead and chrome, and tiny fruits, yellow and red. The branches are joined to blue trunks with little transverse strokes of a paler color. The trunks descend a little below the middle of the church windows. At the top of the trunks and on the branches sit peacocks and tiny, varicolored birds. The trees are being watered by holy figures and angels with dark faces and halos, in simple clothes with heavy folds. A radiant Christ, a pole axe in his hand, descends from a mountain to his church and garden in order to find his withered tree. Will the Lord not let me paint this? Lord, forgive me. . . .

Jealousy is based on sensuality — that is, on sexual attraction — and that attraction, which, for no reason whatsoever, draws you to people who otherwise would hold no interest at all, is a tortuous feeling. It would be interesting to see what would happen if the attraction were to be gratified every time. Perhaps it would then not be aroused so often and would not always be such an insoluble issue, would not be something that can destroy the happiness of an entire life at any moment, destroy the love that we value, would not set all hell loose without giving anything in return. Even when not followed by agonizing consequences, jealousy still disturbs your life, disturbs your social interaction with others. It prevents you from becoming close to those of the opposite sex and often drives you away from your own friends. Perhaps I alone am such a corrupt monster. . . .

Others argue — and argue with

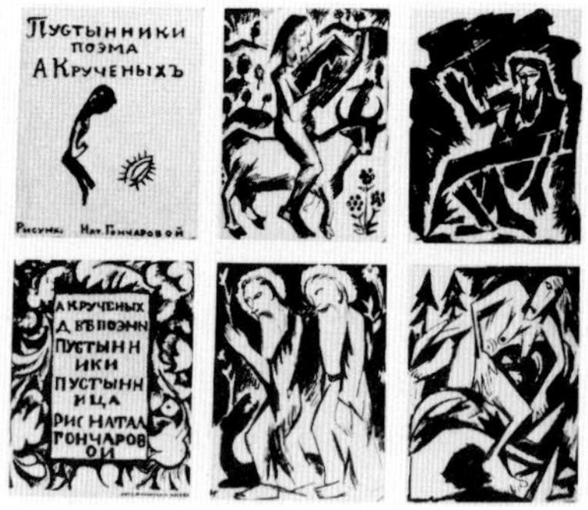

figure 88. Cover and illustrations by Goncharova for Alexei Kruchenykh, *Pustynniki* (Moscow, 1913).

me — that I have no right to paint icons. I believe in the Lord firmly enough. Who knows who believes and how? I'm learning how to fast. I would not do so otherwise, for it feeds too many rumors that tarnish the best feelings and intentions. People say that the look of my icons is not that of the ancient icons. But which ancient icons? Russian, Byzantine, Ukrainian, Georgian? Icons of the first centuries, or of more recent times after Peter the Great? Every nation, every age, has a different style. You can understand the most abstract of things only in the forms that you see most often, and also through whatever works of art you've seen — that is consolidated within some kind of material, through an understanding or, rather, recapitulation by previous artists. Of course, within all that material you perceive only what resonates with you. In a certain sense, everyone is color-blind — hence the differences we see in artists of the same period and even in the most realist of artworks by different peoples, whether Russian, Chinese, or Persian, etc., made during the same period, [or] the differences between the ancient artworks of a people and later ones by the same people. That's the point.

Misha has written me the following note from military camp:

"Do drawings of the sky and the clouds in pencil and watercolor. Make them both literally and also as they might appear, in all cases observing their characteristics. Do this simply so as to seize the most outstanding characteristic at a given moment. In this way, no one drawing will resemble the next, just as it happens in nature that no one motif resembles another. Do drawings of things, the landscape, people just as they appear at a given moment in your imagination; fear absolutely nothing, no deformity of any kind, no fabrication, no fantasy. Try out various styles and methods, emphasizing first one part, then another, now movement, now the very position of the object itself in space and its relationship to others. Change them according to your imagination and instinct, urge yourself to do it precisely that way or in accordance with the idea that you have worked out consciously in your own mind.

"Study the sky in engravings or other kinds of pictures. Study the expression of faces, too, in engravings, paintings, and in life."

I rewrote this so as not to lose it. I will try to recollect what he said and write it all down:

"It is not to an artist's merit to find

himself and then to keep on painting in the same old manner and with the same old colors. It is much better to keep creating new forms and color combinations. You can combine and invent them forever. For example, here is what you can do: spread green and orange pigments over a clean, primed, white canvas, and draw over them with black. The effect will be the same as in popular prints if, whenever passing the brush over the [orange] each time, you use a new brush to continue the line over the white in the same way that black lines in a popular print are covered in certain places by green and other colors. The colors set off the black lines while they cross over onto the background and pass from one object onto another.

"You can do this so that the surfaces of the objects border each other, a dark surface bordering a light one, and vice versa, so that they are not divided by lines (as in Picasso's works) or so that they border each other with thin lines. Thus the thin, hard lines outline an object which is of the same color as its background. In the sky, you can employ the same methods and apply the same colors, both dark and light, bordering them with various lines. Generally speaking, a line that borders an object can be darker than [the] object. So that it stands out, it is best to avoid broad lines and use them only if needed. They serve as a kind of extra (third) line, which can be used like a color separating two objects. You can make bright, almost white, faces with shades of black, green, blue, or red and place them on a dark background. This creates a very strong, almost tragic impression, like the figure of a smoker on a round tobacco tin. You can try this combination on objects in the environment: surround a direct white light and then the color of the object itself with the deepest shade of black.

"Orange, yellow, and red create the brightest effect. It works well to add blue and bright green, which, when in such proximity, become particularly bright. It is better to work on something that takes longer. At any rate, you have to give it some thought.

"You can begin ahead of time, without knowing [where you're going].

"One more thing I forgot to write: you can combine the color of one work with the style of another and thus create a piece unlike the other two.

"Create the theme of a work, the combinations of colors, and the manner or style separately. Consequently and inevitably, observations, and both realistic and fantastic forms, will flow into the work."

Misha asked me to note these things down and, of course, I'll do that.

For the moment that's all I can recall of what Misha told me yesterday and three days ago. I'll write down what he says.

Letter to the Editor (1912)[2]

Dear Mr. Editor,

Since the unofficial opponents at the debate on the new art were granted no

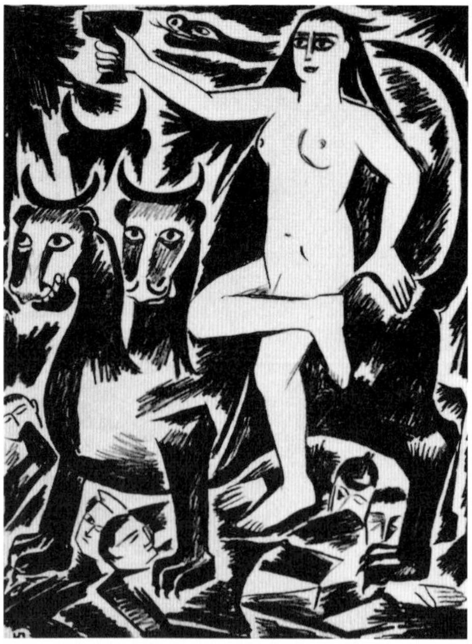

figure 89. *Maiden on the Beast*, 1914. Sheet no. 5 in Goncharova's album of lithographs, *Misticheskie obrazy voiny*, 32.5 x 24.8 cm. Private collection.

more than five minutes to respond (and part of that was lost, what with the noise in the hall and onstage), I did not have the chance to finish what I had begun to say. Consequently, my humble request is that you print the following continuation of my speech.

During the course of his speech, Mr. Kulbin showed photographs of my paintings, *Spring in the Countryside* and *Spring in the Town*, so as to reinforce his highly confused theories about our ill-starred modern art, especially Cubism. Cubism is a positive phenomenon, but it is not altogether a new one, especially as far as Russia is concerned. The Scythians made their stone maidens in this hallowed style. Wonderful painted, wooden dolls are sold at our fairs. These are sculptural works, but in France, too, it was the Gothic and African figure sculptures that served as the springboard for Cubist painting. Over the last decade, Picasso has been the most important, most talented artist working in the Cubist manner, whereas in Russia it has been yours truly. I do not renounce any of my works made in the Cubist manner. At the same time, I just cannot accept any kinship with the flaccid Jack of Diamonds group. The members of that venerable institution seem to think it's enough to join the apologists of the new art, including Cubism, to become an artist of the new persuasion, even if they lack tone in color, the power of observation, and artistic memory. Their mastery of line is pathetic, and it's not worth talking about their textures. Judging by their paintings, these artists have never thought about this or worked on it. In many cases, they are hopeless academics, whose fat bourgeois faces peep out from behind the terrifying mugs of innovators. This simply confirms that pathetic snails will cling to any ship. Andrei Bely had some good things to say about this in his manifesto, when he spoke about decadent literary small-fry.

It's a terrible thing when a formulation of theory begins to replace creative work. I assert that creators of genius have never created theories, but have created works on which theories were later constructed; and after that, works — for the most part of very low quality — were built on [those theories].

What can be said about particular individuals can also be said of entire cities and countries at a certain moment in their artistic existence. In Italy, where there is a total lack of contemporary art, Futurism suddenly appeared, i.e., the art of the future, a mixture of Impressionism and emotionalism. As a theory, Futurism is no worse than any other, but where can the Italians find the means to implement it? Germany also lacks contemporary painting and for the most part has borrowed the history and techniques of her neighbor, France. That even the slightest theory will still exist in the absence of a single popular history of contemporary art is confirmed by the great toiling away at [making] pictures and [applying] paint, even on the part of Signac and Cross.

The Cubist Picasso is great and, in France (above all, Paris), stands at the very center of contemporary painting. In this respect, the destiny of the Russian center of painting, Moscow, coincides with that of Paris. Both cities are besieged by foreign theorists with their big theories and little accomplishments.

I assert that religious art — and art that exalts the state — was and will always be the most majestic, and this is because such art, first and foremost, is not theoretical, but traditional. Hence, the artist could see what he was depicting and why, and, thanks to this, his idea was always clear and definite. It remained only to find the perfect and most well-defined form so as to avoid any misunderstanding. Please note that I have in mind not academic training (since I consider academism to be a transient phenomenon), but rather the eternal successive connection that Cézanne had in mind and that creates genuine art. In contradistinction to what was said at the debate yesterday, therefore, I assert that *what's* depicted is, was, and will be important, and that *how* it's depicted is also important.

I assert that there can be an infinite number of forms to express an object and that they can all be equally beautiful, independent of the theories that coincide with them. It was said at the debate that contemporary art is renouncing beauty as it advances toward ugliness. I assert that this opinion seriously undermines the meaning of beauty, ugliness, and art as phenomena, which in this case have their own laws and do not coincide with life. Ugliness in art is whatever is weak in technique, texture, line, color, and distribution of form and color masses.

Accept my assurances of deep respect.

Open Letter (1913?)[3]

What can I say about women that has not already been said a thousand times? To repeat all of the good and idiotic things that have been said about my sisters a thousand times already is infinitely boring and useless, so I want to say a few words not *about* them, but *to* them: Believe in yourself more, in your strengths and rights before mankind and God, believe that every-

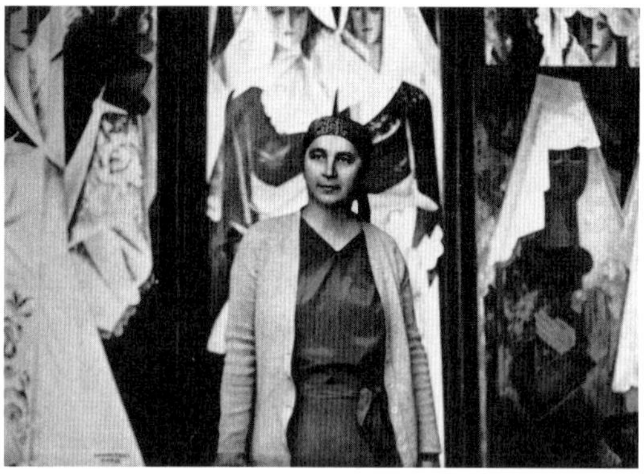

figure 90. Goncharova in front of her painting, *Spanish Ladies*, 1920, Paris

body, including women, has an intellect in the form and image of God, that there are no limits to the human will and mind, that a woman should not only carry within herself thoughts about heroism and great deeds, but should also search for a hero and creator among her male colleagues in order to create heroes and creators in her daughters and sons. Remember, too, that when one colleague is base, lazy, and stupid, another ends up wasting half of his/her effort struggling with that person, leaving only one half for the rest of life.

Letter to Filippo Tommaso Marinetti (1914)[4]

Monsieur Marinetti,
Our country is a beautiful country. It is bigger and younger than yours. Italy used to be a beautiful, young matron [*sic*], then a beautiful, fifty-year old courtesan, and then a beautiful beggar-woman. Being a beggar-woman after such a beautiful career means the end, even if one has a Futurist son or daughter. Our country, of which you are a guest, is still a child. For her everything is in the future as [*illegible*]. [She is] a fantastic, but not exotic, creature [whom] Europe may exploit, but can never comprehend.

Woman is [*illegible*]. They are mother-men and formally are women-men-lovers, but as with the worker, there is no need to despise them. In Russian, the word *chelovek* [human being] designates the human beings of both sexes. Which concerns human relationships and our own nationality. As for the new color [painting], I can tell you that a dozen years ago art in Russia abandoned the museums [while] our grandparents were [still] sketching life around them. For the old and fragile nerves of Italy and Europe, Futurism is very much for the nerves [*sic*], whereas for Russia, however, it hardly exists; it is a new academicism, one with a Romantic character. You see very well that I am right. . . .

Letter to Boris Anrep (1914)[5]

Dear Boris Vasilievich,
Thank you very much for the letter and the invitation, and for thinking of me. If everything works out, I'll be in Paris on business this spring.[6]

Why do you write about the distance separating the artist and his work like that? Is it really so important that an artist remain completely bound together with his work? Man is a complex machine, perpetually moving and changing, and a work, once completed, becomes a static thing with its own individual life, a life that lasts longer than that of the individual who created it: the difference between the two has always existed and always will. If you try and approach your work from the distance of the future, when you will no longer have the painting you created anywhere near you, then all that's left is simply whether the work has been created well or poorly, strongly or weakly. What remains is merely the extrinsic and intrinsic artistic value and absolutely nothing of the extent to which the work expressed the artist, his soul, or his connection with what he created. Nonetheless, the material of the work, and, beyond that, its creative spirit, lies not in the individual, but in the people, in the nation to which the individual belongs, in its earth and nature. It is part of the common, popular soul, like a flower on a huge tree. True, the flower may be torn from the tree and planted in an artificial growing environment, and at first it will perhaps begin to bloom still better, but, even so, it would have been nicer had the flower remained on the tree. For the Russian artist, this tree is Russia and the East, but not Europe, from whence she can and must take military ships, aeronautics, methods for attack and defense. The artist, however, needs to devote his life to indigenous places, to take life from indigenous places.

Please forgive my overly serious tone, but these are things that I think about a lot. A Russian cannot become a European without first creating a division between his [or her] own inner world and the means of expressing [this] in external life — dressing, walking about, or making poetry, music, and painting — all of which possess a certain dryness and restraint, don't express things very well, and provide little gratification. The same might happen if you withdraw into the aesthetic and the archaeological. However, there is also another way of discovering equilibrium, i.e., forget your first love, become the adopted son of a foreign country, and give yourself up to the new country completely. That's what happened with van Gogh, Gauguin, and Picasso, but not with the Russians. Again, please forgive me for the overly serious tone, but there are things in your letter that do not allow me to write lightly or on just any old topic.

We will be happy to help your Englishman as someone who has seen you recently. Your name suffices for us to welcome him, but he hasn't turned up yet. What a shame that it's just a friend of yours and not you yourself. I do ask you to understand that I do not forget you and that your name alone would suffice for M[ikhail] F[edorovich] and I to welcome him as a good person.[7]

My exhibition has been a really great success.[8] Bundles of newspapers featuring articles big and small, one contradicting another. There have been photographs of me, reproductions in journals, flowers [sent to me], interviews, letters (from various ladies), and a lecture about me and my work; there were public scandals and receptions in restaurants, three editions of the catalogue, commissions for portraits, for a carpet, for [stage] décors; and three works were purchased for the Tretiakov Gallery (very early works, to be sure, but all the praise is lavished on my old works, not the new ones — to which two rooms were devoted and which met with little approval, but which caused a furor).[9]

1. These are excerpts from an undated manuscript entitled "Albom" in the Archive of the Khardzhiev-Chaga Cultural Foundation, Amsterdam (in Box 78); translated from the Russian by J. Frank Goodwin. The "Album" is difficult to date with precision, but the fact that Goncharova emphasizes her current interest in icons and refers to a letter that Mikhail Larionov had written from military camp (Larionov was drafted in October 1910 and was in an army camp near Moscow in the summer of 1911) indicates that this section of the "Album" dates from 1911.
2. Goncharova wrote this "Letter to the Editor" on February 13, 1912, the day after a debate organized by the Jack of Diamonds group and held in the Greater Auditorium of the Polytechnic Museum, Moscow. Chaired by Petr Konchalovsky, the debate, dedicated to the new art, consisted of three main lectures — by David Burliuk ("On Cubism and Other Directions in Painting"), Nikolai Kulbin ("The New Art as the Basis of Life"), and, in absentia, Vasily Kandinsky (and read aloud by someone else) — followed by comments by Goncharova, Larionov, and Maximilian Voloshin. Goncharova sent this letter to several newspapers. The manuscript of the text presented here, "Letter to the Editor" ["Pismo k redaktoru 'Russkogo slova'"] (undated), is handwritten in pen on fourteen sheets and is addressed to the editor of *Russkoe slovo* (*Russian word*). *Russkoe slovo* did not publish the letter, although part of it was published in the Moscow newspaper *Protiv techeniia* (*Against the Current*), March 3, 1912. Shorter versions of the letter have also appeared in Eli Eganbiuri's 1913 monograph on Larionov and Goncharova, pp. 18–19, and in Benedikt Livshits's memoirs (Benedikt Livshits, *The One and a Half-Eyed Archer*, translated by John E. Bowlt [Newtonville, Mass., 1977], pp. 82–84). A French translation of the entire letter appeared in Tatiana Loguine, *Gontcharova et Larionov: Cinquante ans à Saint Germain-des-Prés* (Paris: Klincksieck, 1971), pp. 21–23. This English translation by Thea Durfee first appeared in *Experiment* (Los Angeles), no. 1 (1995), pp. 162–63 (NB.: it appears here with some slight editorial changes). The letter is preserved in the Manuscript Division of the Russian State Library, Moscow (inv. no. f. 259, R.S.,13 ed., k. 4).
3. Goncharova's "Open Letter" is handwritten in pen on paper, and, while undated, is probably from 1913, since it is accompanied by a copy of the celebrated group photograph of the contributors to the 1913 *Target* exhibition). It is preserved in the Nikolai Rykovsky Archive at the Manuscript Division of the Russian State Library, Moscow (inv. no. f. 421, no. 1, ed. khr. 33).
4. Goncharova wrote this undated letter, in pencil and in halting French, during Marinetti's visit to Moscow and St. Petersburg in January and February 1914; translated from the French by John E. Bowlt. It is not known whether the letter was ever sent. Clearly Goncharova was incensed by Marinetti's open disdain for women, at least as voiced in his manifestos and speeches. Although Marinetti attracted attention as a social curio, and some of the

Russian intelligentsia welcomed him, he commanded neither respect nor popularity with the more radical wing of the Russian avant-garde. But even if Goncharova and her closest Russian colleagues tried to distance themselves from Marinetti, critics tended to regard both the Italians and the Russians as parts of the same generic Futurism. The Moscow newspaper *Nov* (*New*) even reproduced a photograph of Goncharova to accompany a commentary on Marinetti's visit (see P. Kozhevnikov, "Italianiskii futurizm," January 29, 1914, p. 3). The letter is in the collection of the Khardzhiev-Chaga Cultural Foundation, Amsterdam (in Box 78).

5. This unfinished, undated letter, written in pencil, is thought to have been written in 1914, a conclusion based on Goncharova's reference to the three editions of the catalogue of her solo exhibitions in 1913–14 (two for the Moscow venue, one for the St. Petersburg venue); translated from the Russian by J. Frank Goodwin. It is not known whether the letter was ever sent. Boris Vasilievich Anrep (1883–1969), a painter, sculptor, mosaicist, and writer, was born in Russia but lived mainly in France, England, and Scotland. Before the Revolution, he often returned to St. Petersburg, mixed with the local artists and intellectuals (at one time he was very close to poet Anna Akhmatova), and contributed several articles to the journal *Apollon* (*Apollo*). Anrep put together the Russian section for Roger Fry's *Second Post-Impressionist Exhibition* at the Grafton Galleries, London, in 1912, which included a strong representation by Goncharova and Larionov. Presumably, Anrep's and Goncharova's friendship dates from that time. The letter is in the collection of the Khardzhiev-Chaga Cultural Foundation, Amsterdam (in Box 78).
6. Invited by Sergei Diaghilev, Goncharova and Larionov left for Paris via Rome in April 1914, and they stayed with Anrep for much of their time in Paris.
7. This paragraph has been crossed out in the original. The "Englishman" has not been identified.
8. A reference to Goncharova's solo exhibitions in Moscow (September–November 1913) and St. Petersburg (March–April 1914).
9. In March 1914, the public censor removed twelve "blasphemous" works from the preview of the St. Petersburg venue of Goncharova's exhibition.

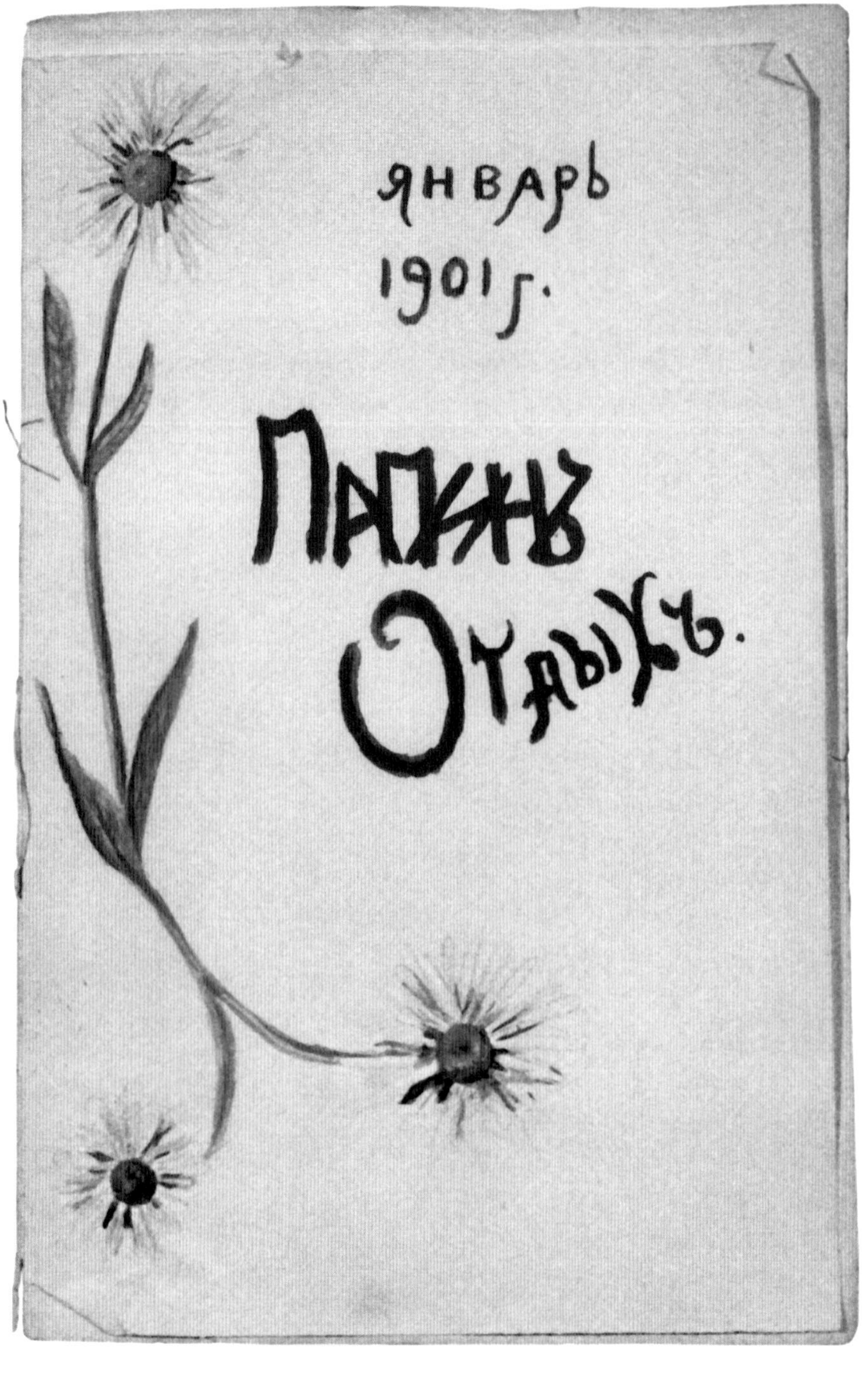

figure 91. Cover for Popova's handmade book, *Pankin otdykh*, 1901.
Watercolor, ink, and pencil on paper, 17.6 x 11.2 cm.
Private collection, Moscow.

LIUBOV POPOVA

Artist's Statement in the Catalogue of the Exhibition $5 \times 5 = 25$ (1921)[1]

All these experiments are visual and should be regarded merely as a series of preparatory experiments toward concrete, materialized constructions.

Department of Contemporary Russian Painting: Explanatory Classification (ca. 1921)[2]

Whether due to the greater age of Western artistic culture or because of the stimuli of concurrent artistic impulses, the history of contemporary Russian painting is experiencing the same evolution and revolution of artistic forms as Western Europe is.

Although Russian painting in its initial stages also coincides with the course of Western painting or evolves parallel with it, its individual deviations seem to expose another root, one nourished by the art of Russia's past and the unquestionable influence of national and psychological character. Consequently, many Russian artists may regard any attempt to accommodate contemporary Russian painting within a precise scheme based on a consecutive development of pictorial ideas (which Western art follows, particularly French art of recent decades) as troublesome, if not as an act of violence. Indigenous national culture or again, perhaps, national, painterly emotion, comes through all too obviously and distinctively.

The two points of derivation—French art as a school and the private psycho-physical impetus—produce a specific kind of painting that always stands out at international exhibitions by virtue of its deviation from the common herd. This also provides instant identification of the artist's nationality.

Nevertheless, let us try to locate and classify the pictorial foundations of this kind of work. In its aspiration toward formal expression, French art of the second half of the nineteenth and early twentieth centuries attained one of its culminating points with Impressionism, whose synthesis of undulating colors was intended to create a [total] image in the eye of the viewer.

Later on, the goal narrowed and consciously so, as [French art] moved away from the object and its concept to purely formal emotions. Cézanne no longer depicted the impression of the object, but only its essence, the essence of its color, volume, and the drawn. . . .

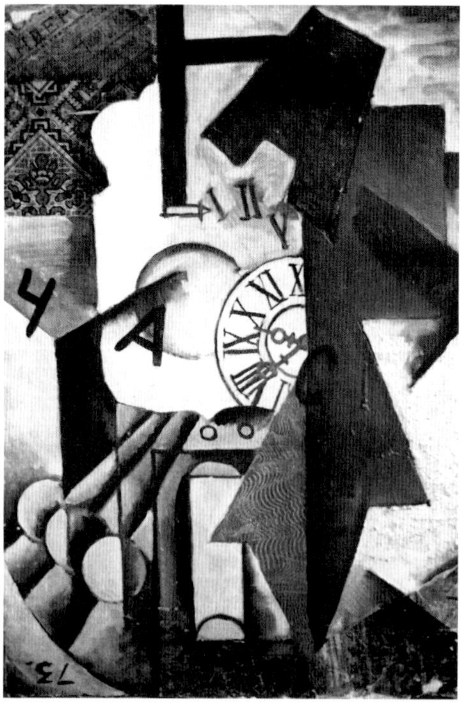

figure 92. Liubov Popova, *Clock*, 1914. Oil and wallpaper on canvas, 88 x 70 cm. Private collection, Moscow.

Impressionism as a New Approach to Color (ca. 1921)[3]

Color assumes a formal significance. With Impressionism, in general, we can speak of a new consciousness and a "new style" in art. What — even at the highest moments of formal art — appeared to be merely a method (its formal significance often manifested itself spontaneously), becomes *content* and *purpose*.

Moments of formal achievement [are] Impressionism, Cubism, Futurism, Suprematism, *Objectivism*.[4]

The latter tendency denotes an abrupt turn, one that is occurring on a completely new level. The goal here is not what results in any one of the spheres of the elements, for another shift of the entire and total constructive consciousness is taking place — from the representation of the object to its concrete, material organization. What happens to the entire object also happens to all its individual parts or elements, as in the case of color.

In Impressionism, color moved away from representation only with the help of the colorizing means of painting. Now, however, color is no longer a means of representation, but assists in its own materialization. Both within the material texture of the material itself (or its imitation) and with the help of texture, abstract color materializes, distinguishes itself from the representation of color, and becomes a goal that exerts an influence through its concrete essence, independently of the method of representation.

But the goal has been torn from its traditional, applied denotation, all the way down to being designated as formal pictorial relations, except that they themselves have become the goal as such, contributing to the construction of a living organism.

On Organizing Anew (ca. 1921)[5]

We have no need to conceal our pride that we are living in this new Great Epoch of Great organizations.

Not a single historical moment will be repeated.

The past is for history. The present and the future are for organizing life, for organizing what is both creative will and creative exigency.

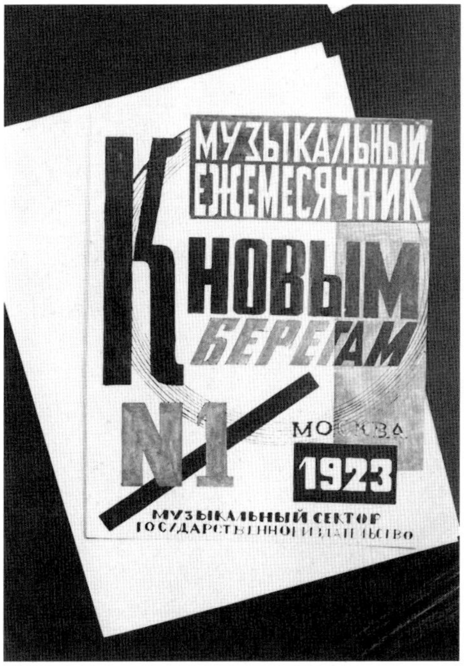

figure 93. Cover design made in 1922 by Popova for the music journal *K novym beregam*, 1923. Gouache and india ink on paper, 24.5 x 18.6 cm. Private collection, Moscow.

We are breaking with the past, because we cannot accept its hypotheses. We ourselves are creating our own hypotheses anew and only upon them, as in our inventions, can we build our new life and new world view.

More than anyone else, the artist knows this intuitively and believes in it absolutely. That is exactly why artists, above all, undertook a revolution and have created — are still creating — a new world view. Revolution in art has always predicted the breaking of the old public consciousness and the appearance of a new order in life.

A real revolution, unprecedented in all the enormity of its significance for the future, is sweeping away all the old conceptions, customs, concepts, qualities, and attachments and is replacing them with new and very different ones, as if borrowed from another planet or from alien creatures. But wasn't art the forerunner of this revolution — art that replaced the old world view with the need to organize — and to such an extent that even the end of "art" was declared? In fact, this [new] form has declared the end not only of the old art, but perhaps of art in general or, if not the end, then an artistic transformation so great that it cannot be accommodated within the old conception of art.

An analysis of the conception of the subject as distinguished from its representational significance lies at the basis of our approach toward reality: at first there was the deformation of the subject, and this was followed by the exposition of its essence, which is the concretization of a given consciousness within given forms. It also marks the beginning of the organization of the artistic media.

As a purpose, this is not new, for there has been no significant era in art when the subject was not deformed in accordance with the external energy of expression or reconstructed from a need to concretize a particular world view.

To the extent that a given confluence of historical conditions for the formation of a certain consciousness is unique, that condition of consciousness in relation to its own past,

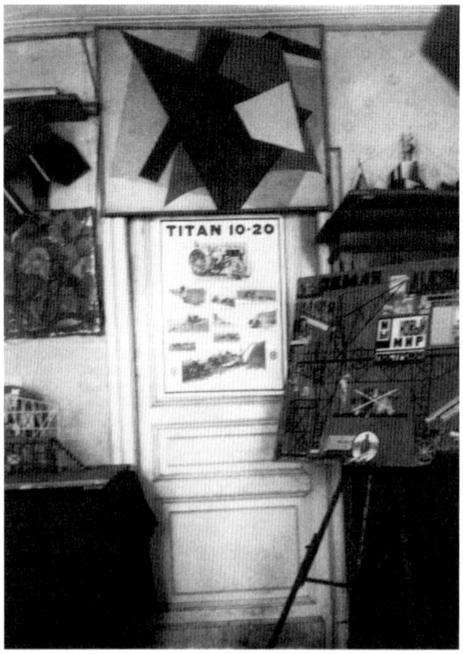

figure 94. Popova's Moscow studio, 1924, showing: (bottom left) her maquette for *The Magnanimous Cuckold* (1922); (above door) *Painterly Architectonics* (1917, Museum of Modern Art, New York); a maquette for her project (with Vsevolod Meierkhold and Alexander Vesnin) for an open-air mass spectacle intended to celebrate the theme of *Struggle and Victory* for the Congress of the Third International in 1921; and (on easel) a set design in collage on plywood for *Earth on End* (1923).

present, and future will also be singular and unique.

That's the first point.

The second point is still more important — above all, the moment of creation: a new organization of elements is created out of the constant, traditional ones, which are so only because, ultimately, we know only one and the same concrete material.

Through a transformed, [more] abstract reality, the artist will be liberated from all the conventional world views that existed hitherto.

In the absolute freedom of non-objectivity and under the precise dictation of its consciousness (which helps the expediency and necessity of the new artistic organization to manifest themselves), [the artist] is now constructing [his] own art, with total conviction.

Our fanaticism is conscious and assured, for the scope of our experiences has taught us to assume our positive place in history.

The more organized, the more essential the new forms in art, the more apparent it will become that our era is a great one and indispensable to humanity.

(Form + color + texture + rhythm + material + etc.) x ideology (the need to organize) = our art.

Note (ca. 1921)[6]

I don't think that non-objective form is the final form; rather, it is the revolutionary condition of form.

One must renounce the object and all the conventionality of the traditional [kind of] representation connected with it. We must feel completely free of everything created before us in order to attend to the emergent need. We can then look differently at the form of the object, which emerges from the work not only transformed, but as an altogether different form.

Not only theoretical work on the concept of volumetric form, line, or color, but also working on the joining of these disparate concepts (their synthesis should produce the concept of a new form) — this is what [we mean by] the construction of pictorial form, liberated, of course, from any excrescence irrelevant to painting.

1. Liubov Popova, untitled statement in the catalogue (unpaginated) of the exhibition *5x5 = 25*, held at the All-Russian Writers' Club, Moscow, in September 1921; translated from the Russian by John E. Bowlt. Popova contributed five works to the exhibition: *Spatial-Volumetrical [Construction]*, *[Construction] of Color Planes*, *Enclosed Spatial Construction*, and two *Spatial-Force [Constructions]*. See Exter essay in the present catalogue, n. 2.
2. Popova, "Otdel noveishei russkoi zhivopisi: Obiasnitelnaia klassifikatsiia"; translated from the Russian by J. Frank Goodwin. The text is from an unfinished, undated manuscript in a private collection, Moscow.
3. Popova, "Impressionizm kak novyi podkhod k tsvetu"; translated from the Russian by J. Frank Goodwin. The text is from an undated manuscript in the Department of Manuscripts, State Tretiakov Gallery, Moscow (inv. no. f. 148, ed. khr. 75, ll. 1-2).
4. The term *obektivizm* refers to the position of the Group for Objective Analysis, founded by Alexei Babichev within Inkhuk in 1921. Countering the extreme attitude of Alexei Gan, Alexander Rodchenko, Georgii and Vladimir Stenberg, Nikolai Tarabukin, et al., who called for the total rejection of studio painting in favor of production art, the Objectivists recognized that art could develop on the basis both of traditional studio painting and sculpture and of industrial design.
5. Popova, "O novoi organizatsii"; translated from the Russian by J. Frank Goodwin. The text is from an undated manuscript in a private collection, Moscow.
6. Popova, untitled text from an undated, unfinished manuscript in a private collection, Moscow; translated from the Russian by J. Frank Goodwin.

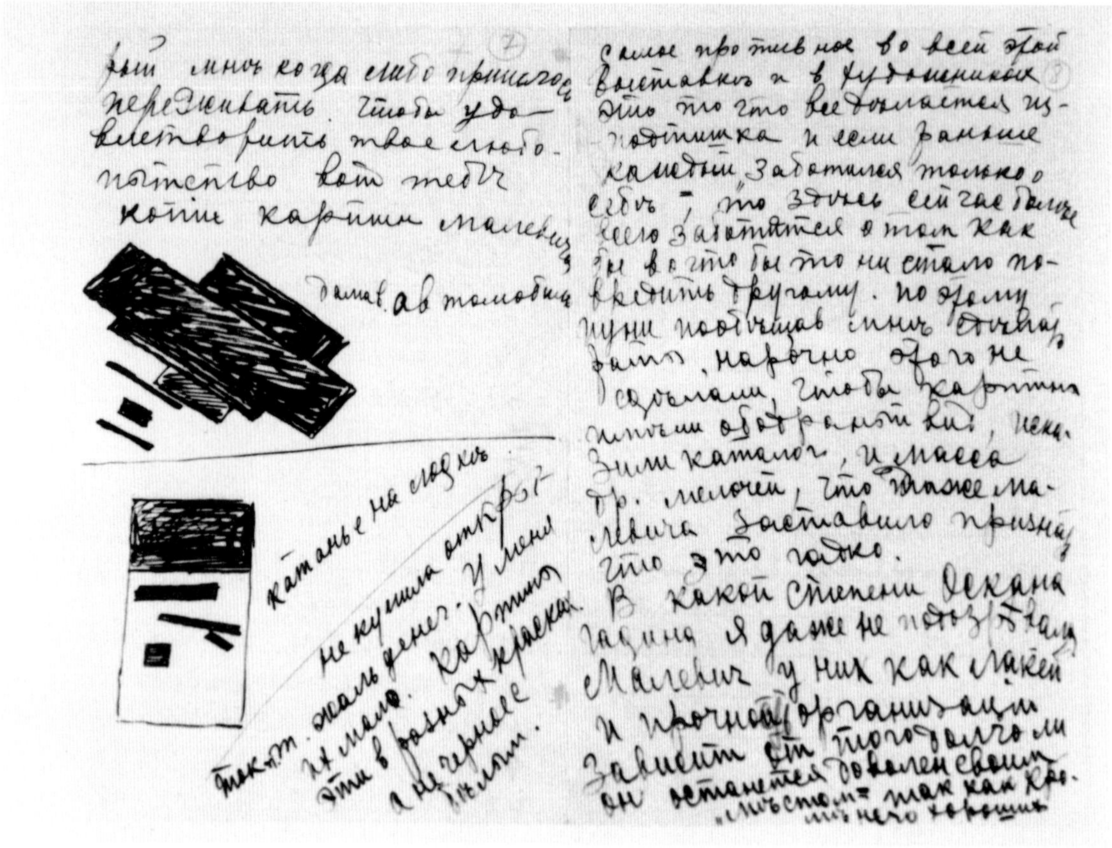

figure 95. Handwritten letter from Rozanova to Alexei Kruchenykh, December, 1915, in connection with the *0.10* exhibition, Petrograd, 1915–16. Archive of the Khardzhiev-Chaga Cultural Foundation, Amsterdam (Box 78). (Translation on page 330.)

Olga Rozanova[1]

Letter to Anna Rozanova (December 9, 1912)[2]

Your portrait [*Portrait of a Lady in Pink*, (*Portrait of Anna Rozanova, the Artist's Sister*) plate 42] has caused a sensation among artists! . . . I met a most interesting guy today, David Burliuk, and now I'm in love with him.[3] We shook hands. He really likes my paintings and says he's discovered a star in me. He particularly liked my portrait of you and the houses in landscapes, too. Burliuk lectures on art. Wanted to photograph my paintings so as to show them to the public on the screen. He lectures in different cities. Good for him! What a great chest he has! But he's a bit impudent. Tomorrow he's lecturing in St. Petersburg. Has given me a complimentary ticket to the lecture. O, David!

. . . The critics come down on me, i.e., the critics from the gutter press. They even wanted to reproduce my *Smithy* and wanted your portrait, but Shkolnik said no.[4]

If you knew just how entertaining these critics are! Burliuk laughs and says, "They come down on me, too. I'm happy that our names are next to each another."

. . . So far my pictures are not selling, but I'm having a great success among artists. One artist from the World of Art group introduced himself to me at the exhibition[5] and said it was a great pleasure to make my acquaintance. [Female] students of Petrov-Vodkin[6] try to ingratiate themselves with me, and Madame Zvantseva[7] herself spoke with me at the exhibition, saying she likes my paintings . . . A lot of new acquaintances. Some of them are interesting, but I'm really immersed in my artistic milieu and artistic interests . . . I'm now reading about art in French, and am hanging out at the exhibition. My paintings occupy the very best place. Alas, David is soon going away!

Letter to Anna Rozanova (December 9, 1913)[8]

. . . Alexei Kruchenykh and I have been coloring books together, books that are selling very well, so we'll earn a lot from them.

I've been hanging out at the Stray Dog cabaret. There was an "Evening of Apache Dance" there recently. An unusual Saturday. I sat through the entire night, from 12:30 a.m. to 7:30 a.m. Thus I got there on the last streetcar that night and left on the first one the next morning. Such are my labors and diversions! I'm going to the Stray

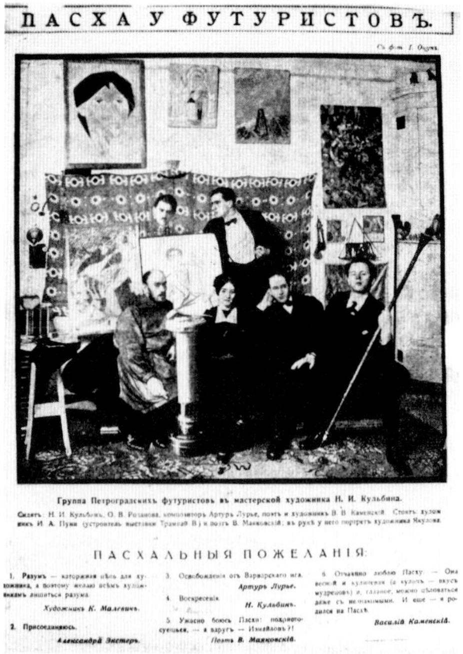
ПАСХА У ФУТУРИСТОВЪ.

Съ фот. I. Оцупа.

Группа Петроградскихъ футуристовъ въ мастерской художника Н. И. Кульбина.

Сидятъ: Н. И. Кульбинъ, О. В. Розанова, композиторъ Артуръ Лурье, поэтъ и художникъ В. В. Каменскій. Стоятъ: художникъ И. А. Пуни (устроитель выставки Трамвай В.) и поэтъ В. Маяковскій; въ рукѣ у него портретъ художника Якулова.

ПАСХАЛЬНЫЯ ПОЖЕЛАНІЯ:

1. Разумъ — каторжная цѣпь для художника, а поэтому желаю всѣмъ художникамъ лишиться разума.

Художникъ К. Малевичъ.

2. Присоединяюсь.

Александра Экстеръ.

3. Освобожденія отъ Варварскаго ига.

Артуръ Лурье.

4. Воскресенія.

Н. Кульбинъ.

5. Ужасно боюсь Пасхи: похристосуешься, — а вдругъ — Измайловъ?!

Поэтъ В. Маяковскій.

6. Отчаянно люблю Пасху. — Она весенняя и куличевая (а куличъ — вкусъ мудрецовъ) и, главное, можно цѣловаться даже съ незнакомыми. И еще — я родился на Пасхѣ.

Василій Каменскій.

figure 96. Ivan Otsup, Photograph captioned *Easter with the Futurists. Group of Petrograd Futurists in the Studio of the Artist N.I. Kulbin*, Petrograd, 1915. Showing (left to right) Nikolai Kulbin, Ivan Puni, Olga Rozanova, Vladimir Mayakovsky, Arthur Lourié, and Vasilii Kamensky. The portrait in front of Puni is Kulbin's of Georgii Yakulov. The photograph has been doctored, for the Puni head has been beheaded from another photograph, stuck on to the drape, and rephotographed to give the impression of collegiality, even though the calisthenic Mayakovsky is about to punch the rubberhead Puni.

Dog again today, although I'm not going to stay there all night this time.

Letter to Alexei Kruchenykh (summer 1915)[9]

. . . Right now, I can do either only exclusively realist or non-objective paintings, but nothing in between, since I don't think that there are any connecting links between these two arts, no rivalry, nothing in common, just as there is no link between the crafts of shoemaking and tailoring and so on. They are not even vaguely similar. I have to confess that objectivity and non-objectivity (in painting) are not two different tendencies in one art, but two different arts. The screen is the only possible medium that can replace the material paints in non-objective painting! No connection whatsoever!!!

Letter to Alexei Kruchenykh (December 1915)[10]

He [Puni] has taken down my *Automobile* and *Devil's Panel* [*Bicyclist*]. When these pieces were brought into the exhibition, my [paintings] proved to be more more original than Puni's. My relations with Oksana [Boguslavskaia] are strained to the limit.[11] There is no tension between me and Ivan Albertovich [Puni], but Oksana is behaving like a stupid old bag and, except for Malevich, there's absolutely no one on Puni's side. In the catalogue, Puni went as far as to sign himself "manager." For reasons of tact, not even Zheverzheev has ever done such a thing,[12] but Oksana says that she has the right to administer everything, since the exhibition is financed with their capital and so on. All this is disgusting. Not worth writing about.

Rostislavov[13] is in ecstasy over my works and has told me that most likely not even I know my own true worth, etc. Now if he would only write that in *Rech* [*Discourse*] — vulgar man. Well, never mind! . . .

I'll say more: all of Suprematism

consists entirely of my collages, combinations of surfaces, lines, discs (particularly discs), and totally without a realistic subject. In spite of all that, that swine doesn't mention my name.

... Malevich has a guilty look when he is with me. He has turned a bit humble. He offers his services politely. Quite unrecognizable. The first day, I deliberately turned my back on him. Did you show Malevich my collages, and when exactly? Unfortunately, I gave [him] only Suprematist reliefs (four), but no painting. My narrative painting is infinitely more Suprematist than Puni's, however.

I saw Zelmanova[14] at the opening. She was delighted, invited me over to her place, and I invited her to mine. I don't know what will come of that. I'll send you photographs and reviews, if there are any. I regret that you are not with me. Kisses to you. Write. Kulbin and Matiushin were not at the opening.

... Malevich remembered that he hadn't yet sent you the package. I reprimanded him for that.

Letter to Alexei Kruchenykh (December 1915)

... On the wall at the exhibition, they [the Suprematists] have titled their paintings, "Suprematist," but not in the catalogue.[15] However, I didn't [title mine that way], since in his review that fool Rostislavov did not include me as a member of the group. In general, he gave a very good review of both the exhibition and of me in particular. Unfortunately, I have only one copy of

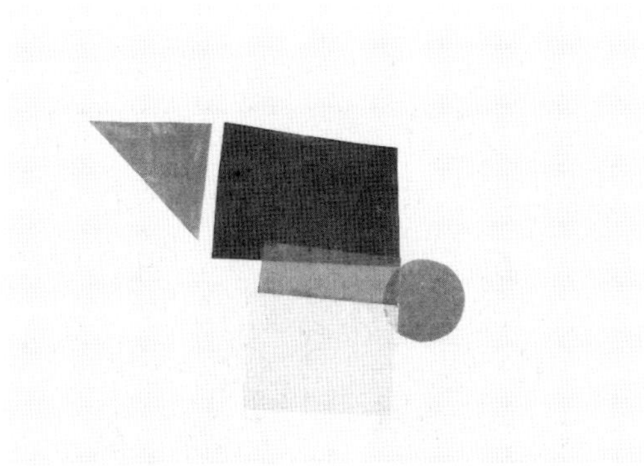

figure 97. Alexei Kruchenykh, *Heavy Weapon*, illustration for his *Vselenskaia voina* (Petrograd, 1916). Paper collage, 22.9 x 30.4 cm. Courtesy of Galerie Gmurzynska, Cologne

the newspaper and don't know how to send it to you. ... There were other stupid and totally hostile reviews in *Petrogradskaia gazeta* [*Petrograd Gazette*], *Listok* [*Sheet*], *Birzhevye vedomosti* [*Stock-Exchange News*], and *Den* [*Day*], but I haven't read them yet.

Attendance at the exhibition is poor. Just over two hundred attended the opening, the worst one I've ever had to endure. So as to satisfy your curiosity, here are my copies of Malevich's pictures, *Lady in an Automobile* [her sketch of the composition follows] and *Boat Ride* [her sketch of the composition follows]. I did not buy any postcards for reasons of thrift. I don't have much money ...

Letter to Alexei Kruchenykh (1916)

I've sent a registered [letter] to Shemshurin with the drawings for the poetry that you asked for.[16] I made the drawings in colored ink. How do you like them? You've probably already received them, haven't you? As I already

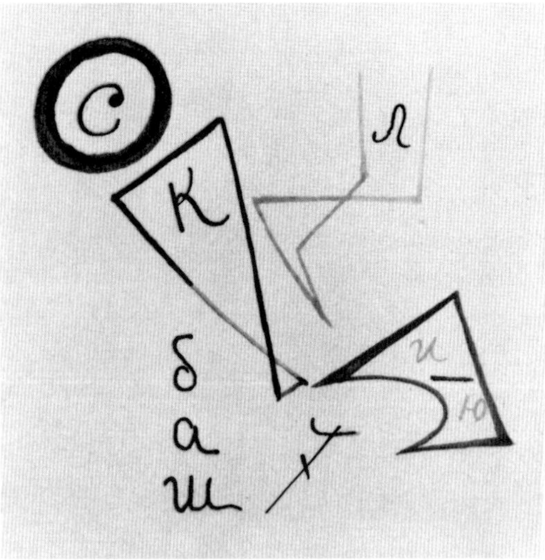

figure 98. Olga Rozanova, *Untitled*, 1917–18. Gouache and india ink on paper, 10.8 x 9.8 cm. Sheet no. 68 in Alexei Kruchenykh's scrapbook, *A. Kruchenykh, 1900–1930*.

wrote, I'm crazy about these verses and the idea of letters of the alphabet floating free in these transrational poems. I simply burst with pleasure when I read and contemplated them.

Cubism, Futurism, Suprematism (1917)[17]

. . . We propose liberating painting from its subservience to the ready-made form of reality and to make it first and foremost a creative, not a reproductive, art.

The savage happily drawing the outlines of a bull or a deer on a piece of stone, the primitive, the academician, the artists of antiquity and of the Renaissance, the Impressionists, the Cubists, and even to some degree the Futurists are all united by the same thing: the object. These artists are intrigued, delighted, amazed, and gladdened by nature. They try to fathom her essence, they aspire to immortalize her. . . .

Cubism killed the love of the everyday appearance of the object, but not the love of the object as a whole. Nature continued to be the guide of aesthetic ideas. The works of the Cubists lack a clearly defined idea of nonobjective art.

Their art is characterized by efforts to complicate the task of depicting reality. Their complaint against the established prescriptions for copying nature turned into a formidable bomb that smashed the decayed metaphysics of figurative art into smithereens — an art that had lost all idea of aim and technique. . . .

In its force and its clarity of perception, Futurism provided art with a unique expression — the fusion of two worlds, the subjective and the objective. Maybe this event is destined never to be repeated.

But the ideological gnosticism of Futurism had no effect on the damned consciousness of the majority who, to this day, continue to reiterate that Futurism marks a radical break in the course of world art, a crisis of art . . .

Our time is one of metal, its soul is initiative and technology: the Futurists brought technology to its full potential. . . .

Until the Futurists came along, artists used to express movement in the following conventional manner: a maximum expression of movement resulted from placing forms on the surface of the canvas parallel to the perimeter of the canvas, and a maximum static expression resulted from placing the forms parallel to the surface of the canvas.

The spectator did not sense movement in the picture. All he [or she] saw was a rendering of movement. . . .

For the Suprematists, the painting has ceased, once and for all, to be a function of the frame.

We do not regard the forms that we use [in painting] as real objects. We do not force them to depend on the up and down directions in the painting. . . . We consider their painterly content. Consequently, the emphasis on symmetry or asymmetry, on static or dynamic elements, is the result of creative thinking and not of the preconceived notions of common logic. The aesthetic value of the non-objective painting lies entirely in its painterly content.

We perceive the color of an object as its hue made visible by the refraction of light (the rainbow, the spectrum). But we can also conceive of color independently of our conception of the object, and beyond the colors of the spectrum.

We can see green, blue, and white mentally. . . .

The unreality of the Cubo-Futurists was a product of their self-destructive desire to convey the total reality of the object via the prism of pure subjectivity. This was so remarkable that "non-existence," created by the artist's will, acquired the value of a new reality, of a kind of abstract absolute that killed any interest in what was actually being observed. . . .

Suprematism rejects the use of real forms for painterly ends. Like leaky vessels, they cannot hold color. Stifled by the chance simplicity or complexity of these forms, which may not always correspond to their respective color content, color just creeps about, faded and dim. . . . We create quality of form in connection with quality of color, and not each separately.

We have chosen the plane as the transmitter of color, since its reflective surface will transmit color the most effectively and with the least mutability. As a result, reliefs, appliqués, textures that imitate material reality, and sculptural effects (for example, a brushstroke creates shadow), which were used in figurative painting (right up to, and including, Futurism), cannot be applied to two-dimensional painting on a plane: such factors influence and change the essence of color. . . .

Just as a change in the atmosphere can create a strong or weak air current in nature, one that can overturn and destroy things, so dynamism in the world of colors is created by the properties of their values, by their weight or lightness, by their intensity or duration. This dynamism is, essentially, very real. It commands attention. It engenders style and justifies construction.

Dynamism liberates painting from the arbitrary laws of taste and establishes the law of pragmatic inevitability. It also liberates painting from utilitarian considerations. . . .

The works of pure painting have the right to exist independently and not in relation to banal interior furnishings. To many, our efforts and endeavors — as well as those of our Cubist and Futurist predecessors — to put painting on a course of self-determination may seem ridiculous, and this is because they are difficult to understand and do not come with glowing recommendations. Nevertheless, we do believe that a time will come when, for many people, our art will become an aesthetic necessity — an art justified by its selfless aspiration to reveal a new beauty.

Translation of figure 95: "[It was the worst opening] I've ever had to endure. In order to satisfy your curiosity, here are my copies of some of Malevich's pictures: *Lady in an Automobile* [first drawing], *Boat Ride* [second drawing]. I didn't buy any postcards. I didn't want to waste my money and I don't have that much. The pictures are painted in various colors, not black and white. The most disgusting aspect of the entire exhibition and of the artists themselves is that everything is being done on the sly. While it used to be that you just looked after yourself, now what you do is to harm someone else, no matter what. For example, Puni and his wife promised to make frames for me and then failed to do so on purpose, so that the paintings would look slipshod. They distorted the catalogue and a myriad other things, so that even Malevich thought it was disgusting. I never imagined that Oksana [Boguslavskaia] could be such a horrible creature. Malevich is like their lackey. How long the organization will last depends on how long he remains satisfied with his 'corner,' since besides him good. . . ."

1. The following documents (except the last) are excerpts from letters that Olga Rozanova wrote between 1912 and 1916. They are preserved in the Archive of the Khardzhiev-Chaga Cultural Foundation, Amsterdam (in Box 78).
2. Letter to Anna Rozanova, the artist's sister, transcribed by Nikolai Khardzhiev.
3. The reference is to poet and painter David Davidovich Burliuk (1862–1967), the "father of Russian Futurism."
4. Iosif Solomonovich Shkolnik (1883–1926), a painter, was secretary of the Union of Youth. In spite of Shkolnik's objections, Rozanova's portrait of Anna was reproduced in the journal *Ogonek* (St. Petersburg), no. 1 (1913), p. 20. Rozanova's oil painting, *Smithy* (1912), is in the collection of the State Russian Museum, St. Petersburg.
5. The reference is to the *Union of Youth* exhibition in St. Petersburg, December 1912–January 1913.
6. Kuzma Sergeevich Petrov-Vodkin (1878–1939), a painter
7. Elizaveta Nikolaevna Zvantseva (1864–1922), a painter, directed an art school in St. Petersburg. Rozanova was a student there in 1911.
8. Letter to Anna Rozanova (1886–1969), transcribed by Nikolai Khardzhiev.
9. Letter to Alexei Eliseevich Kruchenykh (1886–1969), Rozanova's companion.
10. In this letter, Rozanova is describing the *0.10* exhibition at Nadezhda Dobychina's Art Bureau in Petrograd, December 1915 through January 1916, to which she contributed the works mentioned here.
11. Ivan Albertovich Puni (Jean Pougny, 1894–1956) and his wife Ksenia Leonidovna Boguslavskaia (1892–1972) were the organizers of the *0.10* exhibition.

12. Levkii Ivanovich Zheverzheev (1891–1942), a collector and businessman, was a sponsor of the Union of Youth, specifically of the two theatrical productions that it produced in December 1913, *Victory over the Sun* and *Vladimir Maiakovsky*.
13. Alexander Alexandrovich Rostislavov (1860–1920), an art critic.
14. Anna Mikhailovna Zelmanova-Chudovskaia (ca. 1890–1948) was a member of the Union of Youth.
15. Rozanova is referring to the *0.10* exhibition.
16. Andrei Akimovich Shemshurin (1872–1939), a literary critic. Rozanova is probably referring to the Suprematist book illustrations that she was making at this time for *Zaumnaia gniga* [*Transrational Book*]. See Terekhina et al., *Olga Rozanova 1886–1918*, pp. 37–38.
17. These extracts are from Rozanova's text "Kubizm, futurizm, suprematizm," which she wrote for the journal *Supremus* in 1917 (not published); translated from the Russian by John E. Bowlt. The entire text was published in English and German in *Von der Malerei zum Design/From Painting to Design*, exh. cat. (Cologne: Galerie Gmurzynska, 1981), pp. 100–113.

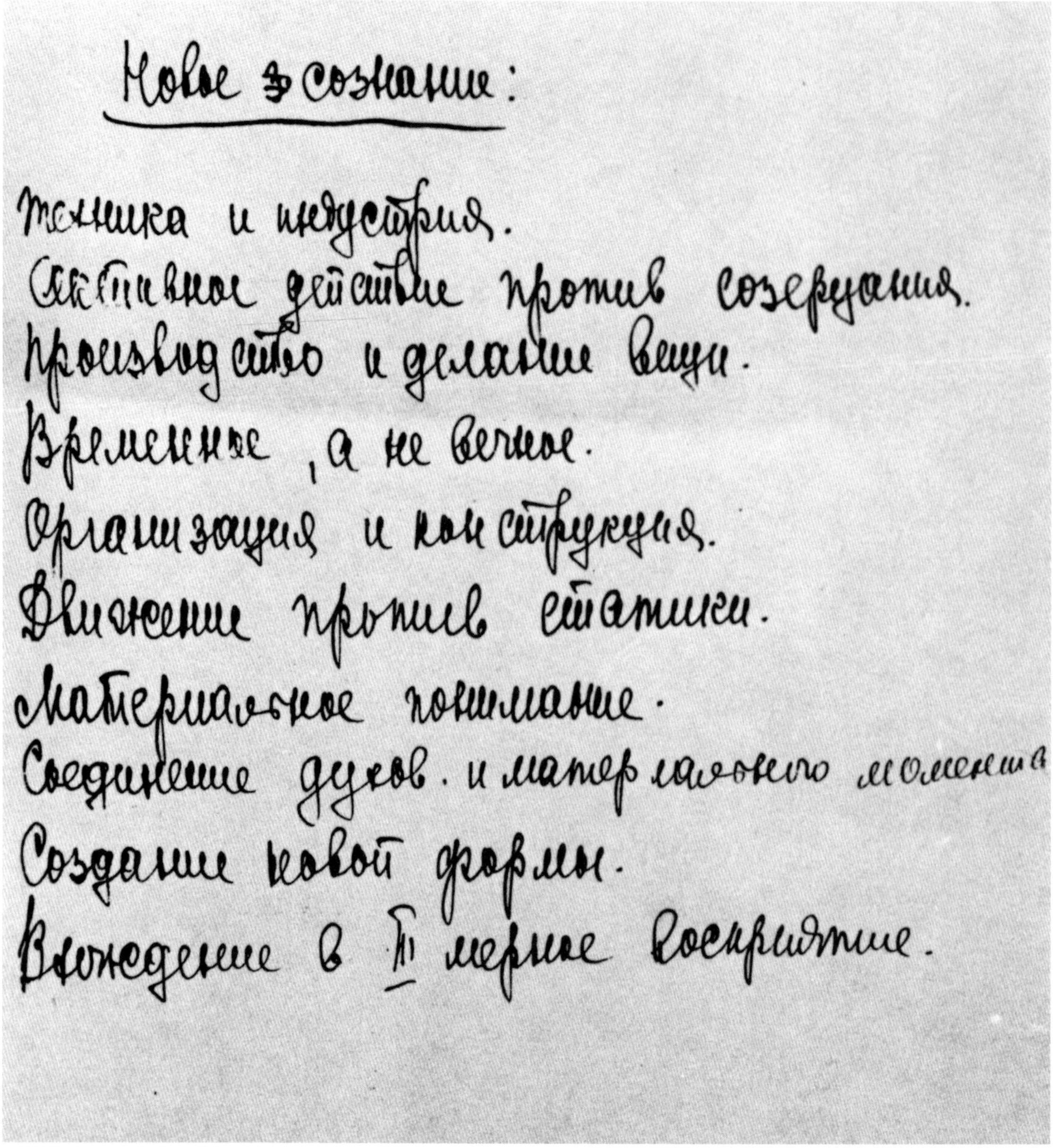
Новое сознание:

Техника и индустрия.
Активное действие против созерцания.
Производство и делание вещи.
Временное, а не вечное.
Организация и конструкция.
Движение против статики.
Материальное понимание.
Соединение духов. и матерьяльного момента
Создание новой формы.
Вхождение в IV мерное восприятие.

figure 99. Handwritten statement by Stepanova, *The New Consciousness.* Undated, private collection. (Translation on page 340.)

varvara stepanova

On Non-Objective Creativity (in Painting) (1919)[1]

In the logical course of its development, painting reached non-objectivity. Not so long ago the defenders of "studio art" — i.e., painting of a particular size, painting in a narrow, professional sense, but a kind of painting bereft of meaning or any spiritual aspiration — rejected the slogan "painting as an end in itself." This is a painting of synthesis, a monumental kind of painting that is just as indispensable as a road sign. However, painting moves not by synthesis, but by analysis and innovation — which is always excessive, but which always stimulates further movement.

Non-objective creativity is a movement of the spirit, a protest against the narrow materialism and naturalism that had begun to control life.

Non-objective creativity is a new world view in all spheres of life and art, and painters were the first to appreciate it. We should note that recently painting has begun to occupy a really major place in the global movement, overtaking all other arts in its development and achievement.

Without knowing one another, painters in different corners of the world have begun to appreciate non-objective art and, perhaps intuitively, to begin waging "war on the object." This has been particularly characteristic for Russia, where most of our smart young painters came to negate the object in painting. Russia has become the home of non-objectivity, and this is understandable, since Russia had long been a country of the spirit.

In Russia the epoch of transition to "non-objectivity" produced good painters who derived much from material life. However, they took not the essence of the object, but its surface, its texture, its relationship to another object, all of which diverted them from the object as such. How very different from French art. Take Cubism. The French artist will take an object, break it up, extrapolate, will think it through and through, and then, on the well-defined surface of the studio painting, present you with the object or a painting in which the object in the painting realizes its highest potential.

The French artist learned to paint by studying the object, while the majority of Russian painters of the transitional period learned not through the object itself but through French paintings of the object. The Russian Cubists offered an elaboration of space, but not of the object; they understood the idea of "breaking up the object" in an abstract sense and passed from the object of the painting to painting [itself].

Color was of great importance to the painting of "Russian Cubism," but the color of paint also led it away from Cubism. [Artists] began to investigate the sphere of color and removed the object. The shift among Russian artists toward non-objectivity came roughly in 1913, although "studio painting" was also promoted at the same time, which, as I mentioned above, completed the moment of transition and took the preceding accomplishments to their limit.

At first, each individual artist understood non-objective creativity differently. Some explored color, others texture or composition. But as non-objective creativity and the consciousness of it deepened, a particular group [of artists] came to the fore, demonstrating a method or system that was able to accommodate non-objective painting. The first method was Suprematism as interpreted in two ways — either as a new formal accomplishment (the square) or as an intensification of painting through color, destined to play the role of a "new Renaissance of painting." The square, of course, was not a discovery, but merely the logical extension of the cube; color began to play a role here, however, when it commandeered the square so as to make a more effective representation. Consequently, color provided the stimulus to the liberation of painting from the object, while the square provided the synthesis.

The Suprematists extolled the square plane of color, which they began to elaborate and build into the picture in a monumental fashion. But the canons of Suprematism did not allow a further shift, since color — formerly the living force of Suprematism — now became just a component auxiliary to the square, the latter assuming preeminence.

Where did this lead? Suprematist compositions, executed not on canvas but in embroidery, where color is purer than in paint on canvas. Made from surfaces colored with the finest methods, they soon rivaled the painted picture, and quite successfully.[2] It is now clear that in its pure form Suprematism is decorative and, as a new style, was meant to be applied — a forceful and astonishing one. Perhaps Suprematism needed to find a better technique than the application of paint to a canvas in order to carry the Suprematist method to its logical conclusion. In Suprematist painting, the colored form is incomplete, and demands that the paint from the tube be at least three times more intense, so that when applied to a composition the color will lose no more than one-fifth of its properties.

Meanwhile, two individuals in particular came forward from the ranks of a second group of painters, who at one time had supported the Suprematist method in their non-objective creativity, finally breaking with the method of Suprematism: they had either removed color at the expense of composition (Udaltsova) or, on the contrary, had intensified it to the point of decorativeness and dissonance (Rozanova). Such was the attempt to accommodate non-objective creativity within the system of Suprematism. At the same time, nonobjective creativity also developed outside the methods of Suprematism, but here individual artists set out on their own, making no attempt to contain their inventions within a particular system (Rodchenko, Kandinsky) or to assign an "-ism" to their achievements. All in all, non-objective creativity in painting is still at its initial stage of development, and it is difficult to find an "-ism" that could characterize it fully. But one thing has become very clear in non-objective painting: the ways in which it is being rendered are certainly not monotonous, and nearly all the non-objective artists are powerful and vivid individuals. Each of them may well create his own school. The non-objective artists are advancing toward new inventions, toward analysis in the work of painting, toward the painting of color (color-painting), toward acuity of composition, and toward the making of monochrome painting (Drevin).... [3]

Diary (1919)[4]

January 5

... *0.10.*[5] Malevich discovers Suprematism, but doesn't say anything until the exhibition. Wishing to ruin the exhibition, he managed to have it called "The last Futurist exhibition."

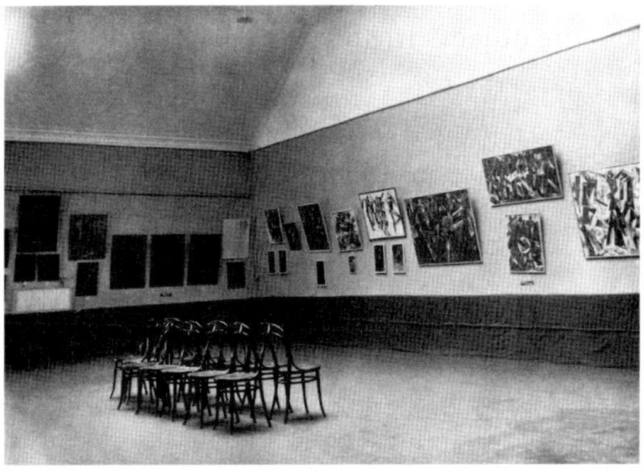

figure 100. Works by Stepanova (on right) and Alexander Rodchenko (on left) at the *Nineteenth State Exhibition*, Moscow, 1920.

Ivan Puni and "Punka" (Boguslavskaia) are helping him.[6] Draconian measures are being taken to prevent Tatlin from exhibiting his reliefs alongside their works. The Moscow group (Udaltsova, Popova, Exter) threatens to "back out" unless the Petrograd group changes these conditions. The Petrograd group agrees, so Tatlin delivers his reliefs ... With Malevich, the atmosphere thickens. You feel that he has discovered something, but he says nothing. Every effort is being made to find out what he's going to call his works ...

A gathering at Exter's (chic hotel room, knickknacks, she herself is eccentric — constantly smoking, fruit, pastries): Udaltsova, Popova, Malevich, Kliun, twelve midnight, but failed to find out anything ... Kliun squeaks on about something and Malevich says nothing. Udaltsova is pale. Exter's face has broken out, Popova's all in stripes.... Malevich declares, "I have discovered Suprematism," and he proceeds to

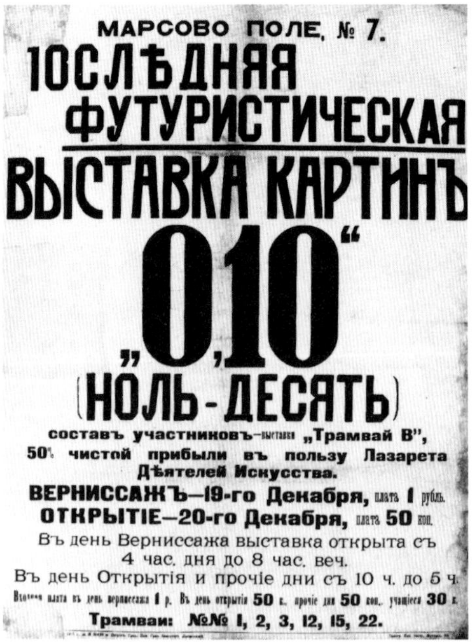

figure 101. Anonymous designer, Poster advertising vernissage (December 19, 1915) and opening (December 20, 1915) of the *Last Futurist Exhibition of Paintings, 0.10 (Zero-Ten)* at Nadezhda Dobychina's Art Bureau, Petrograd. Courtesy of Puni-Archiv, Zurich.

explain . . . Exter refuses to participate in *0.10*, since her works are almost non-objective [anyway] and she doesn't want to be in the Malevich group.

Organizing *0.10*: Tatlin is nervous, curses at "Punka," hangs the works of the Moscow group, and then brings in his reliefs at four in the afternoon. The exhibition opens at five. He curses at "Punka" to keep her from peeking to see what he's carrying in. Finally, the room is partitioned off with screens, but when Tatlin walks by, "Punka" yelps. The Suprematists want to scatter Suprematism throughout the exhibition and at all costs to hang at least part [of their works] in the "Muscovite" room. That's why they hide their works, at first those of Pestel, then of Vasilieva M.,[7] but to no avail, since the Muscovites wouldn't give up their room. Five o'clock: the opening. Tatlin failed to hang his reliefs in time and is now up on a ladder hanging them right in front of the public. The public responds with attention and interest.

"Punka" catches reporters at the entrance. The result is evident in the newspapers: Malevich-Puni, Malevich-Puni . . .

Dinner in the Vienna Restaurant. Malevich and Tatlin quarrel, the latter declaring, "This peasant [Malevich] has insulted me," and demands that their works (his, Udaltsova's, Popova's) be removed from the exhibition. But Udaltsova and Popova do not give their consent, so Tatlin fumes and threatens to remove his own works himself. But he doesn't.

By now Tatlin's policy is clear — he wants to ruin *0.10*, and since the Muscovites have a big room, the exhibition would collapse if they were to remove their works.

Through this exhibition, Malevich ruined the Futurists and Cubists with his Suprematism and by calling the exhibition "the last one." *0.10* pertains to Suprematism in that it derives from Malevich's own words, "I've reached the 0 of form."

A debate rages: on one side, Tatlin, Udaltsova, and Popova; on the other, Kliun, Malevich, and Puni . . . In order to avenge Malevich, Popova hangs a poster in her room reading "Room of

Professional Painters"; Udaltsova lends a hand. Again a scandal breaks out.

Throughout all these ups and downs, Rozanova landed in the middle, neither on Malevich's side nor on Tatlin's. She did get a sinking feeling, as she said herself, when she began to realize that Malevich had discovered something; but she soon sensed what it was all about and hastily painted several Suprematist works for the exhibition.

Rodchenko turns up (he hasn't met Tatlin yet). . . .

Malevich appears at *The Store*[8] . . . *0.10* is written on his forehead, and on his back is a sheet of paper with the declaration "I am an apostle" (of what was not recorded).

Tatlin throws Malevich out of the exhibition, because of the announcement [of it being "the last one"] that he has been putting up everywhere, and because of his promotion of Suprematism . . . Malevich and Kliun take down their works.

Malevich flirts with Rodchenko. About Rodchenko's graphic works,[9] Malevich says, "You yourself still don't know what you're doing" . . . and draws him over to his side. . . . He invites Rodchenko home to talk about Suprematism, and shows him some of the works with small forms. Kliun invites Rodchenko to participate in the *Jack of Diamonds*. Rodchenko uses this to get a better handle on Tatlin, who had been warning Rodchenko about Malevich. Tatlin positively panicked when he learned that Rodchenko was

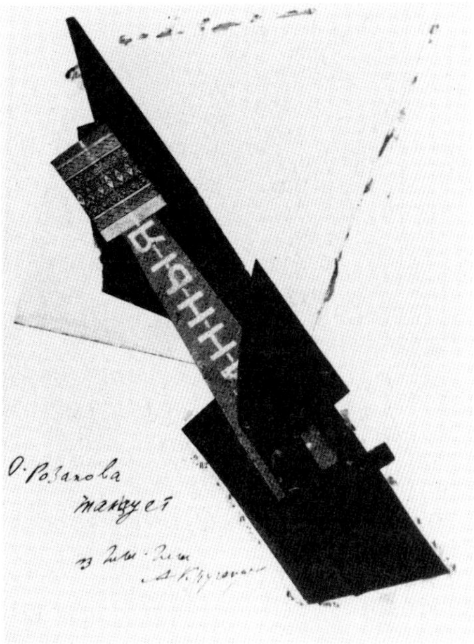

figure 102. Varvara Stepanova, *Rozanova Dancing*, 1918–19, collage and india ink on cardboard, 15.5 x 11 cm. Made by Stepanova for Alexei Kruchenykh's play *Gly-Gly*. Private collection.

being invited to join the *Jack of Diamonds*. Malevich did not present any Suprematist works at *The Store* — thanks to Udaltsova, as it turned out, who insisted that Malevich not exhibit Suprematism there. . . .

January 11

It all began delightfully.

Drevin talked about Olga Rozanova's exhibition. . . .[10]

Opening today . . . Drevin and I, along with Strzeminski (head of the Exhibition Bureau)[11] set off for the exhibition . . . Here we are. Kliun and the boys are hanging up an enormous black square on a white canvas beneath a sign . . . Drevin and I become extremely indignant. We shout at the guys not to put it up, but Kliun shouts "Put it up!" At first the guys were confused, but soon resumed working. . . .

We come down on Kliun for putting Malevich's square under Rozanova['s name] . . . Kliun blames Malevich for everything, says that he (Kliun) has nothing to do with [the exhibition], and that he is doing all this based on a sketch by Malevich.

We go in to the exhibition. Attack Strzeminski and demand to know how he could have allowed Malevich to put this logo onto Rozanova['s sign]. We look at the exhibition. The exhibition shines, simply sings with color.

The square has been raised and is about to be nailed up, but it fits perfectly into the window of the "non-objective" room. I get mad. Drevin and I attack Strzeminski, and he demands that the square be removed . . . Kliun runs to remove the square . . . He moves Rozanova's playing-card paintings and several other works . . . Kliun stammers that there are still a few other decorations for the exhibition which he, Kliun, had been painting all night . . .

We take a look . . . O, what a delight! Malevich has brought in three more enormous canvases with square black forms of colossal dimensions . . . Bad language . . . We protest that such things should not be displayed at a Rozanova exhibition, since she had been on the way to smashing the square . . . We demand that all these "decorations" be left behind for Malevich . . . It becomes apparent that these "decorations" might have covered the entire façade . . .

We managed to prevent the exhibition of "ornaments" . . . Kliun whines that he won't be paid for his work and shows how his fingers had swollen from the cold as he painted them.

All worked up [over this dispute], we set off to see Gan.

Most disgraceful is that Malevich showed no one that he was making such squares for Olga Rozanova. What is there in common between Malevich's square and Rozanova?

Rozanova has what Malevich aspired to, and he used her, as a painter, for his philosophizing. Color in its essence is paint, it is decoration, and that's why, during the heyday of Suprematism, the enthusiasm was for applied art, and there were numerous exhibitions of decorative art. Thus at one such exhibition Anti[12] said of Malevich's works that here was the real sphere of Suprematism, its alpha and omega, not a Suprematism of the form of the square, but a Suprematism of color. Malevich confuses color and the philosophy of the square in Suprematism and now, therefore, wants to pin Rozanova to a Suprematism of the square. Drevin, too, understood Suprematism in this way. According to Drevin, Suprematism is like a textile, and Malevich had created not painting but merely a new style. Malevich provided a graphic scheme or form of the square which, without Malevich's essays and mysticism, has no significance. Furthermore, if Malevich declares that he alone discovered the square, then that is nonsense. Drevin painted with square forms without ever seeing Malevich's works or even knowing of Malevich's existence. Then in 1915, when Malevich promulgated the square, both Kliun and Rozanova contributed to the same exhibition. In remote Kazan, Rodchenko, too, without knowing anything about Suprematism, the square, or knowing of Malevich's existence, created graphic works with square forms. Malevich's trick lies only in his promulgation of the name. Who thought of it and how, I do not know.

The square . . . hung logically in the air and derived from the cube . . .

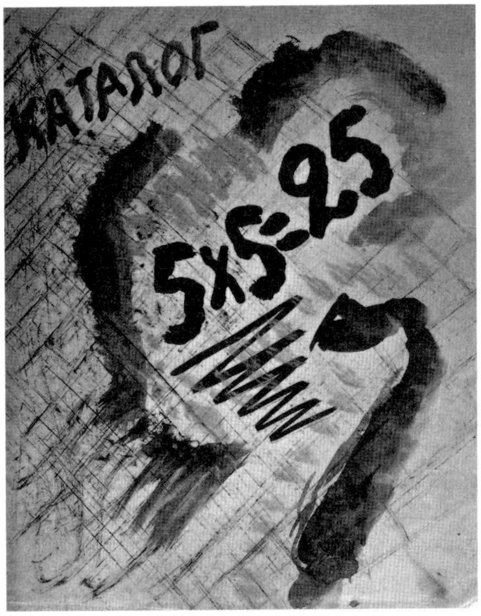

figure 103. Varvara Stepanova, cover for the catalogue of the *5 x 5 = 25* exhibition, 1921. Gouache on paper, 17.7 x 14 cm. Private collection.

February 17
On the exhibition of the Young Leftist Federation of the Professional Union of Artists and Painters. Udaltsova: a great female Cubist artist in Russia and good-looking, too, like a piece of chintz. She breaks up the object along vertical lines (hence a certain monotony). Of course, Udaltsova is quite smart and won't let on. [Her work] is displayed wonderfully. She wins laurels and wants to play a dirty trick on Malevich, since in Cubism he's just a zero ["=0"]. Rodchenko exhibits old works. Kandinsky likes his earliest works, where everything is done to a "t" to the extreme. Gabo says of him: "He has everything in order to paint, but he still hasn't begun" . . . Pevsner, delighted, says: "This guy will show you, he'll go a long away. Look! There's not [even] Suprematism here. That's amazing!"[13]

Kliun likes Anti's texture in tempera. Yes, he really knows what texture's all about.

Kandinsky says that Anti is the only artist whom he likes.

P. Kuznetsov also likes Anti.[14] He walks around all the time expressing amazement: "And that's Rodchenko . . . Yes, yes . . . "

Rozanova has a certain dryness. This trait is characteristic of many Russian artists (Shevchenko, Ledantiu).[15]

The works of Pevzner and Drevin obviously made an impression on Udaltsova through their primitive simplicity.

Artist's Statement in the Catalogue of the Exhibition 5 x 5 = 25 (1921)[16]

In the artist's creativity, composition is a contemplative approach.

Technology and industry have confronted art with the problem of CONSTRUCTION as a dynamic action and as contemplative visuality.

The "sacred" value of the work [of art] as something singular and unique has been eliminated.

As the depository of this "unicum" the museum turns into an archive.

Translation of figure 99: "Technology and industry. Active action vs. contemplation. Production and making things. Temporal, not eternal. Organization and construction. Movement vs. statics. Material conception. Integration of the spiritual and material aspects. Creation of a new form. Coming into a three-dimensional perception."

1. Varvara Stepanova, "O bespredmetnom tvorchestve"; translated from the Russian by J. Frank Goodwin. The text is from a manuscript in a private collection, Moscow. Stepanova published a similar essay, "Bespredmetnoe tvorchestvo" [Non-Objective Creativity], under the pseudonym "V. Agrarykh" in the catalogue of the *Tenth State Exhibition: Non-Objective Creativity and Suprematism*, Moscow, 1919. Another translation of this text is in Lavrentiev and Bowlt, *Stepanova*, p. 170. For other statements by Stepanova in English translation see ibid., pp. 171–83.
2. A number of the Suprematists, particularly Ksenia Boguslavkaia, Kazimir Malevich, and Ivan Puni, applied their Suprematist motifs to embroideries for purses, scarves, belts, etc., contributing their designs to exhibitions such as the *Exhibition of Industrial Art* at the Lemercier Gallery, Moscow, 1915, and the *Exhibition of Contemporary Decorative Art* at the Mikhailova Salon, Moscow, 1916–1917.
3. Alexander Davidovich Drevin (1889–1938), Udaltsova's husband, painted several monochrome paintings in 1921, each of which he titled *Suprematism* or *Painterly Composition*. For reproductions of two of these works, see *The Great Utopia*, cat. nos. 255, 256.
4. These are excerpts from the diary that Stepanova kept intermittently between 1919 and 1921 and then in 1927–28, and from the notes that she made during the 1930s and 1940s; translated from the Russian by J. Frank Goodwin. However, the most interesting entries are the early ones, which document events crucial to the history of the Russian avant-garde: here we read of the various responses to Malevich's Suprematism, to Olga Rozanova's posthumous exhibition, and the preparations for the *Nineteenth State Exhibition*, which was the first time that Stepanova showed her paintings publicly. Extracts from the diaries have been published in various Russian and German sources, including Oleg Melnikov, ed., *Varvara Stepanova: Chelovek ne mozhet zhit bez chuda*, Moscow: Sfera, 1994, pp. 202–58 and the catalogues for the exhibitions *Sieben Moskauer Künstler/Seven Moscow Artists* at the Galerie Gmurzynska, Cologne, 1984, pp. 251–60; and *Rodschenko-Stepanova* at the Osterreichische Museum für angewandte Kunst, Vienna, 1991, pp. 136–41.
5. *0.10: The Last Futurist Exhibition* was presented at Nadezhda Dobychina's Art Bureau in Petrograd from December 1915 through January 1916.
6. According to the catalogue of *0.10*, Ivan Albertovich Puni (Jean Pougny, 1894–1956) and Ksenia Leonidovna Boguslavakaia ("Punka," 1892–1972) were the organizers of the exhibition. Boguslavskaia, in fact, financed the enterprise.

7. Vera Efremova Pestel (1883–1952) and Mariia Ivanovna Vasilieva (Marie Vassilieff, 1884–1957) contributed four and eight Cubist works, respectively, to *0.10*.
8. Tatlin's exhibition *The Store* opened in Moscow in 1916. Tatlin showed reliefs, but Malevich was represented only by pre-Suprematist paintings.
9. Rodchenko's contribution included six non-objective ruler-and-compass compositions.
10. A reference to Rozanova's posthumous exhibition in 1918 in Moscow, i.e., the *First State Exhibition*.
11. Avant-garde Polish artist Wladyslaw Strzeminsku (1893–1952) was living in Russia at this time.
12. Anti was the pseudonym of Alexander Mikhailovich Rodchenko (1890–1956), Stepanova's husband.
13. The brothers Naum Gabo (pseudonym of Naum Neemiia Pevzner, 1890–1977) and Antoine Pevsner (pseudonym of Noton Pevzner, 1886–1962) were responsible for the *Realisticheskii manifest* (*Realist manifesto*), which they published in Moscow in 1920.
14. Pavel Varfomoleevich Kuznetsov (1878–1968) had been leader of the Symbolist Blue Rose group in the early 1900s. By this time, he was painting mainly Kirghizian scenes.
15. Alexander Vasilievich Shevchenko (1882–1948) and Mikhail Vasilievich Le-Dantiu (1891–1917) had been close to Larionov before the Revolution, investigating Neo-Primitivism, Cubism, and Rayonism.
16. Varst (i.e., Varvara Stepanova), untitled statement in the catalogue (unpaginated) of the exhibition *5 x 5 = 25*, held at the All-Russian Writers' Club, Moscow, in September 1921; translated from the Russian by John E. Bowlt.
    Stepanova contributed five works to the exhibition: *Figure (Peasant)* (plate 72), *Two Figures*, *Figure*, *Seated Figure*, and *Figure* (plate 73). See Exter essay, n. 2.

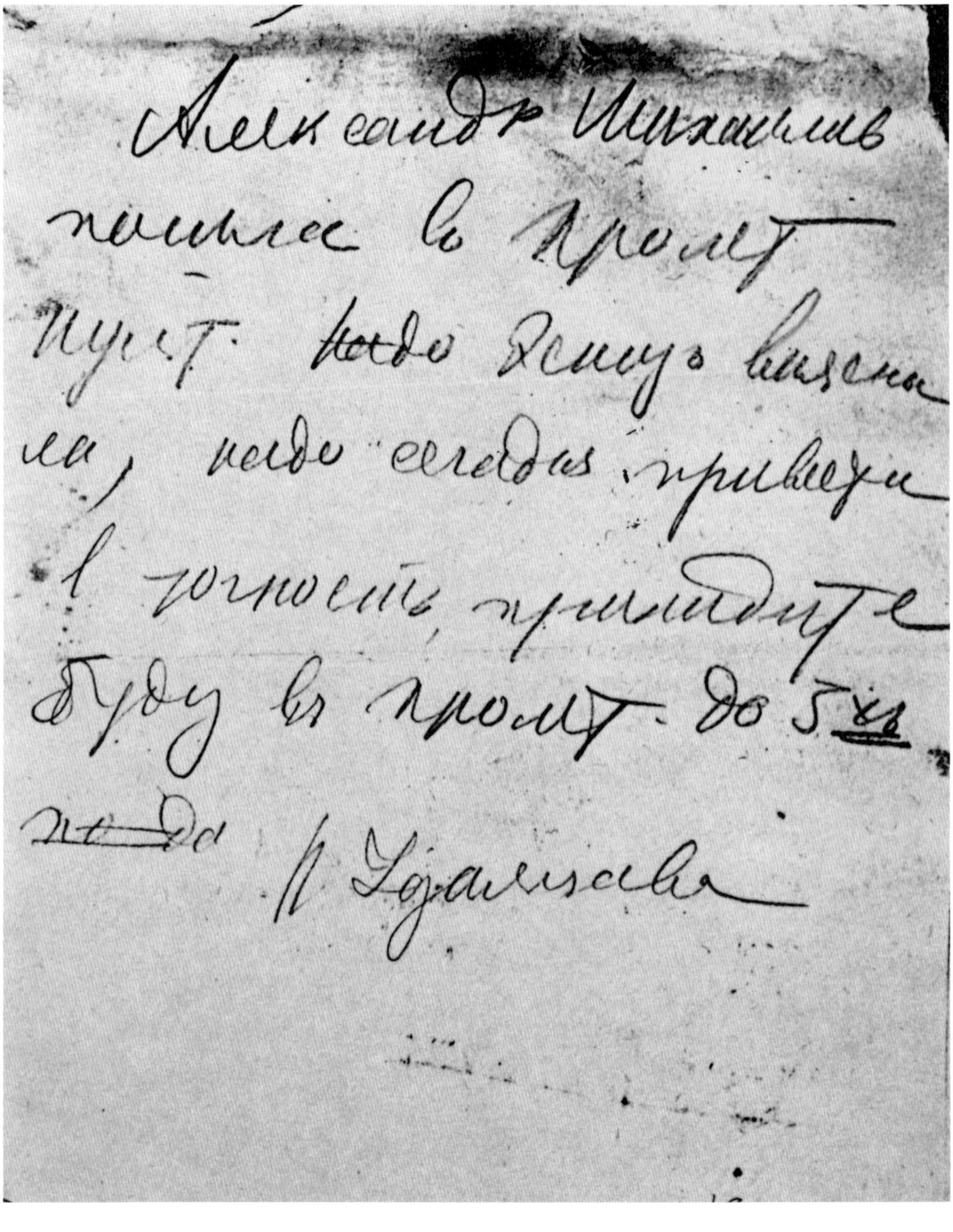
Александр Михайлович
пошла въ Промт
Пуст. ~~надо~~ Ясину вызва-
ла, надо сегодня привези
в точность, приходите
Буду въ Промт. до 5 ч.
~~надо~~ Н. Удальцова

figure 104. Handwritten letter from Udaltsova to Alexander Rodchenko, 1919. Private collection. (Translation on page 347.)

Nadezhda Udaltsova

Extract from Diary (1914)[1]
February 17
Picasso is a classic. He has a classical understanding of planes and space.

My Recollections: My Life in Art (early 1930s)
. . . In November 1912, I went to Paris with Liubov Popova. Sofia Karetnikova and Vera Pestel also traveled with us, although they soon returned to Moscow. After looking around, Popova and I began to search for a studio.

Our intention had been to work with Matisse, but his school was already closed, so we went over to Maurice Denis's studio. But there we ran into a Red Indian with feathers sitting against a red background and we ran away. Someone then told us about La Palette, the studio of Le Fauconnier. We went there and immediately decided that it was what we wanted.

. . . Le Fauconnier, Metzinger, and Segonzac used to visit the studio once a week. Le Fauconnier offered pictorial solutions for the canvas, while Metzinger spoke of Picasso's latest accomplishments. That was still the time of classical Cubism without all the *vie banale* [ordinary life] — which first appeared in the form of wallpaper and appliqués in the works of Braque. Le Fauconnier was a ferocious expert, and many a student trembled before the canvas. Both Le Fauconnier and Metzinger responded positively to my works, and I was so happy when Metzinger told me two weeks later, "Vous avez fait le progrès extraordinaire" ["You have made extraordinary progress"]. How the students looked at me!

. . . A year of life with only art, and [living] in isolation, turned me into a conscious artist and a real individual. For the first time I now sensed my own "I." In my diary for that year, I wrote that Cubism was only a school for me, not a goal. I fully appreciated the extraordinary nature of Cubist achievements in painting — and it was not the decorative aspect that attracted me, but rather the severity of its construction and the severe laws of painting itself . . . Oddly enough, after working through a season in Paris, I felt that I just had to leave, that I could work only in my own country. I felt the need to hide away and not see anything else.

Letter from Liubov Popova to Nadezhda Udaltsova (Paris, March 3 1913)[2]
Dear Nadezhda Andreevna,
Thank you for the letter. There's a lot I

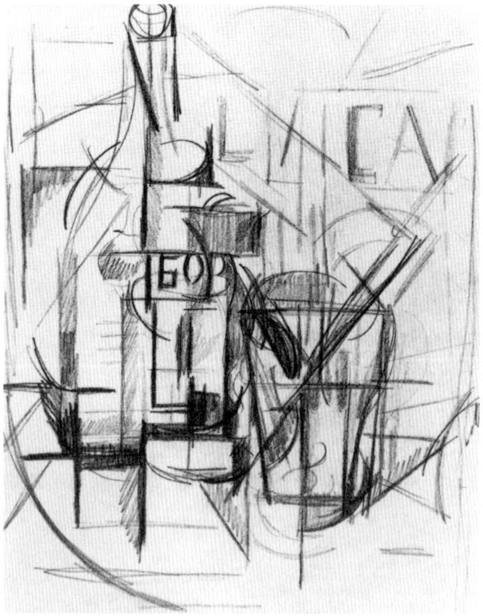

figure 105. Nadezhda Udaltsova, *Study for a Restaurant Table*, 1914, pencil on paper. Private collection.

need to tell you and my head is simply reeling, but at least I can mention the important news. I saw the new Picassos at Uhde's and Kahnweiler's (I sent you *Violin* and *Portrait with a Violin*, only I wasn't sure if I had sent you the right ones, since you did not indicate in your letter which of them you received). They are uncommonly good. I think that they are even more essential than the period of precise form that we all like so much (although that, too, of course, is amazing). *Man with a Guitar* (I sent this to you) at Uhde's is a very large work. I've never seen anything with such a diversity of planes and formal balance. As for its colors, the marble is green and painted photographically, while the rest consists of well-defined white, black, and an entire spectrum of grays.

Letter from Nadezhda Udaltsova to Olga Rozanova (1917)[3]

Olga Vladimirovna,

You asked me my opinion about French art and also expressed your own view that Russian artists are less aesthetic, that their textures are firmer, and their colors stronger. I agree with you completely.

As for the French, you sense their so-called "culture of successive tradition," as we say. That's true, but the same culture also contributes an element of disintegration (into subtlety, prettiness, and a technique that is skillful, but may only be superficial).

Essentially, I just don't understand this constant reference to the great culture of successive tradition. Does the very definition of art not lie, in fact, within the concept of culture? Does there really exist an uncultured art? Art is a phenomenon of culture, whether young or old, it doesn't matter. We try to understand both the primitive art of a savage with a bare minimum of culture and the refined art of a Cubist from the standpoint of art. Art is possible only for those peoples who have the power to create and renew [their art] through a knowledge of other cultures.

Even after receiving a fresh influx of forms from the art of other cultures (Japan, Impressionism, the East, Matisse, the African works of Picasso), much of French art retains an awful proclivity to depersonalize the forms of other cultures and affix the stamp of sickliness upon them. . . .

In my view it's time to oppose [French art] with a different art, an art based on the principle of pure painting, painting as an end in itself, which will generate not profound changes in the human soul, but canvases in which the artist will demonstrate the clear and simple laws of pure color and pure form with inexorable clarity.

If the Futurists have called for a healthy life and have been dreaming of cultivating a strong and healthy soul, then let us produce a strong and healthy art. There has been enough cultivated thought from the big city, enough gloomy iron from the factory and the train station. We have demonstrated that the steam engine and the automobile are just as wonderful as nature and man, but we do not wish to imitate these forms that already exist.

To create something out of iron and wood for us is the same as painting a sunny landscape or a portrait of a girl.

If artists wish to imitate forms that already exist, then let them do so. We say that art should be free and an end in itself.

We shall create things in our work no less expediently than the artists of the other kind of creativity — those who work with technology.

Extract from Diary: The *0.10* Exhibition (1915)

December 6

Tatlin has left. Doesn't write.

December 19

So we've had the inauguration of the exhibition and I think people approve of me, but I feel like leaving, going off again alone and working. I didn't expect such a success from this group of young people.

December 20

I'm very glad no vanity lies within me, that yesterday's success remained outside of me, and, I suppose, has only driven me to bring my own tasks into even higher and clearer relief — and that's why I'm pleased. Just my own tasks.

December 21

. . . I stopped by. Tatlin was waiting. He apologized, kissed my hands and a reconciliation took place. All the same, it's true, I do need to be more independent.

Extract from Diary (1916)

November 29

I've suddenly become interested in decorative designs and in Malevich.

December 8

. . . Pure forms fly in pure, cold space. They are thrown into a headlong race, colliding, separating, or, through their inner dynamism, revealing the static development of color. Form-color. The composition of color relationships.

Letter from Nadezhda Udaltsova to Kazimir Malevich (1917?)

Kazimir Severinovich,

[I've had] many new thoughts about our art recently and I see new possibilities.

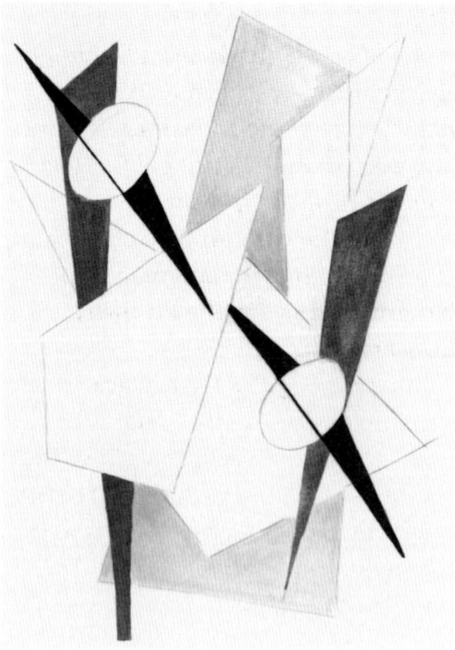

figure 106. Nadezhda Udaltsova, *Untitled*, 1916. Gouache on paper, 34.5 x 25 cm. Private collection.

Just as nine years ago the first form appeared and created the great art of Cubism, so now the new painterly form has become a reality and is creating a new art. It is already establishing a new technique and a new understanding of color. It is revealing the characteristics of color. Our new art will be built on these new laws and we will tell about this new art simply and clearly in our paintings and our articles.

Cézanne once said that everything is built with the geometric forms of volume. We can say that everything is built with geometric forms. We know the qualities of the colors of paints, their depth and intensity. We could compile a mathematical table of the relations between this and that color.

The material we work with is paint, and it is only from paint that we will create a new world of reality.

Nadezhda Udaltsova: Article for Supremus (1917)

A) If the Cubists studied the forms of things and looked for their volume; if the Futurists, crazy about swift movement, aspired to convey this movement as reality; if artists who are chained by love to their material made things of iron and wood or imitated them in painting and pasted together paper and cardboard, then artists of today have arrived at the fundamental basis of painting: color (color-painting).

Color determines form.

From within color reveals one of its distinctive characteristics: its depth, its weight.

Henceforth, the artist will not strive to transform a given form of nature so as to create a wonderful aesthetic work; rather, he will go to the foundation of the art of painting: color. He will produce new forms that have not yet appeared within nature, but that originate within the consciousness of the artist. This is not the study of the forms of nature in the light of this or that painterly idea.

Nature may enter only as a stimulus to this or that correlation of colors and abstract forms.

The world as a result of sensory perception is a falsehood. Art that is constructed on the basis of sensory perception confirms this falsehood. Abstract thought can penetrate beyond the limits of the sensory world.

An abstract form of consciousness can also penetrate beyond those limits.

"The forms of our consciousness evoked through the medium of expression evolve continuously. In addition to the forms we know, new forms should arise." They arise within life; all the forms of technique are summoned to life by necessity.

Art searches for them persistently.

Cubism broke up the object and Futurism smashed it, while Suprematism generates a completely abstract form of viewer perception.

The Suprematist form is confirmed by the necessity of its pictorial existence on a given canvas. In this way, a concrete life is created, a life more affirmative than anything else, than all the living and dead forms of nature. These forms change in perspective, according to light or the influence of the atmosphere and surrounding forms, and only the individual desire of the artist will show them on the canvas in this or that aspect. . . .

B) Art gives new forms to life; or, more precisely, as a more sensitive work of creativity, it designs new forms of life.

Futurism, now obsolete in art, has entered life.

After first discovering new forms of dynamism, the Futurists were struck by the beauty of a new form and strove to convey it in their canvases. We who have experienced the pleasure of passing through these forms can look back calmly and now create a new art: we have a presentiment of a new form of life based not on tremor and excitement before the machine and technology, but on the calm application of these factors of life and on the free creative work of the human soul liberated from the slavery of property.

For us, for our spirit, airplanes are no different than the automobile or the cart, for they are already forms of the everyday.

Unrestrained by the rapture of the moment, our spirit calmly subordinates all forms of human creation. We are not carried away with delight before a newly discovered form of technology, for our free spirit, in its own creative work, rises to infinity.

Translation of figure 104: Alexander Mikhailovich. I went to the Proletkult. What I found out is that the sketch has to be finished by today. Drop by. I'll be in Proletkult until three o'clock.
N. Udaltsova.

1. The following excerpts are from the manuscripts in the Drevin-Udaltsova Archive in Moscow. "My Recollections: My Life in Art" and the 1915–16 diary entries are taken from Ekaterina Drevina and Vasilii Rakitin, *Nadezhda Udaltsova: Zhizn russkoi kubistki. Dnevniki, stati, vospominaniia* (Moscow: RA, 1994), pp. 9–14, 28–42; translated from the Russian by J. Frank Goodwin.
2. The manuscript of this letter is in the Drevin-Udaltsova Archive, Moscow.
3. Udaltsova intended to publish this letter (and her letter to Malevich below) in *Supremus*. Copies of the letters are in a private collection in St. Petersburg and in the Archive of the Khardzhiev-Chaga Cultural Foundation, Amsterdam (inv. no. KAZ-2).

The following list of plates, prepared as this book was going to press, contains information that, in some cases, differs from that found in the catalogue section. In the case of discrepancies, it is the information below that prevails, reflecting scholarly discoveries made in the course of preparations for this exhibition.

Information about the provenance and exhibition history of the works has been supplied by the following individuals: Liudmila Bobrovskaia (Alexandra Exter and Nadezhda Udaltsova), Nina Gurianova and Faina Balakhovskaia (Olga Rozanova), Alexander Lavrentiev and Tatiana Mikhienko (Varvara Stepanova), and Alla Lukanova (Natalia Goncharova and Liubov Popova).

Provenance. Gaps in chronology and ownership still persist. Much research has yet to be done on the issues of itinerary and ownership of works by the artists of the Russian avant-garde.

Exhibitions. While many of the works listed below continue to be included in public exhibitions, only major venues of the 1910s and early 1920s have been listed here. The following abbreviations have been used:

1911. Moscow, *Jack of Diamonds*: *Jack of Diamonds*, Levisson Building, 11 Bolshaia Dmitrovka, Moscow, December 1910–January 1911

1912. Moscow, *Donkey's Tail*: *Donkey's Tail*, Institute of Painting, Sculpture, and Architecture, Moscow, March–April 1912

1912. Moscow, *Union of Youth*: *Union of Youth*, Institute of Painting, Sculpture, and Architecture, Moscow, March–April 1912

1912. St. Petersburg, *Union of Youth*: *Union of Youth*, 73 Nevskii Prospect, St. Petersburg, January–February 1912

1912–13. St Petersburg, *Union of Youth*: *Union of Youth*, 73 Nevskii Prospect, St. Petersburg, December 1912–January 1913

1913–14. St. Petersburg, *Union of Youth*: *Union of Youth*, 73 Nevskii Prospect, St. Petersburg, November 1913– January 1914

1913. Moscow, *Jack of Diamonds*: *Jack of Diamonds*, Art Salon, 11 Bolshaia Dmitrovka, Moscow, February–March 1913

1913. Moscow, *Target*: *Target*, Art Salon, 11 Bolshaia Dmitrovka, Moscow, March–April 1913

1913. St. Petersburg, *Jack of Diamonds*: *Jack of Diamonds*, St. Petersburg, April 1913

1913. Moscow, *Goncharova*: *Exhibition of Paintings by Natalia Sergeevna Goncharova*, 1900–1913, Art Salon, 11 Bolshaia Dmitrovka, Moscow, August–October 1913

1914. Kiev, *Ring*: *Ring*, House of Ilia Kalf on the Kreshchatik Boulevard, Kiev, February 23–March 1914

1914. Moscow, *Jack of Diamonds*: *Jack of Diamonds*, Art Salon, 11 Bolshaia Dmitrovka, Moscow, February 1914

1914. St. Peterburg, *Goncharova*: *Exhibition of Paintings by Natalia Sergeevna Goncharova, 1900–1913* at the Dobychina Bureau, 63 Moika, St. Petersburg, March–April 1914.

1914. Moscow, *No. 4*: *No. 4*, Levisson Building, 11 Bolshaia Dmitrovka, Moscow, March–April 1914

1914. Paris, *Guillaume*: *Exposition Natalia de Gontcharova et Michel Larionov*, Galerie Paul Guillaume, Paris, June 1914.

1915. Petrograd, *Tramway V*: *Tramway V*, Imperial Society for the Encouragement of the Arts, Petrograd, March–April 1915

1915. Moscow, *Exhibition of Painting*: *Exhibition of Painting*, 1915, Art Salon, 11 Bolshaia Dmitrovka, March–May, Moscow, 1915

1915. Petrograd, *0.10.*: *0.10*. The Last Futurist Exhibition, Dobychina Bureau, Petrograd, December 1915–January 1916

1916. Moscow, *The Store*: *The Store*, Petrovka, Moscow, March 1916

1916. Moscow, *Jack of Diamonds*: *Jack of Diamonds*, Art Salon, 11 Bolshaia Dmitrovka, Moscow, November–December 1916

1917. Moscow, *Jack of Diamonds*: *Jack of Diamonds*, Art Salon, 11 Bolshaia Dmitrovka, Moscow, November–December 1917

1918. Moscow, *I State Exhibition: I State Exhibition. Posthumous Exhibition of Paintings, Studies, Sketches, and Drawings by O.V. Rozanova, Art Salon*, Moscow, December 1918

1919. Moscow, *X State Exhibition: X State Exhibition. Non-Objective Creativity and Suprematism*, Art Salon, Moscow, April 1919

1920. Kazan, *First State Exhibition: First State Exhibition of Art and Science in Kazan organized by the Political Section of the Reserve Army, the Kazan Gubernatorial Department of Popular Education, and the Kazan Sub-Section of the All-Russian Collegiate for Museums and the Preservation of Monuments of Art and Antiquity*, Kazan, 1920

1920 Moscow, *XIX State Exhibition: XIX State Exhibition*, Bolshaia Dmitrovka 11, October 2–December 4, 1920.

1921. Moscow, *5 x 5 = 25: 5 x 5 = 25, Club of the All-Russian Union of Poets Moscow*, September and October 1921 (two sessions)

1922. Berlin, *Erste russische Kunstausstellung: Erste russische Kunstausstellung*, Galerie Van Diemen, Berlin, October–November1922

1924. Moscow, *Popova: Posthumous Exhibition of the Artist-Constructor, L. S. Popova, 1889–1924*, Museum of Painterly Culture (formerly the Central Stroganov Industrial Art Institute), Moscow, December 1924

ALEXANDRA EXTER

1. *The Bridge (Sèvres)*, 1912
Oil on canvas, 145 x 115 cm
National Art Museum of Ukraine, Kiev

Provenance: State Museum of Russian Art, Kiev;
State Museum of Ukrainian Visual Art, Kiev
(National Art Museum of Ukraine, Kiev) (1936)
Inv. ZhS-045
Exhibitions: 1913. Moscow, *Jack of Diamonds*
(cat. no. 182)
1913. St. Petersburg, *Jack of Diamonds* (cat. no. 404)

2. *Composition (Genoa)*, 1912–14
Oil on canvas, 115.5 x 86.5 cm
Museum Ludwig, Cologne

Provenance: Alisa Koonen, Moscow;
George Costakis, Moscow;
Galerie Gmurzynska, Cologne;
Museum Ludwig, Cologne (1981) Inv. M1338
Exhibitions: 1914. Moscow, *Jack of Diamonds*
(cat. no. 187 or 192)

3. *City*, 1913
Oil on canvas, 88.5 x 70.5 cm
Regional Picture Gallery, Vologda

Provenance: State Art Fund, Moscow,
Vologda Museum of Local Lore, (1927);
Regional Picture Gallery, Vologda, (1970)
Inv. Zh-614
Exhibitions: Possibly at 1913. St. Petersburg,
Union of Youth (cat. no. 161)
Possibly at 1914. Moscow, *Jack of Diamonds*
(cat. no. 188)
1914. Kiev, *Ring* (cat. no. 14)
Possibly at 1914. Moscow, *No. 4* (cat. no. 234)
Possibly at 1915. Petrograd, *Tramway V* (cat. no. 84)
1922. Berlin, *Erste russische Kunstausstellung*
(cat. no. 32)

4. *Still Life*, ca. 1913
Oil on canvas, 68 x 53 cm
Museo Thyssen-Bornemisza, Madrid

Provenance:Simon Lissim, New York;
Leonard Hutton Galeries, New York (1968) ;
Thyssen-Bornemisza Collection, Lugano (1973);
Museo Thyssen-Bornemisza, Madrid,
Inv. 540(1973.26)
Exhibitions: 1914. Moscow, *Jack of Diamonds*
(cat. no. 193)
1915. Petrograd, *Tramway V* (cat. no. 86, 87, or 89)

5. *Still Life. Bowl of Cherries*, 1914
Oil on canvas, 89 x 72 cm
Rostov Kremlin State Museum Preserve

Provenance: Museum Bureau of IZO NKP;
Museum of Architecture and Art, Rostov-Yaroslavskii
(as of 1998 Rostov Kremlin State Museum Preserve)
(1922), Inv. Zh-142
Exhibitions: 1915. Petrograd, *Tramway V*
(cat. no. 86, 87, or 89)

6. *Composition*, 1914
Oil on canvas, 90.7 x 72.5 cm
State Tretiakov Gallery, Moscow
Gift, George Costakis

Provenance: Private collection, Moscow;
George Costakis, Moscow;
State Tretiakov Gallery, Moscow (1977), Inv. 46984
Exhibitions: Possibly at 1915. Petrograd, *Tramway V* (cat no. 81, as *Paris Boulevards in the Evening*)

7. *Venice*, 1915
Oil on canvas, 123 x 97 cm
Moderna Museet, Stockholm

Provenance: Henschen Collection, Stockholm;
Moderna Museet, Stockholm (1980)
Inv. MOM (173)
Exhibitions: 1922. Berlin, *Erste russische Kunstausstellung* (cat. no. 33)

8. *Cityscape (Composition)*, ca. 1916
Oil on canvas, 117 x 88 cm
Slobodskoi Museum and Exhibition Center

Provenance: Museum Bureau of IZO NKP, Moscow;
Slobodskoi Museum of Local Lore, Slobodskoi (as of 1998 Slobodskoi Museum and Exhibition Center) (1919–20), Inv. SMK-995/54
Exhibitions: *Exhibition of Contemporary Russian Painting*, Dobychina Bureau, 63 Moika, Petrograd, 1916–17 (within cat. nos. 284–88)

9. *Non-Objective Composition*, 1917
Oil on canvas, 71 x 53 cm
Krasnodar District Kovalenko Art Museum

Provenance: State Art Fund, Moscow;
Kuban Art Museum, Krasnodar;
(as of 1940 Krasnodar District Lunacharsky Art Museum; Krasnodar District Kovalenko Art Museum, 1927), Inv. Zh-359
Exhibition: 1922. Berlin, *Erste russische Kunstausstellung* (cat. no. 34)

10. *Composition. Movement of Planes*, 1917–18
Oil on canvas, 92.5 x 76.9 cm
State Museum of Visual Arts, Nizhnii Tagil

Provenance: State Art Fund, Moscow;
Museum of Local Lore, Nizhnii Tagil
(as of 1967 State Museum of Visual Arts, Nizhnii Tagil) (1927), Inv. Zh-485
Exhibition: *XIV Esposizione internazionale d'Arte della città di Venezia*, Venice, 1924 (cat. no. 31 or 32)

11. *Construction of Color Planes*, 1921
Oil on canvas, 89 x 89 cm
State Radischev Art Museum, Saratov

Provenance: State Art Fund, Moscow;
State Radishchev Art Museum, Saratov (1929)
Inv. Zh-685
Exhibition: *XIV Esposizione internazionale d'Arte della città di Venezia*, Venice, 1924 (cat. no. 30)

12. *Construction*, 1922–23
Oil on canvas, 89.8 x 89.2 cm
The Museum of Modern Art, New York.
The Riklis Collection of McCrory Corporation (partial gift)

Provenance: The Riklis Collection of McCrory Corporation, The Museum of Modern Art (1983)

NATALIA GONCHAROVA

13. *Self-Portrait with Yellow Lilies*, 1907
Oil on canvas, 77 x 58.2 cm
State Tretiakov Gallery, Moscow

Provenance: Moscow Soviet Depository of Works of Contemporary Art (until mid-1920s);
Acquired by the State Tretiakov Gallery, Moscow, from the artist in through the mediation of Lev Zhegin (1927), Inv. 8965
Exhibitions: 1913. Moscow, *Goncharova* (cat. no. 339)

14. *Mowers*, 1907–08
Oil on canvas, 98 x 118 cm
Private Collection, Courtesy Gallery Gmurzynska, Cologne

Provenance: Private collection, Cologne
Exhibitions: 1913. Moscow, *Goncharova* (cat. no. 554?)
1914. Paris, *Guillaume* (cat. no. 54)

15. *Pillars of Salt*, 1908
Oil on canvas, 80.5 x 96 cm
State Tretiakov Gallery, Moscow

Provenance:
Moscow Soviet Depository of Works of Contemporary Art (until mid-1920s);
Artist's studio, Paris (after 1928);
Alexandra Tomilina (1964);
State Tretiakov Gallery, Moscow (1988)
Inv. Zh-1579, P-74159
Exhibitions: Probably at *Goncharova's One-day Exhibition*, Society of Free Esthetics, 15 Bolshaia Dmitrovka, Moscow, 24 March, 1910
1913. Moscow, *Goncharova* (cat. no. 441)
1914. St. Petersburg, *Goncharova* (cat. no. 49)

16. *Apocalypse (Elder with Seven Stars)*, 1910
Oil on canvas, 147 x 188 cm
State Tretiakov Gallery, Moscow

Provenance: Moscow Soviet Depository of Works of Contemporary Art (until mid-1920s);
Artist's studio, Paris (after 1928);
Alexandra Tomilina (1964);
State Tretiakov Gallery, Moscow (1988),
Inv. Zh-1585
Exhibitions: 1914. St. Petersburg, *Goncharova* (cat. no. 249)

17. *The Evangelists (in Four Parts)*, 1911
1) *In Blue*; 2) *In Red*; 3) *In Gray*; 4) *In Green*
Oil on canvas, 204 x 58 cm each
State Russian Museum, St. Petersburg

Provenance: Moscow Soviet Depository of Works of Contemporary Art (until mid-1920s);
Artists's studio, Paris (late 1920s);
Alexandra Tomilina (1964);
State Russian Museum, Leningrad (1966),
Inv. Zh-8183-86
Exhibitions: 1914. St. Petersburg, *Goncharova* (cat. no. 247).

18. *Sabbath*, 1912
Oil on canvas, 137.5 x 118 cm
State Museum of the Visual Arts of Tatarstan, Kazan

Provenance: State Art Fund, Moscow (1919);
Museum Bureau of IZO NKP (1920);
State Museum of the Tatar Soviet Republic, Kazan (as of 1962 State Museum of the Visual Arts of Tatarstan, Kazan) (1920), Inv. Zh-772
Exhibitions: 1913. Moscow, *Target* (cat. no. 34)
1913. Moscow, *Goncharova* (cat. no. 605)
1914. St. Petersburg, *Goncharova* (cat. no. 91, 159, or 161)
1920. Kazan, *First State Exhibition* (cat. no. 27)

19. *Peasants Gathering Grapes*, 1912
Oil on canvas, 145 x 130 cm
State Art Museum of Bashkkortostan, Ufa

Provenance: State Art Fund, Moscow (1919);
Museum Bureau of IZO NKP (1920);
State Art Museum of Bashkkortostan, Ufa (1920)
Inv. Zh-1438
Exhibitions: 1912. Moscow, *Donkey's Tail* (cat. no. 34)
1913. Moscow, *Goncharova* (possibly cat. no. 753)
1914. St. Petersburg, *Goncharova* (cat. no. 130).

20. *Electric Lamp*, 1913
Oil on canvas, 125 x 81.5 cm
Centre Georges Pompidou,
Musée national d'art moderne, Paris

Provenance: Galerie Der Sturm, Berlin (1914);
Artist's Studio, Paris (1918);
Alexandra Tomilna, Paris (1964);
Musée National d'Art Moderne, Paris (1966)
Inv. AM 435BP
Exhibitions: 1914. Moscow, *No. 4* (cat. no. 39 or 51)

21. *The Weaver (Loom + Woman)*, 1912–13
Oil on canvas, 153.3 x 99 cm
National Museum and Gallery, Cardiff

Provenance: Mikhail Larionov;
Sotheby's London (1964);
Rogers Collection (1964);
Grosvenor Gallery, London (1972);
National Museum and Gallery, Cardiff (1975)
Inv. A 2056
Exhibitions: 1913. Moscow, *Goncharova* (cat. no. 765)
1914. Paris, *Guillaume* (cat. no. 35)

22. *Airplane over a Train*, 1913
Oil on canvas, 55 x 83.5 cm
State Museum of the Visual Arts of Tatarstan, Kazan

Provenance: State Art Fund, Moscow (1919);
Museum Bureau of IZO NKP (1920);
State Museum of the Tatar Soviet Republic, Kazan (State Museum of the Visual Arts of Tatarstan, Kazan) (1920), Inv. Zh-1243
Exhibitions: 1913. Moscow, *Goncharova* (cat. no. 632)
1914. St. Petersburg, *Goncharova* (cat. no. 29)
Kazan (cat. no. 28)

23. *Rayist Lilies*, 1913
Oil on canvas, 91 x 75.4 cm
State Picture Gallery, Perm

Provenance: State Art Fund, Moscow (1919);
Museum Bureau of IZO NKP, Moscow (1920);
Museum of Local Lore of the City of Ekaterinburg (1920);
(as of 1920 Regional Museum of Local Lore, Sverdlov),
State Picture Gallery, Perm (1935), Inv. Zh-538
Exhibitions: 1913. Moscow, *Target* (cat. no. 45)
1913. Moscow, *Goncharova* (cat. no. 633)

24. *Yellow and Green Forest*, 1913
Oil on canvas, 102 x 85 cm
Staatsgalerie, Stuttgart

Provenance: Galleria del Levante, Milan;
Galerie Beyeler, Basel;
Staatsgalerie, Stuttgart (1965), Inv. LNA 881
Exhibitions: 1912. Moscow, *Donkey's Tail* (cat. no. 73, as *Autumn Study [Spontaneous Perception]*)
Erster Deutscher Herbstsalon, Galerie Der Sturm, Berlin, October–November, 1913 (cat. no. 151)

25. *Cats (rayist percep.[tion] in rose, black, and yellow)*, 1913
Oil on canvas, 84.5 x 83.8 cm
Solomon R. Guggenheim Museum, New York
57.1484

Provenance: From the artist, 1957
Exhibitions: 1913. Moscow, *Target* (cat. no. 49)
1913. Moscow, *Goncharova* (cat. no. 645)
1913. Berlin, Der Sturm, *Erster Deutscher Herbstsalon*, Sept. 20–Nov. 1 (cat. no. 149)
1914. Paris, *Guillaume* (cat. no. 34)

26. *Emptiness*, 1913
Mixed media on canvas, 80 x 106 cm
State Tretiakov Gallery, Moscow

Provenance: Moscow Soviet Depository of Works of Contemporary Art (until mid-1920s);
Artist's studio, Paris (after 1928);
Alexandra Tomilina (1964);
State Tretiakov Gallery, Moscow (1988), Inv. Zh-1543
Exhibitions: 1914. Moscow, *No. 4* (cat. no. 51)

27. *Composition*, 1913–14
Oil on canvas, 103.5 x 97.2 cm
Centre Georges Pompidou,
Musée national d'art moderne, Paris

Provenance: Moscow Soviet Depository of Works of Contemporary Art (until mid-1920s);
Artists's studio, Paris (late 1920s);
Alexandra Tomilina (1964);
State Tretiakov Gallery, Moscow (1988),
Centre Georges Pompidou, Musée national d'art Moderne (1988), Inv. AM 1988–887

LIUBOV POPOVA

28. *Composition with Figures*, 1913
Oil on canvas, 160 x 124.3 cm
State Tretiakov Gallery, Moscow

Provenance: Pavel Popov (Liubov Popova's brother) or his stepson, Moscow.
George Costakis, Moscow;
State Tretiakov Gallery, Moscow (1977), Inv. 1310
Exhibitions: 1914. Moscow, *Jack of Diamonds* (cat. no. 119)
1924. Moscow, *Popova* (cat. no. 17)

29. *Italian Still Life*, 1914
Oil, plaster, and paper collage on canvas, 61.5 x 48 cm
State Tretiakov Gallery, Moscow

Provenance: Museum of Painterly Culture, Moscow;
State Art Fund, Moscow;
State Tretiakov Gallery, Moscow (1927), Inv. Zh-9365
Exhibitions: *V State Exhibition of Paintings* at the Museum of Visual Arts, Volkhonka, Moscow, 1918–19 (within cat. nos. 181–84)
1922. Berlin, *Erste russische Kunstausstellung* (cat. no. 153)
1924. Moscow, *Popova* (cat. no. 29)

30. *Guitar*, 1915
Oil on canvas, 83.5 x 71 cm
Collection of Elena Murina and
Dmitrii Sarabianov, Moscow

Provenance: Pavel Popov (Liubov Popova's brother), Moscow;
Alexander Vesnin, Moscow;
Elena Murina and Dmitrii Sarabianov, Moscow (1960)

31. *The Pianist*, 1914–15 [1915]
Oil on canvas, 106.5 x 88.7 cm
National Gallery of Canada, Ottawa

Provenance: Popova family, Moscow;
Victor Moore, Moscow (1957), (purchased through George Costakis);
National Gallery of Canada, Ottawa (1966)
Inv. NGC 14930

32. *Lady with a Guitar*, 1915
Oil on canvas, 107 x 71.5 cm
State Museum of History, Architecture, and Art, Smolensk

Provenance: Museum of Painterly Culture, Moscow;
Museum Bureau of IZO NKP, Moscow (1920);
State Museum of History, Architecture, and Art, Smolensk (1920), Inv. Zh-855
Exhibitions: 1915. Petrograd, *Tramway V* (cat. no. 45)
1916. Moscow, *The Store* (cat. no. 47)

33. *Traveling Woman*, 1915
Oil on canvas, 158.5 x 123 cm
Art Co. Ltd. (George Costakis Collection)

Provenance: Pavel Popov (Liubov Popova's brother) or his stepson, Moscow;
George Costakis, Moscow;
Art Co. Ltd. (George Costakis Collection) (1984), Inv. 177.78
Exhibitions: 1915. Petrograd, *0.10* (cat. no. 92)
1916. Moscow, *The Store* (cat. no. 51)

34. *Jug on Table. Plastic Painting*, 1915
Oil on cardboard, mounted on panel,
59.1 x 45.3 cm
State Tretiakov Gallery, Moscow,
Gift, George Costakis

Provenance: Pavel Popov (Liubov Popova's brother) or his stepson, Moscow;
George Costakis, Moscow;
State Tretiakov Gallery, Moscow (1977), Inv. P 46736
Exhibitions: 1915. Petrograd, *0.10* (cat. no. 96)
1916. Moscow, *The Store* (cat. no. 54)
1924. Moscow, *Popova* (cat. no. 16)

35. *Birsk*, 1916
Oil on canvas, 106 x 69.5 cm
Solomon R. Guggenheim Museum, New York,
Gift, George Costakis 81.2822.1

Provenance: Pavel Popov (Liubov Popova's brother), Moscow;
George Costakis, Moscow;
Solomon R. Guggenheim Museum, New York (1981)
Exhibitions: 1924. Moscow, Popova

36. *Painterly Architectonics*, 1917
Oil on canvas, 107 x 88 cm
Krasnodar District Kovalenko Art Museum

Provenance: Museum of Painterly Culture, Moscow;
State Tretiakov Gallery, Moscow (until 1929);
Kuban Art Museum, Krasnodar (attributed to Ivan Kliun)
(Krasnodar District Lunacharsky Art Museum;
Krasnodar District Kovalenko Art Museum)
Inv. 403
Exhibitions: 1924. Moscow, *Popova* (within cat. nos. 33–46)

37. *Painterly Architectonics*, 1918
Oil on canvas, 105 x 80 cm
Slobodskoi Museum and Exhibition Center

Provenance: Museum Bureau of IZO NKP, Moscow;
Museum of Local Lore, Slobodskoi, Viatka Region (as of 1998 Slobodskoi Museum and Exhibition Center) (1920), Inv. SMK 995/49
Exhibitions: *X State Exhibition* (within cat. nos. 164–74)

38. *Construction*, 1920
Oil on canvas, 106.8 x 88.7 cm
State Tretiakov Gallery, Moscow

Provenance: Museum of Painterly Culture, Moscow;
State Art Fund, Moscow;
State Tretiakov Gallery, Moscow (1927), Inv. 9389
Exhibitions: 1922. Berlin, *Erste russische Kunstausstellung* (cat. no. 152)

39. *Spatial-Force Construction*, 1921
Oil with marble dust on plywood, 112.7 x 112.7 cm
Art Co. Ltd. (George Costakis Collection)

Provenance: Pavel Popov (Liubov Popova's brother) or his stepson, Moscow;
George Costakis, Moscow;
Art Co. Ltd (Georges Costakis Collection) (1984)
Inv. no. 175.78

40. *Spatial-Force Construction*, 1921
Oil over pencil on plywood, 124 x 82.3 cm
State Tretiakov Gallery, Moscow,
Gift, George Costakis

Provenance: Pavel Popov (Liubov Popova's brother) or his stepson, Moscow;
George Costakis, Moscow;
State Tretiakov Gallery, Moscow (1977),
Inv. Zh 1314 (P 46727)

41. *Spatial-Force Construction*, 1921
Oil with marble dust on plywood, 71 x 64 cm
Art Co. Ltd. (George Costakis Collection)

Provenance: Pavel Popov (Liubov Popova's brother) or his stepson, Moscow;
George Costakis, Moscow;
Art Co. Ltd (George Costakis Collection) (1984),
Inv. 179.78
Exhibitions: 1924. Moscow, *Popova*

OLGA ROZANOVA

42. *Portrait of a Lady in Pink (Portrait of Anna Rozanova, the Artist's Sister)*, 1911
Oil on canvas, 113 x 139 cm
Museum of Visual Arts, Ekaterinburg

Provenance: Museum Bureau of IZO NKP, Moscow;
Museum of Local Lore of the City of Ekaterinburg,
(as of 1920 Regional Museum of Local Lore, Sverdlovsk;
as of 1936 Sverdlovsk Picture Gallery, Sverdlovsk;
Museum of Visual Arts, Ekaterinburg) (1920),
Inv. 390
Exhibitions: 1912, Moscow, *Union of Youth* (cat. no. 67)
1912. St. Petersburg, *Union of Youth* (cat. no. 68)
1912–13. St Petersburg, *Union of Youth* (cat. no. 73)
1918. Moscow, *I State Exhibition* (cat. no. 16)

43. *Fire in the City (Cityscape)*, 1914
Oil on metal, 71 x 71 cm
Art Museum, Samara

Provenance: Museum Bureau of IZO NKP, Moscow,
Art Museum, Samara
(Art Museum, Kuibyshev;
Art Museum, Samara) (1919), Inv. Zh-411
Exhibitions: 1915. Petrograd, *Tramway V* (cat. no. 63)
1916. Moscow, *Jack of Diamonds* (cat. no. 266)
1918. Moscow, *I State Exhibition* (cat. no. 65 or 66?)

44. *Pub (Auction)*, 1914
Oil on canvas, 84 x 66 cm
State Unified Art Museum, Kostroma

Provenance: Museum Bureau of IZO NKP, Moscow;
Museum of Painterly Culture, Kostroma
(as of 1922 Art Museum, Kostroma) (1920),
Inv. NV5
Exhibitions: *Exhibition of Paintings of Leftist Trends*, Dobychina Bureau, Petrograd, 1915 (cat. no. 89)
1918. Moscow, *I State Exhibition* (cat. no. 83)

45. *Jack of Hearts*, 1912(?)–15, from the series *Playing Cards*
Oil on canvas, 80 x 65 cm
Slobodskoi Museum and Exhibition Center

Provenance: Museum Bureau of IZO NKP, Moscow; Museum of Local Lore, Slobodskoi, Viatka Region (as of 1998 Slobodskoi Museum and Exhibition Center) (1920), Inv. SMK 995/14
Exhibitions: *Exhibition of Paintings of Leftist Trends*, Dobychina Bureau, Petrograd, 1915 (cat. no. 84)
1917. Moscow, *Jack of Diamonds* (cat. no. 181, dated 1912)
1918. Moscow, *I State Exhibition* (within cat. nos. 36–47)

46. *King of Clubs*, 1912(?)–1915, from the series *Playing Cards*
Oil on canvas, 72 x 60 cm
Slobodskoi Museum and Exhibition Center

Provenance: Museum Bureau of IZO NKP, Moscow; Museum of Local Lore, Slobodskoi, Viatka Region (as of 1998 Slobodskoi Museum and Exhibition Center) (1920), Inv. SMK 995/23
Exhibitions: *Exhibition of Paintings of Leftist Trends*, Dobychina Bureau, Petrograd, 1915 (cat. no. 81)
1917. Moscow, *Jack of Diamonds* (cat. no. 182, dated 1912)
1918. Moscow, *I State Exhibition* (within cat. nos. 36–47)

47. *Queen of Spades*, 1912(?)–1915, from the series *Playing Cards*
Oil on canvas, 77.5 x 61.5 cm
Regional Art Museum, Ulianovsk

Provenance: Museum Bureau of IZO NKP, Moscow; Regional Art Museum, Simbirsk (as of 1924 Art Museum, Ulianovsk) (1920), Inv. Zh-504
Exhibitions: *Exhibition of Paintings of Leftist Trends*, Dobychina Bureau, Petrograd, 1915 (cat. no. 88)
1917. Moscow, *Jack of Diamonds* (cat. no. 178, dated 1912)
1918. Moscow, *I State Exhibition* (within cat. nos. 36–47)

48. *The "Moderne" Movie Theater (In the Street)*, 1915
Oil on canvas, 101 x 77 cm
Slobodskoi Museum and Exhibition Center

Provenance: Museum Bureau of IZO NKP, Moscow; Museum of Local Lore, Slobodskoi, Viatka Region (as of 1998 Slobodskoi Museum and Exhibition Center) (1920), Inv. SMK 995/48
Exhibitions: 1915. Petrograd, *0.10* (cat. no. 123, called *In the Street*)
1918. Moscow, *I State Exhibition* (cat. no. 90–91, as *In the Street*)

49. *Non-Objective Composition (Flight of an Airplane)*, 1916
Oil on canvas, 118 x 101 cm
Art Museum, Samara

Provenance: Museum Bureau of IZO NKO; Art Museum, Samara (1919, where renamed Flight of an Airplane in the early 1930s; Art Museum, Kuibyshev; Art Museum, Samara), Inv. Zh-418
Exhibitions: 1916. Moscow, *Jack of Diamonds* (within cat. nos. 269–74)
1918. Moscow, *I State Exhibition* (within cat. no. 93–111)

50. *Non-Objective Composition (Suprematism)*, 1916
Oil on canvas, 90 x 74 cm
Museum of Visual Arts, Ekaterinburg

Provenance: Museum Bureau of IZO NKO, Museum of Local Lore of the City of Ekaterinburg, (as of 1920 Regional Museum of Local Lore, Sverdlovsk;
as of 1936 Sverdlovsk Picture Gallery, Sverdlovsk; Museum of Visual Arts, Ekaterinburg) (1920), Inv. Zh-409
Exhibitions: 1916. Moscow, *Jack of Diamonds* (within cat. nos. 269–74)
1918. Moscow, *I State Exhibition* (within cat. nos. 93–111)

51. *Non-Objective Composition (Suprematism)*, 1916
Oil on canvas, 102 x 94 cm
Museum of Visual Arts, Ekaterinburg

Provenance: Museum Bureau of IZO NKO;
Museum of Local Lore of the City of Ekaterinburg
(as of 1920 Regional Museum of Local Lore, Sverdlovsk;
as of 1936 Sverdlovsk Picture Gallery, Sverdlovsk;
Museum of Visual Arts, Ekaterinburg) (1920),
Inv. Zh-411
Exhibitions: 1916. Moscow, *Jack of Diamonds* (within cat. nos. 269–74)
1918. Moscow, *I State Exhibition* (within cat. nos. 93–111)

52. *Color Painting (Non-Objective Composition)*, 1917
Oil on canvas, 62.5 x 40.5 cm
State Russian Museum, St. Petersburg

Provenance: Museum of Artistic Culture, Petrograd (1922);
State Russian Museum, Leningrad (1926),
Inv. ZhB 1579
Exhibitions: 1917. Moscow, *Jack of Diamonds* (within cat. nos. 159–76, under the title *Color Composition*)
1918. Moscow, *I State Exhibition* (within cat. nos. 116–27 under the title *Color Composition*)
1919. Moscow, *X State Exhibition* (cat. no. 181 or 182?)

53. *Non-Objective Composition (Color Painting)*, 1917
Oil on canvas, 71 x 64 cm
Regional Art Museum, Ulianovsk

Provenance: Museum Bureau of IZO NKP, Moscow;
Regional Art Museum, Simbirsk,
(as of 1924 Art Museum, Ulianovsk) (1920),
Inv. 1180-zh
Exhibitions: 1917. Moscow, *Jack of Diamonds* (within cat. nos. 159–76, under the title *Color Composition*)
1918. Moscow, *I State Exhibition* (within cat. nos. 116–27 as *Color Composition*)
1919. Moscow, *X State Exhibition* (cat. no. 181 or 182?)

54. *Green Stripe (Color Painting)*, 1917
Oil on canvas, 71.5 x 49 cm
Rostov Kremlin State Museum Preserve

Provenance: Museum Bureau of IZO NKP;
Museum of Architecture and Art, Rostov-Yaroslavskii
(as of 1998 Rostov Kremlin State Museum Preserve) (1922), Inv. 371
Exhibitions: 1917. Moscow, *Jack of Diamonds* (within cat. nos. 159–76, as *Color Composition*)
1918. Moscow, *I State Exhibition* (within cat. nos. 116–27, as Color Composition)
1919. Moscow, *X State Exhibition* (cat. no. 181 or 182?)

VARVARA STEPANOVA

55. *Illustration for the poem "Rtny Khomle,"* 1918
Watercolor on paper, 23.3 x 17.7 cm
Private collection

Provenance: Artist's family, Moscow;
Private collection , Moscow
Exhibitions: 1919. Moscow, *X State Exhibition*

56. *Illustration for the poem "Rtny Khomle,"* 1918
Watercolor on paper, 23.3 x 17.7 cm
Private collection

Provenance: Artist's family, Moscow;
Private collection, Moscow
Exhibitions: 1919. Moscow, *X State Exhibition*

57. *Illustration for the poem "Rtny Khomle,"* 1918
Watercolor on paper, 23.3 x 17.7 cm
Private collection

Provenance: Artist's family, Moscow;
Private collection, Moscow
Exhibitions: 1919. Moscow, *X State Exhibition*

58. *Illustration for the poem "Rtny Khomle,"* 1918
Watercolor on paper, 23.3 x 17.7 cm
Private collection

Provenance: Artist's family, Moscow;
Private collection , Moscow
Exhibitions: 1919. Moscow, *X State Exhibition*

59. *Illustration for the poem "Zigra Ar,"* 1918
Watercolor on paper, 18.8 x 16 cm
Private collection

Provenance: Artist's family, Moscow;
Private collection, Moscow
Exhibitions: 1919. Moscow, *X State Exhibition*

60. *Illustration for the poem "Zigra Ar,"* 1918
Watercolor on paper, 18.8 x 16 cm
Private collection

Provenance: Artist's family, Moscow;
Private collection, Moscow
Exhibitions: 1919. Moscow, *X State Exhibition*

61. *Illustration for the poem "Zigra Ar,"* 1918
Watercolor on paper, 18.8 x 16 cm
Private collection

Provenance: Artist's family, Moscow;
Private collection, Moscow
Exhibitions: 1919. Moscow, *X State Exhibition*

62. *Illustration for the poem "Zigra Ar,"* 1918
Watercolor on paper, 18.8 x 16 cm
Private collection

Provenance: Artist's family, Moscow;
Private collection, Moscow
Exhibitions: 1919. Moscow, *X State Exhibition*

63. *Illustration for the poem "Zigra Ar,"* 1918
Watercolor on paper, 18.8 x 16 cm
Private collection

Provenance: Artist's family, Moscow;
Private collection, Moscow
Exhibitions: 1919. Moscow, *X State Exhibition*

64. *Illustration for the poem "Zigra Ar,"* 1918
Watercolor on paper, 18.8 x 16 cm
Private collection

Provenance: Artist's family, Moscow;
Private collection, Moscow
Exhibitions: 1919. Moscow, *X State Exhibition*

65. *Dancing Figures on White*, 1920
Oil on canvas, 107.5 x 143.5 cm
State Tretiakov Gallery, Moscow

Provenance: Artist's family, Moscow;
State Tretiakov Gallery, Moscow (1998)
Exhibitions: 1919. Moscow, *X State Exhibition*
Exhibition of Four Artists (Kandinsky, Rodchenko, Stepanova, Shevchenko), Moscow, 1920.

66. *Five Figures on a White Background*, 1920
Oil on canvas, 80 x 98 cm
Private collection

Provenance: Artist's family, Moscow;
Private collection, Moscow
Exhibitions: 1920. Moscow, *XIX State Exhibition*
Exhibition of Four Artists (Kandinsky, Rodchenko, Stepanova, Shevchenko), Moscow, 1920.

67. *Billiard Players*, 1920
Oil on canvas, 68 x 129 cm
Carmen Thyssen-Bornemisza Collection

Provenance: Artist's family, Moscow;
Galerie Gmurzynska, Cologne;
Thyssen-Bornemisza Collection, Lugano (1983);
Carmen Thyssen-Bornemisza Collection, Madrid (1995), Inv. 540.730

68. *Playing Draughts*, 1920
Oil on plywood, 78 x 62 cm
Private collection

Provenance: Artist's family, Moscow;
Private collection, Moscow
Exhibitions: 1920. Moscow, *XIX State Exhibition*
Exhibition of Four Artists (Kandinsky, Rodchenko, Stepanova, Shevchenko), Moscow, 1920

69. *Trumpet Player*, 1920
Oil on canvas, 70 x 57 cm
Private collection

Provenance: Artist's family, Moscow;
Private collection, Moscow
Exhibitions: 1920. Moscow, *XIX State Exhibition*
Exhibition of Four Artists (Kandinsky, Rodchenko, Stepanova, Shevchenko), Moscow, 1920

70. *Musicians*, 1920
Oil on canvas, 106 x 142 cm
Museum of Private Collections,
Pushkin State Museum of Fine Arts, Moscow

Provenance: Artist's family, Moscow;
Museum of Private Collections, State Pushkin Museum of Fine Arts, Moscow (1992), Inv. ZhR-828
Exhibitions: 1919. Moscow, *X State Exhibition*
Exhibition of Four Artists (Kandinsky, Rodchenko, Stepanova, Shevchenko), Moscow, 1920.

71. *Self-Portrait*, 1920
Oil on plywood, 71 x 52.5 cm
Museum of Private Collections,
Pushkin State Museum of Fine Arts, Moscow

Provenance: Artist's family, Moscow;
Museum of Private Collections, Pushkin State Museum of Fine Arts, Moscow (1992), Inv. ZhR 826
Exhibitions: 1920. Moscow, *XIX State Exhibition*
Exhibition of Four Artists (Kandinsky, Rodchenko, Stepanova, Shevchenko), Moscow, 1920.

72. *Figure (Peasant)*, 1921
Oil on canvas, 99.5 x 65.5 cm
Private collection

Provenance: Artist's family, Moscow;
Private collection, Moscow
Exhibitions: 1921. Moscow, *5 x 5 =25* (cat. no. 1)

73. *Figure*, 1921
Oil on canvas, 125 x 71.5 cm
Private collection

Provenance: Artist's family, Moscow;
Private collection, Moscow
Exhibitions: 1921. Moscow, *5 x 5 = 25* (cat. no. 3 or 5)

NADEZHDA UDALTSOVA

74. *Seamstress*, 1912–13
Oil on canvas, 71.5 x 70.5 cm
State Tretiakov Gallery, Moscow

Provenance: Andrei Drevin, the artist's son, Moscow;
George Costakis, Moscow;
State Tretiakov Gallery, Moscow (1977), Inv. Zh-1297

75. *Composition*, 1913
Oil on canvas, 111.5 x 133 cm
Museum of History and Architecture,
Pereiaslavl-Zalesskii

Provenance: Ivanovo Regional Museum;
Museum of History and Architecture, Pereiaslavl-Zalesskii (1923), Inv. 9934
Exhibitions: 1914. Moscow, *Jack of Diamonds* (cat. no. 144)

76. *At the Piano*, 1915
Oil on canvas, 107 x 89 cm
Yale University Art Gallery,
Gift of Collection Société Anonyme

Provenance: 1922. Berlin, Erste russische Kunstausstellung;
Katherine Dreier, New York (1922);
Société Anonyme, New York (1922);
Yale University Art Gallery, New Haven (1941), Inv. 1941.725
Exhibitions: 1915. Petrograd, *0.10* (cat. no. 145, as Music)
1916. Moscow, *The Store* (cat. no. 80)
1922. Berlin, Erste russische Kunstausstellung (cat. no. 235)

77. *Guitar Fugue*, 1914–15
Oil on canvas, 106 x 71 cm
State Tretiakov Gallery, Moscow,
Gift, George Costakis

Provenance: George Costakis, Moscow;
State Tretiakov Gallery, Moscow (1977), Inv. Zh-1296

78. *Artist's Model*, 1914
Oil on canvas, 106 x 71 cm
State Russian Museum, St. Petersburg

Provenance: Museum of Artistic Culture, Petrograd;
State Russian Museum, Leningrad (1926), Inv. Zh-B 1712
Exhibitions: 1915. Petrograd, *Tramway V* (cat. no. 73, as *Artists's Model with Guitar [Architectonic Composition]*)

79. *New*, 1914–15
Oil on canvas, 60 x 48 cm
Vasnetsov Regional Art Museum, Kirov

Provenance: Yaransk Museum of Local Lore of Kirov Region (1923);
Vasnetsov Regional Art Museum, Kirov (1958), Inv. NV/Zh-54

80. *Self-Portrait with Palette*, 1915
Oil on canvas, 72 x 53 cm
State Tretiakov Gallery, Moscow

Provenance:Museum of Painterly Culture;
State Tretiakov Gallery (1929), Inv. 11929
Exhibitions: 1915. Petrograd, *0.10* (cat. no. 150, as *My Representation*).

81. *Red Figure*, 1915
Oil on canvas, 70 x 70 cm
Rostov Kremlin State Museum Preserve

Provenance: Museum Bureau of IZO NKP, Moscow;
Museum of Architecture and Art, Rostov-Yaroslaskii (as of 1998 Rostov Kremlin State Museum Preserve, Rostov) (1922), Inv. Zh-136

82. Study for *Restaurant*, 1915
Oil on canvas, 71 x 53 cm
State Tretiakov Gallery, Moscow

Provenance: Museum of Painterly Culture, Moscow;
State Tretiakov Gallery, Moscow (1929), Inv. 11930
Exhibitions: 1915. Petrograd, *Tramway V* (cat. no. 72)
1916. Moscow, *The Store* (cat. no. 74)

83. *Restaurant*, 1915
Oil on canvas, 134 x 116 cm
State Russian Museum, St. Petersburg

Provenance: Museum of Artistic Culture, Petrograd;
State Russian Museum, Leningrad (1926) Inv. 1334
Exhibitions: 1916. Moscow, *The Store* (cat. no. 73)

84. *Kitchen*, 1915
Oil on canvas, 161 x 165 cm
Museum of Visual Arts, Ekaterinburg

Provenance: Museum Bureau of IZO NKP, Moscow;
Museum of Local Lore of the City of Ekaterinburg, (as of 1920 Regional Museum of Local Lore, Sverdlovsk;
as of 1936 Sverdlovsk Picture Gallery, Sverdlovsk;
Museum of Visual Arts, Ekaterinburg) (1920), Inv. 421
Exhibitions: 1915. Petrograd, *0.10* (cat. no. 146)
V State Exhibition of Paintings [from Impressionism to Non-Objectivity], Moscow, 1919, as cat. no. 268)

85. *Painterly Construction*, 1916
Oil on canvas, 109 x 79 cm
State Tretiakov Gallery, Moscow

Provenance: Museum of Artistic Culture, Moscow;
State Tretiakov Gallery, Moscow (1929), Inv. 11931
Exhibitions: 1916. Moscow, *Jack of Diamonds* (cat. no. 283, 284, or 285)

86. *Untitled*, ca. 1918
Watercolor on paper, 48 x 40 cm
Art Co. Ltd. (George Costakis Collection)

Provenance: Andrei Drevin, the artist's son, Moscow;
George Costakis, Moscow;
Art Co. Ltd. (George Costakis Collection) (1984), Inv. ATH 80.21

87. *Untitled*, 1916
Gouache and pencil on paper, 24.6 x 15.9 cm
Art Co. Ltd. (George Costakis Collection)

Provenance: Andrei Drevin, the artist's son, Moscow;
George Costakis, Moscow;
Art Co. Ltd (George Costakis Collection) (1984), Inv. 200.80

88. *Untitled*, 1916
Gouache on paper, 48 x 38.5
Art Co. Ltd. (George Costakis Collection)

Provenance: Andrei Drevin, the artist's son, Moscow;
George Costakis, Moscow;
Art Co. Ltd. (George Costakis Collection) (1984) Inv. ATH 80.19

89. *Untitled*, 1916
Gouache on paper, 64 x 44.5 cm
Art Co. Ltd. (George Costakis Collection)

Provenance: Andrei Drevin, the artist's son, Moscow;
George Costakis, Moscow;
Art Co. Ltd (George Costakis Collection) (1984), Inv. ATH 80.18

Works on the Russian Avant-Garde

Bowlt, John E., ed. *Russian Art of the Avant-Garde: Theory and Criticism 1902–1934*. Trans. John E. Bowlt. London: Thames and Hudson, 1988.

Compton, Susan. *Russian Avant-Garde Books, 1917–34*. Cambridge, Mass.: The MIT Press, 1993.

——. *The World Backwards: Russian Futurist Books, 1912–16*. London: British Museum, 1978.

Douglas, Charlotte. *Swans of Other Worlds: Kazimir Malevich and the Origins of Abstraction in Russia*. Ann Arbor, Mich.: UMI Research Press, 1980.

Gray, Camilla. *The Great Experiment: Russian Art, 1863–1922*. London: Thames and Hudson, 1962.

Gurianova, Nina and Andrei Sarabianov. *Neizvestnyi russkii avangard*. Moscow: Sovetskii khudozhnik, 1992.

Hagelstein, Virginia M. and Gail H. Roman, eds. *The Avant-Garde Frontier: Russia Meets the West, 1910–1930*. Gainesville, Fla.: University Press of Florida, 1992.

Howard, Jeremy. *The Union of Youth: An Artists' Society of the Russian Avant-Garde*. New York: St. Martin's Press, 1992.

Janecek, Gerald. *The Look of Russian Literature: Avant-Garde Visual Experiments, 1900–1930*. Princeton: Princeton University Press, 1984.

Kafetsi, Anna, et al. *Russian Avant-Garde, 1910–1930: The G. Costakis Collection*. Exh. cat., 2 vols., Athens: The National Gallery and Alexandros Soutzos Museum, 1996.

Karasik, Irina. *Russkii avangard. Muzei v muzee*. St. Petersburg: Palace Editions, 1998.

Kovtoune, Evgeni. *L'Avant-Garde Russe dans les Années 1920–1930*. Bournemouth, England: Parkstone, 1996.

Kovtun, Evgenij. *Sangesi. Die russische Avangarde. Chlebnikow und seine Maler*. Zurich: Stemmle, 1993.

Lodder, Christina. *Russian Constructivism*. New Haven: Yale University Press, 1983.

Margolin, Victor. *The Struggle for Utopia: Rodchenko, Lissitzky, Moholy-Nagy, 1917–1946*. Chicago: University of Chicago Press, 1997.

Milner, John. *Kazimir Malevich and the Art of Geometry*. New Haven: Yale University Press, 1996.

Parton, Anthony. *Mikhail Larionov and the Russian Avant-Garde*. Princeton: Princeton University Press, 1993.

Rudenstine, Angelica, ed. *Russian Avant-Garde Art: The George Costakis Collection*. New York: Abrams, 1981.

Von Geldern, James. *Bolshevik Festivals, 1917–1920*. Berkeley: University of California Press, 1993.

Wood, Paul, et al. *The Great Utopia: The Russian and Soviet Avant-Garde, 1915–1932*. Exh. cat., New York: Guggenheim Museum, 1992.

Works on the Women Artists of the Russian Avant-Garde

Bernier, Georges. *Cherchez la femme*. Exh. cat., Cologne: Galerie Gmurzynska, 1993.

Costlow, Jane T., Stephanie Sandler, and Judith Vowles, eds. *Sexuality and the Body in Russian Culture*. Stanford: Stanford University Press, 1993.

Cunningham, Rebecca. "The Russian Women Artist/Designers of the Avant-Garde." *Theatre Design and Technology* (London), spring 1998, pp. 39–51.

Das Leben zur Kunst machen. Arbeiten auf Papier von Frauen der russischer Avantgarde, Stoffe und Porzellan aus der jungen Sowjetunion. Exh. cat., Zurich: Helmhaus, 1989.

Die Rationale. Rationale Konzepte von Künstlerinnen 1915–1985. Exh. cat., Bonn: Frauen Museum, 1985.

Goussev, Vladimir. *Le Portrait du féminin du XVIIIe début du XXe siècle*. Exh. cat., Leningrad: Khudozhnik RSFSR, 1981.

Gusev, Vladimir, et al. *The Beauty of Russian Women of the Fifteenth–Twentieth Centuries*. Exh. cat., Otaru, Japan: Petersburg Museum, 1995.

Klimov, Evgenii. *Russkie zhenshchiny po izobrazheniiam russkikh khudozhnikov*. Washington, D.C.: Kamkin, 1967.

Lippard, Lucy R., et al. *Künstlerinnen international 1877–1977*. Exh. cat., Berlin: Schloss Charlottenburg, 1977.

Marcadé, Valentine, et al. *L'Avant-Garde au féminin: Moscou, Saint-Petersbourg, Paris (1907–1930)*. Paris: Artcurial, 1983.

Nochlin, Linda and Ann Sutherland-Harris. *Women Painters*. Exh. cat., Los Angeles: Los Angeles County Museum, 1976.

Pioneering Women Artists 1900 to 1940. Exh. cat., New York: Helen Serger, la Boétie, 1980.

Rubinger, Krystyna, ed. *Künstlerinnen der russischen Avantgarde/Women-Artists of the Russian Avant-Garde, 1910–1930*. Exh cat., Cologne: Galerie Gmurzynska, 1979.

Schlagheck, Irma. "Geniale Töchter der russischen Revolution." *Art* (Hamburg), no. 3 (March 1992), pp. 32–47.

Stein, Donna. *Women Artists in the Avant-Garde: 1910–1935*. Exh. cat., New York: Rachel Adler Gallery, 1984.

Stites, Richard. *The Women's Liberation Movement in Russia: Feminism, Nihilism, and Bolshevism, 1860–1930*. Princeton: Princeton University Press, 1978; 2nd ed., 1998.

Toporkov, Andrei L., ed. *Seks i erotika v russkoi traditsionnoi kulture*. Moscow: Ladomir, 1996.

Vachtova, Ludmila, et al. *Künstlerinnen des 20. Jahrhunderts*. Exh. cat., Wiesbaden: Museum Wiesbaden, 1990.

Vergine, Lea. *L'altra meta dell'avanguardia 1910–1940*. Exh. cat., Milan: Gabriele Mazzotta, 1980.
Wismer, Beat, ed. *Karo Dame: Konstruktive, konkrete und radikale Kunst von Frauen von 1914 bis heute*. Baden: Lars Müller, 1995.
Yablonskaya, Myuda. *Women Artists of Russia's New Age, 1900–1935*. London: Thames and Hudson, 1990.

Works on the Artists in the Exhibition
Alexandra Exter
Baty, Gaston. *Alexandra Exter. Théâtre (Maquettes, Décors, Costumes)*. Exh. cat., Galerie Quatre Chemins, Paris, 1929.
Belli, Gabriella., et al. "Interferenze culturali." *Alexandra Exter e il Teatro da Camera*, pp. 13–16. Exh. cat., Archivio del '900, Rovereto, 1991.
Bowlt, John E. "Alexandra Exter." *Alexandra Exter. Marionettes*. Exh. cat., Leonard Hutton Galleries, New York, 1975.
Cohen, Ronny. "Alexandra Exter's Designs for the Theater." *Artforum* (New York) 19, no. 10 (summer 1981), pp. 46–49.
Faucher, Paul. "Préface." *Alexandra Exter. Théatre*. Exh. cat., Musée des Arts et Metiers, Paris, 1937.
Gorbachev, Dmitrii. "Exter in Kiev-Kiev in Exter." *Experiment* (Los Angeles) 1, no. 1 (1995), pp. 299–322.
Kolesnikov, Mikhail. "Alexandra Exter i Vera Mukhina." *Panorama iskusstv* (Moscow) no. 12 (1989), pp. 89–110.
——. "Alexandra Exter. Ot impressionizmak konstruktivizmu." *Sovetskii balet* (Moscow) no. 6, (1987), pp. 61–65.
——. *Alexandra Exter*, pp. 5–24. Exh. cat., Bakhrushin Museum, Moscow, 1988.
Koval, Alexander. "Aus Anlass der Wiederentdeckung von Alexander Exter-Marionetten." *Ausstellung Russische Avantgarde. Alexandra Exter. Michel Andreenko*, pp. 1–3. Exh. cat., Galerie Werner Kunze, Berlin, 1974.
Kovalenko, Georgii. "Exter v Parizhe." *Teatralnaia zhizn*, (Moscow) no. 17 (1990), pp. 20–23.
——. "Alexandra Exter v Parizhe." *Teatr* (Moscow) no. 2 (1992), pp. 103–22.
——. *Alexandra Exter*. Moscow: Galart, 1993.
——. "'Tsvetovaia dinamika' Alexandry Exter (iz byshego sobraniia Kurta Benedikta)." In Vagner, Georgii Karlovich, et al., eds.: *Pamiatniki kultury. Novye otkrytiia*, pp. 356–65. Moscow: Nauka, 1996.
——. "La peinture cubo-futuriste d'Alexandra Exter." *Ligeia* (Paris) no. 21–24 (1998), pp. 104–19.
——. "Teatr i zhivopis Olexandri Exter." *Ukrainskii teatr* (Kiev) no. 4 (1988), pp. 25–27 (in Ukrainian).
Lissim, Simon. "Alexandra Exter As I Knew Her." *Artist of the Theatre, Alexandra Exter*, pp. 9–15. Exh. cat., Center for the Performing Arts, New York Public Library at Lincoln Center, New York, 1974.
Marcadé, *L'avant-garde au féminin: Moscou, Saint-Petersbourg, Paris (1907–1930)*, pp. 13, 27–29.
McClintic, Miranda. "Alexandra Exter, Marionettes and Theatrical Designs." *Alexandra Exter, Marionettes and Theatrical Designs*. Exh. cat., Hirshhorn Museum and Sculpture Garden, Washington, D.C., 1980.
Nakov, André B. "Alexandra Exter." *Alexandra Exter*, pp. 5–48. Galerie Chauvelin, Paris, 1972.
Rubinger, *Künstlerinnen der russischen Avantgarde/Women-Artists of the Russian Avant-Garde, 1910–1930*, pp. 112–30.
Rudenstine, *Russian Avant-garde Art: The George Costakis Collection*, pp. 97–102.
Tairov, Alexander. *Alexandra Exter. Décors de Théâtre*. Galerie Quatre Chemins, Paris, 1930.
Tomilovskaia, Elena. "Alexandra Exter." *Alexandra Exter. Eskizy dekoratsii i kostiumov*. Exh. cat., Bakhrushin Museum, Moscow, 1986.
Tugendkhold, Yakov. *Alexandra Exter*, Berlin: Zaria, 1922.
Vergine, *L'altra metà dell'avanguardia 1910–1940*, pp. 83–85.
Walden, Herwarth. *Ausstellung Alexandra Exter*. Exh. cat., Der Sturm, Berlin, 1927.
Wismer, *Karo Dame: Konstruktive, konkrete und radikale Kunst von Frauen von 1914 bis heute*, pp. 84–87.
Yablonskaya, *Women Artists of Russia's New Age, 1900-1935*, pp. 117–40.
Yakovenko, N. E. "Introduction," *Alexandra Exter (1884–1949)*. Exh. cat., Odessa Art Museum, Odessa, 1989.

Natalia Sergeevna Goncharova
Bakos, Katalin. *Goncsarova*. Budapest: Corvina, 1981.
Belloli, Carlo. "Incidenza internationale di due magistrali protagonisti dell'avanguardia russa." *Nathalie Gontcharova. Michel Larionov*. Exh. cat., Arte Centro, Milan, 1983.
Berlewi, Henryk. *Larionov. Gontcharova*. Exh. cat., Galerie Beyler, Basel, 1961.
Boissel, Jessica, et al. *Nathalie Gontcharova. Michel Larionov*. Exh. cat., Centre Georges Pompidou, Paris, 1995.
Bowlt, John E. "Natalia Goncharova and Futurist Theater." *Art Journal* (New York) 49, no. 1 (spring, 1990), pp. 44–51.

Chamot, Mary and Camilla Gray. *A Retrospective Exhibition of Paintings and Designs for the Theatre. Larionov and Goncharova*. Exh. cat., City Art Gallery, Leeds; City Art Gallery, Bristol; and Arts Council Gallery, London, 1961.

——. *Goncharova. Stage Designs and Paintings*. London: Oresko, 1979.

Chamot, Mary. *Gontcharova*. Paris: La Bibliothèque des Arts, 1972.

Dane, Marie-Claude. *Gontcharova. Larionov*. Exh. cat., Musée d'art moderne de la ville de Paris, Paris, 1963.

Daulte, François. "Introduction." *Larionov. Gontcharova. Rétrospective*. Exh. cat., Musée d'Ixelles, Brussels, 1976.

Durfee, Thea. "Natalia Goncharova: Two Letters." *Experiment* (Los Angeles)1, no. 1 (July, 1995), pp. 159–68.

Eganbiuri, Eli (pseudonym of Ilia Zdanevich). *Mikhail Larionov Natalia Goncharova*. Moscow: Miunster, 1913.

Exposition des oeuvres de Gontcharova et Larionow. L'Art décoratif théâtral moderne. Exh. cat., Galerie Sauvage, Paris, 1918.

Gayraud, Regis, ed. *Nathalie Gontcharova Michel Larionov par Elie Eganebury*. Paris: Clémence Hiver, 1996.

Goldman, John. "Introduction." *Rétrospective Gontcharova*. Exh. cat., Maison de la culture de Bourges, 1973.

Gurianova, Nina. "Voennye graficheskie tsikly N. Goncharovoi i O. Rozanovoi." *Panorama iskusstv* (Moscow) no. 12 (1989), pp. 63–88.

Kovalenko, Georgii. *Natalia Goncharova. Mikhail Larionov. Vospominaniia sovremennikov*. Moscow: Galart, 1995.

Loguine, Tatiana. *Gontcharova et Larionov*. Paris: Klincksieck, 1971.

Marcadé, *L'avant-garde au féminin: Moscou, Saint-Petersbourg, Paris (1907–1930)*, pp. 12–13, 33–36.

Martini and Ronchetti, *Michel Larionov. Nathalie Goncharova*. Exh. cat., Galleria Martini & Ronchetti, 1983.

Omuku, Toshiharu. *Le Paris des années vingt. R. Kawashiva, N. Gontcharova et M. Larionov*. Exh. cat., Shiseido Gallery, Tokyo, 1995.

Orenstein, Gloria. "Natalia Goncharova. Profile of the Artist-Futurist Style." *The Feminist Art Journal* (New York) 3, no. 2 (summer, 1974), pp. 1–6.

Parton, Anthony. "Gontcharova and the 'Ballets Russes.'" *Natalia Gontcharova and the Russian Ballet*. Exh. cat., Julian Barran, Ltd., London, 1996.

Rubinger, *Künstlerinnen der russischen Avantgarde/Women-Artists of the Russian Avant-Garde, 1910–1930*, pp. 132–52.

Rude, Ferdinand. "Nathalie Gontcharova et son temps." *Nathalie Gontcharova*. Exh. cat., Musée des Beaux-Arts, Lyon, 1969.

Rudenstine, *Russian Avant-Garde Art: The George Costakis Collection*, pp. 106–09.

Seuphor, Michel. "Ricordi di tempi eroici." *Larionov-Gontcharova*. Exh. cat., Galleria Schwartz, Milan, 1961.

Sharp, Jane A. "Redrawing the Margins of Russian Vanguard Art: Natalia Goncharova's Trial for Pornography in 1910." In Jane T. Costlow, Stephanie Sandler, and Judith Vowles, eds., *Sexuality and the Body in Russian Culture* (Stanford: Stanford University Press, 1997), pp. 104–06.

Stupples, Peter. "The Stylistic Development of Natalia Gontcharova." *Goncharova*, pp. 11–15. Exh. cat., National Art Gallery, Wellington, New Zealand, 1987.

Tobin, Robert. "Gontcharova/Larionov." *Natalia Goncharova*, pp. 5–7. Exh. cat., Marion Koogler McNay Art Museum, San Antonio, 1987.

Tsvetaeva, Marina. *Nathalie Gontcharova*, Paris: Clémence Hiver, 1990.

Vergine, *L'altra metà dell'avanguardia 1910–1940*, pp. 80–82.

Wismer, *Karo Dame: Konstruktive, konkrete und radikale Kunst von Frauen von 1914 bis heute*, pp. 48–52.

Yablonskaya, *Women Artists of Russia's New Age, 1900–1935*, pp. 52–79.

Liubov Sergeevna Popova

Adaskina, Natalia and Dmitrii Sarabianov. *Lioubov Popova*. Paris: Sers, 1989; English edition, New York: Abrams, 1990.

——. "Formirovanie dizainerskoi kontseptsii L.S. Popovoi. GVYTM-VKHUTEMAS. 1921–1923 goda." *Trudy VNIITE. Tekhnicheskaia estetika*, (Moscow) no. 41 (1983), pp. 43–60.

Adaskina, Natalia. "Rabota L. Popovoi po sozdaniiu 'tsvetovoi distsipliny' Vkhutemasa." Ida Gofman, ed. *Gosudarstvennaia Tretiakovskaia galleria. Materialy i issledovaniia*, pp. 172–87. Leningrad: Khudozhnik RSFSR, 1983.

Bodine, Sarah. "Liubov Sergeevna Popova." *Gouaches and Drawings by Liubov Popova and Kazimir Malevich*, p. 2. Exh. cat., Leonard Hutton Galleries, New York, 1986.

Bowlt, John E. "From Surface to Space: The Art of Liubov Popova." *The Structurist* (Saskatoon) no. 15–16 (1976), pp. 80–88.

——. "Liubov Popova, Painter." In Nadia Jernakoff, ed.: *Transactions of the Association of Russian-American Scholars in US*, special issue devoted to Russian art (New York) 15 (1982), pp. 227–51.

Dabrowski, Magdalena. *Liubov Popova*. Exh. cat., The Museum of Modern Art, New York, 1991–92.Douglas, Charlotte. "Liubov Popova's Spatial Force Constructions." *Liubov Popova*. Exh. cat., Rachel Adler Gallery, New York, 1985.
Law, Alma. "'Le Cocu Magnifique' de Crommelynck." *Les Voies de la création théâtrale* (Paris) no. 7 (1980), pp. 14–43.
Marcade, *L'avant-garde au féminin: Moscou, Saint-Petersbourg, Paris (1907–1930)*, pp. 16, 37–39.
Posmertnaia vystavka proizvedenii L. S. Popovoi. Exh. cat., Museum of Artistic Culture, Moscow, 1924.
Rubinger, *Künstlerinnen der russischen Avantgarde/Women-Artists of the Russian Avant-Garde, 1910–1930*, pp. 174–214.
Rudenstine, *Russian Avant-Garde Art: The George Costakis Collection*, pp. 344–420.
Sarabianov, Dmitrii, et al. *L. S. Popova 1889–1924*. Exh. cat., Tretiakov Gallery, Moscow; Russian Museum, Leningrad, 1990.
——. *Priamaia i obratnaia perspektiva russkogo minimalizma/Gerade und umgekehrte Perspektive des russischen Minimalismus. Liubov Popova/Aleksandr Konstantinov*. Exh. cat., Tsaritsyno Museum, Moscow; Palais Liechtenstein, Feldkirch, 1994.
Sarabianov, Dmitrii. *Liubov Popova*, Moscow: Galart, 1994.
Vergine, *L'altra metà dell'avanguardia 1910–1940*, pp. 104–07.
Vorobiev, Vladimir. "Kak Liubvi Popovoi povezlo." *Russkaia mysl*, (Paris) (4 October 1979), p. 10.
Wismer, *Karo Dame: Konstruktive, konkrete und radikale Kunst von Frauen von 1914 bis heute*, pp. 52–65.
Yablonskaya, *Women Artists of Russia's New Age, 1900–1935*, pp. 99–116.

Olga Vladimirovna Rozanova

Bowlt, John E. "Olga Wladimirowna Rozanova." *Von der Fläche zum Raum/From Surface to Space. Russland/Russia 1916–1924*, pp. 126–31. Exh. cat., Galerie Gmurzynska, Cologne, 1974.
Efros, Abram. "O.V. Rozanova." *Profili*. (Moscow) Federatsiia, 1930, pp. 228–29. First appeared as Rozanova obituary "Vo sled ukhodiashchikshim." *Moskva. Zhurnal literatury i iskusstva* (Moscow) no. 3 (1919), pp. 4–6.
Gurianova, Nina. "Na puti k novomu iskusstvu. Olga Rozanova." *Iskusstvo* (Moscow) no. 1 (January, 1989), pp. 24–30.
——. "Voennye graficheskie tsikly N. Goncharovoi i O. Rozanovoi." *Panorama iskusstv* (Moscow) no. 12 (1989), pp. 63–88.
——. "Olga Rozanova: Colore Libero." *Art e Dossier* (Florence) no. 85 (Dec. 1993), pp. 37–43.
——. *Rozanova, Filonov, Tatlin, Goncharova, Larionov, Malevich, Kulbin*. Moscow: Avant-Garde; Paris: La Hune, 1994.
KhanMagomedov, Selim., et al. *Von der Malerei zum Design/From Painting to Design*. Exh. cat., Galerie Gmurzynska, Cologne, 1981.
Kliun, Ivan. "Introduction." *Pervaia Gosudarstvennaia naia vystavka. Katalog posmertnoi vystavki kartin, etiudov, eskizov i risunkov O.V. Rozanovoi*. Exh. cat., "I State Exhibition," pp. i–vi. Art Salon, Moscow, 1919.
Marcade, *L'avant-garde au féminin: Moscou, Saint-Petersbourg, Paris (1907–1930)*, pp. 14–15, 42–44.
Rubinger, *Künstlerinnen der russischen Avantgarde/Women-Artists of the Russian Avant-Garde, 1910–1930*, pp. 215–56.
Rudenstine, *Russian Avant-Garde Art: The George Costakis Collection*, pp. 453–61.
Terekhina, Vera. "Zhenshchina russkogo avangarda." *Chelovek* (Moscow) no. 6 (1993), pp. 128–31.
——. "Nachalo zhizni tsvetochno aloi. . . ." *Panorama iskusstv* (Moscow) no. 12 (1989), pp. 38–62.
Terekhina, Vera., et al. *Olga Rozanova 1886–1918*. Exh. cat., Helsingin Kaupungin Taidemuseo, Helsinki, 1992.
Vergine, *L'altra metà dell'avanguardia 1910–1940*, pp. 96–101.
Wismer, *Karo Dame: Konstruktive, konkrete und radikale Kunst von Frauen von 1914 bis heute*, pp. 66–73.
Yablonskaya, *Women Artists of Russia's New Age, 1900–1935*, pp. 81–98

Varvara Fedorovna Stepanova

Bowlt, John E. and Alexander Lavrentiev. *Stepanova*, Cambridge, Mass.: The MIT Press, 1988.
Kovtun, Evgenii. "Das Antibuch der Warwara Stepanova/Varvara Stepanova's Anti-book." In John E. Bowlt, et al.: *Von der Fläche zum Raum/From Surface to Space. Russland/Russia 1916–1924*, pp. 57–64, 142–51. Exh. cat., Galerie Gmurzynska, Cologne, 1974.
Lavrentiev, Alexander."V. F. Stepanova o rannem konstruktivizme." *Trudy VNIITE Tekhnicheskaia estetika* (Moscow) no. 21 (1979), pp. 111–17.
——. "Poeziia graficheskogo dizaina v tvorchestve Varvary Stepanovoi." Trudy VNIITE. *Tekhnicheskaia estetika* (Moscow) no. 5 (1980), pp. 22–26.
——. "The Graphics of Visual Poetry in the Work of Varvara Stepanova." *Grafik* (Budapest) no. 1 (1982), pp. 46–51.
Lavrentiev, Alexander and Nicoletta Misler. *Stepanova*, Milan: Idea Books, 1988.

Lavrentiev, Alexander and Varvara Rodchenko, eds. *V. Stepanova: Chelovek ne mozhet zhit bez chuda*. Moscow: Sfera, 1994.
Law, Alma. "'The Death of Tarelkin.' A Constructivist Vision of Tsarist Russia." *Russian History* (Tempe, AZ) 8, parts 1–2 (1982), pp. 145–98.
Quilici, Vieri. "Lo schermo traspaarente." *Rodcenko/Stepanova*, pp. 13–19. Exh. cat., Palazzo dei Priori a Palazzo Cesaroni, Perugia, 1984.
Rubinger, *Künstlerinnen der russischen Avantgarde/Women-Artists of the Russian Avant-Garde, 1910–1930*, pp. 270–84.
Rudenstine, *Russian Avant-Garde Art: The George Costakis Collection*, pp. 467–69.
Sarabianov, Dmitrii, et al. *Sieben Moskauer Künstler/Seven Moscow Artists*. Exh. cat., Galerie Gmurzynska, Cologne, 1984.
Stepanova, Varvara. "Aufzeichnungen/Occasional Notes (1919–1940)." In Selim Khan-Magomedov, et al.: *Von der Malerei zum Design/From Painting to Design*, pp. 122–44. Exh. cat., Galerie Gmurzynska, Cologne, 1981.
Vergine, *L'altra metà dell'avanguardia 1910–1940*, pp. 87–89.
Wismer, *Karo Dame: Konstruktive, konkrete und radikale Kunst von Frauen von 1914 bis heute*, pp. 84–95.
Yablonskaya, *Women Artists of Russia's New Age, 1900–1935*, pp. 141–56.

Nadezhda Andreevna Udaltsova

Drevina, Ekaterina. *Nadezhda Udaltsova*. Moscow: Trilistik, 1997.
Drevina, Ekaterina and Veronika Starodubova, eds. *Alexander Drevin. Nadezhda Udaltsova*. Exh. cat., Union of Artists of the USSR, Moscow: Sovetskii khudozhnik, 1991.
Drevina, Ekaterina and Vasilii Rakitin. *N. Udaltsova. Zhizn russkoi kubistki. Dnevniki, stati, vospominaniia*. Moscow: RA, 1994.
Marcade, *L'avant-garde au féminin: Moscou, Saint-Petersbourg, Paris (1907–1930)*, pp. 40–41.
Miasina, Marianna, ed. "Udaltsova, Nadezhda Andreevna." *Stareishie sovetskie khudozhniki o Srednei Azii i Kavkaze*. Moscow: Sovetskii khudozhnik, 1973.
Rubinger, *Künstlerinnen der russischen Avantgarde/Women-Artists of the Russian Avant-Garde, 1910–1930*, pp. 286–312.
Rudenstine, *Russian Avant-Garde Art: The George Costakis Collection*, pp. 484–87.Sarabianov, Dmitrii, et al., *Sieben Moskauer Künstler/Seven Moscow Artists*. Exh. cat., Galerie Gmurzynska, Cologne, 1984.
Vergine, *L'altra metà dell'avanguardia 1910–1940*, pp. 93–95.
Wismer, *Karo Dame: Konstruktive, konkrete und radikale Kunst von Frauen von 1914 bis heute*, pp. 74–83.
Yablonskaya, *Women Artists of Russia's New Age, 1900–1935*, pp. 157–72.

Royal Academy Trust

Major Benefactors

The Trustees of the Royal Academy Trust would like to thank all those who have been exceedingly generous over a number of years in support of the galleries, the exhibitions, the conservation of the Permanent Collection, the Library, the Royal Academy Schools and the education programme:

H M The Queen
The 29th May 1961 Charitable Trust
The Annie Laurie Aitken Charitable Trust
American Associates of the Royal Academy Trust
The Honorable and Mrs Walter H Annenberg
Barclays Bank
B.A.T. Industries plc
Brenda M Benwell-Lejeune
John Frye Bourne
British Telecom
The Brown Foundation Inc
The Trustees of the Clore Foundation
The John S Cohen Foundation
Sir Harry and Lady Djanogly
The Dulverton Trust
Alfred Dunhill Limited
The John Ellerman Foundation
Esso UK plc
Esmée Fairbairn Charitable Trust
Mr and Mrs Eugene V Fife
Walter Fitch III
Mrs Henry Ford II
The Foundation for Sport and the Arts
Friends of the Royal Academy
The Getty Grant Program
Glaxo Holdings plc
Diane and Guilford Glazer
Jack and Grete Goldhill
Maurice and Laurence Goldman
The Horace W Goldsmith Foundation
Dr Armand Hammer
Mr and Mrs Jocelin Harris
The Philip and Pauline Harris Charitable Trust
The Hayward Foundation
Drue Heinz Trust
Henry J & Drue Heinz Foundation
Heritage Lottery Fund
IBM United Kingdom Limited
The Idlewild Trust
The JP Jacobs Charitable Trust
The Japan Foundation
Mr and Mrs Donald P Kahn
The Kresge Foundation
The Lankelly Foundation
Mr John S Latsis
Mrs Katherine L Lawrence
The Leverhulme Trust
Lex Service plc
The Linbury Trust
Mr & Mrs Sydney Lipworth
John Madejski
Her Majesty's Government
The Manifold Trust
Mr and Mrs John L Marion
Marks and Spencer
Mr and Mrs Jack C Massey
Ronald and the Honourable Rita McAulay
McKinsey and Company Inc
Paul Mellon KBE
The Mercers' Company
The Monument Trust
The Henry Moore Foundation
The Moorgate Trust Fund
Museums and Galleries Improvement Fund
National Westminster Bank
Stavros S Niarchos
The Otemae College
The Peacock Trust
The Pennycress Trust
PF Charitable Trust
The Pilgrim Trust
The Edith and Ferdinand Porjes Trust
Rio Tinto plc
John A Roberts FRIBA
The Ronson Foundation
The Rose Foundation
Rothmans International plc
Mrs Arthur M Sackler
Mrs Jean Sainsbury
The Saison Foundation
The Basil Samuel Charitable Trust
Mrs Louisa S Sarofim
Sea Containers Ltd
Shell UK Limited
Miss Dasha Shenkman
William and Maureen Shenkman
The Archie Sherman Charitable Trust
The Starr Foundation
Alfred Taubman
Mr and Mrs Vernon Taylor Jr
Sir Anthony and Lady Tennant
Eugene & Clare Thaw Charitable Trust
Ware and Edythe Travelstead
The Trusthouse Charitable Foundation
The Douglas Turner Trust
Unilever plc
The Weldon UK Charitable Trust
The Welton Foundation
Garry H Weston
The Honourable and Mrs John C Whitehead
Mr and Mrs Frederick B Whittemore

The Maurice Wohl Charitable Foundation
The Wolfson Foundation
and others who wish to remain anonymous

Benefactors

The Trustees of the Royal Academy Trust would like to thank all those who have recently supported the galleries, the exhibitions, the conservation of the Permanent Collection, the Library, the Royal Academy Schools or the education programme:

Miss B A Battersby
Mr Tom Bendhem
The Charlotte Bonham-Carter Charitable Trust
Mr Keith Bromley
The Dorothy Burns Charity
The Clothworkers' Foundation
The John Coates Charitable Trust
The Ernest Cook Trust
Crabtree & Evelyn
Mr and Mrs Keith Dawson
The Dorner family and friends in memory of Lotte Dorner
The D'Oyly Carte Charitable Trust
The Gilbert & Eileen Edgar Foundation
Miss Jayne Edwardes
The Elephant Trust
Mr M E Flintoff
Mrs Helena Frost
The Worshipful Company of Goldsmiths
Mrs Sue Hammerson
Philip and Pauline Harris Charitable Trust
Mr and Mrs David Haynes
The Hayward Foundation
Mr Tony Howitt
The Leche Trust
Pamela Littman JP
Sir Edwin and Lady Manton
The Richard and Margaret Merrell Foundation
The Worshipful Company of Painter-Stainers
The Austin and Hope Pilkington Trust
The Radcliffe Trust
Mr Charles Saatchi
The Schneer Foundation Inc
Mr Paul Smith CBE
Sotheby's
The South Square Trust
Joseph Strong Frazer Trust
The Celia Walker Art Foundation
The Welton Foundation
and others who wish to remain anonymous

Exhibition Patrons Group

The Exhibition Patrons Group was established in May 1997 to encourage the regular and committed support of individuals who believe in the Royal Academy's mission to promote the widest possible understanding and enjoyment of the visual arts. The Royal Academy is delighted to thank the following for generously supporting the exhibition programme with donations of £1,000 and more:

President
Mr Garry Weston

Co-Chairmen
Sir Trevor Chinn CVO
The Hon Mrs Anne Collins
The Lady Lever of Manchester

Members
The 29th May 1961 Charitable Trust
Mrs Annabel Agace
Mr and Mrs V Alaghband
Mrs Suad Al-Attar
Mr and the Hon Mrs Michael Alen-Buckley
Mr John Asprey
Lord and Lady Attenborough
Mr Stephen Bampfylde
The Duke of Beaufort
Tom Bendhem
Mr and Mrs Thomas J Berger
Mrs Vanessa Bernstein
Sir Victor and Lady Blank
Mr and Mrs George Bloch
Mr Peter Boizot MBE
Mr and Mrs Mark Booth
Alain and Marie Boublil
Mrs Adrian Bowden
Mr Peter Bowring CBE
Ivor Braka
The Britto Foundation
Lady Brown
Jeremy Brown
Mr and Mrs John Burns
Marlene and Neville Burston
Mr Raymond M Burton CBE
Jim and Margaret Butler
Mr and Mrs P H G Cadbury
Mrs Lily Cantor
Mr F A A Carnwath CBE
Jean and Eric Cass
Mrs Rivka Chenevix-Trench
John Chiene
Sir Trevor and Lady Chinn
C H K Charities Limited
Mrs Denise Cohen
The Hon Mrs Anne Collins
Mr and Mrs G L Collins
Neville and Carole Conrad Charitable Trust

David J and Jennifer A Cooke
Corona Extra Beer
Mr Arnold M Crook
Mr and Mrs Andrew Dalton
Ian and Morny Davison
The Marquise de Cérenville
Peter and Kate De Haan
The de Laszlo Foundation
Mr and Mrs Patrick Doherty
Sir Philip Dowson PRA and Lady Dowson
John Drummond, FCSD, HON, DES, RCA
Mr and Mrs Maurice Dwek
EFG Private Bank Limited
Mrs Alyce Faye Eichelberger Cleese
Amelia Chilcott Fawcett
Mary Fedden RA
Mrs Juliet Fenton
Mr and Mrs Bryan Ferry
Mrs Kaye Finegold
Mrs Donatella Flick
Dr Gert-Rudolf Flick
Mr and Mrs Gerald Fogel
Mr and Mrs George Fokschaner
Mrs Helena Frost
A Fulton Company Limited
Mr and Mrs Richard Gapper
The Robert Gavron Charitable Trust
Jacqueline and Michael Gee
Jacqueline and Jonathan Gestetner
Sir Paul and Lady Girolami
M. and Mme Michel Goldet
Sir Nicholas and Lady Goodison's
Charitable Settlement
David and Maggi Gordon
Lady Gosling
David and Catherine Graham
Mrs Mary K Graves
Mrs Michael Green
Mr Robert Alan Green
Mrs Maro Hadjipateras
Mrs Sue Hammerson
Mr and Mrs Jocelin Harris
Michael and Morven Heller
Mr and Mrs Alan Hobart
Anne Holmes-Drewry
Mr and Mrs Allan Hughes
Jasper Jacob Associates
Mr and Mrs Ian Jay
Mr and Mrs Harold Joels
Mr and Mrs David Josefowitz
Mrs Gabrielle Jungels-Winkler
Mr and Mrs Donald P Kahn
Mr and Mrs Joseph Karaviotis
Mr and Mrs James Kirkman
Mr and Mrs Henry L R Kravis
The Kreitman Foundation
Mrs Thomas Kressner
Mr and Mrs Irvine Laidlaw
The Kirby Laing Foundation
Mrs Panagiotis Lemos
Mr George Lengvari
The Lady Lever of Manchester
Mr and Mrs John Lewis
Sir Sydney Lipworth QC and Lady Lipworth
Mr Jonathon E Lyons
Fiona Mactaggart
Sir John and Lady Mactaggart
Mr and Mrs Michael (RA) and José Manser
Mr and Mrs M Margulies
Marsh Christian Trust
R C Martin
Mrs Jack Maxwell
Sir Kit and Lady McMahon
The Mercers' Company
Lt Col L S Michael OBE
Nancy Miller Jong
Mr and Mrs Peter Morgan
Mr Thomas F Mosimann III
Mr Harry Moss
Jim Moyes
Mr and Mrs Carl Anton Muller
Paul and Alison Myners
John Nickson and Simon Rew
Mr Michael Palin
Lord and Lady Palumbo
Mrs Chrysanthy Pateras
Lynda Pearson
The Pennycress Trust
The P F Charitable Trust
Miss Karen Phillipps
Mr Godfrey Pilkington
George and Carolyn Pincus
Mr and Mrs William A Plapinger
The Quercus Trust
Barbara Rae RA
John and Anne Raisman
The Rayne Foundation
Mrs Jean Redman-Brown
Mr T H Reitman
Mr and Mrs Robert E Rhea
Sir John and Lady Riddell
Mr and Mrs John Ritblat
Mr John A Roberts FRIBA
Mr and Mrs Nicolas Rohatyn
Mr and Mrs Ian Rosenberg
Alastair and Sarah Ross Goobey
Mrs Coral Samuel CBE
Mr and Mrs Victor Sandelson
Mr Adrian Sassoon
Ms Pierrette Schlettwein
Dr Lewis Sevitt
The Cyril Shack Trust

The Countess of Shaftesbury
Mr and Mrs D M Shalit
Mrs Stella Shawzin
Mr and Mrs Clive Sherling
Mrs Lois Sieff OBE
Silhouette Eyewear
Mr and Mrs Richard Simmons
Mr Peter Simon
Mrs Roama Spears
James and Alyson Spooner
Mr and Mrs Nicholas Stanley
Mrs Jack Steinberg
Mr and Mrs David Stileman
Swan Trust
Mr and Mrs David Swift
Mr and The Hon Mrs Richard Szpiro
Sir Anthony and Lady Tennant
Eugene V and Clare E Thaw Charitable Trust
Mr and Mrs Julian Treger
Mrs Claire Vyner
The Walter Guinness Charitable Trust
John B Watton
Edna and Willard Weiss
Mr and Mrs Anthony Weldon
Mrs Gerald Westbury
Mrs Linda M Williams
Roger and Jennifer Wingate
Mr and Mrs Rainer Zietz
Mr and Mrs Michael Zilkha
and others who wish to remain anonymous

Benjamin West Group Donors

The Benjamin West Group was founded in March 1998 for American citizens living temporarily or permanently in Britain. The group takes its name from Benjamin West, a founder Member of the Royal Academy and the first American artist to become an Academician who also served as President from 1790 to 1805 and from 1806 to his death in 1820. The Royal Academy is delighted to thank the following members of the group who have also generously contributed donations of £1,000 and more to support the conservation of works touring the United States in the exhibition 'The Royal Academy in the Age of Queen Victoria 1837–1901: Paintings and Sculpture from the Permanent Collection'.

Patron
The Hon Raymond G H Seitz

Chairman
The Hon Barbara S Thomas

Donors
Mr Paul Abecassis
Mrs Wendy Becker Payton
Bernadette J Berger
Mr and Mrs Charles Brocklebank
Mr and Mrs Paul Collins
Mrs Joan Curci
Miss Elizabeth Gage
Mr and Mrs John Gore
Mrs Robin Hambro
Lady Harvie-Watt
Mr and Mrs Peter Holstein
Mr Paul Josefowitz
Mr and Mrs Richard Kaufman
Mr and Mrs Philip Mengel
Mr and Mrs Donald Moore
Mr Neil Osborn and Ms Holly Smith
Sir William and Lady Purves
Mrs Robert Rose
Albert and Marjorie Scardino
Mrs Sylvia B Scheuer
Mr and Mrs Paul Shang
Barbara and Allen Thomas
Mr Fred M Vinton

American Associates of the Royal Academy Trust

Benefactors
American Express
Mrs Russell B Aitken
Chase Manhattan Bank
Mr Walter Fitch III
Mrs Henry Ford II
The Honorable Amalia L de Fortabat
Glaxo Wellcome
The Horace W Goldsmith Foundation
Mr and Mrs Lewis P Grinnan Jr
Mrs Henry J Heinz II
Mr and Mrs Donald Kahn
Mr and Mrs Jon B Lovelace
Mr and Mrs John L Marion
Mrs Jack C Massey
Mr and Mrs Michael Meehan II
Mr Charles J Meyers
Mrs Nancy B Negley
Mrs Arthur M Sackler
Mrs Louisa S Sarofim
The Starr Foundation
The Honorable John C Whitehead
Mr and Mrs Frederick B Whittemore
Mrs William W Wood Prince
and others who wish to remain anonymous

Sponsors
The Honorable and Mrs Walter H Annenberg
Mr and Mrs Samuel R Blount
Mrs Jan Cowles
Mrs Donald Findlay

Mr D Francis Finlay
Mr James Kemper
Ms Stephanie Krieger
Mrs Linda Noe Laine
Mrs Janice H Levin
Mr and Mrs Vernon Taylor Jr
Prince Charitable Trusts
Mrs Sylvia Scheuer
US Trust Company of New York
and others who wish to remain anonymous

Patrons
Mr and Mrs John W Annan
Mr and Mrs Robert J Arnold
Mr and Mrs Stephen D Bechtel Jr
Mrs Helen Benedict
Mr and Mrs James Benson
Mrs Bette Berry
Mr Donald A Best
Ms Jan Blaustein Scholes
Mr and Mrs Henry W Breyer III
Mrs Mildred C Brinn
Mrs Caroline Chapin
Mrs Helene Chiang
Mr William L Clark
Ms Dorothea F Darlington
Ms Anne S Davidson
Mrs Charles H Dyson
Mrs John W Embry
Lady Warwick Fairfax
Mrs A Barlow Ferguson
Mrs Robert Ferst
Mr Ralph A Fields
Mr Richard E Ford
Mr and Mrs Lawrence S Friedland
Mrs Roswell L Gilpatric
Mr and Mrs Ralph W Golby
Mrs Betty N Gordon
Mrs Melville Wakeman Hall
Mr and Mrs Gurnee F Hart
Mr and Mrs Gustave M Hauser
The Honorable Marife Hernandez
Mr Robert J Irwin
Ms Betty Wold Johnson and Mr Douglas Bushnell
Ms Barbara R Jordan
The Honorable and Mrs Eugene Johnston
Mr William W Karatz
Mr and Mrs Stephen M Kellen
Mr Gary A Kraut
Mrs Katherine K Lawrence
Mr and Mrs William M Lese
Dr and Mrs Peter Linden
Mrs John P McGrath
Mrs Mark Millard
Mr Achim Moeller
Mrs Robin Heller Moss
Mr Paul D Myers
Ms Diane A Nixon
Mr and Mrs Jeffrey Pettit
Mr Robert S Pirie
Dr and Mrs Meyer P Potamkin
The Honorable and Mrs Charles H Price II
Mrs Signe E Ruddock
Mrs Frances G Scaife
Mrs Frederick M Stafford
Mr and Mrs Robert L Sterling Jr
Mrs Kenneth Straus
Mr Arthur O Sulzberger and Ms Alison S Cowles
Mrs Frederick Supper
Mrs Royce Dean Tate
Mr and Mrs A Alfred Taubman
Ms Britt Tidelius
Mrs Susan E Van de Bovenkamp
Mrs Bruce E Wallis
Mrs Sara E White
Mrs Joseph R Wier
Mrs Mary Louise Whitmarsh
Mr Robert W Wilson
Mr and Mrs Kenneth Woodcock
and others who wish to remain anonymous

Friends of the Royal Academy

Patron Friends
Mrs Denise Adeane
Mr Paul Baines
Mr P F J Bennett
Mr and Mrs Sidney Corob
Mr Michael Godbee
Mrs M C Godwin
Mr David Ker
Dr Abraham Marcus
Mr Thomas Mosimann
Mr and Mrs David Peacock
Mr and Mrs Derald H Ruttenberg
Mr Nigel J Stapleton
Mr Robin Symes
Mrs K L Troughton
Mrs Cynthia H Walton
Mrs Roger Waters
The Hon Mrs Simon Weinstock
Miss Elizabeth White
Mr David Wolfers
Mrs I Wolstenholme
and others who wish to remain anonymous

Supporting Friends
Mr Richard B Allan
Mr Peter Allinson
Mr Ian Anstruther
Mr John R Asprey
Mrs Yvonne Barlow

Mr J M Bartos
Mrs Wendy Becker-Payton
Mrs Susan Besser
Mrs C W T Blackwell
Mr Christopher Boddington
Mr Peter Boizot MBE DL
Mrs J M Bracegirdle
Mr Cornelius Broere
Mrs Gertraud Brutsche
Mrs Anne Cadbury OBE JP DL
Mr W L Carey-Evans
Miss E M Cassin
Mr R A Cernis
Mrs Norma Chaplin
Mr S Chapman
Mr W J Chapman
Mr and Mrs John Cleese
Mrs Ruth Cohen
Mrs D H Costopoulos
Mr and Mrs Chris Cotton
Mrs Saeda H Dalloul
Mr John Denham
Miss N J Dhanani
The Marquess of Douro
Mr Kenneth Edwards
Mrs Nicholas Embiricos
Mr and Mrs John R Farmer
Mr Ian S Ferguson
Mrs R H Goddard
Mr Gavin Graham
Mrs Richard Grogan
Miss Julia Hazandras
Mr Malcolm P Herring
Mr R J Hoare
Mr Charles Howard
Mrs O Hudson
Mrs Manya Igel
Mr S Isern-Feliu
Mrs Jane Jason
Mr Harold Joels
Mr and Mrs S D Kahan
Mrs P Keely
Mr and Mrs J Kessler
Mr D H Killick
Mr N R Killick
Mr Peter W Kininmonth
Mrs Joan Lavender
Mr and Mrs David Leathers
Mr Owen Luder CBE, PRIBA, FRSA
Miss Julia MacRae
Mr Donald A Main
Ms Rebecca Marek
The Hon Simon Marks
Mrs Janet Marsh
Mr J B H Martin
Mrs Gillian M S McIntosh
Mr J Moores
Mrs A Morgan
Miss Kim Nicholson
Mrs E M Oppenheim Sandelson
Mr Brian Oury
Mrs J Pappworth
Mrs M C S Philip
Mrs Anne Phillips
Mr Ralph Picken
Mr William Plapinger
Mr Benjamin Pritchett-Brown
Mr Clive Richards
Mr F Peter Robinson
Mr D S Rocklin
Mrs A Rodman
Mr and Mrs O Roux
The Hon Sir Steven Runciman CH
Dr Susan Saga
Sir Robert and Lady Sainsbury
Mr G Salmanowitz
Mr Anthony Salz
Mr and Mrs Julian Schild
Dr I B Schulenburg
Mrs Bernard L Schwartz
Mrs Lisa Schwartz
Mrs D Scott
Mr and Mrs Richard Seymour
Mr Mark Shelmerdine
Mr R J Simmons CBE
Mr John H M Sims
Miss L M Slattery
Dr and Mrs M L Slotover
Mrs P Spanoghe
Professor Philip Stott
Mr James Stuart
Mr J A Tackaberry
Mr G C A Thorn
Mrs Andrew Trollope
Mr and Mrs Vignoles
Mrs Catherine I Vlasto
Mr and Mrs Ludovic de Walden
Miss J Waterous
Mrs Claire Weldon
Mr Frank S Wenstrom
Mrs Ann S Wilberding
Mr David Wilson
Mr W M Wood
Mr R M Woodhouse
Ms Karen S Yamada
Dr Alain Youell
Mrs Pia Zombanakis
and others who wish to remain anonymous

Corporate Membership of the Royal Academy of Arts

Launched in 1988, the Royal Academy's Corporate Membership Scheme has proved highly successful. With 109 members it is now the largest membership scheme in Europe. Corporate membership offers company benefits to staff and clients and access to the Academy's facilities and resources. Each member pays an annual subscription to be a Member (£6,000) or Patron (£20,000). Participating companies recognise the importance of promoting the visual arts. Their support is vital to the continuing success of the Academy.

Corporate Membership Scheme

Corporate Patrons
Arthur Andersen
Bloomberg LP
BP AMOCO p.l.c.
Debenhams Retail plc
The Economist Group
GE Group
Glaxo Wellcome plc
Merrill Lynch Mercury
Morgan Stanley International
Rover Group Limited

Honorary Corporate Patrons
Ernst & Young

Corporate Members
Alliance & Leicester plc
Apax Partners & Co. Ltd.
Athenaeum Hotel
Aukett Associates
AXA Sun Life plc
Bacon and Woodrow
Bank of America
Bankers Trust
Banque Nationale de Paris
Barclays plc
Bear, Stearns International Ltd
BG plc
BICC plc
BMP DDB Limited
Bovis Europe
BT plc
British Airways plc
British Alcan Aluminium plc
British American Tobacco plc
The Brunswick Group
Bunzl plc
CB Hillier Parker
CJA (Management Recruitment Consultants) Limited
Christie's
Chase Manhattan Bank
Chubb Insurance Company of Europe
Clayton Dubilier and Rice Limited (CDR)
Clifford Chance
Colefax and Fowler Group
Cookson Group plc
Credit Agricole Indosuez
Credit Suisse First Boston
The Daily Telegraph plc
Deutsche Bank AG
Diageo plc
De Beers
E D & F Man Limited Charitable Trust
Esprit Telecom
Eversheds
Foreign & Colonial Management Ltd
Gartmore Investment Management plc
Granada Group PLC
Hay Management Consultants Limited
H J Heinz Company Limited
HSBC plc
ICI
John Lewis Partnership
King Sturge and Co.
Kleinwort Benson Charitable Trust
Korn/Ferry International
KPMG
Kvaerner Construction Ltd
Land Securities PLC
Lex Service PLC
Linklaters & Paines
Marks & Spencer
Marsh Ltd
McKinsey & Co.
Mitchell Madison Group
MoMart Limited
Newton Investment Management Ltd
Ove Arup Partnership
Paribas
Pearson plc
The Peninsular and Oriental Steam Navigation Company
Pentland Group plc
PricewaterhouseCoopers
Provident Financial plc
The Rank Group Plc
Robert Fleming & Co. Ltd
Rothmans UK Holdings Limited
The Royal Bank of Scotland
Sainsbury's PLC
Salomon Smith Barney
Schroders plc
Sea Containers Ltd.

SG
Slaughter and May
SmithKline Beecham
The Smith & Williamson Group
Sotheby's
Sun Life and Provincial Holdings plc
TI Group plc
Trowers & Hamlins
Unilever UK Limited
United Airlines
Wilde Sapte

Honorary Corporate Members
All Nippon Airways Co. Ltd
A. T. Kearney Limited
Goldman Sachs International Limited
London First
Old Mutual
Reuters Limited
Yakult UK Limited

Corporate Associates
Bass PLC
The General Electric Company plc
Macfarlanes
Save and Prosper Foundation

Sponsors of Past Exhibitions

The President and Council of the Royal Academy thanks sponsors of past exhibitions for their support. Sponsors of major exhibitions during the last ten years have included the following:

Alitalia
Italian Art in the 20th Century, 1989
Allied Trust Bank
Africa: The Art of a Continent, 1995*
Anglo-American Corporation of South Africa
Africa: The Art of a Continent, 1995*
A.T. Kearney
Summer Exhibition 99, 1999
The Banque Indosuez Group
Pissarro: The Impressionist and the City, 1993
Banque Indosuez and W I Carr
Gauguin and The School of Pont-Aven: Prints and Paintings, 1989
BBC Radio One
The Pop Art Show, 1991
BMW (GB) Limited
Georges Rouault: The Early Years, 1903–1920, 1993
David Hockney: A Drawing Retrospective, 1995*
British Airways
Africa: The Art of a Continent, 1995
BT
Hokusai, 1991
Cantor Fitzgerald
From Manet to Gauguin: Masterpieces from Swiss Private Collections, 1995
The Capital Group Companies
Drawings from the J Paul Getty Museum, 1993
Chilstone Garden Ornaments
The Palladian Revival: Lord Burlington and His House and Garden at Chiswick, 1995
Christie's
Frederic Leighton 1830–1896, 1996
Sensation: Young British Artists from The Saatchi Collection, 1997
Classic FM
Goya: Truth and Fantasy, The Small Paintings, 1994
The Glory of Venice: Art in the Eighteenth Century, 1994
Corporation of London
Living Bridges, 1996
The Dai-Ichi Kangyo Bank Limited
222nd Summer Exhibition, 1990
The Daily Telegraph
American Art in the 20th Century, 1993
De Beers
Africa: The Art of a Continent, 1995
Deutsche Morgan Grenfell
Africa: The Art of a Continent, 1995
Diageo plc
230th Summer Exhibition, 1998
Digital Equipment Corporation
Monet in the '90s: The Series Paintings, 1990
The Drue Heinz Trust
The Palladian Revival: Lord Burlington and His House and Garden at Chiswick, 1995
Denys Lasdun, 1997
Tadao Ando: Master of Minimalism, 1998
John Soane, Architect: Master of Space and Light, 1999
The Dupont Company
American Art in the 20th Century, 1993
The Economist
Inigo Jones Architect, 1989
Edwardian Hotels
The Edwardians and After: Paintings and Sculpture from the Royal Academy's Collection, 1900–1950, 1990
Elf
Alfred Sisley, 1992
Ernst & Young
Monet in the 20th Century, 1999
Fiat
Italian Art in the 20th Century, 1989
Financial Times
Inigo Jones Architect, 1989

Fondation Elf
Alfred Sisley, 1992
Ford Motor Company Limited
The Fauve Landscape: Matisse, Derain, Braque and Their Circle, 1991
Friends of the Royal Academy
Victorian Fairy Painting, 1997
Gamlestaden
Royal Treasures of Sweden, 1550–1700. 1989
The Jacqueline and Michael Gee Charitable Trust
LIFE? or THEATRE? The Work of Charlotte Salomon, 1999
Générale des Eaux Group
Living Bridges, 1996
Glaxo Wellcome plc
Great Impressionist and other Master Paintings from the Emil G Buhrle Collection, Zurich, 1991
The Unknown Modigliani, 1994
Goldman Sachs International
Alberto Giacometti, 1901–1966. 1996
Picasso: Painter and Sculptor in Clay, 1998
The Guardian
The Unknown Modigliani, 1994
Guinness PLC (see Diageo plc)
Twentieth-Century Modern Masters: The Jacques and Natasha Gelman Collection, 1990
223rd Summer Exhibition, 1991
224th Summer Exhibition, 1992
225th Summer Exhibition, 1993
226th Summer Exhibition, 1994
227th Summer Exhibition, 1995
228th Summer Exhibition, 1996
229th Summer Exhibition, 1997
Guinness Peat Aviation
Alexander Calder, 1992
Harpers & Queen
Georges Rouault: The Early Years, 1903–1920. 1993
Sandra Blow, 1994
David Hockney: A Drawing Retrospective, 1995*
Roger de Grey, 1996
The Headley Trust
Denys Lasdun, 1997
The Henry Moore Foundation
Alexander Calder, 1992
Africa: The Art of a Continent, 1995
Ibstock Building Products Ltd
John Soane, Architect: Master of Space and Light, 1999
The Independent
The Art of Photography 1839–1989. 1989
The Pop Art Show, 1991
Living Bridges, 1996
Industrial Bank of Japan, Limited
Hokusai, 1991
Intercraft Designs Limited
Inigo Jones Architect, 1989
Donald and Jeanne Kahn
John Hoyland, 1999
The Kleinwort Benson Group
Inigo Jones Architect, 1989
Land Securities PLC
Denys Lasdun, 1997
Logica
The Art of Photography, 1839–1989. 1989
The Mail on Sunday
Royal Academy Summer Season, 1992
Royal Academy Summer Season, 1993
Marks & Spencer
Royal Academy Schools Premiums, 1994
Royal Academy Schools Final Year Show, 1994*
Martini & Rossi Ltd
The Great Age of British Watercolours, 1750–1880. 1993
Paul Mellon KBE
The Great Age of British Watercolours, 1750–1880. 1993
Mercury Communications
The Pop Art Show, 1991
Merrill Lynch
American Art in the 20th Century, 1993*
Midland Bank plc
The Art of Photography 1839–1989. 1989
RA Outreach Programme, 1992–1996
Lessons in Life, 1994
Minorco
Africa: The Art of a Continent, 1995
Mitsubishi Estate Company UK Limited
Sir Christopher Wren and the Making of St Paul's, 1991
Natwest Group
Nicolas Poussin 1594–1665. 1995
The Nippon Foundation
Hiroshige: Images of Mist, Rain, Moon and Snow, 1997
Olivetti
Andrea Mantegna, 1992
Park Tower Realty Corporation
Sir Christopher Wren and the Making of St Paul's, 1991
Peterborough United Football Club
Art Treasures of England: The Regional Collections, 1997
Premiercare (National Westminster Insurance Services)
Roger de Grey, 1996*
RA Exhibition Patrons Group
Chagall: Love and the Stage, 1998
Kandinsky, 1999
Redab (UK) Ltd
Wisdom and Compassion: The Sacred Art of Tibet, 1992

Reed Elsevier plc
Van Dyck 1599–1641, 1999
Reed International plc
Sir Christopher Wren and the Making of St Paul's, 1991
Republic National Bank of New York
Sickert: Paintings, 1992
The Royal Bank of Scotland
Braque: The Late Works, 1997*
Premiums, 1997
Premiums, 1998
Premiums, 1999
Royal Academy Schools Final Year Show, 1996
Royal Academy Schools Final Year Show, 1997
Royal Academy Schools Final Year Show, 1998
The Sara Lee Foundation
Odilon Redon: Dreams and Visions, 1995
Sea Containers Ltd
The Glory of Venice: Art in the Eighteenth Century, 1994
Silhouette Eyewear
Egon Schiele and His Contemporaries: From the Leopold Collection, Vienna, 1990
Wisdom and Compassion: The Sacred Art of Tibet, 1992
Sandra Blow, 1994
Africa: The Art of a Continent, 1995
Société Générale, UK
Gustave Caillebotte: The Unknown Impressionist, 1996*
Société Générale de Belgique
Impressionism to Symbolism: The Belgian Avant-Garde 1880–1900. 1994
Spero Communications
Royal Academy Schools Final Year Show, 1992
Texaco
Selections from the Royal Academy's Private Collection, 1991
Thames Water Plc
Thames Water Habitable Bridge Competition, 1996
The Times
Wisdom and Compassion: The Sacred Art of Tibet, 1992
Drawings from the J Paul Getty Museum, 1993
Goya: Truth and Fantasy,
The Small Paintings, 1994
Africa: The Art of a Continent, 1995
Time Out
Sensation: Young British Artists from The Saatchi Collection, 1997
Tractabel
Impressionism to Symbolism: The Belgian Avant-Garde 1880–1900. 1994
Unilever
Frans Hals, 1990
Union Minière
Impressionism to Symbolism: The Belgian Avant-Garde 1880–1900. 1994
Vistech International Ltd
Wisdom and Compassion: The Sacred Art of Tibet, 1992
*Yakult UK Ltd**
RA Outreach Programme, 1997–2000

* Recipients of a Pairing Scheme Award, managed by Arts + Business.
Arts + Business is funded by the Arts Council of England and the Department for Culture, Media and Sport.

Other Sponsors/Supporters

Sponsors/supporters of exhibitions, events, publications and other items in the past two years:

Asia House
Atlantic Group plc
Elizabeth Blackadder RA
British Airways Plc
BT Amoco p.l.c.
Champagne Taittinger
Corona Beer
Country Life
Bernard Dunstan RA PPRWA
Foster and Partners
Green's Restaurant
Mr and Mrs David Haynes
HSBC Holdings plc
Michael Hopkins & Partners
Hulton Getty Picture Collection
John Doyle Construction
Allen Jones RA
KLM UK
The Leading Hotels of the World
Met Bar
Mikimoto
Morgan Stanley Dean Witter
Old Mutual
Polaroid (UK) Limited
Richard and Ruth Rogers
Royal & Sun Alliance Insurance Group plc
Salomon Smith Barney
Strutt & Parker
Time Out
ZFL

PHOTO CREDITS

by figure number
2. Courtesy private collection; 5. Courtesy Puni-Archiv, Zurich; 8. Archive of the Institute of Modern Russian Culture, Los Angeles; 10. © Estate of Vera Mukhina/Licensed by VAGA, New York, NY. Photo: Courtesy Harry N. Abrams, Inc.; 11. Courtesy Art Resource. © Erich Lessing; 12. Courtesy Georgii Kovalenko; 14. Courtesy private collection; 18. © State Russian Museum, St. Petersburg; 20. © National Museum of American Art, Smithsonian Institution; 22. © State Russian Museum, St. Petersburg; 23. Courtesy Galart, Moscow; 24. Courtesy private collection; 26. Courtesy Herman Berninger, Zurich; 27. © 1999 The Museum of Modern Art, New York; 33. Courtesy private pollection; 35. Rheinisches Bildarchiv, Cologne. 38. Photo by David Heald; 41. Courtesy Galart, Moscow; 42. Courtesy Alexandra Galitzin Archive, Museum of Russian Culture, San Francisco; 43. © State Russian Museum, St. Petersburg; 45. Archive of the Institute of Modern Russian Culture, Los Angeles; 46. Courtesy Bakhrushin State Theater Museum, Moscow. 48. Courtesy Galart, Moscow; 49. Courtesy Osterreichisches Theatermuseum, Vienna; 54. © State Russian Museum, St. Petersburg; 55. Courtesy private collection; 57. Courtesy private collection; 58. Archive of the Institute of Modern Russian Culture, Los Angeles; 61. Archive of the Institute of Modern Russian Culture, Los Angeles; 62. Courtesy Maxim Fedorovsky, Berlin; 64. © State Russian Museum, St. Petersburg; 65. Courtesy Art Co. Ltd. (George Costakis Collection); 69. Courtesy private collection; 74. Courtesy private collection; 77. Courtesy Ekaterina Drevina; 78. Courtesy Dmitrii Sarabianov, Moscow; 82. Courtesy Vasilii Rakitin; 84. Archive of the Institute of Modern Russian Culture, Los Angeles; 91. Courtesy Mariia Zubova, Moscow; 94. Courtesy private collection; 100. Courtesy private collection.

by plate number
2. Rheinisches Bildarchiv, Cologne; 6, 13, 15, 16, 26, 28, 29, 34, 38, 40, 65, 74, 77, 80, 82, 85. ©State Tretiakov Gallery, Moscow; 12. © 1999 The Museum of Modern Art, NY; 14. Karl Arendt, AFD, Cologne; 17. © State Russian Museum, St. Petersburg; 20. Photothèque des collections du Mnam/Cci; 21. © National Museum and Gallery, Cardiff; 27. Photothèque des collections du Mnam/Cci.; 33, 39, 41: © Art Co. Ltd. (George Costakis Collection);70, 71: © Museum of Private Collections, Pushkin Museum of Fine Arts, Moscow; 78. © State Russian Museum, St. Petersburg; 83. © State Russian Museum, St. Petersburg, courtesy Harry N. Abrams, Inc.; 86–89: © Art Co. Ltd. (George Costakis Collection).